Behavior Research Fund
Monographs

CHILDREN'S BEHAVIOR
PROBLEMS. II

THE UNIVERSITY OF CHICAGO PRESS
CHICAGO, ILLINOIS

*

THE BAKER & TAYLOR COMPANY
NEW YORK

THE CAMBRIDGE UNIVERSITY PRESS
LONDON

CHILDREN'S BEHAVIOR PROBLEMS

A STATISTICAL STUDY BASED UPON 2,113 BOYS
AND 1,181 GIRLS EXAMINED CONSECUTIVELY AT THE
ILLINOIS INSTITUTE FOR JUVENILE RESEARCH

LUTON ACKERSON

*Departments of Psychology, New York University, The College of the
City of New York, and Brooklyn College, Formerly Research
Psychologist, Illinois Institute for Juvenile Research
and Behavior Research Fund, Chicago*

II

RELATIVE IMPORTANCE AND INTERRELATIONS
AMONG TRAITS

Behavior Research Fund

THE UNIVERSITY OF CHICAGO PRESS
CHICAGO · ILLINOIS

FOREWORD

It is a distinct pleasure to be permitted to prepare a Foreword to the second volume of Children's Behavior Problems. The author has labored under most difficult circumstances to complete a well-conceived study—one which has utilized a wealth of material accumulated in a child-guidance clinic over a period of many years. This second volume by no means exhausts the possibilities for contribution to the growing understanding of children's problems.

The author is to be congratulated on the completion of these studies of "Relative Importance and Interrelations among Traits" of Children's Behavior Problems.

Paul L. Schroeder, M.D.

April 17, 1942

EDITOR'S PREFACE

In this volume Dr. Luton Ackerson continues[1] his statistical analysis of the data upon children's behavior problems extracted from the case records of the Illinois Institute of Juvenile Research.

Dr. Ackerson, in truly scientific spirit, stresses the fact that this is an exploratory study undertaken without a conceptual framework or hypothesis and with the disinterested objective of finding how some 125 behavior problems are intercorrelated with one another—a monumental undertaking that would have deterred a less intrepid and persevering investigator.

The author admits certain difficulties involved in translating case data into statistically manipulable categories that generally lower but may sometimes increase the correlations. These difficulties are: (1) the selective factor involved in the admission of cases to the Institute, (2) the difficulty of ascertaining in quantitative terms the reliability and objectivity of subjective case-record information, (3) the preconceived notions of parents in making reports and of the staff examiners in diagnosing problems, (4) the lack of completeness of the case studies, (5) the inadequate definition of categories, (6) the use of categorical trait names instead of measured variates, and (7) the inadequate representation of desirable and presumably indifferent traits in the data.

No revolutionary discoveries are reported by the writer. The majority of the correlations are low, some moderatly high, and a few quite high. Many of the rather high correlations are evidently due to the fact that what is essentially one characteristic appears under two or more different names in the case records.

_____

[1] His early research upon the same data was published under the title Behavior Problems of Children: A Statistical Study Based upon 5,000 Children Examined Consecutively at the Illinois Institute for Juvenile Research, Vol. I: Incidence, Genetic, and Intellectual Factors (Chicago: University of Chicago Press, 1931).

Certain other correlations are, however, quite revealing. For example, Dr. Ackerson differentiates between "personality problems" and "conduct problems" and gives each individual a "personality-total" score and a "conduct-total" score. He then ascertains that, although these two total scores correlate for boys .50 with each other, the "personality-total" score has a correlation of only .19 with stealing, .18 with police arrests, and .09 with gang membership, but that "conduct total" show scores of .55 with stealing, .53 with police arrest, and .35 with gang membership. Evidently "stealing" is not significantly related to personality behavior problems but is associated with other conduct problems.

From this study can be drawn two points of value for future research. First of all, for statistical studies of a high order of determinacy a schedule of problems should be substituted for or be a supplement to the customary case-study recording. It is highly important that the same items be checked uniformly upon a standardized list. In the second place, helpful for further research is the series of intercorrelations mentioned above, in drawing up a smaller list of "problems" than the 125 problems of this investigation.

ERNEST W. BURGESS

ACKNOWLEDGMENTS

To the late Dr. Herman M. Adler and to Professor L. L. Thurstone the writer is indebted for the preliminary arrangements for a comprehensive statistical study of children's personality and conduct problems based upon the material in a children's behavior clinic, of which this monograph represents a second volume. Our greatest debt of gratitude is unquestionably due the hundred or more present and former staff members of the Illinois Institute for Juvenile Research, who originally gathered this material and who, in addition to their full duties attendant upon the clinic care of cases, have held to the ideal of placing their work as completely as possible in record form suitable for research by others as well as by themselves. The devotion to research as one of the prime obligations of the Institute during the thirteen years of Dr. Adler's directorship has thus built up, not only a rich accumulation of well-kept case data, but also an attitude of encouraging original study continued under his chief-of-staff and successor, Dr. Paul L. Schroeder.

To Mrs. Myrtle Strom Mink the writer is indebted for advice in the interpretation of the social-history material; to Mrs. Muriel Highlander Lyon for varied assistance throughout all portions of the work; to Mr. William Melville and Mrs. Bessie Kight for clerical help; to Miss Margaret O'Connor and Miss Reba Gray for the statistical computations; to Mrs. Lilian Davis for critical aid with the manuscript; and to Mr. John C. Weigel for arranging the many affairs of personnel, equipment, and publication. A portion of the expense has been borne by the Behavior Research Fund and by the Work Projects Administration.

L. A.

CONTENTS

CONTENTS

CONTENTS

LIST OF FIGURES

LIST OF TABLES

        The remaining Tables (6-130) bear titles corresponding to
the headings of chapters ix-lx, in which they appear.

PART I

INTRODUCTORY

CHAPTER I

THE PURPOSE

This volume deals with intercorrelations among children's traits, most of which are here grouped as "personality difficulties" and "conduct difficulties." The ultimate aim of our study, of which this book represents a second volume, is a quantitative investigation into the many causal factors underlying undesirable behavior manifestations in children.

The principle of multiple causality is the basis of our procedure.

> It is assumed . . . . that behavior traits are correlated with a large number of factors either inherent in the child himself or arising in his environment, and that these correlations may vary in magnitude from zero to significantly high values either in a positive or in a negative direction. Thus the individual's behavior pattern is conceived as the resultant of many contributing factors of differing degrees of potency. The labor of this investigation consists in reducing to quantitative terms the degree of correlation or casual contribution.[1]

In accordance with such an empirical plan of attack the list of behavior traits studied was chosen on the basis of how frequently they were noted among our cases rather than according to any prevalent beliefs concerning their relative importance or seriousness. Specifically, all the traits whose incidences among our 2,113 White boys and 1,181 White girls seemed large enough to justify extensive statistical computations were selected for correlational analysis. Among characteristics or conditions other than behavior traits, only a few are discussed in the present inquiry. A more exhuastive examination of these non-behavior factors was not feasible at the present time.

Although our chief objective is the evaluation of causal factors, little will be said in this volume about causation in a

---

[1] L. Ackerson, <u>Children's Behavior Problems</u>, Vol. I: <u>Incidence, Genetic and Intellectual Factors</u> (University of Chicago Press, 1931). Pp. xxi + 268. Hereinafter referred to as Vol. I.

strict sense, for the calculation of correlations does not, of course, afford a final description of causality. It can under proper application state the amount of relationship and thus the amount of causation among a set of traits or conditions, this being its exclusive function, but it can never state the direction of causation. For if a correlation is obtained between trait A and B, the meaning may be (1) that trait A is the cause of trait B or (2) that trait B is the cause of trait A or (3) that both traits A and B, singly or jointly, are the effects of a third cause or group of causes, C. A fourth possibility, which is not usually stated specifically by writers on statistical technology but which is the most important one for research workers desiring to elicit unequivocal conclusions from actual data is (4) that a combination of two or more of the aforementioned factors may be present, e.g., traits A and B may react reciprocally upon each other and at the same time be influenced by a third cause or group of causes, C.

A concrete illustration will make Point 4 clear. Between the notations staying out late at night and sex delinquency (coitus) among our 1,181 girl cases we have found the substantial correlation (Pearson's tetrachoric r with age partialed out) of .44 ± .04. In this instance the causal interpretation is complex. The fact of staying away from home late at night probably exposes some girls to special temptations or opportunities for sex misconduct and may therefore stand as a direct causal influence. At the same time it is probable that girls of whom heterosexual activity has become a characteristic (the "aggressive" sex delinquents) may tend to stay away from home at night in search of conditions or companions peculiarly associated with misconduct of this type, so that the fact of sex delinquency thus may be to this extent the contributing cause. And at the same time both staying out late at night and sex delinquency may be effects of an outside cause or group of causes: e.g., if family control is inadequate and the girl is "allowed to run wild"; if the girl is on terms of hostility with other members of the family (e.g., the step-parent hypothesis), and may tend to stay away from home and seek the quasi-friendship associated with illicit sex relations; if the girl is "infatuated" with some man, i.e., "sexually suggestible by one individual," as one sociological writer has expressed it, and responds to his requests that she "go out with him"; if the girl

"craves excitement" or a "gay life," which to her imply such activities as "booze parties" or "picking up a fellow who has a car";
if the girl in "looking for a job" arrives in such predisposing
employment as "music shows," night clubs, or "taxi dancing acade-
mies"; or if the girl was engaging in prostitution, in which the
economic motive may have had some part. Many other outside factors could readily be cited, which in certain instances or under
certain conditions may be operative as causes of either "late
habits" or sex misconduct.

        Thus it becomes apparent that a strict determination of
what is cause and what is effect lies outside the scope of correlational statistics as they are employed in this study. Therefore,
with a view toward simplifying the presentation of our findings,
the material of this volume will be considered only as correlations
or associations between traits. The interpretation of this material from the standpoint of assigning causal influences would require additional data bearing perhaps more directly upon questions
of causation. Many readers will probably not be content with considering correlations merely as correlations but will desire to
make their own interpretation of causal factors implied therein.
There is no reason why they should not do so, under the cautions
noted above.

                The Utility of Correlation Coefficients

        If this volume expressly refrains from discussion of causa-
tion, in order to avoid at this time the interpretive intricacies
involved in assigning cause-and-effect status, and covers only the
eliciting of correlations, what is the utility of this lengthy
presentation of correlation coefficients?

        1. Although correlations cannot by themselves point out
what is cause and what is effect, they do serve a useful function
in locating where causation of some kind exists. Statistical correlation is but the quantification of John Stuart Mill's "method
of concomitant variations,"[2] which has long been recognized by lo-
gicians as an instrument of causal analysis. The approach in our

_____

        [2]W. Brown and G. H. Thomson, The Essentials of Mental Measurement
(London: Cambridge University Press, 1921), p. 97.

study has been largely empirical. In view of the nature of the
case material available to us and in view of the relatively small
body of proved research information now existing, upon which one
could base the hypotheses necessary for a more refined research
investigation in this field, it was felt that a systematic explora-
tion of a large number of frequently appearing behavior difficulties would be the most efficacious plan of attack. From such an
empirical analysis it is to be expected that certain relations will
be elicited and specific hypotheses suggested, which can be investigated in more crucial studies especially set up for this purpose.
In thus circumscribing the field in which causal factors may be
looked for, the routine calculation of correlation coefficients
contributes directly to the study of causation.

2. The study of causation is valued not merely as an end
in itself but rather as a means toward the ultimate aim of prognosis and therapeusis or prophylaxis, to use the medical terms, or
the aim of prediction and guidance, to employ the psychologist's
words. The usual logic has been that when we have identified the
causes of certain conditions we may proceed more intelligently to
devise methods of treatment or prevention. Now it has often hap-
pened that effective methods of treatment have been discovered
more or less by chance, without any complete working-out of the
intermediate implications of causal analysis or etiology. For example, much of the use of specific drugs in the cure of physical
disease has been the result of fortuitous discovery, without any
clear understanding of the reason for their efficacy. In reference
to our data, then, it is possible that in many instances a study of
the intercorrelations between behavior traits and related traits
or conditions may lead directly to the invention of practical methods of treatment or prevention, although an adequate knowledge of
the underlying causal mechanism is lacking.

3. An extensive list of correlation coefficients, it is
hoped, will possess some practical utility both for workers in a
clinic and for parents or guardians in the following manner: A
high correlation coefficient between two traits means that the two
traits tend to be associated in the same individual. Therefore,
if the presence of one trait in a given child has been ascertained,
high correlation coefficients may often serve as clues to the presence of other traits not so easily ascertainable. A more detailed

discussion of this possibility will be given in chapter vii.

4. A similar possibility is that of prediction. If one of
two traits which have been found from previous studies to be substantially intercorrelated is present in a given child, while the
other trait has been ascertained to be absent, the question may
well be raised whether the second trait may become present at a
later time. Since a time factor is here admitted as a further com-
plication, one's estimate of probabilities may be aided by a consideration of Volume I, Part III, in which the relation of behavior
traits to the age factor was presented. A more complete explanation of this possibility of prediction is reserved for chapter vii.

Volume I dealt with the relation of children's behavior
difficulties to sex differences, to racial (Negro-White) differences, to the developmental factor as represented by simple chronological age, and to the factor of intelligence as represented by
mental age and intelligence quotient as obtained from an individual
psychometric examination.

In the present volume, Part II deals with the correlations
of 161 frequently noted behavior traits and other case-record notations, with three criteria designed to indicate the degree of
the child's deviation from the conventional norm of acceptable behavior: (1) personality-total, i.e., the unweighted summation of
all the personality problems reported for a given child, (2) conduct-total, similarly the unweighted summation of all the conduct
problems reported for each child, and (3) arrest by police or appearance in juvenile court for reason of misconduct. A study of
these correlations will throw light on the problem of the relative
"seriousness" or "ominousness" of various behavior difficulties
and may serve to point out which traits call for special attention.

Part III deals with 122 tables of correlation coefficients
classifiable as follows: Tables 9 and 10, chronological age and
intelligence quotient (IQ). These two tables cover much of the
material of Volume I, Part III, but in the present volume the relationships are expressed in terms of correlation coefficients.
Tables 11-116, inclusive, frequently appearing behavior traits.
Tables 117-30, inclusive, case-record notations in the physical
and psychophysical, the home and familial, and the educational and
vocational fields which would not be considered as "behavior
traits."

CHAPTER II

THE DATA

All the correlations reported in the present volume are
based upon two groups of cases, 2,113 White boys and 1,181 White
girls, except where otherwise explicitly stated. The boys and
girls were never combined. They were children between their sixth
and eighteenth birthdays, who were or had been in the regular public schools and whose intelligence quotients as obtained in the
routine clinic examination (usually the 1916 Stanford-Binet) were
50 or more. Negro children, who comprised 408 out of the 5,000
cases originally covered in this investigation, were excluded because it was found that in our population they appeared to show a
somewhat different sort of behavior complex than the White children (see Vol. I, chap. v). Children below 6 years of age and below 50 IQ were excluded from the total 5,000 consecutive cases,
because it was found that our children below these age and intelligence levels manifested so few behavior problems (see Vol. I,
Part III) that their inclusion would only inflate the correlation
coefficients computed upon them. To "partial out" age and intelligence quotient would probably not overcome this difficulty suc-
cessfully because of the frequent tendency toward curvilinearity
of regression of trait on age or IQ, as shown in the curves in Volume I. There was excluded also a group of 90 boys and 98 girls of
adolescent ages who were referred by "scholarship associations,"
primarily for advice as to whether their capacities justified the
expenditure of the agencies' funds on their further education. The
reason for this exclusion was that in the nature of things it was
probable that their parents might be tempted to underemphasize any
undesirable behavior traits which could militate against their obtaining scholarship grants. It is probable, moreover, that these
children represent a very superior group in respect to personality
traits and family morale, since they were planning on a high-school
course which, even with the scholarship association's assistance
of twenty-five dollars a month or less, would entail a considerable

8

financial sacrifice to the family.[1]

While these same factors of heterogeneity in motivation and selection could be urged for excluding some of the remaining cases, it was felt that they were too few in number to warrant their intentional omission. And, furthermore, too great a homogeneity in the material is not desirable, since a situation of complete homogeneity in any factors would render a correlational study of those factors impossible.

This arbitrary exclusion of cases described in the preceding paragraphs was made for the purpose of decreasing to some extent the divergence between our group of cases and an ideally unselected group of children of the same ages. That any sort of real approximation to unselected children of these ages has been achieved by these exclusions cannot, of course, be asserted. The many qualifying conditions surrounding the data, as far as the writer can see them, will be explained and discussed in detail in subsequent pages devoted to a description of our data and its source (chap. iv).

An extensive account of the source of our material and the circumstances under which it was obtained, together with the numerous factors influencing its validity, has been given in Volume I. Hence a brief résumé will be sufficient for the present.

All the children of this study have been examined at the Illinois Institute for Juvenile Research. A group of 5,000 consecutive cases who had a complete examination (psychiatric, psychological, physical, social, and, when requested, recreational) during the years 1923-27 provided the data.

The 2,113 White boys and 1,181 White girls concerned in this volume, it is well to repeat, were between their sixth and eighteenth birthdays at the time of their first admission, and their intelligence quotients were above 50 (Figs. 1 and 2).

The reasons for their being referred for examination may be found in Volume I, Tables 1-13. Most of the examinees provided a complex of reasons leading to their examination, so that one must

---

[1] A description of the group of scholarship children may be found in M. Raymaker (Worthington), "A Study of High School Scholarship Students," Institution Quarterly, XVI (Springfield, Ill.: Department of Public Welfare, 1925), 62-65.

not fall into the error of supposing that all in any group of children were referred specifically because of the trait under discussion. For example, our children with a notation of <u>stealing</u> include not only cases in which stealing was a major reason for their
appearance in a behavior clinic but also cases in which stealing
was only an incidental problem among many others. There appeared
to be no practicable means of distinguishing "major" and "minor"
reasons within our material.

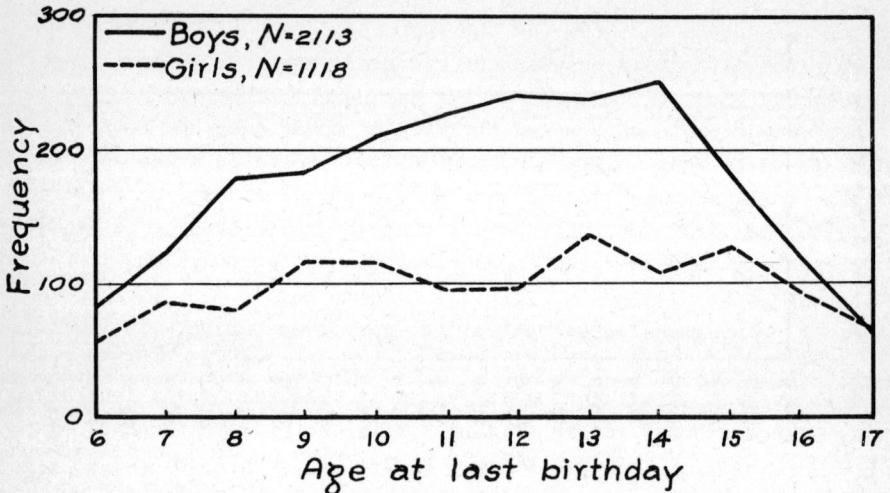

Fig. 1.—Frequency Distribution of Chronological Ages

The character of the material may be roughly described as
follows: The largest single group of children was referred because
of behavior difficulties ranging from such relatively minor problems as <u>finicky food habits</u> to such serious problems as <u>suspected
insanity</u>, <u>illegitimate pregnancy</u>, or <u>alleged murder</u>. The majority
of these behavior difficulties concern the home, neighborhood, or
school milieu. Only a fraction of the 3,294 cases discussed in
this volume—about 22 per cent of the boys and 15 per cent of the
girls—had a notation of police arrest or juvenile-court appearance for reasons of bad conduct, so that this group must not be
thought of as "delinquents," a term which is best restricted to
children who have been under police detention. That juvenile behavior difficulties are to a considerable extent prophetic of social or personal maladjustment in later life may be assumed. In

fact, the justification of the support by the Illinois State Department of Public Welfare of the Institute's clinical and research
activities among these younger children lies in the possibility
for prevention of such serious manifestations as criminalism or
mental disease in later life which is afforded by this early care
and study of childhood conduct and personality trends.

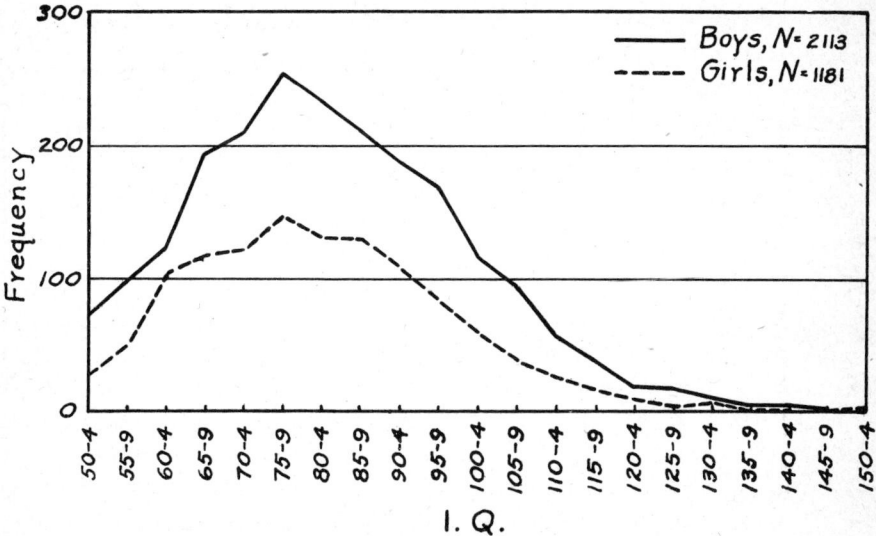

Fig. 2.—Frequency Distribution of Intelligence Quotients

The second largest single group of children presented problems of low intelligence and poor work in their school studies.
Since our present group of cases includes only the children with
intelligence quotients above 50, only a few of this group were referred for routine examination for commitment to a state school
for mental defectives. Retardation in school (which would probably
amount to two years or more by the age of 16) was noted in over
40 per cent of our 3,294 cases. In only a minority of instances,
however, did inadequate intelligence or poor school work appear to
be a principal reason leading to their being referred for examination.

Another large group presented problems of educational or
vocational guidance not necessarily associated with low intelligence or general inadequacy in school work.

The remainder were referred for miscellaneous reasons, e.g., physical defects with which may be associated gross behavior difficulties, such as enuresis, convulsions, post-encephalitic conditions, endocrine disfunction, and the like, and various problems of foster-home placement and problems of future supervision.

It must be remembered that these descriptions do not represent any discrete or "official" classification of cases, since most of the children could be placed in two or more of these broad descriptive classes.

Most of the children live in or near Chicago. Their economic and cultural status ranged from very poor to very high but, in general, would be considered below average. A substantial fraction were of foreign-born parentage. Their intelligence level was generally below average (Fig. 2), although the grossly feeble-minded cases were excluded from our study.

The largest portion of the information was obtained from the child's parents, usually the mother, in a personal interview conducted by the psychiatric social worker. In the interview a social-history outline[2] was followed which "includes all the major points which should be covered in every case and which allows for expansion here and there according to the individual problems considered." Additional preliminary information was obtained from any social agencies with which the child or family had had a previous contact. In some cases supplementary information was obtained from other relatives or "friends of the family," from teachers, club-leaders, employers, etc. The rest of the information was obtained in the clinical examination itself, to which the psychiatrist was the chief contributor.

The data employed in this study are almost entirely in the form of categorical case notations, only four items—the personality-total, the conduct-total, chronological age (CA), and intelligence quotient (IQ)—being in the form of continuous or measured variates. These categorical notations should be strictly interpreted as "noted or not noted" rather than as "present or absent."

---

[2] M. S. Mink and H. M. Adler, "A Suggested Outline for History-Taking in Cases of Behavior Disorders in Children," Welfare Magazine, VII (1926), 5-22. See also P. L. Schroeder, Child Guidance Procedures: Methods and Techniques Employed at the Institute for Juvenile Research (New York: Appleton-Century, 1937). Pp. viii + 362.

This caution is necessary in view of the fact that we cannot be
sure that the absence of a specific notation means that the trait
was non-existent in the child, since the amount or intensity of
the interviewing was not necessarily uniform in each case (see pp.
35-38). Furthermore, in many of the more secretive or subjective
behavior traits we cannot rely absolutely on the verity of the informant's observations and interpretations (see pp. 30-31). In
the categorical notations as used in this volume no distinction
was made between cases in which the grounds for a notation were
well established and those in which the grounds were less certain.
Our reasons for grouping the questioned and episodical instances
with the unquestioned cases rather than on the "not-noted" side of
the dichotomization are discussed on pages 31-32.

Our extensive use of these categorical and subjective case
notations as research material raises many queries concerning not
only the validity of the tetrachoric and bi-serial correlation
methods necessary in treating such data but also the meaning of
statistical results based upon such material. The next two chapters will attempt to discuss these technical problems in detail.

CHAPTER III

STATISTICAL METHODS IN CATEGORICAL DATA

The method of presenting the data of this volume is almost
entirely by the comparison of correlation coefficients. These have
been arranged in descending order, as far as possible, to facilitate comparisons with one another. Boys and girls are kept separate.

Pearson's Bi-serial and Tetrachoric Correlation Coefficients

Pearsonian correlation was used throughout. For the intercorrelations among the four quantitative variates—personality-
total, conduct-total, chronological age, and intelligence quotient
—product-moment coefficients were computed. For the correlations
of these four quantitative variates with the categorical notations,
Pearson's[1] bi-serial r was employed. For the intercorrelations
among the categorical notations Pearson's[2] tetrachoric r, together
with Everitt's tables of the tetrachoric functions,[3] was used.
Probable errors of bi-serial r were obtained by Soper's[4] Formula 23
and his tables. Probable errors of tetrachoric r were obtained by

---

[1]A brief description of this bi-serial method may be found in I, 136.
Its original presentation was given by K. Pearson, "On a New Method of Determin-
ing Correlation between a Measured Character A, and a Character B, of Which the
Percentage of Cases wherein B Exceeds (or Falls Short of) a Given Intensity Is
Recorded for Each Grade of A," Biometrika, VII (1907), 96-105.

[2]"On the Correlation of Characters Not Quantitatively Measurable,"
Philosophical Transactions of the Royal Society, London, CXCV, Ser. A (1900),
1-47.

[3]K. Pearson (ed.), Tables for Statisticians and Biometricians, Part I
(2d ed.; London: Cambridge University Press, 1924), pp. l-lv and Tables XXIX
and XXX. Since the time when the tetrachoric coefficients of this study were
computed, a very efficient method has been devised for obtaining tetrachoric r's
(L. Chesire, M. Saffir, and L. L. Thurstone, Computing Diagrams for the Tetrachoric Correlation Coefficient [University of Chicago Bookstore, 1933]), which
yields coefficients of sufficient accuracy for almost all practical needs.

[4]H. E. Soper, "On the Probable Error of the Bi-serial Expression for
the Correlation Coefficient," Biometrika, X (1914), 384-90.

Formula 213 in Kelley's textbook[5] and by his Table LI. For the
coefficients smaller than .20 the computation of probable errors
was omitted, partly because such probable errors would be very
large in comparison with their coefficients and partly as a means
of indicating that in view of the many possible distorting influences upon the coefficients (to be described in chap. iv) little
interpretation should be made of coefficients below this size.

A brief explanation of these two coefficients may be desirable. Bi-serial r is computed from a tabulation such as the
accompanying table, which shows the relation of depressed spells
to chronological age among 2,113 boys, bi-serial r being .22 ± .03
(Table 9, pp. 128-29).

	Chronological Age											
	6	7	8	9	10	11	12	13	14	15	16	17
Depressed spells noted.........	5	3	6	8	9	14	18	16	19	24	20	7
Depressed spells not noted.....	82	119	170	181	200	215	225	223	234	161	99	55

This procedure assumes rectilinearity of regression in the
continuous variate (chronological age) and normality of distribution in the dichotomized variate (depressed spells). The former
assumption can be satisfactorily investigated for each tabulation
by drawing up incidence curves[6] and observing their form. In the
case of chronological age (CA) and intelligence quotient (IQ) it
was obvious in Volume I, Part III, that in our data curvilinearity
is the rule rather than rectilinearity. Our reasons for employing
bi-serial r for these variates in spite of its admitted inadequacy
are explained on later pages in this chapter.

The use of Pearson's[7] bi-serial η and "coefficient of class

---

[5]T. L. Kelley, Statistical Method (New York: Macmillan, 1923), p.
258. The original presentation was given by K. Pearson, "On the Probable Error of a Coefficient of Correlation as Found from a Fourfold Table," Biometrika, IX (1913), 22-27.

[6]I, 114-18, and Figs. 15-47.

[7]K. Pearson, "On a New Method of Determining Correlation When One Variable Is Given by Alternative Categories and the Other by Multiple Categories,"
Biometrika, VII (1910), 248-57.

heterogeneity or divergence"[8] (a two-row contingency coefficient),
which make no requirements as to the form of regression in the continuous variates, did not appear serviceable in our material.
These coefficients become seriously magnified by cell-frequencies
of zero; and it was found after a brief experimentation that the
large number of zero cell-frequencies in our data tended to exag-
gerate these types of coefficients beyond the limits of credibil-
ity.

It appeared best to compute bi-serial r's routinely for
each two-row tabulation and to accompany them with a verbal caution to the reader that these are only an inadequate substitute
for the regular n x n-fold scatter diagrams and product-moment coefficients and correlation ratios, which will not be obtainable
until personality and conduct traits can be subjected to a satisfactory quantitative measurement.

There follows a specimen tetrachoric tabulation of the in-
terrelation of stealing and truancy from home among 2,113 boys, r_t
being .64 $\pm$ .02 (Table 56, p. 312).

	Stealing Noted	Stealing Not Noted
Truancy from home noted.........	375	128
Truancy from home not noted......	440	1,170

As a means of economizing work in the computation of tetrachoric r's, the following system was observed: The equation was
first written out to the second power of r_t and solved. If the obtained coefficient fell between .30 and .49, the successive two
terms up to the fourth power were added; and, for initial values
of r_t of .50 or larger, the equation was carried out to the sixth
power. It was found empirically that such short cuts seldom left
the final r_t as far as .01 away from what would have been obtained
with full carrying-out of computations.

Furthermore, in all coefficients in this volume, except

---

[8] K. Pearson, "On the Coefficient of Class Heterogeneity or Divergence,"
ibid., V (1906), 198-203.

those for chronological age and intelligence quotient (Tables 9
and 10, pp. 128 and 130), chronological age was "partialed out,"[9]
a process which in general had little effect upon the coefficients,
since the correlations of age with the two notations in question
were usually negligible. As a time-saving device, the partial coefficients were obtained from tables showing the limits between
which the partial r's would fall for various correlations with age.
This short-cut process could only very seldom yield final coefficients differing as much as .01 from a stricter computation.

Among our r_t's in Tables 6-130 it is possible, then, that,
on account of the two short cuts just described, a few may differ
as much as .02 from what would have been obtained under the strict-
est conditions of calculation; but, in view of the exploratory and
tentative character of this research, this slight deviation from
strict numerical accuracy is negligible.

Mention should also be made of the fact that the formula
for the probable error of tetrachoric r is technically incorrect
for our partial coefficients, involving as they do both tetrachoric
and bi-serial methods. For such coefficients the probable error
formula for tetrachoric r would give too large a value, while that
for bi-serial r would give too small a value. Since the technically correct formula for this purpose has not yet been derived,
it seems preferable to overstate rather than to understate the degree of unreliability attaching to these coefficients, and therefore the probable error for tetrachoric r was employed.

A correlation coefficient, it must be remembered, carries
only a part of the implications of a relationship between traits.
Wherever space permits, the tabulation upon which it is based
should accompany it. The coefficient by itself, to be sure, probably represents the most essential element of the relationship.
Because of its ease of computation it serves as a convenient measure of the amount of correlation between traits, and because of its
compactness and universalized meaning it lends itself to use in
comparative studies. These are the two uses made of it in this
volume. But the worker who wishes more precise or complete information will need to refer to the original tabulations, at times

---

[9]G. U. Yule and M. G. Kendall, _An Introduction to the Theory of Sta-
tistics_ (11th ed.; London: Charles Griffin, 1937), p. 269 (14.13).

even to the original protocols. He may wish to inquire into any
irregularities in the relationship, whether it is rectilinear or
curvilinear or whether a given population is homogeneous or heterogeneous, or he may wish to go beyond the abstract correlation coefficient to some more specific or practical application, such as
eliciting clues to the presence of other important characteristics
or the possibilities of predicting future behavior (see pp. 69-77
and Vol. I, chap. xii). When the role of the correlation coefficient in the <u>total</u> research process is considered, it is evident
that obtaining the coefficient marks only the beginning stage and
is not an end unto itself.

In order that bi-serial r and tetrachoric r may approximate the value of the standard product-moment r, the requirements
underlying the two formulas should be fulfilled. These requirements are rectilinearity of regression in the case of quantitative
variates and normality of distribution in the case of categorical
notations, i.e., both formulas were derived from the product-moment
formula on these assumptions. That is, we must assume that, if
adequate measurements of the trends underlying the categorical notations could be obtained, they would be found to be normally dis-
tributed. In the absence of actual graduated measurement of trait
notations such as ours, the fact of normality cannot, of course,
be proved. The extensive employment of tetrachoric and bi-serial
correlation in data of this kind, with its implicit acceptance of
normality, is attributable to three lines of reasoning: (1) if
many contributing factors of varying degree of potency may be effective in bringing about the presence of a given behavior trait
and if this trait may be present in varying degrees of intensity,
the resulting distribution of this trait in a population will be
of graduated character and will tend toward normality of form;[10]
(2) distributions actually obtained on measurable traits similar
to ours usually show a symmetrical or bell-shaped form resembling
Gaussian distribution, so that in the absence of specific knowledge as to the form of distribution, an assumption of normal or
Gaussian distribution is better than that of any other <u>one</u> form;[11]

---

[10]A simple explanation of this point may be found in E. L. Thorndike,
<u>Mental and Social Measurements</u> (New York: Teachers College, Columbia Univer-
sity, 1912), pp. 80-84.

[11]<u>Ibid.</u>, pp. 94-105.

and (3) if the form of distribution is not grossly irregular, one may consider that, if an actual measurement device were constructed, it could be arbitrarily "scaled" to yield a normal or Gaussian distribution.

It should be remembered that the value of a bi-serial r or a tetrachoric r is not affected in any constant direction by the location of the point of dichotomization. The ideal point of dichotomization is near the centroid of the distribution. The effect of extreme dichotomies is a reduction in the reliability, which is (theoretically, at least) taken care of by the accompanying probable error.

Now a strict mathematical normality cannot be expected in actual research data. The question is whether the state of affairs of a specific research approaches sufficiently to a Gaussian distribution to warrant an acceptable interpretation of bi-serial and tetrachoric correlations in terms of the standard product-moment coefficient, with which we are more generally familiar. An empirical test was obtained by comparing tetrachoric r's with product-moment r's when both were computed from the same scatter diagrams found in statistical literature. In case of distributions approximating the normal, the two coefficients were generally similar, as one might suppose. But upon scatter diagrams whose variates showed extreme skewness and with extreme dichotomies, the discrepancy between the product-moment r and the tetrachoric r became so great at times that the two types of coefficients bore little resemblance to each other except in sign. It should be remembered, furthermore, that, when distortions from a true underlying normality of distribution are present, one cannot know in any instance whether they have the effect of increasing or of decreasing the r_t in comparison with a corresponding product-moment coefficient. It is probable, however, that in our categorical data the departure from strict normality was seldom so great as to invalidate entirely the meaning of our tetrachoric and bi-serial correlations within the latitude of interpretation of this study.

Other Correlation Methods for Categorical Dada

As a means of escaping bothersome questions concerning assumptions as to the form of distribution of categorical notations,

some workers have avoided Pearson's tetrachoric and bi-serial correlation coefficients in favor of methods which make no such assumptions. Some workers have also preferred procedures less labo-
rious of computation, but this can hardly be a worth-while advantage in working with material intended for publication, since the
availability of simplified methods of calculation described above
minimizes this difference in labor of calculation. Some of these
methods are coefficiential, such as Yule's <u>coefficient of associa-
tion</u> (Q) or his coefficient <u>of colligation</u> (ω) or the fourfold contingency coefficients,[12] and some are quantitative indices; such
as P (probability).[13]

    While all these methods afford a measure of correlation or
association between categorical notations, it must be pointed out
that the values obtained by their use bear little or no functional
relation to those of the standard product-moment correlation coefficient but must be interpreted, each within its own system of
numerical indices. This lack of standardized or universalized
meaning in the Q, ω, and fourfold-C coefficients seems to the
writer to constitute an important objection to their use. While
there is an undeniable strength of position in employing techniques
requiring no special assumptions in dealing with a categorical and
subjective notation when one can neither prove nor disprove the
validity of such techniques, it should be remembered, nevertheless,
that, while these techniques impose no assumptions, at the same
time they tell us little. Even at their poorest, the Pearson tetrachoric and bi-serial techniques can do as much as the Q, ω, and
fourfold-C coefficients. For if one disregards the assumptions
and is willing to consider the coefficients as a unique system
without thought of any relation or resemblance to the product-
moment family of coefficients, one still has a "coefficient of association," whose derivation is equally plausible with Q, ω, or
fourfold-C. The <u>raison d'être</u> for assumption of normality of

[12]These coefficients are described in Kelley, <u>op. cit.</u>, pp. 259-71.

[13]K. Pearson, "On the Criterion that a Given System of Deviations from
the Probable in the Case of a Correlated System of Variables Is Such that It Can
Be Reasonably Supposed To Have Arisen from Random Sampling," <u>Philosophical Maga-
zine</u>, L, Ser. V (London, 1900), 157-75, and "On the Probability that Two Independent Distributions of Frequency Are Really Samples from the Same Population,"
<u>Biometrika</u>, VIII (1911), 250-54; R. A. Fisher, <u>Statistical Methods for Research
Workers</u> (7th ed.; Edinburgh: Oliver & Boyd, 1938), pp. 81-85.

distribution is that the coefficients may be understood as an approximation to the values obtained from product-moment correlation.
Therefore, the use of Pearson tetrachoric and bi-serial methods af-
fords not only the meaning of a "coefficient of association" but
gains the additional advantage of a fair likelihood that the coefficients may approximate the values of the universalized product-
moment correlation.

Yule's Q and ω coefficients have been vigorously criticized
by Heron and by Pearson and Heron[14] on the grounds not only of
their incomparability with the standard product-moment coefficient
but also of their greater instability under changes in the point
of dichotomization.

A fourfold mean-square-contingency coefficient, C, has several disadvantages: (1) its values do not approximate product-
moment correlation except under special circumstances; (2) its
values are without sign, i.e., they measure merely the divergence
of a given fourfold table from one which would occur in the complete absence of interdependence or association between the two
traits under discussion and cannot indicate whether the inferen-
tial relation or association is "positive" or "negative"; and
(3) the maximum value obtainable by a contingency calculation on
a 2 x 2-fold table according to Yule and Kendall[15] is .707, so that
very high correlations cannot be adequately measured by a fourfold
C.

The methods of expressing the amount of correlation—or,
more precisely, non-independence—between traits in terms of probability indices, such as P (the probability that a distribution as
divergent as the obtained one, or more so, could have occurred
purely from random sampling in actually uncorrelated material),
and the more conventionalized "critical ratio" (the ratio of a difference between percentages to the standard error of that difference) are faultless enough from the standpoint of sheer statistical
logic. But, from the standpoint of simple interpretation or understanding, these probability indices possess marked disadvantages

---

[14] D. Heron, "The Danger of Certain Formulae Suggested as Substitutes
for the Correlation Coefficient," Biometrika, VIII (1911), 109-22; K. Pearson
and D. Heron, "On Theories of Association," Biometrika, IX (1913), 159-315.

[15] Op. cit., pp. 68-69.

in comparison with correlation coefficients of the product-moment
family, such as Pearson's bi-serial r and tetrachoric r. The latter coefficients may take values ranging from zero to $\pm$ 1.00, while
probability indices may take values ranging from zero to infinity.
Because of their compact range of values, the meaning of individual
correlation coefficients becomes appreciable upon the briefest experience with them.

A more important drawback of a probability index is that
it is a function not only of the underlying differences in the
traits of the two groups but also of the number of cases upon which
it is computed.[16]   In fact, if a true trait-difference exists at
all between two groups, whatever its amount, the index may be sys-
tematically raised to infinity by the simple expedient of increasing the number of cases. In actual practice, then, the probability
index or "critical ratio" often becomes more a measure of the number of cases involved than a measure of the true underlying trait-
difference. For this reason, such an index must be interpreted
only with reference to the number of cases upon which it is based.
Therefore, such indices cannot be used in comparisons unless the
experimental populations are of uniform size. For example, in the
present volume it would have been impossible, by the probability
methods, to make comparisons between the boys' and the girls' correlations, since their populations were 2,113 and 1,181, respectively. The chief utility of these probability methods lies in
establishing the degree of assurance that a difference actually
exists.

Correlation coefficients, on the other hand, are not func-
tionally related in any meaningful extent to the number of cases
upon which they are computed beyond the conventionalized minimum
of 20 or 30 cases[17] but measure purely the underlying correlation.
This does not mean, of course, that the use of correlation coefficients evades entirely the implications of probability, "the

_____

[16] Fisher, op. cit., pp. 94-95.

[17] Even on smaller samples the systematic distortion in the central or
expected values of product-moment coefficients is for most practical purposes
negligible. See H. E. Soper et al., "On the Distribution of the Correlation Coefficient in Small Samples," Appen. II to the papers of "Student" and R. A.
Fisher, in Biometrika, XI (1917), 328-413, esp. Table A.

fundamental problem of practical statistics,"[18] since they, like
all other measures of trend or relationship based upon samplings
of variate material, must be interpreted with some regard to their
accompanying probable errors. But the correlation coefficient
coupled with its probable error forms a compact quantitative expression which varies only within somewhat narrow limits with increase in the number of cases. The fact of this comparative stability of bi-serial and tetrachoric r under varying conditions of
mere sampling constitutes an important advantage of these coefficients over the use of probability indices.

Although the tetrachoric coefficient has been in use among
the English biometricians since 1900 and is described fully in most
of the advanced statistics textbooks, it is only in recent years
that more than a limited use has been made of this method of treating categorical data among other workers in the social sciences.

---

[18] K. Pearson, "The Fundamental Problem of Practical Statistics," Biometrika, XIII (1920), 1-16.

CHAPTER IV

THE VALUE OF CASE-RECORD NOTATIONS AS RESEARCH DATA

The preceding chapter described the statistical methods
employed in this study and attempted to point out to what extent
they conform to the requirements of our case-record data. In this
chapter it is desirable to turn to a discussion of this case material from another standpoint, namely, its validity.[1]

In dealing scientifically with the gross patterns of individual human behavior, the problem of validity is a more critical
matter than in the physical and biological sciences. For in the
latter sciences many of the most important basic concepts can be
clarified once for all by the simple expedient of an arbitrary definition of terms or units of measurement, and the validity or meaning of such terms is automatically established. In human behavior,
on the other hand, workers cannot so readily resort to arbitrary
definition to clarify concepts. Overt behavior manifestations are
a matter of familiar knowledge, however superficial, to the lay-
man and have already acquired firmly established popular names.
The social scientist, therefore, has not the same opportunity to
define once for all the phenomena with which he works but must frequently conform to this established usage of terms, however ambiguous or misleading it may be. While the question of validity involves more than an agreement on the definition of terms, concepts,
or units of measurement, the fact remains that much of the problem
of validity, as it is encountered in actual researches, would dis-
appear if a universalized system of concepts were available.

The evaluation of case-record notations as research data
raises the following points of validity, which will be discussed
at some length in subsequent pages: the selective factors influencing the admission of children to clinic examination; the

---

[1] A critical discussion of our use of case-record data is given in a
review of Vol. I by Ruth E. Arrington, Journal of Criminal Law and Criminology,
XXIII (1932), 515-16.

reliability and objectivity of this sort of data, as psychometricians use these terms; the prejudicial effect upon correlation coefficients arising from prevalent beliefs or biases on the part of
informants or examiners; differential completeness of the case-
record information; inadequate defining of terms and ambiguous and
overlapping grouping of notations; the use of categorical trait
names instead of measured variates; and the inadequate representation in most case-record data of the desirable or indifferent
traits, as distinguished from undesirable traits, i.e., the under-
representation of "assets" in the child's behavior makeup and the
overrepresentation of "liabilities."

The Selective Factors Influencing the Admission of Children to Clinic Examination

A glance at Figures 1 and 2 (chap. ii) indicates that our
cases at the outset form a selected group on the basis of age and
intelligence level. The age distributions in our material do not
show an even distribution of cases at each age level, as one would
expect among unselected children of this age range, but show increasing frequencies from 6 years up to about 13 or 14 years and
decreasing frequencies beyond these levels through the seventeenth
year. In our correlational results, chronological age has been
"partialed out," but because of the frequent curvilinearity of regression of behavior problem on chronological age (Vol. I, Part
III) the selective influence of age is probably not adequately
cared for by the simple expedient of partial correlation.

The average intelligence quotient of our cases falls in
the eighties. The exact average IQ of unselected children of these
ages is still a matter of controversy, but in any event one can be
sure that the cases of this study include a disproportionate number of children of below-average intelligence. A further selection
enters through the fact that children with IQ's below 50 were arbitrarily excluded from the present study (see p. 9)—a factor which
is probably of little import to our present problem.

In all probability there has also been a marked selection
on the basis of cultural and economic status. These factors ranged
from very low to very high among our cases but in the main would
be considered well below average. The major portion were born in
the Chicago metropolitan area. Over half of the parents were

foreign born, the largest foreign-born groups coming from "Russia,"
Poland, Italy, Germany, Austria, Hungary, and Rumania.

Probably the most serious selective factor, in the estimation of most readers, arises from the overweighting of cases manifesting marked personality and conduct difficulties.

There were enough children referred for other reasons than
behavior difficulties, however, to prevent our material from being
entirely homogeneous—for example, children referred because of
difficulty in school studies or for vocational guidance or for advice regarding foster-home placement. But in general the divergence between our material and a group of ideally unselected children is probably sufficient to alter significantly the values of
our correlation coefficients from what would have been obtained
upon unselected material if it had been available.

A mitigating circumstance, however, lies in the fact that
the selection on the basis of severity of behavior problems is
probably a regular one and not an erratic one. The frequency distributions of behavior difficulties (Figs. 3 and 4) are generally
regular and continuous. Therefore, one may hope that our correlation coefficients based upon this selected material may bear enough
resemblance to the true state of affairs to suggest trends which
may at some time be ascertained more precisely upon more representative material. Inasmuch as the effect of selection in our data
appears to be a more or less regular "restriction of range," the
expected result is a diminution in the size of the obtained correlation coefficients. The effect of selective factors alone, then,
in contrast to some other influences to be described later, is an
understatement rather than an overstatement of the true prevailing
trends.

The problem of avoiding selective influences in the gathering of research data is one of the most difficult problems con-
fronting the worker in the social sciences. When the material involves intimate facts in the behavior of people and their children,
no mere matter of diligence, perseverance, or sincerity on the part
of the worker will induce most persons to tell openly of such "family skeletons" as police records, psychoses, pauperism, illegitimate pregnancies, and the like, even under the confidential conditions of a psychiatric clinic. It is entirely possible that at
some future time people will take a more objective attitude toward

undesirable or unsanctioned behavior among members of their families, but for the present the researcher who desires to study the
more intimate and confidential facts of human behavior must content himself with material obtainable from informants who are willing to offer this information in return for the assistance which
child guidance and mental-hygiene clinics can give them in their
own problems.   The task before the researcher, then, is to elicit
information of more general applicability from material admittedly
subject to selective influences.   From such data, trends may be
discernible which may be substantiated from other sources.

The Unknown Factors of Reliability and Objectivity

"Reliability" and "objectivity" are used in this chapter
in the strict sense as used by psychometricians.   "Reliability" is
the correlation or agreement between the results of independent observations upon the same phenomena made by the same observer.   "Objectivity" is the correlation or agreement between the results of
observations upon the same phenomena by different observers.   The
fact that psychometricians have appropriated these words which are
in common use and have restricted them to a very specific statistical meaning has aroused considerable objection on the ground that
these words have already acquired in popular usage a much broader
connotation which commonly includes the idea of dependability,
trustworthiness, or truthfulness, to which psychometricians have
given the separate technical term, "validity."   The psychometri-
cian's use of the concepts "reliability" and "objectivity" concern
strictly only the consistency of different takings of the measures
and not their truthfulness.   In deference to this objection against
the terms, and as a collective term to include the ideas both of
reliability and of objectivity, we shall employ the word "consistency" in this discussion to refer jointly to both ideas.

The well-made research based upon variate and "fallible"
data should include the formal presentation of reliability or objectivity coefficients.[2]   These serve at least three essential purposes.

---

[2] A valuable discussion of this point is given by T. L. Kelley, "The Reliability of Test Scores," Journal of Educational Research, III (1921), 370-79.

1. In the case of an obtained zero-relationship between two variates, the researcher cannot know whether the underlying correlation is actually negligible, regardless of the adequacy with which the two variates in question have been measured or, on the other hand, whether the present measurement of the two variates was so faulty that they could not yield any outside correlations of significant size, even though actually the two variates are substantially correlated.

2. In case a consistency correlation is found to be zero, the researcher may either drop the given variate from further consideration or improve its method of measurement until its consistency is large enough to "support" outside correlations.

3. Knowing both the correlation between two variates and the consistency correlations of each variate, the researcher may infer the <u>theoretical maximum correlation</u> which would be obtained if the two variates were perfectly measured, i.e., the so-called "correction for attenuation"[3] or, similarly, the theoretical correlation which would be obtained under given degrees of improvement in the consistency of measurement of the two variates.

It has become evident to the reader that the attitude taken in this discussion toward reliability and objectivity is that these are very definite mathematical indices, to be computed in very specific ways, and not mere impressionistic and categorical expressions. The assertion that a certain datum is reliable or not reliable, or objective or not objective, is next to meaningless. What we wish to know, rather, is whether its reliability or objectivity coefficient is as high as .90, or only .50, or as low as .30. Having this information, we are enabled to conclude whether the research data in a given instance are suitable for the purpose in view. While the use of these consistency correlations fits most conveniently into a straightforward coefficiential correlation methodology, it must be remembered that the same factors of reliability and objectivity function just as importantly in other types of correlational research, whether by group differences, probability indices, or graphical representation in curves and the like.

---

[3]C. Spearman, "Demonstration of Formula for the True Measurement of Correlation," <u>American Journal of Psychology</u>, XVIII (1907), 161-69, and "The Coefficient of Correlation Calculated from Faulty Data," <u>British Journal of Psychology</u>, III (1910), 271-95.

In the material of this study, which is composed almost entirely of subjective notations made by parents and examining staff, the lack of consistency correlations is painfully conspicuous. From our case material there appeared to be no feasible method of obtaining these correlations. Ordinarily, there was only one person who served as the source of information. In the home and developmental history of the child it was possible occasionally to obtain interviews from both parents of the child. A cursory comparison of such paired interviews, one from each parent, disclosed that in the great majority of instances the two parents agreed substantially in their accounts of the child's behavior. There were a few instances, however, in which the parents gave contradictory information on the same items. The amount of agreement or disagreement between the two parents, however, cannot be taken as an adequate measure of the objectivity of these case notations, since in most instances they have probably been considerably influenced by each other in their attitude toward the child's behavior, so that their statements really represent a joint belief or consensus of opinion. To ascertain the amount of agreement between the mother and some informant outside of the family would not obviate this difficulty. Since the largest part of our data concerns the child's behavior in the home and neighborhood, other informants are not likely to possess much knowledge beyond that which the child's parents have given them, so that these two sources of information would not be ideally independent sources. In short, there seemed to be no satisfactory source of parallel information to employ as a measure of the objectivity of the mother's statements.

The other principal source of our data was the case notations of the examining staff. It would not be impossible to make a fairly adequate study of the objectivity of this type of data. The difficulties, however, would be large: (1) the expense of providing parallel staff members, (2) the tendency of members of the same clinic to conform to certain schools of thought or modes of practice, and (3) the fact that the child-guidance field is still so largely uncharted and systems of interpretation of human behavior still in such a state of flux that studies of subjective case notations made at this stage may within a few years become obsolescent.

The study by Willard C. Olson presents encouraging evidence as to the reliability and objectivity of categorial and semi-

categorical case notations. He employed a cross-on-a-line rating
scale modified by the inclusion of five landmarks in each trait,
each rating being weighted according to a previously derived criterion of relative importance or seriousness. Thirty-five behavior
traits were separately rated on 182 school children in Grades I-IV.
Repeated ratings were obtained from their teachers. The reliability or consistency correlations for the 35 separate traits ranged
from .33 to .81. The intellectual traits were rated most reliably
(average r = .69), followed by social traits (average r = .61),
then the physical traits (average r = .55) and, least reliably,
the emotional traits (average r = .51).

> Traits with readily observable trait actions were rated
> most reliably. Thus for the trait, "Is he slovenly or neat in
> personal appearance?" (r = .81.) Similarly for the trait, "Is
> he quiet or talkative?" (r = .80.) On the other hand, traits
> that called for more elusive interpretations of behavior were
> rated less reliably. "Does he lack nerve, or is he coura-
> geous?" (r = .33) and "Does he give in or does he assert him-
> self?" (r = .37) are examples of traits with low reliability.[4]

These reliability coefficients are not so high as one could wish
but are in the main high enough to justify their use in correlational studies. While they were obtained under conditions quite
different from those of our study, there is no reason to suppose
that the consistency of our case notations, if it were obtainable,
would be found to be greatly different.

The many ways in which the subjectivity factor may show
itself in our case notations scarcely need describing. The informants, usually the child's mother, vary all the way from those pos-
sessing a good knowledge and understanding of their children's behavior and adequate language to express themselves down to mothers
unaware of the true state of affairs and with poor powers of dis-
cernment and interpretation. Parents differ also in their standards of noting a behavior item as important. An overanxious mother
will probably remark many more behavior problems in her children
than a more easygoing or less protective mother. Therefore, we
cannot assume that the line of demarcation between such traits as
overinterest in the opposite sex and a merely normal sex interest

---

[4]Problem Tendencies in Children: A Method for Their Measurement and
Description (Minneapolis: University of Minnesota Press, 1930), pp. 25-32 and
Table XXVI.

is uniform for each child in our series. A quarrelsome or scold-
ing mother may by her actions engender or enhance behavior traits
in her children, which under more skilful parentcraft might not
have emerged to the same conspicuous degree. Thus the notations
concerning a child's behavior really measure not only the child's
intrinsic personality and conduct but also the attitude or behavior
of other persons toward him. In short, the effect of the subjectivity factor on the part of informants is to bring about a lack
of uniformity in the conditions under which the data are gathered.

Three other problems arise in connection with the subjectivity factor: (1) prejudicial attitudes or beliefs on the part
of the informant or the examining staff, (2) the varying completeness of the case material, and (3) inadequate defining or grouping
of terms by the indexers. These are important and distinctive
enough to warrant separate discussion in later pages.

There are two elements in the situation, however, which
tend to counteract to some extent the lack of uniformity occurring
through variability among the informants. One is the fact that
the interviews are conducted by experienced psychiatric social
workers or by students in training under their supervision. Their
aim is to elicit as far as possible the truth underlying the informant's statements. The other is the fact that the members of
the examining staff are obliged to come to some conclusion and
make recommendations concerning the child's future care. For that
reason the case record is not considered complete until the staff
is satisfied that adequate information covering the child's social,
mental, emotional, and physical status has been obtained. There
arises the danger that an interviewer, if markedly domineering or
biased, may inject an additional element of subjectivity into this
sort of data. It seems more probable, however, in view of the uncertain quality of most informants, that case information obtained
and recorded by a trained interviewer, such as a psychiatric social
worker, will lie closer to the truth than data based upon the un-
checked statement of the child's parents.

A further factor in the reliability and objectivity of our
case notations concerns the items about which the informant or
staff member is uncertain. For example, if the mother suspects
that the child steals but has had no convincing evidence, should
the child be placed among the "stealing noted" group or among the

"stealing not noted" group, or should he be placed in a separate
"question of stealing" group? It was possible to make an empirical test of the matter. For some of the more frequently noted
traits, such as <u>stealing</u>, <u>stubbornness</u>, <u>sex delinquency (coitus</u>),
or <u>psychoneurotic trends</u>, subclassifications were made for "<u>ques-
tion of</u>" and occasionally for "<u>episode of</u>." Parallel bi-serial
and tetrachoric correlation coefficients and also incidence curves
were computed with the "<u>question of</u>" cases placed first on one side
of the dichotomy and then on the other side. It was quickly found
that the coefficients and curves obtained from pooling the questioned and episodical cases with the "noted at present" group usually showed a slightly higher correlation than by considering them
in the "not noted" side of the dichotomization. This fact was
taken as an indication in favor of including them in the "noted as
present" group. The diminishing of the size of the correlations
consequent upon the other system of grouping was interpreted as
due to a neutralizing effect upon the underlying correlation, which
would result if a case were placed on the wrong side of the dichotomization.

A further source of attenuation in the obtained correlations arises from the fact that the "not noted" category includes
both the cases in which the trait was absent (or present only to
an inconsiderable degree) and cases in which the item was unknown
or unrecorded. In the specific list of traits discussed in this
volume,[5] however, this element of uncertainty is probably not of
great importance, since these more frequently appearing traits
were fairly diligently inquired into at the time the case information was obtained. Furthermore, in the present research the aim
is exploratory and only marked relationships are sought for. Therefore, any trends which are so tenuous as to be blurred seriously by
these crudities of measurement are too slight to be given attention
in this study. In a more conclusive <u>ad hoc</u> investigation of some
specific question or hypothesis such a tolerant attitude toward im-
perfections in one's data would be quite undesirable and inexcus-
able. In anything approaching a refined study based upon case-
record notations it would be necessary to distinguish rigidly between "unknown" and "negative" items.

_____

[5]Chap. v.

The effect of a lack of reliability or objectivity in the measures, as described in the preceding paragraphs is an "attenuation,"[6] or constant tendency toward reduction in the size of correlation coefficients based upon such data. The error arising from this factor alone (in contrast with the effect of certain factors to be discussed in subsequent pages) is fortunately one of understatement, rather than of overstatement, of existing trends.

While there is no entirely satisfactory substitute for consistency correlations as obtained from a routine calculation upon repeated measures, there exists, however, an indirect indicator of the presence of reliability or objectivity which has some degree of utility in actual research situations. If r_{ab} represents the correlation between traits $\underline{A}$ and $\underline{B}$, and if $r_{a_1a_2}$ and $r_{b_1b_2}$ represent the consistency correlations of the two traits, Kelley[7] has shown that the maximum correlation of r_{ab} cannot, except as a matter of chance, exceed $\sqrt{r_{a_1a_2} \times r_{b_1b_2}}$. If any trait, then, manifests a tendency toward substantial correlation with other traits, it is highly probable that the trait in question possesses a workable amount of reliability and objectivity, for, if either consistency correlation under the radical were zero, the intercorrelation between these two traits could not be expected to attain a significant size unless some fortuitous combination of subtle factors were present.

While the fact of substantial outside correlations argues in favor of the consistency or stability of the data, the fact of zero outside correlations does not necessarily mean that the reliability or objectivity of the data is low. In the latter case the meaning is indeterminate. A zero outside correlation may also mean simply that the two traits are actually uncorrelated, regardless of the adequacy of their measurement. Because of this uncertainty of meaning, little interpretation is made in this volume concerning low and zero correlation coefficients. In view, furthermore, of the large probable errors attaching to these tetrachoric and biserial coefficients, we have arbitrarily chosen .20 as the lower

---

[6] C. Spearman, "The Proof and Measurement of Association between Two Things," American Journal of Psychology, XV (1904), 72-101.

[7] Loc. cit.

limit of significance. Coefficients below this size are presented
with little comment or interpretation.

Prejudicial Trends in the Data

        While the effect of the factors of selection and instabil-
ity of measurement on correlations is in general to reduce their
magnitude toward zero, as we have pointed out in the preceding two
sections, the effect of the two factors to be described in the next
two sections—the factor of prejudices or biases in the data and
the factor of varying completeness in the case information—is usually an increase in the size of obtained correlations or, in the
case of negative correlations, a swing toward zero or toward the
positive direction. Both of these problems arise from the subjectivity in the source of information based, as it is, so largely
upon the personal beliefs or opinions of parents and examiners.

        If there is a widespread belief among parents or staff
members that two traits are associated or that one trait is a cause
of another, this prejudicial influence may enlarge an obtained cor-
relative coefficient between case-record notations of the two
traits. For example, we note the relatively substantial correlations between enuresis and masturbation of .24 and .19 among boys
and girls, respectively (see Table 97). Now it is entirely possible that these two traits are intrinsically correlated, but the
possibility also exists that these coefficients also comprise a
prejudicial effect arising from the fact that many parents believe,
whether correctly or not, that masturbation actually causes bed-
wetting, so that such parents of an enuretic child may search more
diligently for evidences of masturbation, and, in view of its all-
but-universal prevalence among children, are more likely to obtain
these evidences than in the case of children whose parents have no
special reason to suspect masturbation.

        Such prejudicial or biased factors probably exist through-
out our data. As a further example, one may be suspicious of our
high correlations of bad companions (Table 82) with police arrest
and the more conspicuous conduct problems, such as stealing, truancy from home, or heterosexual sex misconduct among girls. While
clinical studies have indicated certainly that bad companions is an
important causal factor in misbehavior, it is also probable that

our obtained coefficients have been somewhat enlarged by the additional bias arising from the well-known fact that parents tend to
blame other people's children for leading their own children into
trouble.

A further example will show how this prejudicial factor
may enter into data obtained from the clinical examination. In
our question of encephalitis, less than half of the cases were definitely so diagnosed, while the majority of cases were "questioned,"
i.e., the medical history or neurological signs alone were insuffi-
cient to establish the diagnosis. In such instances, then, the examining psychiatrist often makes a tentative diagnosis on the basis
of the behavior manifestations themselves. Therefore, in our correlations of question of encephalitis (Table 117) with the very behavior traits commonly thought to arise as a result of this neuro-
pathology, such as question of change of personality, emotional
instability, "nervous," or temper, it is probable that the coefficients have been enlarged or influenced toward the direction of
positiveness because of this prejudicial factor.

Let us turn to another defect in typical case-record notations, which tends to enlarge our coefficients or to influence
their magnitude unduly toward the positive direction.

Differential Completeness of the Case-Record Information

While the recorders of the case-record information have
made all reasonable effort to obtain information which would be
adequate for the clinical treatment of our cases, one cannot assume that the extent of this information is uniform for all the
3,294 children of this study. Some parents are better acquainted
with their children's activities than others and consequently possess more information to give to the recorders. Some parents have
stricter standards of what constitutes undesirable behavior and
are therefore prone to enumerate a longer inventory of personality
and conduct problems than are parents with a more liberal and easygoing attitude toward their children's behavior. Of similar effect
is the great variation among parents themselves in their actual
treatment of their children. It is a matter of frequent observation that some parents actually evoke undesirable behavior reactions

in their children through unwise management, so that in such instances the child's behavior becomes largely an index of his parent's attitude and conduct. Furthermore, varying facility in the
use of language may work against uniformity in the amount of case
data obtained, e.g., a stupid or uneducated informant or an immi-
grant parent unproficient in the American language or a parent who
is naturally bashful or taciturn, in contrast with university-bred
mothers with active interest in child study.

For the sake of completeness, we might mention another possible source of nonuniformity in extent of case data, namely, varying willingness of the informants to co-operate in the giving of
case information. This factor is probably not very serious in our
material. Usually the parents have themselves been eager to obtain
whatever aid the Institute can offer, since the home has been the
party most affected. In any instances in which the parents were
not frank with the staff, the case was usually discontinued before
completion and consequently does not appear in this study.

As a counteracting influence, the history-taker, ordinarily
a graduate psychiatric social worker or an apprentice working under
her supervision—a person specially trained in the technique of interviewing—aims to elicit the essential facts concerning the
child's life-history. She is an active getter of information and
not a mere passive recorder. An outline is followed in the interview which covers the personality and conduct items commonly
thought to be important in the explanation of the child's behavior.[8]
Among the 162 specific behavior and non-behavior items considered
in this volume practically all are expressly called for in this
history outline or else are clinical concepts which the examiners
are very likely to investigate. For that reason it seems probable
to the writer that the correlations covered in the present volume
are not seriously distorted by the prejudicial or dilating effect
of variability in the extent of data-recording. A comparison of the
cases in which extensive social-service care was given with the
cases in which only a routine examination was made showed that
among the frequently appearing traits which are included in the
present study most of the entries were made at the first visit.

---

[8] M. S. Mink and H. M. Adler, "A Suggested Outline for History-taking
in Cases of Behavior Disorders in Children," Welfare Magazine, XVII (1926), 5-22.

New data elicited usually concerned such less frequently appearing trait notations as inability to get along with other children, self-indulgent attitude, overdependence on mother, lack of shame or concern over misdeeds, gluttony or overeating, cheating on school work and the like, which are not discussed in this volume. The personality-total and the conduct-total, i.e., the unweighted summation of the total number of personality and conduct problems reported for each child, are the only items in the present volume which would be seriously affected in respect to their correlation coefficients.

Let us illustrate the statistical mechanism by which the factor of varying fulness in the case-record information may magnify correlation coefficients artificially. Among the traits discussed in this study, seclusiveness is a more recondite and subjective entity than, for example, truancy from home or finicky food habits. The parent, then, who is discerning enough to mention seclusiveness is also more likely to be acute enough to note such other traits as daydreaming, sensitiveness, depressed spells, and the like, if they are present. On the other hand, a parent who is unable to think about behavior in fine terms would tend to omit any statement about either seclusiveness or sensitiveness, even if both traits are present in a child. In the one instance, therefore, a child may be noted as both seclusive and sensitive, while a hypothetical duplicate of that child may in the other instance receive neither notation. In a tetrachoric table made up of a group of such cases, therefore, too many individuals tend to be diverted into both the "noted-noted" cell and the "unnoted-unnoted" cell and too few into the other two cells. The effect on the correlation coefficient of this distortion in the fourfold table is an unwarranted thrust toward the positive direction, i.e., positive coefficients become artificially enlarged and negative coefficients become reduced toward zero.

The correlation coefficients in this volume will not be equally influenced by this factor. Some of the traits are relatively objective and observable, while others are of a more secretive or interpretive nature. It is probable that the correlation coefficients involving our personality-total and conduct-total were the most seriously influenced. While the items going to make up these totals were for the most part those which have been most

diligently inquired into by the history-taker and the clinic examiners, a substantial fraction were rarely appearing items which
would be given by unusually well-informed or talkative informants.

There is, of course, no direct evidence that this factor
of varying completeness of the case-record information was operative in our material. On the other hand, however, it seems significant to the writer that there are too many positive correlation coefficients, and too few negative ones.

Inadequate Defining and Ambiguous Grouping of Terms

A prime need is a terminology of trait names which are objectively definable, elementary, and, where possible, exclusive.
Such an attainment seems to be next to hopeless.[9] In this study
it was necessary to make a more or less arbitrary grouping of the
descriptive terms as found in the case records. The actual statements by the informants include thousands of terms, many of which
may be considered as redundant and synonymous. In indexing these
many trait names an attempt was made to fix upon a system of nomen-
clature which conformed as far as possible to current usage in the
literature and in the clinic routine.

The question arose at the outset as to the fineness or
coarseness of the grouping of terms. It is necessary, on the one
hand, to establish categories sufficiently fine so that the traits
included therein are reasonably homogeneous. On the other hand,
the categories should be broad enough to include all traits which
are really homogeneous entities, regardless of the variation in
terminology between different informants. In this research there
was also the practical consideration that one should fix categories
sufficiently broad, whenever permissible, to yield groups large
enough for adequate statistical treatment. (After all, an original
sample of 5,000 cases in this research has proved to be none too
large.) In our inventorying, the aim was to choose as fine a classification as possible, to err on the side of an overfineness of

---

[9]Some of the difficulties have been discussed in Vol. I, Part II, and
in the author's article, "On the Feasibility of Inventorying Children's Behavior
Traits," Journal of Juvenile Research, XVI (1932), 32-39.

grouping rather than an overcoarseness. And in the light of subsequent examination of our data, it is probable that our standard
of classification has attempted often to make impossibly fine dis-
tinctions, i.e., has attempted to place under separate rubrics many
items which scarcely represent actual differences in behavior.[10]
In some instances it seemed advisable to regroup some of the finer
categories into larger classifications.[11]

The distortion in the bi-serial and tetrachoric correlation
coefficients due to inaccurate defining of terms and to improper
grouping of traits is under some conditions an unwarranted diminution of their values and under other circumstances an undue enlarge-
ment.

Too fine a classification means that what is essentially
the same trait is incorrectly placed under two or more rubrics.
In a bi-serial or tetrachoric tabulation, then, we have the anom-
alous situation that the same sort of cases are placed on both
sides of the dichotomization. The effect will be to neutralize
the force of any true underlying correlation, with the result of
attenuation in the coefficient, i.e., a reduction toward zero.

If the categories are too coarse, i.e., if a given rubric
is not a homogeneous affair but actually covers two or more dissimilar traits,[12] the effect on the correlation coefficients may
be either an attenuation or a dilation   As an illustration, let
us suppose that a too coarse category A comprises two somewhat dissimilar traits a and b, that is, two traits whose intercorrelation
is not high. If trait a is substantially correlated with any outside trait X, while trait b is only negligibly correlated with
trait X, the effect of combining a and b into trait A is in general
a reduction in the correlation coefficient toward zero; i.e., when
one throws together two or more groups of somewhat dissimilar cases
into a composite and computes correlation coefficients on that composite, the usual result is a coefficient whose magnitude is

---

[10]Vol. I, Tables 1-13.   [11]Vol. I, Table 13.

[12]This problem has been discussed by Henry B. Elkind and Carl R. Doer-
ing, "The Application of Statistical Method to the Study of Mental Disease,"
American Journal of Psychiatry, VII (1928), 789-808, under the name of "mixed
or hidden classification," which they describe as "the inclusion of known and
unknown attributes in our classifications which are mixed in such proportions
that they influence the result in which we are interested."

intermediate to the coefficients which would be obtained by treating each component trait separately.

In a few instances, however, the effect of clubbing together two or more groups of cases may be to elicit a higher correlation from the composite than from any of its components. Such may be the outcome when both a and b are substantially correlated with the outside trait X but are intercorrelated either negligibly or negatively with each other.

An empirical estimate of the effect of finer and coarser categories in our data may be made by comparing the correlations for the larger classifications indicated as "grouped, etc.," in the tables discussed in Part III. For example, grouped: depressed, etc. (Table 13) is a composite of depressed (Table 11) and unhappy (Table 12); grouped: dull, slow, etc. (Table 41), comprises slow, dull (Table 38), listless (Table 39), and lack of initiative (Table 40); grouped: "nervous," etc. (Table 48), comprises "nervous" (Table 45), restless (Table 46), irritable (Table 47), and changeable moods (Table 35); grouped: disobedient, etc. (Table 66), comprises disobedient (Table 61), incorrigible (Table 62), defiant (Table 63), stubborn (Table 64), and contrary (Table 65); grouped: fighting, etc. (Table 73), comprises fighting (Table 69), quarrelsome (Table 70), violence (Table 71), and threatening violence (Table 72); grouped: temper, etc. (Table 78), comprises temper tantrums (Table 76), temper display (Table 77), and irritable (Table 47); and grouped: lack of interest in school, etc. (Table 93), comprises lack of interest in school (Table 91) and inattentive in school (Table 92). A comparison of the corresponding correlations in the "grouped" categories with those in the more specialized categories shows that the broader categories as a rule yield coefficients which are either intermediate in size or else slightly larger than those for the component categories. It seems probable to the writer from such a comparison that the classifications of behavior attempted in this study have been too fine rather than too coarse.

In deciding upon how restricted a classification one should employ in studies of this kind, it is probable that we must rely chiefly upon our subjective interpretation of the meanings of these trait names, in spite of our desire for refined objective methods of discrimination.

There are, however, two statistical devices which will assist one in making decisions in specific instance. One method
consists of comparing the correlation coefficients of each
trait against a large number of "outside" traits or conditions.
If the two traits are found to show important divergences in
their correlation with other traits, then this procedure establishes the fact with certainty that the two traits in question should be considered separate entities. On the other hand,
if the two traits show generally similar outside correlations,
this criterion is not in practice so serviceable. If we could
be sure that our outside traits or conditions included all the
important ones conceivable, then it would be possible to conclude that these two traits were for all practical purposes
identical. But the question will always arise whether any series has not failed to include certain other important traits
or facts which would have shown divergent correlations. Therefore, if the purpose is to eliminate a category on the ground
that it so closely resembles another accepted category, this
procedure does not by itself constitute a decisive criterion,
but it possesses some utility in reinforcing one's evidence obtained from other sources.

Some illustrations from our material will make this method
clear. We have set up two similar and overlapping rubrics,
temper tantrums and temper display. The question arises
whether these are different enough to justify separate treatment. Temper tantrums in their "classic" form involve such
bizarre behavior as banging one's head against a wall or floor,
biting one's own hands, or running around in circles, while in
temper display the behavior usually consists in an excessive
emotional discharge such as hitting or swearing, which bears
more directly upon the apparent purpose of the child. On the
other hand, it can be urged that both are expressions of the
same desire, i.e., to coerce others into yielding to the child's
wishes and that the overt differences which I have just mentioned are really superficial. To test this point, the correlations of the traits against a list of about 120 other
traits or conditions (mental, emotional, physical, educational,
familial, and social) were compared. (These coefficients were
chiefly Pearson's tetrachoric-r's with chronological age "partialed" out.) The product-moment correlation of these coefficients was .66 $\pm$ .03. Now this intercolumnar correlation is
so low in comparison with others in our material that it seems
safe to conclude that these two notations should be placed under separate categories.

Another example in our material will illustrate the less
decisive alternative. The question arose whether the two notations bad companions and running with a gang should be considered as separate categories. Running with a gang according
to our definition implies bad companions, the main difference
being that a gang involves some degree of organization or duration while bad companions may be a more sporadic and transient
affair. The intercolumnar correlation was found to be .81 $\pm$
.02. In this instance the evidence of such a computation suggests that the latter pair, bad companions and running with a
gang, are definitely more similar than the former pair, temper
tantrums and temper display. Whether this intercolumnar correlation of .81 is high enough to warrant one's grouping both
notations into one category is another question. If a brief

list is desired, the correlation may be considered sufficiently high to justify the elimination of a separate rubric, but in view of the persistent belief that the influence of youthful city gang associations tends to continue beyond the eighteen-year age limit of our group[13] it was concluded that important differences may exist which were not adequately represented in our series of 120 outside traits.

The other statistical device consists in comparing the out-side correlations for the traits taken separately with those for a coarser grouping comprising all the similar notations. If the coarser grouping should produce lower correlation coefficients than the more restricted notations considered separately, the coarser grouping should be avoided because such a result probably means that heterogeneous traits have been included in that coarser grouping. If, on the other hand, the coarser grouping yields generally larger correlation coefficients than the finer grouping, this evidence is to some extent in favor of the coarser grouping. This does not constitute a decisive criterion, however, since a compositing of traits in this manner may approximate the outcome of Yulean multiple correlation in which the addition of fresh variables tends to increase the multiple correlation coefficient and never to decrease it.

An example in our material will illustrate the procedure. Among the five categories <u>disobedience</u>, <u>defiant attitude</u>, <u>incorrigibility</u>, <u>contrariness</u>, and <u>stubbornness</u> the question arose whether there may be some redundancy. A broader grouping was set up to include all cases showing any one of these five traits, and a series of 117 outside correlations were computed. The broader grouping, in the main, yielded larger coefficients, as one might expect, but there were marked differences among the five traits. The specific notation <u>contrariness</u> (or negativism) gave thirty-three coefficients higher than those for the composite category out of a total of 117 coefficients and therefore should be considered as a separate category. <u>Incorrigibility</u> and <u>stubbornness</u> similarly gave twenty-six and twenty-five coefficients, respectively, higher than those for the composite category, and therefore should be retained as separate categories. <u>Disobedience</u> and <u>defiant attitude</u>, on the other hand, showed only seventeen coefficients each higher than those for the composite category, and therefore became candidates for elimination as far as this criterion is concerned. This analysis of this troublesome group of overlapping notations is, of course, very incomplete. An additional refinement would consist in repeating the process of compositing after eliminating the more obviously independent traits one by one. The possibility of applying some form of the Spearman common-factor techniques to this problem is also suggested.[14]

---

[13]F. M. Thrasher, <u>The Gang: A Study of 1,313 Gangs in Chicago</u> (Chicago: University of Chicago Press, 1927). Pp. xxi + 571.

[14]Quoted from the author's article, "On the Feasibility of Inventorying Children's Behavior Traits," <u>op. cit.</u>, pp. 32-39.

An <u>overlapping</u> in the meaning of trait names also presented
a difficulty in the original indexing of the case material and a
distortion in certain correlation coefficients. For example, we
have made separate categories for <u>depressed</u>, <u>discouraged attitude</u>,
<u>spells of depression or discouragement</u>, on the one hand, and <u>un-
happy or discontented attitude or appearance</u>, on the other. These
two traits are very similar and may often be used synonymously in
the original data. In cases in which both notations are applicable
both should be used. But often it is probable that an explicit
mention of the one by the informant tends to exclude mention of the
other apparently redundant trait name. Consequently, the tetrachoric tabulation concerning the correlation between two such overlapping trait notations will have too few entries in the "noted-
noted" cell, e.g., in the cell containing the children in whom both
"depressed" and "unhappy" should be entered, and as a consequence
the correlation coefficient shows too low a value. In Tables 6-130
there are many instances in which the correlations between similar
and probably overlapping trait names are too low to be credible:
the correlations between <u>depressed</u> and <u>unhappy</u> (Table 11 or Table
12) were .40 + .05 for boys and .33 + .08 for girls; those between
<u>seclusive</u> and <u>repressed</u> (Table 31 or Table 32) were .16 and .40 +
.07; those between <u>egocentric</u> and <u>selfish</u> (Table 51 or Table 52)
were .21 + .04 and .45 + .05; those between <u>disobedient</u> and <u>stub-
born</u> (Table 61 or Table 64) were .30 + .03 and .37 + .04; and those
between <u>lack of interest in school</u> and <u>inattentiveness in school</u>
(Table 91 or Table 92) were .06 and .28 + .06. The data for the
intercorrelation of <u>temper tantrums</u> and <u>temper display</u> (Table 76
or Table 77) appeared from inspection to be so unsatisfactory that
the coefficients were not reproduced here. The correlation coefficients between any two such overlapping trait notations as these
in our tables, therefore, are probably too low to be representative
of the true relationship existing between those traits.

In short, in such material as ours, we do not have unadul-
terated or simon-pure, objectively determined categories, so in any
series of correlation coefficients we are really obtaining some
sort of "team" or "sums-and-differences" correlations in which the
intercorrelations and weightings of the component elements are obscure. The effect, therefore, of inadequate defining and classifi-

cation of trait names upon our correlation coefficients may be in
some instances a deceptive diminution, in other instances a deceptive magnification, and in some instances—let us hope—a negligible influence.

The Use of Categorical Trait Names instead of
Measured Variates

The discussion of the bi-serial and tetrachoric methods of
correlation in chapter iii[15] has indicated the inferiority of categorical data in respect to correlational methodology. The next few
paragraphs will indicate how this deficiency obscures the interpretation of correlation coefficients based upon such dichotomized
data.

The ideal statistical material should be in measured and
continuous or graduated units, since such data permit drawing up
a scatter diagram in which one can observe in detail the statistical behavior of variates in whose correlation we are interested.
For example, we may wish to know such factors as normality of distribution, linearity of regression, kurtosis, scedasticity, and
whether there are any unusual concentrations or any lacunae in any
portions of the distribution. In a bi-serial tabulation one of the
traits is compressed into a "noted" and "not noted" dichotomization
and in a tetrachoric tabulation both variates are so compressed
that such refined information is not ascertainable.

The most complete and meaningful representation of the
correlation between two traits is the actual scatter diagram. The
product-moment coefficient is a secondary symbol to bring out in a
concise and comparative manner the amount of the relationship.
Since scatter diagrams are space-filling affairs, they are seldom
presented in publication, but the correlation coefficients are employed to represent in economical fashion the essence of the scatter diagram. While the product-moment coefficient is thus a substitute device, the bi-serial and tetrachoric coefficients become
in turn only a makeshift for the standard product-moment coefficient. The only justification for the use of such inadequate
methods of correlation in research is the lack of satisfactory

---

[15] Esp. pp. 14-19.

quantitative data permitting more complete and precise treatment, and the results obtained from such correlation methods should be regarded as only tentative and exploratory.

The obscurity in the form of correlations obtained from the use of categorical trait names instead of measured variates makes difficult the interpretation of certain apparently inconsistent correlations which will be noticed in Tables 6-130. These are among the correlations obtained from presumably "opposite" traits,[16] e.g., unpopular (Table 27) and popular (Table 28), oversuggestible (Table 42) and stubborn (Table 64), slovenly (Table 89) and clean (Table 90), and "leader" (Table 107) and "follower" (Table 108). Here we occasionally find that both members of a pair of "opposite" traits correlate positively and substantially with the same "outside" trait. For example, "leader" correlates .26 $\pm$ .04 with running with a gang among boys (Table 83), while "follower" correlates .21 $\pm$ .04 with the same notation. Now one explanation may lie in a possible curvilinearity of regression of running with a gang on the combined trait "leader-follower," i.e., boys who participate in gang activities tend to be either leaders or followers (since a gang must have some of each kind in order to maintain its organization), while boys who are neither leaders nor followers do not tend to become implicated in gang activities. Another possible explanation may be that these and other "opposites" are not really the opposite poles of a single underlying trait. It may be that the true antithesis of "leader" is not "follower," but "indifference," i.e., the incapacity or unwillingness either to lead or to follow. Thus it may be that the same individuals who under one situation are leaders may under other conditions take the role of follower, while the true "opposite" is represented by the child who neither leads nor follows.

Inadequate Representation of Desirable and Indifferent Traits in Case Data

The examination in typical children's behavior clinics tends to cover the undesirable or "ominous" personality and conduct

---

[16]See I, 134-35 and this volume, final paragraphs of chaps. xx, xxv, xlvi, and liii.

traits with considerable thoroughness. Much less attention is
given the desirable and presumably "indifferent" traits. This results in an under-representation of the "assets" in the child's
behavior makeup in comparison with the "liabilities."

Among the 96 behavior traits specially studied in this volume, 90 may be considered as unquestionably undesirable, while only
6 desirable or presumably indifferent traits (popular, clean, sex
denied entirely, "leader," "follower," and attractive manner) appeared to have been inquired into diligently enough to warrant inclusion in our study.

This inadequate representation of the desirable and indifferent traits cannot affect the individual correlation coefficients
presented in this study. But it precludes the possibility of interpreting a series of correlations of one trait with all the other
frequently noted traits selected for this study in any comprehensive manner. As they stand, the correlations present only one side
of the picture—the relation of certain traits to undesirable
traits. In an exploratory study such as the present one it would
have been very meaningful to have had in one series the correlations with all other traits of frequent occurrence, in order to
obtain a more comprehensive view of the significance of traits in
the light of their correlations with other traits.

                      Summary and Discussion

The points discussed in this chapter may be summarized as
follows:

1. The selective factors operative in the admission of
children to clinic examination tend in general toward a restriction
of range and therefore toward an attenuation in the correlation coefficients or a reduction toward zero.

2. The factors of unreliability and subjectivity, which are
undoubtedly very considerable in our material, tend likewise to reduce the correlations toward zero. Unfortunately, there appeared
to be no feasible method of obtaining a measure of these factors,
whereby one could estimate the theoretical correlation which would
be found to exist under conditions of perfect reliability or objectivity.

3. The effect of prejudicial or biased trends in the data,

i.e., the preconceived notions of the parents or staff examiners that certain traits either do or do not occur together, is usually to swing the correlation toward the positive direction. Positive correlations are thus enlarged, negative correlations are reduced, and low negative correlations may at times be distorted into low positive correlations.

4. The effect of variations in the completeness of the case-record information is likewise a swing toward the positive direction.

5. The effect of an inadequate defining or ambiguous grouping of terms upon correlations is usually an attenuation or reduction toward zero but under some circumstances may be an increase in the size of the correlation.

6. The use of categorical trait names instead of measured variates need not distort the value of the correlation coefficient if the distribution of the trait underlying the categorical notation approaches sufficiently to the normal or Gaussian. The serious defect in categorical notations is that the actual form of the distribution is so obscured that one is unable to ascertain its form.

7. The inadequate representation of desirable and presumably indifferent traits in our case data does not have any effect upon the individual correlation coefficients but precludes the possibility of obtaining a comprehensive view of the meaning of a trait in terms of its correlations with other traits.

We see, then, that in typical case-record data there are many uncontrolled factors, some of which magnify the obtained correlation coefficient, while others diminish it. These factors tend to neutralize to some extent the distorting effect each has upon the other. But one cannot estimate whether the net result still leaves the coefficient too high or too low. For that reason we are allowing a considerable margin of safety in our interpretation of the correlations in this volume by confining the discussion only to coefficients greater than .20. This does not imply that correlations below this size are without meaning. Many of the underlying relationships between traits which must be taken into consideration in the actual care of children presenting behavior difficulties are probably no larger than this. If the results of a research are intended to be applied in a practical manner in some

highly organized or collectivized society in which millions of
children would be affected, statistically significant coefficients
smaller than .20 would be of definite social importance. But since
we cannot be more sure of our data, it is better to jettison this
portion of our material and confine our attention to correlations
well above zero.

This chapter has been intended as a critique of clinical
case records as research material. Workers have long been aware
of their many inadequacies, and this chapter has attempted to ana-
lyze in greater detail the difficulties and to point out how they
function in actual studies.

The shortcomings of such data will be equally operative in
other research methodologies, it should be pointed out, and not
only in studies employing the method of Pearsonian correlation.
Such devices as group differences, contingency, the probability
methods, or graphical representation require fewer assumptions and
make less claim to refinement of procedure, but the same distorting influences are at work. The advantage of refined correlational
methods, even though the data are defective, is that the effect of
such deficiencies becomes more obvious.

It is unnecessary and injurious, however, to become so ob-
sessed with the presumptive defects of case data as to conclude
that they are valueless for research purposes. To the writer the
findings obtained from our material have enough plausibility to
reassure him that this sort of material has a large field of utility for research needs under the proper restrictions of interpretation. Greater use should be made of the case-record material
which accumulates rapidly in all behavior clinics. Such data do
not permit precise, unequivocal, controlled conditions comparable
to the classic researches in the older physical and biological
sciences. Researchers in the social sciences must necessarily employ to a lesser extent the adequately standardized and objective
data because at present few of the complex functions of gross human behavior have been reduced to satisfactory measurement. The
social scientist must be ready for the present to work with data
admittedly inadequate and must couch much of his interpretation in
terms of _trends_, _probabilities_, _multiple causal factors_, _correla-
tions_, and the like. The correlation coefficients presented in
this volume, then, must not be considered as final psychologic,

sociologic, or biometric constants but must be regarded as provisional, until future studies can be made under improved conditions of selection and improved methods of gathering and recording such data.

Any betterment in the technique of constructing case records will necessarily enhance research results obtained therefrom. Improvement may take place in two respects.

1. More complete and more verified information for case records will meet with the enthusiastic approval of research workers. But from the standpoint of clinic routine there are important limitations to the amount of effort and time which can be spent on each case: first, the available staff personnel in comparison with "case load" and, second, the amount of time which can be required of an informant. A behavior clinic supported from state or municipal funds or by "community chests" is expected to take care of all appropriate cases brought to it, and this demand for service often relegates the purely research aspects to a position of secondary importance. It is also desirable to complete the interview with a parent within one sitting or with as few subsequent sittings as possible. In clinics endowed for the specific purpose of research or for intensive work upon a relatively small number of cases the possibility of accumulating fuller case data is much greater. Actually there has been a tendency for case records to contain more and more material, owing to the fact that, as our knowledge of children's behavior has increased, we have realized more and more that the causal factors are numerous and complex.

The use of a formal printed schedule or questionnaire would automatically insure uniformity and a certain degree of completeness of information. But the objections are many. They are likely to take away the spontaneity and rapport of the interviewing process. They may tend to elicit superficial judgments as to the presence or absence of a trait. They may slur over any special items which are of particular importance in the individual case. They do not enable the interviewer to make adequate emphasis of conspicuous elements in the situation. They would be uneconomical of time in actual clinic practice, since large sections of such a universalized schedule would comprise items not applicable to the individual case. Probably the best use of a formal schedule is in a special study of a specific problem covering a restricted series of cases.

2. The second desideratum is an increase in measurement devices. These, however, accumulate slowly. Many worthy attempts have been made to derive home-rating and neighborhood-rating scales, scales for evaluating parental occupation, for evaluating the occupational capacities of children, and for measuring various personality traits. It seems probable to the writer that some of these have been developed well beyond the experimental stage and already deserve inclusion in the clinic routine. As a matter of fact, however, few of them have at the time of writing attained sufficient credence to place them there. In actual practice the preference still remains on the side of subjective estimates, whether rightly or wrongly.

CHAPTER V

THE BEHAVIOR TRAITS DISCUSSED IN THIS VOLUME

As a convenience in listing the items discussed in this
volume, a division of them may be made into three groups. In the
accompanying tables these items are listed, together with their
frequencies among 2,113 boys and 1,181 girls. For example (Table 1),
police arrest was noted in 457 cases among 2,113 boys and in 179
cases among 1,181 girls. The wording in which these are given is
a concise one intended to save space in the large number of subsequent tables. A more complete and exact description is given at
the head of each section in which are collected the coefficients
concerning a given trait or condition.

The 111 items in Table 1 were employed in correlations with
all items in Tables 1 and 3. These are chiefly the often noted
personality and conduct problems in our case data, together with
a few other traits or conditions. These coefficients will be found
on later pages in Parts II and III.

TABLE 1

TRAITS FOR WHICH CORRELATIONS WITH ALL TRAITS
IN TABLES 1 AND 3 WERE COMPUTED

	Frequencies	
	Boys	Girls
Personality-total......................	(2,113)	(1,181)
Conduct-total..........................	(2,113)	(1,181)
Police arrest..........................	457	179
Chronological age......................	(2,113)	(1,181)
Intelligence quotient..................	(2,113)	(1,181)
Depressed..............................	149	73
Unhappy................................	95	64
Grouped: depressed, etc...............	219	125
Crying spells..........................	473	297
Sensitive (general)....................	163	92
Sensitive over specific fact...........	322	156
Worry over specific fact...............	100	40
Grouped: sensitive or worrisome, etc...	490	255

TABLE 1—Continued

	Frequencies	
	Boys	Girls
Bashful...............................	316	218
Apprehensive..........................	322	149
Inferiority feelings..................	202	62
Mental conflict.......................	102	45
Psychoneurotic........................	87	64
"Spoiled child".......................	250	112
Complaining of bad treatment by other children...........................	121	....
Object of teasing.....................	312	91
Unpopular.............................	110	54
Popular...............................	138	76
Absent-minded.........................	134	62
Daydreaming...........................	195	94
Repressed.............................	138	45
Seclusive.............................	254	106
Queer.................................	118	67
Question of change of personality.......	123	65
Changeable moods......................	219	144
Emotional instability.................	104	85
Question of hypophrenia...............	454	283
Slow, dull...........................	541	285
Listless.............................	178	87
Lack of initiative...................	132	63
Grouped: dull, slow, etc.............	704	364
Oversuggestible......................	354	174
Distractible.........................	264	116
Preference for younger children........	164	78
Restless.............................	559	258
"Nervous"............................	344	197
Irritable............................	448	175
Grouped: "nervous," etc..............	987	488
Restless in sleep....................	324	146
Irregular sleep habits...............	123	64
Egocentric...........................	287	147
Selfish..............................	130	73
Grouped: egocentric, etc.............	405	211
Excuse-forming.......................	237	99
Conduct prognosis bad................	78	47
Stealing.............................	815	271
Truancy from home....................	503	189
Staying out late at night............	319	140
Truancy from school..................	675	143
Refusal to attend school.............	145	46
Disobedient..........................	459	207
Incorrigible.........................	501	212
Stubborn.............................	420	220
Contrary.............................	88	51
Defiant..............................	178	95
Grouped: disobedient, etc............	992	482
Lying................................	637	340

TABLE 1—Continued

	Frequencies	
	Boys	Girls
Fantastical lying	104	75
Fighting	291	89
Quarrelsome	292	186
Violence	281	87
Threatening violence	102	....
Grouped: fighting, etc	644	273
Destructive	227	55
Teasing other children	210	....
Temper tantrums	221	127
Temper display	250	93
Grouped: temper, etc	736	312
Swearing (general)	137	....
Grouped: swearing, etc	278	90
Smoking	190	....
Bad companions	370	132
Gang	219	....
Leading others into bad conduct	138	50
Loitering	174	61
Lazy	182	81
Inefficient in work, play, etc	106	75
Irresponsible	118	70
Slovenly	337	205
Clean	318	171
Lack of interest in school	279	107
Inattentive in school	223	81
Grouped: lack of interest in school, etc	467	172
Disturbing influence in school	348	89
Rude	320	180
Masturbation	559	154
Sex delinquency (coitus)	70	218
Sex denied entirely	142	47
Overinterest in sex matters	86	81
Overinterest in opposite sex	....	175
Victim of sex abuse	....	104
Enuresis	576	250
Nail-biting	300	246
Finicky food habits	236	105
Boastful, "show-off"	251	77
Bossy	112	86
"Leader"	152	78
"Follower"	202	103
Sullen	243	97
Sulky	112	68
Hatred or jealousy of sibling	95	58
Retardation in school	878	474
Poor work in school	632	319
Exclusion from school	204	71
Attractive manner	307	165
Stuttering	83	....

    The 36 items in Table 2 were employed only in correlations with personality-total, conduct-total, police arrest, chronological age, and intelligence quotient (Tables 6-10). They are similar in nature to the items in Table 1 but of less frequent occurrence, so that it was felt that extensive statistical analysis was not warranted.

TABLE 2

TRAITS FOR WHICH ONLY THE CORRELATIONS WITH
PERSONALITY-TOTAL, CONDUCT-TOTAL, POLICE
ARREST, CHRONOLOGICAL AGE, AND INTEL-
LIGENCE QUOTIENT WERE COMPUTED

	Frequencies	
	Boys	Girls
Dementia praecox	50	.....
Incipient psychosis	41	.....
Psychopathic personality	91	41
"Night terrors"	62	34
Talking to self without apparent reason	46	25
Lack of affection	50	.....
Tiring easily	69	38
"Sugar hunger"	72	.....
Resentful attitude	78	51
Failure to adjust in foster-home	50	50
Disturbing influence in home	78	48
Irregular employment record	72	39
Stealing an automobile	58	.....
Robbing a building, home, etc	70	.....
Truancy from institution	123	.....
Swearing at mother, teacher, etc	57	.....
Bad language	83	40
Obscene language	90	.....
Bullying	75	.....
Cruelty to younger children	71	.....
Cruelty to animals	53	.....
Fire-setting	44	.....
Sneaky	70	37
Gambling	51	.....
Begging	68	.....
Gluttony	81	35
Sex attack on opposite sex	60	.....
"Annoying" girls	69	.....
Mutual masturbation (same sex)	80	.....
Homosexual (same age)	73	.....
Passive pederasty	49	.....
Exhibitionism	46	.....
Bowel incontinence	50	19
Thumb-sucking	58	40
Illegitimate parentage	65	45
Immoral sister	53	60

The 14 items in Table 3 were employed only in correlations with the items in Table 1. The coefficients will be found in Tables 6-130. These consist in miscellaneous, frequently noted physical, educational, and familial conditions which would not be considered as behavior problems or difficulties. They scarcely belong logically with the other traits discussed in these pages but were included in this volume for comparative purposes.

TABLE 3

MISCELLANEOUS TRAITS OR CONDITIONS FOR WHICH
CORRELATIONS ONLY WITH THE ITEMS
OF TABLE 1 WERE COMPUTED

	Frequencies	
	Boys	Girls
Underweight..................................	349	193
Headaches....................................	118	86
Former convulsions...........................	155	54
Neurological defect..........................	191	120
Question of encephalitis.....................	70	37
Lues...	106	86
Speech defect................................	180	92
Vocational guidance..........................	238	169
Irregular attendance at school...............	162	102
Feeble-minded sibling........................	110	103
Brother in penal detention...................	137	103
Vicious home conditions......................	85	68
Immoral home conditions......................	107	101
Discord between parents......................	525	285

The 162 traits discussed in this volume were selected from the total number of traits listed in Volume I, Tables 1-13, on the basis of frequency of occurrence among our cases rather than because of any imputed special significance.

CHAPTER VI

THE EXPLORATORY AND THE AD HOC APPROACHES
IN RESEARCH

The choice of trait notations indicates the exploratory character of this study. On the basis of sampling, consisting of 5,000 cases, it was found that the 162 notations described in the preceding chapter occurred often enough to warrant a systematic correlational treatment. Only to a slight extent did any a priori considerations of intrinsic importance or interest enter into the selection of these 162 trait notations. If our sampling had consisted of 10,000 cases or 25,000 cases instead of 5,000, the number of behavior items studied would have been correspondingly larger.

The reader will note the absence of any specific hypothesis guiding this study, unless we consider the principle of multiple etiology itself to be a hypothesis, i.e., the principle that the causes of children's behavior problems are numerous and of varying degrees of potency from child to child and in the mass (see pp. 3-4). In planning this research the writer has sought to avoid the espousing of any special theories concerning either interrelations or causality, though there would be no lack of excellent theories to choose from if it were so desired. It was felt that the conditions peculiar to this research, i.e., an extensive provision of card-sorting and calculating machinery and clerical assistance at the outset of the work enabled one to plan on a comprehensive factual investigation into many possible components of behavior traits rather than to set up an intensive examination of any specific question which one might set. To have adopted some definite "working hypothesis" would have restricted unnecessarily the scope of the inquiry, in addition to exposing one to the ever present danger that such a priori attitudes may interfere with an impartial and unprejudiced appreciation of the actual facts present in the data.

Another practical reason for adopting an empirical and

exploratory approach in this inquiry is that the major part of the
case data had already been gathered and little additional information concerning our children could be obtained except with considerable inconvenience and expense. While the original case material
has attempted to be fairly complete, often comprising over a hundred typed pages of information concerning a case, the items covered usually varied from child to child according to the individual
requirements for diagnosis and recommendations. For that reason
seldom were the data sufficiently uniform or complete over a large
series of cases to afford the opportunity of framing a precise crucial research concerning a specific relationship.

In the research designed for an intensive or conclusive
study of a clear-cut theorem, on the other hand, the worker usually
desires to gather his data ad hoc, i.e., for the special purposes
of his problem. He typically formulates a working hypothesis and
then seeks only the data which presumably are pertinent to that
hypothesis and ignores any data which appear irrelevant. This distinction between the two modes of research, which may be designated
as the ad hoc approach and the exploratory or empirical approach,
is briefly stated by Wilder D. Bancroft:

> The first of the two general methods of research is that
> in which one first gets one's working hypothesis and then ac-
> cumulates data to test it. The second general method is that
> in which one accumulates data until the general theory under-
> lying them becomes obvious.[1]

The slogan of the former is "First get your working hypotheses,"
he says, the plural being used advisedly because it is always better to have several working hypotheses if possible. The slogan of
the latter is "First get your facts."

The ad hoc study is especially appropriate in the more ma-
ture fields of science, as in the physical and medical sciences,
where there already exists an abundance of well-established knowledge and where there are many ramifications in which the "next
step" to be taken is obvious. The desideratum here is a final and
unequivocal answer to some well-defined query.

In an ad hoc study the hypothesis varies in specificity.
In some instances the researcher may have a "hunch" or supposition
that a certain relationship exists. This may at times come a priori

[1] "The Methods of Research," Rice Institute Pamphlet, XV (1928), 171-72.

from speculation or reading but is more likely to be based upon
some fragmentary research or upon less formal observation of the
phenomena within a field with which the worker is familiar. He
then sets up a research or series of researches to test the truth
of this thesis. If his hunch is not verified by the test, the
worker may feel that his work is "unsuccessful" (though actually
it may yield many valuable by-products if he is shrewd enough to
see them). Such unitary researches require considerable imagination or "genius" on the part of the worker. If we can credit the
many semipopular accounts of what may be termed the "classical"
researches in the progress of science, many examples of this procedure will be readily recalled by the reader. In other instances
the researcher may allow himself a greater latitude. He may set
his research to ascertain the answer to a certain question according to this formula: Is the given relationship positive, negative,
or indifferent, or, to speak in terms of coefficiential correlation, what is the sign and amount of this relationship? Regardless of what the answer turns out to be, the research, if properly
planned and carried out, is successful. Examples are numerous,
especially in the dissertations of advanced students and in the
current scientific journals: What is the effect of adenoids and
diseased tonsils on children's intelligence or Is the "only child"
more likely to manifest personality difficulties than the child
with siblings? Or in other instances the research may permit of
a less strictly defined answer, e.g., how do foundling children
turn out? In examples such as this the approach may be considered
as either ad hoc or exploratory, and there is no need for attempt-
ing to force such a borderline instance into a rigid category.

     In the typical exploratory or empirical research the hy-
pothesis guiding the investigation is couched in general, noncommittal terms, which may often seem lacking in clarity to the reader.
The worker gathers a wide range of material and tries to include
everything which may have a bearing upon his field of study and
does not attempt to justify in detail every item in his data schedule. He depends chiefly upon his martialing of the data to bring
to light any underlying relationships or principles of which he may
or may not have been cognizant in advance of actual trial. In
other words, he relies more upon his instruments or research procedures to elicit the truth than upon his own previous insight into

the problems which he is studying.

An exploratory research is especially appropriate in a relatively young field of scientific inquiry, partly because here
there is little experimentally determined groundwork upon which to
base a more specific hypothesis and partly because in such virgin
soil whatever the researcher does is likely to yield valuable new
information. Such studies are likely to raise more questions, however, than they answer. It is safe to say that in the early study
of anatomy, physiology, and medicine and in the identification of
disease processes, such as "Addison's disease," the approach was
exploratory in the main, partly because at that time the techniques
of research had not been brought to the more or less formal science
which we have at the present day.

For similar reasons an important new discovery or invention
in research methodology will bring about a large amount of empirical investigation. The query naturally arises as to whether the
new techniques are able to throw new light upon the persistent
problems within a science. For example, the discovery of serum
therapy in medicine initiated a mass of largely exploratory experimentation to ascertain its usefulness in almost every important
disease. Other examples may be cited: the large amount of statistical investigation in the social and biological sciences following upon Karl Pearson's devising of correlation methods or, at
this time of writing, the numerous "common-factor" studies in psychology and education following upon Spearman's and Thurstone's devising of new techniques.

The two approaches differ in the location of the "hunch"[2]
or "leap of the imagination over gaps in the evidence" to the discovery of the generalization underlying the data. In the exploratory inquiry this comes late in the process. It ordinarily comes
a posteriori as a result of surveying the data and the indications
brought out by the manipulations thereof. The worker would prefer
an objective procedure in which the conclusions become self-evident,
but often the interpretation of the underlying trends is a matter

---

[2] For an interesting questionnaire study of the circumstances under
which the "scientific hunch" occurs, based upon the replies from 232 "scientists
of admitted leadership," see Washington Platt and Ross A. Baker, "The Relation
of the Scientific 'Hunch' to Research," <u>Journal of Chemical Education</u>, VIII
(1931), 1969-2002.

of considerable insight and scientific imagination, if the investigator aims at something more than a mere enumeration of research "findings." In the ad hoc procedure, on the other hand, the hunch or "working hypothesis" precedes and determines the program of the study. This hypothesis, as we have said, is probably obtained from a tentative or inadequately supported conclusion from earlier studies made by the worker or by others or may at times appear to be a sort of "happy inspiration" obtained largely from a priori speculation.

While this brief chapter has been devoted to a differentiation of these two approaches in so far as it may serve to explain the exploratory aims of the present study, a caution is probably necessary lest the contrast be pushed too far. The researcher himself should, of course, be fully aware of the distinction in planning and carrying out his work and especially in preparing his report for publication. But in actual work it is probable that almost every empirical study has been planned with some anticipation of the sort of outcome which may be expected and that most ad hoc researches have been outlined to permit a degree of flexibility in order to be on the watch for the almost inevitable "unexpected" in research. How would one describe Charles Goring's classic, The English Convict?[3] From the introductory pages one may surmise that much of his original plan was specifically to submit to actual test Lombroso's belief in the existence of a differentiable "criminal type"; but in the body of his report he follows more the form of an exploratory research, with conclusions which would scarcely have been expected in advance of actual analysis of his data.

In a comprehensive research program involving a laboratory staff of several workers, both approaches have their usefulness, according to which portion of the undertaking each worker is concerned with. In such situations the course of a research program is a continuous process. Exploratory or empirical studies are undertaken to uncover new leads or clues, which will serve as working hypotheses for the more final and decisive ad hoc studies.

The interdependence of the two modes is thus best explained as a developmental schema. In a relatively new field of study or

---

[3]The English Convict: A Statistical Study (London: H.M. Stationery Office, 1913). Pp. 440.

when a new instrument of research is to be applied, the exploratory procedure is the favored one. In a more developed field, in which the fundamental principles are pretty well known and the desire is to close up certain "loose ends" in our knowledge, the ad hoc procedure is naturally to be preferred. The empirical investigation is thus a more primitive and contributing project, usually following a somewhat routine course. The ad hoc aims at a final conclusive answer and usually offers a greater opportunity for the researcher's personal insight and resourcefulness. The well-wrought ad hoc research follows as a model the familiar type of theorem in elementary geometry, in which the student demonstrates not only that if the given conditions are fulfilled the proposition is true but also that unless all the essential conditions are present the proposition is not necessarily true.

Each method is subject to its own misuse. This is, of course, due not so much to any fault in either method as to the limitations of the researcher himself.

The empirical worker may rely too exclusively upon his objective manipulation of the data to elicit automatically any unforseen generalizations. He may forget that the ultimate interpretation of meaning is a subjective process and that his objective methods are after all merely the instrumentation. His report may become a mere fact-finding survey, useful enough in itself, which misses, however, its opportunities for original discovery of new principles. It may at times degenerate into routine presenting of an undigested and indigestible mass of data, from which neither the researcher himself nor the reader may gain much useful knowledge.

The ad hoc method, in contrast, is peculiarly liable to the defects of oversubjectivity. The worker may so restrict his attention to his guiding query that he may overlook valuable implications or by-products of his study. Often the by-product may be more important than the main quest itself. At worst, the ad hoc research may lapse into a strongly prejudicial effort merely to prove one's hypothesis. One must at times marvel at the regularity with which the researches undertaken in certain laboratories, closely identified with definite beliefs or opinions, all seem to come out with results in conformity with that point of view, even though there may be other equally competent laboratories

with a contrary point of view, whose researches likewise all seem
to eventuate in conformity with the contrary point of view.

To contrast the two approaches from the standpoint of "efficiency" or convenience is a consideration of secondary importance
since the choice of method must be guided mainly by the requirements of the data and the research situation, as we have attempted
to show in the preceding pages. The prime utility of the ad hoc
study is in affording the final answer to some specific question,
while the utility of the empirical survey lies in disclosing new
facts or queries in a relatively unexplored field. Because of its
adaptability to problems of restricted scope, the ad hoc method is
greatly favored by students, teachers, and other workers who are
limited in time and resources. The exploratory researches usually
necessitate a more formidable plan of work and, as a consequence,
are likely to be undertaken only in laboratories or institutes able
to provide sufficient equipment and personnel.

The foregoing pages have attempted to make clear why the
writer has so definitely chosen the exploratory approach instead o
of the more conclusive ad hoc approach. The reasons may be summarized as follows: (1) Children's behavior problems comprise a
field of study almost untouched by formal researches. (2) Consequently, there is not a large amount of experimentally established
groundwork upon which to base specific ad hoc researches. (3) The
Pearson correlation methods have been utilized to a relatively
small degree in this field, which is so well adapted to a systematic correlational analysis. (4) The data were already gathered,
and only to a small extent could they be amplified to satisfy the
needs of the more final and crucial ad hoc studies. (5) The original plans for this research project were sufficiently elaborate
to permit a comprehensive exploratory survey of the many factors
which are presumably of importance in the field.

CHAPTER VII

EXPLANATION AND INTERPRETATION OF THE TABLES

The remaining chapters of this book are filled with tables
of correlation coefficients. For each of the 125 traits listed in
Tables 1 and 3 of chapter v there is such a table.

Construction of the Tables

In order to facilitate the reader's comprehension of the
trends shown in the 125 tables of correlations, these coefficients
have been arranged as far as possible in descending order of magnitude or, more strictly, from high positive values through zero
to increasingly negative values, according to the boys' correlations.

Within each table the correlations for personality-total,
conduct-total, and police arrest are placed first because of their
peculiar interest in this study.

Under the subheading "Larger Correlations (Positive)" are
listed in descending order of magnitude the positive boys' correlations down through .20. Since the girls' coefficients do not
necessarily follow the boys' ranking, their position is indicated
by the rank order in parentheses. For example, in Table 6, personality-total (p. 89), the symbol "(1)" after violence means that
.64 ± .03 is the largest positive correlation obtained among girls,
"(2)" means that .61 ± .03 is the second largest positive correlation among girls, "(3-4)" means that there were two coefficients of
.59 and that these take the third and fourth places in order of decreasing magnitude, "(16-19)" means that there were four coefficients of .50, and that they fell in the sixteenth, seventeenth,
eighteenth, and nineteenth places in order of decreasing magnitude,
and so on. Following these are listed the girls' coefficients of
positive values of .20 or above, for which the corresponding correlations for the boys are less than ± .20.

Under the subheading "Larger Correlations (Negative)" are

63

placed negative coefficients of -.20 or greater. These are similarly arranged in descending order of negativeness, first, according to the boys and, following these, according to the girls.

The "Not Calculable (N.C.)" are placed next, because, in meaning, these correlations belong with the negative. (In these instances the frequency for the "noted-noted" cell of the tetrachoric tabulation was 0, and a tetrachoric correlation coefficient on such a tabulation is unobtainable.) For example, in Table 11, depressed (p. 136), none of the children noted as depressed had a notation of feeble-minded sibling. The association between these two notations, therefore, would be considered as negative.

Under the subheading "Other Correlations (Positive to Negative)" are placed all other coefficients with values falling between +.19 and -.19. They are arranged according to the boys' correlations in descending order from .19 down through 0, and then in increasing order of negativeness up through -.19.

The "Omitted" correlations are placed at the end of each table. These correlations were not computed, either because for some technical reason such a coefficient would be meaningless (as in Table 13, grouped: depressed, etc. [p. 144], where it would be absurd to correlate a pooled category against the component items of that pool) or because for some reason the indexing of a certain pair of items is so unsatisfactory that a coefficient would be greatly misleading (as, in Table 76, temper tantrums, probably tended to exclude a notation of temper display).[1]

A blank space in the tables indicates that a coefficient was not computed, usually because of paucity of cases or because the item would not be applicable to both sexes, e.g., "annoying" girls (Tables 6, 7, 8, 9, or 10).

Probable errors, it will be recalled, were not computed for coefficients smaller than .20 or -.20 except for personality-total, conduct-total, and police arrest. In view of the many distorting factors in our data, as described in chapter iv, it appears inadvisable to take much notice of correlations below this size, beyond merely reporting them.

---

[1]Pp. 38-44.

The Interpretation of Correlation Coefficients

The substance of this monograph must be sought in these
tables of correlations. Readers who have learned to think in terms
of correlation coefficients will welcome this concise method of
statement. Altogether there are about seven thousand coefficients
for the boys, and a similar number for the girls, so there is no
feasible method of presenting this diffuse material except in tab-
ular form. Since the tables are so constructed as to be self-explanatory, any interpretative or exegetical comment by the writer
becomes somewhat superfluous. The reader is invited to make his
own interpretation according to his own background or individual
interests. Probably few readers will attempt to read the tables
consecutively but will prefer to use them for reference as to some
specific relationship or to specific groups of correlations.

How must correlation coefficients be read? Everyone is
familiar with the fact that a coefficient of 0 means that no correlation or concomitant variation exists between the traits in
question; and that intermediate values between 0 and +1.00 represent a _positive_ correlation, i.e., a high degree of the one trait
is accompanied more or less by a high degree of the other trait,
and a low degree of one trait by a low degree of the other; and
that coefficients between 0 and -1.00 represent _negative_ correlation, i.e., high values in one of the traits tend to be associated
with low values in the other. Some statisticians have ventured to
classify correlation coefficients in the abstract as to whether
they are "high," "substantial," "low," or "negligible." Such an
evaluation of a correlation without reference to the material on
which it is based would seem almost meaningless. A correlation
coefficient per se is merely a unit of measurement of relationship
analogous to measures of weight, temperature, angular distance, and
the like. It would be futile to state whether 10 kilograms is a
large or a small weight, without specifying whether we are dealing
with coal or with platinum; with gross body weight or with a tumor.

The fundamental understanding of a correlation coefficient
from the mathematical standpoint, of course, is in terms of _alien-
ation_,[2] i.e., the reduction in variability (σ) of the "dependent"

---

[2]T. L. Kelley, _Statistical Method_ (New York: Macmillan, 1923), pp.
173-74.

or "predicted" variable associated with differing values of the
correlation, according to the factor $\sqrt{1 - r^2}$. Upon our material,
however, such an interpretation has little meaning, since only a
small part of our correlations exceed .50 and an r of .50 reduces
the variability of the dependent variable only to .866 of the variability which would be present in the case of zero correlation—
an amount which is scarcely palpable. On the other hand, in comparison with what clinic workers and social scientists must make
use of, relationships as high as .50 represent fairly respectable
"findings." It is necessary for them to think in terms of low correlations and low probabilities.

With reference to our material, then, correlations greater
than .50 are considered "high" on the basis of their rarity. Correlations in our study falling between .40 and .49 may similarly
be considered "large," those between .30 and .39 "substantial," and
those between .20 and .29 "moderate." Correlations smaller than
.20 must be considered of little significance because of the many
distorting factors at work in our data. Among negative correlations, those larger than -.20 occurred so infrequently that they
must be considered important.

An individual correlation coefficient represents by a simple quantitative symbol the relation between two traits or conditions. It is the mathematical equivalent of the type of statement
which one hears commonly among clinical observers, e.g., "Whenever
we see a patient with condition A, we may expect the existence also
of condition B," or "trait A is usually associated with trait B,"
or, to illustrate a negative relationship, "the presence of trait
A in a patient usually precludes the likelihood of trait B" or
"trait A seldom occurs in combination with trait B." The many correlation coefficients in this monograph are intended to serve the
same purposes as clinical observations of this type. The advan-
tages of a coefficiential expression lie not only in its more precise, quantitative form but also in the fact that in a routine procedure of computing an r the weight of contrary instances are not
so likely to be overlooked as in the subjective observations arising out of clinical experience. The important limitations of correlation coefficients, in comparison with clinical observations, is
that they are not based similarly upon the recognition of process
with temporal sequences and consideration of cause-and-effect

relationships but merely state the extent of concomitant variation.
They are themselves entirely noncommittal as to temporal or causal
implications.[3]   Their meaning or utility must be supplied by the
reader from his own background and for his own purposes.

At this point it may be desirable to discuss briefly the
relation of a "control group" to researches of this kind. The formal description of a control group belongs rather to a research
employing the method of "group differences," i.e., a comparison of
two groups equivalent in every respect except in the trait which
is the basis of comparison. In a study employing correlation coefficients, the control group is comprehended in the computation of
the coefficient without a formal mention of the fact. In a bi-
serial tabulation for the correlation of depressed spells with
chronological age among boys (p. 15) there are 149 cases consti-
tuting the "marked" group in which depressed spells were not noted.
In a group-differences methodology one would compare such facts as
the means, variability, or distribution of ages for each of the two
groups. In the tetrachoric tabulation for the correlation of truancy from home with stealing (p. 16) we may consider the 503 boys
noted as truant from home as the marked group, the 1,610 boys not
noted as truant from home as the control, and compare the incidence
of stealing in each group. Or we may divide these cases into the
marked group of 815 boys with a notation of stealing and compare
the incidence of truancy from home in each group. In our data
either method would have been applicable. The method of Pearsonian
correlation was chosen because of its conciseness in presenting a
large amount of material and because of the fact that correlation
coefficients represent a more universalized mode of expression of
relationships and fluctuate less with the number of cases (p. 22).
If brevity were not so necessary, the method of group differences
would be desirable because it would permit a closer analysis of
the component parts of a tabulation which a correlation coefficient may obscure.

The question may arise as to whether such a control group
is adequate. It may be urged that a proper control group should
be obtained entirely outside a clinic population, since the fact
of admission to a behavior clinic implies the presence of selective

---

[3]Pp. 3-7.

factors (pp. 25-27). Now the ideal control group should match
the marked group in every respect except the one under study. If
the marked group is a series of clinic cases, the control group
likewise should be obtained from the same clinic population, in
order that whatever selective factors are present in the one group
may also be present in the other.

At face value the tables of correlation coefficients may
be considered as an effort to describe children's behavior difficulties in terms of correlated behavior problems. The correlations
for each of the 111 variates and traits listed in Table 1 have been
computed with one another and with the 14 traits or conditions
listed in Table 3. A reading of such tables of correlation coefficients as though they were cursive bits of descriptive writing
will yield a considerable amount of information, which could be
obtained otherwise only through extensive personal clinical observation.

This list is a fairly comprehensive one as far as undesirable behavior is concerned, and in actual experience few behavior
difficulties will be encountered which are not included in this
list. Unfortunately, the desirable and indifferent behavior traits
are seriously underrepresented here because of the prevailing tendency of children's behavior child-guidance clinics to concentrate
attention upon the manifestly undesirable traits (pp. 45-46). For
that reason the tables afford a description of only one side of the
story.

In the tables one will note that among the girls' coefficients there is a larger number of high correlations, both positive
and negative, than among the boys' coefficients. The writer does
not profess to know the reason. On the one hand, the fact that the
girls' coefficients are based upon a smaller number of cases (N =
1,181) than the boys' coefficients (N = 2,113) will permit a larger
number of extreme values. (It is a simple fact in statistics not
always appreciated by actual researchers that the smaller the number of cases, the more likelihood that occasional high values will
arise purely because of this inadequacy of sampling.) If one considers these correlations in relation to their probable errors,
specifically the ratio of coefficient to its $P.E.$, the difference
is not so striking. It is possible also that, among our clinic
population, selective factors may have served to introduce a greater

amount of heterogeneity into the girls' population than into the
boys', so that part of this difference in range of values may be
an artifact due to differential selective influences. On the other
hand, it is also possible that actually there is a greater amount
of heterogeneity among girls on the basis of undesirable behavior
than among boys: it may be that girls who become "bad actors" in
some respects have a greater tendency to become so in many respects
and that therefore the correlation coefficients obtained from such
material are enlarged because of the factor of heterogeneity. These
are only conjectures. It should be repeated that the writer does
not claim to know the reason.

Suggestions, Clues, Predictive Values

        But the tables of correlation coefficients in this mono-
graph have more than a descriptive utility. Each coefficient represents a relationship between two traits, and many of them indicate important concepts. The mere statement of a correlation is,
of course, not the final goal of a research procedure but may be
considered as a valuable landmark or guidepost. Our ultimate desire is to be able to trace the process by which certain inherent
tendencies of the individual together with environmental factors
acting upon him produce a given type of behavior. Here we cannot
expect to isolate some one unitary or essential cause, as physi-
cians do in the case of certain infective bodily diseases, but must
be prepared to find that the causal factors are multiplex and of
differing degrees of potency. It is in the locating of causal factors and measurement of their potency that correlation coefficients
serve their unique purpose. In the total procedure, then, the computation of correlations is but a preliminary or exploratory, though
useful, step. They indicate the directions which further research
should take and suggest relationships which warrant special inquiry
in more completely elaborated ad hoc researches.

        In addition to the suggestions for further research to be
found in such a collection of correlation coefficients, there are
two uses of value in actual clinic practice, that of clues to behavior trends not readily observable and that of prediction of future behavior or condition.

        As an illustration of the use as clues, let us consider

the substantial tetrachoric correlation of .64 ± .02 (with age
"partialed out") between stealing and truancy from home among our
2,113 boys (p. 16 and Table 56, p. 312). Now stealing is likely
to take place more or less in secret, so that its presence in an
individual child may often not be known except as a result of special inquiry. Truancy from home, on the other hand, is an overt
occurrence well enough known to the child's parents. In view of
the high correlation of .64 ± .02 in our clinic population, the
presence of truancy from home raises the question of the presence
of stealing. A more meaningful interpretation would be obtained
directly from the full tetrachoric tabulations, which unfortunately
could not be reproduced here in any great number because of lack
of space. In this instance, out of 503 home truants, 375, or 75
per cent, had a notation of stealing, while of 1,610 non-truants
only 440, or 27 per cent, had a notation of stealing. Thus the
"expectancy" for stealing is almost three times as great among home
truants as among non-truants within our clinic population. What
this expectancy may be among children in general not subjected to
the selective factors, whatever these may be, attendant upon examination in a children's behavior clinic, cannot be easily inferred;
but this relation is large enough to imply that the presence of the
one trait indicates the advisability of an inquiry into the presence of the other.

A more adequate conjecture or estimate would be obtained
by considering the joint evidence of several traits or notations.[4]
We note from Table 56 that stealing among boys correlates substantially also with truancy from school (.62 ± .02), lying (.61 ± .02),
and bad companions (.57 ± .02). Obviously, the ascertained presence of several of these traits or notations increases the probability of the presence of stealing. For example, we have noted
that, of the boys with a case-record notation of truancy from home,
75 per cent had a notation of stealing. Out of the 324 boys with
notations both of truancy from home and truancy from school, 265
boys, or 82 per cent, had a notation of stealing. Out of 182 boys
with three notations—truancy from home, truancy from school, and
lying—87 per cent had a notation of stealing. Out of 76 boys with

---

[4] R. L. Jenkins and Luton Ackerson, "The Study of the Type as a Statistical Method," Journal of Juvenile Research, XVII (1933), 1-9.

the four notations <u>truancy from home</u>, <u>truancy from school</u>, <u>lying</u>, and <u>bad companions</u>, 93 per cent had a notation of <u>stealing</u>.

Another illustration of the use as clues or indicators of the presence of less easily observable traits which may be had from a scrutiny of the tables of correlation coefficients in subsequent pages is in reference to <u>sex delinquency (coitus</u>), which among girls is an item of information often desired in the examination but relatively difficult to ascertain. The correlation coefficients of <u>sex delinquency (coitus</u>) among the girls (Table 96, p. 470) were as follows: with <u>truancy from home</u>, .48 ± .04; with <u>oversuggestibility</u>, .38 ± .04; and with <u>overinterest in opposite sex</u>, .38 ± .04. Among 189 girls with a case-record notation of <u>truancy from home</u> 87 girls, or 46 per cent, had a notation of <u>sex delinquency (coitus</u>). Out of 67 girls with notations of both <u>truancy from home</u> and <u>staying out late at night</u>, 51 per cent had notations of <u>sex delinquency (coitus</u>). Out of 19 girls with the three notations <u>truancy from home</u>, <u>staying out late at night</u>, and <u>oversuggestibility</u>, about 58 per cent had also a notation of <u>sex delinquency (coitus</u>). Out of 5 girls with the four notations <u>truancy from home</u>, <u>staying out late at night</u>, <u>oversuggestibility</u>, and <u>overinterest in opposite sex</u>, 4 girls (80 per cent) had also a notation of <u>sex delinquency (coitus</u>).

Within our material, it should be remarked in passing, the probabilities could not be increased indefinitely by this cumulative process. As the number of notations increased, the number of cases decreased (as in the example cited in the last paragraph) to the point where mere fluctuations of sampling blurred the trends. The procedure appeared empirically to be satisfactory, up the the accumulation of three notations, but often unsafe if four or more notations were considered. But in an application of this cumulative process to actual children, among whom paucity of cases cannot enter as a disturbing statistical factor, there is no reason why the cumulative effect of each added notation, which, as in the preceding illustrations, is highly correlated with the notation under discussion, should not increase the probabilities indefinitely. In practice, however, it is likely that the increment in the probabilities to be gained by the addition of fresh notations beyond the first five or six will become almost negligible. The technical reason is that the intercorrelations among the notations themselves are usually as high as with the notation under discussion and by analogy with "team correlation," high "outside correlations" cannot be obtained if the intercorrelations are also high.[5]

Although the material in this monograph does not enable the reader to calculate the actual probabilities, as in the two illustrations cited above, an application of the Spearman sums-and-differences formula[6] will enable one to infer whether the addition of further notations to the composite can be depended upon to increase the probabilities that a given trait or condition is present. If we consider the notations to represent actual continuous measures and if these are reduced to "standard measures,"[7] i.e., measures so calibrated that their standard deviation becomes unity, this formula becomes delightfully simplified. For example, the correlation of a trait (1) with the combination of two other traits (2 and 3) becomes

$$r_{1(2+3)} \text{(in the case of equal } \sigma\text{'s)} = \frac{r_{12} + r_{13}}{\sqrt{2 + 2r_{23}}}.$$

The correlation of a trait (1) with the combination of three others (2, 3, and 4) becomes

$$r_{1(2+3+4)} \text{(in the case of equal } \sigma\text{'s)} = \frac{r_{12} + r_{13} + r_{14}}{\sqrt{3 + 2(r_{23} + r_{24} + r_{34})}}.$$

The general formula for the correlation of a trait with the combination of any number of traits similarly becomes

$$r_{1(2+3+4+\ldots+n)} \text{(in the case of equal } \sigma\text{'s)}$$

$$= \frac{r_{12} + r_{13} + r_{14} + \ldots + r_{1n}}{\sqrt{(n-1) + 2(r_{23} + r_{24} + \ldots + r_{2n} + r_{34} + \ldots + r_{3n} + \ldots + r_{(n-1)n})}},$$

wherein n denotes the ordinal number of the last notation to be added to the composite.

---

[5] C. L. Hull, "The Joint Yield from Teams of Tests," Journal of Educational Psychology, XIV (1923), 396-404, or Aptitude Testing (Yonkers: World Book Co., 1928), chap. viii.

[6] C. Spearman, "Correlations of Sums and Differences," British Journal of Psychology, V (1913), 419, or Kelley, op. cit., Formula 147.

[7] Kelley, op. cit., pp. 114-17.

There is no method, of course, of transmuting these correlation coefficients into probabilities. Nor should one expect that
the results of this sort of formulaic computation would parallel
exactly the probabilities obtained from an actual counting of cases,
as in the two illustrations described above. But an empirical comparison of the results of the sums-and-differences formula showed
that, whenever the team correlation increased definitely with the
addition of a fresh notation, the probabilities also increased.
For example, in the two illustrations cited above, the correlations
of stealing among boys with truancy from home and with truancy from
school were .64 and .62 respectively, and with the composite of the
two the team correlation was .70. When a third notation, lying,
was added, the correlation with the three became .76; and, when bad
companions was added, the team correlation of stealing with the
composite of four notations was .79. In the other illustration
the correlations of sex delinquency (coitus) among girls with truancy from home and staying out late at night were .48 and .44 respectively, and with the composite of the two the correlation was
.53. When a third notation—oversuggestibility—was added, the
team correlation was .59; and, when overinterest in opposite sex
was added, the correlation of sex delinquency (coitus) with the
composite of four notations was .60.

Whenever the addition of a fresh notation brought about
a decrease in the sums-and-differences correlation, inferences
could not be made as to the effect upon the probabilities. Of
the two instances cited below (pp. 76-77), in which the team correlation showed decreases with the addition of certain notations,
in one instance (police arrest among boys) the probabilities continued to increase, while in the other (police arrest among girls)
the probabilities showed a decrease.

The question arose as to the probable results of re-sorting
the cards into fourfold tables for cumulative teams of notations
and computing Pearson tetrachoric correlations therefrom. An empirical test quickly showed that this method was not feasible.
Among the four instances cited (pp. 70-72 and 76-77), it was found
that the tetrachoric coefficient usually increased for the composite of two notations but, beyond this, usually decreased with successive additions of further notations. At least three factors may
co-operate in bringing about this irregularity. (1) It may be that

the requirement of normality in tetrachoric correlation is not fulfilled. As far as one notation is concerned, the assumption of
normality of distribution is not implausible (pp. 18-19); but,
when several notations are compounded, the form of the distribution may become complex and irregular. (2) Or it may be that in
such a combination the point of dichotomization becomes equivocal,
so that the resultant grouping of cases may tend to neutralize the
effect of the underlying correlation. An analysis of the structure
of a tetrachoric tabulation will make this clear. On the one side
of the dichotomization one would have, for example, the boys with
all three notations—truancy from home, truancy from school, and
lying—while on the other side of the dichotomization one would
have the boys with any two, one, or none of these notations. Now
it is possible that many of the boys with two or even one of these
notations differ so slightly from those with all three notations
that when they are placed in the opposite dichotomy they will tend
to counteract the statistical influence of the other boys with all
three notations and thus reduce the correlation coefficient. In
addition to this effect, there is often a marked decrease in the
number of cases in the marked dichotomy, so that any increase in
the value of the correlation coefficient resulting from this regrouping of cases on this side of the dichotomization may be more
than counterbalanced by the increased number of cases on the other.
Or, to speak in terms of the actual tetrachoric tabulation (p. 16),
the compounding of additional notations may often increase the ratio of cases in the upper left quadrant to cases in the lower left
quadrant, thereby tending to increase the correlation coefficient
as far as the left half of the tabulation alone is concerned. On
the other hand, such a regrouping will also tend to increase to a
small extent the ratio of cases in the upper right quadrant to
cases in the lower right quadrant. Even though this increase
in ratio in the right half of the tabulation will usually be much
less than the increase in the left half, this smaller ratio may
nevertheless acquire a predominant influence in the total tabulation because of the large shift of cases from the left half to the
right half which usually results from such a regrouping. (3) A
third probable factor may be the unsatisfactory amount of validity
or consistency (pp. 27-33) in the case notations, e.g., it is
probable that in many instances where only two of a given set of

notations are present the third should also have been present if
the true facts were known. The effect of this weakness in the data
is, of course, ordinarily a reduction in the correlation toward
zero. While this possibility of inadequate validity and consistency exists also when we are dealing with one notation, this "attenuation" effect probably becomes multiplied when several notations are involved.

The use of the information comprised in the tables of correlation coefficients as predictions of future behavior is of the
same nature as their use as clues, but with the time element added.
Let us cite two illustrations, police arrest among boys and among
girls (Table 8, p. 107). Among boys the correlations with police
arrest were as follows: with truancy from home, .68 + .02; with
stealing, .63 + .02; with bad companions, .59 + .02; with truancy
from school, .57 + .02; and with staying out late at night, .52 +
.03. Out of 503 boys with a notation of truancy from home, 270
boys, or 54 per cent, had a notation of police arrest. Now in the
case of an individual boy who truants from home but has not yet
been under police detention, the probability is greater that at
some future time he will have a police arrest than the boy with
no such notation in his history. (It should be noted that the histories of our children are not yet "completed" in point of time,
so that the probabilities as here given are undoubtedly understated
as far as our clinic populations are concerned.) In interpreting
these probabilities two cautions are necessary. (1) Our population
is unquestionably a selected one on the basis of admission to a behavior clinic, and it is impossible to conjecture how closely these
percentages correspond to what would be found among unselected children. Our percentages cannot be applied strictly to any other population except that of a behavior clinic with an intake similar to
that of this one. (2) Since a time consideration is involved, the
question arises as to which behavior trait antedates the other. In
the present instance one can readily believe that truancy from home
usually occurs prior to police arrest, partly because in many cases
the truancy was one of the specific reasons for the police arrest.
The data of this monograph do not aid the reader in concluding
which comes first. That must be decided from other criteria. Frequently either one of two behavior traits may be antecedent and
predisposing to the other interchangeably, e.g., stealing may be

prophetic of truancy from home, and, vice versa, truancy from home may be prophetic of stealing.[8]

The joint evidence of several notations will, within certain limits, increase the possibility of prediction. Out of 372 boys with notations of both truancy from home and stealing, 227 boys, or 61 per cent, had notations of police arrest. When bad companions was added to the composite, the probability arose to 72 per cent of 157 boys. When truancy from school was added, the probability arose to 73 per cent of 120 boys. When staying out late at night was added, the occurrence of notations of police arrest among 54 boys with all five notations arose to 78 per cent.

The use of Spearman sums-and-differences correlations (p. 72) upon this series showed irregular results. For the combination of truancy from home and stealing the sums-and-differences correlation with police arrest among boys arose to .72, and when bad companions was added this correlation increased to .75. But with the addition of truancy from school this correlation decreased to .64, and with the addition of staying out late at night this correlation arose again only to .75.

Let us examine another instance, that of police arrest among girls. Among the highest correlations (Table 8, p. 107) were: with sex delinquency (coitus), .76 ± .02; with truancy from home, .67 ± .03; with oversuggestibility, .57 ± .03; and with staying out late at night, .49 ± .04. Out of 218 girls with a notation of sex delinquency (coitus), 126 girls, or 58 per cent, had a notation of police arrest. Out of 87 girls with the two notations—sex delinquency (coitus) and truancy from home—62 girls, or 71 per cent, had a notation of police arrest. When oversuggestibility was added, the probability arose to about 77 per cent of 22 girls. When staying out late at night was added to the composite, the number of cases with all four notations dropped to 11, of whom 7, or about 64 per cent, had a notation of police arrest.

The Spearman sums-and-differences correlations (p. 72) were also irregular. The team correlation of police arrest with

---

[8]An attempt to indicate which traits are likely to appear at different age levels among children on the basis of incidences is given in Vol. I, Figs. 48 and 52. An excellent study of sequences in offenses among juvenile delinquents is reported by Ruth E. Burkey, "A Statistical Study of the Sequence of Successive Delinquencies," Journal of Juvenile Research, XVI (1932), 133-44.

the composite of two notations was .83; with three notations, .89; and for the composite of four notations the sums-and-differences correlation dropped to .86.

In selecting notations to be added to a composite from which one desires either clues to other traits not so easily ascertainable or <u>prediction</u> as to future behavior or condition, these rules should be followed: (1) The notations should be correlated as high as possible with the unascertained trait or condition. (2) The notations should be intercorrelated as low as possible, or even negatively, with the other traits in the composite. (3) Whenever feasible, preference should be given to notations of relatively frequent occurrence in order to avoid too great a reduction in the number of cases.

PART II

THE RELATIVE IMPORTANCE AMONG TRAITS

CHAPTER VIII

ON CRITERIA OF "SERIOUSNESS" AMONG
BEHAVIOR DIFFICULTIES

In our effort toward a systematic study of children's behavior difficulties our first step has been a canvass of the data
for the purpose of obtaining a comprehensive inventory of the problems actually reported by parents and by examining staff. This inventory resulted in an extensive list of about 300 behavior items
found to occur oftener than 0.5 per cent among our total 5,000
cases.[1] Out of this list, 135 items which are ordinarily designated as "personality" or "conduct" difficulties and 26 miscellaneous traits or conditions, which occurred often enough to warrant
separate statistical treatment, were selected for the investigation
reported in Part II of this monograph.

The next step is an evaluation of what, for the lack of
better terms, may be called the relative "seriousness" or "ominousness" among these traits. In clinical work with children and also
in planning research projects the question arises as to which of
the many behavior problems warrant special attention and which are
of negligible importance. Is a notation of <u>truancy from home</u> more
serious than a notation of <u>stealing</u>? Is <u>seclusiveness</u> more serious
than <u>disobedience</u>? How much importance should be attached to <u>enu-
resis</u>, a frequently noted item in children's behavior clinics?

Ideal criteria of importance or seriousness lie beyond the
potentialities of our data. A socially minded worker would wish
to estimate seriousness in terms of the social injury resulting
from a given pattern of behavior. A more individualistically
minded worker would think in terms of the injury or frustration
to the child himself. Others would estimate it according to its
prognostic implications, i.e., which of two behavior traits augurs

---

[1]This inventory is published in Tables 1-13 of Vol. I. See also the
author's "On the Feasibility of Inventorying Children's Behavior Traits," <u>Jour-
nal of Juvenile Research</u>, XVI (1932), 32-39.

the less favorable outcome in the future as the child grows to ma-
turity? Several researchers have attempted to evaluate relative
seriousness by asking authorities in children's work to rate various traits as to their importance, leaving to each rater his own
subjective conception of what he considers importance or seriousness to mean, i.e., the criterion of "consensus of opinion." Our
problem was to find some feasible criteria capable of research
treatment by quantitative methods.

        As objective and measurable criteria of importance or ser-
iousness, we have employed three devices—the personality-total,
the conduct-total, and the notation of a police arrest. The personality-total consists of the unweighted enumeration of all the
undesirable personality traits noted for each child. For example,
if he is noted as seclusive only, his personality-total is 1; if
he also daydreams, his total is 2; if he also has inferiority feelings, his total is 3; and so on. The conduct-total is similarly
constructed. If he steals only, his conduct-total is 1; if he is
also truant from home, his total is 2; if he is also noted as quarrelsome, his conduct-total is 3; and so on. A refinement may have
been given these totals by weighting the various component traits
according to their importance, for undoubtedly all the components
are not of equal importance, e.g., in the conduct sphere, stealing
is of greater concern than finicky food habits. There was no feasible technique of ascertaining such differential weightings in
our data, however, without resorting to subjectivity, which our
methods have tried to avoid as far as possible. It is unlikely,
moreover, that such a weighting of the component traits would have
changed our correlational findings to any considerable extent. The
third criterion is the fact of a police arrest or detention by reason of misconduct. Among our cases this notation was present among
about one-fifth of the boys and about one-seventh of the girls.

        The assumption underlying these criteria is that any traits
which are highly correlated with the extent of personality or conduct deviation as measured by the number of reported behavior difficulties or which are highly associated with the fact of a police
arrest or juvenile-court appearance are more "serious" or "ominous,"
whether as causes or merely as symptoms, than traits only negligibly correlated with these criteria.

        Our grouping of behavior problems into personality and

conduct categories does not profess to rest upon any etiological
basis but merely follows the customary usage of these terms by
child workers.   In so far as a distinction can be made, a personality problem is commonly thought to be a comparatively intrinsic
trait in an individual, which in an overdeveloped or exaggerated
form is associated with a diagnosis of psychosis or psychopathy
or similar mental disorder.   It is not ordinarily considered to be
deserving of punishment or amenable to it.   A conduct problem, on
the other hand, in an extreme form is usually associated with commitment to a correctional institution in the case of adults and
with a spanking or other overt disciplinary expedient among younger
children.[2]   The reader who wishes to learn more exactly our arbitrary grouping of traits in order to understand the composition of
the personality-total and the conduct-total may refer to Volume I,
in which the personality problems are listed in Tables 1 and 2 and
the conduct problems in Tables 3 and 4.

The question may well be asked concerning the validity of
these three criteria, i.e., What is the evidence that they may be
accepted as working measures of "seriousness" or "ominousness."

Among the clinic's staff members who were acquainted with
the children of our series in a professional capacity it was observed that a child who was commonly considered a "personality
case" usually showed a relatively high personality-total, while
one considered primarily a "conduct case" usually showed a large
conduct-total.   Similarly, a child spoken of as "not a behavior
problem" usually showed a small inventory of personality and conduct problems.   The formal counting-up of his behavior problems
thus gave a result which agreed generally with the opinion of the
examiners.[3]

The correlations of these totals with the fact of a police
arrest indicate the same contrasts.   For conduct-total these coefficients were .53 ± .02 and .31 ± .03 for boys and girls respectively, while for personality-total these coefficients were only

---

[2]For a further discussion on this point see I, 41-42.

[3]In this connection it may be appropriate to note that the boy with the
largest conduct-total among our entire 5,000 cases, the 63 items of which were
listed under Case I.P. in Vol. I (pp. 8-10), is at the time of writing (1939)
serving his second state penitentiary sentence for serious property offenses,
the two incarcerations having been in widely separated states.

.18 ± .02 and .11 ± .03 respectively. The correlations of the two
totals with the separate behavior notations in Tables 6 and 7 (pp.
89 and 98) showed similar differences. The high correlations for
personality-total were usually with traits commonly described as
personality problems, e.g., incipient psychosis (unspecified), diagnosis or question of dementia praecox, queer behavior, depressed
spells, talking to self without apparent reason, and the like;
while the high coefficients for the conduct-total were with such
conspicuous conduct difficulties as swearing, disturbing influence
in the home, destructiveness, "annoying" girls, truancy from home,
disobedience, and stealing. The fact that personality-total is
correlated most highly with incipient psychosis (.76 ± .03 among
boys) and diagnosis or question of dementia praecox (.60 ± .03
among boys) gives strong support to the validity of our personality-
total, since the recognized psychoses represent the maximum degree
of personality disorder.[4]

The validity of the notation of police arrest is scarcely
open to question. Our information concerning this item is complete
up to the time of the child's examination at the clinic. It includes only those children who have been under police arrest or
detention (whether "booked" on formal complaints or not) for reasons of misconduct. It does not include the children brought to
the juvenile court by their parents only for advice, unless the
child was actually placed under arrest or detention. Its high correlations were with such obvious misconduct as stealing an automobile, truancy from home, stealing (unspecified), robbing a building, home, etc., bad companions, and the like. An attenuating factor is in all likelihood present in the correlations with police
arrest, since our children's histories are uncompleted in point of
time and a substantial fraction of these children may be expected
to encounter a police arrest in subsequent years. While the "par-
tialing out" of chronological age in these coefficients (the correlations of police arrest with age being .29 ± .02 and .56 ± .02
for boys and girls respectively) may tend to standardize their

---

[4]The technical point should be noted here that in the correlations of a
given total with a specific behavior notation which it comprises, the specific
notation was excluded from that total; e.g., the correlation (bi-serial r) of
personality-total with queer behavior means the correlation of queer behavior
with the aggregate number of personality problems other than queer behavior.

meaning on the basis of "with age constant," it is very probable
that they are definitely reduced in size in comparison with what
would have been obtained if one could have employed life-histories
fully complete in point of time.

The use of three parallel criteria may seem confusing, but
there appeared to be no satisfactory basis for combining them into
a single criterion measure. A glance at their intercorrelations
(Table 4) shows that they are not highly enough intercorrelated to

TABLE 4*

PERSONALITY-TOTAL, CONDUCT-TOTAL, AND
POLICE ARREST

| | | | | Personality-Total | | |
| | | | | Intercorrelations | | |
	Range	Means	Standard Deviations	Personality-Total	Conduct-Total	Police Arrest
Boys......	0 to 46	6.5	5.2	....	.50 + .01	.18 + .02
Girls.....	0 to 49	6.0	5.4	....	.61 ∓ .01	.11 ∓ .03
				Conduct-Total		
Boys......	0 to 63	9.4	7.8	.50 + .01	....	.53 + .02
Girls.....	0 to 50	7.6	7.2	.61 ∓ .01	....	.31 ∓ .03
				Police Arrest[†]		
Boys......	....	.....	......	.18 + .02	.53 + .02	....
Girls.....	....	.....	......	.11 ∓ .02	.31 ∓ .03	....

*Means, standard deviations, ranges, and intercorrelations
(age "partialed out"), N's = 2,113 boys and 1,181 girls.

†Categorical data.

to be considered as duplicating one another. The data of Table 5
show similarly that the three criteria tend to show differing correlations with the specific behavior traits covered in this study.

The study by E. K. Wickman[5] obtained direct ratings of the

---

[5]Children's Behavior and Teachers' Attitudes (New York: Commonwealth
Fund, 1929). Pp. 247.

TABLE 5*

RANK-ORDER AGREEMENT BETWEEN THE "OUTSIDE"
CORRELATION COEFFICIENTS FOR EACH
OF THE THREE CRITERIA

| | Boys | | |
	Personality-Total	Conduct-Total	Police Arrest
Personality-total............	....	.33 + .05	-.05 + .06
Conduct-total................	.33 + .05	....	.70 + .03
Police arrest................	-.05 + .06	.70 + .05	....
	Girls		
Personality-total............	....	.76 + .03	.13 + .06
Conduct-total................	.76 + .03	....	.51 + .05
Police arrest................	.13 + .06	.51 + .05	....

*The coefficients given are Spearman rank-differences-squared correlations between the columns of coefficients in Tables 6, 7, and 8 in subsequent pages.

relative seriousness of behavior problems among school children in the form of rankings by a group of 511 teachers and a group of 30 mental hygienists (8 psychiatrists, 4 psychologists, 13 psychiatric social workers, and 5 visiting teachers), all "actually and solely engaged in the study and treatment of behavior disorders of children" in child-guidance clinics (p. 121). He found that there was no agreement between the rankings of these traits by the two groups, the rank-order correlation coefficient being -.11 (p. 122). He concludes that "teachers stress the importance of problems relating to sex, dishonesty, disobedience, disorderliness, and failure to learn. . . . . Mental hygienists, on the other hand, consider . . . . unsocial forms of behavior . . . . [withdrawing, recessive characteristics] most serious and discount the stress which teachers lay on anti-social conduct." A perusal of Wickman's Charts XVI and XVIII, which list the relative rankings of the seriousness of traits by teachers and by mental hygienists respectively and a comparison with our own Tables 6 (p. 89) and 7 (p. 98) bring to light the fact that our conduct-total and police-arrest criteria resemble the teachers' rankings, while our personality-

total criterion corresponds rather with the mental hygienists'
rankings.

A similar distinction between conduct problems and personality problems in respect to the differing attitudes of parents or
college students, on the one hand, and mental hygienists, on the
other, was found by R. M. Stogdill[6] in his studies.

At some future time, as our knowledge of behavior difficulties increases, it may be possible to construct a single comprehensive over-all criterion measure; but for the present, in the
writer's estimation, the most defensible policy is to treat each
criterion as lying in a different plane.

---

[6]"Attitude of Parents, Students, and Mental Hygienists toward Children's
Behavior," Journal of Social Psychology, IV (1933), 486-89, and "The Measurement
of Attitudes toward Children," Abstracts of Doctors' Dissertations (Columbus:
Ohio State University Press, 1935), XVI, 189-201.

CHAPTER IX

THE PERSONALITY-TOTAL CRITERION

The personality-total is the unweighted sum of all the personality problems reported for an individual child, as we have explained in the preceding chapter. Among our 2,113 White boys the
number of personality problems noted per child ranged from 0 to 46,
with a mean of 6.5 and a standard deviation of 5.2 (Table 4, p. 85).
Among our 1,181 White girls the range was 0-49, the mean, 6.0, and
the standard deviation, 5.4. The distribution of the personality-
total is shown in Figure 3.

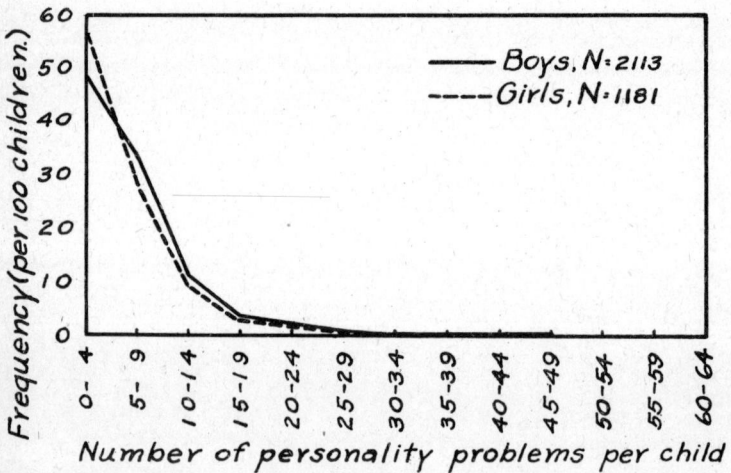

Fig. 3.—Percentage Frequency Distribution of
Personality-Totals

In Table 6 it will be noted that the personality-total is
strongly correlated with the conduct-total in our data, both among
boys and among girls, the product-moment coefficients being .50
$\pm$ .01 and .61 $\pm$ .01 respectively. It is probable that in our data
these two coefficients are artificially enlarged because of a.

88

TABLE 6

CORRELATIONS WITH "PERSONALITY-TOTAL"

	Boys	Girls
Conduct-total	.50 ± .01	.61 ± .01
Police arrest	.18 ± .02	.11 ± .03
	Larger Correlations (Positive)	
Incipient psychosis	.76 ± .03	....
Dementia praecox	.60 ± .03	....
Queer	.52 ± .03	.61 ± .03 (2)*
Grouped: depressed, etc	.50 ± .02	.57 ± .03 (6)
Talking to self without apparent reason	.47 ± .04	....
Contrary	.45 ± .03	.38 ± .04 (51-52)
Question of change of personality	.45 ± .03	.53 ± .03 (12-13)
Hatred or jealousy of sibling	.43 ± .03	.45 ± .04 (28-30)
Inferiority feelings	.43 ± .02	.59 ± .03 (3-4)
Grouped: sensitive or worrisome, etc	.43 ± .02	.50 ± .02 (16-19)
Boastful, "show-off"	.42 ± .02	.56 ± .03 (7-8)
Inefficient in work, play, etc	.42 ± .03	.50 ± .03 (16-19)
Depressed	.42 ± .03	.55 ± .03 (9)
Grouped: "nervous," etc	.42 ± .02	.48 ± .02 (23-26)
Bad language	.41 ± .03	.42 ± .04 (37-40)
Fantastical lying	.41 ± .03	.41 ± .03 (41-43)
Question of encephalitis	.41 ± .03	.52 ± .04 (14-15)
Disturbing influence in home	.40 ± .03	.58 ± .04 (5)
Unpopular	.39 ± .03	.50 ± .04 (16-19)
Daydreaming	.38 ± .02	.49 ± .03 (20-22)
Psychoneurotic	.38 ± .03	.49 ± .04 (20-22)
Cruelty to animals	.37 ± .04	....
"Annoying" girls	.37 ± .03	....
"Nervous"	.37 ± .02	.35 ± .03 (55-59)
Worry over specific fact	.37 ± .03	.37 ± .04 (52-53)
Grouped: temper, etc	.36 ± .02	.42 ± .02 (37-40)
Teasing other children	.35 ± .02	.42 ± .04 (37-40)
Tiring easily	.35 ± .03	.33 ± .05 (65-68)
Mental conflict	.35 ± .03	.43 ± .04 (33-36)
Complaining of bad treatment by other children	.35 ± .03	.34 ± .05 (60-64)
Threatening violence	.34 ± .03	....
Seclusive	.33 ± .02	.31 ± .03 (71-73)
Sensitive (general)	.33 ± .03	.34 ± .03 (60-64)
Grouped: swearing, etc	.33 ± .02	.43 ± .03 (33-36)
Bossy	.32 ± .03	.50 ± .03 (16-19)
Rude	.32 ± .02	.39 ± .03 (47-49)
Masturbation	.32 ± .02	.30 ± .03 (74-76)
"Night terrors"	.32 ± .02	.48 ± .04 (23-26)
Neurological defect	.32 ± .02	.39 ± .03 (47-49)
Exclusion from school	.32 ± .02	.16
Gluttony	.31 ± .03	.43 ± .04 (33-36)

*Rank order of girls' correlations.

TABLE 6—Continued

	Boys	Girls
Violence	.31 ± .02	.64 ± .03 (1)
Overinterest in sex matters	.31 ± .03	.35 ± .04 (55-59)
Sensitive over specific fact	.31 ± .02	.34 ± .03 (60-64)
Emotional instability	.31 ± .03	.45 ± .03 (28-30)
Unhappy	.31 ± .03	.33 ± .04 (65-68)
Headaches	.31 ± .03	.25 ± .04 (83-86)
Grouped: disobedient, etc	.31 ± .02	.40 ± .02 (44-46)
Destructive	.30 ± .02	.40 ± .04 (44-46)
Failure to adjust in foster-home	.30 ± .04	.54 ± .04 (10-11)
Swearing (general)	.30 ± .03	.59 ± .04 (3-4)
Thumb-sucking	.30 ± .04	.33 ± .04 (65-68)
Absent-minded	.30 ± .03	.18
Changeable moods	.30 ± .02	.49 ± .03 (20-22)
Psychopathic personality	.30 ± .03	.46 ± .04 (27)
Grouped: fighting, etc	.30 ± .02	.48 ± .02 (23-26)
Lazy	.29 ± .02	.17
Stubborn	.29 ± .02	.36 ± .03 (54)
Sullen	.29 ± .02	.34 ± .03 (60-64)
Temper tantrums	.29 ± .02	.54 ± .03 (10-11)
Irritable	.29 ± .02	.27 ± .03 (81-82)
Spoiled child	.29 ± .02	.27 ± .03 (81-82)
Bowel incontinence	.28 ± .04	....
Cruelty to younger children	.28 ± .03	
Nail-biting	.28 ± .02	.24 ± .03 (87-77)
Resentful attitude	.28 ± .03	.56 ± .04 (7-8)
Abused feeling or manner	.28 ± .03	.48 ± .04 (23-26)
Quarrelsome	.27 ± .02	.44 ± .02 (31-32)
Crying spells	.27 ± .02	.38 ± .02 (50-51)
Object of teasing	.27 ± .02	.30 ± .03 (74-76)
Finicky food habits	.26 ± .02	.41 ± .03 (41-43)
Disturbing influence in school	.26 ± .02	.52 ± .03 (14-15)
Lack of interest in school	.26 ± .02	.32 ± .03 (69-70)
Grouped: lack of interest in school, etc	.26 ± .02	.33 ± .03 (65-68)
Overinterest in opposite sex	.26 ± .03	.31 ± .03 (71-73)
Restless in sleep	.26 ± .02	.35 ± .03 (55-59)
Fire-setting	.25 ± .04	....
Selfish	.25 ± .03	.44 ± .03 (31-32)
Temper display	.25 ± .02	.16
Distractible	.25 ± .02	.41 ± .03 (41-43)
Restless	.25 ± .02	.34 ± .03 (60-64)
Grouped: egocentric, etc	.25 ± .02	.39 ± .03 (47-49)
Begging	.24 ± .03	....
Disobedient	.24 ± .02	.31 ± .03 (71-73)
Irresponsible	.24 ± .03	.29 ± .04 (77-79)
Lying	.24 ± .02	.35 ± .02 (55-59)
Exhibitionism	.24 ± .04	
Incorrigible	.23 ± .02	.35 ± .03 (55-59)
Irregular employment record	.23 ± .03	.37 ± .04 (52-53)
Loitering	.23 ± .03	.06
Passive pederasty	.23 ± .04	....
Sex attack on opposite sex	.23 ± .04	....
Irregular sleep habits	.23 ± .03	.42 ± .04 (37-40)

TABLE 6—Continued

	Boys	Girls
Slovenly	.22 + .02	.25 ± .03 (83-86)
Swearing at mother, teacher, etc.	.22 + .04	....
Bullying	.21 ± .03	....
Gambling	.21 ± .04	....
Smoking	.21 ± .03	....
Sneaky	.21 ± .04	.28 ± .05 (80)
Sulky	.21 ± .03	.29 ± .04 (77-79)
Poor work in school	.21 ± .02	.18
Defiant	.20 ± .03	.53 ± .03 (12-13)
Leading others into bad conduct	.20 ± .03	.45 ± .04 (28-30)
Illegitimate parentage	.20 ± .04	.06
Obscene language	.20 ± .03	....
Stealing an automobile	.20 ± .04	....
Fighting	.18	.43 ± .03 (33-36)
Egocentric	.11	.30 ± .03 (74-76)
Stealing	.19	.29 ± .03 (77-79)
Inattentive in school	.18	.25 ± .04 (83-86)
Excuse-forming	.13	.25 ± .03 (83-86)
Staying out late at night	.16	.24 ± .03 (87-88)
Bad companions	.14	.22 ± .03 (89-91)
Truancy from home	.11	.22 ± .03 (89-91)
Conduct prognosis bad	.19	.22 ± .05 (89-91)
Repressed	.06	.21 ± .04 (92)
Enuresis	.17	.20 ± .03 (93)
	Larger Correlations (Negative)	
Feeble-minded sibling	-.20 ± .03	-.12

Other Correlations (Positive to Negative)

Apprehensive, .19 and .16; Listless, .19 and .16; Discord between parents, .19 and .08; Robbing a building, home, etc., .18 (boys); Truancy from institution, .18 (boys); Former convulsions, .18 and .11; Speech defect, .18 and .11; Refusal to attend school, .17 and .08; Truancy from home, .17 and .19; Mutual masturbation (same sex), .17 (boys); Homosexual (same age), .16 (boys); "Sugar hunger," .16 (boys); Attractive manner, .16 and .05; Clean, .15 and .14; Grouped: dull, slow, etc., .15 and .07; Lack of initiative, .14 and -.03; Bashful, .13 and .05; Vicious home conditions, .13 and .06; Preference for younger children, .12 and .13; Follower, .12 and .07; Victim of sex abuse, .11 (girls); Lack of affection, .10 (boys); Stuttering, .10 (boys); Gang, .09 (boys); Underweight, .09 and .11; Sex delinquency (coitus), .08 and .08; Irregular attendance at school, .07 and -.02; Leader, .05 and .16; Sex denied entirely, .04 and .17; Question of hypophrenia, .04 and -.05; Popular, .03 and .12; Vocational guidance, .02 and .02; Oversuggestible, .01 and .13; Immoral home conditions, .00 and -.03; Slow, dull, -.04 and -.07; Immoral sister, -.07 and -.06; Lues, -.07 and .06; Brother in penal detention, .08 and .12; Retardation in school, -.12 and .13

prejudicial effect due to varying completeness in the case-record
data.[1] It can be supposed that the informants who tend to give extensive information concerning the child in the personality sphere
of his activity also tend to give extensive data in the conduct
sphere, and, similarly, informants who give only a brief account
of a child's personality problems are likely to give only limited
information as to his conduct difficulties. The personality-total
showed relatively low correlations with police arrest, the bi-serial
correlations being .18 $\pm$ .02 and .11 $\pm$ .03 for boys and girls respectively.

          (In computing the correlations of a specific behavior trait
with either the personality-total or the conduct-total of which it
would form a component, it was necessary in each instance to exclude the specific behavior notation concerned in the correlation
in order to avoid a spurious correlation due to identity of material if both variates were used in the correlation. For example,
such a correlation coefficient as that of queer behavior with personality-total among boys, .52 $\pm$ .03, means the bi-serial correlation of queer behavior with the total number of personality problems noted for each child other than the notation queer behavior
itself.)

          The highest correlations (bi-serial r) among boys with the
personality-total criterion of relative seriousness or "ominousness" were with the notations staff diagnosis or question of incipient psychosis or psychosis not elsewhere specified, .76 $\pm$ .03,
and staff diagnosis or question of dementia praecox or schizophre-
nia (simple, hebephrenic, catatonic, paranoid, or unspecified),
.60 $\pm$ .03; the corresponding coefficients for girls could not be
reliably calculated because of the paucity of girls' cases in our
data. Among girls the highest coefficients were for violence, .64
$\pm$ .03, and queer behavior, .61 $\pm$ .03, the corresponding coefficients for boys being .31 $\pm$ .02 and .52 $\pm$ .03 respectively. The
"larger grouping," depressed spells or unhappiness (undifferentiated), yielded relatively high correlations in the .50's among both
sexes.

          Eight notations among girls yielded high correlations in

_____

[1]Chap. iv, pp. 35-38.

the .50's among girls, and almost equally large coefficients in
the .40's among boys: diagnosis or question of encephalitis, question of change of personality, disturbing influence in home, depressed mood or spells, sensitiveness or worrisomeness (undifferentiated), inferiority feelings, boastful or "show-off" manner,
and inefficiency in work, play, etc. Four behavior notations among
girls yielded high correlations in the .50's and relatively substantial coefficients in the .30's among boys: unpopularity, bossy
manner, swearing in general, and failure to adjust in foster-home.
Among girls four additional behavior problems yielded high correlations in the .50's and among boys moderate correlations in the
.20's: temper tantrums, defiant attitude, resentful attitude, and
disturbing influence in school.

Fairly large correlations in the .40's were found among
both sexes for fantastical lying, bad language, hatred or jealousy
of sibling, and the "larger grouping," "nervousness" or restlessness (including irritable temperament and changeable moods, undifferentiated), and also for the notation talking to self without apparent reason, for which only the boys' coefficient was computed.
Contrariness yielded almost equally large correlations of .45 $\pm$ .03
and .38 $\pm$ .04 among boys and girls respectively. Twelve behavior
problems among girls yielded fairly large correlations in the .40's
and among boys substantial correlations in the .30's: staff notation or question of psychopathic personality or psychopathic trends,
staff notation of psychoneurosis or psychoneurotic trends (unspecified), mental conflict, daydreaming, staff notation of emotional
instability, changeable moods, "night terrors," teasing other children, disobedience or incorrigibility (including defiant attitude,
stubbornness, and contrariness, undifferentiated), destructiveness,
fighting or quarrelsomeness (including violence, undifferentiated),
and gluttony or overeating. Eight behavior problems among girls
similarly yielded large correlations in the .40's and moderate coefficients ranging from .18 to .28 among boys: abused feeling or
manner, quarrelsomeness, fighting, selfishness, leading others into
bad conduct, distractibility, irregular sleep habits, and finicky
food habits.

Thirteen miscellaneous notations yielded substantial correlations in the .30's with personality-total among both sexes:
"nervousness," unhappiness, worry over some specific fact or

episode, sensitiveness in general, sensitiveness over some specif-
fact or episode, seclusiveness, complaining of bad treatment by
other children, rudeness, thumb-sucking, tiring easily, masturbation, overinterest in sex matters, and neurological defect (unspecified). Three additional conduct problems for which only the boys
correlations could be reliably computed also yielded substantial
correlations in the .30's: threatening violence, cruelty to animals, and "annoying" girls. Three miscellaneous notations among
boys yielded substantial correlations in the .30's, and low or moderate coefficients ranging from .16 to .25 among girls: absent-
mindedness, exclusion from school, and headaches. Thirteen miscellaneous case-record notations among girls yielded substantial correlations in the .30's and moderate correlations in the .20's amor
boys: restlessness, restlessness in sleep, crying spells, egocentricity or selfishness (including self-indulgent attitude [undif-
ferentiated]), disobedience, incorrigibility, stubbornness, sullen
ness, lying, object of teasing by other children, lack of interest
in school, overinterest in the opposite sex, and irregular employment record.

    Seven behavior difficulties among both sexes showed moder-
ate correlations in the .20's with the personality-total criterior
of seriousness or "ominousness": irritable temperament, sulkiness
"spoiled child," sneakiness, slovenliness, irresponsibility, and
nail-biting. A large series of thirteen behavior traits for which
only the boys' correlations were computed (the girls' cases being
too few) also showed moderate coefficients in the .20's: cruelty
to younger children, fire-setting, bullying, swearing at mother,
teacher, etc., stealing an automobile or horse, begging on the
street, smoking, gambling, obscene language, sex attack or abuse
(actual or attempted) upon child of opposite sex, passive pederasty, exhibitionism or "indecent exposure," and bowel incontinence
Five miscellaneous notations among boys showed moderate correlations in the .20's but low positive coefficients below .20 among
girls: temper display (other than "tantrums"), laziness, loitering or wandering, poor work in school, and illegitimate parentage.
Ten miscellaneous notations among girls showed moderate correlations ranging from .20 to .30, but low positive coefficients below
.20 among boys: repressed manner, excuse-forming attitude, egocentricity, stealing, bad companions, truancy from home, staying

out late at night, inattentiveness in school, staff notation of unfavorable conduct prognosis, and enuresis (continuing beyond third
birthday).

The only negative correlation of moderate size was for
feeble-minded sibling among boys, -.20 ± .03, the corresponding
coefficient for girls being a low negative, -.12.

Among the following notations the correlations with the
personality-total were found to be quite negligible (less than
± .10):   running with a gang, sex delinquency (coitus), slow or
dull manner, question of hypophrenia (suspected feeble-mindedness),
immoral home conditions, immoral sister, and question or diagnosis
of lues or former lues.

Among the thirteen sex notations considered in this chapter
the highest correlation with the personality-total criterion of
seriousness was the substantial one of .37 ± .03 among boys for
"annoying" girls. Moderate to substantial coefficients ranging
from .26 to .35 among both sexes were found for overinterest in
the opposite sex, overinterest in sex matters, and masturbation.
Four sex notations for which only the boys' correlations were computed showed moderate correlations in the .20's: sex attack or
abuse (actual or attempted) upon child of the opposite sex, passive
pederasty, exhibitionism or "indecent exposure," and obscene language. The remaining five sex notations (sex delinquency or coitus, mutual masturbation with child of same sex, homosexual practices with child of similar age, victim of sex attack or abuse by
older person, and sex misbehavior denied entirely) showed only low
or negligible correlations, ranging from .04 to .17.

Among the twelve physical, psychophysical, or "constitutional" notations considered in this chapter, the highest correlations were with diagnosis or question of encephalitis, with coefficients of .41 ± .03 and .52 ± .04 for boys and girls respectively.
Neurological defect (unspecified) yielded corresponding substantial
coefficients of .32 ± .02 and .39 ± .03. Moderate or substantial
corresponding correlations of .31 ± .03 and .25 ± .04 were found
for headaches. Enuresis (continuing beyond third birthday) among
girls and bowel incontinence (computed for boys only) showed moderate correlations in the .20's. Low or negligible coefficients
ranging from -.07 to .18 were found for the remaining seven notations in this field: underweight condition (10 per cent or more),

"sugar hunger," former convulsions or convulsions in infancy, lues
(present or former), speech defect, stuttering, and question of hy
pophrenia (if mental defect may be classifiable as a "constitutional" disability).

Among the seven home or familial notations considered in
this chapter, only two correlations of moderate size were found,
both among boys: .20 ± .04 with illegitimate parentage and the
curious negative one of -.20 ± .03 with feeble-minded sibling.
Discord between parents among boys showed the low but statisticall
significant correlation of .19 ± .02.   All other coefficients in
this field, including those for vicious home conditions, immoral
home conditions, immoral sister, and brother with police arrest or
under penal detention were low or negligible, ranging from -.12 to
.13.

The correlation coefficients for boys and girls in Table 6
were generally similar to each other, the girls' correlations usually averaging somewhat larger.   In other words, notations which
from a personality standpoint appeared to be important among boys
also appeared to be important in this respect among girls, and vic
versa.   The rank-order correlation (Spearman's rank-differences-
squared formula) for the boys' and girls' coefficients was found
to be .78 ± .02.

CHAPTER X

THE CONDUCT-TOTAL CRITERION

The conduct-total is the unweighted sum of all conduct problems reported for an individual child, as we have explained in chapter viii. Among our 2,113 White boys the number of conduct notations ranged from 0 to 63, with a mean of 9.4 and a standard deviation of 7.8 (Table 4, p. 85). Among our 1,181 White girls the range was from 0 to 50, the mean 7.6, and the standard deviation 7.2. The distribution of the conduct-total is shown in Figure 4.

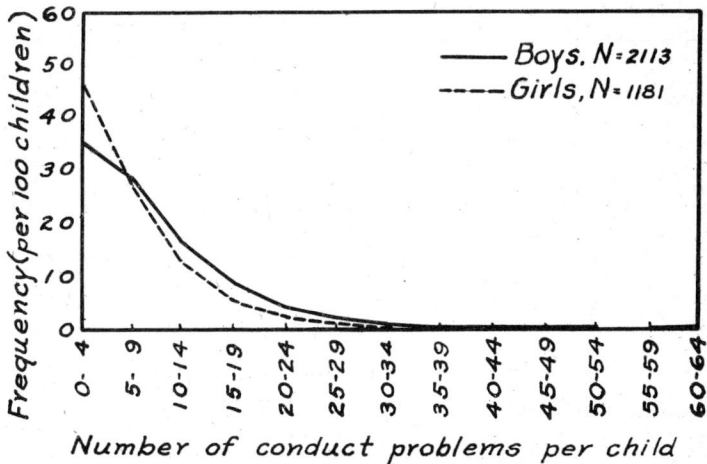

Fig. 4.—Percentage Frequency Distribution
of Conduct-Totals

It will be noted in Table 7 that among boys the conduct-total showed large correlations with the other two criteria, personality-total and police arrest, the coefficients being .50 ± .01 and .53 ± .02 respectively. Among girls the correlations with personality-total were comparatively large (.61 ± .01), but they were of lesser magnitude (.31 ± .03) with the police-arrest criterion. In other words, the extent of conduct deviation among girls appears

TABLE 7

CORRELATIONS WITH "CONDUCT-TOTAL"

	Boys	Girls
Personality-total..............................	.50 + .01	.61 + .01
Police arrest.................................	.53 + .02	.31 + .03
	Larger Correlations (Positive)	
Grouped: swearing, etc.......................	.61 ± .02	.76 + .02 (3)*
Disturbing influence in home.................	.60 ± .03	.69 ± .03 (4)
Psychopathic personality.....................	.60 ± .03	.61 ± .04 (13-14)
Destructive..................................	.59 ± .02	.54 ± .04 (21-23)
"Annoying" girls.............................	.56 ± .03	....
Truancy from home............................	.56 ± .02	.42 ± .03 (49-52)
Grouped: disobedient, etc...................	.56 ± .01	.64 ± .02 (9-11)
Stealing....................................	.55 ± .01	.51 ± .02 (27-28)
Begging.....................................	.54 ± .03	....
Violence....................................	.54 ± .02	.79 ± .02 (2)
Incorrigible................................	.53 ± .02	.59 ± .02 (15)
Grouped: fighting, etc.....................	.53 ± .02	.65 ± .02 (7-8)
Bad language................................	.52 ± .03	.66 ± .04 (6)
Obscene language............................	.52 ± .03	....
Threatening violence........................	.52 ± .03	....
Failure to adjust in foster-home............	.51 ± .04	.62 ± .03 (12)
Leading others into bad conduct.............	.51 ± .02	.65 ± .03 (7-8)
Swearing (general)..........................	.51 ± .02	.86 ± .03 (1)
Cruelty to animals..........................	.50 ± .03	....
Cruelty to younger children.................	.50 ± .03	....
Smoking.....................................	.49 ± .02	....
Unpopular...................................	.49 ± .03	.64 ± .03 (9-11)
Exclusion from school.......................	.49 ± .02	.56 ± .03 (17-18)
Boastful, "show-off"........................	.48 ± .02	.52 ± .03 (25-26)
Contrary....................................	.48 ± .03	.34 ± .04 (65)
Lying.......................................	.48 ± .02	.56 ± .02 (17-18)
Rude..	.48 ± .02	.55 ± .02 (19-20)
Staying out late at night...................	.48 ± .02	.51 ± .03 (27-28)
Disturbing influence in school..............	.46 ± .02	.48 ± .03 (33-35)
Fantastical lying...........................	.46 ± .03	.49 ± .03 (31-32)
Gambling....................................	.45 ± .04	....
Swearing at mother, teacher, etc............	.45 ± .04	....
Truancy from institution....................	.45 ± .03	....
Truancy from school.........................	.45 ± .02	.44 ± .03 (41-43)
Homosexual (same age).......................	.44 ± .03	....
Excuse-forming..............................	.44 ± .02	.53 ± .03 (24)
Defiant.....................................	.43 ± .02	.68 ± .03 (5)
Disobedient.................................	.43 ± .02	.49 ± .02 (31-32)
Fighting....................................	.43 ± .02	.55 ± .03 (19-20)
Loitering...................................	.43 ± .02	.27 ± .04 (80-82)
Grouped: egocentric, etc...................	.42 ± .02	.47 ± .02 (36-38)

*Rank order of girls' correlations.

TABLE 7—Continued

	Boys	Girls
Teasing other children	.41 ± .02	.50 ± .04 (29-30)
Stealing an automobile	.41 ± .04	....
Egocentric	.41 ± .02	.48 ± .03 (33-35)
Bad companions	.40 ± .02	.35 ± .03 (61-64)
Conduct prognosis bad	.40 ± .03	.46 ± .04 (39-40)
Passive pederasty	.39 ± .04	....
Lack of affection	.39 ± .04	....
Grouped: temper, etc	.39 ± .02	.50 ± .02 (29-30)
Temper tantrums	.38 ± .02	.57 ± .03 (16)
Exhibitionism	.38 ± .04	....
Irregular sleep habits	.38 ± .03	.32 ± .04 (68-71)
Fire-setting	.37 ± .04	....
Gluttony	.36 ± .03	.32 ± .05 (68-71)
Incipient psychosis	.36 ± .04	....
Complaining of bad treatment by other children	.36 ± .03	.39 ± .05 (56-57)
Gang	.35 ± .02	....
Sullen	.35 ± .02	.33 ± .03 (66-67)
Grouped: "nervous," etc	.35 ± .02	.41 ± .02 (53-54)
Quarrelsome	.34 ± .02	.46 ± .03 (39-40)
Overinterest in sex matters	.34 ± .03	.42 ± .03 (49-52)
Restless	.34 ± .02	.43 ± .02 (44-48)
Robbing a building, home, etc	.33 ± .03	....
Overinterest in opposite sex	.33 ± .03	.47 ± .03 (36-38)
Talking to self without apparent reason	.33 ± .04	....
Masturbation	.32 ± .02	.41 ± .03 (53-54)
Hatred or jealousy of sibling	.32 ± .03	.33 ± .04 (66-67)
Abused feeling or manner	.32 ± .03	.61 ± .04 (13-14)
Queer	.32 ± .03	.64 ± .03 (9-11)
Grouped: lack of interest in school, etc	.32 ± .02	.36 ± .03 (59-60)
Irregular employment record	.31 ± .03	.52 ± .05 (25-26)
Mutual masturbation (same sex)	.31 ± .03	....
Sex attack on opposite sex	.31 ± .04	....
Spoiled child	.31 ± .02	.38 ± .03 (58)
Refusal to attend school	.30 ± .03	.22 ± .04 (88-89)
Resentful attitude	.30 ± .03	.54 ± .04 (21-23)
Slovenly	.30 ± .02	.30 ± .03 (72-75)
Irritable temperament	.30 ± .02	.29 ± .03 (76)
Bowel incontinence	.29 ± .04	....
Question of change of personality	.29 ± .03	.54 ± .03 (21-23)
Mental conflict	.29 ± .03	.40 ± .04 (55)
Unhappy	.29 ± .03	.35 ± .04 (61-64)
Bossy	.28 ± .03	.43 ± .03 (44-48)
Emotional instability	.28 ± .03	.44 ± .03 (41-43)
Irresponsible	.27 ± .03	.32 ± .04 (68-71)
Daydreaming	.27 ± .02	.48 ± .03 (33-35)
Changeable moods	.26 ± .02	.43 ± .03 (44-48)
Dementia praecox	.26 ± .04	....
Oversuggestible	.26 ± .02	.22 ± .03 (88-89)
Inferiority feelings	.26 ± .02	.25 ± .04 (84)
Sneaky	.25 ± .03	.42 ± .04 (49-52)
Stubborn	.25 ± .02	.43 ± .02 (44-48)
Restless in sleep	.25 ± .02	.39 ± .03 (56-57)

TABLE 7—Continued

	Boys	Girls
Inefficient in work, play, etc................	.24 ± .03	.35 ± .04 (61-64)
Sulky...	.24 ± .03	.27 ± .04 (80-82)
"Night terrors"...............................	.24 ± .04	.47 ± .04 (36-38)
Grouped: depressed, etc......................	.24 ± .02	.42 ± .03 (49-52)
Bullying......................................	.23 ± .03	....
Distractible.................................	.23 ± .02	.44 ± .03 (41-43)
Inattentive in school........................	.22 ± .02	.24 ± .04 (85-86)
Lazy...	.22 ± .03	.17
Crying spells................................	.22 ± .02	.30 ± .02 (72-75)
"Sugar hunger"...............................	.22 ± .04	....
Selfish......................................	.21 ± .03	.35 ± .04 (61-64)
Leader.......................................	.21 ± .03	.19
Illegitimate parentage.......................	.21 ± .04	.10
Lack of interest in school...................	.20 ± .02	.28 ± .03 (77-79)
Question of encephalitis.....................	.20 ± .04	.36 ± .04 (59-60)
Depressed....................................	.17	.43 ± .03 (44-48)
Worry over specific fact.....................	.11	.32 ± .05 (68-71)
Object of teasing............................	.18	.30 ± .03 (72-75)
Headaches....................................	.14	.30 ± .03 (72-75)
Finicky food habits..........................	.10	.28 ± .03 (77-79)
Grouped: sensitive or worrisome, etc........	.16	.28 ± .03 (77-79)
Sensitive over specific fact.................	.19	.27 ± .03 (80-82)
Thumb-sucking................................	.15	.26 ± .05 (83)
"Nervous"....................................	.19	.24 ± .04 (85-86)
Psychoneurotic...............................	.06	.23 ± .04 (87)
Victim of sex abuse..........................	....	.21 ± .03 (90)

Other Correlations (Positive to Negative)

Nail-biting, .19 and .17; Temper display, .19 and .08; Absent-minded, .18 and .09; Sex delinquency (coitus), .17 and .16; Seclusive, .17 and .17; Former convulsions, .17 and .00; Enuresis, .16 and .18; Irregular attendance at school, .15 and .01; Popular, .13 and .08; Sensitive (general), .12 and .16; Attractive manner, .12 and .08; Vicious home conditions, .12 and .18; Poor work in school, .11 and .08; Preference for younger children, .10 and .15; Brother in penal detention, .10 and -.01; Tiring easily, .09 and .12; Apprehensive, .09 and .16; Listless, .08 and .15; Repressed, .08 and .09; Slow, dull, .07 and -.07; Follower, .07 and .03; Neurological defect, .07 and .12; Clean, .06 and .04; Immoral sister, .04 and .02; Lack of initiative, .02 and -.06; Sex denied entirely, .02 and -.00; Discord between parents, .02 and .16; Immoral home conditions, .01 and .10; Grouped: dull, slow, etc., -.02 and -.03; Bashful, -.02 and -.07; Speech defect, -.03 and .00; Lues, -.03 and .12; Question of hypophrenia, -.03 and -.03; Underweight, -.04 and -.02; Stuttering, -.05 (boys); Retardation in school, -.08 and -.14; Vocational guidance, -.10 and -.17; Feeble-minded sibling, -.15 and -.16

to be more closely related to personality problems than among boys. On the other hand, conduct problems among girls do not seem to be so closely associated with the fact of a police arrest.

(In computing the correlations of a specific conduct notation with the conduct-total, that specific notation was not counted
in the conduct-total. For example, the correlation of stealing
with the conduct-total among boys, .55 ± .01, means the bi-serial
correlation of stealing with the total number of conduct problems
other than the notation of stealing itself.)

The largest correlation with the conduct-total criterion
of seriousness or "ominousness" was the extremely high one of .86
± .03 among girls for swearing in general, the corresponding coefficient among boys (.51 ± .02) also being relatively large.
(This coefficient of .86 ± .03, it may be remarked in passing, is
the largest correlation found among all the 14,000-odd coefficients
computed in this study.) Violence among girls yielded the unusually large correlation of .79 ± .02, the corresponding coefficient
among boys being .54 ± .02. Staff diagnosis or question of psychopathic personality (unspecified) and disturbing influence in school
yielded very high correlations in the .60's among both sexes. Five
notations among girls yielded very high correlations in the .60's
and among boys almost equally large coefficients in the .50's:
leading others into bad conduct, failure to adjust in foster-home,
fighting or quarrelsomeness (including violence, undifferentiated),
bad language, and disobedience or incorrigibility (including defiant attitude, stubbornness, and contrariness, undifferentiated).
Unpopularity and defiant attitude among girls similarly yielded
high correlations in the .60's and among boys fairly large coefficients in the .40's. Queer behavior and abused feeling or manner
among girls also yielded very high correlations in the .60's and
among boys substantial correlations in the .30's.

High correlations in the .50's were found among both sexes
for three conduct difficulties—stealing, incorrigibility, and destructiveness—and also for six conduct difficulties for which only
the boys' coefficients were computed: threatening violence, cruelty to younger children, cruelty to animals, begging on the street,
obscene language, and "annoying" girls. Truancy from home yielded
the meaningful correlations of .56 ± .02 and .42 ± .03 among boys
and girls respectively. Eight behavior problems among girls
yielded high correlations in the .50's and among boys almost
equally large coefficients in the .40's: fighting, teasing other
children, rudeness, staying out late at night, lying, excuse-forming

attitude, boastful or "show-off" manner, and exclusion from school.
Four notations among girls yielded large correlations in the .50's
and among boys fairly substantial coefficients ranging from .29 to
.38: temper tantrums, resentful attitude, question of change of
personality, and irregular employment record.

Fairly large correlations in the .40's with the conduct-
total criterion of seriousness or "ominousness" were found for six
conduct difficulties among both sexes: disobedience, disturbing
influence in school, truancy from school, fantastical lying, egocentricity, and staff notation of unfavorable conduct prognosis,
and also for six conduct problems for which only boys' coefficients
were computed: stealing an automobile or horse, truancy or running
away from an institution, swearing at mother, teacher, etc., gambling, smoking, and homosexual practices (unspecified) with child
of similar age. Three conduct problems among boys yielded large
correlations in the .40's and among girls moderate or substantial
coefficients ranging from .27 to .35: contrariness, bad companions, and loitering or wandering. Five conduct difficulties among
girls yielded large correlations in the .40's and among boys substantial coefficients in the .30's: quarrelsomeness, restlessness,
masturbation, overinterest in the opposite sex, and overinterest in
sex matters. Ten personality and conduct problems among girls similarly yielded fairly large correlations in the .40's and among
boys low or moderate coefficients raning from .17 to .29: stubbornness, bossy manner, changeable moods or attitudes, staff notation of emotional instability, depressed mood or spells, daydreaming, mental conflict, distractibility, sneakiness, and "night terrors."

Moderate correlations in the .30's among both boys and
girls were found for the following eight behavior problems: sullenness, complaining of bad treatment by other children, hatred or
jealousy of sibling, "spoiled child," slovenliness, lack of interest or inattentiveness in school studies, employment, etc. (undifferentiated), irregular sleep habits, and gluttony or overeating,
and also for the following ten behavior problems for which only
the boys' correlations were computed: robbing a building, home,
etc., running with a gang, fire-setting, lack of affection for
other people, staff diagnosis or question of incipient psychosis
or psychosis not elsewhere specified, talking to self without

apparent reason, sex attack or abuse on younger person of opposite
sex, mutual masturbation with child of same sex, passive pederasty,
and exhibitionism or "indecent exposure." Among boys irritable
temperament and refusal to attend school similarly yielded substantial correlations in the .30's and among girls moderate coefficients in the .20's. Among girls seven miscellaneous case-record
notations yielded substantial correlations in the .30's and among
boys moderate coefficients in the .20's: selfishness, inefficiency
in work, play, etc., irresponsibility, restlessness in sleep, unhappiness, crying spells, and diagnosis or question of encephalitis. Three additional case-record notations among girls yielded
substantial correlations in the .30's but among boys low positive
coefficients below .20: worry over some specific fact or episode,
object of teasing by other children, and headaches.

     Moderate correlations in the .20's among both boys and
girls were found for five behavior problems: sulkiness, inattentiveness in school, lack of interest in school, oversuggestibility,
and inferiority feelings and also for four traits for which only
the boys' correlations were computed: bullying, staff diagnosis
or question of dementia praecox (unspecified), "sugar hunger," and
bowel incontinence and also for the notation victim of sex attack
or abuse by older child or person, for which only the girls' correlation was computed. Three miscellaneous notations among boys similarly showed moderate correlations in the .20's but low coefficients, ranging from .10 to .19, among girls: laziness, "leader,"
and illegitimate parentage. Among girls five behavior problems
showed moderate correlations in the .20's but among boys low positive correlations below .20: "nervousness," sensitiveness over
some specific fact or episode, staff diagnosis or question of psychoneurosis (unspecified) or psychoneurotic trends, finicky food
habits, and thumb-sucking.

     With the following notations the correlations were found
to be quite negligible (less than $\pm$ .10): repressed manner, "follower," slow or dull manner, lack of initiative, bashfulness, question of hypophrenia or suspected feeble-mindedness, underweight
condition (10 per cent or more), speech defect, stuttering, clean
habits, sex misconduct denied entirely, and immoral sister.

     Among the thirteen sex notations considered in this chapter
the highest correlations with the conduct-total criterion of seri-

ousness or "ominousness" were found for the two conduct difficulties for which only the boys' coefficients were computed: "annoying" girls, .56 ± .03, and obscene language, .52 ± .03. Three additional notations for which only the boys' correlations were computed yielded very substantial coefficients ranging from .38 to
.44: passive pederasty, homosexual practices (unspecified) with
child of similar age, and exhibitionism or "indecent exposure."
Three sex behavior problems among girls yielded relatively large
correlations in the .40's and substantial coefficients in the .30's
among boys: overinterest in the opposite sex, overinterest in sex
matters, and masturbation. Two sex difficulties for which only the
boys' correlations were computed—sex attack or abuse (actual or
attempted) upon younger child of opposite sex and mutual masturbation with child of the same sex—yielded respective coefficients
of .31 ± .04 and .31 ± .03. Victim of sex attack or abuse by older
child or person among girls showed the moderate correlation of .21
± .03, the corresponding coefficient for boys not being calculated
because of paucity of boys' cases. Sex delinquency (coitus) showed
the low but statistically significant correlations of .17 ± .04 and
.16 ± .03 among boys and girls respectively. For sex misconduct
denied entirely the correlations were quite negligible, .02 and
-.00.

Among the twelve physical, psychophysical, or "constitutional" factors considered in this chapter, the largest correlation with conduct-total was for diagnosis or question of encephalitis among girls, .36 ± .04, the corresponding coefficient among
boys being moderate, .20 ± .04. Headaches among girls showed the
significant correlation of .30 ± .03, the corresponding coefficient
among boys being low, .14. Two notations for which only the boys'
coefficients were computed—bowel incontinence and "sugar hunger"—
showed moderate correlations in the .20's. The remaining eight notations in this field—neurological defect (unspecified), lues
(present or former), former convulsions or convulsions in infancy,
enuresis (continuing beyond third birthday), underweight condition
(10 per cent or more), speech defect, stuttering, and question of
hypophrenia (if mental deficiency may be truly classified as a constitutional defect)—all showed only low or negligible correlations, ranging from -.05 to .18.

Among the seven home or familial case-record notations

considered in this chapter the only coefficient of moderate size
with conduct-total was for illegitimate parentage among boys, .21
± .04, the corresponding correlation among girls being low, .10.
For the remaining six notations in this field—discord between parents, vicious home conditions, immoral home conditions, brother
with police arrest or in penal detention, immoral sister, and
feeble-minded sibling—all correlations were low or negligible,
ranging from -.16 to .18.

The correlation coefficients for boys and girls in Table 7
were generally similar to each other. The rank-order correlation
(Spearman's rank-differences-squared formula) of the two columns
of coefficients in this table was found to be .89 ± .01. In other
words, the notations which appeared to be important from a conduct
standpoint among one sex also appeared to be similarly important
among the other sex.

Among boys the correlations with the conduct-total bore
little resemblance to those with the personality-total. The rank-
order correlation among the boys' coefficients for the two criteria
was only .33 ± .05 (Table 5, p. 86). In other words, a notation
which among boys appeared serious from a personality standpoint was
not necessarily serious from a conduct standpoint. Among girls the
rank order of coefficients was more similar for the two criteria,
the intercolumnar correlation of these coefficients being 76 ±
.03, that is, notations which among girls appeared to be important
according to the one criterion also appeared to be important according to the other criterion.

CHAPTER XI

THE POLICE-ARREST CRITERION

The notation of police arrest in a child's case record
covered any arrest by police for reason of misconduct, whether the
child was formally "booked" on charges or not. In many instances
a commitment to a penal or correctional institution or to a "parental school" resulted, and in other instances the child was dis-
missed. It did not include cases in which a child was placed in
the "detention home" because of inadequate guardianship by parents.
Nor did it include a few instances in which an irresponsible child
"wandered away" from his home or his guardians and "became lost"
and was taken in charge by police officers for safekeeping until
his parents arrived, though some of these instances bordered closely
on "truancy." The behavior implied in a police arrest thus varied
in seriousness from patent juvenile criminality down to instances
of "pickup" for some minor prank or truancy.

Among our children, aged 6 to 17 years inclusive, this notation appeared in 457, or 21.6 per cent, of the 2,113 boys and in
179, or 15.2 per cent, of the 1,181 girls.

Police arrest showed only low correlations with personality-
total, the bi-serial r coefficients being .18 $\pm$ .02 and .11 $\pm$ .03
for boys and girls respectively (Table 8). Among boys the correlation with conduct-total was high, .53 $\pm$ .02, while among girls
the correlation was of less, though substantial, size, .31 $\pm$ .03.

The largest correlation with police arrest was the unusually high one of .76 $\pm$ .02 with sex delinquency (coitus) among
girls, the corresponding boys' coefficient being low but positive,
.18 $\pm$ .05. Very high correlations in the .60's were found for truancy from home among both sexes and also for the two conduct problems for which only the boys' correlations were computed, stealing
an automobile and robbing a building, home, etc. Stealing among
boys yielded the very large coefficient of .63 $\pm$ .02 and among
girls the substantial one of .37 $\pm$ .04. Three conduct problems
among boys yielded high correlations in the .50's and among girls

106

TABLE 8

CORRELATIONS WITH "POLICE ARREST"

	Boys	Girls
Personality-total..............................	.18 ± .02	.11 ± .03
Conduct-total.................................	.53 ± .02	.31 ± .03
	Larger Correlations (Positive)	
Stealing an automobile........................	.69 ± .03	....
Truancy from home.............................	.68 ± .02	.67 ± .03 (2)*
Stealing......................................	.63 ± .02	.37 ± .04 (8)
Robbing a building, home, etc.................	.63 ± .04	....
Bad companions................................	.59 ± .02	.40 ± .04 (7)
Truancy from school...........................	.57 ± .02	.42 ± .04 (6)
Staying out late at night.....................	.52 ± .03	.49 ± .04 (4)
Begging.......................................	.46 ± .04	....
Gang..	.45 ± .03	....
Truancy from an institution...................	.42 ± .04	....
Loitering.....................................	.41 ± .03	.23 ± .06 (20-21)
Leading others into bad conduct...............	.40 ± .04	.27 ± .06 (15-17)
Incorrigible..................................	.38 ± .03	.28 ± .04 (12-14)
Passive pederasty.............................	.37 ± .05	
Psychopathic personality......................	.37 ± .04	.26 ± .07 (18)
Oversuggestible...............................	.36 ± .03	.57 ± .03 (3)
Gambling......................................	.36 ± .05	
Smoking.......................................	.35 ± .03	....
Irregular employment record...................	.33 ± .05	.13
Sex attack on opposite sex....................	.33 ± .05	
Exclusion from school.........................	.33 ± .03	.22 ± .06 (22-26)
Brother in penal detention....................	.33 ± .04	.00
Grouped: disobedient, etc....................	.33 ± .02	.27 ± .04 (15-17)
Fantastical lying.............................	.31 ± .04	.22 ± .06 (22-26)
Swearing at mother, teacher, etc..............	.31 ± .05	....
Mutual masturbation (same sex)................	.31 ± .04	
Destructive...................................	.30 ± .03	.15
Refusal to attend school......................	.30 ± .04	.07
Boastful, "show-off"..........................	.29 ± .03	.10
Violence......................................	.29 ± .03	.18
Conduct prognosis bad.........................	.29 ± .05	.47 ± .06 (5)
Bad language..................................	.28 ± .04	.27 ± .07 (15-17)
Obscene language..............................	.28 ± .04	
Overinterest in opposite sex..................	.28 ± .05	.18
Contrary......................................	.27 ± .04	-.02
Overinterest in sex matters...................	.27 ± .04	.28 ± .05 (12-14)
Excuse-forming................................	.27 ± .03	.22 ± .05 (22-26)
Incipient psychosis...........................	.27 ± .06	....
Threatening violence..........................	.26 ± .04	....
Lying...	.25 ± .03	.31 ± .04 (10)
Psychoneurotic................................	.24 ± .04	-.14

*Rank order of girls' correlations.

TABLE 8—Continued

	Boys	Girls
Irregular sleep habits	.24 ± .04	.13
Disturbing influence in school	.23 ± .03	-.03
Sullen	.23 ± .03	.09
"Annoying" girls	.23 ± .05	....
Exhibitionism	.23 ± .06	....
Grouped: fighting, etc.	.23 ± .03	.08
Grouped: swearing, etc.	.23 ± .03	.18
Complaining of bad treatment by other children	.22 ± .04	.19
Disobedient	.21 ± .03	.18
Defiant	.20 ± .04	.14
Fighting	.20 ± .03	.22 ± .05 (22-26)
Fire-setting	.20 ± .06	....
Sneaky	.20 ± .05	.34 ± .07 (9)
Homosexual (same age)	.20 ± .05	....
Masturbation	.20 ± .03	.21 ± .05 (27-28)
Egocentric	.20 ± .03	.09
Emotional instability	.20 ± .04	.23 ± .05 (20-21)
Irregular attendance at school	.20 ± .04	-.22 ± .05
Sex delinquency (coitus)	.18	.76 ± .02 (1)
Immoral home conditions	-.00	.30 ± .05 (11)
Failure to adjust in foster-home	.18	.28 ± .06 (12-14)
Lues	.00	.24 ± .05 (19)
Irritable	.04	.22 ± .04 (22-26)
Gluttony	.12	.21 ± .07 (27-28)
Rude	.19	.20 ± .04 (29)
Larger Correlations (Negative)		
Vocational guidance	-.35 ± .03	-.34 ± .04
Lazy	-.05	-.30 ± .05
Bashful	-.05	-.28 ± .04
Finicky food habits	.01	-.26 ± .05
Inattentive in school	.06	-.26 ± .05
Poor work in school	-.04	-.26 ± .04
Enuresis	.07	-.25 ± .04
Underweight	-.12	-.22 ± .04
Sensitive (general)	-.02	-.21 ± .05
Grouped: "nervous," etc.	.02	-.20 ± .04

Other Correlations (Positive to Negative)

Disturbing influence in home, .19 and .04; Slovenly, .19 and -.02; Victim of sex abuse, .19 (girls); Vicious home conditions, .18 and .15; Swearing (general), .17 and .09; Mental conflict, .16 and .07; Sulky, .16 and .07; Lack of interest in school, .15 and .08; Resentful attitude, .15 and .01; Cruelty to younger children, .14 (boys); Teasing other children, .14 and .04; Apprehensive, .14 and .13; Question of change of personality, .14 and .12; Dementia praecox, .14 (boys); Grouped: egocentric, etc., .14 and .07; Grouped: lack of interest in school, etc., .14 and -.01; Bowel incontinence, .13 (boys); Crying spells, .13 and .07; Discord between parents, .13 and -.01; Leader, .13 and .07; Bully-

TABLE 8—Continued

ing, .12 (boys); Quarrelsome, .11 and .08; Irresponsible, .10 and .08; Nail-
biting, .10 and .06; Hatred or jealousy of sibling, .10 and -.11; Clean, .10
and -.03; Popular, .10 and .12; Spoiled child, .09 and .04; Stuttering, .09
(boys); Grouped: temper, etc., .09 and -.06; Inefficient in work, play, etc.,
.08 and .00; Stubborn, .08 and .09; Temper tantrums, .08 and .03; Listless,
.08 and -.01; Queer, .08 and .19; Follower, .08 and .05; Cruelty to animals,
.07 (boys); Daydreaming, .07 and .14; Sensitive over specific fact, .07 and
.03; Sex denied entirely, .07 and -.16; Former convulsions, .07 and -.19; Temper display, .06 and .06; Restless, .06 and .09; Restless in sleep, .06 and
.07; Worry over specific fact, .06 and .00; Immoral sister, .06 and .04; Lack
of affection, .05 (boys); Attractive manner, .05 and -.08; Feeble-minded sibling, .05 and .09; Inferiority feelings, .04 and -.02; Headaches, .04 and -.07;
"Sugar hunger," .03 (boys); Seclusive, .03 and -.03; Unpopular, .03 and .08;
Repressed, .03 and -.14; Question of encephalitis, .03 and .07; Bossy, .02 and
-.08; Absent-minded, .02 and -.16; Changeable moods, .02 and .03; Object of
teasing, .02 and -.10; Grouped: sensitive or worrisome, etc., .02 and -.02;
Talking to self without apparent reason, .01 (boys); Unhappy, .01 and -.02;
Abused feeling or manner, .00 and .04; Illegitimate parentage, -.00 and .05; "k曰
"Night terrors," -.00 and .07; "Nervous," .00 and -.00; Grouped: depressed,
etc., -.02 and -.00; Retardation in school, -.03 and -.05; Question of hypo-
phrenia, -.03 and -.15; Depressed, -.03 and -.01; Thumb-sucking, -.03 and -.01;
Preference for younger children, -.05 and -.14; Distractible, -.05 and .07;
Neurological defect, -.06 and -.19; Slow, dull, -.08 and -.16; Speech defect,
-.09 and -.08; Grouped: dull, slow, etc., -.12 and -.10; Selfish, -.12 and .15;
Tiring easily, -.14 and -.12; Lack of initiative, -.15 and -.12

fairly high coefficients in the .40's: associating with bad companions, staying out late at night, and truancy from school. Oversuggestibility among girls yielded the high correlation of .57 ±
.03, with a corresponding substantial coefficient among boys of
.36 ± .03.

          Three conduct problems for which only the boys' correla-
tions were computed—running with a gang, truancy or running away
from an institution, and begging—yielded large coefficients in
the .40's. Leading others into bad conduct and loitering or wandering among boys yielded large correlations in the .40's but among
girls moderate coefficients in the .20's. Staff notation of unfavorable conduct prognosis among girls yielded the large correlation of .47 ± .06 but among boys the moderate coefficient of .29 ±
.05.

          Six conduct problems for which only the boys' correlations
were computed yielded substantial coefficients in the .30's: gambling or crap-shooting, swearing at mother, teacher, etc., smoking,
sex attack or abuse of younger child of opposite sex, passive pederasty, and mutual masturbation with child of same sex. Four

behavior notations among boys yielded substantial correlations in
the .30's and among girls moderate coefficients in the .20's: incorrigibility, exclusion from school, fantastical lying, and staff
notation of psychopathic personality (unspecified). Four case-
record notations—refusal to attend school, irregular employment
record, destructiveness, and brother in penal detention--yielded
substantial correlations in the .30's among boys but low coefficients below .20 among girls. Lying and sneakiness among girls
yielded substantial correlations in the .30's and among boys moderate coefficients in the .20's. For immoral home conditions the
respective correlations for girls and boys were .30 $\pm$ .05 and -.00

     Police arrest showed moderate correlations in the .20's
among both sexes for the following six behavior traits: fighting,
bad language, excuse-forming attitude, emotional instability, over
interest in sex matters, and masturbation and also for the following seven, for which only the boys' coefficients were calculated:
threatening violence, fire-setting, staff notation of incipient
psychosis (unspecified), obscene language, "annoying" girls, exhibitionism or indecent exposure, and homosexual practices with chil
of same age. Thirteen undesirable case-record notations showed
moderate correlations in the .20's among boys but low coefficients
below .20 among girls: violence, disturbing influence in school,
disobedience, defiant attitude, contrariness, sullenness, egocentricity, boastful or "show-off" manner, complaining of bad treatment by other children, irregular sleep habits, staff notation of
psychoneurotic trends (unspecified), overinterest in opposite sex,
and irregular attendance at school. Five miscellaneous notations
among girls showed moderate correlations in the .20's but low correlations below .20 among boys: irritable temperament, rudeness,
failure to adjust in foster-home, gluttony, and lues (present or
former).

     Among girls there were several significant negative corre-
lations ranging from -.20 to -.30: laziness, inattentiveness in
school, poor work in school, bashfulness, sensitiveness in general
"nervousness" or restlessness (including irritable temperament and
changeable moods, undifferentiated), finicky food habits, enuresis
and underweight condition. The notation "request for vocational
guidance" showed correlations in the -.30's for both sexes.

     Among the thirteen sex notations considered in chapters

ix-xii of this volume there were many correlations of significant
size. The most conspicuous was for sex delinquency (coitus) among
girls, .76 + .02. (This is one of the largest correlations found
among the approximately fourteen thousand correlation coefficients
comprising the data of this volume). This unusually high correlation indicates that heterosexual misbehavior is the major cause
among girls for referral to a juvenile court and that known sex
misconduct among girls is liable to lead to an appearance in the
juvenile court. Among boys the corresponding correlation, .18 +
.05, was low but positive. Three sex behavior problems among boys
—passive pederasty, mutual masturbation with child of the same
sex, and sex attack or abuse (actual or attempted) upon younger
child of opposite sex—yielded substantial coefficients in the
.30's, the corresponding coefficients for girls not being computed
because of the paucity of cases. Three sex behavior notations
showed moderate correlations ranging from .18 to .28 among both
sexes: overinterest in the opposite sex, overinterest in sex matters, and masturbation and also four notations for which only the
boys' coefficients were computed: obscene language, exhibitionism
or "indecent exposure," homosexual practices (actual or attempted)
with child of similar or younger age, and "annoying" girls. Victim of sex attack or abuse by older child or person (which was calculated only for girls, since the boys' cases were too few) showed
the low but significant correlation of .19 + .05. For the notation
sex misbehavior denied entirely the correlations were low and not
significant, .07 + .04 and -.16 + .06 for boys and girls respectively.

        Among the twelve physical or psychophysical notations there
was only one positive coefficient of moderate size in the .20's,
lues (present or former) among girls, the boys' coefficient being
zero. Among our children the lues may be either congenitally acquired ("inherited") or acquired through sexual behavior of the
patient herself, so that this correlation includes to a large extent the correlation of police arrest with sex delinquency (coitus).
The correlation of lues with sex delinquency (coitus) (Table 96,
p. 470) among girls was .23 + .05; if we "partial out" sex delinquency (coitus), the resulting correlation of lues with police arrest is reduced to the negligible coefficient of -.06. The only
additional correlations of significant size in this field were the

negative ones in the -.20's with enuresis and underweight condition among girls, the corresponding coefficients for boys being negligible. The remaining eight notations showed only low coefficients ranging from -.19 to .13: question or diagnosis of encephalitis, neurological defect (unspecified), headaches, former convulsions, and speech defect, and the following for which only the boys' correlations were computed: stuttering, bowel incontinence, and "sugar hunger." Question of hypophrenia (if it be permissible to include it among psychophysical notations) showed negligible correlations of -.03 and -.15 with police arrest for boys and girls respectively.

Among the seven notations concerning home or familial conditions there were two correlations of substantial size in the .30's: brother in penal detention among boys and immoral home conditions among girls. Vicious (not "immoral") home conditions showed the low but suggestive correlations of .18 ± .05 and .15 ± .06 among boys and girls respectively. All other notations in this field (illegitimate parentage, immoral sister, feeble-minded sibling, and discord between parents) showed negligible correlations ranging from -.01 to .13 with police arrest among both sexes.

The following thirty-one miscellaneous notations showed negligible correlations less than ± .10 with the police-arrest criterion of seriousness or "ominousness" among both boys and girls: stubbornness, temper tantrums, temper display, bossy manner, "nervousness," restlessness, restlessness in sleep, "night terrors," "spoiled child," inferiority feelings, sensitiveness over some specific fact, worry over some specific fact, depressed mood or spells, unhappiness, changeable moods or attitudes, seclusiveness, abused feeling or manner, unpopularity, inefficiency in work, play, etc., listlessness, "follower," distractibility, retardation in school, attractive manner, thumb-sucking, speech defect, question or diagnosis of encephalitis, headaches, illegitimate parentage, immoral sister, and feeble-minded sibling and also four additional notations for which only the boys' correlations were computed: cruelty to animals, lack of affection for others, talking to self without apparent reason, and stuttering.

We may summarize the trends shown by these correlations in this chapter as follows:

1. Behavior notations which constitute specific charges for

arrest are highly correlated with <u>police arrest</u>, as one would suppose, e.g., stealing, truancy, and incorrigibility and, among
girls, heterosexual misconduct.

2. Traits which are characteristic of aggressive "bad actors" are highly associated with <u>police arrest</u>, e.g., bad companions and running with a gang, staying out late at night, begging,
gambling, smoking, irregular employment record, leading others into
bad conduct, and psychopathic personality.

3. Heterosexual misconduct among girls appears to be highly
associated with <u>police arrest</u>, but among boys the relation is almost negligible, except in the instances where the misconduct includes an attempt to make a forced attack upon the opposite sex.
<u>Passive pederasty</u>, on the other hand, among boys is perceptibly
associated with <u>police arrest</u>. This form of misconduct is not of
itself often the specific cause of the police arrest, but probably
the trait is symptomatic of a grave degree of behavior deviation
in that the child may have fallen into a form of homosexual prostitution or may have come under the influence of older aggressive
boys or men who have induced him to submit to passive homosexual
practices.

4. Among the several notations implying unfavorable home
or family conditions, the correlations with <u>police arrest</u> are small
or negligible, e.g., immoral or vicious home conditions, brother
or sister with police arrest or in penal or correctional institution, immoral sister, illegitimate parentage, and discord between
parents. Such a finding is contrary to general expectation; and,
since our data did not afford an exhaustive investigation into
these factors, no discussion will be made of these correlation coefficients beyond merely reporting them.

The correlation coefficients for the girls bore only a moderate resemblance to those for the boys. The rank-order correlation of the two columns of coefficients in Table 8 was found to be
only .64 $\pm$ .04.

The correlation coefficients with the <u>police-arrest</u> criterion resembled fairly closely those for the <u>conduct-total</u> criterion,
the rank-order intercolumnar correlations being .70 $\pm$ .03 and .51 $\pm$
.05 for boys and girls respectively. With the correlation coefficients for the <u>personality-total</u> criterion there was no resemblance,
the intercolumnar correlations being -.05 $\pm$ .06 and .13 $\pm$ .06 for
boys and girls respectively.

CHAPTER XII

SUMMARY AND CONCLUSIONS TO PART II

1. The three criteria of importance or seriousness among
children's behavior traits employed in this study were accepted
because of their objectivity and measurability even though they
fall short of ideal criteria which could be conceived of if one
resorts to subjective and theoretical terms.

2. The personality-total is the unweighted summation of
the specific personality problems noted for each of our 2,113 White
boys and 1,181 White girls. The conduct-total is similarly derived
from the specific conduct notations. The police-arrest criterion
is self-explanatory.

3. Because of the relatively moderate and low intercorrelations among these three criteria, it was deemed inadvisable to
combine them into one criterion measure.

4. The personality-total criterion showed results somewhat
similar to the conduct-total as far as the girls' correlations were
concerned, but with only a slight similarity as far as the boys'
correlations were concerned. It showed no similarity to the police-arrest criterion among either sex.

5. The conduct-total criterion showed considerable resemblance to the police-arrest criterion, especially with respect to
the boys' correlations.

6. The correlations for the boys were substantially similar to those for the girls in all three criteria.

7. The notations diagnosis or question of dementia praecox
and incipient or undiagnosed psychosis (computed only for boys)
showed the relatively high bi-serial correlations of .76 $\pm$ .03 and
.60 $\pm$ .03 with the personality-total criterion, but low correlations with the other two criteria.

8. The notations queer behavior, depressed mood or spells,
unhappy appearance or manner, question of change of personality,
changeable moods, and mental conflict yielded high correlations
with personality-total among both sexes and with conduct-total

114

among girls. With police arrest their correlations were negligible
or zero.

9. Hatred or jealousy of sibling, inferiority feelings, and
daydreaming showed substantial correlations with personality-total,
low correlations with conduct-total, and almost no correlation with
police arrest.

10. Sensitiveness, worrisomeness, and diagnosis or question
of psychoneurotic trends showed substantial correlations with personality-total, but low or negligible correlations with the other
two criteria.

11. Boastfulness or "show-off" manner and disturbing influence in the home showed substantial correlations with both personality-total and conduct-total, but low or zero correlations with
the police-arrest criterion.

12. Violence, fighting, swearing, resentful attitude, and
unpopularity showed especially high correlations with both personality-total and conduct-total among girls. Among boys these correlations were also substantial. Against the police-arrest criterion corresponding correlations ranged from moderate down to
negligible in size.

13. Diagnosis or question of psychopathic personality (unspecified) showed high correlations with personality-total and conduct-total and substantial correlations with police arrest. Curiously enough, in spite of its name, it appears to be more associated with overt conduct problems than with personality problems.

14. Diagnosis or question of encephalitis (present or former) and inefficiency in work, play, etc., show high correlations
with personality-total, moderate correlations with conduct-total,
but negligible or zero relationships with police arrest.

15. The following showed high correlations for both conduct-total and police arrest, but moderate or low correlations with
personality-total: truancy from home, truancy from school, staying out late at night, and (calculated for boys only) stealing an
automobile.

16. The following showed high correlations with conduct-
total and moderate correlations with personality-total and police
arrest among both boys and girls: disobedience, incorrigibility,
lying, leading others into bad conduct, diagnosis or question of
psychopathic personality, and bad language. Similar correlations

were shown by the following four notations, which were calculated only for boys: threatening violence, begging (on the street), "annoying" girls, and obscene language.

17. The following behavior notations showed high or at least substantial correlations with conduct-total, moderate to substantial correlations with personality-total, but low or negligible correlations with police arrest for both boys and girls: fighting, swearing, destructiveness, rudeness, and unpopularity. Similar tendencies were shown by cruelty to younger children and cruelty to animals, which were calculated for boys only.

18. Egocentricity (in behavior or attitude) showed relatively large bi-serial correlations of .41 ± .02 and .48 ± .03 for boys and girls respectively for conduct-total, but only very moderate or negligible correlations with either personality-total or police arrest for either sex. Lack of affection for others (calculated for boys only) yielded a moderate correlation with conduct-total, but negligible correlations with the other two criteria.

19. Gambling, smoking, and swearing at mother, teacher, etc. (calculated for boys only) showed moderately high correlations with conduct-total, moderate correlations with police arrest, but fairly low correlations with personality-total.

20. With the police-arrest criterion of seriousness, among both boys and girls, the conspicuous correlations were for such conduct difficulties as stealing, robbery, burglary, truancy from home or from school, associating with bad companions or running with a gang, and staying out late at night. Among girls, the outstanding correlations were for sex delinquency (coitus) and over-suggestibility, both of which showed only low or moderate correlations among the boys.

21. The following case notations showed correlations ranging from moderate to fairly substantial but not high for both sexes with all three criteria of "seriousness" or "ominousness": staff notation of unfavorable conduct prognosis, exclusion from school, contrariness, sneakiness, emotional instability, fantastical lying, irregular sleep habits, masturbation, and overinterest in sex matters. The following five notations (calculated only for boys) showed similar trends: complaining of bad treatment by other children, fire-setting (arson), sex attack on opposite sex, passive pederasty, and exhibitionism (including "indecent exposure").

22. The following long list of traits showed correlations for either sex ranging from moderate to fairly substantial with the personality-total and conduct-total but small or negligible with the police-arrest criterion: temper tantrums, hatred or jealousy of sibling, "spoiled child," violence, fighting, quarrelsomeness, irritable manner, defiant manner, stubbornness, disturbing influence in school, bossy manner, restlessness, restlessness in sleep, egocentric behavior or attitude, selfishness, resentful attitude, sullenness, sulkiness, unhappy manner or appearance, crying spells, changeable moods, question of change of personality, mental conflict, queer behavior, daydreaming, "night terrors," irresponsibility, slovenliness, lack of interest in school, inattentiveness in school, and thumb-sucking. Among the less frequently occurring notations, which were calculated only for the boys, the following showed similar trends: bullying, teasing other children, talking to self without apparent reason, bowel incontinence, and "sugar hunger."

23. Traits associated with mental deficiency and those indicating an unaggressive type of personality tended to show a negligible or even slightly negative correlation with all three criteria of "seriousness" or "ominousness." These were: question of hypophrenia (suspected mental deficiency), slow or dull manner, retardation in school, preference for younger children as playmates, mentally defective sibling, listlessness, lack of initiative, "follower," repressed manner, apprehensiveness, and bashfulness. Bashfulness, in fact, among girls showed a negative tetrachoric correlation of $-.28 \pm .04$ with the police-arrest criterion, i.e., bashful girls tended to have greater immunity from police arrest or detention than the nonbashful ones. In a later chapter (Table 10, p. 130) it will be noted that intelligence (IQ) as measured by formal psychometrics (usually the Stanford-Binet of 1916) shows only low or negligible correlations with the three over-all criteria, though with certain specific behavior difficulties it will later be shown that the correlations with formal IQ were occasionally of substantial size.

24. In addition, the following personality traits and physical or home-life conditions showed negligible or occasionally even negative correlations with all three criteria: popularity, "leader," attractive manner, clean habits, sex misbehavior denied

entirely, discord between parents, vicious (as distinguished from
"immoral") home conditions, immoral sister, irregular attendance
at school, former convulsions, enuresis or bed-wetting (present or
former), underweight condition, speech defect, and (calculated for
boys only) stuttering. The fact that such unfavorable home conditions as discord between parents and vicious home conditions in our
data showed only low or negligible correlations with our over-all
criteria of the extent of personality and conduct deviation among
children is contrary to the belief held by many social workers. In
view of the many inadequacies in our original data, as described
in chapter v, the present writer considers it unwise to press the
importance of these findings in this controversial topic but prefers to consider them as tentative until more detailed ad hoc studies are available.

25. The case notation brother with police arrest or in penal detention showed among boys the substantial tetrachoric correlation of .33 $\pm$ 04 with the police-arrest criterion, but all other
correlations with our three over-all criteria for both sexes were
negligible.

26. Exclusion or suspension from school showed moderate to
high correlations with all three criteria, especially with conduct-
total.

27. Immoral (as distinguished from "vicious") home conditions among our girls showed the significant tetrachoric correlation of .30 $\pm$ .05 with police arrest, but only negligible correlations with the other two criteria.

28. "Nervousness," which in our data was a vague and poorly
defined term, showed moderate correlations among our girls with all
three criteria, but among boys only with the personality-total criterion. The boys' correlations with the other two criteria were
low or zero.

29. A brief consideration of the "seriousness" of the half-
dozen most frequently appearing overt conduct difficulties in our
case-record data elicits the following. Stealing among both sexes
showed moderate correlations with both conduct-total and police arrest, but only low or moderate correlations with personality-total.
Lying, fighting, and incorrigibility showed high correlations among
both sexes with the conduct-total criterion, and moderate or substantial correlations with personality-total and police arrest.

Truancy from home and truancy from school among both sexes showed generally high correlations with both conduct-total and police arrest, but low correlations with personality-total.

30. Sex behavior problems in our material tended in the main to be intercorrelated with one another to a substantial or high degree, but only to a moderate or negligible extent with non-sex case notations. Sex delinquency (defined strictly as coitus with opposite sex) among girls showed the unusually high tetrachoric correlation of .76 ± .02 with police arrest, but all other correlations for either boys or girls with our three criteria of "seriousness" were all but negligible. Sex attack or sex abuse, actual or attempted, upon child of opposite sex and "annoying" girls, i.e., lifting their dresses or requesting sexual intercourse (both calculated only for boys) showed moderate to substantial correlations with all three criteria. Masturbation (including questionable and former masturbation), which was noted in about 28 per cent of our 2,113 White boys and in about 13 per cent of our 1,181 White girls, showed moderate correlations ranging from .20 to .41 with all three criteria, similar correlations being found for mutual masturbation with child of same sex and age, which was calculated for boys only. The three sex notations passive pederasty with older person, homosexual activities (unspecified) with child of similar age, and exhibitionism (including "indecent exposure"), which were calculated for boys only, yielded moderate to substantial correlations ranging from .16 to .44 with all three criteria. Manifesting a precocious or excessive interest in the opposite sex and manifesting a precocious or excessive interest in sex matters also yielded moderate to substantial correlations ranging from .18 to .47 with all three criteria of "seriousness" or "ominousness."

31. Among sex notations not considered as personality or conduct difficulties the correlations with our three criteria of "seriousness" generally were of low magnitude. Victim of actual or attempted rape or sex abuse by older person (not a relative), calculated for girls only, yielded a bi-serial correlation of .21 ± .03 with the conduct-total and a tetrachoric correlation of .19 ± .05 with police arrest and a negligible correlation with personality-total. Staff diagnosis or question of lues among our cases usually denoted a congenital or "innocently acquired" syphilis and its correlations with our three criteria of "seriousness" were very

negligible for both sexes, except for its correlation of .24 + .05
among girls with <u>police arrest</u>. In this case it is probable that
the infection was often acquired through "sex delinquency," which
in our data was highly correlated with the fact of a police arrest
or detention among girls. The correlations for <u>immoral</u> (as distinguished from "vicious") <u>home conditions</u> were similarly negligible
for both sexes except for the tetrachoric correlation of .30 + .05
with <u>police arrest</u> among girls. For the notation <u>immoral sister</u>
<u>(or half-sister)</u> all correlations for both boys and girls with our
three criteria were practically zero. Among our boys from <u>ille-
gitimate parentage</u>, the bi-serial correlations with <u>personality-
total</u> and <u>conduct-total</u> were .20 + .04 and .21 + .04 respectively,
while with <u>police arrest</u> the boys' tetrachoric correlation came out
at zero; among our girls, all three correlations were practically
zero. The notation <u>sex misbehavior denied entirely</u> among boys
yielded approximately zero correlations, while among girls the correlations with <u>personality-total</u> and <u>police-arrest</u> criteria were
.17 + .04 and -.16 + .06 respectively, while its correlation with
<u>conduct-total</u> was zero.

     32. Four other behavior items, which were mentioned fre-
quently in the social histories may be briefly noted here. <u>Enure-
sis</u> (bed-wetting continuing beyond the third birthday) among girls
yielded the <u>negative</u> tetrachoric correlation of -.25 + .04 with the
<u>police-arrest</u> criterion. All other correlations for both sexes
with the three criteria were positive but low. <u>Thumb-sucking</u> (including finger- and knuckle-sucking) and <u>nail-biting</u> both showed
moderate correlations with <u>personality-total</u> but low positive correlations with <u>conduct-total</u> and negligible correlations with <u>po-
lice arrest</u>. <u>Finicky or capricious food habits</u> among girls yielded
the fairly substantial bi-serial correlation of .41 + .03 with <u>per-
sonality-total</u> and the moderate correlations of .28 + .03 and .26
+ .05 with the <u>conduct-total</u> and <u>police-arrest</u> criteria respectively. Among boys its bi-serial correlation was .26 + .02 with
<u>personality-total</u>, but with the <u>conduct-total</u> and <u>police-arrest</u>
criteria its correlations were negligible.

     The foregoing several chapters of Part II have attempted
to survey the relative "seriousness" or "ominousness" of typical
children's behavior traits as measured by over eight hundred correlation coefficients computed with our three criteria. It has

been necessary to limit discussion to only the outstanding indications in this diffuse material.   The reader who desires a closer understanding of the importance or significance of specific behavior traits is advised to consult the more detailed correlational analyses which are presented and described in Part III, which concerns the intercorrelations of over a hundred behavior notations with one another.

PART III

INTERRELATIONS AMONG TRAITS

INTRODUCTORY

The essential contribution of Part III consists in a series of one hundred and twenty-five tables of correlation coefficients. These represent the intercorrelations of 111 behavior traits, chiefly personality problems and conduct difficulties, with one another and their correlations with a selection of 14 miscellaneous physical and educational conditions and home-life circumstances. The "meat" of the succeeding chapters lies in these tables, which consist of about 14,000 correlation coefficients. To the reader who has learned to appreciate the conciseness and universality of correlation coefficients as a means of expressing relationships, the writer's interpretative comments will seem superfluous and repetitious.

In chapter v we described the construction of the tables. In chapter vii we attempted to explain how the correlation coefficients in this study may be interpreted in terms of their practical and social significance. As a description of a behavior trait in terms of its correlates, their purpose is obvious. Their use as clinical clues to other behavior traits not so easily ascertainable or as predictions of expected future behavior was described in considerable detail in chapter vii.

It should be recalled that the cases considered in this volume were White children between the ages of 6 and 17, inclusive, and with intelligence quotients ranging from 50 to over 150. The exclusion of the very young and the very mentally defective, together with several small groups of other non-typical cases, as described in chapter ii, was made in an effort to obtain a group of children more representative of "normal" children. Chronological age was "partialed out" for all tables except those for chronological age and intelligence quotient.

125

CHAPTER XIII

CHRONOLOGICAL AGE AND INTELLIGENCE (IQ)

The relations of children's behavior problems to the factors of age and of intelligence as measured by intelligence quotient (usually from the Stanford-Binet of 1916) were described in
Part III of Volume I by means of charts showing the incidence of
a given trait for each age and intelligence level, as well as occasionally by means of correlation coefficients. It seemed apparent from those charts that the relationships tended to be curvilinear rather than rectilinear. Furthermore, the effect of age and
intelligence is so intertwined that their correlations with the de-
velopment of behavior difficulties cannot be adequately represented
by the usual graphical or coefficiential methods. Our statement of
this apparent relation was as follows:

> Our hypothesis is that the interaction of the age factor
> and the intelligence factor produces the resultant effect of
> increasing the number of behavior problems within the lower
> age and IQ ranges, and of inhibiting them within the upper age
> and IQ ranges within our group of children below 18 years of
> age. It is probable also that either the age factor or the
> intelligence factor alone, if the other factor were held con-
> stant, would likewise produce this "waxing and waning" effect.
> The process, so far as developmental factors are concerned, is
> probably a matter of learning and "unlearning."[1]

The reader who compares the material of this chapter with
that of Volume I should bear in mind another qualifying circumstance. In the correlations discussed in the present chapter children below 6 years of age and those whose IQ fell below 50 were excluded, and as a result the correlation coefficients of this chapter will tend to be lower because of the reduction in range or variability.

This chapter will thus discuss the relation of age and intelligence quotient to other traits in a briefer manner. The factor of non-curvilinearity of regression probably must be taken into

---

[1]See I, 254-55.

consideration in interpreting all the coefficients in this chapter.

The mean age for our 2,113 boys in the present study was 12.0 years, with a standard deviation of 2.9. For the 1,181 girls the corresponding constants were 12.2 and 3.1 respectively.

The correlation coefficients for chronological age or maturation (Table 9) in general were low. The largest was found to be for diagnosis or question of dementia praecox (calculated only for boys) with a substantial bi-serial r of .40 ± .02. Diagnosis or question of incipient psychosis (unspecified), which was calculated only for boys, also showed the moderate correlation of .24 ± .02. Diagnosis or question of psychopathic personality showed the low but positive correlations of .15 and .18 for boys and girls respectively. For diagnosis or question of psychoneurotic trends, however, our correlations were about zero. In addition to the psychiatric notations above, heterosexual behavior items, as one might suppose, tend to become more numerous with increasing age or maturation, especially among girls. Sex delinquency (coitus) among girls yielded the relatively high bi-serial r of .52 ± .02 and among boys the moderate correlation of .24 ± .02. Similar correlations of lesser size were found for overinterest in opposite sex. Among girls several other conduct difficulties frequently associated with heterosexual behavior also show moderate to substantial correlations with age. These were staff notation of unfavorable conduct prognosis, staying out late at night, truancy from home, and associating with bad companions. Masturbation among girls, however, showed a moderate negative correlation of -.21 ± .04 and also a negligible negative correlation among boys.

Several behavior notations associated with immaturity showed low to moderate negative correlations with chronological age: speech defect (other than stuttering), enuresis (still continuing), bowel incontinence, thumb-sucking, restlessness, distractibility, destructiveness, fire-setting (calculated for boys only), fighting, disturbing influence in school, and apprehensiveness.

Among numerous notations which showed zero relationships with age or maturation were inferiority feelings, mental conflict, hatred or jealousy of sibling, "spoiled child," daydreaming, queer behavior, sensitiveness (general), boastful or "show-off" manner, staff diagnosis or question of psychoneurotic trends, irritable behavior, changeable moods, emotional instability, sulkiness,

TABLE 9

CORRELATIONS WITH "CHRONOLOGICAL AGE"

	Boys	Girls
Personality-total.........................	.03 ± .01	.04 ± .02
Conduct-total.............................	-.12 ± .01	-.07 ± .02
Police arrest.............................	.29 ± .02	.56 ± .02
	Larger Correlations (Positive)	
Irregular employment record..............	.66 ± .03	.60 ± .04 (1)*
Vocational guidance.......................	.49 ± .02	.53 ± .02 (2)
Dementia praecox..........................	.40 ± .02	....
"Annoying" girls.........................	.34 ± .02	....
Stealing an automobile...................	.32 ± .04	....
Incipient psychosis......................	.24 ± .02	....
Sex delinquency (coitus).................	.24 ± .02	.52 ± .02 (3)
Worry over specific fact.................	.23 ± .03	.14
Gambling..................................	.23 ± .04	....
Retardation in school....................	.22 ± .02	.28 ± .02 (7-8)
Depressed.................................	.22 ± .03	.23 ± .04 (10-11)
Conduct prognosis bad....................	.21 ± .03	.35 ± .04 (4)
Smoking...................................	.20 ± .03	....
Overinterest in opposite sex............	.15	.31 ± .03 (5)
Staying out late at night...............	.06	.30 ± .03 (6)
Truancy from home........................	.08	.28 ± .03 (7-8)
Resentful attitude.......................	.07	.25 ± .04 (9)
Bad companions...........................	.08	.23 ± .03 (10-11)
Lazy......................................	.15	.20 ± .04 (12-13)
Grouped: depressed, etc.................	.19	.20 ± .03 (12-13)
	Larger Correlations (Negative)	
Speech defect.............................	-.25 ± .03	-.18
Enuresis still continuing................	-.25 ± .02	-.30 ± .03
Restless..................................	-.23 ± .02	-.30 ± .03
Distractible.............................	-.23 ± .02	-.25 ± .03
Thumb-sucking.............................	-.21 ± .02	-.23 ± .05
Bowel incontinence.......................	-.14	-.29 ± .06
Destructive...............................	-.17	-.25 ± .04
Disturbing influence in school..........	-.06	-.24 ± .04
Apprehensive.............................	-.10	-.22 ± .03
Masturbation still continuing...........	-.06	-.21 ± .04
Fighting..................................	-.14	-.20 ± .04

Other Correlations (Positive to Negative)

Lack of initiative, .19 and .01; Robbing a building, home, etc., .19 (boys); Question of change of personality, .16 and .04; Popular, .16 and .07;

*Rank order of girls' correlations.

TABLE 9—Continued

Seclusive, .15 and .11; Psychopathic personality, .15 and .18; Gang, .15 (boys);
Swearing at mother, teacher, etc., .14 (boys); Preference for younger children, .13
.13 and -.01; Rude, .12 and .14; Victim of sex abuse, .11 (girls); Grouped:
sensitive or worrisome, etc., .11 and .06; Unhappy, .11 and .15; Question of
encephalitis, .11 and -.06; Lack of affection, .11 (boys); Inefficient in work,
play, etc., .11 and .16; Inferiority feelings, .10 and .07; Sensitive over specific fact, .10 and .04; Truancy from institution, .10 (boys); Truancy from
school, .09 and .07; Listless, .09 and .14; Headaches, .09 and .14; Lack of interest in school, .08 and .09; Sullen, .08 and .12; Refusal to attend school,
.07 and .18; Sex denied entirely, .07 and .01; "Sugar hunger," .07 (boys);
Clean, .07 and -.01; Neurological defect, .07 and -.11; Bullying, .06 (boys);
Queer, .06 and .04; Abused feeling or manner, .06 and .16; Oversuggestible, .06
and .16; Poor work in school, .05 and -.00; Stuttering, .05 (boys); Exclusion
from school, .05 and -.07; Irregular sleep habits, .05 and .01; Tiring easily,
.05 and -.11; Threatening violence, .05 (boys); Loitering, .05 and .05; Bossy,
.05 and -.16; Daydreaming, .04 and .08; Sex attack on opposite sex, .04 (boys);
Homosexual (same age), .04 (boys); Irresponsible, .04 and .19; Grouped: lack
of interest in school, etc., .03 and .01; Attractive manner, .03 and -.10; Immoral sister, .03 and .05; Former convulsions, .03 and -.08; Sensitive, .03 and
.06; Stealing, .03 and .06; Grouped: dull, slow, etc., .03 and .11; Boastful,
"show-off," .02 and -.04; Overinterest in sex matters, .02 and -.09; Psychoneurotic, .02 and .03; Irritable, .02 and .00; Object of teasing, .01 and -.14;
Irregular attendance at school, 1.00 and .08; Disturbing influence in home,
-.00 and .12; Defiant, -.01 and .06; Leading others into bad conduct, -.01 and
.09; Temper display, -.01 and .18; Swearing (general), -.01 and .06; Sulky,
-.01 and .04; Brother in penal detention, -.01 and .05; Leader, -.01 and -.11;
Follower, -.01 and -.00; Grouped: swearing, etc., -.01 and .03; Emotional instability, -.01 and .06; Obscene language, -.02 (boys); Lying, -.02 and .12;
Absent-minded, -.02 and -.16; Mutual masturbation (same sex) -.02 (boys);
Changeable moods, -.02 and .03; Nail-biting, -.03 and -.05; Selfish, -.03 and
-.04; Passive pederasty, -.03 (boys); Talking to self without apparent reason,
-.03 (boys); Finicky food habits, -.04 and -.12; Contrary, -.04 and .05; Teasing other children, -.04 and .11; Exhibitionism, -.04 (boys); Slow, dull, -.04
and .16; "Nervous," -.04 and .15; Gluttony, -.05 and -.17; Egocentric, -.05 and
.10; Underweight, -.05 and -.10; Lues, -.05 and -.03; Grouped: egocentric,
etc., -.05 and .10; Improvement in behavior, -.05 and -.16; Mental conflict,
-.05 and -.02; Inattentive in school, -.06 and -.14; Slovenly, -.06 and .13;
Stubborn, -.06 and -.06; Excuse-forming, -.06 and .10; Restless in sleep,
-.06 and -.15; Question of hypophrenia, -.06 and .03; Grouped: temper, etc.,
-.06 and .00; Grouped: disobedient, etc., -.06 and .04; Bashful, -.07 and
-.12; Disobedient, -.08 and -.08; Incorrigible, -.08 and -.07; Hatred or jealousy of sibling, -.08 and .04; Bad language, -.09 and -.04; Quarrelsome, -.09
and -.04; Crying spells, -.09 and -.11; Spoiled child, -.09 and -.09; "Night
terrors," -.10 and -.12; Grouped: "nervous," etc., -.10 and .16; Sneaky, -.11
and -.09; Complaining of bad treatment by other children, -.11 and -.15; Repressed, -.11 and -.15; Fantastical lying, -.12 and -.02; Temper tantrums, -.12
and -.12; Grouped: fighting, etc., -.12 and -.07; Failure to adjust in foster-
home, -.13 and -.02; Unpopular, -.03 and -.06; Violence, -.14 and -.11; Discord
between parents, -.15 and .01; Cruelty to younger children, -.15 (boys); Illegitimate parentage, -.16 and -.14; Feeble-minded sibling, -.16 and -.07; Vicious
home conditions, -.17 and -.05; Begging, -.17 (boys); Cruelty to animals, -.17
(boys); Immoral home conditions, -.18 and -.03; Fire-setting, -.19 (boys)

contrariness, clean habits, attractive manner, "follower," nail-
biting, stealing, truancy from school, lack of interest in school,
poor work in school, disobedience, defiant attitude, incorrigibility, stubbornness, bad language, swearing (general), quarrelsomeness, selfishness, egocentric attitude or behavior, loitering,
overinterest in sex matters, and the following six sex notations
which were calculated for boys only: sex attack or abuse of little
girl, exhibitionism (including "indecent exposure"), mutual masturbation with same sex, homosexual behavior with child of same
age, passive pederasty, and obscene language.

The correlations for girls with the factor of age or maturation tended to be of larger size in the notations concerning
heterosexual behavior, but in other respects the coefficients for
both boys and girls tended to resemble each other.

Intelligence quotient (Table 10) was measured usually by
the Stanford-Binet of 1916, but in certain cases by a Kuhlmann-
Binet or by an Army or Arthur performance test. (In computing IQ

TABLE 10

CORRELATIONS WITH "INTELLIGENCE QUOTIENT"

	Boys	Girls
Personality-total.............................	.15 + .01	.16 + .02
Conduct-total.................................	.13 + .01	.12 + .02
Police arrest.................................	-.02 + .02	-.07 + .03
	Larger Correlations (Positive)	
Repressed.....................................	.27 + .03	.24 + .04 (7)*
Attractive manner.............................	.25 + .02	.15
Hatred or jealousy of sibling.................	.24 + .03	.23 + .04 (8-12)
Daydreaming...................................	.23 + .03	.26 + .03 (5)
Bossy...	.23 + .03	.27 + .04 (4)
Grouped: sensitive or worrisome, etc.........	.23 + .02	.14
Mental conflict...............................	.23 + .03	.23 + .04 (8-12)
Inferiority feelings..........................	.22 + .02	.18
Boastful, "show-off"..........................	.22 + .02	.25 + .04 (6)
Sex attack on opposite sex....................	.21 + .04	....
Popular.......................................	.21 + .03	.11

*Rank order of girls' correlations.

TABLE 10—Continued

	Boys	Girls
Worry over specific fact......................	.21 + .03	.11
Psychoneurotic................................	.20 + .03	.16
Leader..	.18	.32 + .04 (1)
Egocentric....................................	.18	.29 + .03 (2)
Grouped: egocentric, etc.....................	.18	.28 + .03 (3)
Abused feeling or manner......................	.12	.23 + .04 (8-12)
Thumb-sucking.................................	.00	.23 + .05 (8-12)
Sneaky..	.05	.23 + .05 (8-12)
Spoiled child.................................	.15	.22 + .03 (13)
Selfish.......................................	.15	.20 + .03 (14)
	Larger Correlations (Negative)	
Retardation in school.........................	-.70 + .01	-.70 + .02
Question of hypophrenia.......................	-.57 + .02	-.53 + .02
Slow, dull....................................	-.26 + .04	-.24 + .03
Feeble-minded sibling.........................	-.16	-.28 + .03
Grouped: dull, slow, etc.....................	-.19	-.21 + .02

Other Correlations (Positive to Negative)

Clean, .19 and .16; Lazy, .19 and .09; Sensitive (general), .19 and .13; Sensitive over specific fact, .19 and .16; Discord between parents, .19 and .07; Finicky food habits, .18 and .09; "Sugar hunger," .18 (boys); Defiant, .16 and .19; Unhappy, .16 and .16; Rude, .16 and .13; Masturbation, .16 and .09; Contrary, .15 and .12; Inefficient in work, play, etc., .15 and .07; Lack of affection, .15 (boys); Failure to adjust in foster-home, .14 and .06; Inattentive in school, .14 and .13; Quarrelsome, .14 and .10; Psychopathic personality, .14 and .16; Grouped: "nervous," etc., .14 and .14; Grouped: depressed, etc., .14 and .17; Unpopular, .13 and .14; Restless in sleep, .13 and .14; Tiring easily, .13 and .14; Stubborn, .13 and .14; Fantastical lying, .12 and .14; Disturbing influence in home, .12 and .04; Immoral home conditions, .12 and .02; Changeable moods, .12 and .18; Overinterest in sex matters, .12 and .19; Mutual masturbation (same sex), .12 (boys); Truancy from institution, .12 (boys); Grouped: lack of interest in school, etc., .11 and .06; Restless, .11 and .13; "Night terrors," .11 and .17; Teasing other children, .11 and .10; Temper tantrums, .10 and .08; Lying, .10 and .12; Resentful attitude, .10 and .16; Irresponsible, .10 and .10; Lues, .10 and -.03; Irritable, .10 and .14; Depressed, .10 and .13; Crying spells, .10 and .12; Bad language, .09 and -.09; Cruelty to animals, .09 (boys); Lack of interest in school, .09 and -.01; Bashful, .09 and .05; "Nervous," .09 and .08; Enuresis, .09 (boys); Overinterest in opposite sex, .09 and -.04; Destructive, .08 and .13; Grouped: disobedient, etc., .08 and .09; Nail-biting, .08 and .05; Excuse-forming, .08 and .13; Emotional instability, .07 and .10; Begging, .07 (boys); Illegitimate parentage, .07 and .16; Grouped: temper, etc., .07 and .10; Sex denied entirely, .07 and .02; Incipient psychosis, .06 (boys); Sex delinquency (coitus), .06 and -.13; Grouped: fighting, etc., .06 and .11; Vocational guidance, .06 and -.02; Slovenly, .06 and -.04; Vicious home conditions, .06 and -.15; Question of change of personality, .05 and .02; Absent-minded, .05 and .01; Stealing, .05 and .02; Fire-setting, .05 (boys); Bad companions, .05 and .10; Homosexual (same age), .04

TABLE 10—Continued

(boys); Lack of initiative, .04 and .07; Neurological defect, .04 and .11;
Fighting, .04 and .10; Disobedient, .04 and .10; Bullying, .04 (boys); Queer,
.03 and .13; Irregular sleep habits, .03 and .10; Passive pederasty, .03 (boys);
Complaining of bad treatment by other children, .03 and -.03; Truancy from home,
.02 and -.03; Question of encephalitis, .02 and .05; Seclusive, .02 and .12;
Incorrigible, .02 and .03; Grouped: swearing, etc., .02 and -.06; Headaches,
.02 and .01; Gluttony, .02 and -.03; Sulky, .01 and .10; Listless, .01 and -.11;
Loitering, .01 and -.13; Obscene language, .01 (boys); Gambling, .00 (boys);
Swearing at mother, teacher, etc., .00 (boys); Leading others into bad conduct,
-.00 and -.00; Cruelty to younger children, -.00 (boys); Immoral sister, -.01
and -.06; Exhibitionism, -.01 (boys); Sullen, -.01 and .03; Staying out late at
night, -.01 and -.05; Smoking, -.01 (boys); Disturbing influence in school,
-.01 and .04; Brother in penal detention, -.02 and -.06; Dementia praecox, -.02
(boys); Violence, -.02 and .04; Temper display, -.02 and .05; Bowel incontinence, -.02 and .02; Gang, -.02 (boys); Stuttering, -.03 (boys); Swearing (general), -.03 and .04; Refusal to attend school, -.03 and -.08; Distractible,
-.04 and .06; Stealing an automobile, -.04 (boys); Object of teasing, -.05 and
-.08; Threatening violence, -.05 (boys); Apprehensive, -.06 and -.01; Underweight, -.06 and -.07; Poor work in school, -.06 and -.13; Follower, -.07 and
-.04; Irregular employment record, -.07 and -.04; Truancy from school, -.07 and
.02; Former convulsions, -.07 and -.07; Robbing a building, home, etc., -.08
(boys); Irregular attendance at school, -.08 and -.12; Victim of sex abuse,
-.09 (girls); Speech defect, -.09 and -.15; Exclusion from school, -.10 and
-.03; Talking to self without reason, -.10 (boys); Preference for younger children, -.12 and -.19; Conduct prognosis bad, -.18 and -.12; Oversuggestible,
-.19 and -.14

among older children the denominator of 16 years' chronological
age was used during the years in which these children were examined.) As explained in earlier pages, the range of IQ within this
group was from 50 to over 150. The mean IQ of our 2,113 boys was
83.0 and the standard deviation, 17.1. For the 1,181 girls the
corresponding constants were 81.6 and 16.1 respectively. This
group thus forms an artificial and truncated distribution with respect to intelligence, and it is probable that the correlations
based on it are likely to be reduced in size toward zero because
of the effect of these restrictions of range.[2]

With the personality-total and the conduct-total the product-moment correlations were all low but positive, indicating that
the more intelligent children in our clinic population tended to
manifest a slightly larger number of behavior difficulties than
the less intelligent. Since these relationships, however, were
shown in Part III of Volume I to be of a curvilinear character,

[2] T. L. Kelley, Statistical Method (New York: Macmillan, 1923), pp.
314-16.

they are not adequately measured by the coefficients of the product-moment family, including bi-serial r and tetrachoric r, which
presuppose only a rectilinear relationship. The interested reader,
therefore, is referred to our previous volume, in which the data
were more closely analyzed by separation into more restricted and
homogeneous age and intelligence groupings, and wherein the relationships were represented graphically. These qualifications must
probably be considered also in interpreting the remainder of the
correlations in Table 10.

With police arrest the coefficients were of negligible size
and negative sign.

The correlations (bi-serial r) of intelligence quotient
with the separate behavior and other notations were generally of
low magnitude, probably owing in some measure to the technical factors of curvilinearity of regression in these relationships and
restriction of range, as described above. Only a few coefficients
were larger than $\pm$ .20.

The highest coefficients were negative: for retardation
in school, -.70 $\pm$ .01 and -.70 $\pm$ .02, among boys and girls respectively, and for question of hypophrenia or suspected mental deficiency (not a staff notation), -.57 $\pm$ .02 and -.53 $\pm$ .02. Slow,
dull manner also yielded negative correlations of moderate size.

Among the positive correlations the largest were of only
moderate size: repressed manner, hatred or jealousy of sibling,
daydreaming, bossy manner, mental conflict, and boastful or "show-
off" manner. In addition, the following showed moderate correlations in the .20's among boys but lesser correlations among girls:
attractive manner, sensitiveness or worrisomeness (undifferentiated), inferiority feelings, popularity, psychoneurotic trends, and
(calculated among boys only) sex attack or abuse of young girl.
The following showed moderate correlations ranging from .20 to .32
among girls, but lower correlations among boys: "leader," egocentricity, selfishness, abused feeling or manner, sneakiness, "spoiled
child," and thumb-sucking.

Three other behavior notations which are frequently found
in the case histories of mental defectives showed low negative correlations with IQ among our cases: oversuggestibility, preference
for younger children as playmates, and object of teasing by other
children. If these correlation coefficients seem lower than might

be expected, it must be recalled that this group is a somewhat artificial one with restricted range, as explained previously, and
our coefficients involving these three notations would probably be
much larger if a selection of all IQ ranges were used.

    An interesting comparison may be made between the correla-
tions of Table 10 and the corresponding coefficients in Table 37
(p. 241) for question of hypophrenia (suspected mental deficiency).
The latter notation was not made by the professional staff of the
clinic, nor was it based directly upon a psychometric score. It
was the subjective opinion or conjecture made by a parent, teacher,
family friend, or social-agency worker prior to the child's admission to the clinic. Although one series was based upon objective
psychometric ratings while the other was a matter of subjective
"lay" opinion, it is evident that the corresponding coefficients
usually showed similar trends (although the coefficients would be
of opposite sign because of the antithetic meaning of the two notations). Retardation in school with its very high bi-serial correlations of -.70 for both boys and girls curiously enough showed
a closer agreement with IQ than with question of hypophrenia, with
which its tetrachoric correlations were .55 $\pm$ .02 and .48 $\pm$ .03 for
boys and girls respectively.[3]

----

[3]A brief summary and comparison of these two series of correlations
may be found in the author's "Behavior Traits of High-Grade Mental Defectives
(a Statistical Study)," Proceedings of the Fifty-ninth Annual Session of the
American Association on Mental Deficiency, Chicago, XL (1935), 435-43. See
also the concluding paragraph of chap. xxv.

CHAPTER XIV

DEPRESSED MOOD OR SPELLS; UNHAPPY APPEARANCE
OR MANNER; CRYING SPELLS

Depressed or discouraged attitude or spells of depression
or discouragement in our study was considered as a more profound
emotional state than unhappy or discontented appearance or manner.
The notation crying spells or crying easily was used to designate
merely an overt behavior pattern without regard to the depth of
any underlying emotion. A fundamental difference between the three
notations is in their genetic aspects as shown in our Volume I
(Fig. 48, pp. 204-7). Among 2,779 White boys and 1,675 White girls
of ages ranging from infancy to 17.9 years of age and of IQ ranges
from about 0 to over 150, crying spells or crying easily appeared
characteristic during the earlier years of age, unhappiness or dis-
content during an older age, and depressed spells during a still
later age. All three traits yielded numerous substantial correlations with other behavior problems, especially of "personality"
type, and should be considered important notations from a clinical
standpoint, though of little significance as far as overt juvenile
delinquency is concerned, as one may infer from their lack of correlation with police arrest. Our justification for treating depressed and unhappy as two separate behavior entities lies in the
fact that their correlations with other traits showed many divergences and also that the combining of the two groups of cases under one rubric (as shown in Table 13, p. 144) did not appreciably
increase the size of the resulting correlation coefficients, which
would have occurred if these two notations were really the same
entity.[1]

The notation depressed, discouraged attitude; spells of
depression or discouragement appeared among 149 of our 2,113 White
boys, or in 7.1 per cent, and among 73 of our 1,181 White girls,

_____

[1]See chap. iv, pp. 38-44.

or in 6.2 per cent. It was of marked clinical importance as an indicator of personality deviation, its bi-serial correlations with
the personality-total being .42 + .03 and .55 + .03 among boys and
girls respectively. Among girls it was of considerable significance also as an indicator of conduct difficulties, the correlation with the conduct-total being .43 + .03, but among boys its relation with the conduct-total was of little importance, the corresponding bi-serial correlation being only .17 + .03. It appears
to have no relation with our police-arrest criterion of overt juvenile delinquency, since its tetrachoric correlations among both
sexes were practically zero.

        Its highest correlation as shown in Table 11 was with
changeable moods among girls, .51 + .05, the corresponding correlation among boys, .28 + .04, being of moderate size. Six personality notations yielded substantial or large correlations ranging

TABLE 11

CORRELATIONS WITH "DEPRESSED"

	Boys	Girls
Personality-total.............................	.42 + .03	.55 + .03
Conduct-total.................................	.17 + .03	.43 + .03
Police arrest.................................	-.03 + .04	-.01 + .06
	Larger Correlations (Positive)	
Grouped: sensitive or worrisome, etc.........	.44 + .03	.50 + .04 (2)*
Worry over specific fact......................	.41 + .04	.43 + .08 (6-7)
Unhappy.......................................	.40 + .05	.33 + .08 (16)
Psychoneurotic................................	.38 + .06	.46 + .07 (4)
Sensitive over specific fact.................	.36 + .04	.41 + .05 (8-9)
Daydreaming...................................	.34 + .03	.34 + .06 (14-15)
Sensitive (general)..	.31 + .05	.47 + .06 (3)
Changeable moods..............................	.28 + .04	.51 + .05 (1)
Question of change of personality............	.28 + .05	.34 + .07 (14-15)
"Nervous".....................................	.28 + .04	.09
Crying spells................................	.27 + .04	.37 + .05 (11)
Unpopular.....................................	.25 + .06	.23 + .08 (35-38)
Grouped: "nervous," etc......................	.25 + .05	.26 + .04 (32-33)
Hatred or jealousy of sibling................	.24 + .06	.31 + .08 (17-22)
Restless......................................	.24 + .04	.22 + .06 (39-42)
Seclusive.....................................	.24 + .04	.36 + .06 (12-13)

*Rank order of girls' correlations.

TABLE 11—Continued

	Boys	Girls
Inferiority feelings..........................	.24 ± .05	.39 ± .08 (10)
Inefficient in work, play, etc...............	.23 ± .06	.41 ± .07 (8-9)
Rude..	.22 ± .04	.17
Listless......................................	.21 ± .05	.23 ± .07 (34-37)
Mental conflict...............................	.21 ± .06	.31 ± .08 (17-22)
Emotional instability.........................	.21 ± .06	.26 ± .07 (32-33)
Neurological defect...........................	.21 ± .05	.19
Question of encephalitis......................	.20 ± .07	.08
Queer...	.18	.44 ± .07 (5)
Stubborn......................................	.14	.43 ± .05 (6-7)
Defiant.......................................	.13	.36 ± .06 (12-13)
Grouped: disobedient, etc....................	.13	.31 ± .06 (17-22)
Repressed.....................................	.08	.31 ± .08 (17-22)
Temper tantrums...............................	.01	.31 ± .06 (17-22)
Bossy...	-.02	.31 ± .07 (17-22)
Grouped: temper, etc.........................	.12	.30 ± .06 (23-24)
Distractible..................................	.04	.30 ± .06 (23-24)
Violence......................................	.09	.29 ± .07 (25-28)
Sullen..	.07	.29 ± .07 (25-28)
Sulky...	.06	.29 ± .07 (25-28)
Selfish.......................................	.19	.29 ± .04 (25-28)
Boastful, "show-off"..........................	.18	.28 ± .07 (29)
Restless in sleep.............................	.17	.27 ± .06 (30-31)
Contrary......................................	.09	.27 ± .08 (30-31)
Sex denied entirely...........................	-.02	.25 ± .08 (34)
Slovenly......................................	.15	.23 ± .06 (35-38)
Grouped: egocentric, etc....................	.18	.23 ± .05 (35-38)
Absent-minded.................................	.12	.22 ± .08 (39-42)
Masturbation..................................	.13	.22 ± .06 (39-42)
Leading others into bad conduct...............	.06	.22 ± .08 (39-42)
Fantastical lying.............................	.17	.21 ± .07 (43-45)
Lazy..	.14	.21 ± .07 (43-45)
Egocentric....................................	.07	.21 ± .06 (43-45)
Irregular sleep habits........................	.08	.20 ± .08 (46)
	Larger Correlations (Negative)	
Retardation in school.........................	-.14	-.26 ± .06
Question of hypophrenia.......................	-.00	-.23 ± .04
	Not Calculable	
Feeble-minded sibling.........................	(n.c.)	(n.c.)

Other Correlations (Positive to Negative)

Grouped: dull, slow, etc., .19 and .08; Irritable, .18 and .19; Discord between parents, .17 and .01; Overinterest in opposite sex, .17 (girls); Nail-biting, .16 and .17; Sex delinquency (coitus), .16 and .01; Slow, dull,

TABLE 11—Continued

.16 and .01; Grouped: fighting, etc., .16 and .19; Attractive manner, .15 and
.05; Disobedient, .14 and -.03; Refusal to attend school, .14 and -.13; Finicky
food habits, .13 and .17; Smoking, .13 (boys); Lack of interest in school, .12
and .07; Teasing other children, .12 (boys); Spoiled child, .12 and .14; Immoral home conditions, .12 and .15; Grouped: swearing, etc., .12 and .07;
Swearing (general), .11 (boys); Threatening violence, .11 (boys); Bashful, .11
and .14; Victim of sex abuse, .11 (girls); Disturbing influence in school, .10
and .13; Incorrigible, .10 and .15; Object of teasing, .10 and .14; Clean, .10
and .15; Grouped: lack of interest in school, etc., .10 and .09; Fighting, .09
and .12; Temper display, .09 and .17; Complaining of bad treatment by other
children, .09 (boys); Apprehensive, .08 and .09; Headaches, .08 and .09; Irregular attendance at school, .08 and -.03; Vicious home conditions, .08 and -.02;
Lying, .07 and .14; Quarrelsome, .07 and .18; Overinterest in sex matters, .07
and .16; Exclusion from school, .07 and .10; Speech defect, .06 and -.05; Lack
of initiative, .05 and .01; Preference for younger children, .05 and -.05; Former convulsions, .05 and .05; Excuse-forming, .04 and .13; Underweight, .04 and
-.00; Enuresis, .03 and .18; Poor work in school, .03 and .05; Irresponsible,
.02 and .18; Loitering, .01 and .01; Conduct prognosis bad, .01 and .12; Stuttering, .01 (boys); Follower, .01 and -.19; Vocational guidance, .01 and -.00;
Destructive, -.02 and .17; Inattentive in school, -.02 and .08; Oversuggestible,
-.02 and .08; Popular, -.03 and -.13; Bad companions, -.04 and .07; Stealing,
-.07 and .18; Truancy from school, -.08 and .02; Leader, -.08 and .09; Lues,
-.09 and -.01; Gang, -.09 (boys); Staying out late at night, -.11 and .09; Truancy from home, -.11 and .07; Brother in penal detention, -.12 and -.13
         Omitted—Grouped: depressed, etc.

from .31 to .47 among both sexes: <u>unhappiness</u>, <u>sensitiveness in
general</u>, <u>sensitiveness over some specific fact or episode</u>, <u>worry
over some specific fact or episode</u>, <u>daydreaming</u>, and <u>staff notation or question of psychoneurotic trends</u>. <u>Queer behavior</u> and
<u>stubbornness</u> among girls yielded large correlations in the .40's,
but among boys low positive correlations below .20.

Six personality problems yielded substantial correlations
in the .30's among girls and moderate correlations in the .20's
among boys: <u>crying spells</u>, <u>inferiority feelings</u>, <u>mental conflict</u>,
<u>seclusiveness</u>, <u>question of change of personality</u>, and <u>hatred or
jealousy of sibling</u>. An additional five personality and conduct
difficulties yielded substantial correlations in the .30's among
girls but low correlations below .20 among boys: <u>repressed man-
ner</u>, <u>disobedience or incorrigibility</u> (including <u>defiant attitude</u>,
<u>stubbornness</u>, and <u>contrariness</u>, undifferentiated), <u>temper tantrums</u>,
<u>bossy manner</u>, and <u>distractibility</u>.

With <u>depressed mood or spells</u> four personality notations
showed moderate correlations in the .20's among both sexes: <u>emo-
tional instability</u>, <u>unpopularity</u>, <u>listlessness</u>, and "<u>nervousness</u>"

or restlessness (including irritable temperament and changeable
moods, undifferentiated). Question of encephalitis and neurological defect (unspecified) showed moderate correlations in the .20's
among boys but low positive coefficients below .20 among girls.
Sixteen miscellaneous behavior notations among girls showed moderate correlations in the .20's, but low coefficients, ranging
from -.02 to .19, among boys: sullenness, sulkiness, slovenliness,
laziness, absent-mindedness, fantastical lying, boastful or "show-
off" manner, selfishness, egocentricity, contrariness, leading
others into bad conduct, violence, irregular sleep habits, restlessness in sleep, masturbation, and sex misbehavior denied entirely.

Two case-record notations showed significant negative correlations in the -.20's, both among girls: retardation in school
and question of hypophrenia.

The tetrachoric correlation of depressed mood or spells
with the notation feeble-minded sibling could not be calculated
for either boys or girls because there were no instances in our
data in which a child's case record showed both notations.

Among the six sex notations (which are being considered
throughout Part III) there were found only two positive correlations of moderate size in the .20's, both among boys—masturbation
and sex misbehavior denied entirely—all other correlations in this
field being low or negligible.

Among the seven physical or psychophysical notations the
only correlations of moderate size in the .20's were for question
of encephalitis and neurological defect (unspecified), both among
boys.

Among the four home or familial notations all correlations
with depressed mood or spells were low or negligible.

The notation unhappy or discontented attitude, appearance,
or manner appeared in 95 boys' cases, or 4.5 per cent, and among
64 of our girls' cases, or 5.4 per cent. Its correlations as shown
in Table 12 were somewhat similar to those for depressed mood or
spells but slightly lower. The most conspicuous difference is that
among our boys unhappiness tended to show more significant correlations with overt conduct problems than were found for depressed
mood or spells.

Among both sexes unhappiness showed fairly substantial

TABLE 12

CORRELATIONS WITH "UNHAPPY"

	Boys	Girls
Personality-total.........................	.31 ± .03	.33 + .04
Conduct-total.............................	.29 ± .03	.35 + .04
Police arrest.............................	.01 ± .05	-.02 + .06
	Larger Correlations (Positive)	
Inferiority feelings......................	.43 ± .05	.25 ± .08 (20-23)*
Depressed.................................	.40 ± .05	.33 ± .08 (5-6)
Seclusive.................................	.38 ± .05	.28 ± .07 (12-13)
Sensitive over specific fact..............	.38 ± .04	.34 ± .06 (2-4)
Daydreaming...............................	.36 ± .05	.36 ± .07 (1)
Grouped: sensitive or worrisome, etc......	.26 ± .04	.32 ± .05 (7-9)
Sensitive (general).......................	.26 ± .06	.21 ± .07 (27-29)
Nail-biting...............................	.25 ± .05	.07
Bad companions............................	.24 ± .05	.07
Sullen....................................	.24 ± .05	.31 ± .07 (10)
Discord between parents...................	.23 ± .04	.11
Incorrigible..............................	.23 ± .04	.22 ± .06 (26)
Inefficient in work, play, etc...........	.22 ± .07	.13
Truancy from home.........................	.22 ± .04	.13
Hatred or jealousy of sibling.............	.22 ± .07	.18
Restless..................................	.22 ± .04	.08
Staying out late at night.................	.21 ± .05	.11
Lack of interest in school................	.20 ± .05	.17
Lazy......................................	.20 ± .06	.16
Temper display............................	.20 ± .04	.02
Question of change of personality.........	.20 ± .06	.19
Repressed.................................	.20 ± .06	.32 ± .09 (7-9)
Grouped: swearing, etc....................	.20 ± .05	.32 ± .07 (7-9)
Excuse-forming............................	.05	.28 ± .07 (12-13)
Contrary..................................	.18	.34 ± .08 (2-4)
Irresponsible.............................	.17	.34 ± .07 (2-4)
Sulky.....................................	.04	.33 ± .08 (5-6)
Queer.....................................	-.02	.30 ± .08 (11)
Overinterest in sex matters...............	.18	.27 ± .07 (14-16)
Leading others into bad conduct...........	.18	.27 ± .09 (14-16)
Boastful, "show-off"......................	.07	.27 ± .07 (14-16)
Bossy.....................................	.16	.26 ± .07 (17-19)
Apprehensive..............................	.10	.26 ± .06 (17-19)
Grouped: fighting, etc....................	.10	.26 ± .05 (17-19)
Grouped: disobedient, etc.................	.19	.25 ± .05 (20-23)
Mental conflict...........................	.14	.25 ± .09 (20-23)
Changeable moods..........................	.03	.25 ± .06 (20-23)
Rude......................................	.16	.24 ± .06 (24)
Victim of sex abuse.......................	....	.23 ± .07 (25)
Violence..................................	.07	.21 ± .07 (27-29)

*Rank order of girls' correlations.

TABLE 12—Continued

	Boys	Girls
Defiant..	.16	.21 + .07 (27-29)
Masturbation...................................	.15	.20 + .06 (30-33)
Overinterest in opposite sex...................	....	.20 + .06 (30-33)
Crying spells..................................	.17	.20 + .05 (30-33)
Underweight....................................	.12	.20 + .06 (30-33)
		Larger Correlations (Negative)
Lack of initiative............................	.15	-.25 + .08
Loitering.....................................	.12	-.25 + .08
Refusal to attend school......................	.17	-.22 + .09

Other Correlations (Positive to Negative)

Lying, .19 and .15; Complaining of bad treatment by other children, .18 (boys); Spoiled child, .18 and -.00; Threatening violence, .18 (boys); Destructive, .18 and .11; Disobedient, .17 and .17; Slovenly, .17 and .09; Worry over specific fact, .16 and -.04; Swearing (general), .16 (boys); Fantastical lying, .15 and -.16; Irregular sleep habits, .15 and .10; Attractive manner, .15 and .02; Grouped: "nervous," etc., .14 and .16; Grouped: temper, etc., .14 and .07; Neurological defect, .14 and .12; Poor work in school, .14 and .09; Stealing, .13 and .06; Stubborn, .13 and .07; Listless, .13 and .13; Former convulsions, .13 and -.07; Grouped: egocentric, etc., .13 and .10; Speech defect, .12 and -.10; Bashful, .12 and .08; Quarrelsome, .11 and .19; Egocentric, .11 and .17; Immoral home conditions, .11 and .07; Grouped: dull, slow, etc., .11 and .01; Grouped: lack of interest in school, etc., .11 and .14; Object of teasing, .10 and .12; "Nervous," .10 and .18; Psychoneurotic, .10 and .04; Smoking, .10 (boys); Disturbing influence in school, .10 and .10; Finicky food habits, .10 and .12; Clean, .09 and .09; Sex denied entirely, .09 and .11; Headaches, .09 and .10; Vocational guidance, .08 and .17; Sex delinquency (coitus), .08 and .01; Preference for younger children, .07 and -.01; Follower, .07 and -.03; Emotional instability, .06 and .16; Conduct prognosis bad, .06 and -.03; Unpopular, .06 and .09; Irritable, .06 and .14; Truancy from school, .05 and .08; Absent-minded, .04 and .07; Teasing other children, .04 (boys); Selfish, .04 and -.15; Enuresis, .04 and -.01; Slow, dull, .03 and .02; Vicious home conditions, .03 and .13; Lues, .02 and .02; Restless in sleep, .02 and -.01; Gang, .01 (boys); Temper tantrums, .01 and .14; Popular .01 and .05; Fighting, -.01 and .19; Irregular attendance at school, -.01 and -.04; Distractible, -.02 and .12; Oversuggestible, -.03 and .12; Leader, -.03 and .06; Stuttering, -.05 (boys); Brother in penal detention, -.05 and -.03; Exclusion from school, -.08 and .08; Feeble-minded sibling, -.09 and -.08; Inattentive at school, -.10 and -.00; Question of encephalitis, -.10 and .01; Retardation in school, -.11 and -.12; Question of hypophrenia, -.16 and -.03
    Omitted—Depressed, etc.

bi-serial correlations ranging from .29 to .35 with personality-total and conduct-total, but its tetrachoric correlations with police arrest were practically zero.

Its largest correlations (in the .40's) were with depressed mood or spells and inferiority feelings among boys, the corresponding coefficients for girls being of lesser size—.33 ± .08 and .25 ± .08 respectively.

Three personality problems—sensitiveness over some specific fact or episode, daydreaming, and seclusiveness—yielded substantial correlations ranging from .28 to .38 among both sexes. Among girls three notations—repressed manner, sullenness, and swearing or bad language (undifferentiated)—yielded substantial correlations in the .30's and among boys moderate correlations in the .20's. Among girls an additional four behavior traits yielded substantial correlations in the .30's, but low coefficients below .20 among boys: queer behavior, sulkiness, irresponsibility, and contrariness.

Unhappiness showed moderate correlations in the .20's among both sexes with sensitiveness in general and incorrigibility. Two notations, for which only the girls' coefficients were computed—overinterest in the opposite sex and victim of sex abuse by older child or person—also showed moderate correlations in the .20's. Twelve miscellaneous case-record notations showed moderate correlations in the .20's among boys but low positive coefficients below .20 among girls: question of change of personality, lack of interest in school, inefficiency in work, play, etc., laziness, hatred or jealousy of sibling, restlessness, temper display, bad companions, staying out late at night, truancy from home, nail-biting, and discord between parents. Fourteen miscellaneous notations showed moderate correlations in the .20's among girls but low positive coefficients below .20 among boys: crying spells, changeable moods or attitudes, mental conflict, excuse-forming attitude, apprehensiveness, boastful or "show-off" manner, bossy manner, rudeness, disobedience or incorrigibility (including defiant attitude, stubbornness, and contrariness, undifferentiated), leading others into bad conduct, fighting or quarrelsomeness (including violence, undifferentiated), masturbation, overinterest in sex matters, and underweight condition.

Unhappiness showed three negative correlations of moderate size in the .20's, all among girls: lack of initiative, loitering or wandering, and refusal to attend school.

Among the six sex notations unhappiness showed four corre-

lations of moderate size in the .20's, all among girls: masturbation, overinterest in sex matters, overinterest in the opposite
sex, and victim of sex abuse by older child or person.

Among the seven physical or psychophysical notations the
only correlation of significant size was with underweight condition among girls, .20 + .06.

Among the four home or familial notations the only correlation of significant size with unhappiness was for discord between
parents among boys, .23 + .04.

When our cases showing a notation of either depressed mood
or spells or unhappiness were grouped together under one rubric or
combined into a broad grouping,[2] there were 219 such cases, or 10.4
per cent, among our 2,113 White boys and 125 cases, or 10.6 per
cent, among our 1,181 White girls. The resulting correlations, as
shown in Table 13, were not greatly different from those found when
such notation was discussed separately.

Yielding substantial to large correlations ranging from
about .20 to .47 for both notations and among both sexes were the
following: sensitiveness or worrisomeness (undifferentiated), inferiority feelings, daydreaming, seclusiveness, hatred or jealousy
of sibling, and question of change of personality. Six notations
yielded substantial correlations with depressed mood or spells but
moderate or low correlations with unhappiness: psychoneurotic
trends, mental conflict, unpopularity, changeable moods or attitudes, restlessness, and inefficiency in work, play, etc. On the
other hand, four notations showed meaningful correlations with unhappiness but were negligibly associated with depressed mood or
spells: repressed manner, sullenness, incorrigibility, and swearing or bad language (undifferentiated).

Crying spells or crying easily was found among 473 boys,
or 22.4 per cent, and among 297 girls, or 25.1 per cent, and is
thus one of the most frequently appearing case-record notations
found among the children studied in our clinic,[3] especially among

---

[2]The reasons for this grouping were given in I, 44 and 86, Table 13,
Item J.

[3]I, 46.

TABLE 13

CORRELATIONS WITH "GROUPED: DEPRESSED, ETC."

	Boys	Girls
Personality-total..........................	.50 ± .02	.57 ± .03
Conduct-total.............................	.24 ± .02	.42 ± .03
Police arrest.............................	-.02 ± .03	-.00 ± .05
	Larger Correlations (Positive)	
Grouped: sensitive or worrisome, etc.........	.44 ± .03	.47 ± .04 (1)*
Sensitive over specific fact.................	.41 ± .03	.45 ± .04 (2)
Inferiority feelings.........................	.37 ± .04	.38 ± .06 (6-7)
Worry over specific fact.....................	.37 ± .05	.35 ± .07 (9-12)
Daydreaming..................................	.36 ± .05	.39 ± .05 (5)
Psychoneurotic...............................	.34 ± .05	.35 ± .06 (9-12)
Sensitive (general).........................	.31 ± .05	.38 ± .05 (6-7)
Seclusive....................................	.30 ± .04	.37 ± .05 (8)
Crying spells...............................	.27 ± .03	.30 ± .04 (8-10)
Restless.....................................	.27 ± .03	.19
Inefficient in work, play, etc..............	.25 ± .05	.29 ± .06 (11-13)
Hatred or jealousy of sibling...............	.25 ± .05	.25 ± .07 (19-20)
Question of change of personality...........	.25 ± .05	.29 ± .06 (11-13)
"Nervous"....................................	.24 ± .04	.16
Unpopular....................................	.23 ± .05	.22 ± .07 (27-33)
Mental conflict..............................	.22 ± .05	.33 ± .07 (13-14)
Changeable moods.............................	.21 ± .04	.44 ± .05 (3-4)
Discord between parents......................	.21 ± .03	.07
Listless.....................................	.20 ± .04	.14
Emotional instability.......................	.20 ± .05	.22 ± .06 (27-33)
Queer..	.11	.44 ± .06 (3-4)
Contrary.....................................	.13	.35 ± .07 (9-12)
Bossy..	.12	.35 ± .06 (9-12)
Defiant......................................	.14	.33 ± .06 (13-14)
Sulky..	.08	.32 ± .06 (15)
Irresponsible................................	.12	.31 ± .06 (16-17)
Violence.....................................	.08	.31 ± .05 (16-17)
Stubborn.....................................	.15	.30 ± .04 (8-10)
Leading others into bad conduct.............	.14	.30 ± .07 (8-10)
Grouped: fighting, etc.....................	.15	.29 ± .04 (11-13)
Boastful, "show-off"........................	.14	.27 ± .06 (14-17)
Sullen.......................................	.17	.27 ± .06 (14-17)
Masturbation.................................	.16	.27 ± .05 (14-17)
Repressed....................................	.13	.27 ± .07 (14-17)
Overinterest in sex matters.................	.15	.26 ± .06 (18)
Grouped: "nervous," etc....................	.14	.25 ± .04 (19-20)
Distractible................................	-.03	.24 ± .05 (21-23)
Excuse-forming...............................	.05	.24 ± .06 (21-23)
Quarrelsome..................................	.07	.24 ± .05 (21-23)
Grouped: swearing, etc.....................	.17	.23 ± .06 (24-26)

*Rank order of girls' correlations.

TABLE 13—Continued

	Boys	Girls
Rude	.19	.23 ± .05 (24-26)
Temper tantrums	.02	.23 ± .05 (24-26)
Victim of sex abuse	....	.22 ± .06 (27-33)
Irritable	.18	.22 ± .05 (27-33)
Slovenly	.16	.22 ± .05 (27-33)
Lazy	.15	.22 ± .06 (27-33)
Grouped: temper, etc.	.15	.22 ± .04 (27-33)
Incorrigible	.17	.20 ± .05 (34-35)
Grouped: disobedient, etc.	.16	.20 ± .04 (34-35)
	Larger Correlations (Negative)	
Feeble-minded sibling	-.22 ± .05	-.25 ± .06
Refusal to attend school	.09	-.25 ± .07
Retardation in school	-.13	-.22 ± .04

Other Correlations (Positive to Negative)

Nail-biting, .19 and .15; Complaining of bad treatment by other children, .19 (boys); Neurological defect, .18 and .17; Overinterest in opposite sex, .18 (girls); Grouped: dull, slow, etc., .17 and .01; Fantastical lying, .17 and .10; Spoiled child, .17 and .10; Irregular sleep habits, .16 and .15; Swearing (general), .16 (boys); Lack of interest in school, .16 and .13; Immoral home conditions, .15 and .14; Question of encephalitis, .15 and .02; Disobedient, .15 and .11; Selfish, .15 and .17; Smoking, .15 (boys); Threatening violence, .15 (boys); Attractive manner, .14 and .07; Restless in sleep, .14 and .17; Finicky food habits, .14 and .13; Grouped: egocentric, etc., .14 and .18; Lying, .13 and .16; Sex delinquency (coitus), .13 and .03; Bashful, .13 and .12; Object of teasing, .12 and .13; Lack of initiative, .12 and -.08; Slow, dull, .12 and -.01; Temper display, .12 and .14; Speech defect, .12 and -.06; Clean, .10 and .13; Apprehensive, .10 and .18; Teasing other children, .10 (boys); Destructive, .10 and .19; Grouped: lack of interest in school, etc., .10 and .13; Former convulsions, .10 and .07; Disturbing influence in school, .09 and .13; Egocentric, .08 and .19; Fighting, .08 and .18; Bad companions, .08 and .09; Headaches, .08 and .09; Vicious home conditions, .07 and .07; Underweight, .07 and .10; Loitering, .07 and -.07; Poor work in school, .07 and .08; Preference for younger children, .06 and .05; Absent-minded, .06 and .13; Truancy from home, .06 and .10; Staying out late at night, .06 and .13; Enuresis, .06 and .13; Irregular attendance at school, .05 and -.04; Conduct prognosis bad, .05 and .03; Exclusion from school, .04 and .11; Vocational guidance, .03 and .09; Stealing, .02 and .12; Stuttering, .01 (boys); Sex denied entirely, .01 and .18; Oversuggestible, -.00 and .13; Follower, -.00 and -.09; Truancy from school, -.01 and .03; Popular, -.02 and -.05; Lues, -.02 and -.04; Inattentive in school, -.05 and .04; Gang, -.06 (boys); Leader, -.06 and .12; Question of hypophrenia, -.07 and -.13; Brother in penal detention, -.12 and -.06

Omitted—Depressed; Unhappy

the younger ones. Among girls it showed substantial bi-serial correlations in the .30's with both personality-total and conduct-
total, while among boys the corresponding coefficients were of moderate size in the .20's (Table 14). With police arrest its tetrachoric coefficients were low.

TABLE 14

CORRELATIONS WITH "CRYING SPELLS"

	Boys	Girls
Personality-total..............................	.27 ± .02	.38 ± .02
Conduct-total.................................	.22 ± .02	.30 ± .02
Police arrest.................................	.13 ± .03	.07 ± .04
	Larger Correlations (Positive)	
Sensitive (general)...........................	.43 ± .03	.50 ± .04 (1)*
Grouped: sensitive or worrisome, etc.........	.40 ± .03	.49 ± .03 (2)
Sensitive over specific fact..................	.33 ± .03	.35 ± .04 (9)
Irritable.....................................	.32 ± .03	.30 ± .04 (19-20)
Grouped: "nervous," etc......................	.32 ± .02	.47 ± .03 (3)
Question of change of personality.............	.30 ± .04	.32 ± .05 (14-16)
Grouped: temper, etc.........................	.30 ± .02	.38 ± .03 (5-6)
Depressed.....................................	.27 ± .04	.51 ± .05 (7-8)
Grouped: depressed, etc......................	.27 ± .03	.30 ± .04 (19-20)
Question of encephalitis......................	.26 ± .05	.32 ± .06 (14-16)
Emotional instability.........................	.25 ± .04	.38 ± .05 (5-6)
Apprehensive..................................	.24 ± .03	.33 ± .04 (12-13)
Sex denied entirely...........................	.24 ± .04	.15
Bossy...	.23 ± .04	.17
Sulky...	.23 ± .04	.20 ± .05 (44-48)
Changeable moods..............................	.23 ± .03	.43 ± .04 (4)
"Nervous".....................................	.23 ± .03	.37 ± .04 (7-8)
Inefficient in work, play, etc...............	.22 ± .04	.23 ± .05 (34-35)
Bashful.......................................	.21 ± .03	.22 ± .04 (36-39)
Unpopular.....................................	.21 ± .04	.34 ± .05 (10-11)
Worry over specific fact......................	.21 ± .04	.26 ± .06 (24-26)
Grouped: fighting, etc.......................	.21 ± .03	.29 ± .04 (21)
Nail-biting...................................	.20 ± .03	.21 ± .04 (40-43)
Complaining of bad treatment by other children	.20 ± .04	....
Follower......................................	.20 ± .03	.19
Temper tantrums...............................	.17	.34 ± .04 (10-11)
Irregular sleep habits........................	-.02	.33 ± .05 (12-13)
Quarrelsome...................................	.18	.32 ± .04 (14-16)
Restless......................................	.16	.31 ± .03 (17-18)
Fantastical lying.............................	.05	.31 ± .05 (17-18)
Hatred or jealousy of sibling.................	.16	.28 ± .05 (22-23)

*Rank order of girls' correlations.

TABLE 14—Continued

	Boys	Girls
Queer..	.18	.28 ± .05 (22-23)
Daydreaming.....................................	.16	.26 ± .05 (24-26)
Inferiority feelings...........................	.19	.26 ± .05 (24-26)
Headaches.......................................	.17	.25 ± .05 (27-30)
Restless in sleep..............................	.19	.25 ± .04 (27-30)
Object of teasing..............................	.11	.25 ± .05 (27-30)
Psychoneurotic..................................	.16	.25 ± .05 (27-30)
Leading others into bad conduct...............	.00	.24 ± .06 (31-33)
Violence..	.12	.24 ± .05 (31-33)
Grouped: swearing, etc........................	.08	.24 ± .05 (31-33)
Conduct prognosis bad..........................	.09	.23 ± .06 (34-35)
Irresponsible...................................	.05	.22 ± .05 (36-39)
Rude..	.02	.22 ± .04 (36-39)
Distractible....................................	.08	.22 ± .04 (36-39)
Spoiled child...................................	.17	.21 ± .04 (40-43)
Selfish...	.15	.21 ± .04 (40-43)
Disturbing influence in school................	.09	.21 ± .05 (40-43)
Finicky food habits............................	.14	.20 ± .05 (44-48)
Sullen..	.11	.20 ± .05 (44-48)
Unhappy...	.17	.20 ± .05 (44-48)
Grouped: egocentric, etc.....................	.09	.20 ± .04 (44-48)

Other Correlations (Positive to Negative)

Overinterest in sex matters, .19 and .12; Mental conflict, .18 and .19; Stealing, .16 and .15; Temper display, .16 and .15; Disobedient, .14 and .13; Enuresis, .14 and .17; Swearing (general), .14 (boys); Neurological defect, .14 and .14; Grouped: disobedient, etc., .14 and .16; Refusal to attend school, .13 and .00; Masturbation, .13 and .15; Former convulsions, .13 and .11; Grouped: lack of interest in school, etc., .13 and .09; Contrary, .12 and .12; Destructive, .12 and .13; Fighting, .12 and .13; Lack of interest in school, .12 and .10; Stubborn, .12 and .15; Absent-minded, .12 and .18; Lues, .12 and .01; Incorrigible, .11 and .10; Stuttering, .11 (boys); Defiant, .10 and .19; Truancy from school, .10 and .07; Preference for younger children, .10 and .16; Poor work in school, .10 and .08; Discord between parents, .10 and -.01; Lying, .09 and .16; Slovenly, .09 and .11; Excuse-forming, .09 and .19; Seclusive, .09 and .16; Loitering, .08 and -.01; Staying out late at night, .08 and .11; Threatening violence, .08 (boys); Truancy from home, .08 and .03; Listless, .08 and .09; Grouped: dull, slow, etc., .08 and -.02; Bad companions, .07 and .12; Inattentive in school, .07 and -.01; Underweight, .07 and .08; Speech defect, .07 and .03; Lazy, .06 and .03; Smoking, .06 (boys); Attractive manner, .06 and .10; Teasing other children, .05 (boys); Sex delinquency (coitus), .05 and -.05; Slow, dull, .05 and .01; Egocentric, .05 and .19; Lack of initiative, .05 and -.04; Oversuggestible, .05 and .15; Repressed, .05 and .15; Popular, .05 and .09; Exclusion from school, .04 and .15; Leader, .04 and .19; Boastful, "show-off," .03 and .17; Clean, .03 and .06; Overinterest in opposite sex, .03 (girls); Gang, -.01 (boys); Retardation in school, -.01 and -.09; Question of hypophrenia, -.04 and .06; Vocational guidance, -.05 and -.08; Immoral home conditions, -.05 and -.06; Irregular attendance at school, -.06 and -.08; Vicious home conditions, -.06 and -.10; Victim of sex abuse, -.06 (girls); Feeble-minded sibling, -.14 and -.13; Brother in penal detention, -.16 and -.18

Its highest correlations were with <u>sensitiveness in general</u>, the coefficients being .43 + .03 and .50 + .04 among boys and girls respectively. Its next highest correlation was with the notation <u>"nervousness" or restlessness</u> (including <u>irritable temperament</u> and <u>changeable moods</u>, undifferentiated) with corresponding coefficients of .32 + .02 and .47 + .03 for boys and girls.

Three additional behavior traits yielded substantial correlations in the .30's among both sexes: <u>sensitiveness over some specific fact or episode</u>, <u>question of change of personality</u>, and <u>temper tantrums or display</u> (including <u>irritable temperament</u>, undifferentiated). Among girls five notations yielded substantial correlations in the .30's and among boys moderate coefficients in the .20's: <u>depressed mood or spells</u>, <u>emotional instability</u>, <u>apprehensiveness</u>, <u>unpopularity</u>, and <u>question of encephalitis</u>. An additional four behavior problems among girls yielded substantial correlations in the .30's but low coefficients below .20 among boys: <u>quarrelsomeness</u>, <u>irregular sleep habits</u>, <u>restlessness</u>, and <u>fantastical lying</u>.

<u>Crying spells</u> showed moderate correlations ranging from .19 to .26 among both sexes for the six behavior notations, <u>worry over some specific fact or episode</u>, <u>sulkiness</u>, <u>inefficiency in work, play, etc.</u>, <u>bashfulness</u>, <u>nail-biting</u>, and <u>"follower"</u> and also for the notation <u>complaining of bad treatment by other children</u>, which was calculated only for boys. Among girls the following twenty-one miscellaneous notations showed moderate correlations in the .20's but among boys low positive coefficients below .20: <u>unhappiness</u>, <u>inferiority feelings</u>, <u>staff notation of psychoneurotic trends</u>, <u>daydreaming</u>, <u>queer behavior</u>, <u>sullenness</u>, <u>"spoiled child,"</u> <u>finicky food habits</u>, <u>hatred or jealousy of sibling</u>, <u>object of teasing by other children</u>, <u>distractibility</u>, <u>irresponsibility</u>, <u>disturbing influence in school</u>, <u>rudeness</u>, <u>leading others into bad conduct</u>, <u>violence</u>, <u>swearing or bad language</u> (undifferentiated), <u>egocentricity or selfishness</u> (undifferentiated), <u>restlessness in sleep</u>, <u>staff notation of unfavorable conduct prognosis</u>, and <u>headaches</u>.

Among the six sex notations the only significant correlation with <u>crying spells</u> was for <u>sex misbehavior denied entirely</u> among boys, .24 + .04.

Among the seven physical or psychophysical notations the only significant correlations were with <u>question of encephalitis</u>,

the respective coefficients for boys and girls being .26 $\pm$ .05 and
.32 $\pm$ .06.

Among the four home or familial notations all correlations
with crying spells were low or negligible.

CHAPTER XV

SENSITIVENESS AND WORRISOMENESS

Sensitiveness or worrisomeness, whether considered as a
general habit of mind or as a concern over a specific fact or episode, appeared frequently among our clinical cases. About 23 per
cent of our 2,113 White boys and about 22 per cent of our 1,181
White girls were so described. Curiously enough, the trait was
remarked slightly more often among boys than among girls. In general the notations were correlated substantially with personality
problems and occasionally also with conduct problems. With police
arrest, however, the correlations were substantially zero, except
that among girls the specific notation sensitiveness (general)
showed a significant negative tetrachoric correlation of -.25 $\pm$
.05. These case notations should, however, be considered of definite clinical importance, especially from the standpoint of personality deviation. The four tables of this chapter comprise different aspects of this general behavior trait.

Sensitiveness as a general trait was noted in about 8 per
cent of our children. Its highest correlations (Table 15) were
among girls, the tetrachoric coefficients ranging from .43 to .50
for crying spells, depressed mood or spells, and inferiority feelings, with substantial correlations also among boys. The highest
correlation among boys was also for crying spells (.43 $\pm$ .03).
Among both sexes the following yielded substantial correlations in the .30's: sensitiveness over specific fact, changeable moods, and finicky or capricious food habits. Other meaningful correlations among both sexes were for psychoneurotic trends,
seclusiveness, and for "nervousness" or restlessness (undifferentiated) with coefficients ranging from .25 to .36. Among girls
the following additional notations yielded substantial correlations
ranging from .30 to .37, while the boys' correlations were of doubtful significance though of positive sign: sulkiness, hatred or
jealousy of sibling, boastful or "show-off" manner, and irregular
sleep habits.

150

TABLE 15

CORRELATION WITH "SENSITIVE (GENERAL)"

	Boys	Girls
Personality-total..........................	.33 ± .03	.34 ± .03
Conduct-total.............................	.12 ± .03	.16 ± .04
Police arrest.............................	-.02 ± .04	-.21 ± .05
	Larger Correlations (Positive)	
Crying spells.............................	.43 ± .03	.50 ± .04 (1)*
Sensitive over specific fact...............	.37 ± .04	.30 ± .05 (13)
Changeable moods...........................	.33 ± .04	.35 ± .05 (7)
Finicky food habits........................	.31 ± .04	.33 ± .06 (9)
Depressed..................................	.31 ± .05	.47 ± .06 (2)
Grouped: depressed, etc...................	.31 ± .04	.38 ± .05 (4)
Seclusive..................................	.30 ± .04	.28 ± .06 (15-16)
Worry over specific fact...................	.29 ± .05	.28 ± .08 (15-16)
Lack of initiative........................	.27 ± .05	.18
Psychoneurotic.............................	.26 ± .06	.31 ± .07 (10-12)
Unhappy....................................	.26 ± .06	.21 ± .07 (25-29)
Grouped: "nervous," etc..................	.25 ± .03	.36 ± .04 (6)
Bossy......................................	.25 ± .05	.20 ± .07 (30-34)
Inefficient in work, play, etc............	.24 ± .05	.26 ± .07 (18-20)
Inferiority feelings.......................	.24 ± .04	.43 ± .07 (3)
Spoiled child..............................	.24 ± .04	.26 ± .06 (18-20)
Restless in sleep.........................	.23 ± .04	.13
Attractive manner..........................	.22 ± .04	.19
Speech defect..............................	.21 ± .05	.04
"Nervous"..................................	.21 ± .04	.25 ± .04 (21-22)
Clean......................................	.20 ± .04	.29 ± .05 (14)
Sulky......................................	.12	.37 ± .07 (5)
Hatred or jealousy of sibling.............	.19	.34 ± .07 (8)
Irregular sleep habits....................	.09	.31 ± .07 (10-12)
Boastful, "show-off"......................	.16	.31 ± .07 (10-12)
Excuse-forming............................	.03	.27 ± .06 (17)
Irritable.................................	.19	.26 ± .05 (18-20)
Repressed.................................	.16	.25 ± .08 (21-22)
Daydreaming...............................	.19	.24 ± .06 (23)
Queer.....................................	.15	.23 ± .07 (24)
Grouped: egocentric, etc.................	.15	.21 ± .05 (25-29)
Egocentric................................	.12	.21 ± .06 (25-29)
Sullen....................................	.11	.21 ± .06 (25-29)
Contrary..................................	.10	.21 ± .08 (25-29)
Fantastical lying.........................	.16	.20 ± .07 (30-34)
Absent-minded.............................	.02	.20 ± .07 (30-34)
Bashful...................................	.19	.20 ± .05 (30-34)
Popular...................................	.12	.20 ± .07 (30-34)

*Rank order of girls' correlations.

TABLE 15—Continued

	Boys	Girls
	Larger Correlations (Negative)	
Brother in penal detention...................	-.04	-.31 + .06
Truancy from home...........................	-.03	-.25 + .05

Other Correlations (Positive to Negative)

Object of teasing, .19 and .18; Mental conflict, .19 and .09; Selfish, .18 and .17; Lack of interest in school, .17 and .02; Temper tantrums, .17 and .15; Complaining of bad treatment by other children, .16 (boys); Apprehensive, .15 and .05; Unpopular, .15 and -.01; Grouped: temper, etc., .14 and .18; Question of change of personality, .14 and .13; Overinterest in sex matters, .14 and .10; Lazy, .13 and .10; Former convulsions, .13 and .09; Neurological defect, .12 and .09; Stuttering, .12 (boys); Disobedient, .11 and .12; Restless, .13 and .13; Grouped: lack of interest in school, etc., .11 and .04; Question of encephalitis, .10 and .15; Quarrelsome, .10 and .18; Smoking, .10 (boys); Enuresis, .09 and .14; Nail-biting, .09 and .11; Refusal to attend school, .09 and .13; Emotional instability, .09 and .13; Preference for younger children, .09 and .12; Poor work in school, .09 and .09; Vocational guidance, .09 and .10; Headaches, .08 and .12; Masturbation, .08 and .06; Stubborn, .07 and .17; Irregular attendance at school, .07 and .04; Immoral home conditions, .07 and -.17; Grouped: dull, slow, etc., .06 and .07; Grouped: disobedient, etc., .06 and .10; Discord between parents, .06 and -.02; Lying, .05 and .01; Sex denied entirely, .05 and .18; Vicious home conditions, .05 and -.07; Grouped: fighting, etc., .05 and .14; Defiant, .03 and .13; Disturbing influence in school, .03 and .06; Lues, .03 and -.08; Fighting, .02 and .09; Inattentive in school, .01 and .04; Listless, .01 and .05; Distractible, .01 and .14; Oversuggestible, .01 and .10; Grouped: swearing, etc., .01 and -.09; Gang, .00 (boys); Rude, .00 and .16; Irresponsible, -.00 and .06; Slovenly, -.01 and .04; Teasing other children, -.02 (boys); Stealing, -.02 and -.06; Swearing (general), -.02 (boys); Sex delinquency (coitus), -.02 and -.18; Slow, dull, -.02 and .02; Follower, -.03 and .03; Violence, -.03 and .05; Threatening violence, -.03 (boys); Loitering, -.03 and -.05; Destructive, -.03 and -.08; Temper display, -.04 and .05; Exclusion from school, -.04 and .02; Question of hypophrenia, -.05 and -.08; Incorrigible, -.06 and -.06; Overinterest in opposite sex, -.06 (girls); Leader, -.07 and .05; Underweight, -.07 and .07; Truancy from school, -.08 and .05; Conduct prognosis bad, -.10 and -.17; Bad companions, -.10 and .04; Retardation in school, -.12 and -.14; Feeble-minded sibling, -.12 and -.18; Leading others into bad conduct, -.14 and .01; Victim of sex abuse, -.14 (girls); Staying out late at night, -.15 and -.05

Omitted—Grouped: sensitive or worrisome, etc.

The following showed moderate correlations of .20 to .29 among both sexes: worry over specific fact or episode, unhappiness, bossy manner, inefficiency in work, play, etc., "spoiled child," and clean habits or appearance. Four notations showed moderate correlations ranging from .20 to .27 among boys, with lesser though positive correlations among girls: lack of initiative,

restlessness in sleep, attractive manner, and speech defect (other
than stuttering). Among girls there were a dozen correlations
ranging from .20 to .27, the corresponding coefficients for boys
ranging only from .02 to .19; these were for irritable manner or
disposition, excuse-forming attitude, contrariness, sullenness,
egocentricity, queer behavior, fantastical lying, daydreaming, repressed manner, bashfulness, absent-mindedness, and popularity.

Only two significant negative correlations with sensitiveness (general) were found. Among girls the correlations for brother
in penal detention was -.31 ± .06 and for truancy from home -.25 ±
.05, the boys' correlations being negligible.

For the six sex notations all coefficients were of almost
negligible size. The largest were among girls: a negative correlation of -.18 for sex delinquency (coitus) and a positive one of
.18 for sex misbehavior denied entirely. Since our cases were too
few to establish "statistical significance" in case of tetrachoric
correlations of less than ± .20, one can report these coefficients
only as suggesting that sexually abstinent girls tend to be sensitive, while sexually delinquent ones tend to be less sensitive in
general than others.

Discord between parents and enuresis showed quite negligible correlations with sensitiveness (general).

Sensitiveness over some specific fact or episode appeared
almost twice as often among our cases as sensitiveness in general.
It was noted in 15 per cent of our 2,113 boys and in 13 per cent
of our 1,181 girls and was one of the most frequent notations in
the personality field.

The usual sources of this specialized sensitiveness were
in order of frequency: school problems such as poor work in school,
retardation in school, being in "ungraded room" or in room with
younger or smaller children, special educational defect, exclusion
from school because of poor work in studies, low intelligence,
memory defect, etc.; physical deficiencies such as poor physique,
short stature, loss of limb, crippled condition, obesity, convul-
sive attacks, wearing glasses, deafness or hearing defect, speech
defect or stuttering, unattractive personal appearance or poor
complexion, enuresis or bowel incontinence, etc.; sex misbehavior
such as masturbation, sexual intercourse, homosexual behavior,

illegitimate pregnancy, and, among girls, menstruation; home or
familial conditions such as the fact that relatives do not visit
or write to patient or that he has no relatives, death of parent
or near-relative, rejection or desertion by both parents or the
fact of adoption or other circumstances concerning patient's parentage, poor clothing, poor financial condition of family or of
self or the fact that the family receives aid from charity organi-
zations, parent's criminality, immorality, alcoholism, viciousness,
venereal disease, etc., and discord between parents or foster-parents; and miscellaneous source such as misdeeds in general, unpopularity or inability to make friends or sensitiveness over being
an object of teasing by other children, race or nativity, and religion.[1]

Its correlations (Table 16) were very similar to those for
sensitiveness in general. Its three highest correlations among
both sexes were for inferiority feelings, mental conflict, and depressed spells or unhappiness (undifferentiated), the tetrachoric
coefficients ranging from .41 to .50. Four personality traits
showing coefficients ranging from .30 to .41 among both sexes were:
unhappiness, sensitiveness in general, crying spells, and object
of teasing by other children. The notations daydreaming and hatred
or jealousy of sibling showed correlations in the .30's for girls
and in the .20's for boys.

Seven traits showed moderate correlations in the .20's for
both sexes: worry over some specific fact or episode, masturbation, overinterest in sex matters, psychoneurotic trends, bashfulness, seclusiveness, and probably "spoiled child." Among boys enuresis, repressed manner, attractive manner, and clean habits showed
correlations ranging from .20 to .23 and lesser though positive
correlations among girls. Eighteen notations showed correlations
among girls ranging from .20 to .30 but lesser though generally
positive coefficients among boys: emotional instability, changeable moods, queer behavior, "nervousness" or restlessness (undifferentiated), unpopularity, preference for younger children as
playmates, irresponsibility, lack of interest in school, egocentricity, selfishness, bossy manner, stubbornness, defiant attitude,

---

[1] Vol. I, Tables 1 and 2, Items 62, 72, 86, 88, 99, 104, 118, 120, 122,
123, 126, 131, 132, 133, 138, 139, and 144.

TABLE 16

CORRELATION WITH "SENSITIVE OVER SPECIFIC FACT"

	Boys	Girls
Personality-total..............................	.31 ± .02	.34 + .03
Conduct-total.................................	.19 ± .02	.27 + .03
Police arrest.................................	.07 ± .03	.03 + .05
	Larger Correlations (Positive)	
Inferiority feelings..........................	.49 + .03	.50 + .05 (1)*
Mental conflict...............................	.48 + .04	.46 + .06 (2)
Grouped: depressed, etc.......................	.41 + .03	.45 + .04 (3)
Unhappy.......................................	.38 + .04	.34 + .06 (7)
Sensitive (general)..........................	.37 + .04	.30 + .05 (10-11)
Depressed.....................................	.36 + .04	.41 + .05 (4-5)
Crying spells................................	.33 + .03	.35 + .04 (6)
Object of teasing............................	.30 + .03	.41 + .05 (4-5)
Bashful.......................................	.29 + .03	.22 + .04 (23-25)
Psychoneurotic................................	.27 + .05	.20 + .06 (32-36)
Worry over specific fact......................	.27 + .05	.27 + .07 (12-14)
Spoiled child.................................	.27 + .03	.19
Seclusive.....................................	.25 + .03	.23 + .05 (18-22)
Daydreaming...................................	.24 + .04	.33 + .05 (8)
Masturbation..................................	.23 + .03	.27 + .05 (12-14)
Hatred or jealousy of sibling.................	.23 + .05	.31 + .06 (9)
Attractive manner.............................	.23 + .03	.15
Enuresis......................................	.22 + .03	.09
Clean...	.22 + .03	.12
Overinterest in sex matters..................	.21 + .05	.21 + .06 (26-31)
Repressed.....................................	.20 + .04	.17
Bossy...	.16	.30 + .05 (10-11)
Selfish.......................................	.11	.27 + .04 (12-14)
Lying...	.10	.26 + .04 (15-16)
Emotional instability.........................	.11	.26 + .06 (15-16)
Changeable moods..............................	.07	.24 + .05 (17)
Grouped: fighting, etc.......................	.03	.23 + .04 (18-22)
Neurological defect...........................	.10	.23 + .05 (18-22)
Stealing......................................	.11	.23 + .05 (18-22)
Leading others into bad conduct...............	.05	.23 + .07 (18-22)
Defiant.......................................	.01	.22 + .05 (23-25)
Irresponsible.................................	-.04	.22 + .06 (23-25)
Grouped: egocentric, etc.....................	.04	.21 + .04 (26-31)
Grouped: "nervous," etc......................	.12	.21 + .04 (26-31)
Queer...	.11	.21 + .06 (26-31)
Stubborn......................................	.17	.21 + .04 (26-31)
Lack of interest in school...................	.16	.21 + .05 (26-31)
Egocentric....................................	-.00	.20 + .05 (32-36)
"Nervous".....................................	.15	.20 + .05 (32-36)

*Rank order of girls' correlations.

TABLE 16—Continued

	Boys	Girls
Unpopular..	.09	.20 ± .07 (32-36)
Preference for younger children...............	.02	.20 ± .06 (32-36)
		Larger Correlations (Negative)
Retardation in school.........................	-.14	-.28 ± .04

Other Correlations (Positive to Negative)

Headaches, .18 and .17; Complaining of bad treatment by other children, .18 (boys); Victim of sex abuse, .18 (girls); Question of change of personality, .17 and .19; Irregular sleep habits, .17 and .17; Lack of initiative, .17 and -.19; Speech defect, .17 and .07; Discord between parents, .17 and .07; Lazy, .16 and -.01; Sulky, .16 and .15; Listless, .15 and .01; Inefficient in work, play, etc., .14 and .18; Apprehensive, .14 and .07; Boastful, "show-off," .13 and .11; Rude, .13 and .01; Staying out late at night, .13 and .03; Sex delinquency (coitus), .13 and .01; Grouped: disobedient, etc., .13 and .13; Teasing other children, .12 (boys); Absent-minded, .12 and .10; Popular, .12 and .00; Underweight, .12 and .10; Grouped: lack of interest in school, etc., .12 and .18; Finicky food habits, .11 and .05; Listless, .11 and .09; Leader, .11 and .11; Nail-biting, .10 and .17; Temper display, .10 and .07; Conduct prognosis bad, .10 and -.08; Stuttering, .10 (boys); Question of encephalitis, .10 and .11; Vocational guidance, .10 and -.10; Sullen, .09 and .17; Temper tantrums, .09 and .16; Gang, .08 (boys); Distractible, .08 and .05; Grouped: temper, etc., .08 and .09; disobedient, .07 and .04; Irritable, .07 and .02; Sex denied entirely, .07 and .11; Poor work in school, .07 and .07; Immoral home conditions, .07 and .15; Grouped: swearing, etc., .07 and .15; Bad companions, .06 and .11; Refusal to attend school, .06 and .19; Smoking, .06 (boys); Contrary, .05 and .01; Threatening violence, .05 (boys); Restless in sleep, .05 and .14; Grouped: dull, slow, etc., .05 and -.05; Overinterest in opposite sex, .05 (girls); Incorrigible, .04 and .09; Quarrelsome, .04 and .16; Truancy from home, .04 and .05; Vicious home conditions, .04 and -.00; Swearing (general), .03 (boys); Violence, .02 and .14; Destructive, .01 and .11; Loitering, .01 and -.13; Slovenly, .01 and .06; Truancy from school, .01 and .16; Follower, .01 and .06; Oversuggestible, .01 and .02; Disturbing influence in school, -.00 and .10; Inattentive in school, -.00 and .09; Fantastical lying, -.01 and .12; Excuse-forming, -.01 and .14; Exclusion from school, -.01 and .11; Irregular attendance at school, -.01 and .04; Slow, dull, -.04 and -.02; Lues, -.04 and .02; Fighting, -.05 and .11; Brother in penal detention, -.08 and .04; Feeble-minded sibling, -.13 and .19; Question of hypophrenia, -.16 and -.08
     Omitted—Grouped: sensitive or worrisome, etc.

fighting, stealing, lying, leading others into bad conduct, and neurological defect (unspecified).

Only one "statistically significant" negative coefficient was found, retardation in school, with values of -.14 and -.28 ± .04 for boys and girls respectively.

Boys appeared to be somewhat sensitive over <u>enuresis (present or former</u>), the tetrachoric <u>r</u> being .22 ± .03, but seemingly do not worry about it. It does not appear to be associated with <u>sensitiveness in general</u>, however. Our girls seemed quite unconcerned over bed-wetting, though it was noted among 21 per cent of them.

Among the sex notations, two showed moderate correlations in the .20's among both sexes: <u>masturbation</u> and <u>overinterest in sex matters</u>. For <u>victim of sex abuse by older person</u> the correlation of .18 (calculated for girls only) may be suggestive but is scarcely "statistically significant" upon our small number of cases. For <u>sex delinquency (coitus</u>), <u>overinterest in opposite sex</u> (calculated for girls only), and <u>sex misbehavior denied entirely</u>, the correlations were of negligible size though positive in sign.

Although a great variety of conditions in the child's life served as sources of its concern or sensitiveness (<u>vide supra</u>), in many instances the presence of such conditions seemed only slightly associated with <u>sensitiveness over some specific fact</u>, e.g., <u>poor work in school</u>, <u>exclusion from school</u>, <u>underweight condition</u>, <u>speech defect</u>, <u>stuttering</u> (calculated for boys only), <u>police arrest</u>, <u>immoral home conditions</u>, <u>vicious home conditions</u>, <u>brother in penal detention</u>, and <u>discord between parents</u>. Some tendency toward a moderate association was shown by the following potential sources (with their respective coefficients for boys and girls): <u>neurological defect (unspecified</u>) (.10 and .23 ± .05), misdeeds as measured by <u>conduct-total</u> (.19 ± .02 and .27 ± .03), and <u>unpopularity</u> (.09 and .20 ± .07).

Among boys the significant correlations with <u>sensitiveness over some specific fact or episode</u> were found only in the case of personality difficulties, but among girls there were also a number of moderate correlations with conduct problems as well as with personality problems.

<u>Worry over some specific fact or episode</u> was noted slightly more often among our boys than among the girls, the percentages of incidence being 4.7 and 3.4 respectively. The usual sources of this worrisomeness were, in order of frequency: sex misbehavior (masturbation, homosexual behavior, sexual intercourse, illegitimate pregnancy), physical deficiencies (poor health, short stature,

etc., unattractive personal appearance and poor complexion), poor
health or insanity of parent, foster-parent, or guardian, race or
nativity, religion, low intelligence, memory defect, deafness or
hearing defect, "feelings of guilt," "castration complex," and
"stool hypochondriasis."[2] Like <u>sensitiveness in general</u> and <u>sen-
sitiveness over some specific fact</u>, it showed many substantial correlations with other personality problems among both sexes and
among girls with a number of conduct problems also. It should be
considered a significant symptom from a clinical standpoint. With
<u>police arrest</u>, however, its associations were practically zero.

      The highest correlations for <u>worry over some specific fact
or episode</u> (Table 17) were with <u>mental conflict</u>, the coefficients
being .49 $\pm$ .06 and .50 $\pm$ .09 for boys and girls respectively.
Other substantial correlations ranging from .33 to .44 for either
sex were for <u>psychoneurotic trends</u>, <u>depressed spells or unhappi-
ness</u> (undifferentiated), <u>inferiority feelings</u>, and among girls
<u>overinterest in sex matters</u>, <u>masturbation</u>, <u>seclusiveness</u>, and <u>clean
habits</u>.

      Seven notations showing moderate correlations in the .20's
for both sexes were <u>sensitiveness (general)</u>, <u>sensitiveness over
specific fact</u>, <u>crying spells</u>, "nervousness" or restlessness (undifferentiated), <u>irregular sleep habits</u>, <u>daydreaming</u>, and <u>attrac-
tive manner</u>. A few notations showed moderate correlations in the
.20's for boys but negligible correlations for the girls: <u>appre-
hensiveness</u>, <u>bashfulness</u>, <u>object of teasing by other children</u>, <u>vi-
cious home conditions</u>, and (calculated for boys only) <u>teasing other
children</u>. Seventeen personality and conduct difficulties showed
moderate correlations ranging from .20 to .34 among our girls but
lesser or even negligible correlations among the boys: <u>truancy
from school</u>, <u>exclusion from school</u>, <u>associating with bad companions</u>,
<u>violence</u>, <u>destructiveness</u>, <u>stubbornness</u>, <u>defiant attitude</u>, <u>leading
others into bad conduct</u>, <u>sulkiness</u>, <u>bossy manner</u>, <u>unpopularity</u>,
<u>hatred or jealousy of sibling</u>, <u>changeable moods</u>, <u>question of change
of personality</u>, <u>queer behavior</u>, <u>distractibility</u>, and <u>finicky food
habits</u>. Similar differences between the boys' and girls' cases
were shown for <u>headaches</u>, <u>neurological defect</u>, and <u>question of en-
cephalitis</u>. <u>Preference for younger children as playmates</u> showed

      [2]Vol. I, Tables 1 and 2, Items 90, 129, 134, 139, and 144.

TABLE 17

CORRELATIONS WITH "WORRY OVER SPECIFIC FACT"

	Boys	Girls
Personality-total...........................	.37 ± .03	.37 ± .04
Conduct-total...............................	.11 ± .03	.32 ± .05
Police arrest...............................	.06 ± .04	.00 ± .07
		Larger Correlations (Positive)
Mental conflict.............................	.49 ± .06	.50 ± .09 (1)*
Psychoneurotic..............................	.44 ± .06	.37 ± .09 (4-5)
Depressed...................................	.41 ± .05	.43 ± .08 (2)
Grouped: depressed, etc....................	.37 ± .05	.35 ± .07 (7)
Inferiority feelings........................	.35 ± .07	.33 ± .09 (10-11)
"Nervous"...................................	.29 ± .04	.15
Sensitive (general).........................	.29 ± .05	.28 ± .08 (16)
Masturbation................................	.28 ± .04	.33 ± .07 (10-11)
Overinterest in sex matters.................	.27 ± .07	.40 ± .08 (3)
Sensitive over specific fact................	.27 ± .05	.27 ± .07 (17-21)
Vicious home conditions.....................	.26 ± .07	-.17
Teasing other children......................	.25 ± .05	....
Attractive manner...........................	.25 ± .05	.20 ± .07 (36-38)
Seclusive...................................	.24 ± .05	.37 ± .07 (4-5)
Clean.......................................	.24 ± .05	.34 ± .07 (8-9)
Grouped: "nervous," etc...................	.24 ± .04	.27 ± .06 (17-21)
Irregular sleep habits......................	.22 ± .06	.22 ± .09 (27-32)
Crying spells...............................	.21 ± .04	.26 ± .06 (22-24)
Apprehensive................................	.20 ± .05	.09
Bashful.....................................	.20 ± .03	-.10
Daydreaming.................................	.20 ± .05	.22 ± .08 (27-32)
Object of teasing...........................	.20 ± .04	.09
Headaches...................................	.07	.36 ± .08 (6)
Distractible................................	.04	.34 ± .07 (8-9)
Bossy.......................................	.14	.32 ± .08 (12)
Destructive.................................	-.11	.30 ± .10 (13-14)
Bad companions..............................	-.01	.30 ± .07 (13-14)
Restless....................................	.15	.29 ± .06 (15)
Stubborn....................................	-.04	.27 ± .06 (17-21)
Truancy from school.........................	-.13	.27 ± .07 (17-21)
Unpopular...................................	.17	.27 ± .10 (17-21)
Neurological defect.........................	.16	.26 ± .08 (22-24)
Exclusion from school.......................	-.12	.26 ± .09 (22-24)
Hatred or jealousy of sibling...............	.05	.24 ± .10 (25)
Changeable moods............................	.07	.23 ± .07 (26)
Question of encephalitis....................	.02	.22 ± .11 (27-32)
Leading others into bad conduct.............	.05	.22 ± .10 (27-32)
Defiant.....................................	-.04	.22 ± .08 (27-32)
Finicky food habits.........................	.05	.21 ± .08 (33-35)
Question of change of personality...........	.19	.21 ± .09 (33-35)

*Rank order of girls' correlations.

TABLE 17—<u>Continued</u>

	Boys	Girls
Violence	.04	.21 + .09 (33-35)
Queer	.04	.20 + .09 (36-38)
Sulky	.14	.20 + .09 (36-38)
	Larger Correlations (Negative)	
Retardation in school	-.36 + .04	-.34 + .05
Preference for younger children	-.24 + .06	.22 + .08 (27-32)
Question of hypophrenia	-.23 + .04	-.10
Brother in penal detention	-.17	-.26 + .08
Feeble-minded sibling	-.08	-.26 + .08
Listless	.13	-.25 + .08
Popular	.05	-.20 + .09
	Not Calculable	
Irresponsible	.01	(n.c.)

Other Correlations (Positive to Negative)

Fantastical lying, .19 and .11; Egocentric, .19 and .18; Grouped: egocentric, etc., .19 and .15; Sex delinquency (coitus), .18 and .15; Complaining of bad treatment by other children, .18 (boys); Irritable, .17 and .17; Restless in sleep, .17 and .12; Discord between parents, .17 and .05; Absent-minded, .16 and .11; Emotional instability, .16 and .14; Spoiled child, .16 and .19; Unhappy, .16 and -.04; Boastful, "show-off," .15 and .11; Lack of initiative, .15 and -.15; Inefficient in work, play, etc., .14 and .16; Selfish, .14 and .12; Grouped: lack of interest in school, etc., .14 and .10; Inattentive in school, .14 and .18; Grouped: dull, slow, etc., .13 and -.17; Victim of sex abuse, .13 (girls); Grouped: temper, etc., .12 and .17; Nail-biting, .11 and .16; Refusal to attend school, .10 and .03; Temper display, .10 and .03; Excuseforming, .10 and .04; Grouped: swearing, etc., .10 and .19; Contrary, .09 and .03; Enuresis, .09 and .09; Quarrelsome, .09 and -.01; Leader, .09 and .05; Immoral home conditions, .09 and -.03; Overinterest in opposite sex, .09 (girls); Lack of interest in school, .08 and .01; Follower, .07 and -.04; Poor work in school, .07 and -.03; Irregular attendance at school, .07 and .15; Underweight, .06 and .16; Lying, .05 and .12; Rude, .05 and .07; Slow, dull, .05 and .07; Repressed, .05 and .18; Former convulsions, .05 and .03; Smoking, .04 (boys); Grouped: fighting, etc., .04 and .07; Disobedient, .03 and .13; Disturbing influence in school, -.00 and .17; Threatening violence, -.00 (boys); Fighting, -.01 and .10; Loitering, -.01 and .16; Vocational guidance, -.01 and .13; Stealing, -.03 and .10; Sullen, -.03 and -.04; Conduct prognosis bad, -.03 and -.00; Grouped: disobedient, etc., -.03 and .10; Incorrigible, -.04 and .03; Sex denied entirely, -.04 and -.09; Lues, -.04 and .01; Lazy, -.05 and -.00; Slovenly, -.05 and .02; Oversuggestible, -.05 and .15; Temper tantrums, -.07 and .11; Speech defect, -.07 and .09; Gang, -.08 (boys); Truancy from home, -.10 and -.02; Swearing (general), -.11 (boys); Stuttering, -.15 (boys); Staying out late at night, -.16 and .02

Omitted—Grouped: sensitive or worrisome, etc.

the small _positive_ correlation of .22 $\pm$ .09 among girls but the
negative correlation of -.24 $\pm$ .06 among boys.

There were several significant negative correlations. _Re-
tardation in school_ among both sexes yielded the substantial negative correlations of -.36 $\pm$ .04 and -.34 $\pm$ .05 among boys and
girls respectively. _Question of hypophrenia_ showed negative correlations of -.23 $\pm$ .04 and -.10 for boys and girls respectively.
The four notations _brother in penal detention_, _feeble-minded sib-
ling_, _listlessness_, and _popularity_ showed moderate negative correlations ranging from -.20 to -.26 among girls but lesser or negligible correlations among boys.

Sex difficulties appear to be slightly associated with
worry over some specific fact or episode.

When the children with one or more notations of _sensitive-
ness (general)_, _sensitiveness over some specific fact_, and _worry
over some specific fact_ (together with a handful of cases in which
the notation of _worrisomeness in general_ occurred too infrequently
to justify separate statistical treatment) were combined into one
group, there were 490 boys and 255 girls so described. The correlations for _sensitiveness or worrisomeness_ (thus undifferentiated),
as shown in Table 18, were usually larger than the corresponding

TABLE 18

CORRELATIONS WITH "GROUPED: SENSITIVE OR WORRISOME, ETC."

	Boys	Girls
Personality-total................................	.43 $\pm$ .02	.50 $\pm$ .02
Conduct-total....................................	.16 $\pm$ .02	.28 $\pm$ .03
Police arrest....................................	.02 $\pm$ .03	-.02 $\pm$ .04
	Larger Correlations (Positive)	
Mental conflict.................................	.52 $\pm$ .03	.49 $\pm$ .05 (3-4)*
Inferiority feelings...........................	.49 $\pm$ .03	.50 $\pm$ .05 (1-2)
Depressed.......................................	.44 $\pm$ .03	.50 $\pm$ .04 (1-2)
Grouped: depressed, etc........................	.44 $\pm$ .03	.47 $\pm$ .04 (5)
Crying spells...................................	.40 $\pm$ .03	.49 $\pm$ .03 (3-4)
Psychoneurotic..................................	.39 $\pm$ .04	.35 $\pm$ .05 (7)

*Rank order of girls' correlations.

TABLE 18—Continued

	Boys	Girls
Unhappy....................................	.36 ± .04	.32 ± .05 (10-13)
Spoiled child.............................	.27 ± .03	.21 ± .05 (33-37)
Overinterest in sex matters..............	.27 ± .04	.29 ± .05 (16-17)
Bashful...................................	.27 ± .03	.21 ± .04 (33-37)
Daydreaming...............................	.27 ± .03	.31 ± .05 (14)
Object of teasing.........................	.27 ± .03	.37 ± .05 (6)
Seclusive.................................	.27 ± .03	.28 ± .05 (18-20)
Masturbation..............................	.27 ± .03	.28 ± .04 (18-20)
Grouped: "nervous," etc..................	.25 ± .02	.32 ± .03 (10-13)
"Nervous".................................	.25 ± .03	.28 ± .04 (18-20)
Attractive manner.........................	.25 ± .03	.17
Clean.....................................	.24 ± .03	.24 ± .04 (28-32)
Lack of initiative.......................	.24 ± .04	-.01
Changeable moods..........................	.23 ± .03	.33 ± .04 (9)
Finicky food habits......................	.22 ± .03	.19
Inefficient in work, play, etc...........	.21 ± .04	.21 ± .05 (33-37)
Hatred or jealousy of sibling............	.20 ± .04	.34 ± .05 (8)
Complaining of bad treatment by other children	.20 ± .04	....
Bossy.....................................	.19	.32 ± .05 (10-13)
Emotional instability....................	.11	.32 ± .05 (10-13)
Sulky.....................................	.16	.30 ± .05 (15)
Repressed.................................	.17	.29 ± .10 (16-17)
Question of change of personality........	.18	.25 ± .05 (21-22)
Sullen....................................	.09	.25 ± .05 (21-22)
Irregular sleep habits...................	.17	.24 ± .05 (23)
Queer.....................................	.10	.23 ± .05 (24-27)
Leading others into bad conduct..........	-.02	.23 ± .06 (24-27)
Headaches.................................	.16	.23 ± .05 (24-27)
Neurological defect......................	.14	.23 ± .05 (24-27)
Grouped: egocentric, etc................	.11	.22 ± .04 (28-32)
Defiant...................................	.04	.22 ± .05 (28-32)
Restless..................................	.15	.22 ± .04 (28-32)
Preference for younger children..........	.01	.22 ± .05 (28-32)
Egocentric................................	.09	.21 ± .04 (33-37)
Selfish...................................	.17	.21 ± .04 (33-37)
Grouped: fighting, etc..................	.03	.20 ± .04 (38-41)
Truancy from school......................	-.05	.20 ± .04 (38-41)
Excuse-forming............................	.02	.20 ± .05 (38-41)
Restless in sleep........................	.15	.20 ± .04 (38-41)

	Larger Correlations (Negative)	
Retardation in school....................	-.17	-.28 ± .03
Feeble-minded sibling....................	-.16	-.21 ± .05

Other Correlations (Positive to Negative)

Enuresis, .19 and .13; Speech defect, .18 and .11; Apprehensive, .18 and .12; Popular, .18 and .06; Lack of interest in school, .17 and .16; Irritable, .16 and .13; Stubborn, .15 and .19; Lazy, .15 and .01; Grouped: lack of interest in school, etc., .14 and .12; Grouped: temper, etc., .14 and .18;

TABLE 18—Continued

Boastful, "show-off," .14 and .19; Listless, .13 and -.03; Nail-biting, .13 and
.19; Discord between parents, .13 and .05; Absent-minded, .12 and .18; Stuttering, .12 (boys); Sex delinquency (coitus), .11 and -.01; Teasing other children, .11 (boys); Grouped: disobedient, etc., .11 and .10; Vocational guidance, .10 and .03; Question of encephalitis, .10 and .15; Fantastical lying,
.10 and .18; Lying, .10 and .18; Temper tantrums, .10 and .17; Victim of sex
abuse, .10 (girls); Distractible, .09 and .15; Quarrelsome, .09 and .17; Vicious home conditions, .08 and -.05; Grouped: dull, slow, etc., .08 and -.02;
Disobedient, .08 and .06; Rude, .08 and .10; Leader, .07 and .10; Follower,
.07 and .03; Poor work in school, .07 and .10; Contrary, .06 and .12; Stealing,
.06 and .11; Temper display, .06 and .10; Sex denied entirely, .06 and .06; Overinterest in opposite sex, .06 (girls); Conduct prognosis bad, .05 and -.07; Smoking, .05 (boys); Immoral home conditions, .05 and .07; Underweight, .04 and .06;
Former convulsions, .04 and .04; Inattentive in school, .04 and .06; Refusal to
attend school, .04 and .15; Grouped: swearing, etc., .03 and .09; Irregular attendance at school, .03 and .05; Gang, .02 (boys); Slovenly, .02 and .07; Violence, .02 and .14; Oversuggestible, .02 and .08; Threatening violence, .01
(boys); Staying out late at night, .01 and .01; Disturbing influence in school,
.01 and .17; Lues, .01 and -.01; Bad companions, .00 and .16; Loitering, -.00
and -.04; Incorrigible, -.01 and .01; Swearing (general), -.01 (boys); Slow,
dull, -.01 and -.01; Destructive, -.02 and .16; Fighting, -.03 and .15; Truancy
from home, -.04 and -.02; Irresponsible, -.05 and .13; Exclusion from school,
-.06 and .13; Brother in penal detention, -.14 and -.06; Question of hypophrenia,
-.15 and -.09

          Omitted—Sensitive (general); Sensitive over specific fact; Worry over
specific fact

correlations for each of the three traits when considered separately. This fact, together with the tendency for high interrela-
tion among these three notations, indicates their close similarity.

          The bi-serial correlations with the personality-total for
both boys and girls were relatively high, .43 ± .02 and .50 ± .02
respectively. For the conduct-total the correlation for girls was
substantial, .28 ± .03, but relatively low among the boys, .16 ±
.02. Their significance from a clinical standpoint is thus established, but from the sheer standpoint of "juvenile delinquency"
their importance is slight in view of their generally negligible
correlations with police arrest.

          The highest correlations for sensitiveness or worrisomeness
(undifferentiated) were for mental conflict, inferiority feelings,
depressed spells or unhappiness (undifferentiated), and crying
spells, with correlations ranging from .52 ± .03 down to .40 ± .03.
Psychoneurotic trends yielded substantial correlations of .39 ±
.04 and .35 ± .05 for boys and girls respectively. The following
five personality traits showed correlations ranging from .30 to .37

among girls, and coefficients in the .20's for boys: <u>object of</u>
<u>teasing by other children</u>, <u>hatred or jealousy of sibling</u>, <u>change-</u>
<u>able moods</u>, "<u>nervousness" or worrisomeness</u> (undifferentiated), and
<u>daydreaming</u>. In addition, three notations, <u>bossy manner</u>, <u>emotional</u>
<u>instability</u>, and <u>sulkiness</u>, yielded tetrachoric correlations rang-
ing from .30 to .32 among girls but among boys lower correlations
ranging from .11 to .19.

The following personality notations showed moderate correlations in the .20's for both boys and girls: <u>masturbation</u>, <u>over-</u>
<u>interest in sex matters</u>, <u>seclusiveness</u>, <u>bashfulness</u>, <u>inefficiency</u>
<u>in work, play, etc</u>., <u>clean habits</u>, "<u>spoiled child</u>," and (calculated
for boys only) <u>complaining of bad treatment by other children</u>. The
three notations <u>finicky food habits</u>, <u>lack of initiative</u>, and <u>at-</u>
<u>tractive manner</u> among boys showed moderate correlations of .22 to
.25 but lower or negligible correlations among girls. The following seventeen personality, conduct, and other notations among our
girls showed moderate correlations in the .20's but low or negligible correlations among the boys: <u>repressed manner</u>, <u>queer behav-</u>
<u>ior</u>, <u>sullenness</u>, <u>question of change of personality</u>, <u>egocentricity</u>,
<u>selfishness</u>, <u>defiant attitude</u>, <u>fighting or quarrelsomeness</u> (undif-
ferentiated), <u>truancy from school</u>, <u>leading others into bad conduct</u>,
<u>excuse-forming attitude</u>, <u>restlessness</u>, <u>irregular sleep habits</u>,
<u>restlessness in sleep</u>, <u>preference for younger children as play-</u>
<u>mates</u>, <u>headaches</u>, and <u>neurological defect (unspecified)</u>.

Two notations showed significant negative correlations
among girls: <u>retardation in school</u> (-.28 + .03) and <u>feeble-minded</u>
<u>sibling</u> (-.21 + .05). the corresponding coefficients for boys also
being negative (-.17 and -.16 respectively).

Among the six sex notations studied, only two—<u>masturbation</u>
and <u>overinterest in sex matters</u>—showed significant correlations
with <u>sensitiveness or worrisomeness</u> (undifferentiated). The correlations for <u>sex delinquency (coitus)</u>, <u>sex misbehavior denied en-</u>
<u>tirely</u>, and the two notations which were calculated for girls only
—<u>victim of sex abuse</u> and <u>overinterest in opposite sex</u>—showed negligible correlations of positive sign.

Physical or constitutional defects such as <u>underweight con-</u>
<u>dition</u>, <u>speech defect</u> and <u>stuttering</u>, <u>former convulsions</u>, <u>lues</u>,
<u>question of encephalitis</u>, and <u>enuresis</u> showed only moderate or low
positive correlations, while <u>neurological defect (unspecified)</u>

among girls showed the moderate positive correlation of .23 $\pm$ .05.

Unfavorable home conditions such as discord between parents, vicious or immoral home conditions, and brother in penal detention showed negligible association with sensitiveness or worrisomeness (undifferentiated).

CHAPTER XVI

BASHFULNESS AND APPREHENSIVENESS

. The case notations of <u>bashfulness</u> and <u>apprehensiveness</u> appeared from the data of this chapter to be of quite minor clinical importance as far as our three criteria of "seriousness" are concerned. In fact, among girls the negative tetrachoric correlation of -.28 ± .04 indicates that bashful girls are less likely to be involved in "juvenile delinquency" than their less bashful sisters.

<u>Bashfulness, shyness, or becoming embarrassed easily</u>, etc., was a frequently appearing item among our cases. It was noted among 316 of our 2,113 White boys and among 218 of our 1,181 White girls, the respective percentages being 15.0 and 18.5.

Its highest correlations were of barely substantial size in the .30's: <u>inferiority feelings</u> and <u>seclusiveness</u> among girls and <u>apprehensiveness</u> among boys, the corresponding coefficients for the other sex being of moderate size in the .20's (Table 19).

TABLE 19

CORRELATIONS WITH "BASHFUL"

	Boys	Girls
Personality-total............................	.13 ± .02	.05 ± .03
Conduct-total................................	-.02 ± .02	-.07 ± .03
Police arrest................................	-.05 ± .03	-.28 ± .04
	Larger Correlations (Positive)	
Apprehensive.................................	.30 ± .03	.26 ± .04 (3)*
Lack of initiative..........................	.29 ± .04	.19
Sensitive over specific fact................	.29 ± .03	.22 ± .04 (5-6)
Grouped: sensitive or worrisome, etc........	.27 ± .03	.21 ± .04 (7)
Seclusive...................................	.25 ± .03	.31 ± .05 (2)
Follower....................................	.22 ± .04	.23 ± .05 (4)

*Rank order of girls' correlations.

TABLE 19—Continued

	Boys	Girls
Inferiority feelings..........................	.21 ± .05	.32 ± .06 (1)
Listless......................................	.21 ± .04	.04
Crying spells.................................	.21 ± .03	.22 ± .04 (5-6)
Worry over specific fact......................	.20 ± .03	-.10
Sensitive (general)..........................	.19	.20 ± .05 (8)
	Larger Correlations (Negative)	
Irregular sleep habits........................	-.20 ± .04	.06
Exclusion from school.........................	-.20 ± .04	-.13
Question of encephalitis......................	-.10	-.22 ± .07
Rude..	-.05	-.20 ± .04

Other Correlations (Positive to Negative)

Queer, .19 and .07; Underweight, .19 and .16; Grouped: dull, slow, etc., .18 and .14; Preference for younger children, .18 and .08; Vocational guidance, .16 and .09; Spoiled child, .16 and -.05; Unpopular, .16 and -.08; Irritable, .16 and .08; Lazy, .16 and -.07; Hatred or jealousy of sibling, .15 and .04; Clean, .15 and .03; Speech defect, .15 and .02; Restless in sleep, .14 and .08; Daydreaming, .14 and .16; Teasing other children, .14 (boys); Repressed, .13 and .14; Grouped: depressed, etc., .13 and .12; Unhappy, .12 and .08; Stubborn, .12 and -.03; Feeble-minded sibling, .12 and .02; Selfish, .11 and .11; Depressed, .11 and .14; "Nervous," .11 and .10; Mental conflict, .11 and .06; Poor work in school, .11 and .06; Neurological defect, .11 and .05; Slow, dull, .10 and .07; Lack of interest in school, .09 and .05; Grouped: "nervous," etc., .09 and .08; Oversuggestible, .08 and .00; Absent-minded, .08 and -.03; Masturbation, .08 and -.07; Inefficient in work, play, etc., .08 and .02; Finicky food habits, .07 and .14; Question of change of personality, .07 and -.03; Distractible, .07 and -.04; Question of hypophrenia, .07 and .10; Headaches, .07 and .02; Discord between parents, .07 and .11; Grouped: lack of interest in school, etc., .06 and .04; Grouped: temper, etc., .06 and .00; Immoral home conditions, .06 and -.04; Stuttering, .06 (boys); Object of teasing, .06 and .07; Sulky, .06 and .06; Enuresis, .05 and .02; Conduct prognosis bad, .05 and -.07; Popular, .05 and .06; Vicious home conditions, .04 and -.05; Changeable moods, .04 and .07; Nail-biting, .04 and .01; Bossy, .04 and -.04; Sullen, .03 and -.05; Leader, .03 and -.08; Irregular attendance at school, .02 and -.06; Lues, .02 and .13; Attractive manner, .02 and .10; Inattentive in school, .02 and -.02; Irresponsible, .01 and -.03; Slovenly, .01 and .03; Grouped: egocentric, etc., .01 and -.03; Psychoneurotic, .00 and .16; Quarrelsome, .00 and -.03; Refusal to attend school, .00 and .00; Temper display, -.00 and .04; Leading others into bad conduct, -.01 and .04; Excuse-forming, -.02 and -.07; Egocentric, -.02 and -.10; Former convulsions, -.03 and .03; Complaining of bad treatment by other children, -.03 (boys); Temper tantrums, -.03 and -.12; Fantastical lying, -.03 and -.03; Boastful, "show-off," -.03 and .11; Destructive, -.04 and -.04; Grouped: disobedient, etc., -.04 and -.08; Retardation in school, -.05 and -.05; Restless, -.05 and -.05; Overinterest in sex matters, -.05 and .07; Threatening violence, -.05 (boys); Victim of sex abuse, -.05 (girls); Contrary, -.05 and -.09; Loitering, -.06 and -.18; Lying, -.06 and -.09; Brother in penal detention, -.06 and .04; Grouped: swearing, etc., -.07 and -.11; Bad companions, -.07 and -.11; Swearing (general), -.08 (boys); Emotional instability, -.08 and -.04; Sex delinquency (coitus), -.09 and -.19;

TABLE 19—Continued

Stealing, -.09 and -.13; Defiant, -.09 and .06; Overinterest in opposite sex,
-.09 (girls); Incorrigible, -.10 and -.17; Staying out late at night, -.10 and
-.13; Grouped: fighting, etc., -.10 and -.07; Violence, -.11 and .01; Disturbing influence in school, -.12 and -.06; Fighting, -.12 and -.11; Gang, -.12
(boys); Sex denied entirely, -.13 and -.07; Truancy from home, -.13 and .19;
Disobedient, -.13 and -.06; Truancy from school, -.14 and -.04; Smoking, -.18
(boys)

The following personality problems showed moderate correlations in
the .20's among both sexes: sensitiveness or worrisomeness (especially sensitiveness over specific fact), "follower," and crying
spells. The three notations lack of initiative, listlessness, and
worry over specific fact also showed moderate tetrachoric correlations in the .20's among boys but lesser or negligible correlations
among girls.

Several minor negative correlations ranging from -.20 to
-.22 were found: among boys for irregular sleep habits and exclusion from school and among girls for question of encephalitis and
rudeness.

Among the six sex correlations the only one of probable
significant size was the interesting negative one of -.19 ± .04
with sex delinquency (coitus) among girls, all other coefficients
in this field being negligible.

It will be noted that whatever correlations existed with
bashfulness were almost entirely confined to personality difficulties. Conduct problems showed only a negligible relationship.

A similar personality problem, apprehensiveness, which occurred in 322 of our boys and in 149 of our girls, showed a tendency for slightly larger correlation with other traits. Its highest correlations, as shown in Table 20, among both boys and girls
were with bashfulness, crying spells, and "nervousness." The following nine notations showed moderate correlations ranging from
.20 to .26 among boys but lesser or negligible correlations among
girls: psychoneurotic trends, queer behavior, seclusiveness, repressed manner, worry over some specific fact, oversuggestibility,
sulkiness, headaches, and (computed for boys only) teasing other
children. The following behavior difficulties yielded moderate
correlations ranging from .30 down to .20 among girls but less than

TABLE 20

CORRELATIONS WITH "APPREHENSIVE"

	Boys	Girls
Personality-total.............................	.19 ± .02	.16 ± .03
Conduct-total.................................	.09 ± .02	.16 ± .03
Police arrest.................................	.14 ± .03	.13 ± .05
	Larger Correlations (Positive)	
Bashful.......................................	.30 ± .03	.26 ± .04 (5-6)*
Sulky...	.26 ± .04	-.06
Psychoneurotic................................	.26 ± .05	.08
Queer...	.25 ± .04	.13
Crying spells.................................	.24 ± .03	.33 ± .04 (2)
"Nervous".....................................	.22 ± .05	.36 ± .04 (1)
Teasing other children........................	.21 ± .04	....
Oversuggestible...............................	.21 ± .03	.13
Seclusive.....................................	.21 ± .04	.14
Repressed.....................................	.21 ± .04	.19
Headaches.....................................	.21 ± .04	-.14
Worry over specific fact......................	.20 ± .05	.09
Irregular sleep habits........................	.01	.30 ± .06 (3)
Question of change of personality.............	.11	.28 ± .06 (4)
Unhappy.......................................	.10	.26 ± .06 (5-6)
Victim of sex abuse...........................	....	.25 ± .05 (7-8)
Restless in sleep.............................	.13	.25 ± .05 (7-8)
Grouped: lack of interest in school, etc.....	.01	.22 ± .05 (9)
Lack of interest in school...................	-.00	.21 ± .05 (10)
Bossy...	.05	.20 ± .06 (11-15)
Unpopular.....................................	.11	.20 ± .07 (11-15)
Inferiority feelings..........................	.17	.20 ± .06 (11-15)
Grouped: "nervous," etc......................	.15	.20 ± .04 (11-15)
Grouped: swearing, etc.......................	.01	.20 ± .06 (11-15)

*Rank order of girls' correlations.

Other Correlations (Positive to Negative)

Grouped: sensitive or worrisome, etc., .18 and .12; Absent-minded, .18 and .05; Overinterest in sex matters, .16 and .03; Refusal to attend school, .16 and .19; Contrary, .15 and .08; Excuse-forming, .15 and .04; Sensitive (general),..15 and .05; Vocational guidance, .15 and .02; Grouped: dull, slow, etc., .15 and .03; Former convulsions, .14 and .03; Complaining of bad treatment by other children, .14 (boys); Sensitive over specific fact, .14 and .07; Object of teasing, .14 and .14; Lack of initiative, .14 and -.02; Changeable moods, .14 and .17; Hatred or jealousy of sibling, .14 and .16; Violence, .14 and .13; Neurological defect, .13 and .14; Question of hypophrenia, .12 and .10; Preference for younger children, .12 and .04; Listless, .12 and -.10; Bad companions, .11 and .13; Irritable, .11 and -.02; Follower, .11 and .12; Grouped: depressed, etc., .10 and .18; Sex denied entirely,.10 and -.10; Spoiled child, .10 and .09;

TABLE 20—Continued

Slow, dull, .10 and .08; Finicky food habits, .10 and .11; Nail-biting, .09 and .15; Masturbation, .09 and .10; Conduct prognosis bad, .09 and -.02; Attractive manner, .09 and -.02; Irregular attendance at school, .09 and -.03; Grouped: temper, etc., .09 and .08; Speech defect, .08 and -.06; Emotional instability, .08 and .16; Depressed, .08 and .09; Staying out late at night, .08 and .17; Destructive, .08 and .09; Daydreaming, .07 and .05; Poor work in school, .07 and .12; Underweight, .07 and .10; Clean, .06 and .11; Temper display, .06 and .02; Swearing (general), .06 (boys); Enuresis, .06 and .07; Inefficient in work, play, etc., .05 and .12; Irresponsible, .05 and .05; Rude, .05 and .14; Slovenly, .05 and .08; Truancy from school, .05 and .19; Mental conflict, .05 and .18; Grouped: fighting, etc., .04 and .10; Grouped: disobedient, etc., .04 and .11; Retardation in school, .04 and -.04; Sullen, .04 and .10; Lazy, .04 and -.02; Inattentive in school, .03 and .13; Gang, .03 (boys); Temper tantrums, .03 and .17; Stuttering, .03 (boys); Loitering, .02 and .06; Boastful, "show-off," .02 and .18; Smoking, .01 (boys); Stubborn, .01 and -.01; Exclusion from school, .01 and .05; Discord between parents, .01 and .03; Vicious home conditions, .01 and .19; Popular, .00 and .12; Lues, -.00 and -.10; Restless, -.00 and .14; Overinterest in opposite sex, -.00 (girls); Fighting, -.01 and .06; Lying, -.01 and .12; Immoral home conditions, -.01 and -.06; Stealing, -.02 and .13; Incorrigible, -.02 and .08; Fantastical lying, -.02 and .08; Disturbing influence in school, -.02 and .19; Defiant, -.03 and .19; Threatening violence, -.03 (boys); Question of encephalitis, -.03 and .16; Brother in penal detention, -.03 and -.11; Truancy from home, -.05 and .14; Sex delinquency (coitus), -.05 and -.00; Leading others into bad conduct, -.06 and .14; Disobedient, -.08 and .06; Quarrelsome, -.08 and .08; Distractible, -.08 and .18; Selfish, -.09 and .09; Egocentric, -.10 and -.05; Grouped: egocentric, etc., -.10 and .01; Leader, -.11 and -.02; Feeble-minded sibling, -.14 and .11

.20 among boys: question of change of personality, unhappiness, irregular sleep habits, restlessness in sleep, lack of interest or inattentiveness in school (undifferentiated), inferiority feelings, unpopularity, "nervousness" or restlessness (undifferentiated), swearing or bad language (undifferentiated), bossy manner, and (computed for girls only) victim of sex abuse.

No significant negative correlations were found.

Sex notations, with the lone exception of victim of sex abuse, showed negligible correlations.

Apprehensiveness, like bashfulness, we may note in conclusion, showed a few moderate correlations with personality problems but almost no association with conduct problems.

CHAPTER XVII

STAFF NOTATIONS OF "INFERIORITY FEELINGS"
AND "MENTAL CONFLICT"

The staff notations of <u>inferiority feelings</u> and <u>mental conflict</u> were among the most frequent of "diagnostic terms" employed in the clinical examination of our children. Among boys these two personality problems appeared to be fairly closely associated, as one may infer from their tetrachoric correlation of .53 ± .04; but among girls the association appeared to be only moderate, the correlation being .20 ± .09. Both should be considered as relatively serious behavior problems from a clinical standpoint and in view of their substantial to high bi-serial correlations of .35 to .59 with the <u>personality-total</u> and their lesser though significant correlations of .25 to .40 with the <u>conduct-total</u>. From the standpoint of "juvenile delinquency," however, their importance appeared to be almost negligible, since the tetrachoric coefficients ranged only from -.02 to .16 with the fact of a <u>police arrest or detention</u>.

<u>Staff notation or question of "inferiority" feeling or "complex," or feeling of inadequacy</u> was found among 202 of our 2,113 White boys and 62 of our 1,181 White girls, the respective percentages being 9.6 and 5.2. Its incidence among boys is thus seen to be definitely larger than among girls.

Its highest correlation (Table 21) was .53 ± .04 among boys with <u>mental conflict</u>, in contrast with its scarcely significant correlation of .20 ± .09 among girls. Its other high correlations were for <u>sensitiveness or worrisomeness</u> (undifferentiated) and for <u>sensitiveness over some specific fact</u> with tetrachoric coefficients of .49 or .50. <u>Unhappy appearance or manner</u> among boys was associated to the very substantial extent of .43 ± .05 with <u>inferiority feelings</u>, but the coefficient of .25 ± .08 among girls was of only moderate significance.

TABLE 21

CORRELATIONS WITH "INFERIORITY FEELINGS"

	Boys	Girls
Personality-total..............................	.43 ± .02	.59 ± .03
Conduct-total..................................	.26 ± .02	.25 ± .04
Police arrest.................................	.04 ± .04	-.02 ± .06
	Larger Correlations (Positive)	
Mental conflict................................	.53 ± .04	.20 ± .09 (37-40)*
Sensitive over specific fact..................	.49 ± .03	.50 ± .05 (1-2)
Grouped: sensitive or worrisome, etc.........	.49 ± .03	.50 ± .05 (1-2)
Unhappy..	.43 ± .05	.25 ± .08 (21-24)
Object of teasing.............................	.38 ± .03	.30 ± .07 (12)
Grouped: depressed, etc.......................	.37 ± .04	.38 ± .06 (7)
Hatred or jealousy of sibling.................	.36 ± .05	.43 ± .08 (4-5)
Worry over specific fact......................	.35 ± .07	.33 ± .09 (9)
Daydreaming....................................	.31 ± .04	.37 ± .07 (8)
Unpopular......................................	.29 ± .05	.29 ± .08 (13-15)
Boastful, "show-off"..........................	.28 ± .04	.28 ± .08 (16-19)
Queer..	.27 ± .05	.28 ± .08 (16-19)
Lazy...	.27 ± .04	.04
Spoiled child.................................	.26 ± .04	.17
Bossy..	.25 ± .05	.09
Complaining of bad treatment by other children	.25 ± .05	....
Sensitive (general)...........................	.24 ± .04	.43 ± .07 (4-5)
Psychoneurotic................................	.24 ± .06	.16
Depressed.....................................	.24 ± .05	.39 ± .08 (6)
Masturbation..................................	.24 ± .03	.11
Rude..	.23 ± .04	.17
Seclusive.....................................	.23 ± .04	.48 ± .06 (3)
Question of change of personality.............	.22 ± .05	.16
Bashful.......................................	.21 ± .05	.32 ± .06 (10-11)
Temper display................................	.20 ± .04	.09
Swearing (general)............................	.20 ± .05	....
Quarrelsome...................................	.20 ± .04	.21 ± .06 (34-36)
Lying...	.20 ± .03	.20 ± .05 (37-40)
"Nervous".....................................	.17	.32 ± .06 (10-11)
Fighting......................................	.11	.29 ± .04 (13-15)
Irregular sleep habits........................	.05	.29 ± .08 (13-15)
Grouped: "nervous," etc.......................	.19	.28 ± .05 (16-19)
Restless in sleep.............................	.07	.28 ± .06 (16-19)
Crying spells.................................	.19	.26 ± .05 (20)
Defiant.......................................	.10	.25 ± .07 (21-24)
Irritable.....................................	.12	.25 ± .06 (21-24)
Grouped: fighting, etc........................	.17	.25 ± .05 (21-24)
Restless......................................	.16	.24 ± .06 (25-28)
Changeable moods..............................	.11	.24 ± .06 (25-28)
Absent-minded.................................	.19	.24 ± .08 (25-28)
Inefficient in work, play, etc...............	.08	.24 ± .08 (25-28)

*Rank order of girls' correlations.

TABLE 21—Continued

	Boys	Girls
Poor work in school	.17	.23 ± .05 (29)
Grouped: temper, etc.	.18	.22 ± .05 (30-33)
Neurological defect	.06	.22 ± .07 (30-33)
Distractible	.16	.22 ± .07 (30-33)
Overinterest in sex matters	.15	.22 ± .08 (30-33)
Violence	.12	.21 ± .07 (34-36)
Repressed	.17	.21 ± .09 (34-36)
Apprehensive	.17	.20 ± .06 (37-40)
Finicky food habits	.11	.20 ± .07 (37-40)
	Larger Correlations (Negative)	
Feeble-minded sibling	-.09	-.33 ± .07
Vicious home conditions	.05	-.27 ± .08
Loitering	.01	-.24 ± .08
Retardation in school	-.11	-.21 ± .05
	Not Calculable	
Contrary	(n.c.)	.23 ± .05

Other Correlations (Positive to Negative)

Fantastical lying, .19 and .00; Disturbing influence in school, .19 and .18; Lack of interest in school, .18 and .11; Nail-biting, .18 and .13; Grouped: egocentric, etc., .18 and .11; Grouped: swearing, etc., .17 and -.04; Egocentric, .16 and .18; Stuttering, .16 (boys); Underweight, .15 and .09; Lack of initiative, .15 and .11; Sex delinquency (coitus), .15 and -.09; Enuresis, .15 and .10; Conduct prognosis bad, .14 and -.07; Clean, .14 and .10; Grouped: lack of interest in school, etc., .14 and .13; Threatening violence, .13 (boys); Selfish, .13 and .17; Leading others into bad conduct, .13 and .17; Destructive, .13 and .17; Teasing other children, .12 (boys); Emotional instability, .12 and .17; Attractive manner, .12 and .10; Grouped: disobedient, etc., .12 and .08; Disobedient, .10 and .04; Stealing, .10 and .07; Stubborn, .10 and .07; Exclusion from school, .10 and .08; Speech defect, .09 and .02; Excuse-forming, .09 and .17; Temper tantrums, .09 and .17; Sullen, .09 and -.13; Incorrigible, .09 and .06; Inattentive in school, .08 and .15; Preference for younger children, .08 and .05; Discord between parents, .08 and .08; Smoking, .07 (boys); Staying out late at night, .06 and .12; Oversuggestible, .05 and .09; Sulky, .05 and .09; Bad companions, .04 and -.01; Irresponsible, .04 and .13; Slovenly, .04 and .07; Grouped: dull, slow, etc., .03 and .05; Truancy from home, .03 and .02; Refusal to attend school, .02 and .18; Listless, .02 and .02; Immoral home conditions, .02 and -.01; Irregular attendance at school, .01 and -.01; Headaches, .01 and -.19; Question of encephalitis, .00 and .01; Leader, -.01 and .06; Follower, -.02 and .08; Truancy from school, -.02 and .06; Slow, dull, -.03 and -.01; Brother in penal detention, -.03 and -.14; Popular, -.04 and -.06; Sex denied entirely, -.04 and .04; Vocational guidance, -.06 and .15; Question of hypophrenia, -.06 and -.07; Gang, -.07 (boys); Former convulsions, -.08 and .08; Overinterest in opposite sex, -.11 (girls); Victim of sex abuse, -.15 (girls); Lues, -.16 and .08

The following five personality difficulties among both sexes yielded substantial coefficients in the .30's: <u>hatred or jealousy of sibling</u>, <u>depressed spells or unhappiness</u> (undifferentiated), <u>worry over some specific fact</u>, <u>daydreaming</u>, and <u>object of teasing by other children</u>. Four personality traits yielded substantial correlations ranging from .43 down to .32 among girls but moderate coefficients in the .20's for boys: <u>sensitiveness in general</u>, <u>depressed spells</u>, <u>seclusiveness</u>, and <u>bashfulness</u>.

Five behavior problems yielded moderate correlations ranging from .20 to .29 among both sexes: <u>unpopularity</u>, <u>queer behavior</u>, <u>boastful or "show-off" manner</u>, <u>quarrelsomeness</u>, and <u>lying</u>. The following ten notations showed moderate correlations in the .20's among boys but lesser though positive ones among girls: <u>laziness</u>, <u>"spoiled child,"</u> <u>complaining of bad treatment by other children</u>, <u>psychoneurotic trends</u>, <u>bossy manner</u>, <u>rudeness</u>, <u>masturbation</u>, <u>temper display</u>, <u>question of change of personality</u>, and (computed for boys only) <u>swearing (general)</u>. A large list of twenty behavior and other notations showed moderate or substantial correlations ranging from .32 down to .20 among girls but low positive correlations below .20 among boys: <u>"nervousness,"</u> <u>irregular sleep habits</u>, <u>restlessness in sleep</u>, <u>irritable manner or disposition</u>, <u>restlessness</u> (in general), <u>changeable moods</u>, <u>fighting</u>, <u>defiant attitude</u>, <u>temper tantrums or temper display</u> (undifferentiated), <u>violence</u>, <u>crying spells</u>, <u>absent-mindedness</u>, <u>repressed manner</u>, <u>inefficiency in work, play</u>, etc., <u>distractibility</u>, <u>poor work in school</u>, <u>apprehensiveness</u>, <u>overinterest in sex matters</u>, <u>finicky food habits</u>, and <u>neurological defect (unspecified)</u>. The trait <u>contrariness</u> among girls showed the moderate correlation of .23 $\pm$ .05, but among our 2,113 boys there were no instances whatever in which a "contrary" child also showed "inferiority feelings," and therefore a tetrachoric coefficient could not be calculated.

Four case-record notations showed <u>negative</u> correlations ranging from -.33 to -.21 among girls but negligible correlations among boys: <u>feeble-minded sibling</u>, <u>vicious home conditions</u>, <u>loitering</u> (including wandering or "bumming" on streetcars, etc., or loafing in poolrooms, dance halls, etc.), and <u>retardation in school</u>.

Among the six sex notations there were only two instances in which <u>inferiority feelings</u> showed statistically significant correlations in our data. These were for <u>masturbation</u> among boys

(.24 ± .03) and for <u>overinterest in sex matters</u> among girls (.22 ± .08).

Among physical and psychophysical deficiencies in our data, non-significant correlations were found for <u>enuresis</u>, <u>underweight condition</u>, and <u>lues</u> among both sexes. <u>Neurological defect</u> (unspecified) among girls yielded the moderate correlation of .22 ± .07. <u>Speech defect</u> and <u>stuttering</u> (undifferentiated) likewise appeared to be unassociated with <u>inferiority feelings</u>. These findings are contrary to general belief among clinic workers. Again we must point out that because of the paucity of data our results are presented as suggestive rather than as conclusive.

<u>Question of hypophrenia</u> (or suspected mental deficiency) and <u>slow or dull manner</u> yielded negligible negative correlations, but it will be recalled that intelligence quotient (IQ) yielded <u>positive</u> bi-serial correlations of .22 ± .02 and .18 among boys and girls respectively (see Table 10, p. 130). It appears, then, that intelligent children do not seem to suffer from <u>inferiority feelings</u>, while the less intelligent ones, whom one might suppose to be especially warranted in being so affected, actually seem no more affected than others. <u>Poor work in school</u> showed a moderate positive association, especially among girls, but <u>retardation in school</u> (defined to mean at least a prospective two years of retardation by the age of fourteen) showed an equally moderate <u>negative</u> relationship. <u>Exclusion or suspension from school</u> for any cause showed a negligible relationship. We may conclude that children in general do not develop an "inferiority" when their intelligence is low or their school achievement poor.

<u>Unpopularity</u> seemed to be a moderate cause of an "inferiority." <u>Popularity</u> showed corresponding correlations of negative sign.

Among home conditions which would presumably give rise to "inferiorities" the only significant indication was the <u>negative</u> coefficient of -.27 ± .08 among girls for <u>vicious home conditions</u>. The three notations <u>discord between parents</u>, <u>immoral home conditions</u>, and <u>brother in penal detention</u> were quite unassociated with "inferiorities."

<u>Inferiority feelings</u> are hardly productive of an <u>excuse-forming attitude</u>, since the low positive correlations of .09 and .17 can scarcely be considered as significant.

Staff notation of mental or emotional conflict or "complex" or marked emotional disturbance concerning certain subjects was employed as a diagnostic term in 102 of our boys and 45 of our girls, the respective percentages of incidence being 4.8 and 3.8.

Its highest correlations (Table 22) was with inferiority feelings, the tetrachoric coefficients for boys and girls, respectively, being .53 ± .04 and .20 ± .09. In its correlations with

TABLE 22

CORRELATIONS WITH "MENTAL CONFLICT"

	Boys	Girls
Personality-total..............................	.35 ± .03	.43 ± .04
Conduct-total.................................	.29 ± .03	.40 ± .04
Police arrest.................................	.16 ± .04	.07 ± .07
	Larger Correlations (Positive)	
Inferiority feelings..........................	.53 ± .04	.20 ± .09 (40-44)*
Grouped: sensitive or worrisome, etc.........	.52 ± .03	.49 ± .05 (2)
Worry over specific fact......................	.49 ± .06	.50 ± .09 (1)
Sensitive over specific fact.................	.48 ± .04	.46 ± .06 (3)
Psychoneurotic................................	.39 ± .06	.19
Bossy...	.28 ± .06	.30 ± .08 (16-18)
Queer...	.26 ± .06	.32 ± .09 (12)
Absent-minded.................................	.25 ± .06	.30 ± .09 (16-18)
Masturbation..................................	.24 ± .04	.27 ± .07 (21-24)
Boastful, "show-off"..........................	.22 ± .05	.01
Seclusive.....................................	.22 ± .05	.24 ± .08 (31)
Stuttering....................................	.22 ± .07	....
Grouped: depressed, etc......................	.22 ± .05	.33 ± .07 (8-11)
Hatred or jealousy of sibling................	.21 ± .07	.27 ± .09 (21-24)
Question of change of personality............	.21 ± .06	.29 ± .09 (19)
Depressed.....................................	.21 ± .06	.31 ± .08 (13-15)
Repressed.....................................	.21 ± .06	.21 ± .10 (36-39)
Lack of interest in school...................	.20 ± .05	.11
Overinterest in sex matters..................	.20 ± .07	.42 ± .08 (4)
Sex delinquency (coitus).....................	.20 ± .07	.23 ± .06 (32-33)
Leading others into bad conduct..............	.05	.36 ± .09 (5)
Exclusion from school........................	.03	.35 ± .08 (6)
Headaches.....................................	.01	.34 ± .08 (7)
Preference for younger children..............	.13	.33 ± .08 (8-11)
Destructive..................................	.12	.33 ± .09 (8-11)
Violence......................................	.07	.33 ± .08 (8-11)
Daydreaming...................................	.18	.31 ± .08 (13-15)
Enuresis......................................	.03	.31 ± .06 (13-15)

*Rank order of girls' correlations.

TABLE 22—Continued

	Boys	Girls
Temper tantrums................................	.12	.30 ± .07 (16-18)
Inattentive in school.........................	.12	.28 ± .08 (20)
Spoiled child.................................	-.03	.27 ± .07 (21-24)
Emotional instability.........................	.16	.26 ± .08 (25)
Fantastical lying.............................	.18	.25 ± .08 (26-30)
Grouped: fighting, etc.......................	.18	.25 ± .06 (26-30)
Unhappy.......................................	.14	.25 ± .09 (26-30)
Grouped: swearing, etc.......................	.11	.25 ± .08 (26-30)
Object of teasing.............................	.09	.25 ± .08 (26-30)
Unpopular.....................................	.10	.23 ± .10 (32-33)
Restless......................................	.15	.22 ± .06 (34-35)
Stubborn......................................	-.00	.22 ± .06 (34-35)
Fighting......................................	.16	.21 ± .04 (36-39)
Disobedient...................................	.05	.21 ± .06 (36-39)
Victim of sex abuse...........................	....	.21 ± .08 (36-39)
Grouped: lack of interest in school, etc.....	.19	.20 ± .07 (40-44)
Stealing......................................	.17	.20 ± .10 (40-44)
Inefficient in work, play, etc...............	.16	.20 ± .09 (40-44)
Grouped: disobedient, etc...................	.03	.20 ± .06 (40-44)
	Larger Correlations (Negative)	
Popular.......................................	-.24 ± .06	.01
Retardation in school.........................	-.09	-.36 ± .05
Feeble-minded sibling.........................	-.13	-.29 ± .08
Temper display................................	.00	-.26 ± .08
	Not Calculable	
Conduct prognosis bad.........................	.02	(n.c.)

Other Correlations (Positive to Negative)

Sensitive (general), .19 and .09; Irresponsible, .18 and .03; Crying spells, .18 and .19; Swearing (general), .17 (boys); Irregular sleep habits, .17 and -.04; Grouped: "nervous," etc., .17 and .19; Lazy, .16 and -.00; Gang, .16 (boys); Lack of initiative, .16 and -.04; Grouped: egocentric, etc., .16 and .07; Quarrelsome, .15 and .18; Selfish, .15 and .02; "Nervous," .15 and .13; Disturbing influence in school, .14 and .10; Slovenly, .14 and .15; Truancy from home, .14 and -.06; Excuse-forming, .14 and -.05; Listless, .14 and .05; Discord between parents, .14 and .10; Irritable, .13 and .06; Sex denied entirely, .13 and -.11; Contrary, .12 and .01; Sullen, .12 and .13; Egocentric, .12 and .19; Bad companions, .11 and .06; Rude, .11 and .12; Bashful, .11 and .06; Poor work in school, .11 and .06; Clean, .11 and .10; Grouped: temper, etc., .11 and .09; Grouped: dull, slow, etc., .10 and -.12; Overinterest in opposite sex, .10 (girls); Threatening violence, .09 (boys); Vicious home conditions, .09 and -.06; Complaining of bad treatment by other children, .08 (boys); Follower, .08 and .12; Attractive manner, .08 and -.01; Neurological defect, .08 and .17; Vocational guidance, .07 and -.07; Incorrigible, .07 and -.00; Refusal to attend school, .07 and .13; Sulky, .07 and .17; Immoral home conditions, .07 and -.06;

TABLE 22—Continued

_____

Nail-biting, .05 and .06; Teasing other children, .05 (boys); Apprehensive, .05 and .18; Leader, .05 and .08; Lues, .04 and .11; Truancy from school, .03 and .12; Speech defect, .03 and .03; Finicky food habits, .02 and -.07; Slow, dull, .02 and -.10; Defiant, .01 and .14; Staying out late at night, .01 and .13; Restless in sleep, .01 and .19; Underweight, .01 and .17; Oversuggestible, -.00 and .02; Smoking, -.01 (boys); Changeable moods, -.01 and .15; Distractible, -.05 and .09; Former convulsions, -.05 and .08; Question of encephalitis, -.09 and .18; Question of hypophrenia, -.10 and -.18; Irregular attendance at school, -.15 and -.15; Loitering, -.17 and -.17; Brother in penal detention, -.17 and -.15

other traits <u>mental conflict</u> showed many similarities to <u>inferiority feelings</u>.

Mental conflict yielded its highest tetrachoric correlations with <u>sensitiveness or worrisomeness</u> (undifferentiated), <u>worry over specific fact</u>, and <u>sensitiveness over specific fact</u>, the coefficients ranging from .46 to .52. <u>Staff notation of psychoneurotic trends</u> yielded the meaningful correlation of .39 ± .06 among boys and a low correlation of .19 among girls. Among girls the following five behavior problems showed substantial correlations ranging from .30 to .42 but among boys only moderate correlations in the .20's: <u>overinterest in sex matters</u>, <u>depressed spells</u>, <u>queer behavior</u>, <u>absent-mindedness</u>, and <u>bossy manner</u>. The following nine notations also showed substantial correlations in the .30's for girls but negligible correlations below .20 for boys: <u>daydreaming</u>, <u>preference for younger children as playmates</u>, <u>destructiveness</u>, <u>violence</u>, <u>temper tantrums</u>, <u>leading others into bad conduct</u>, <u>exclusion from school</u>, <u>enuresis</u>, and <u>headaches</u>.

The following six behavior difficulties showed moderate correlations in the .20's for both sexes: <u>question of change of personality</u>, <u>repressed manner</u>, <u>seclusiveness</u>, <u>hatred or jealousy of sibling</u>, <u>masturbation</u>, and <u>sex delinquency (coitus)</u>. <u>Stuttering</u> (computed for boys only) showed a moderate correlation of .22 ± .07. Two behavior problems among boys—<u>boastfulness or "show-off" manner</u> and <u>lack of interest in school</u>—showed correlations of .22 ± .05 and .20 ± .05 respectively but negligible correlations among girls. A large list of fifteen case notations showed moderate correlations in the .20's among the girls but low or negligible correlations among the boys: <u>emotional instability</u>, <u>restlessness</u>, <u>unhappiness</u>, <u>"spoiled child,"</u> <u>unpopularity</u>, <u>object of teasing by</u>

other children, inattentiveness in school, inefficiency in work,
play, etc., stealing, fantastical lying, swearing or bad language
(undifferentiated), fighting, disobedience, stubbornness, and victim of sex abuse by older child or person.

Four significant negative correlations were found. Popularity among boys yielded the significant negative correlation of
-.24 + .06 with mental conflict but only .01 among girls. Retar-
ation in school, feeble-minded sibling, and temper display among
girls yielded negative correlations ranging from -.26 to -.36, the
corresponding correlations for boys being zero or a negligible negative.

The staff notation of unfavorable conduct prognosis showed
a zero correlation among boys, while among our 1,181 girls a tetrachoric correlation was not calculable since there were no instances
in which a girl with mental conflict was so described.

Sex problems tended to be more significantly associated
with mental conflict than with inferiority feelings. Among girls
the tetrachoric correlation for overinterest in sex matters was
very substantial, .42 + .08, the corresponding correlation for boys
being only .20 + .07. Sex delinquency (coitus), masturbation, and
(calculated only for girls) victim of sex abuse showed moderate
correlations in the .20's. Sex misbehavior denied entirely (for
both boys and girls) and overinterest in opposite sex (calculated
for girls only) showed quite negligible correlations.

Enuresis, which showed no correlation with inferiority
feelings, was correlated to the significant extent of .31 + .06
among girls with mental conflict, though the corresponding coefficient for boys was practically zero. Underweight condition, speech
defect, neurological defect, and lues were only negligibly correlated with mental conflict. Question of hypophrenia and retardation in school tended to be negatively associated with mental conflict, but intelligence quotient (IQ), as we have seen in Table 10
(p. 130), showed the moderate positive correlation of .23 for both
sexes with mental conflict.

The four undesirable home conditions—discord between parents, vicious home conditions, immoral home conditions, and brother
in penal detention—were negligibly correlated with mental conflict.

  We may conclude this chapter by noting that such personality problems as sensitiveness or worrisomeness, depressed or unhappy moods, queer, seclusive or absent-minded behavior, daydreaming, psychoneurotic trends, hatred or jealousy of sibling, object
of teasing by other children and unpopularity and masturbation
tended to be associated with both <u>inferiority feelings</u> and <u>mental
conflict</u> but that children so affected do not assume a <u>boastful</u> or
"<u>show-off</u>" manner as a compensatory mechanism. Among boys the positive correlations appeared to be almost entirely with personality
problems, while among the girls there were many moderate correlations also with conduct problems.[1]

---

[1] A more extensive discussion of the correlations with staff notation of
<u>inferiority feelings</u> (Table 21) may be found in the author's article "Inferiority
Attitudes and Their Correlations among Children Examined in a Behavior Clinic,"
accepted for publication (1941) by the <u>Journal of Genetic Psychology</u>.

CHAPTER XVIII

PSYCHONEUROTIC TRENDS AND "SPOILED CHILD"

In spite of their supposed interdependence, psychoneurotic trends and "spoiled child" do not appear to be very closely related since the tetrachoric correlations between these traits were only .29 ± .05 and .08 among boys and girls respectively. Their correlations with other behavior problems appeared in some cases to be similar but in other cases to be quite unlike.

Staff diagnosis or question of psychoneurosis or psychoneurotic or neurotic trends (unspecified), hysteria, neurasthenia, psychasthenia, etc., was noted in 87 of our 2,113 White boys and in 64 of our 1,181 White girls, the percentages of incidence being 4.1 and 5.4 respectively. It was one of the most frequently employed diagnostic terms found in the case records during the years in which these children were examined. This notation as used in the present chapter varied all the way from an unqualified psychiatric diagnosis down to a clinical description of a relatively minor personality trait. It was substantially correlated with personality-total but only moderately and irregularly associated with conduct-total or police arrest (Table 23).

The highest correlation with psychoneurotic trends was for emotional instability among girls, .47 ± .06, the corresponding coefficient for boys being also substantial, .29 ± .07.

The three personality problems—depressed spells, sensitiveness or worrisomeness (undifferentiated), and worry over some specific fact—yielded substantial to high correlations ranging from .35 to .46 among both sexes. Mental conflict among boys showed a very substantial correlation of .39 ± .06, but among girls the coefficient was only .19. The vague notation "nervousness" showed substantial correlations of .33 to .35 among both sexes.

Three important personality difficulties yielded substantial correlations ranging from .38 down to .32 among girls but moderate coefficients in the .20's for the boys: question of change

TABLE 23

CORRELATIONS WITH "PSYCHONEUROTIC"

	Boys	Girls
Personality-total...........................	.38 ± .03	.49 ± .04
Conduct-total...............................	.06 ± .03	.23 ± .04
Police arrest...............................	.24 ± .04	-.14 ± .06
	Larger Correlations (Positive)	
Worry over specific fact....................	.44 ± .06	.37 ± .09 (4)*
Mental conflict.............................	.39 ± .06	.19
Grouped: sensitive or worrisome, etc........	.39 ± .04	.35 ± .05 (5-9)
Depressed...................................	.38 ± .06	.46 ± .07 (2)
Grouped: depressed, etc....................	.34 ± .05	.35 ± .06 (5-9)
"Nervous"...................................	.33 ± .05	.35 ± .06 (5-9)
Stuttering..................................	.29 ± .07	....
Emotional instability.......................	.29 ± .07	.47 ± .06 (1)
Spoiled child...............................	.29 ± .05	.08
Queer.......................................	.28 ± .06	.23 ± .08 (19-22)
Seclusive...................................	.28 ± .05	.10
Grouped: "nervous," etc....................	.27 ± .04	.38 ± .05 (3)
Sensitive over specific fact...............	.27 ± .05	.20 ± .06 (26-27)
Apprehensive................................	.26 ± .05	.08
Sensitive (general).........................	.26 ± .06	.31 ± .07 (13-14)
Question of change of personality..........	.24 ± .06	.35 ± .08 (5-9)
Inferiority feelings........................	.24 ± .06	.16
Irritable...................................	.23 ± .05	.11
Changeable moods............................	.22 ± .05	.35 ± .06 (5-9)
Restless in sleep..........................	.21 ± .05	.19
Overinterest in sex matters.................	.21 ± .07	.08
Egocentric..................................	.17	.32 ± .06 (10-12)
Irregular sleep habits......................	.12	.32 ± .08 (10-12)
Grouped: egocentric, etc...................	.12	.32 ± .05 (10-12)
Selfish.....................................	.03	.31 ± .04 (13-14)
Boastful, "show-off"........................	.04	.30 ± .07 (15)
Temper tantrums.............................	.13	.27 ± .06 (16)
Crying spells...............................	.16	.25 ± .05 (17)
Unpopular...................................	.02	.24 ± .08 (18)
Neurological defect.........................	.10	.23 ± .07 (19-22)
Masturbation................................	.15	.23 ± .06 (19-22)
Bossy.......................................	.02	.23 ± .07 (19-22)
Leading others into bad conduct.............	-.08	.22 ± .09 (23)
Restless....................................	.14	.21 ± .05 (24-25)
Finicky food habits.........................	.13	.21 ± .07 (24-25)
Grouped: temper, etc.......................	.18	.20 ± .05 (26-27)
	Larger Correlations (Negative)	
Question of hypophrenia.....................	-.29 ± .04	-.21 ± .05

*Rank order of girls' correlations.

TABLE 23—Continued

	Boys	Girls
Lues...	-.26 ± .07	-.19
Retardation in school.........................	-.25 ± .04	-.26 ± .05
Brother in penal detention....................	-.22 ± .06	-.34 ± .07
Feeble-minded sibling.........................	-.16	-.23 ± .07
Speech defect.................................	.03	-.21 ± .07
	Not Calculable	
Lack of initiative...........................	.19	(n.c.)

Other Correlations (Positive to Negative)

Headaches, .19 and .16; Immoral home conditions, .19 and .02; Overinterest in opposite sex, .19 (girls); Hatred or jealousy of sibling, .18 and .18; Sex delinquency (coitus), .17 and -.05; Listless, .17 and .15; Disobedient, .15 and .16; Grouped: fighting, etc., .14 and .08; Refusal to attend school, .14 and .04; Daydreaming, .12 and .13; Quarrelsome, .11 and .14; Object of teasing, .11 and .05; Grouped: disobedient, etc., .10 and .12; Unhappy, .10 and .04; Nail-biting, .10 and -.01; Complaining of bad treatment by other children, .09 (boys); Sex denied entirely, .08 and -.05; Enuresis, .07 and -.07; Question of encephalitis, .07 and .18; Violence, .06 and .19; Staying out late at night, .06 and -.03; Rude, .06 and .13; Victim of sex abuse, .06 (girls); Conduct prognosis bad, .05 and .18; Clean, .04 and .06; Defiant, .03 and .09; Former convulsions, .03 and .07; Vicious home conditions, .03 and -.05; Grouped: lack of interest in school, etc., .02 and .02; Exclusion from school, .02 and .12; Temper display, .02 and -.00; Slovenly, .02 and .05; Inattentive in school, .02 and -.02; Destructive, .02 and .08; Contrary, .02 and .09; Swearing (general), .01 (boys); Preference for younger children, .01 and -.08; Excuse-forming, .01 and .03; Bashful, .00 and .16; Fighting, .00 and -.04; Stubborn, -.00 and .16; Grouped: swearing, etc., -.01 and .10; Grouped: dull, slow, etc., -.01 and -.16; Underweight, -.01 and .05; Threatening violence, -.01 (boys); Lack of interest in school, -.01 and .05; Fantastical lying, -.01 and .19; Inefficient in work, play, etc., -.02 and .10; Lazy, -.02 and -.02; Teasing other children, -.02 (boys); Absent-minded, -.02 and .05; Discord between parents, -.03 and .04; Popular, -.03 and .15; Sulky, -.03 and .08; Irresponsible, -.04 and .13; Vocational guidance, -.04 and .02; Leader, -.05 and -.01; Bad companions, -.05 and .03; Smoking, -.06 (boys); Sullen, -.06 and .08; Loitering, -.08 and -.02; Lying, -.08 and .04; Truancy from home, -.08 and .05; Repressed, -.08 and -.18; Poor work in school, -.08 and -.01; Stealing, -.09 and .03; Incorrigible, -.10 and .02; Gang, -.10 (boys); Truancy from school, -.11 and —.03; Follower, -.12 and -.08; Attractive manner, -.12 and -.11; Irregular attendance at school, -.12 and .02; Oversuggestible, -.13 and .19; Distractible, -.14 and .12; Disturbing influence in school, -.16 and -.04; Slow, dull, -.19 and -.12

of personality, changeable moods, and sensitiveness in general. Four additional behavior problems showed substantial correlations of .30-.32 among girls but low positive coefficients of less than .20 among boys: egocentricity, selfishness, boastful or "show-off" manner, and irregular sleep habits.

Queer behavior (among both sexes) and stuttering (calculated for boys only) showed correlations in the .20's. Seven personality problems showed moderate correlations in the .20's among
boys but lesser though positive correlations below .20 among girls:
"spoiled child," inferiority feelings, seclusiveness, apprehensiveness, irritable temperament, restlessness in sleep, and overinterest in sex matters. The following nine behavior and other notations showed moderate correlations in the .20's among girls but low
or negligible ones among boys: temper tantrums, crying spells,
unpopularity, leading others into bad conduct, bossy manner, restlessness, finicky food habits, masturbation, and neurological defect (unspecified).

Several negative correlations of significant size were
found. Brother in penal detention among our girls showed the substantial negative association of -.34 + .07 with psychoneurotic
trends, the corresponding coefficient for our boys of -.22 + .06
also being of significant size. Feeble-minded sibling showed similar negative association though of lesser size, the coefficient
for girls being -.23 + .07 and for boys -.16. Among our cases,
then, children who have a delinquent brother or a mentally defective sibling appeared to be less psychoneurotic than were the children with more normal siblings. Question of hypophrenia and retardation in school showed similarly negative tetrachoric correlations ranging from -.21 to -.29 among both sexes. With intelligence as measured by intelligence quotient (IQ), it will be recalled from our Table 10 (p. 130) that there were slight positive
bi-serial correlations of .20 + .03 and .16 among boys and girls
respectively. Lues yielded negative coefficients of -.26 + .07
and -.19 for boys and girls respectively. Speech defect (other
than stuttering) showed a moderate negative correlation of -.21 +
.07 among our girls but practically zero correlation among boys.

Among girls the tetrachoric correlation of lack of initiative with psychoneurotic trends was not calculable because there
were no instances in which these two notations were made in the
case of the same girl. Among boys the correlation was .19.

Among our six sex notations there were only two instances
of statistically significant correlations with psychoneurotic
trends: among boys the correlation for overinterest in sex matters

was .21 $\pm$ .07, the corresponding coefficient for girls being quite
negligible; and among girls the correlation for masturbation was
.23 $\pm$ .06, the corresponding coefficient for boys being only .15.
Sex delinquency (coitus) among boys showed the low positive correlation of .17, while the girls' coefficient was quite negligible.
Overinterest in opposite sex, which was calculated for girls only,
yielded the low correlation of .19. Victim of sex abuse and sex
misbehavior denied entirely yielded practically zero correlations.

     Neurological defect among girls showed the moderate corre-
lation of .23 $\pm$ .07. Stuttering among boys showed the moderate
correlation of .29 $\pm$ .07, the corresponding coefficient for girls
being omitted because of paucity of cases. Lues among boys and
speech defect (other than stuttering) among girls showed moderate
negative correlations in the .20's. Enuresis, underweight condition, and question of encephalitis showed negligible correlations
below .20 among both sexes.

     Discord between parents and vicious home conditions among
both sexes and immoral home conditions among girls showed practically zero correlations with psychoneurotic trends. Among boys
the correlation for immoral home conditions was slightly positive,
.19. Brother in penal detention, however, showed moderate to substantial negative coefficients, as noted above.

     Question of "spoiled" or overindulged child was noted in
250 (or 11.8 per cent) of our boys and in 112 (or 9.5 per cent) of
our girls. It was correlated to a substantial but not high extent
with the personality-total and the conduct-total but negligibly
with police arrest.

     Its highest correlation (Table 24) was among girls, .42 $\pm$
.06, with violence, the correlation among boys being only .16. The
next highest correlation was for boastful or "show-off" manner,
.32 $\pm$ .04 and .38 $\pm$ .06 among boys and girls respectively. Fantastical lying yielded correlations of .31 $\pm$ .05 and .30 $\pm$ .06 for
boys and girls respectively. Among girls three behavior problems
yielded substantial correlations ranging from .30 to .38, while
among boys the coefficients were of moderate size in the .20's:
"nervousness" or restlessness (undifferentiated), bossy manner,
and temper tantrums. Six additional behavior traits also showed
substantial correlations in the .30's for girls but low positive

TABLE 24

CORRELATIONS WITH "SPOILED CHILD"

	Boys	Girls
Personality-total...............................	.29 ± .02	.27 ± .03
Conduct-total..................................	.31 ± .02	.38 ± .03
Police arrest..................................	.09 ± .03	.04 ± .05
	Larger Correlations (Positive)	
Boastful, "show-off"...........................	.32 ± .04	.38 ± .06 (2-3)*
Fantastical lying..............................	.31 ± .05	.30 ± .06 (13-14)
Psychoneurotic.................................	.29 ± .05	.08
Seclusive......................................	.29 ± .04	.09
Hatred or jealousy of sibling.................	.28 ± .05	.19
Grouped: "nervous," etc......................	.28 ± .03	.31 ± .04 (11-12)
Bossy...	.27 ± .05	.38 ± .06 (2-3)
Finicky food habits...........................	.27 ± .04	.27 ± .06 (16-24)
Sensitive over specific fact.................	.27 ± .03	.19
Grouped: disobedient, etc...................	.27 ± .03	.28 ± .04 (15)
Grouped: sensitive or worrisome, etc.........	.27 ± .03	.21 ± .05 (35-37)
Teasing other children.......................	.26 ± .04	....
"Nervous".....................................	.26 ± .03	.35 ± .05 (5)
Inferiority feelings..........................	.26 ± .04	.17
Rude..	.25 ± .04	.27 ± .05 (16-24)
Sensitive (general)...........................	.24 ± .04	.26 ± .06 (25-27)
Contrary......................................	.23 ± .05	.15
Stubborn......................................	.23 ± .03	.20 ± .05 (38-39)
Attractive manner............................	.23 ± .04	.20 ± .05 (38-39)
Popular.......................................	.22 ± .09	.07
Destructive...................................	.21 ± .04	.10
Irritable.....................................	.21 ± .03	.26 ± .05 (25-27)
Distractible..................................	.21 ± .04	.27 ± .06 (16-24)
Object of teasing.............................	.21 ± .03	.19
Grouped: temper, etc.........................	.21 ± .03	.27 ± .04 (16-24)
Disturbing influence in school...............	.20 ± .03	.26 ± .06 (25-27)
Inefficient in work, play, etc...............	.20 ± .05	.18
Loitering.....................................	.20 ± .04	.01
Temper tantrums...............................	.20 ± .04	.34 ± .05 (6)
Irregular sleep habits........................	.20 ± .05	.25 ± .07 (28-29)
Violence......................................	.16	.42 ± .06 (1)
Selfish.......................................	.13	.36 ± .04 (4)
Defiant.......................................	.17	.33 ± .06 (7-9)
Question of encephalitis......................	.06	.33 ± .08 (7-9)
Question of change of personality............	.19	.33 ± .06 (7-9)
Grouped: egocentric, etc....................	.08	.32 ± .05 (10)
Sullen..	.16	.31 ± .06 (11-12)
Emotional instability.........................	.10	.30 ± .06 (13-14)
Mental conflict...............................	-.03	.27 ± .07 (16-24)
Daydreaming...................................	.18	.27 ± .06 (16-24)

*Rank order of girls' correlations.

TABLE 24—Continued

	Boys	Girls
Changeable moods	.18	.27 ± .05 (16-24)
Leading others into bad conduct	.07	.27 ± .07 (16-24)
Disobedient	.16	.27 ± .05 (16-24)
Egocentric	.04	.25 ± .05 (28-29)
Irresponsible	.13	.24 ± .07 (30-31)
Refusal to attend school	.17	.24 ± .08 (30-31)
Neurological defect	.10	.23 ± .06 (32)
Inattentive in school	.19	.22 ± .06 (33-34)
Absent-minded	.17	.22 ± .07 (33-34)
Grouped: fighting, etc	.14	.21 ± .05 (35-37)
Crying spells	.17	.21 ± .04 (35-37)
	Larger Correlations (Negative)	
Lues	-.27 ± .05	-.05
Feeble-minded sibling	-.17	-.45 ± .05
Brother in penal detention	-.11	-.36 ± .05
Grouped: dull, slow, etc	.01	-.29 ± .04
Retardation in school	-.14	-.24 ± .04

Other Correlations (Positive to Negative)

Restless, .19 and .19; Lying, .18 and .17; Unhappy, .18 and -.00; Incorrigible, .17 and .19; Sulky, .17 and .10; Grouped: lack of interest in school, etc., .17 and .19; Grouped: depressed, etc., .17 and .10; Lazy, .16 and .11; Bashful, .16 and -.05; Queer, .16 and .10; Unpopular, .16 and .17; Worry over specific fact, .16 and .19; Gang, .15 (boys); Threatening violence, .15 (boys); Masturbation, .15 and .01; Lack of initiative, .15 and .00; Poor work in school, .15 and .10; Excuse-forming, .19 and -.01; Bad companions, .13 and .14; Enuresis, .13 and .10; Stealing, .13 and .05; Restless in sleep, .13 and .17; Grouped: swearing, etc., .13 and .02; Nail-biting, .12 and .13; Irregular attendance at school, .12 and .01; Depressed, .12 and .14; Discord between parents, .12 and .02; Complaining of bad treatment by other children, .12 (boys); Sex denied entirely, .12 and .17; Lack of interest in school, .11 and .13; Slovenly, .11 and -.03; Staying out late at night, .11 and .19; Leader, .11 and .12; Quarrelsome, .10 and .12; Apprehensive, .10 and .09; Oversuggestible, .10 and .03; Truancy from school, .09 and .16; Headaches, .09 and .04; Fighting, .08 and .18; Smoking, .08 (boys); Swearing (general), .08 (boys); Listless, .08 and -.01; Truancy from home, .07 and .07; Conduct prognosis bad, .07 and .12; Temper display, .06 and .09; Repressed, .06 and .04; Preference for younger children, .06 and .09; Clean, .06 and .06; Vocational guidance, .06 and .13; Former convulsions, .05 and .08; Stuttering, .04 (boys); Underweight, .04 and .14; Exclusion from school, .03 and .09; Overinterest in sex matters, .02 and .17; Overinterest in opposite sex, .02 (girls); Follower, .01 and .01; Victim of sex abuse, .01 (girls); Question of hypophrenia, -.01 and -.08; Speech defect, -.03 and .06; Sex delinquency (coitus), -.06 and -.08; Vicious home conditions, -.07 and -.19; Slow, dull, -.08 and .08; Immoral home conditions, -.08 and -.18

correlations below .20 for the boys: selfishness, defiant attitude, sullenness, question of encephalitis, question of change of
personality, and emotional instability.

The following ten notations showed moderate correlations
in the .20's for both boys and girls: sensitiveness or worrisomeness (undifferentiated), irritable temperament, irregular sleep
habits, distractibility, disobedience or incorrigibility (including stubbornness, contrariness, and defiant attitude [undifferen-
tiated]), rudeness, disturbing influence in school, finicky food
habits, attractive manner, and (calculated for boys only) teasing
other children. Ten traits showed moderate correlations with
"spoiled child" in the .20's for the boys but low positive correlations below .20 for the girls: psychoneurotic trends, inferiority feelings, sensitiveness over specific fact, seclusiveness,
hatred or jealousy of sibling, object of teasing by other children,
inefficiency in work, play, etc., destructiveness, loitering or
loafing, and popularity. A group of eleven notations showed moderate correlations ranging from .27 down to .21 among the girls
but negligible or low positive correlations below .20 for the boys:
mental conflict, daydreaming, absent-mindedness, inattentativeness
in school, changeable moods, crying spells, irresponsibility, leading others into bad conduct, refusal to attend school, fighting or
quarrelsomeness (undifferentiated), and neurological defect (unspecified).

Several negative correlations of significant size were
found, the highest being for girls, -.45 ± .05 for feeble-minded
sibling, while the corresponding boys' correlation was only -.17.
The next highest negative correlation, also among the girls, was
-.36 ± .05 for brother in penal detention, the corresponding correlation for boys being -.11. (These correlations are indeed curious and again raise the question of the validity of much of our
case-record data. One can see no reason a priori why families with
a mentally deficient child or a delinquent son appear to be more
free of "spoiled children" than the remainder of the families included in our data or why any tendency toward this immunity seems
to be so much greater in the case of daughters than in the case of
sons.) Girls showed similar negative correlations of -.24 ± .04
and -.29 ± .04 with retardation in school and with dull, slow,
listless, or unambitious manner (undifferentiated) respectively,

the corresponding coefficients for boys being of lesser size.
Another curious negative correlation is that for <u>lues</u> among boys,
-.27 ± .05, the corresponding coefficient for girls being quite
negligible, -.05.

Among the six sex notations all correlations with "<u>spoiled
child</u>" were low but positive, ranging from .01 to .17, the highest
correlations, oddly enough, being for <u>sex misbehavior denied en-
tirely</u>.

<u>Underweight condition</u>, <u>enuresis</u>, and <u>speech defect</u> (other
than stuttering) also showed low or negligible correlations.

Among our four undesirable home conditions—<u>discord between
parents</u>, <u>vicious</u> and <u>immoral home conditions</u>, and <u>brother in penal
detention</u>—all correlations were low or negligible, except for
<u>brother in penal detention</u> among girls with its substantial <u>nega-
tive</u> coefficient of -.36 ± .05.

CHAPTER XIX

COMPLAINING OF BAD TREATMENT AND OBJECT OF
TEASING (BY OTHER CHILDREN)

Complaining of bad treatment by other children (which was
calculated for boys only because of the paucity of girls' cases)
was correlated more substantially with object of teasing by other
children than with any other of the 111 behavior traits considered
in this study, the tetrachoric r being .43 $\pm$ .04 (Table 25). Their
correlations with other traits showed many similarities. Complaining of bad treatment by other children appears to be of substantial

TABLE 25

CORRELATIONS WITH "COMPLAINING OF BAD TREATMENT
BY OTHER CHILDREN"
(Boys Only)

Personality-total	.35 $\pm$ .03
Conduct-total	.36 $\pm$ .03
Police arrest	.22 $\pm$ .04

Larger Correlations (Positive)

Object of teasing	.42 $\pm$ .04
Unpopular	.38 $\pm$ .06
Question of change of personality	.29 $\pm$ .06
Seclusive	.29 $\pm$ .05
Changeable moods	.26 $\pm$ .05
Queer	.26 $\pm$ .06
Disturbing influence in school	.25 $\pm$ .04
Inferiority feelings	.25 $\pm$ .05
Exclusion from school	.25 $\pm$ .05
Grouped: disobedient, etc.	.25 $\pm$ .04
Contrary	.24 $\pm$ .06
Fantastical lying	.24 $\pm$ .03
Fighting	.24 $\pm$ .04
Lying	.24 $\pm$ .04
Truancy from home	.24 $\pm$ .04
Headaches	.24 $\pm$ .06
Quarrelsome	.23 $\pm$ .04
Violence	.23 $\pm$ .05
"Nervous"	.23 $\pm$ .04
Question of encephalitis	.23 $\pm$ .07
Grouped: swearing, etc.	.23 $\pm$ .05
Disobedient	.22 $\pm$ .04

TABLE 25—Continued

Slovenly	.22 ± .04
Emotional instability	.22 ± .06
Grouped: fighting, etc.	.22 ± .06
Incorrigible	.21 ± .04
Irregular sleep habits	.21 ± .06
Destructive	.20 ± .05
Rude	.20 ± .04
Temper tantrums	.20 ± .05
Threatening violence	.20 ± .06
Crying spells	.20 ± .04
Grouped: "nervous," etc.	.20 ± .04
Grouped: sensitive or worrisome, etc.	.20 ± .04

Other Correlations (Positive to Negative)

Lack of interest in school, .19; Refusal to attend school, .19; Truancy from school, .19; Masturbation, .19; Hatred or jealousy of sibling, .19; Grouped: lack of interest in school, etc., .19; Grouped: depressed, etc., .19; Boastful, "show-off," .18; Teasing other children, .18; Staying out late at night, .18; Distractible, .18; Sensitive over specific fact, .18; Worry over specific fact, .18; Unhappy, .18; Inattentive in school, .18; Inefficient in work, play, etc., .17; Stealing, .17; Grouped: temper, etc., .17; Swearing (general), .16; Daydreaming, .16; Sensitive (general), .16; Bossy, .15; Sulky, .15; Excuse-forming, .15; Egocentric, .15; Vicious home conditions, .15; Apprehensive, .14; Conduct prognosis bad, .14; Poor work in school, .14; Grouped: egocentric, etc., .14; Lazy, .13; Nail-biting, .13; Stubborn, .13; Irritable, .13; Former convulsions, .13; Defiant, .12; Leading others into bad conduct, .12; Overinterest in sex matters, .12; Spoiled child, .12; Clean, .12; Irresponsible, .11; Question of hypophrenia, .11; Stuttering, .11; Bad companions, .10; Loitering, .10; Restless in sleep, .10; Irregular attendance at school, .10; Sullen, .09; Temper display, .09; Depressed, .09; Psychoneurotic, .09; Oversuggestible, .08; Mental conflict, .08; Attractive manner; Restless, .07; Speech defect, .07; Brother in penal detention, .07; Follower, .07; Discord between parents, .07; Smoking, .07; Sex denied entirely, .06; Selfish, .05; Slow, dull, .04; Leader, .04; Neurological defect, .04; Finicky food habits, .03; Enuresis, .03; Gang, .01; Listless, .01; Preference for younger children, .01; Grouped: dull, slow, etc., .01; Retardation in school, .00; Repressed, -.01; Absent-minded, -.02; Sex delinquency (coitus), -.03; Bashful, -.03; Lack of initiative, -.03; Lues, -.05; Underweight, -.07; Vocational guidance, -.07; Immoral home conditions, -.07; Feeble-minded sibling, -.11; Popular, -.14

or at least moderate importance as a clinical notation, as may be inferred from its correlations with <u>personality-total</u>, <u>conduct-total</u>, and <u>police arrest</u>, with correlation coefficients ranging from .36 down to .22. It was noted among 121 of our 2,113 White boys, i.e., in 5.7 per cent of cases.

Another correlation of substantial size was with unpopularity (.38 ± .06). There were about thirty notations showing correlations ranging from .29 down to .20, the more meaningful among the personality problems being for question of change of personality, seclusiveness, changeable moods, queer behavior, inferiority feelings, emotional instability, and "nervousness" and among conduct problems such aggressive behavior difficulties as disturbing influence in school, disobedience (together with incorrigibility and contrariness), fighting and quarrelsomeness, violence and destructiveness, temper tantrums, swearing or bad language (undifferentiated), truancy from home, and lying.

Among the four sex notations studied among the boys, masturbation showed a low positive tetrachoric r of .19, the other coefficients being of negligible size.

Among the seven physical or psychophysical notations, question of encephalitis showed the moderate correlation of .23 ± .07, all other correlations in this field being of negligible size.

The tetrachoric correlation of complaining of bad treatment by other children with teasing other children was .18 (calculated for boys only). This suggests a trend toward a compensatory relation between the two, i.e., boys who tease others may tend to complain that others mistreat them.

Object of teasing or of unpleasant nicknaming by other children was noted among 312 instances, or 14.8 per cent, of our boys and among 91 instances, or 7.7 per cent, of the girls and was one of the most frequent of personality problems in our data. It was especially characteristic of younger children, as one may suppose.[1] It was particularly characteristic of less intelligent children, especially among those of adolescent age.[2] It was moderately correlated with the personality-total among both sexes and among girls also with the conduct-total, with bi-serial coefficient ranging from .27 to .30. There was almost no correlation with police arrest.

---

[1] I, 151, Fig. 27, and 205, Fig. 48, and this volume, Table 9 (p. 128).
[2] I, 151, Fig. 27, and this volume, Table 10 (p. 130).

Among boys its highest correlation was with <u>complaining of
bad treatment by other children</u>, .42 ± .04 (Table 26). Among girls
the highest correlations were with <u>disturbing influence in school</u>

TABLE 26

CORRELATIONS WITH "OBJECT OF TEASING"

	Boys	Girls
Personality-total.............................	.27 ± .02	.30 + .03
Conduct-total.................................	.18 ± .02	.30 ∓ .03
Police arrest.................................	.02 ± .03	-.10 ± .05
	Larger Correlations (Positive)	
Complaining of bad treatment by other children	.42 ± .04	....
Inferiority feelings..........................	.38 ± .03	.30 ± .07 (12)*
Queer.........................:...............	.30 ± .04	.35 ± .07 (6)
Sensitive over specific fact..................	.30 ± .03	.41 ± .05 (3)
Unpopular.....................................	.30 ± .04	.33 ± .07 (9-10)
Masturbation..................................	.29 ± .03	.09
Emotional instability.........................	.27 ± .04	.11
Grouped: sensitive or worrisome, etc.........	.27 ± .03	.37 ± .05 (4)
Question of encephalitis......................	.26 ± .05	.30 ± .08 (13-14)
Question of change of personality............	.26 ± .04	.25 ± .07 (21-23)
Daydreaming...................................	.24 ± .04	.04
Temper display...............................	.21 ± .04	.19
Violence......................................	.21 ± .03	.36 ± .06 (5)
"Nervous".....................................	.21 ± .03	.15
Spoiled child................................	.21 ± .03	.19
Headaches.....................................	.20 ± .04	.12
Preference for younger children..............	.20 ± .04	.22 ± .07 (26-28)
Worry over specific fact......................	.20 ± .04	.09
Fighting......................................	.20 ± .03	.43 ± .03 (2)
Disturbing influence in school...............	.18	.45 ± .06 (1)
Exclusion from school........................	.17	.34 ± .07 (7-8)
Bossy..	.10	.34 ± .06 (7-8)
Grouped: "nervous," etc.....................	.13	.33 ± .04 (9-10)
Distractible.................................	.12	.31 ± .06 (11)
Grouped: fighting, etc......................	.14	.30 ± .05 (13-14)
Grouped: lack of interest in school, etc.....	.09	.29 ± .05 (15)
Inattentive in school........................	.06	.28 ± .07 (16-17)
Restless.....................................	.05	.28 ± .05 (16-17)
Neurological defect..........................	.19	.27 ± .06 (18)
Defiant......................................	.04	.26 ± .06 (19-20)
Grouped: swearing, etc......................	.17	.26 ± .06 (19-20)
Mental conflict..............................	.09	.25 ± .08 (21-23)
Crying spells................................	.11	.25 ± .05 (21-23)
Repressed....................................	.14	.23 ± .08 (24-25)

*Rank order of girls' correlations.

TABLE 26—Continued

	Boys	Girls
Grouped: disobedient, etc.	.09	.23 ± .04 (24-25)
Lues	-.06	.22 ± .07 (26-28)
Lack of interest in school	.08	.22 ± .06 (26-28)
Contrary	.16	.21 ± .08 (29-31)
Former convulsions	.05	.21 ± .08 (29-31)
Speech defect	.15	.21 ± .06 (29-31)
Changeable moods	.09	.20 ± .06 (32-36)
Sullen	.08	.20 ± .06 (32-36)
Sulky	.10	.20 ± .07 (32-36)
Incorrigible	.00	.20 ± .05 (32-36)
Fantastical lying	.12	.20 ± .07 (32-36)
	Larger Correlations (Negative)	
Immoral home conditions	-.16	-.23 ± .06
Vocational guidance	-.05	-.22 ± .05

Other Correlations (Positive to Negative)

Sensitive (general), .19 and .18; Poor work in school, .19 and .14; Hatred or jealousy of sibling, .18 and .13; Question of hypophrenia, .17 and .18; Stuttering, .16 (boys); Seclusive, .16 and .01; Threatening violence, .16 (boys); Destructive, .16 and .06; Boastful, "show-off," .16 and .13; Grouped: temper, etc., .14 and .18; Lack of initiative, .14 and -.11; Apprehensive, .14 and .14; Swearing (general), .14 (boys); Inefficient in work, play, etc., .13 and .08; Grouped: dull, slow, etc., .13 and .05; Grouped: depressed, etc., .12 and .13; Lazy, .12 and .07; Disobedient, .11 and .17; Irresponsible, .11 and .15; Refusal to attend school, .11 and -.01; Stubborn, .11 and .12; Slow, dull, .11 and .06; Psychoneurotic, .11 and .05; Irregular sleep habits, .11 and .14; Restless in sleep, .11 and .17; Unhappy, .10 and .12; Conduct prognosis bad, .10 and .08; Oversuggestible, .10 and -.04; Depressed, .10 and .14; Absent-minded, .10 and -.01; Quarrelsome, .10 and .13; Lying, .09 and .18; Teasing other children, .09 (boys); Slovenly, .09 and .09; Temper tantrums, .09 and .05; Overinterest in opposite sex, .09 (girls); Enuresis, .08 and .14; Leading others into bad conduct, .07 and .08; Nail-biting, .07 and .19; Staying out late at night, .07 and .14; Excuse-forming, .07 and .16; Irritable, .06 and .15; Bashful, .06 and .07; Loitering, .06 and -.04; Finicky food habits, .05 and .14; Rude, .05 and .10; Listless, .05 and -.01; Egocentric, .04 and -.07; Truancy from school, .03 and .17; Overinterest in sex matters, .03 and .03; Vicious home conditions, .03 and -.07; Grouped: egocentric, etc., .03 and -.10; Sex denied entirely, .02 and -.13; Underweight, .02 and .07; Stealing, .02 and .19; Bad companions, .02 and .14; Retardation in school, .01 and .05; Irregular attendance at school, .01 and .06; Smoking, -.00 (boys); Follower, -.00 and .13; Attractive manner, -.00 and .08; Sex delinquency (coitus), -.01 and -.08; Selfish, -.02 and .06; Clean, -.02 and -.09; Truancy from home, -.03 and .15; Discord between parents, -.07 and -.06; Feeble-minded sibling, -.07 and .00; Brother in penal detention, -.07 and .07; Popular, -.07 and .10; Victim of sex abuse, -.07 (girls); Gang, -.08 (boys); Leader, -.09 and -.19

(.45 ± .06), fighting (.43 ± .03), and sensitiveness over some specific fact (.41 ± .05), the corresponding coefficients for boys being .18, .20 ± .03, and .30 ± .03 respectively.

Among both sexes three personality difficulties yielded
substantial tetrachoric correlations ranging from .30 to .38: inferiority feelings, queer behavior, and unpopularity. Among girls
three notations yielded substantial correlations in the .30's with
corresponding moderate coefficients for boys in the .20's: sensitiveness or worrisomeness (undifferentiated), violence, and question of encephalitis. The following five notations also showed
substantial correlations in the .30's for girls but low coefficients ranging from .10 to .18 among boys: exclusion from school,
bossy manner, fighting or quarrelsomeness (undifferentiated), "nervousness" or restlessness (undifferentiated), and distractibility.

Two personality problems showed moderate correlations in
the .20's for both boys and girls—question of change of personality and preference for younger children as playmates. The following seven notations showed moderate correlations in the .20's for
boys but low positive correlations below .20 for girls: masturbation, emotional instability, daydreaming, "nervousness," "spoiled
child," temper display other than "tantrums," and headaches. The
following sixteen case notations showed moderate coefficients among
the girls, ranging from .29 down to .20, but low or negligible coefficients below .20 among boys: inattentiveness in school, lack
of interest in school studies or employment, restlessness, crying
spells, mental conflict, repressed manner, changeable moods, swearing or bad language (undifferentiated), disobedience (including incorrigibility, defiant manner, and contrariness), sulkiness, sullenness, fantastical lying, speech defect (other than stuttering),
neurological defect (unspecified), former convulsions, and lues.

Only two case notations showed significant negative correlations, both among girls: immoral (other than vicious) home conditions, -.23 ± .06, and vocational or educational guidance, -.22
± .05, the corresponding coefficients among boys being also negative or of small size.

Among the six sex notations the only significant correlation with object of teasing by other children was masturbation
among boys, .29 ± .03, the other correlations being quite negligible.

Among physical defects, substantial correlations were found for <u>question or diagnosis of encephalitis (present or former</u>), the coefficients for girls and boys respectively being .26 $\pm$ .05 and .30 $\pm$ .08, for <u>neurological defect (unspecified</u>) with the respective coefficients of .19 and .27 $\pm$ .06, for <u>lues</u> with respective coefficients of -.06 and .22 $\pm$ .07, and for <u>speech defect</u> (other than <u>stuttering</u>) with respective coefficients of .15 and .21 $\pm$ .06. Low or negligible correlations were found for <u>underweight condition</u>, <u>enuresis (present or former</u>), and, oddly enough, for <u>stuttering</u> (which was calculated for boys only).

Among unfavorable home conditions there were the interesting negative coefficients of -.16 and -.23 $\pm$ .06 with <u>immoral home conditions</u> for boys and girls respectively, but for <u>vicious home conditions</u>, <u>brother in penal detention</u>, and <u>discord between parents</u> the correlations were negligible.

Our boys who are themselves <u>object of teasing by other children</u> apparently do not tend to "compensate" therefor by teasing other children, as we may infer from the quite negligible tetrachoric correlation of -.06 between these notations. (This correlation unfortunately could not be calculated for girls because of the paucity of cases.)

CHAPTER XX

UNPOPULARITY AND POPULARITY

Unpopularity among schoolmates or playmates, or marked lack of popularity appears to be among the more meaningful behavior problems from a clinical standpoint, as indicated by its very substantial or high bi-serial correlations ranging from .39 to .64 with both personality-total and conduct-total. It is curious, however, that in view of its negligible tetrachoric correlations with police arrest it appears to be of no significance as far as overt "juvenile delinquency" is concerned. It was noted among 110 of our 2,113 White boys (5.2 per cent) and among 54 of our 1,181 White girls (4.6 per cent).

Its highest correlations (Table 27) were among girls, the coefficients ranging from .54 down to .49 for the five conduct difficulties, bossy manner, lying, boastful or "show-off" manner, and

TABLE 27

CORRELATIONS WITH "UNPOPULAR"

	Boys	Girls
Personality-total...........................	.39 ± .03	.50 ± .04
Conduct-total...............................	.49 ± .03	.64 ± .03
Police arrest...............................	.03 ± .04	.08 ± .06
	Larger Correlations (Positive)	
Disturbing influence in school..............	.42 ± .04	.49 ± .06 (5-6)*
Fighting....................................	.39 ± .04	.28 ± .04 (35-36)
Complaining of bad treatment by other children	.38 ± .06	....
Grouped: fighting, etc.....................	.37 ± .08	.53 ± .05 (2)
Quarrelsome.................................	.36 ± .04	.52 ± .05 (3)
Bossy.......................................	.36 ± .06	.54 ± .06 (1)
Teasing other children......................	.35 ± .05	....
Lying.......................................	.34 ± .04	.50 ± .05 (4)
Boastful, "show-off"........................	.33 ± .04	.49 ± .07 (5-6)

*Rank order of girls' correlations.

197

TABLE 27—Continued

	Boys	Girls
Fantastical lying	.32 ± .06	.38 ± .07 (12-15)
Inefficient in work, play, etc.	.31 ± .06	.33 ± .08 (25-28)
Grouped: swearing, etc.	.31 ± .05	.42 ± .07 (9)
Grouped: egocentric, etc.	.30 ± .04	.33 ± .06 (25-28)
Grouped: disobedient, etc.	.30 ± .04	.37 ± .05 (16-18)
Object of teasing	.30 ± .04	.33 ± .07 (25-28)
Threatening violence	.29 ± .06	....
Violence	.29 ± .05	.40 ± .07 (10)
Excuse-forming	.29 ± .05	.24 ± .07 (44-45)
Egocentric	.29 ± .05	.38 ± .06 (12-15)
Inferiority feelings	.29 ± .05	.29 ± .08 (32-34)
Contrary	.27 ± .06	.13
Destructive	.27 ± .05	.17
Smoking	.27 ± .05	....
Queer	.27 ± .06	.35 ± .08 (21-22)
Grouped: lack of interest in school, etc.	.26 ± .04	.23 ± .06 (46-49)
Irregular sleep habits	.26 ± .06	.08
Daydreaming	.26 ± .05	.26 ± .07 (40-42)
Temper tantrums	.26 ± .05	.35 ± .07 (21-22)
Swearing (general)	.26 ± .06	....
Disobedient	.26 ± .04	.36 ± .06 (19-20)
Loitering	.25 ± .05	.09
Depressed	.25 ± .06	.23 ± .08 (46-49)
"Nervous"	.25 ± .05	.14
Grouped: temper, etc.	.25 ± .04	.38 ± .05 (12-15)
Selfish	.23 ± .06	.25 ± .04 (43)
Sullen	.23 ± .05	.14
Grouped: "nervous," etc.	.23 ± .04	.38 ± .05 (12-15)
Grouped: depressed, etc.	.23 ± .05	.22 ± .07 (50-54)
Distractible	.22 ± .05	.26 ± .07 (40-42)
Question of change of personality	.22 ± .06	.43 ± .08 (7-8)
Rude	.22 ± .05	.30 ± .06 (30-31)
Leading others into bad conduct	.22 ± .06	.43 ± .08 (7-8)
Irresponsible	.22 ± .06	.13
Inattentive in school	.22 ± .03	.22 ± .08 (50-54)
Lack of interest in school	.21 ± .05	.14
Lazy	.21 ± .05	.29 ± .08 (32-34)
Crying spells	.21 ± .04	.34 ± .05 (23-24)
Seclusive	.21 ± .05	.15
Oversuggestible	.20 ± .04	.05
Irritable	.20 ± .04	.19
Staying out late at night	.20 ± .05	.20 ± .07 (55-58)
Incorrigible	.19	.39 ± .06 (11)
Stealing	.18	.37 ± .05 (16-18)
Exclusion from school	.15	.37 ± .08 (16-18)
Changeable moods	.16	.36 ± .06 (19-20)
Overinterest in opposite sex	....	.34 ± .06 (23-24)
Restless	.16	.33 ± .06 (25-28)
Emotional instability	.10	.32 ± .07 (29)
Restless in sleep	.18	.30 ± .06 (30-31)
Defiant	-.01	.29 ± .07 (32-34)
Nail-biting	.18	.28 ± .06 (35-36)

TABLE 27—Continued

	Boys	Girls
Leader	.12	.27 ± .08 (37-39)
Worry over specific fact	.17	.27 ± .10 (37-39)
Stubborn	.16	.27 ± .06 (37-39)
Conduct prognosis bad	.16	.26 ± .09 (40-42)
Psychoneurotic	.02	.24 ± .08 (44-45)
Preference for younger children	.06	.23 ± .08 (46-49)
Mental conflict	.10	.23 ± .10 (46-49)
Enuresis	.08	.22 ± .06 (50-54)
Sulky	.05	.22 ± .08 (50-54)
Question of encephalitis	.09	.22 ± .10 (50-54)
Apprehensive	.11	.20 ± .07 (50-54)
Sensitive over specific fact	.09	.20 ± .07 (50-54)
Poor work in school	.19	.20 ± .06 (50-54)
		Larger Correlations (Negative)
Attractive manner	.02	-.23 ± .06
Lack of initiative	-.01	-.22 ± .09
		Not Calculable
Popular	(n.c.)	(n.c.)
Feeble-minded sibling	(n.c.)	.11

Other Correlations (Positive to Negative)

Overinterest in sex matters, .18 and .18; Masturbation, .17 and .18; Spoiled child, .16 and .17; Bashful, .16 and -.08; Temper display, .16 and .10; Absent-minded, .15 and -.09; Sensitive (general), .15 and -.01; Refusal to attend school, .14 and -.00; Slovenly, .13 and .15; Truancy from home, .13 and .16; Stuttering, .13 (boys); Discord between parents, .13 and -.00; Grouped: sensitive or worrisome, etc., .12 and .17; Clean, .12 and -.08; Truancy from school, .12 and .17; Neurological defect, .11 and .15; Underweight, .08 and .13; Unhappy, .06 and .09; Former convulsions, .06 and .04; Bad companions, .04 and .10; Sex denied entirely, .03 and .08; Question of hypophrenia, .02 and .11; Finicky food habits, .02 and .11; Follower, .01 and -.11; Headaches, .01 and .01; Speech defect, .01 and .13; Vicious home conditions, .01 and .06; Hatred or jealousy of sibling, -.01 and .16; Brother in penal detention, -.04 and -.04; Irregular attendance at school, -.05 and .07; Slow, dull, -.05 and -.02; Victim of sex abuse, -.05 (girls); Vocational guidance, -.06 and -.17; Grouped: dull, slow, etc., -.08 and -.02; Sex delinquency (coitus), -.09 and .18; Listless, -.09 and .17; Repressed, -.10 and .09; Retardation in school, -.10 and -.05; Gang, -.11 (boys); Immoral home conditions, -.16 and -.11

disturbing influence in school. Swearing or bad language (undifferentiated) also yielded substantial coefficients of .42 ± .07 for girls and .31 ± .05 for boys. Three other behavior traits

yielded substantial coefficients in the .40's for the girls but
moderate correlations in the .20's for the boys: <u>violence</u>, <u>lead-
ing others into bad conduct</u>, and <u>question of change of personality</u>.

　　　Five behavior traits yielded substantial correlations in
the .30's for both boys and girls: <u>fantastical lying</u>, <u>egocentric-
ity or selfishness</u> (undifferentiated), <u>inefficiency in work, play</u>,
etc., <u>disobedience or incorrigibility</u> (including <u>stubbornness</u>, <u>con-
trariness</u>, and <u>defiant attitude</u>, undifferentiated), and <u>object of
teasing by other children</u>. Two notations which were calculated
for boys only—<u>teasing other children</u> and <u>complaining of bad treatment by other children</u>—also yielded substantial coefficients in
the .30's. <u>Fighting</u> yielded a substantial correlation of .39 ± .04
among boys and a moderate correlation of .28 ± .04 among girls.
The following five behavior traits among girls yielded substantial
correlations in the .30's but among boys moderate coefficients in
the .20's: <u>queer behavior</u>, <u>rudeness</u>, <u>"nervousness" or restless-
ness</u> (undifferentiated), <u>crying spells</u>, and <u>temper tantrums</u>. The
following seven notations among girls yielded substantial correlations in the .30's but low positive correlations below .20 for the
boys: <u>incorrigibility</u>, <u>stealing</u>, <u>exclusion from school</u>, <u>restless-
ness</u>, <u>restlessness in sleep</u>, <u>changeable moods</u>, and <u>emotional in-
stability</u>. <u>Overinterest in the opposite sex</u>, for which only the
girls' correlation was computed, yielded a substantial coefficient
of .34 ± .06.

　　　The following nine behavior traits showed moderate correlations in the .20's for both sexes: <u>inferiority feelings</u>, <u>de-
pressed spells</u>, <u>daydreaming</u>, <u>inattentiveness in school</u>, <u>distract-
ibility</u>, <u>excuse-forming attitude</u>, <u>laziness</u>, <u>selfishness</u>, and <u>stay-
ing out late at night</u>. Three conduct difficulties for which only
the boys' coefficients were computed—<u>threatening violence</u>, <u>swear-
ing (general)</u>, and <u>smoking</u>—also showed moderate correlations in
the .20's.

　　　The following eleven conduct and personality difficulties
showed moderate correlations in the .20's among boys but low positive correlations below .20 among the girls: <u>contrariness</u>, <u>de-
structiveness</u>, <u>"nervousness,"</u> <u>irritable temperament</u>, <u>irregular
sleep habits</u>, <u>loitering or loafing</u>, <u>sullenness</u>, <u>lack of interest
in school work</u>, <u>irresponsibility</u>, <u>seclusiveness</u>, and <u>oversuggest-
ibility</u>. The following fifteen notations among girls showed mod-

erate correlations in the .20's, but low coefficients below .20
for the boys: defiant attitude, stubbornness, sulkiness, psychoneurotic trends, mental conflict, worry over specific fact, sensitiveness over some specific fact, apprehensiveness, preference for
younger children as playmates, poor work in school, enuresis, nail-
biting, staff diagnosis of unfavorable conduct prognosis, "leader,"
and question or diagnosis of encephalitis.

Two negative coefficients of significant magnitude were
found among the girls' correlations: attractive manner, -.23 +
.06, and lack of initiative, -.22 + .09, the corresponding boys'
correlations being negligible.

Among the six sex notations there was only one coefficient
of significant size, overinterest in opposite sex (calculated for
girls only), .34 + .06.

Among the seven physical or psychophysical notations there
were among the girls two correlations of moderate size: enuresis,
.22 + .06, and question or diagnosis of encephalitis, .22 + .10.
The boys' coefficients for these two notations and all coefficients
for underweight condition, neurological defect (unspecified), headaches, speech defect, and (calculated for boys only) stuttering
were positive but of negligible size, ranging from .01 to .15.

For the four undesirable home or familial conditions the
coefficients were of negligible size.

In order that comparisons could be made with the usual "behavior difficulties," the notation popularity among schoolmates or
playmates or "patient is well liked" is included as one of the frequently appearing behavior traits not considered as undesirable.
It was noted among 138 of our boys and 76 of our girls. Its correlations with our three criteria of "seriousness" or "ominousness"
were all of nonsignificant size, ranging from .03 to .13 (Table
28). It yielded only a few correlations of significant size. Its
highest correlations among both sexes were with the "desirable"
traits, attractive manner and "leader," the coefficients ranging
from .32 to .40. Another substantial correlation was the negative
one of -.39 + .04 with daydreaming among boys, the girls' coefficient being negligible, .06. Apparently children who are popular,
especially boys, do not need to resort to daydreaming. (With unpopularity the correlations with daydreaming were positive,

TABLE 28

CORRELATIONS WITH "POPULAR"

	Boys	Girls
Personality-total...........................	.03 ± .03	.12 ± .04
Conduct-total...............................	.13 ± .03	.08 ± .04
Police arrest..............................	.10 ± .04	.12 ± .06
	Larger Correlations (Positive)	
Attractive manner...........................	.36 ± .04	.36 ± .05 (2)*
Leader.....................................	.32 ± .05	.40 ± .07 (1)
Finicky food habits.........................	.25 ± .05	.02
Spoiled child..............................	.22 ± .09	.07
Clean......................................	.17	.25 ± .06 (3)
Sensitive (general)........................	.12	.20 ± .07 (4)
	Larger Correlations (Negative)	
Daydreaming................................	-.39 + .04	.06
Feeble-minded sibling......................	-.25 + .12	.06
Mental conflict............................	-.24 + .06	.01
Vicious home conditions....................	-.05	-.29 ± .07
Conduct prognosis bad......................	-.09	-.27 ± .08
Worry over specific fact...................	.05	-.20 ± .09
	Not Calculable	
Unpopular..................................	(n.c.)	(n.c.)
Lues.......................................	(n.c.)	.02
Loitering..................................	.13	(n.c.)

*Rank order of girls' correlations.

Other Correlations (Positive to Negative)

Sex delinquency (coitus), .18 and -.01; Grouped: sensitive or worrisome, etc., .18 and .06; Defiant, .17 and .12; Smoking, .17 (boys); Staying out late at night, .17 and .04; Boastful, "show-off," .16 and .18; Refusal to attend school, .16 and .18; Sulky, .16 and .17; Irresponsible, .15 and .02; Masturbation, .13 and .01; Irregular sleep habits, .13 and .15; Question of encephalitis, .13 and .14; Vocational guidance, .13 and .06; Teasing other children, .12 (boys); Overinterest in sex matters, .12 and .04; Restless in sleep, .12 and .03; Sensitive over specific fact, .12 and .00; Fighting, .11 and .12; Stealing, .11 and -.01; Destructive, .09 and -.02; Incorrigible, .09 and .05; Slovenly, .09 and -.01; Lack of initiative, .09 and -.07; Exclusion from school, .09 and .03; Truancy from home, .09 and .03; Stuttering, .09 (boys); Inattentive in school, .08 and .05; Inefficient in work, play, etc., .08 and -.00; Lying, .08 and .02; Slow, dull, .08 and -.13; Grouped: disobedient, etc., .08 and .07;

TABLE 28—Continued

Bad companions, .07 and .10; Disobedient, .07 and .05; Gang, .07 (boys); Temper tantrums, .07 and .16; Stubborn, .07 and .02; Absent-minded, .07 and -.05; Changeable moods, .07 and .03; Irritable, .07 and .13; Question of change of personality, .06 and .19; Listless, .06 and -.10; Grouped: temper, etc., .06 and .12; Grouped: lack of interest in school, etc., .06 and .03; Lazy, .05 and -.02; Sullen, .05 and .03; Truancy from school, .05 and -.12; Hatred or jealousy of sibling, .05 and .08; Bashful, .05 and .06; Crying spells, .05 and .09; Restless, .05 and .03; Repressed, .05 and -.08; Nail-biting, .04 and -.07; Rude, .04 and .04; Sex denied entirely, .04 and .13; Grouped: "nervous," etc., .04 and .07; Grouped: fighting, etc., .04 and .03; Fantastical lying, .03 and .01; Swearing (general), .03 (boys); Violence, .03 and .11; Disturbing influence in school, .02 and .12; Enuresis, .02 and -.03; "Nervous," .02 and .06; Poor work in school, .02 and -.01; Quarrelsome, .01 and -.09; Unhappy, .01 and .05; Apprehensive, .00 and .12; Excuse-forming, .00 and .14; Oversuggestible, .00 and -.01; Neurological defect, .00 and .02; Headaches, -.00 and .11; Speech defect, -.00 and -.03; Discord between parents, -.00 and -.10; Grouped: swearing, etc., -.00 and .01; Lack of interest in school, -.01 and -.04; Immoral home conditions, -.01 and -.19; Distractible, -.02 and .18; Grouped: depressed, etc., -.02 and -.05; Leading others into bad conduct, -.03 and .17; Depressed, -.03 and -.13; Psychoneurotic, -.03 and .15; Emotional instability, -.03 and .11; Overinterest in opposite sex, -.03 (girls); Temper display, -.04 and -.06; Inferiority feelings, -.04 and -.06; Preference for younger children, -.04 and -.06; Grouped: dull, slow, etc., -.04 and -.09; Selfish, -.05 and .07; Egocentric, -.06 and .19; Grouped: egocentric, etc., -.06 and .15; Contrary, -.07 and .11; Threatening violence, -.07 (boys); Object of teasing, -.07 and .10; Underweight, -.07 and -.10; Question of hypophrenia, -.08 and -.14; Follower, -.08 and .10; Victim of sex abuse, -.08 (girls); Queer, -.11 and .04; Former convulsions, -.13 and .04; Bossy, -.14 and .12; Complaining of bad treatment by other children, -.14 (boys); Irregular attendance at school, -.14 and -.07; Brother in penal detention, -.14 and -.19; Retardation in school, -.18 and -.12; Seclusive, -.19 and -.14

.26 $\pm$ .05 and .26 $\pm$ .07 for boys and girls respectively.)

Popularity showed some statistically significant positive correlations in the .20's with three undesirable behavior traits: finicky food habits and "spoiled child" among boys, and sensitiveness in general among girls, the corresponding coefficients for the other sex being low but positive. With the notation clean, neat habits or appearance the correlations were .17 and .25 $\pm$ .06 for boys and girls respectively.

Additional meaningful correlations of negative sign for boys and girls, respectively, were for mental conflict, -.24 $\pm$ .06 and .01, for worry over specific fact, .05 and -.20 $\pm$ .09, and for staff notation of unfavorable conduct prognosis, -.09 and -.27 $\pm$ .08.

Among the six sex notations the correlations with popularity were of negligible size, unless one considers that the positive

correlation of .18 for sex delinquency (coitus) among boys is meaningful. Among the seven physical or psychophysical notations all
correlations were negligible. Among the four undesirable home or
familial notations (discord between parents, vicious and immoral
home conditions, and brother in penal detention) the only significant coefficient was with vicious home conditions among girls, -.29
+ .07.

A comparison of the corresponding coefficients in Tables
27 and 28 for the presumably antithetical notations unpopularity
and popularity brings to light the curious statistical phenomenon
which has been previously mentioned,[1] i.e., the fact that many of
the corresponding correlations for such antithetical pairs of
traits as unpopularity-popularity, slovenliness-cleanliness, and
"leader"-"follower" were not of opposite sign and of similar magnitude, as would be supposed if strictly objectively measurable
traits were being used but were often of the same sign (though of
different magnitude). Among the 116 pairs of corresponding coefficients for the boys in Table 27 (unpopularity) and Table 28 (popularity) there were 80 of like sign and only 36 of unlike sign.
Among 113 pairs of girls' coefficients there were 77 of like sign
and only 36 of unlike sign. The intercolumnar correlations (Pearson's product-moment) were -.08 + .06 for the boys and .14 + .06
for the girls. Now, if these two notations, unpopularity and popularity, were truly antithetical in meaning and could be considered as opposite ends of the same scale, just as "long" and "short"
are the opposite ends on a scale of stature, and if the correlations between the putative trait unpopularity-popularity with other
traits are based upon rectilinearity of regression, we should expect the corresponding correlations in Tables 27 and 28 to be of
unlike sign and of substantially the same magnitude, and intercolumnar correlations based upon these coefficients should approach
a negative unity.

In our previous discussion of this phenomenon of inconsistency between the correlation of coefficients of presumably antagonistic traits two possible theories were suggested—one a possible non-rectilinearity of specific notations on the trait unpop-

_____

[1]See I, 134-35 and 249-50, and this volume, p. 45.

ularity-popularity and the other that the traits unpopularity and
popularity may not be truly opposite poles of a single underlying
trait. It may be that the true "opposite" of unpopularity is "indifference." A third possibility is that this lack of negativeness in correlation described in the preceding paragraph may be
due to the existence of unmeasured prejudicial factors in the data
as discussed in chapter iv.

CHAPTER XXI

DAYDREAMING AND ABSENT-MINDEDNESS

Daydreaming and absent-mindedness do not appear to be fun-
damentally similar traits in spite of their apparent, superficial
resemblance. Their intercorrelations for boys and girls respectively were only .29 + .05 and .33 + .07. Their correlations with
several other traits or notations were higher than with each other.

Daydreaming or fantasying was of substantial but not serious importance clinically, as may be inferred from its bì serial
correlations with the personality- and the conduct-total, which
range from .27 to .49 (Table 29). With police arrest ("juvenile
delinquency") its relations were non-significant. It was noted
among 195 of our 2,113 White boys (9.2 per cent) and among 94 of
our 1,181 White girls (8.0 per cent).
Daydreaming yielded its largest correlations (tetrachoric
r) among girls, .42 + .06 with inefficiency in work, play, etc., and
.42 + .06 for boastful or "show-off" manner, the corresponding coefficients for boys being .26 + .05 and .18 respectively. Other
substantial correlations in the .30's for both boys and girls were
for depressed spells, unhappy appearance or manner, inferiority
feelings, queer behavior, and fantastical lying. Among boys masturbation yielded a correlation of .37 + .03 with a corresponding
correlation among girls of .25 + .05. Hatred or jealousy of sibling among boys showed a correlation of .30 + .05, but its coefficient among girls was negligible, .07. Among girls the following
five personality difficulties yielded substantial correlations in
the .30's with moderate coefficients in the .20's for boys: sensitiveness or worrisomeness (undifferentiated) and sensitiveness
over specific fact, seclusiveness, changeable moods, and absent-
mindedness. Another seven behavior problems also showed substantial correlations in the .30's among girls but negligible coefficients ranging from .18 down to -.00 among boys: violence, rudeness, defiant attitude, disturbing influence in school, emotional

TABLE 29

CORRELATIONS WITH "DAYDREAMING"

	Boys	Girls
Personality-total	.38 ± .02	.49 ± .03
Conduct-total	.27 ± .02	.48 ± .03
Police arrest	.07 ± .04	.14 ± .05
		Larger Correlations (Positive)
Masturbation	.37 ± .03	.25 ± .05 (31-33)*
Grouped: depressed, etc	.36 ± .04	.39 ± .05 (3-4)
Unhappy	.36 ± .05	.36 ± .07 (10)
Depressed	.34 ± .03	.34 ± .06 (11-12)
Fantastical lying	.32 ± .05	.30 ± .07 (20)
Queer	.31 ± .05	.39 ± .06 (3-4)
Inferiority feelings	.31 ± .04	.37 ± .07 (6-9)
Hatred or jealousy of sibling	.30 ± .05	.07
Absent-minded	.29 ± .05	.33 ± .07 (13-16)
Grouped: sensitive or worrisome, etc	.27 ± .03	.31 ± .05 (17-19)
Inefficient in work, play, etc	.26 ± .05	.42 ± .06 (1-2)
Irresponsible	.26 ± .05	.09
Changeable moods	.26 ± .04	.37 ± .05 (6-9)
Listless	.26 ± .04	.20 ± .06 (55-58)
Unpopular	.26 ± .05	.26 ± .07 (27-30)
Grouped: lack of interest in school, etc	.26 ± .03	.16
Grouped: "nervous," etc	.25 ± .03	.28 ± .04 (22-24)
Seclusive	.25 ± .04	.37 ± .06 (6-9)
Lack of initiative	.25 ± .05	.21 ± .07 (46-54)
Inattentive in school	.24 ± .03	.03
Object of teasing	.24 ± .04	.04
Sensitive over specific fact	.24 ± .04	.33 ± .05 (13-16)
"Nervous"	.23 ± .04	.22 ± .05 (40-45)
Distractible	.23 ± .05	.16
Sex delinquency (coitus)	.22 ± .06	-.01
Repressed	.22 ± .05	.21 ± .08 (46-54)
Restless in sleep	.21 ± .04	.26 ± .05 (27-30)
Contrary	.20 ± .06	.20 ± .08 (55-58)
Stubborn	.20 ± .04	.23 ± .05 (36-39)
Threatening violence	.20 ± .05	....
Worry over specific fact	.20 ± .05	.22 ± .08 (40-45)
Clean	.20 ± .04	.01
Boastful, "show-off"	.18	.42 ± .06 (1-2)
Violence	.03	.38 ± .06 (5)
Rude	.02	.37 ± .05 (6-9)
Emotional instability	.04	.34 ± .06 (11-12)
Disturbing influence in school	-.00	.33 ± .06 (13-16)
Defiant	.08	.33 ± .06 (13-16)
Mental conflict	.18	.31 ± .08 (17-19)
Lying	.12	.31 ± .04 (17-19)

*Rank order of girls' correlations.

TABLE 29—Continued

	Boys	Girls
Question of encephalitis.	-.02	.29 ± .08 (21)
Grouped: fighting, etc.	.05	.28 ± .05 (22-24)
Finicky food habits	.15	.28 ± .06 (22-24)
Spoiled child	.18	.27 ± .06 (25-26)
Grouped: disobedient, etc.	.14	.27 ± .04 (25-26)
Crying spells	.16	.26 ± .05 (27-30)
Overinterest in sex matters	.19	.26 ± .07 (27-30)
Quarrelsome	.10	.25 ± .05 (31-33)
Irritable	.16	.25 ± .05 (31-33)
Sensitive (general)	.19	.24 ± .06 (34-35)
Incorrigible	.05	.24 ± .05 (34-35)
Enuresis	.13	.23 ± .05 (36-39)
Question of change of personality	.14	.23 ± .07 (36-39)
Restless	.12	.23 ± .05 (36-39)
Grouped: swearing, etc.	.09	.22 ± .06 (40-45)
Leader	-.02	.22 ± .07 (40-45)
Egocentric	.07	.22 ± .06 (40-45)
Excuse-forming	.07	.22 ± .06 (40-45)
Slovenly	.05	.21 ± .05 (46-54)
Stealing	.12	.21 ± .05 (46-54)
Truancy from school	.06	.21 ± .06 (46-54)
Irregular sleep habits	.10	.21 ± .07 (46-54)
Headaches	.17	.21 ± .07 (46-54)
Grouped: temper, etc.	.12	.21 ± .05 (46-54)
Grouped: egocentric, etc.	.12	.21 ± .05 (46-54)
Attractive manner	.17	.20 ± .05 (55-58)
Sullen	.14	.20 ± .06 (55-58)
	Larger Correlations (Negative)	
Popular	-.39 ± .04	.06
Brother in penal detention	-.22 ± .05	-.32 ± .06
Retardation in school	-.21 ± .03	-.21 ± .04
Feeble-minded sibling	-.09	-.21 ± .04

Other Correlations (Positive to Negative)

Lack of interest in school, .19 and .19; Lazy, .19 and .09; Grouped: dull, slow, etc., .18 and .14; Poor work in school, .18 and .06; Preference for younger children, .18 and .03; Nail-biting, .17 and .08; Teasing other children, .17 (boys); Refusal to attend school, .16 and .12; Complaining of bad treatment by other children, .16 (boys); Neurological defect, .15 and .11; Bashful, .14 and .16; Overinterest in opposite sex, .14 (girls); Vicious home conditions, .13 and .02; Bossy, .13 and .16; Selfish, .12 and .09; Staying out late at night, .12 and .18; Psychoneurotic, .12 and .13; Immoral home conditions, .11 and .18; Temper tantrums, .11 and .19; Underweight, .10 and .06; Speech defect, .09 and -.14; Destructive, .09 and .11; Bad companions, .09 and .05; Victim of sex abuse, .09 (girls); Exclusion from school, .08 and .17; Apprehensive, .07 and .05; Swearing (general), .07 (boys); Sulky, .07 and .18; Smoking, .07 (boys); Loitering, .07 and -.05; Temper display, .06 and .14; Slow, dull, .06 and -.01; Conduct prognosis bad, .05 and .11; Oversuggestible, .05 and .08; Truancy from

TABLE 29—Continued

home, .04 and .15; Former convulsions, .04 and .04; Follower, .04 and -.01; Discord between parents, .03 and .16; Vocational guidance, .03 and -.04; Leading
others into bad conduct, .03 and .16; Fighting, .02 and .16; Disobedient, .02
and .13; Stuttering, .01 (boys); Gang, -.05 (boys); Lues, -.05 and .11; Irregular attendance at school, -.06 and -.00; Question of hypophrenia, -.11 and
-.15; Sex denied entirely, -.16 and .13

instability, mental conflict, and lying.

Nine behavior problems showed moderate correlations in the
.20's for both sexes: "nervousness," restlessness in sleep, listlessness, lack of initiative or ambition, unpopularity, worry over
some specific fact or episode, repressed manner, contrariness,
stubbornness, and also one calculated for boys only, threatening
violence. Another six notations showed moderate correlations in
the .20's for boys but low coefficients ranging from -.01 to .16
among girls: irresponsibility, inattentiveness in school, distractibility, object of teasing by other children, sex delinquency (coitus), and clean habits. Among girls the following twenty-four notations showed moderate correlations in the .20's, with lesser coefficients ranging from -.02 to .19 among the boys: sensitiveness
in general, incorrigibility, quarrelsomeness, swearing or bad language (undifferentiated), excuse-forming attitude, stealing, truancy from school, temper display or temper tantrums (undifferentiated), egocentricity, irritable manner or disposition, sullenness,
slovenliness, restlessness, irregular sleep habits, "spoiled child,"
crying spells, question of change of personality, overinterest in
sex matters, enuresis, finicky food habits, headaches, question or
diagnosis of encephalitis, attractive manner, and "leader."

The largest negative correlations with daydreaming were as
follows: popularity among boys, -.39 + .04, with a corresponding
coefficient for girls of .06, and brother in penal detention, with
moderate or substantial negative correlations of -.22 + .05 and
-.32 + .06 for boys and girls respectively. Retardation in school
showed moderate correlations of -.21 for both sexes. The notation,
feeble-minded sibling, among girls showed the moderate correlation
of -.21 + .04 and a corresponding coefficient of -.09 among boys.

Sex notations showed several significant correlations with
daydreaming. Masturbation among boys showed the substantial coefficient of .37 + .03 and a moderate coefficient of .25 + .05 among

girls. Sex delinquency (coitus) among boys showed the moderate
correlations of .22 + .06, but its correlation among girls was
practically zero (-.01). Overinterest in sex matters among girls
showed the moderate correlation of .26 + .07 and among boys the
scarcely significant coefficient of .19. Sex misbehavior denied
entirely showed the interesting but statistically non-significant
coefficients of -.16 and .13 for boys and girls respectively.
Overinterest in opposite sex and victim of sex abuse by older child
or person, which were calculated for girls only, showed and the
negligible coefficients of .14 and .09 respectively.

Among our physical or psychophysical notations, only two
coefficients were of significant size, both among girls, .23 + .05
for enuresis (present or former) and .29 + .08 for question or diagnosis of encephalitis. All other coefficients in this field,
including those for underweight condition, lues, neurological defect (unspecified), speech defect, and stuttering, were low or
negligible in size. Brother in penal detention, as we have seen,
yielded moderate or substantial negative correlations, while the
other familial notations—discord between parents and vicious and
immoral home conditions—showed negligible correlations.

Absent-mindedness, forgetfulness, or poor memory appear to
be of relatively little importance clinically, unless possibly in
the case of the boys, in which one finds the fairly substantial
bi-serial correlation of .30 + .03 with personality-total (Table
30). All other criteria of "importance or seriousness" showed low
correlations falling between -.16 and .18. It was noted among 134
boys, or 6.3 per cent, and among 62 girls, or 5.2 per cent.

Its highest correlation was with inefficiency in work,
play, etc., with tetrachoric correlations of .47 + .05 and .42 +
.06 for boys and girls respectively. Distractibility among boys
yielded the fairly high correlation of .40 + .04 and among girls
the substantial correlation of .35 + .07. Queer behavior and headaches also yielded substantial correlations in the .30's among
boys and moderate correlations in the .20's among girls. Listlessness and irresponsibility also yielded substantial correlations in
the .30's among boys but low coefficients below .20 for girls.
Among the girls four notations—daydreaming, mental conflict, "nervousness," and question or diagnosis of encephalitis—yielded

TABLE 30

CORRELATIONS WITH "ABSENT-MINDED"

	Boys	Girls
Personality-total..........................	.30 ± .03	.18 ± .04
Conduct-total.............................	.18 ± .03	.09 ± .04
Police arrest.............................	.02 ± .04	-.16 ± .06
	Larger Correlations (Positive)	
Inefficient in work, play, etc...............	.47 ± .05	.42 ± .06 (1)*
Distractible................................	.40 ± .04	.35 ± .07 (11)
Queer......................................	.37 ± .05	.29 ± .08 (7-8)
Headaches..................................	.32 ± .05	.24 ± .07 (12-14)
Grouped: dull, slow, etc...................	.32 ± .03	.19
Listless...................................	.31 ± .05	.05
Irresponsible..............................	.30 ± .05	.17
Question of change of personality............	.29 ± .05	.26 ± .08 (9-10)
Daydreaming................................	.29 ± .05	.33 ± .07 (3)
Restless...................................	.29 ± .04	.10
Seclusive..................................	.29 ± .04	-.13
Poor work in school..........................	.27 ± .04	.21 ± .05 (20-21)
Mental conflict.............................	.25 ± .06	.30 ± .09 (6)
Question of encephalitis.....................	.25 ± .02	.31 ± .09 (4-5)
Lack of initiative..........................	.24 ± .05	.22 ± .08 (16-19)
Lazy.......................................	.22 ± .05	-.04
Slow, dull.................................	.22 ± .04	.29 ± .05 (7-8)
"Nervous"...................................	.22 ± .04	.35 ± .06 (2)
Emotional instability.......................	.22 ± .06	.18
Grouped: "nervous," etc....................	.22 ± .03	.26 ± .05 (9-10)
Contrary...................................	.21 ± .06	-.06
Neurological defect.........................	.21 ± .05	.09
Attractive manner..........................	.20 ± .04	-.00
Grouped: temper, etc......................	.20 ± .04	.02
Restless in sleep...........................	.13	.31 ± .06 (4-5)
Inferiority feelings........................	.19	.24 ± .08 (12-14)
Preference for younger children...............	.13	.24 ± .08 (12-14)
Former convulsions..........................	.01	.23 ± .09 (15)
Depressed..................................	.12	.22 ± .08 (16-19)
Spoiled child..............................	.17	.22 ± .07 (16-19)
Exclusion from school.......................	.00	.22 ± .08 (16-19)
Oversuggestible............................	.05	.21 ± .06 (20-21)
Sullen.....................................	.01	.20 ± .07 (22-23)
Sensitive (general)........................	.02	.20 ± .07 (22-23)
	Larger Correlations (Negative)	
Discord between parents.....................	.02	-.20 ± .05
	Not Calculable	
Leading others into bad conduct..............	.04	(n.c.)

*Rank order of girls' correlations.

TABLE 30—Continued

Other Correlations (Positive to Negative)

Slovenly, .19 and -.03; Stubborn, .19 and .09; Temper display, .19 and -.09; Teasing other children, .18 (boys); Apprehensive, .18 and .05; Changeable moods, .18 and .02; Irritable, .18 and .06; Follower, .18 and .03; Loitering, .17 and -.10; Sulky, .17 and .14; Worry over specific fact, .16 and .11; Unpopular, .15 and -.09; Question of hypophrenia, .15 and .08; Grouped: disobedient, etc., .15 and .06; Inattentive in school, .13 and .17; Underweight, .13 and .08; Boastful, "show-off," .12 and .16; Refusal to attend school, .12 and .16; Masturbation, .12 and .15; Crying spells, .12 and .18; Sensitive over specific fact, .12 and .10; Speech defect, .12 and .08; Grouped: sensitive or worrisome, etc., .12 and .18; Disobedient, .11 and .05; Fantastical lying, .11 and .16; Vocational guidance, .11 and -.08; Object of teasing, .10 and -.01; Grouped: lack of interest in school, etc., .10 and .15; Destructive, .09 and .17; Swearing (general), .09 (boys); Overinterest in opposite sex, .09 (girls); Conduct prognosis bad, .09 and .11; Victim of sex abuse, .09 (girls); Finicky food habits, .08 and -.04; Nail-biting, .08 and .08; Selfish, .08 and .12; Bashful, .08 and -.03; Lues, .08 and .03; Lying, .07 and .14; Violence, .07 and .01; Stuttering, .07 (boys); Popular, .07 and -.05; Staying out late at night, .06 and -.18; Truancy from school, .06 and .03; Overinterest in sex matters, .06 and .13; Excuseforming, .06 and -.12; Irregular attendance at school, .06 and -.00; Grouped: swearing, etc., .06 and .04; Grouped: depressed, etc., .06 and .13; Stealing, .05 and .13; Enuresis, .04 and .14; Incorrigible, .04 and .12; Truancy from home, .04 and .06; Unhappy, .04 and .07; Bossy, .03 and -.13; Disturbing influence in school, .03 and .08; Rude, .03 and .08; Vicious home conditions, .03 and -.13; Grouped: egocentric, etc., .03 and .10; Lack of interest in school, .02 and .08; Clean, .02 and .16; Repressed, .01 and .18; Leader, .01 and -.09; Immoral home conditions, .01 and -.07; Temper tantrums, .00 and .04; Sex denied entirely, .00 and -.18; Quarrelsome, -.01 and -.09; Egocentric, -.02 and .03; Psychneurotic, -.02 and .05; Complaining of bad treatment by other children, -.02 (boys); Gang, -.04 (boys); Grouped: fighting, etc., -.04 and .01; Hatred or jealousy of sibling, -.04 and .19; Brother in penal detention, -.05 and -.07; Irregular habits, -.06 and -.02; Defiant, -.06 and .01; Bad companions, -.08 and -.00; Fighting, -.08 and .17; Feeble-minded sibling, -.08 and -.09; Retardation in school, -.09 and .08; Smoking, -.10 (boys); Threatening violence, -.11 (boys); Sex delinquency (coitus), -.16 and -.03

substantial correlations in the .30's and among boys moderate correlations in the .20's. Restlessness in sleep also yielded a substantial correlation of .31 + .06 among girls but a low coefficient of .13 among boys.

Four behavior notations showed moderate correlations in the .20's with absent-mindedness among both sexes: question of change of personality, poor work in school, slow or dull manner, and lack of initiative or ambition. Eight notations showed moderate correlations in the .20's for boys but low coefficients below .20 for girls: seclusiveness, laziness, restlessness, emotional instability, temper tantrums or display (including irritable temperament, undifferentiated), contrariness, neurological defect (unspecified),

and <u>attractive manner</u>.   Nine additional notations showed moderate
correlations in the .20's for girls but low positive coefficients
below .20 for boys: <u>inferiority feelings</u>, <u>depressed spells</u>,
"<u>spoiled child</u>," <u>sensitiveness in general</u>, <u>preference for younger
children as playmates</u>, <u>oversuggestibility</u>, <u>sullenness</u>, <u>exclusion
from school</u>, and <u>former convulsions</u>.

The only considerable negative correlation with <u>absent-
mindedness</u> was among girls, -.20 + .05 for <u>discord between parents</u>,
the boys' coefficient being about zero.

Our six sex items showed only negligible relationships with
<u>absent-mindedness</u>, the coefficients falling between -.18 and .15.

Among our seven physical or psychophysical notations, <u>ques-
tion or diagnosis of encephalitis</u> showed the suggestive correlations
of .25 + .02 and .31 + .09 for boys and girls respectively. <u>Neu-
rological defect (unspecified)</u> among boys also yielded a moderate
correlation of .21 + .05. All other coefficients in this field
were low or negligible.

Among our four home or familial notations only one was of
statistically significant size, the <u>negative</u> coefficient of -.20
+ .05 among girls for <u>discord between parents</u>.

CHAPTER XXII

SECLUSIVENESS AND REPRESSED MANNER

The notations <u>seclusiveness</u> and <u>repressed manner</u> among girls indicate a somewhat similar behavior in view of their very substantial inter-correlation of .40 $\pm$ .07 (Table 31), but among boys this correlation was low, .16.

TABLE 31

CORRELATION WITH "SECLUSIVE"

	Boys	Girls
Personality-total...........................	.33 ± .02	.31 ± .03
Conduct-total...............................	.17 ± .02	.17 ± .03
Police arrest...............................	.03 ± .03	-.03 ± .05
	Larger Correlations (Positive)	
Queer.......................................	.39 ± .04	.25 ± .07 (14)*
Unhappy.....................................	.38 ± .05	.28 ± .07 (10-13)
Listless....................................	.34 ± .04	.41 ± .06 (2)
Sensitive (general)........................	.30 ± .04	.28 ± .06 (10-13)
Grouped: depressed, etc...................	.30 ± .04	.37 ± .05 (4-6)
Absent-minded...............................	.29 ± .04	-.13
Spoiled child..............................	.29 ± .04	.09
Complaining of bad treatment by other children	.29 ± .05	....
Psychoneurotic.............................	.28 ± .05	.10
Grouped: sensitive or worrisome, etc........	.27 ± .03	.28 ± .05 (10-13)
Contrary...................................	.26 ± .05	.28 ± .07 (10-13)
Selfish....................................	.25 ± .05	.19
Bashful....................................	.25 ± .03	.31 ± .05 (9)
Daydreaming................................	.25 ± .04	.37 ± .06 (4-6)
Sensitive over specific fact..............	.25 ± .03	.23 ± .05 (17)
Depressed..................................	.24 ± .04	.36 ± .06 (7)
Worry over specific fact..................	.24 ± .05	.37 ± .07 (4-6)
Grouped: dull, slow, etc..................	.24 ± .03	.34 ± .04 (8)
Question of change of personality.........	.23 ± .05	.20 ± .07 (19-22)
Lack of initiative........................	.23 ± .05	.18
Inferiority feelings......................	.23 ± .04	.48 ± .06 (1)
Inefficient in work, play, etc............	.22 ± .05	.17

*Rank order of girls' correlations.

TABLE 31—Continued

	Boys	Girls
Mental conflict	.22 ± .05	.24 ± .08 (15-16)
Hatred or jealousy of sibling	.21 ± .05	.13
Apprehensive	.21 ± .04	.14
Unpopular	.21 ± .05	.15
Repressed	.16	.40 ± .07 (3)
Lazy	.19	.24 ± .06 (15-16)
Sullen	.18	.22 ± .06 (18)
Finicky food habits	.02	.20 ± .06 (19-22)
Irregular sleep habits	.16	.20 ± .07 (19-22)
Grouped: "nervous," etc	.13	.20 ± .04 (19-22)
	Larger Correlations (Negative)	
Leader	-.19	-.20 ± .07

Other Correlations (Positive to Negative)

Headaches, .19 and -.01; Stubborn, .17 and .17; Distractible, .17 and .16; Irresponsible, .16 and .01; Lack of interest in school, .16 and .12; Loitering, .16 and -.03; Irritable, .16 and .11; Object of teasing, .16 and .01; Poor work in school, .16 and .19; Preference for younger children, .15 and -.04; Vocational guidance, .15 and .12; Refusal to attend school, .14 and .18; Quarrelsome, 114 and .03; Irregular attendance at school, .14 and .06; Grouped: lack of interest in school, .14 and .15; Defiant, .13 and .19; Underweight, .13 and .11; Speech defect, .13 and .11; Discord between parents, .13 and .19; Inattentive in school, .12 and .11; "Nervous," .12 and .05; Grouped: egocentric, etc., .12 and .11; Slovenly, .11 and .09; Sulky, .11 and .08; Threatening violence, .11 (boys); Violence, .11 and .15; Slow, dull, .11 and .18; Grouped: disobedient, etc., .11 and .08; Leading others into bad conduct, .10 and .03; Smoking, .10 (boys); Clean, .10 and .08; Neurological defect, .10 and .12; Vicious home conditions, .10 and -.11; Grouped: fighting, etc., .10 and .03; Nailbiting, .09 and -.04; Overinterest in sex matters, .09 and .14; Changeable moods, .09 and .16; Crying spells, .09 and .16; Feeble-minded sibling, .09 and -.04; Grouped: temper, etc., .09 and .03; Sex denied entirely, .09 and .14; Fantastical lying, .08 and -.03; Temper display, .08 and -.07; Truancy from home, .08 and .01; Restless, .08 and .17; Question of hypophrenia, .07 and .06; Victim of sex abuse, .07 (girls); Boastful, "show-off," .06 and .08; Disobedient, .06 and -.08; Teasing other children, .06 (boys); Rude, .06 and .05; Restless in sleep, .06 and .01; Emotional instability, .06 and .11; Grouped: swearing, etc., .06 and .10; Lying, .05 and .05; Masturbation, .05 and .02; Bossy, .03 and .10; Enuresis, .03 and .05; Incorrigible, .03 and .02; Gang, .03 (boys); Destructive, .02 and .03; Staying out late at night, .02 and -.03; Truancy from school, .02 and .05; Excuse-forming, .02 and .04; Egocentric, .02 and .09; Attractive manner, .02 and -.09; Temper tantrums, .01 and -.00; Brother in penal detention, .01 and -.04; Immoral home conditions, .01 and -.04; Exclusion from school, -.00 and .15; Bad companions, -.01 and .00; Conduct prognosis bad, -.01 and .06; Stealing, -.02 and .06; Oversuggestible, -.02 and .17; Disturbing influence in school, -.03 and -.01; Swearing (general), -.03 (boys); Stuttering, -.03 (boys); Former convulsions, -.03 and -.04; Question of encephalitis, -.03 and .06; Lues, -.03 and -.07; Retardation in school, -.06 and -.07; Follower, -.06 and -.01; Fighting, -.07 and -.11; Sex delinquency (coitus), -.09 and -.04; Overinterest in opposite sex, -.13 (girls); Popular, -.19 and -.14

The notation seclusiveness, unresponsiveness, ("patient prefers to play alone or be by himself") appears to be of substantial importance from the standpoint of personality deviation but of almost negligible interest in the conduct sphere. It was noted among 254 of our 2,113 White boys, or 12.0 per cent, and among 106 of our 1,181 White girls, or 9.0 per cent. It was of relatively frequent occurrence among our clinic cases.

Its highest correlation was among girls, .48 + .06 with inferiority feelings, the corresponding coefficient among boys being only moderate, .23 + .05. Two other notations also yielded fairly high correlations among girls, .41 + .06 for listlessness and .40 + .07 for repressed manner, the corresponding coefficients among boys being .34 + .04 and .16 respectively. Among boys the highest correlations were for queer behavior, .39 + .04, and for unhappy appearance or manner, .38 + .05, the corresponding correlations for girls being of moderate size, .25 + .07 and .28 + .07 respectively. Sensitiveness in general yielded the substantial correlations of .30 + .04 among boys and .28 + .06 among girls. The following five personality problems showed substantial correlations with seclusiveness in the .30's among girls and moderate correlations in the .20's among boys: daydreaming, depressed spells, worry over some specific fact, bashfulness, and dull or slow manner (including listlessness and lack of initiative, undifferentiated).

Four behavior problems showed moderate correlations in the .20's for both sexes: sensitiveness over some specific fact, mental conflict, question of change of personality, and contrariness. Ten behavior traits showed moderate correlations in the .20's for boys but low or negligible coefficients falling between -.13 and .19 for girls: psychoneurotic trends, apprehensiveness, "spoiled child," hatred or jealousy of sibling, inefficiency in work, play, etc., absent-mindedness, lack of initiative, selfishness, unpopularity, and (calculated for boys only) complaining of bad treatment by other children. Five behavior notations showed moderate correlations in the .20's for girls but low positive correlations below .20 for boys: laziness, sullenness, finicky food habits, "nervousness" or restlessness (undifferentiated), and irregular sleep habits.

The only negative correlations of statistically significant size were for "leader" with coefficients of -.19 and -.20 + .07

among boys and girls respectively.

Among the sex notations, physical and psychophysical notations, and home or familial conditions all coefficients, 31 in number, were too low to be of "statistical significance" within our
data.

Staff notation or question of repressed or suppressed manner appeared to be of negligible significance as far as its correlations with out three criteria of "importance or seriousness" are
concerned. It was noted among 138 of our boys, or 6.5 per cent,
and among only 45 of our girls, or 3.8 per cent.

Its highest correlation was found among girls, .40 ± .07
with seclusiveness, the corresponding coefficient for boys being
only .16 (Table 32). Among girls the three personality problems,

TABLE 32

CORRELATIONS WITH "REPRESSED"

	Boys	Girls
Personality-total..............................	.06 ± .03	.21 ± .04
Conduct-total..................................	.08 ± .03	.09 ± .05
Police arrest..................................	.03 ± .04	-.14 ± .07
	Larger Correlations (Positive)	
Daydreaming....................................	.22 ± .05	.21 ± .08 (14-18)*
Sullen...	.21 ± .05	.20 ± .08 (19)
Apprehensive...................................	.21 ± .04	.19
Mental conflict................................	.21 ± .06	.21 ± .10 (14-18)
Unhappy..	.20 ± .06	.32 ± .09 (2)
Sensitive over specific fact...................	.20 ± .04	.17
Seclusive......................................	.16	.40 ± .07 (1)
Depressed......................................	.08	.31 ± .08 (3)
Contrary.......................................	.18	.30 ± .09 (4)
Boastful, "show-off"..........................	.05	.29 ± .07 (5-7)
Grouped: sensitive or worrisome, etc.........	.17	.29 ± .10 (5-7)
Grouped: dull, slow, etc.....................	.04	.29 ± .06 (5-7)
Grouped: depressed, etc......................	.13	.27 ± .07 (8)
Sensitive (general)...........................	.16	.25 ± .08 (9)
Listless.......................................	.15	.24 ± .08 (10)
Fighting.......................................	-.02	.23 ± .04 (11-13)
Object of teasing..............................	.14	.23 ± .08 (11-13)
Queer..	-.02	.23 ± .09 (11-13)

*Rank order of girls' correlations.

TABLE 32—Continued

	Boys	Girls
Hatred or jealousy of sibling.................	.18	.21 ± .09 (14-18)
Inferiority feelings...........................	.17	.21 ± .09 (14-18)
Clean..	.10	.21 ± .08 (14-18)
Destructive....................................	.02	.20 ± .08 (19-20)
		Larger Correlations (Negative)
Emotional instability..........................	-.26 ± .06	.06
Feeble-minded sibling..........................	-.10	-.30 ± .08
Speech defect..................................	.05	-.30 ± .08
Follower.......................................	.04	-.29 ± .08
Temper display.................................	-.11	-.24 ± .08
Leader...	-.02	-.24 ± .08
Question of hypophrenia........................	-.12	-.22 ± .06
Selfish..	.04	-.21 ± .04
		Not Calculable
Question of encephalitis.......................	(n.c.)	.08
Loitering......................................	-.01	(n.c.)
Conduct prognosis bad..........................	-.09	(n.c.)

Other Correlations (Positive to Negative)

Masturbation, .19 and .04; Lazy, .15 and .10; Question of change of personality, .14 and .12; Sulky, .14 and .11; Lying, .13 and .05; Bashful, .13 .14; Immoral home conditions, .13 and .17; Preference for younger children, .12 and .00; Refusal to attend school, .10 and -.08; Fantastical lying, .10 and -.08; Teasing other children, .09 (boys); Rude, .09 and .03; Stealing, .09 and .03; Overinterest in sex matters, .09 and .06; Victim of sex abuse, .08 (girls); Bad companions, .07 and -.03; Finicky food habits, .07 and .15; Enuresis, .07 and .12; Changeable moods, .07 and .03; Restless in sleep, .07 and .09; Sex denied entirely, .07 and .12; Lues, .07 and .11; Discord between parents; .06 and .16; Spoiled child, .06 and .04; Oversuggestible, .06 and -.00; Temper tantrums, .06 and .18; Stubborn, .06 and .02; Slovenly, .06 and -.01; Quarrelsome, .05 and .08; Violence, .05 and -.04; Sex delinquency (coitus), .05 and -.08; Crying spells, .05 and .15; Worry over specific fact, .05 and .18; Popular, .05 and -.08; Vicious home conditions, .04 and -.06; Neurological defect, .04 and .06; Attractive manner, .04 and .03; Lack of initiative, .04 and .13; Slow, dull, .04 and .18; Nail-biting, .04 and .06; Irresponsible, .04 and -.17; Bossy, .03 and .15; Inattentive in school, .03 and .16; Gang, .03 (boys); Stuttering, .03 (boys); Grouped: swearing, etc., .03 and .10; Grouped: lack of interest in school, etc., .02 and .17; Grouped: fighting, etc., .02 and .11; Poor work in school, .02 and .09; Overinterest in opposite sex, .02 (girls); Defiant, .01 and .04; Inefficient in work, play, etc., .01 and .11; Lack of interest in school, .01 and .12; Smoking, .01 (boys); Truancy from home, .01 and -.01; Absent-minded, .01 and .18; Irregular sleep habits, .01 and .05; "Nervous," .01 and .15; Grouped: "nervous," etc., .01 and .09; Grouped: egocentric, etc., .01 and .05; Brother in penal detention, .00 and -.15; Truancy from school, .00 and .09; Leading others into bad conduct, .00 and .12; Excuse-forming, -.00 and

TABLE 32—Continued

.09; Headaches, -.01 and .07; Complaining of bad treatment by other children, -.01 (boys); Egocentric, -.02 and .13; Vocational guidance, -.02 and .01; Irregular attendance at school, -.02 and .14; Swearing (general), -.03 (boys); Disobedient, -.03 and .04; Incorrigible, -.04 and -.00; Restless, -.04 and -.00; Grouped: disobedient, etc., -.04 and .04; Underweight, -.05 and .14; Former convulsions, -.06 and -.13; Threatening violence, -.06 (boys); Irritable, -.07 and .06; Distractible, -.07 and .05; Exclusion from school, -.07 and .03; Grouped: temper, etc., -.07 and .07; Psychoneurotic, -.08 and -.18; Staying out late at night, -.08 and -.19; Disturbing influence in school, -.08 and .01; Retardation in school, -.10 and -.13; Unpopular, -.10 and .09

unhappiness, depressed spells, and contrariness, yielded substantial correlations ranging from .30 to .32, while among boys the corresponding correlations ranged from .08 to .20.

Three personality notations—daydreaming, mental conflict, and sullenness—showed moderate correlations ranging from .20 to .22 among both sexes. Apprehensiveness and sensitiveness over some specific fact showed moderate correlations of .21 + .04 and .20 + .04 among boys and slightly lower correlations of .19 and .17 among girls. Eleven notations showed moderate correlations in the .20's among girls but low correlations ranging from -.02 to .18 among boys: sensitiveness in general, inferiority feelings, queer behavior, hatred or jealousy of sibling, dull or slow manner (undifferentiated), listlessness, object of teasing by other children, fighting, destructiveness, boastful or "show-off" manner, and clean habits or appearance.

With repressed manner eight case notations showed negative correlations larger than -.20. For emotional instability the coefficients were -.26 + .06 and .06 for boys and girls respectively. Among girls both notations speech defect and feeble-minded sibling yielded correlations of -.30, with negligible coefficients for boys. The following five behavior traits yielded negative coefficients among girls ranging from -.21 to -.29 with negligible coefficients among boys: temper display, selfishness, question of hypophrenia, "leader," and "follower."

In three instances a tetrachoric r could not be calculated: there were no instances in which repressed children also were thought to have suffered from encephalitis or noted as given to loitering or wandering, or considered by the examining staff to manifest an unfavorable conduct prognosis.

All six sex notations showed negligible correlations with
repressed manner. Among physical or psychophysical notations
speech defect among girls yielded a negative correlation of -.30
+ .08, the other coefficients being negligible. Among home or familial conditions there were no significant relationships discovered.

CHAPTER XXIII

QUEER BEHAVIOR AND CHANGE OF PERSONALITY

The two closely interrelated notations "queerness"—patient
considered by others as mentally peculiar, very erratic, or "crazy"—
etc., and question of change of personality, mental status, or behavior dating from some specific time or episode, which were of
very frequent occurrence among our cases, appear to be of major
seriousness from a clinical standpoint, especially in the sphere
of personality deviation. In the conduct sphere their importance
is also substantial, though not as an indicator of "juvenile delinquency" in the strict sense. Both notations were more characteristic of the older children among our group, especially question
of change of personality.[1] Their correlations with chronological
age, however, and with intelligence quotient (IQ), though positive,
were low.[2]

Queer behavior was noted among 118, or 5.6 per cent, of our
2,113 White boys and among 67, or 5.7 per cent, of our 1,181 White
girls.

Among boys its bi-serial correlation of .52 ± .03 with the
personality-total was the highest of the 160 coefficients computed
with this criterion,[3] being exceeded only by the correlations with
the notations staff diagnosis or question of incipient psychosis
(unspecified) and staff diagnosis or question of dementia praecox,
which were of definitely pathological nature (Table 33). Among
girls its bi-serial r of .61 ± .03 was the second highest coefficient, being exceeded by only one other coefficient among the 134
computed with this criterion. With the conduct-total criterion the
boys' bi-serial r of .32 ± .03 indicated a mediocre association,
but among girls its correlation of .64 ± .03 indicated a very meaningful relationship, being exceeded by only 8 of the 134 coeffi-

---

[1]I, 205-6, Fig. 48.

[2]Tables 9 (p. 128) and 10 (p. 130).   [3]Table 6 (p. 89).

TABLE 33

CORRELATIONS WITH "QUEER"

	Boys	Girls
Personality-total............................	.52 ± .03	.61 ± .03
Conduct-total................................	.32 ± .03	.64 ± .03
Police arrest................................	.08 ± .04	.19 ± .06
	Larger Correlations (Positive)	
Question of change of personality............	.40 ± .05	.53 ± .06 (1)*
Seclusive....................................	.39 ± .04	.25 ± .07 (47-48)
Absent-minded................................	.37 ± .05	.29 ± .08 (34-38)
"Nervous"....................................	.32 ± .04	.35 ± .05 (18-23)
Daydreaming..................................	.31 ± .05	.39 ± .06 (10-12)
Inefficient in work, play, etc..............	.30 ± .06	.29 ± .07 (34-38)
Question of encephalitis.....................	.30 ± .10	.29 ± .09 (34-38)
Object of teasing............................	.30 ± .04	.35 ± .07 (18-23)
Hatred or jealousy of sibling...............	.30 ± .06	.21 ± .08 (54-59)
Contrary....................................	.29 ± .06	.29 ± .08 (34-38)
Emotional instability.......................	.28 ± .06	.34 ± .07 (24-26)
Psychoneurotic...............................	.28 ± .06	.23 ± .08 (49-53)
Refusal to attend school....................	.28 ± .05	.11
Unpopular....................................	.27 ± .06	.35 ± .08 (18-23)
Inferiority feelings........................	.27 ± .05	.28 ± .08 (39-42)
Grouped: temper, etc.......................	.26 ± .04	.21 ± .05 (54-59)
Grouped: "nervous," etc....................	.26 ± .04	.37 ± .05 (13-15)
Complaining of bad treatment by other children	.26 ± .06	....
Mental conflict.............................	.26 ± .06	.32 ± .09 (29-32)
Listless....................................	.26 ± .05	.18
Threatening violence........................	.26 ± .06	....
Stubborn....................................	.26 ± .04	.25 ± .06 (47-48)
Apprehensive................................	.25 ± .04	.13
Changeable moods............................	.25 ± .05	.43 ± .06 (5)
Irritable...................................	.25 ± .04	.09
Quarrelsome.................................	.24 ± .04	.33 ± .06 (27-28)
Grouped: fighting, etc.....................	.24 ± .04	.36 ± .05 (16-17)
Headaches...................................	.24 ± .06	.18
Swearing (general)..........................	.24 ± .06	....
Grouped: swearing, etc....................	.21 ± .05	.33 ± .07 (27-28)
Grouped: dull, slow, etc..................	.21 ± .04	.09
Violence....................................	.20 ± .05	.46 ± .06 (2)
Restless in sleep...........................	.20 ± .04	.39 ± .06 (10-12)
Grouped: depressed, etc....................	.11	.44 ± .06 (3-4)
Depressed...................................	.18	.44 ± .07 (3-4)
Leading others into bad conduct.............	-.02	.41 ± .08 (6)
Boastful, "show-off"........................	.16	.40 ± .07 (7-9)
Irregular sleep habits......................	.16	.40 ± .07 (7-9)
Grouped: disobedient, etc..................	.18	.40 ± .04 (7-9)
Defiant.....................................	.00	.39 ± .06 (10-12)

*Rank order of girls' correlations.

TABLE 33—Continued

	Boys	Girls
Overinterest in opposite sex....................	....	.37 ± .06 (13-15)
Temper tantrums...............................	.19	.37 ± .06 (13-15)
Destructive...................................	.19	.36 ± .08 (16-17)
Disturbing influence in school................	.13	.35 ± .07 (18-23)
Fantastical lying.............................	.18	.35 ± .07 (18-23)
Fighting......................................	.13	.35 ± .04 (18-23)
Stealing......................................	.11	.34 ± .05 (24-26)
Lying...	.10	.34 ± .05 (24-26)
Distractible..................................	.15	.32 ± .06 (29-32)
Sulky...	-.01	.32 ± .07 (29-32)
Rude..	.19	.32 ± .06 (29-32)
Unhappy.......................................	-.02	.30 ± .08 (33)
Restless......................................	.07	.29 ± .05 (34-38)
Exclusion from school.........................	.18	.28 ± .07 (39-42)
Crying spells.................................	.18	.28 ± .05 (39-42)
Incorrigible..................................	.15	.28 ± .06 (39-42)
Slovenly......................................	.07	.27 ± .06 (43-44)
Oversuggestible...............................	-.09	.27 ± .06 (43-44)
Masturbation..................................	.19	.26 ± .06 (45-46)
Bossy...	.06	.26 ± .07 (45-46)
Disobedient...................................	.07	.23 ± .06 (49-53)
Sensitive (general)..........................	.15	.23 ± .07 (49-53)
Repressed.....................................	-.02	.23 ± .09 (49-53)
Grouped: sensitive or worrisome, etc.........	.10	.23 ± .05 (49-53)
Bad companions................................	-.00	.21 ± .06 (54-59)
Excuse-forming................................	-.05	.21 ± .07 (54-59)
Sensitive over specific fact..................	.11	.21 ± .06 (54-59)
Neurological defect...........................	.16	.21 ± .07 (54-59)
Grouped: egocentric, etc.....................	.13	.20 ± .06 (60-65)
Speech defect.................................	.04	.20 ± .07 (60-65)
Worry over specific fact......................	.04	.20 ± .09 (60-65)
Overinterest in sex matters...................	.19	.20 ± .07 (60-65)
Loitering.....................................	.13	.20 ± .08 (60-65)
Irresponsible.................................	.14	.20 ± .08 (60-65)
	Larger Correlations (Negative)	
Leader..	-.29 ± .05	.03
Feeble-minded sibling.........................	-.23 ± .06	-.04

Other Correlations (Positive to Negative)

Bashful, .19 and .07; Victim of sex abuse, .19 (girls); Temper display, .18 and -.14; Underweight, .16 and .00; Spoiled child, .16 and .10; Truancy from home, .16 and .19; Lazy, .16 and .17; Inattentive in school, .15 and -.04; Egocentric, .15 and .18; Grouped: lack of interest in school, etc., .15 and .15; Nail-biting, .14 and .18; Finicky food habits, .13 and .04; Staying out late at night, .13 and .19; Slow, dull, .13 and -.01; Lack of initiative, .13 and .19; Immoral home conditions, .12 and -.04; Former convulsions, .12 and -.00; Teasing other children, .11 (boys); Sullen, .11 and .18; Stuttering, .10 (boys); Lack of interest in school, .10 and .18; Preference for younger children, .09

TABLE 33—Continued

and -.09; Question of hypophrenia, .09 and .02; Selfish, .08 and .19; Attractive manner, .07 and -.05; Vocational guidance, .07 and .03; Poor work in school, .06 and .08; Sex denied entirely, .06 and .10; Conduct prognosis bad, .06 and .09; Enuresis, .05 and .08; Smoking, .05 (boys); Sex delinquency (coitus), .04 and .17; Discord between parents, .03 and .11; Vicious home conditions, .02 and .16; Truancy from school, .02 and .13; Lues, .00 and .10; Irregular attendance at school, -.03 and -.09; Follower, -.06 and -.10; Brother in penal detention, -.06 and -.10; Retardation in school, -.08 and -.18; Gang, -.09 (boys); Clean, -.09 and .07; Popular, -.11 and .04

cients calculated with this criterion of seriousness.[4] For <u>police arrest</u> the tetrachoric correlations of .08 + .04 and .19 + .06 among boys and girls respectively indicated a low or negligible degree of relationship.

Among the separate notations its highest correlations among both boys and girls were .40 + .05 and .53 + .06 respectively with <u>question of change of personality</u>. Among girls there were seven additional high coefficients ranging from .40 to .46: <u>violence, leading others into bad conduct</u>, <u>boastful or "show-off" manner, disobedience or incorrigibility</u> (undifferentiated), <u>irregular sleep habits, depressed spells,</u> and <u>changeable moods or attitudes,</u> the corresponding correlations for boys ranging from -.02 to .25.

Three personality difficulties yielded substantial correlations ranging from .30 to .39 among both sexes: <u>daydreaming, "nervousness,"</u> and <u>object of teasing by other children.</u> <u>Overinterest in opposite sex</u> (calculated for girls only) also yielded the substantial coefficient of .37 + .06. Five notations yielded substantial coefficients ranging from .30 to .39 among boys and moderate coefficients in the .20's for girls: <u>seclusiveness, absent-mindedness, inefficiency in work, play,</u> etc., <u>hatred or jealousy of sibling,</u> and <u>question or diagnosis of encephalitis.</u> Six behavior traits among girls yielded substantial correlations in the .30's but moderate correlations in the .20's among boys: <u>unpopularity, mental conflict, emotional instability, restlessness in sleep, quarrelsomeness,</u> and <u>swearing or bad language</u> (undifferentiated). The following twelve conduct and personality difficulties yielded substantial correlations in the .30's among girls but low correlations below .20 for the boys: <u>defiant attitude, temper</u>

[4] Table 7 (p. 98).

tantrums, destructiveness, fighting, disturbing influence in school, stealing, lying, fantastical lying, rudeness, sulkiness, distractibility, and unhappiness.

The following five behavior traits showed moderate correlations in the .20's for both sexes: psychoneurotic trends, inferiority feelings, contrariness, stubbornness, and temper tantrums or display (undifferentiated). Complaining of bad treatment by other children and threatening violence, for which only the boys' coefficients were computed, also showed moderate correlations in the .20's. Six behavior notations among boys also showed moderate correlations in the .20's but low positive correlations ranging from .09 to .18 among girls: refusal to attend school, irritable temperament or disposition, apprehensiveness, listlessness, dull or slow manner (undifferentiated) and headaches. A large group of twenty-one miscellaneous notations showed moderate correlations in the .20's among girls but low or negligible correlations below .20 for the boys: restlessness, incorrigibility, disobedience, exclusion from school, bad companions, excuse-forming attitude, egocentricity or selfishness (undifferentiated), bossy manner, crying spells, sensitiveness in general, sensitiveness over some specific fact, worry over some specific fact, oversuggestibility, slovenliness, irresponsibility, loitering or wandering, repressed manner, masturbation, overinterest in sex matters, neurological defect (unspecified), and speech defect (other than stuttering).

Only two statistically significant negative correlations were found with queer behavior, both among boys: -.29 + .05 for "leader" and -.23 + .06 for feeble-minded sibling. The corresponding coefficients for girls were negligible.

Among the six sex notations, overinterest in opposite sex (calculated for girls only) yielded the substantial correlation of .37 + .06 with queer behavior. Among girls overinterest in sex matters and masturbation also showed the moderate correlations of .20 + .07 and .26 + .06 respectively. The other notations in this field—sex delinquency (coitus), sex misbehavior denied entirely, and (calculated for girls only) victim of sex abuse—showed low coefficients ranging from .04 to .19.

Among the seven physical or psychophysical notations there were three instances in which correlations of moderate size were found. Question or diagnosis of encephalitis yielded correlations of .30 ± .10 and .29 ± .09 for boys and girls respectively. Among girls neurological defect (unspecified) and speech defect (other than stuttering) showed moderate correlations of .21 ± .07 and .20 ± .07 respectively. The other notations in this field—enuresis, underweight condition, lues, and stuttering (calculated for boys only)—showed low positive coefficients ranging from .00 to .16.

The four home or familial notations—discord between parents, vicious and immoral home conditions, and brother in penal detention—showed only non-significant correlations ranging from -.10 to .16.

Question of change of personality was noted in 123 cases, or 5.8 per cent of our boys, and among 65 cases, or 5.5 per cent of our girls. With personality-total its bi-serial correlations of .45 ± .03 and .53 ± .03 for boys and girls respectively indicate a high degree of clinical importance. Among girls its correlation with conduct-total was also high, .54 ± .03, but among boys only moderate, .29 ± .03. With the police-arrest criterion of "juvenile delinquency" its tetrachoric correlations were low and of little meaning.

Its highest correlations were with question or diagnosis of encephalitis for both boys and girls, the tetrachoric coefficients being .65 ± .05 and .66 ± .07 respectively (Table 34).

TABLE 34

CORRELATIONS WITH "QUESTION OF CHANGE OF PERSONALITY"

	Boys	Girls
Personality-total	.45 ± .03	.53 ± .03
Conduct-total	.29 ± .03	.54 ± .03
Police arrest	.14 ± .04	.12 ± .06
	Larger Correlations (Positive)	
Question of encephalitis	.65 ± .05	.66 ± .07 (1)*
Changeable moods	.62 ± .04	.36 ± .06 (16-18)
Queer	.40 ± .05	.53 ± .06 (2)
Neurological defect	.36 ± .05	.42 ± .06 (4)

*Rank order of girls' correlations.

TABLE 34—Continued

	Boys	Girls
Irregular sleep habits........................	.34 ± .05	.35 ± .08 (19-21)
Grouped: temper, etc.......................	.33 ± .04	.38 ± .07 (9-11)
Irritable.....................................	.33 ± .04	.26 ± .06 (43-45)
Contrary......................................	.32 ± .06	.15
Emotional instability........................	.31 ± .06	.41 ± .07 (5)
Crying spells................................	.30 ± .04	.32 ± .05 (28-31)
Absent-minded................................	.29 ± .05	.26 ± .08 (43-45)
Complaining of bad treatment by other children	.29 ± .06	....
Grouped: "nervous," etc.....................	.29 ± .03	.36 ± .05 (16-18)
Depressed....................................	.28 ± .05	.34 ± .07 (22-23)
Object of teasing............................	.26 ± .04	.25 ± .07 (46-48)
Headaches....................................	.26 ± .06	.29 ± .07 (34-37)
Grouped: depressed, etc.....................	.25 ± .05	.29 ± .06 (34-37)
Disobedient..................................	.24 ± .04	.32 ± .05 (28-31)
Smoking......................................	.24 ± .05	....
Psychoneurotic...............................	.24 ± .06	.35 ± .08 (19-21)
Restless in sleep............................	.24 ± .04	.36 ± .06 (16-18)
Seclusive....................................	.23 ± .05	.20 ± .07 (59)
Finicky food habits..........................	.22 ± .05	.09
Listless.....................................	.22 ± .05	.15
Unpopular....................................	.22 ± .06	.43 ± .08 (3)
Inferiority feelings.........................	.22 ± .05	.16
Grouped: disobedient, etc...................	.22 ± .04	.37 ± .05 (12-15)
Mental conflict..............................	.21 ± .06	.29 ± .09 (34-37)
Restless.....................................	.21 ± .04	.27 ± .05 (40-42)
"Nervous"....................................	.21 ± .04	.32 ± .06 (28-31)
Refusal to attend school.....................	.20 ± .05	.23 ± .09 (50-52)
Unhappy......................................	.20 ± .06	.19
Temper tantrums..............................	.19	.40 ± .06 (6)
Lack of interest in school...................	.17	.39 ± .06 (7-8)
Distractible.................................	.05	.39 ± .06 (7-8)
Exclusion from school........................	.04	.38 ± .07 (9-11)
Leading others into bad conduct..............	.03	.38 ± .08 (9-11)
Incorrigible.................................	.18	.37 ± .05 (12-15)
Grouped: lack of interest in school, etc.....	.13	.37 ± .06 (12-15)
Grouped: swearing, etc......................	.19	.37 ± .07 (12-15)
Violence.....................................	.09	.35 ± .07 (19-21)
Truancy from home............................	.13	.34 ± .04 (22-23)
Spoiled child................................	.19	.33 ± .06 (24-27)
Destructive..................................	.11	.33 ± .08 (24-27)
Disturbing influence in school...............	.08	.33 ± .07 (24-27)
Fantastical lying............................	.06	.33 ± .07 (24-27)
Defiant......................................	.19	.32 ± .07 (28-31)
Staying out late at night....................	.03	.30 ± .06 (32-33)
Fighting.....................................	.05	.30 ± .05 (32-33)
Loitering....................................	.18	.29 ± .08 (34-37)
Conduct prognosis bad........................	.07	.28 ± .09 (38-39)
Apprehensive.................................	.11	.28 ± .06 (38-39)
Inefficient in work, play, etc...............	.08	.27 ± .07 (40-42)
Rude...	.10	.27 ± .06 (40-42)
Grouped: fighting, etc......................	.15	.26 ± .05 (43-45)
Lying..	.04	.25 ± .05 (46-48)

TABLE 34—Continued

	Boys	Girls
Grouped: sensitive or worrisome, etc.........	.18	.25 ± .05 (46-48)
Selfish...	.16	.24 ± .04 (49)
Overinterest in opposite sex...................	....	.23 ± .06 (50-52)
Daydreaming....................................	.14	.23 ± .07 (50-52)
Stubborn.......................................	.16	.22 ± .06 (53-54)
Truancy from school...........................	.16	.22 ± .06 (53-54)
Irresponsible.................................	.16	.21 ± .08 (55-58)
Stealing......................................	.11	.21 ± .05 (55-58)
Worry over specific fact......................	.19	.21 ± .09 (55-58)
Grouped: egocentric, etc.....................	.09	.21 ± .06 (55-58)
	Larger Correlations (Negative)	
Feeble-minded sibling.........................	-.22 ± .06	.06
Follower......................................	-.21 ± .05	.06
Brother in penal detention...................	.03	-.24 ± .07
Lues..	.11	-.20 ± .07

Other Correlations (Positive to Negative)

Teasing other children, .19 (boys); Sensitive over specific fact, .17 and .19; Masturbation, .17 and .17; Sullen, .17 and .19; Quarrelsome, .17 and .16; Temper display, .15 and .09; Swearing (general), .14 (boys); Sensitive (general) .14 and .13; Repressed, .14 and .12; Victim of sex abuse, .14 (girls); Attractive manner, .14 and .06; Irregular attendance at school, .14 and .06; Grouped: dull, slow, etc., .13 and .04; Speech defect, .13 and .13; Threatening violence, .13 (boys); Nail-biting, .12 and .13; Gang, .12 (boys); Sulky, .12 and .17; Discord between parents, .11 and -.02; Slovenly, .10 and .15; Poor work in school, .09 and .06; Preference for younger children, .09 and .14; Boastful, "show-off," .08 and .14; Egocentric, .08 and .13; Underweight, .07 and -.02; Lack of initiative, .07 and -.12; Bashful, .07 and -.03; Popular, .06 and .19; Clean, .05 and .02; Excuse-forming, .05 and .15; Bossy, .04 and .19; Sex denied entirely, .03 and .17; Sex delinquency (coitus), .03 and .13; Bad companions, .02 and .19; Slow, dull, .02 and -.02; Question of hypophrenia, .02 and .15; Inattentive in school, .01 and .08; Former convulsions, .00 and .07; Overinterest in sex matters, -.00 and .13; Vicious home conditions, -.02 and .17; Lazy, -.02 and .09; Enuresis, -.04 and .07; Stuttering, -.05 (boys); Vocational guidance, -.05 and .00; Hatred or jealousy of sibling, -.06 and .12; Oversuggestible, -.08 and .16; Leader, -.09 and .07; Immoral home conditions, -.13 and .06; Retardation in school, -.15 and -.10

These correlations (which incidentally are also the highest coefficients found for question or diagnosis of encephalitis, as will be noted later in Table 117 [p. 542]) establish its importance as a clinical item, since it is an outstanding symptom of encephalitis

or encephalitic residual.[5] <u>Changeable moods</u> also showed the very
high correlation of .62 $\pm$ .04 among boys and a substantial correlation among girls of .36 $\pm$ .06.

 <u>Queer behavior</u> among girls yielded the high correlation of
.53 $\pm$ .06 and among boys a very substantial correlation of .40 $\pm$
.05. <u>Neurological defect (unspecified)</u> and <u>emotional instability</u>
among girls also yielded fairly high correlations of .42 $\pm$ .06 and
.41 $\pm$ .07 respectively, with corresponding substantial correlations
among boys of .36 $\pm$ .05 and .31 $\pm$ .06. <u>Unpopularity</u> and <u>temper
tantrums</u> among girls also yielded fairly high correlations of .43
$\pm$ .08 and .40 $\pm$ .06 respectively, with lower corresponding coefficients of .22 $\pm$ .06 and .19 among boys.

 <u>Irregular sleep habits</u> and <u>crying spells</u> yielded substantial correlations in the .30's for both sexes with <u>question of
change of personality</u>. <u>Irritable temperament</u> and <u>contrariness</u>
among boys also yielded substantial correlations in the .30's but
somewhat lower corresponding coefficients for girls (.26 $\pm$ .06 and
.15). Five personality and conduct problems yielded substantial
correlations in the .30's for girls and moderate coefficients in
the .20's for boys: <u>psychoneurotic trends</u>, "<u>nervousness</u>," <u>rest-
lessness in sleep</u>, <u>depressed mood or spells</u>, and <u>disobedience</u>.
Fifteen additional conduct and personality problems yielded substantial correlations in the .30's for girls but low positive coefficients ranging from .03 to .19 among boys: <u>distractibility</u>,
<u>lack of interest in school</u>, <u>exclusion from school</u>, <u>disturbing in-
fluence in school</u>, <u>leading others into bad conduct</u>, <u>incorrigibility</u>,
<u>destructiveness</u>, <u>violence</u>, <u>fighting</u>, <u>defiant attitude</u>, <u>truancy from
home</u>, <u>staying out late at night</u>, <u>swearing or bad language</u> (undifferentiated), <u>fantastical lying</u>, and "<u>spoiled child</u>."

 The following seven notations showed correlations in the
.20's with <u>question of change of personality</u> for both sexes: <u>ab-
sent-mindedness</u>, <u>mental conflict</u>, <u>seclusiveness</u>, <u>object of teasing
by other children</u>, <u>restlessness</u>, <u>refusal to attend school</u>, and
<u>headaches</u>. The two notations which were calculated for boys only,
<u>smoking</u> and <u>complaining of bad treatment by other children</u>, and one
calculated for girls only, <u>overinterest in the opposite sex</u>, also

---

[5]L. Jenkins and Luton Ackerson, "The Behavior of Encephalitic Children,"
<u>American Journal of Orthopsychiatry</u>, IV (1934), 499-507.

showed moderate coefficients in the .20's. The following four behavior difficulties among boys showed moderate correlations in the
.20's but low positive coefficients below .20 for the girls: inferiority feelings, unhappiness, listlessness, and finicky food
habits. The following fourteen behavior problems among girls
showed moderate correlations in the .20's but low positive correlations below .20 for boys: sensitiveness or worrisomeness (undifferentiated), worry over specific fact, daydreaming, apprehensiveness, loitering or wandering, inefficiency in work, play, etc.,
irresponsibility, rudeness, selfishness, stubbornness, truancy from
school, stealing, lying, and staff notation of unfavorable conduct
prognosis.

Among four notations there were negative correlations of
moderate size with question of change of personality, ranging from
-.20 to -.24: feeble-minded sibling and "follower" among boys and
brother in penal detention and lues among girls, the corresponding
coefficients for the other sex being low, ranging from .03 to .11.

Among our six sex notations the only significant negative
correlation was the moderate one of .23 + .06 with overinterest in
opposite sex, which was calculated for girls only.

Among the physical or psychophysical notations there were
three instances of meaningful correlation. Question or diagnosis
of encephalitis, as we have seen, yielded the remarkably high tetrachoric coefficients of .65 + .05 and .66 + .07 for boys and girls
respectively. Neurological defect (unspecified) yielded the very
significant correlations of .36 + .05 and .42 + .06 for boys and
girls respectively. These two neurological notations, it will be
recalled, also showed meaningful correlations with queer behavior,
as well as with question of change of personality. Diagnosis or
question of lues among girls showed the barely significant negative
correlation of -.20 + .07, this coefficient being not quite thrice
its probable error. For enuresis, underweight condition, speech
defect, and stuttering (calculated for boys only), the correlations
were low for both sexes, ranging from -.05 to .13.

Among home and familial conditions the only correlation of
significant size was the negative coefficient among girls of -.24
+ .07 for brother in penal detention.

CHAPTER XXIV

CHANGEABLE MOODS AND EMOTIONAL INSTABILITY

Changeable, excitable moods and attitudes in our study was a case notation based upon a statement of the parent or other lay informant, while staff notation or question of emotional instability was a formal statement resulting from the clinical examination and was usually made by the psychiatrist. These two notations showed substantial to fairly high correlations ranging from .26 to .49 with both personality-total and conduct-total and are thus of some importance as clinical indications. With the police-arrest criterion the correlations with changeable moods were negligible, but those with emotional instability were of moderate size in the .20's.

Among our 2,113 White boys changeable moods was noted in 219 instances, or 10.4 per cent. Among our 1,181 White girls it was noted in 144 cases, or 12.2 per cent.

Its highest correlation was among boys, .62 ± .04 with question of change of personality, the girls' coefficient also being substantial, .36 ± .06 (Table 35). Its next highest coefficient

TABLE 35

CORRELATIONS WITH "CHANGEABLE MOODS"

	Boys	Girls
Personality-total..............................	.30 ± .02	.49 ± .03
Conduct-total.................................	.26 ± .02	.43 ± .03
Police arrest.................................	.02 ± .03	.03 ± .05
	Larger Correlations (Positive)	
Question of change of personality.............	.62 ± .04	.36 ± .06 (14-17)*
Irritable.....................................	.43 ± .03	.35 ± .04 (18-21)

*Rank order of girls' correlations.

TABLE 35—Continued

	Boys	Girls
Grouped: temper, etc.	.39 ± .03	.43 ± .04 (3-6)
"Nervous"	.34 ± .03	.40 ± .04 (9)
Sensitive (general)	.33 ± .04	.35 ± .05 (18-21)
Restless	.30 ± .03	.43 ± .04 (3-6)
Depressed	.28 ± .04	.51 ± .05 (1)
Rude	.27 ± .04	.34 ± .04 (22)
Temper display	.27 ± .04	.27 ± .06 (41-44)
Threatening violence	.27 ± .05	....
Grouped: fighting, etc.	.27 ± .03	.28 ± .04 (36-40)
Daydreaming	.26 ± .04	.37 ± .05 (13)
Complaining of bad treatment by other children	.26 ± .05	....
Contrary	.25 ± .05	.36 ± .06 (14-17)
Queer	.25 ± .05	.43 ± .06 (3-6)
Restless in sleep	.25 ± .04	.33 ± .05 (23-26)
Finicky food habits	.24 ± .04	.12
Temper tantrums	.24 ± .04	.39 ± .05 (10-11)
Inefficient in work, play, etc.	.23 ± .05	.31 ± .06 (29-30)
Violence	.23 ± .04	.31 ± .06 (29-30)
Crying spells	.23 ± .03	.43 ± .04 (3-6)
Excuse-forming	.23 ± .04	.27 ± .05 (41-44)
Grouped: sensitive or worrisome, etc.	.23 ± .03	.33 ± .04 (23-26)
Fantastical lying	.22 ± .03	.42 ± .05 (7-8)
Masturbation	.22 ± .03	.20 ± .05 (60-64)
Psychoneurotic	.22 ± .05	.35 ± .06 (18-21)
Nail-biting	.21 ± .04	.26 ± .04 (45)
Grouped: disobedient, etc.	.21 ± .03	.23 ± .04 (53-57)
Grouped: depressed, etc.	.21 ± .04	.44 ± .05 (2)
Quarrelsome	.20 ± .04	.25 ± .05 (46-49)
Neurological defect	.20 ± .04	.33 ± .05 (23-26)
Boastful, "show-off"	.15	.42 ± .05 (7-8)
Question of encephalitis	.09	.39 ± .07 (10-11)
Grouped: swearing, etc.	.16	.38 ± .05 (12)
Unpopular	.16	.36 ± .06 (14-17)
Selfish	.12	.36 ± .04 (14-17)
Bossy	.10	.35 ± .05 (18-21)
Irregular sleep habits	.19	.33 ± .06 (23-26)
Grouped: egocentric, etc.	.13	.32 ± .04 (27-28)
Emotional instability	.12	.32 ± .06 (27-28)
Sulky	.17	.30 ± .06 (31-32)
Fighting	.16	.30 ± .04 (31-32)
Destructive	.18	.29 ± .06 (33-35)
Leading others into bad conduct	.07	.29 ± .07 (33-35)
Exclusion from school	.07	.29 ± .06 (33-35)
Distractible	.12	.28 ± .05 (36-40)
Egocentric	.09	.28 ± .05 (36-40)
Overinterest in opposite sex	....	.28 ± .05 (36-40)
Sullen	.05	.28 ± .05 (36-40)
Defiant	.16	.27 ± .05 (41-44)
Spoiled child	.18	.27 ± .05 (41-44)
Stubborn	.15	.25 ± .04 (46-49)
Conduct prognosis bad	.12	.25 ± .07 (46-49)
Unhappy	.03	.25 ± .06 (46-49)

TABLE 35—Continued

	Boys	Girls
Headaches..	.17	.24 ± .06 (50-52)
Inferiority feelings............................	.11	.24 ± .06 (50-52)
Sensitive over specific fact....................	.07	.24 ± .05 (50-52)
Incorrigible....................................	.11	.23 ± .04 (53-57)
Preference for younger children................	.12	.23 ± .06 (53-57)
Leader..	.12	.23 ± .06 (53-57)
Worry over specific fact........................	.07	.23 ± .07 (53-57)
Sex denied entirely.............................	-.13	.21 ± .07 (58-59)
Clean...	.07	.21 ± .05 (58-59)
Object of teasing..............................	.09	.20 ± .06 (60-64)
Hatred or jealousy of sibling..................	.06	.20 ± .07 (60-64)
Lack of interest in school.....................	.02	.20 ± .05 (60-64)
Disturbing influence in school.................	.16	.20 ± .06 (60-64)
	Larger Correlations (Negative)	
Brother in penal detention.....................	-.12	-.25 ± .05
	Not Calculable	
Feeble-minded sibling..........................	(n.c.)	-.07

Other Correlations (Positive to Negative)

Absent-minded, .18 and .02; Follower, .17 and .04; Irresponsible, .16 and .08; Teasing other children, .16 (boys); Slovenly, .16 and .08; Smoking, .16 (boys); Former convulsions, .16 and -.02; Inattentive in school, .15 and .09; Overinterest in sex matters, .15 and .03; Speech defect, .15 and .07; Swearing (general), .14 (boys); Apprehensive, .14 and .17; Disobedient, .13 and .12; Lying, .12 and .18; Stealing, .12 and .18; Enuresis, .11 and .01; Repressed, .07 and .03; Popular, .07 and .03; Gang, .06 (boys); Underweight, .06 and -.01; Lack of initiative, .05 and .05; Vicious home conditions, .05 and -.14; Bashful, .04 and .07; Refusal to attend school, .11 and -.03; Oversuggestible, .11 and .07; Listless, .09 and .07; Seclusive, .09 and .16; Grouped: lack of interest in school, etc., .09 and .18; Discord between parents, .08 and .04; Attractive manner, .04 and .02; Lazy, .03 and .01; Truancy from home, .03 and .17; Victim of sex abuse, .03 (girls); Poor work in school, .03 and .04; Grouped: dull, slow, etc., .02 and -.04; Sex delinquency (coitus), -.00 and .03; Bad companions, -.01 and .07; Staying out late at night, -.01 and .18; Mental conflict, -.01 and .15; Loitering, -.02 and .09; Truancy from school, -.02 and -.01; Slow, dull, -.04 and -.05; Stuttering, -.05 (boys); Vocational guidance, -.07 and -.01; Immoral home conditions, -.09 and -.02; Question of hypophrenia, -.10 and -.05; Lues, -.12 and .01; Retardation in school, -.13 and -.13; Irregular attendance at school, -.14 and -.01

Omitted—Grouped: "nervous," etc.

was among girls, .51 + .05, with depressed spells, the corresponding coefficient for boys, .28 + .04, being only moderate. Four behavior difficulties yielded substantial to fairly high correlations ranging from .30 to .43 among both sexes: irritable temperament, "nervousness," restlessness, and sensitiveness in general. The following thirteen case notations yielded substantial correlations ranging from .30 to .43 among girls and moderate correlations in the .20's for boys: daydreaming, queer behavior, inefficiency in work, play, etc., psychoneurotic trends, fantastical lying, restless in sleep, sensitiveness or worrisomeness (undifferentiated), crying spells, contrariness, rudeness, violence, temper tantrums, and neurological defect (unspecified). Ten case notations showed substantial correlations ranging from .30 to .42 among girls but low positive coefficients ranging from .09 to .19 among boys: question or diagnosis of encephalitis, boastful or "show-off" manner, swearing or bad language (undifferentiated), bossy manner, fighting, selfishness, unpopularity, sulkiness, emotional instability, and irregular sleep habits.

Changeable moods showed moderate correlations in the .20's among both sexes for the following six behavior problems: temper display, quarrelsomeness, disobedience or incorrigibility (undifferentiated), excuse-forming attitude, nail-biting, and masturbation. Also overinterest in the opposite sex (computed for girls only) and two other notations, threatening violence and complaining of bad treatment by other children (calculated for boys only), showed moderate correlations in the .20's. Finicky food habits among boys showed the moderate correlation of .24 + .04 but among girls the low correlation of .12. Among girls a large group of twenty-four case notations showed moderate correlations in the .20's but low coefficients ranging from -.13 to .18 among boys: destructiveness, defiant attitude, stubbornness, incorrigibility, sullenness, leading others into bad conduct, exclusion from school, disturbing influence in school, lack of interest in school, distractibility, egocentricity, hatred or jealousy of sibling, "spoiled child," unhappiness, inferiority feelings, sensitiveness over specific fact, worry over specific fact, preference for younger children as playmates, object of teasing by other children, sex misbehavior denied entirely, staff notation of unfavorable conduct prognosis, headaches, "leader," and clean habits.

The only considerable negative correlation with changeable moods was the moderate one of -.25 + .05 among girls with brother in penal detention, the corresponding boys' coefficient being -.12.

Among the sex notations masturbation showed moderate correlations in the .20's for both sexes. Overinterest in opposite sex, which was calculated for girls only, yielded a moderate correlation of .28 + .05. Sex misbehavior denied entirely among girls showed the moderate correlation of .21 + .07, while among boys the correlation was negative, -.13. Sex delinquency (coitus), overinterest in sex matters, and (calculated for girls only) victim of sex abuse yielded only negligible correlations.

Among the seven physical or psychophysical case notations the only significant indications were for question or diagnosis of encephalitis, which yielded the coefficients of .39 + .07 among girls with a negligible coefficient of .09 among boys, and for neurological defect (unspecified), which yielded coefficients of .20 + .04 and .33 + .05 for boys and girls respectively.

Among home or familial notations the only correlation of significant size with changeable moods was the negative one of -.25 + .05 among girls for brother in penal detention.

Staff notation or question of emotional instability or emotional lability yielded correlations bearing considerable similarity to those for changeable moods, one point of difference, however, being that emotional instability among both sexes showed moderate correlations in the .20's with the police-arrest criterion, while changeable moods indicated an essentially zero relationship. Emotional instability was noted among 104, or 4.9 per cent, of our boys and among 85, or 7.2 per cent, of our girls.

Its highest correlation among both sexes was with question or diagnosis of encephalitis, the tetrachoric coefficients being .46 + .06 and .48 + .08 (Table 36). Staff notation of unfavorable conduct prognosis among boys also yielded the fairly high correlation of .40 + .06 with the substantial correlation of .32 + .07 among girls. Three personality notations also yielded similar correlations ranging from .47 down to .41 among girls: psychoneurotic trends, question of change of personality, and restlessness, the corresponding coefficients for boys ranging from .31 down to .21. Violence and "nervousness" or restlessness (including irritable

TABLE 36

CORRELATIONS WITH "EMOTIONAL INSTABILITY"

	Boys	Girls
Personality-total............................	.31 ± .03	.45 ± .03
Conduct-total................................	.28 ± .03	.44 ± .03
Police arrest................................	.20 ± .04	.23 ± .05
	Larger Correlations (Positive)	
Question of encephalitis.....................	.46 ± .06	.48 ± .08 (1)*
Conduct prognosis bad........................	.40 ± .06	.32 ± .07 (12-16)
Grouped: temper, etc........................	.36 ± .04	.28 ± .05 (24-25)
Grouped: "nervous," etc.....................	.35 ± .04	.32 ± .04 (12-16)
Violence.....................................	.32 ± .05	.30 ± .06 (20-22)
Question of change of personality...........	.31 ± .06	.41 ± .07 (3-4)
Psychoneurotic...............................	.29 ± .07	.47 ± .06 (2)
Neurological defect..........................	.29 ± .05	.25 ± .06 (34-38)
Queer..	.28 ± .06	.34 ± .07 (9-11)
Staying out late at night....................	.28 ± .05	.12
Irritable....................................	.27 ± .04	.26 ± .05 (28-33)
Object of teasing...........................	.27 ± .04	.11
Crying spells...............................	.25 ± .04	.38 ± .05 (5-6)
Loitering....................................	.25 ± .05	.08
Quarrelsome..................................	.24 ± .05	.27 ± .05 (26-27)
Temper display..............................	.23 ± .04	.00
Incorrigible................................	.23 ± .04	.29 ± .05 (23)
Complaining of bad treatment by other children	.22 ± .06	....
Absent-minded...............................	.22 ± .06	.18
Fighting....................................	.22 ± .05	.25 ± .07 (34-38)
Fantastical lying...........................	.21 ± .03	.31 ± .07 (17-19)
Inefficient in work, play, etc..............	.21 ± .06	.36 ± .07 (7-8)
Temper tantrums.............................	.21 ± .05	.34 ± .06 (9-11)
"Nervous"...................................	.21 ± .05	.25 ± .04 (34-38)
Restless....................................	.21 ± .04	.41 ± .05 (3-4)
Vicious home conditions.....................	.21 ± .07	-.20 ± .07
Grouped: fighting, etc.....................	.21 ± .06	.24 ± .05 (39-41)
Depressed...................................	.21 ± .06	.26 ± .07 (28-33)
Grouped: depressed, etc....................	.20 ± .05	.22 ± .06 (43-45)
Grouped: disobedient, etc..................	.20 ± .04	.17
Exclusion from school.......................	.20 ± .05	.38 ± .07 (5-6)
Boastful, "show-off"........................	.18	.36 ± .07 (7-8)
Daydreaming.................................	.04	.34 ± .06 (9-11)
Grouped: sensitive or worrisome, etc.......	.11	.32 ± .05 (12-16)
Unpopular...................................	.10	.32 ± .07 (12-16)
Changeable moods............................	.12	.32 ± .06 (12-16)
Destructive.................................	.05	.31 ± .07 (17-19)
Leading others into bad conduct.............	.11	.31 ± .08 (17-19)
Spoiled child...............................	.10	.30 ± .06 (20-22)
Irregular sleep habits......................	.17	.30 ± .07 (20-22)

*Rank order of girls' correlations.

TABLE 36—Continued

	Boys	Girls
Irresponsible...............................	.05	.28 ± .07 (24-25)
Headaches..................................	.08	.27 ± .07 (26-27)
Grouped: swearing, etc....................	.11	.26 ± .07 (28-33)
Mental conflict............................	.16	.26 ± .08 (28-33)
Sensitive over specific fact...............	.11	.26 ± .06 (28-33)
Rude.......................................	.06	.26 ± .05 (28-33)
Disturbing influence in school............	.13	.25 ± .07 (34-38)
Distractible..............................	.16	.25 ± .06 (34-38)
Egocentric................................	.18	.24 ± .06 (39-41)
Lying.....................................	.13	.24 ± .05 (39-41)
Overinterest in opposite sex..............	....	.23 ± .05 (42)
Excuse-forming............................	.08	.22 ± .06 (43-45)
Bossy.....................................	.07	.22 ± .07 (43-45)
	Larger Correlations (Negative)	
Repressed.................................	-.26 ± .06	.06
Lack of initiative........................	.06	-.30 ± .07
	Not Calculable	
Brother in penal detention................	(n.c.)	-.06

Other Correlations (Positive to Negative)

Stealing, .18 and .09; Refusal to attend school, .17 and .04; Worry over specific fact, .16 and .14; Contrary, .16 and .08; Bad companions, .15 and .17; Slovenly, .15 and .07; Irregular attendance at school, .14 and -.01; Masturbation, .14 and .16; Defiant, .14 and .18; Speech defect, .13 and .07; Inferiority feelings, .12 and .17; Overinterest in sex matters, .12 and .13; Restless in sleep, .11 and -.02; Grouped: egocentric, etc., .11 and .17; Stuttering, .10 (boys); Sulky, .10 and .14; Stubborn, .10 and .15; Gang, .10 (boys); Finicky food habits, .10 and .06; Truancy from home, .09 and .18; Sensitive (general), .09 and .13; Leader, .08 and .11; Apprehensive, .08 and .16; Threatening violence, .08 (boys); Swearing (general), .08 (boys); Disobedient, .08 and .19; Sullen, .07 and .17; Lues, .07 and -.01; Immoral home conditions, .07 and -.01; Unhappy, .06 and .16; Seclusive, .06 and .11; Lack of interest in school, .05 and .08; Truancy from school, .05 and .13; Oversuggestible, .05 and .06; Discord between parents, .05 and .01; Former convulsions, .04 and -.05; Sex delinquency (coitus), .04 and .17; Lazy, .03 and .09; Follower, .03 and -.06; Grouped: lack of interest in school, etc., .03 and .07; Smoking, .02 (boys); Enuresis, .02 and .08; Listless, .01 and -.02; Question of hypophrenia, .01 and -.07; Poor work in school, -.01 and -.02; Attractive manner, -.02 and .10; Inattentive in school, -.03 and -.04; Popular, -.03 and .11; Victim of sex abuse, -.03 (girls); Hatred or jealousy of sibling, -.04 and .15; Underweight, -.04 and .10; Nail-biting, -.06 and .13; Feeble-minded sibling, -.07 and .15; Preference for younger children, -.07 and .06; Bashful, -.08 and -.04; Vocational guidance, -.08 and -.04; Clean, -.10 and .07; Retardation in school, -.10 and -.17; Selfish, -.11 and .08; Grouped: dull, slow, etc., -.13 and -.16; Teasing other children, -.13 (boys); Slow, dull, -.17 and -.15; Sex denied entirely, -.18 and -.03

temperament and changeable moods, undifferentiated) yielded substantial correlations in the .30's for both boys and girls. The
following six notations among girls yielded substantial correlations in the .30's, with corresponding moderate coefficients in
the .20's for boys: crying spells, temper tantrums, queer behavior, fantastical lying, inefficiency in work, play, etc., and exclusion from school. The following nine behavior problems also
yielded substantial correlations in the .30's for girls but low
positive coefficients below .20 for boys: changeable moods,
"spoiled child," boastful or "show-off" manner, daydreaming, sensitiveness or worrisomeness (undifferentiated), unpopularity, destructiveness, leading others into bad conduct, and irregular sleep
habits.

　　　　The following seven case notations showed moderate correlations in the .20's with emotional instability for both sexes:
irritable temperament, "nervousness," quarrelsomeness, fighting,
incorrigibility, depressed spells, and neurological defect (unspecified), and also complaining of bad treatment by other children,
which was computed for boys only. The following six notations
among boys also showed moderate correlations in the .20's but low
coefficients below .20 for the girls: temper display, staying out
late at night, loitering or wandering, absent-mindedness, object
of teasing by other children, and vicious home conditions. The
following twelve notations among girls also showed moderate correlations below .20 for the boys: mental conflict, sensitiveness
over specific fact, excuse-forming attitude, irresponsibility, egocentricity, bossy manner, rudeness, distractibility, lying, swearing or bad language (undifferentiated), disturbing influence in
school, and headaches. Overinterest in opposite sex, for which
only the girls' correlation was computed, also showed a moderate
correlation of .23 $\pm$ .05.

　　　　There were three negative correlations of significant size
with emotional instability: among boys repressed manner showed the
moderate coefficient of -.26 $\pm$ .06, the corresponding correlation
among girls being only .06. Lack of initiative or ambition among
girls yielded a correlation of -.30 $\pm$ .07, while among boys its
correlation was .06. Vicious home conditions showed a curious divergence in its correlations, the coefficient for girls being a
negative -.20 $\pm$ .07, while among boys it was a positive .21 $\pm$ .07.

Among the six sex notations the only correlation of significant size was .23 $\pm$ .05 for <u>overinterest in opposite sex</u> (calculated for girls only). For <u>masturbation</u> the two coefficients of .14 and .16 may be suggestive but were below the conventional standard of "statistical significance."

Among the seven physical or psychophysical notations we have already noted the striking correlations of .46 $\pm$ .06 and .48 $\pm$ .08 with <u>question or diagnosis of encephalitis</u> and also the moderate correlations of .29 $\pm$ .05 and .25 $\pm$ .06 with <u>neurological defect (unspecified)</u>. The other five notations in this field (<u>enuresis</u>, <u>underweight condition</u>, <u>diagnosis or question of lues</u>, <u>speech defect</u>, and <u>stuttering</u>) showed only negligible correlations with <u>emotional instability</u>.

Among the four home or familial notations the only coefficients of significant size were the two seemingly contradictory correlations with <u>vicious home conditions</u> (.21 $\pm$ .07 and -.20 $\pm$ .07 for boys and girls respectively).

CHAPTER XXV

SUSPECTED MENTAL DEFICIENCY (HYPOPHRENIA)

Question of mental deficiency, hypophrenia, or inadequate intelligence in the present data is not a staff notation but indicates the "lay" opinion expressed by a parent, friend, teacher, employer, or a social agency not equipped with psychological or psychiatric service sufficient to render a formal diagnosis. This notation does not always indicate a patent mental deficiency but may occasionally mean an intellectual capacity too low for the given school studies or employment of the patient at the time of examination. For example, a fourth-year high-school student may be handicapped by "inadequate intelligence" and still be far from "mentally deficient." (In fact, among the 3,294 boys and girls considered in the present volume, 23 with IQ's of 100 or more were so noted, one of whom achieved a Stanford-Binet IQ above 125.) The coefficients in Table 37 should therefore be carefully contrasted with those for intelligence quotient (IQ).[1]

Question of hypophrenia was noted among 454 of our 2,113 White boys, or 21.5 per cent, and among 283 of our 1,181 White girls, or 24.0 per cent, and was one of the most frequent reasons for which children were referred for examination in this clinic.[2]

The correlations of question of hypophrenia with our three criteria of seriousness or "ominousness" (personality-total, conduct-total, and police arrest) were very low, ranging from -.15 to .04 (Table 37). In this connection it should be pointed out that question of hypophrenia was not counted in the personality-total because its inclusion would probably have weighted the personality total too much in the direction of low intelligence, especially since another similar notation, slow or dull manner, was already included in the personality-total. Following the conventional

---

[1] Table 10, p. 130.

[2] H. M. Adler, Eleventh Annual Report of the Criminologist, 1927-1928 (Springfield, Ill.: Department of Public Welfare, 1928), p. 83, Table V.

TABLE 37

CORRELATIONS WITH "QUESTION OF HYPOPHRENIA"

	Boys	Girls
Personality-total............................	.04 ± .02	-.05 ± .03
Conduct-total................................	-.03 ± .02	-.03 ± .03
Police arrest................................	-.03 ± .03	-.15 ± .04
	Larger Correlations (Positive)	
Retardation in school........................	.55 ± .02	.48 ± .03 (1)*
Slow, dull...................................	.29 ± .03	.24 ± .04 (6)
Conduct prognosis bad........................	.26 ± .05	.04
Grouped: dull, slow, etc.....................	.23 ± .03	.20 ± .03 (9)
Speech defect................................	.22 ± .04	.15
Feeble-minded sibling........................	.20 ± .04	.27 ± .05 (3)
Poor work in school..........................	.20 ± .06	.23 ± .03 (7)
Preference for younger children..............	.18	.32 ± .05 (2)
Exclusion from school........................	.15	.26 ± .05 (4)
Underweight..................................	.04	.25 ± .04 (5)
Lues...	.16	.22 ± .05 (8)
	Larger Correlations (Negative)	
Psychoneurotic...............................	-.29 ± .04	-.21 ± .05
Worry over specific fact.....................	-.23 ± .04	-.10
Grouped: egocentric, etc....................	-.17	-.28 ± .04
Immoral home conditions......................	-.19	-.24 ± .05
Depressed....................................	-.00	-.23 ± .04
Vocational guidance..........................	-.10	-.23 ± .04
Repressed....................................	-.12	-.22 ± .06
Overinterest in sex matters..................	-.01	-.22 ± .05
Selfish......................................	-.06	-.22 ± .04
Hatred or jealousy of sibling................	-.10	-.21 ± .06
Egocentric...................................	-.19	-.21 ± .04

*Rank order of girls' correlations.

Other Correlations (Positive to Negative)

Object of teasing, .17 and .18; Absent-minded, .15 and .08; Irregular attendance at school, .14 and -.08; Former convulsions, .14 and -.10; Oversuggestible, .14 and .02; Distractible, .14 and .18; Threatening violence, .14 (boys); Violence, .13 and .11; Headaches, .12 and -.05; Apprehensive, .12 and .10; Complaining of bad treatment by other children, .11 (boys); Loitering, .10 and .15; Swearing (general), .09 (boys); Lack of initiative, .09 and .10; Queer, .09 and .02; Question of encephalitis, .09 and .08; Incorrigible, .07 and .07; Temper display, .07 and -.06; Bashful, .07 and .10; Seclusive, .07 and .06; Enuresis, .05 and .16; Fantastical lying, .05 and -.02; Follower, .05 and .09; Brother in penal detention, .04 and -.10; Restless in sleep, .04 and .02; Sulky,

TABLE 37—Continued

.04 and .01; Grouped: fighting, etc., .03 and .02; Neurological defect, .03
and .09; Leading others into bad conduct, .03 and .14; Teasing other children,
.02 (boys); Question of change of personality, .02 and .15; "Nervous," .02 and
.01; Stuttering, .02 (boys); Grouped: temper, etc., .02 and .02; Emotional instability, .01 and -.07; Slovenly, .01 and .08; Disobedient, .01 and .04; Destructive, .00 and .11; Temper tantrums, .00 and .02; Inefficient in work, play,
etc., -.00 and .04; Refusal to attend school, -.00 and -.07; Sullen, -.00 and
.05; Listless, -.00 and .08; Grouped: swearing, etc., -.01 and .03; Vicious
home conditions, -.01 and .16; Spoiled child, -.01 and -.08; Sex delinquency
(coitus), -.01 and -.08; Staying out late at night, -.01 and -.04; Disturbing
influence in school, -.01 and .12; Contrary, -.02 and -.01; Fighting, -.02 and
-.06; Lack of interest in school, -.02 and .04; Irregular sleep habits, -.02
and .06; Unpopular, -.02 and .11; Masturbation, -.03 and .00; Truancy from
school, -.03 and -.06; Truancy from home, -.03 and -.05; Quarrelsome, -.03 and
.06; Nail-biting, -.03 and .06; Overinterest in opposite sex, -.03 (girls); Crying spells, -.04 and .06; Irritable, -.04 and -.04; Attractive manner, -.04 ·
and -.18; Grouped: "nervous," etc., -.04 and .04; Grouped: lack of interest
in school, etc., -.05 and -.03; Sensitive (general), -.05 and -.08; Restless,
-.05 and .05; Finicky food habits, -.06 and -.15; Lying, -.06 and -.08; Grouped:
disobedient, etc., -.06 and -.01; Inferiority feelings, -.06 and -.07; Grouped:
depressed, etc., -.07 and -.13; Stubborn, -.07 and -.08; Gang, -.07 (boys); Inattentive in school, -.07 and -.15; Bad companions, -.07 and -.16; Boastful,
"show-off," -.08 and -.05; Rude, -.08 and .12; Stealing, -.08 and -.08; Popular, -.08 and -.14; Victim of sex abuse, -.09 (girls); Mental conflict, -.10
and -.18; Changeable moods, -.10 and -.05; Lazy, -.10 and .06; Irresponsible,
-.10 and .01; Bossy, -.11 and -.05; Daydreaming, -.11 and -.15; Excuse-forming,
-.11 and -.05; Sex denied entirely, -.11 and -.01; Leader, -.11 and .19; Discord between parents, -.11 and -.11; Clean, -.12 and -.17; Smoking, -.13 (boys);
Defiant, -.19 and -.11; Grouped: sensitive or worrisome, etc., -.15 and -.09;
Unhappy, -.16 and -.03; Sensitive over specific fact, -.16 and -.08

beliefs, we have listed it as "physical or constitutional defect"
in our indexing of the original case-record material.[3]

The highest correlations with question of hypophrenia among
both sexes were with intelligence quotient (IQ), which yielded the
negative bi-serial r of -.57 + .02 and -.53 + .02 as noted in chapter xiii. The next highest correlations were the positive tetrachoric r's of .55 + .02 and .48 + .03 for boys and girls respectively with retardation in school.

With the specific behavior and other notations there were
relatively few correlations of statistically significant size. The
coefficients were about equally divided between positive and negative signs. The following three notations among both sexes yielded
moderate positive coefficients ranging from .20 to .29: slow or

---

[3] I, 73-76, Table 6.

dull manner, poor work in school, and feeble-minded sibling. Moderate negative correlations of -.29 + .04 and -.21 + .05 were found for psychoneurotic trends among boys and girls respectively.

Speech defect and staff notation of unfavorable conduct prognosis among boys showed moderate positive correlations in the .20's but corresponding low correlations below .20 among girls. Worry over some specific fact or episode among boys showed the moderate negative correlation of -.23 + .04 and among girls the low negative coefficient of -.10. The following four notations among girls showed moderate positive correlations ranging from .22 to .32 but low positive correlations below .20 for boys: preference for younger children as playmates, exclusion from school, underweight condition, and lues. The following eight notations showed moderate negative tetrachoric correlations in the -.20's among girls, the corresponding coefficients for boys being negative and low, ranging from -.01 to -.19: selfishness, egocentricity, hatred or jealousy of sibling, depressed spells, repressed manner, overinterest in sex matters, immoral home conditions, and "request for vocational guidance."

Among our six sex notations the only correlation of significant size with question of hypophrenia was the negative of -.22 + .05 among girls with overinterest in sex matters. All the other correlations in this field were a low negative, ranging from .00 to -.11.

Among the seven physical or psychophysical traits there were three instances in which the correlations were of statistically significant size. Among girls underweight condition and lues showed moderate correlations of .25 + .04 and .22 + .05 respectively. Speech defect (other than stuttering) showed the moderate correlation of .22 + .04 for boys. The remaining coefficients in this field were low, ranging from .02 to .16.

Among the four home or familial notations there was only one coefficient of significant size, -.24 + .05 among girls for immoral home conditions, the other correlations in this field ranging from -.19 to .16.

Since question of hypophrenia is the "opposite" of intelligence quotient (IQ), a comparison of the coefficients (chiefly tetrachoric r's) in Table 37 with those for IQ (chiefly bi-serial r's)

is interesting. The intercolumnar product-moment correlations were
-.81 ± .02 and -.57 ± .04 for boys and girls respectively. Among
the 120 pairs of boys' coefficients, 83 pairs were of unlike sign
and only 37 were of like sign. Among 115 pairs of coefficients
among girls, 69 were of unlike sign, and 46 were of like sign. If
both measures were truly valid measures of intelligence (or lack
of intelligence), the intercolumnar correlations should approach
a negative unity. In view of the inadequacies in both measures,
especially those due to the subjectivity of the "lay" notation of
<u>question of mental deficiency or inadequate intelligence</u>, these
intercolumnar correlations are probably as satisfactory as may be
expected. (This phenomenon of inconsistency in the correlations
of antithetical traits has been discussed in I, 134-35 and 249-50,
and this volume, pp. 45 and 204-5.)

CHAPTER XXVI

SLOW OR DULL MANNER; LISTLESSNESS;
LACK OF INITIATIVE

The three generally similar personality problems—slow or dull manner, listlessness or indifferent attitude, and lack of initiative or ambition—showed a moderate degree of intercorrelation with one another and also general similarity in their correlations with "outside" traits. All three appear to be of little importance as far as their correlations with our three criteria of "seriousness" indicate, the correlation coefficients ranging from -.16 to .19.

Slow or dull manner was noted among 541 of our 2,113 White boys, or 25.6 per cent, and 285 of our 1,181 White girls, or 24.1 per cent. It was one of the most often noted of behavior traits among our case records. It was significantly correlated with low intelligence, the correlation with intelligence quotient for boys and girls being, respectively, -.26 ± .04 and -.24 ± .03 (Table 10, p. 130).[1]

Of the many correlations computed, only a comparative few were of statistically significant size. Its largest correlations were for listlessness among both boys and girls, the respective coefficients being .31 ± .03 and .28 ± .05, and for retardation in school with corresponding correlations of .24 ± .03 and .30 ± .03 (Table 38). Other correlations of moderate size in the .20's among both sexes were for question of hypophrenia, distractibility, and absent-mindedness. Poor work in school and speech defect among boys showed moderate correlations in the .20's, with corresponding low correlations below .20 among girls. Four notations among girls showed moderate correlations in the .20's, the corresponding coefficients for boys ranging from .07 to .18: lack of initiative,

---

[1] See also I, 151-52, 194, Table 36, and 199, Table 48.

TABLE 38

CORRELATIONS WITH "SLOW, DULL"

	Boys	Girls
Personality-total...........................	-.04 ± .02	-.07 ± .03
Conduct-total...............................	.07 ± .02	-.07 ± .03
Police arrest...............................	-.08 ± .03	-.16 ± .04
	Larger Correlations (Positive)	
Listless....................................	.31 ± .03	.28 ± .05 (3-4)*
Question of hypophrenia.....................	.29 ± .03	.24 ± .04 (6)
Poor work in school........................	.26 ± .03	.11
Retardation in school......................	.24 ± .03	.30 ± .03 (1)
Distractible...............................	.24 ± .03	.20 ± .05 (9)
Absent-minded..............................	.22 ± .04	.29 ± .05 (2)
Speech defect..............................	.21 ± .03	.17
Lack of initiative........................	.18	.28 ± .05 (3-4)
Feeble-minded sibling......................	.07	.26 ± .05 (5)
Preference for younger children............	.13	.23 ± .05 (7-8)
Inefficient in work, play, etc.............	.18	.23 ± .05 (7-8)

*Rank order of girls' correlations.

Other Correlations (Positive to Negative)

Lazy, .18 and .14; Depressed, .13 and .01; Queer, .13 and -.01; Grouped: depressed, etc., .12 and -.01; Follower, .11 and .12; Seclusive, .11 and .18; Oversuggestible, .11 and .10; Object of teasing, .11 and .06; Apprehensive, .10 and .08; Bashful, .10 and .07; Question of encephalitis, .10 and -.07; Slovenly, .09 and .08; Popular, .08 and -.13; Neurological defect, .08 and .02; Sullen, .07 and .08; Irresponsible, .07 and -.03; Daydreaming, .06 and -.01; Sex denied entirely, .06 and -.19; Headaches, .06 and -.08; Former convulsions, .06 and .15; Underweight, .06 and .06; Vicious home conditions, .05 and .03; Worry over specific fact, .05 and .07; Crying spells, .05 and .01; Stubborn, .05 and -.04; Repressed, .04 and .18; Complaining of bad treatment by other children, .04 (boys); Vocational guidance, .03 and -.01; Lues, .03 and .02; Unhappy, .03 and .02; Restless in sleep, .03 and .06; Restless, .03 and .11; Hatred or jealousy of sibling, .03 and .18; Enuresis, .03 and .05; Question of change of personality, .02 and -.02; Sulky, .02 and .03; Mental conflict, .02 and -.10; Stuttering, .02 (boys); Discord between parents, .01 and -.01; Brother in penal detention, .01 and -.07; Excuse-forming, .01 and .00; Truancy from school, .01 and -.13; Swearing (general), .01 (boys); Refusal to attend school, .01 and -.07; Inattentive in school, .01 and -.08; Threatening violence, .00 (boys); Irregular attendance at school, .00 and .03; Grouped: lack of interest in school, etc., .00 and .03; Irregular sleep habits, -.00 and .09; Loitering, -.00 and .01; Teasing other children, -.01 (boys); Conduct prognosis bad, -.01 and .06; Grouped: sensitive or worrisome, etc., -.01 and -.01; Immoral home conditions, -.02 and -.01; Attractive manner, -.02 and -.11; Sensitive (general), -.02 and .02; Stealing, -.02 and -.11; Selfish, -.02 and -.09; Lack of interest in school, -.02 and .13; Lying, -.03 and -.05; "Nervous," -.03 and -.01; Inferiority feel-

TABLE 38—Continued

ings, -.03 and -.01; Grouped: "nervous," etc., -.03 and -.02; Sensitive over specific fact, -.04 and -.02; Changeable moods, -.04 and -.05; Masturbation, -.04 and -.05; Staying out late at night, -.04 and -.13; Leading others into bad conduct, -.04 and -.04; Fantastical lying, -.04 and -.03; Defiant, -.04 and -.06; Bossy, -.04 and .01; Smoking, -.05 (boys); Irritable, -.05 and -.01; Unpopular, -.05 and -.02; Grouped: egocentric, etc., -.05 and -.06; Grouped: swearing, etc., -.06 and .03; Overinterest in sex matters, -.06 and -.14; Temper display, -.06 and .07; Disobedient, -.06 and -.13; Destructive, -.07 and .00; Nail-biting, -.07 and -.08; Quarrelsome, -.07 and .03; Grouped: disobedient, etc., -.07 and -.03; Grouped: temper, etc., -.07 and .06; Grouped: fighting, etc., -.08 and .03; Exclusion from school, -.08 and -.06; Spoiled child, -.08 and .08; Fighting, -.08 and .05; Bad companions, -.08 and -.15; Finicky food habits, -.09 and -.12; Rude, -.09 and -.12; Truancy from home, -.09 and -.04; Egocentric, -.09 and -.10; Sex delinquency (coitus), -.09 and .01; Contrary, -.10 and -.07; Disturbing influence in school, -.11 and .05; Violence, -.11 and .09; Clean, -.11 and .06; Victim of sex abuse, -.11 (girls); Overinterest in opposite sex, -.11 (girls); Gang, -.12 (boys); Incorrigible, -.12 and -.10; Temper tantrums, -.14 and .05; Leader, -.17 and -.14; Emotional instability, -.17 and -.15; Boastful, "show-off," -.17 and -.03; Psychoneurotic, -.19 and -.12

   Omitted—Grouped: dull, slow, etc.

inefficiency in work, play, etc., preference for younger children as playmates, and feeble-minded sibling.

  Among the seventeen notations given special discussion (sex, physical or psychophysical, and home or familial) only one notation showed a meaningful correlation—speech defect (other than stuttering), the coefficients for boys and girls being .21 $\pm$ .03 and .17 respectively.

  Listlessness or attitude of indifference was noted among 178 boys, or 8.4 per cent, and among 87 girls, or 7.4 per cent.
  Its highest correlation was among girls, .41 $\pm$ .06 with seclusiveness, the corresponding coefficients for boys also being substantial, .34 $\pm$ .04 (Table 39). Laziness among boys yielded the substantial coefficient of .36 $\pm$ .04, the corresponding coefficient among girls, .24 $\pm$ .07, being moderate. Two personality notations showed substantial correlations of .31 each among boys, slow or dull manner and absent-mindedness, the corresponding coefficients for girls being .28 $\pm$ .05 and .05 respectively. Two additional substantial correlations in the .30's were found among girls, contrariness and leading others into bad conduct, the boys' correlations being negligible, .08 and -.07 respectively.
  Six notations showed moderate correlations in the .20's

TABLE 39

CORRELATIONS WITH "LISTLESS"

	Boys	Girls
Personality-total............................	.19 ± .03	.16 ± .04
Conduct-total................................	.08 ± .03	.15 ± .04
Police arrest................................	.08 ± .04	-.01 ± .06
	Larger Correlations (Positive)	
Lazy...	.36 ± .04	.24 ± .07 (7-12)*
Seclusive....................................	.34 ± .04	.41 ± .06 (1)
Absent-minded................................	.31 ± .05	.05
Slow, dull...................................	.31 ± .03	.28 ± .05 (4-5)
Inefficient in work, play, etc..............	.28 ± .05	.28 ± .07 (4-5)
Lack of initiative..........................	.27 ± .05	.24 ± .07 (7-12)
Question of encephalitis.....................	.27 ± .06	.03
Queer..	.26 ± .05	.18
Daydreaming..................................	.26 ± .04	.20 ± .06 (17-19)
Question of change in personality...........	.22 ± .05	.15
Bashful......................................	.21 ± .04	.04
Depressed....................................	.21 ± .05	.23 ± .07 (13)
Distractible................................	.21 ± .04	.24 ± .06 (7-12)
Poor work in school.........................	.21 ± .03	.24 ± .05 (7-12)
Grouped: depressed, etc.....................	.20 ± .04	.14
Grouped: "nervous," etc.....................	.20 ± .03	.02
Headaches....................................	.20 ± .05	.12
Irresponsible...............................	.20 ± .05	-.16
Contrary.....................................	.08	.36 ± .07 (2)
Leading others into bad conduct.............	-.07	.30 ± .08 (3)
Violence.....................................	.04	.25 ± .07 (6)
Repressed....................................	.15	.24 ± .08 (7-12)
Inattentive in school.......................	.18	.24 ± .07 (7-12)
Slovenly.....................................	.13	.22 ± .05 (14)
Conduct prognosis bad.......................	.07	.21 ± .08 (15-16)
Grouped: lack of interest in school, etc.....	.17	.21 ± .05 (15-16)
Neurological defect.........................	.16	.20 ± .06 (17-19)
Preference for younger children.............	.09	.20 ± .07 (17-19)
	Larger Correlations (Negative)	
Attractive manner...........................	.06	-.34 ± .05
Worry over specific fact....................	.13	-.25 ± .08

*Rank order of girls' correlations.

Other Correlations (Positive to Negative)

Psychoneurotic, .17 and .15; Irritable, .15 and -.11; Sensitive over specific fact, .15 and .01; Mental conflict, .14 and .05; Restless in sleep, .14 and .06; Refusal to attend school, .14 and -.06; Lack of interest in school,

TABLE 39—Continued

.14 and .16; Restless, .13 and .17; Unhappy, .13 and .13; Stuttering, .13 (boys); Speech defect, .13 and .15; Discord between parents, .13 and -.08; Grouped: sensitive or worrisome, etc., .13 and -.03; Underweight, .12 and -.06; Apprehensive, .12 and -.10; Teasing other children, .12 (boys); Finicky food habits, .12 and .10; Enuresis, .11 and .18; Masturbation, .11 and .00; Overinterest in opposite sex, .11 (girls); Grouped: temper, etc., .10 and -.00; Changeable moods, .09 and .07; "Nervous," .09 and -.04; Spoiled child, .08 and -.01; Crying spells, .08 and .09; Smoking, .08 (boys); Sulky, .07 and .09; Sullen, .07 and .15; Irregular sleep habits, .07 and -.04; Immoral home conditions, .07 and .02; Popular, .06 and -.10; Loitering, .05 and .02; Object of teasing, .05 and -.01; Oversuggestible, .05 and .19; Grouped: egocentric, etc., .04 and .11; Grouped: fighting, etc., .04 and .05; Egocentric, .04 and .03; Threatening violence, .04 (boys); Nail-biting, .04 and -.17; Defiant, .04 and .11; Fighting, .03 and .16; Quarrelsome, .03 and .01; Overinterest in sex matters, .03 and -.10; Vocational guidance, .03 and .07; Inferiority feelings, .02 and .02; Former convulsions, .02 and -.12; Sex delinquency (coitus), .02 and .01; Rude, .02 and .05; Sensitive (general), .01 and .05; Emotional instability, .01 and -.02; Complaining of bad treatment by other children, .01 (boys); Brother in penal detention, .01 and .05; Feeble-minded sibling, .01 and .13; Stealing, .00 and .08; Selfish, .00 and .11; Destructive, .00 and .09; Excuse-forming, -.00 and -.03; Victim of sex abuse, -.00 (girls); Question of hypophrenia, -.00 and .08; Follower, -.00 and .05; Temper display, -.01 and -.07; Stubborn, -.01 and .17; Fantastical lying, -.01 and .02; Disturbing influence in school, -.02 and .10; Staying out late at night, -.02 and -.09; Swearing (general), -.02 (boys); Exclusion from school, -.02 and .05; Retardation in school, -.02 and -.01; Clean, -.02 and .13; Grouped: swearing, etc., -.02 and .05; Vicious home conditions, -.03 and -.00; Hatred or jealousy of sibling, -.03 and .04; Boastful, "showoff," -.03 and .14; Bad companions, -.04 and -.13; Temper tantrums, -.04 and .07; Sex denied entirely, -.05 and .15; Truancy from home, -.05 and -.10; Lying, -.07 and .02; Disobedient, -.07 and .03; Incorrigible, -.08 and -.03; Grouped: disobedient, etc., -.08 and .16; Irregular attendance at school, -.09 and -.07; Unpopular, -.09 and .17; Gang, -.09 (boys); Truancy from school, -.10 and -.09; Lues, -.14 and -.02; Leader, -.15 and -.14; Bossy, -.16 and -.10
     Omitted—Grouped: dull, slow, etc.

with listlessness for both sexes: inefficiency in work, play, etc., lack of initiative, daydreaming, poor work in school, distractibility, and depressed spells. Seven notations showed moderate correlations in the .20's for the boys but low correlations ranging from -.16 to .18 among girls: question or diagnosis of encephalitis, queer behavior, question of change of personality, bashfulness, irresponsibility, "nervousness" or restlessness (undifferentiated), and headaches. Seven notations among girls showed moderate correlations in the .20's, with low positive correlations below .20 for the boys: inattentiveness in school, slovenliness, repressed manner, preference for younger children as playmates, violence, staff notation of unfavorable conduct prognosis, and neurological defect (unspecified).

There were two negative correlations of significant size,

both among girls, <u>attractive manner</u>, -.34 + .05, and <u>worry over</u>
<u>some specific fact</u>, -.25 + .08, the corresponding coefficients for
boys being low, .06 and .13 respectively.

Among the sex notations and also among the home or familial conditions there were no coefficients of significant size.

Among physical notations we have noted the moderate correlations of .27 + .06 for <u>question or diagnosis of encephalitis</u>
among boys and .20 + .06 with <u>neurological defect (unspecified)</u>
among girls.

<u>Lack of initiative or ambition</u> ("patient is unaggressive,
<u>lacks energy</u>") was noted among 132 boys, or 6.2 per cent, and among
63 girls, or 5.3 per cent.

Its highest correlation was noted among boys, .39 + .04,
with <u>inattentiveness in school</u>, the corresponding coefficient among
girls being negligible (Table 40).

TABLE 40

CORRELATIONS WITH "LACK OF INITIATIVE"

	Boys	Girls
Personality-total	.14 ± .03	-.03 ± .04
Conduct-total	.02 ± .03	-.06 ± .04
Police arrest	-.15 ± .04	-.12 ± .06
	Larger Correlations (Positive)	
Inattentive in school	.39 ± .04	.09
Bashful	.29 ± .04	.19
Sensitive (general)	.27 ± .05	.18
Listless	.27 ± .05	.24 ± .07 (5)*
Inefficient in work, play, etc	.26 ± .06	.11
Daydreaming	.25 ± .05	.21 ± .07 (8)
Grouped: sensitive or worrisome, etc	.24 ± .04	-.01
Absent-minded	.24 ± .05	.22 ± .08 (6-7)
Lazy	.23 ± .05	.27 ± .04 (2)
Selfish	.23 ± .06	.01
Seclusive	.23 ± .05	.18
Poor work in school	.23 ± .04	.22 ± .05 (6-7)
Vocational guidance	.23 ± .05	.14
Slow, dull	.18	.28 ± .05 (1)

*Rank order of girls' correlations.

TABLE 40—Continued

	Boys	Girls
Follower..	.16	.25 ± .07 (3-4)
Irregular sleep habits.........................	.00	.25 ± .08 (3-4)
		Larger Correlations (Negative)
Swearing (general).............................	-.29 ± .03	....
Disturbing influence in school................	-.25 ± .04	-.04
Sex delinquency (coitus).......................	-.20 ± .07	-.03
Emotional instability..........................	.06	-.30 ± .07
Grouped: swearing, etc.........................	-.13	-.29 ± .07
Unhappy..	.15	-.25 ± .08
Overinterest in opposite sex...................	....	-.23 ± .06
Bossy..	.09	-.22 ± .07
Unpopular......................................	-.01	-.22 ± .09
Grouped: temper, etc...........................	.09	-.20 ± .05
Conduct prognosis bad..........................	-.09	-.20 ± .09
		Not Calculable
Psychoneurotic.................................	.19	(n.c.)
Sex denied entirely............................	.05	(n.c.)
Question of encephalitis.......................	.01	(n.c.)
Boastful, "show-off"..........................	-.05	(n.c.)
Destructive....................................	-.15	(n.c.)

Other Correlations (Positive to Negative)

Irresponsible, .19 and .08; Clean, .18 and .06; Lack of interest in school, .17 and .06; Sensitive over specific fact, .17 and -.19; Preference for younger children, .17 and .10; Stuttering, .17 (boys); Grouped: "nervous," etc., .16 and .00; Neurological defect, .16 and -.12; Mental conflict, .16 and -.04; Worry over specific fact, .15 and -.15; Inferiority feelings, .15 and .11; Spoiled child, .15 and .00; Discord between parents, .14 and .09; Object of teasing, .14 and -.11; Apprehensive, .14 and -.03; Irritable, .13 and -.12; Distractible, .13 and .04; Oversuggestible, .13 and .17; Queer, .13 and .19; Grouped: lack of interest in school, etc., .13 and .03; Grouped: depressed, etc., .12 and -.08; Speech defect, .12 and .01; Slovenly, .12 and .12; Stubborn, .11 and -.02; Violence, .09 and -.18; Question of hypophrenia, .09 and .10; Popular, .09 and -.07; Attractive manner, .08 and .04; Finicky food habits, .08 and .11; Enuresis, .08 and .05; Question of change of personality, .07 and -.12; Restless, .06 and .01; Loitering, .05 and -.11; Refusal to attend school, .05 and -.18; Temper tantrums, .05 and -.13; Changeable moods, .05 and .05; Crying spells, .05 and -.04; Irregular attendance at school, .05 and -.02; Depressed, .05 and .01; Repressed, .04 and .13; Staying out late at night, .04 and -.06; "Nervous," .03 and -.05; Hatred or jealousy of sibling, .02 and .13; Nail-biting, .02 and .03; Headaches, .01 and -.10; Former convulsions, .01 and -.06; Grouped: egocentric, etc., .01 and -.07; Restless in sleep, .00 and .11; Masturbation, .00 and -.13; Sulky, .00 and -.04; Threatening violence, -.00 (boys); Feeble-minded sibling, -.00 and .03; Grouped: disobedient, etc., -.01 and -.03; Leader, -.01 and -.11; Contrary, -.02 and .03; Sullen, -.02 and -.13; Temper display, -.02 and -.12; Truancy from school, -.02 and -.11;

TABLE 40—Continued

Immoral home conditions, -.03 and .07; Underweight, -.03 and -.11; Complaining of bad treatment by other children, -.03 (boys); Victim of sex abuse, -.03 (girls); Lues, -.05 and -.03; Excuse-forming, -.05 and -.01; Teasing other children, -.05 (boys); Fighting, -.05 and .02; Defiant, -.05 and .05; Lying, -.06 and -.02; Quarrelsome, -.06 and -.06; Truancy from home, -.06 and -.03; Retardation in school, -.06 and -.06; Grouped: fighting, etc., -.07 and -.07; Overinterest in sex matters, -.07 and -.17; Rude, -.07 and -.13; Egocentric, -.08 and .12; Leading others into bad conduct, -.09 and -.06; Incorrigible, -.09 and -.14; Fantastical lying, -.09 and .11; Bad companions, -.10 and -.15; Disobedient, -.10 and -.06; Gang, -.11 (boys); Stealing, -.12 and -.01; Brother in penal detention, -.13 and .03; Smoking, -.14 (boys); Exclusion from school, -.16 and .07; Vicious home conditions, -.17 and -.13
        Omitted—Grouped: dull, slow, etc.

Five behavior traits showed moderate correlations in the .20's for both sexes: listlessness, laziness, absent-mindedness, daydreaming, and poor work in school. Six notations showed moderate correlations in the .20's among boys but low correlations ranging from -.01 to .19 among girls: inefficiency in work, play, etc., bashfulness, seclusiveness, sensitiveness in general, selfishness, and "request for vocational guidance." Three notations among girls showed moderate correlations in the .20's but low positive correlations below .18 for boys: slow or dull manner, irregular sleep habits, and "follower."

There was a large group of behavior notations showing moderate negative correlations ranging from -.20 to -.30 with lack of initiative. Among boys these were disturbing influence in school, sex delinquency (coitus), and (calculated for boys only) swearing (general). Among girls similar negative coefficients were found for emotional instability, unhappiness, unpopularity, bossy manner, temper tantrums or display (undifferentiated), swearing or bad language (undifferentiated), staff notation of unfavorable conduct prognosis, and (calculated for girls only) overinterest in opposite sex.

There were five notations for which tetrachoric correlations could not be computed among girls because there were no instances in which girls noted as lacking initiative had a notation in the following items: psychoneurotic trends, boastful or "show-off" manner, destructiveness, sex misbehavior denied entirely, and question or diagnosis of encephalitis.

Among the six sex notations there were two instances in

which significant correlations were found, both being negative: for sex delinquency (coitus) among boys, -.20 + .07, and for over-interest in opposite sex, which was calculated only among the girls, -.23 + .06.

Among the physical, psychophysical, and home or familial notations there were no correlations of significant size.

When the cases falling under the rubrics slow or dull manner, listlessness, and lack of initiative or ambition were combined into one large grouping, there were 704 boys, or 33.3 per cent, and 364 girls, or 30.8 per cent, so noted. The correlation coefficients based upon this broader grouping, as shown in Table 41, are generally similar to those previously presented in Table 38 (slow

TABLE 41

CORRELATIONS WITH "GROUPED: DULL, SLOW, ETC."

	Boys	Girls
Personality-total...............................	.15 ± .02	.07 ± .03
Conduct-total..................................	-.02 ± .02	-.03 ± .03
Police arrest.................................	-.12 ± .03	-.10 ± .04
	Larger Correlations (Positive)	
Absent-minded.................................	.32 ± .03	.19
Poor work in school...........................	.29 ± .02	.21 ± .03 (8)*
Lazy...	.28 ± .03	.18
Distractible.................................	.27 ± .03	.22 ± .04 (7)
Inefficient in work, play, etc...............	.26 ± .04	.30 ± .05 (2)
Seclusive....................................	.24 ± .03	.34 ± .04 (1)
Question of hypophrenia......................	.23 ± .03	.20 ± .03 (9)
Queer.......................................	.21 ± .04	.09
Speech defect...............................	.21 ± .03	.11
Repressed...................................	.04	.29 ± .06 (3)
Preference for younger children..............	.16	.27 ± .05 (4)
Feeble-minded sibling........................	.04	.25 ± .04 (5)
Retardation in school.......................	.17	.24 ± .03 (6)
	Larger Correlations (Negative)	
Spoiled child...............................	.01	-.29 ± .04
Overinterest in sex matters.................	-.06	-.22 ± .05

*Rank order of girls' correlations.

TABLE 41—Continued

Other Correlations (Positive to Negative)

Depressed, .19 and .08; Bashful, .18 and .14; Daydreaming, .18 and .14; Grouped: depressed, etc., .17 and .01; Apprehensive, .15 and .03; Irresponsible, .15 and -.03; Worry over specific fact, .13 and -.17; Object of teasing, .13 and .05; Question of change of personality, .13 and .04; Slovenly, .13 and .15; Question of encephalitis, .13 and -.08; Headaches, .12 and -.02; Follower, .12 and .15; Oversuggestible, .12 and .15; Unhappy, .11 and .01; Neurological defect, .11 and .01; Grouped: lack of interest in school, etc., .10 and .10; Mental conflict, .10 and -.12; Lack of interest in school, .09 and .17; Vocational guidance, .09 and .08; Grouped: sensitive or worrisome, etc., .08 and -.02; Disobedient, .08 and -.14; Crying spells, .08 and -.02; Restless in sleep, .07 and .09; Stubborn, .07 and -.02; Inattentive in school, .07 and .03; Enuresis, .07 and .04; Discord between parents, .06 and -.01; Underweight, .06 and -.02; Sensitive (general), .06 and .07; Sex denied entirely, .06 and -.07; Sensitive over specific fact, .05 and -.05; Temper display, .05 and .03; Refusal to attend school, .05 and -.12; Grouped: "nervous," etc., .04 and .01; Selfish, .04 and -.07; Sullen, .04 and .07; Irregular sleep habits, .04 and .07; Inferiority feelings, .03 and .05; Excuse-forming, .03 and .02; Threatening violence, .03 (boys); Teasing other children, .03 (boys); Former convulsions, .03 and -.15; Irregular attendance at school, .02 and -.01; Finicky food habits, .02 and -.02; Sulky, .02 and .06; Changeable moods, .02 and -.04; Irritable, .02 and -.04; Attractive manner, .02 and -.11; Stuttering, .01 (boys); Complaining of bad treatment by other children, .01 (boys); Loitering, .01 and .00; Vicious home conditions, .01 and -.00; Immoral home conditions, .00 and -.02; Brother in penal detention, .00 and .01; Truancy from school, .00 and -.09; Restless, -.00 and .11; Conduct prognosis bad, -.00 and .16; Lues, -.00 and .03; "Nervous," -.01 and -.02; Grouped: temper, etc., -.01 and -.00; Psychoneurotic, -.01 and -.16; Swearing (general), -.01 (boys); Masturbation, -.01 and -.12; Hatred or jealousy of sibling, -.01 and -.09; Grouped: egocentric, etc., -.02 and -.03; Bossy, -.02 and -.07; Clean, -.03 and .07; Stealing, -.03 and -.02; Fantastical lying, -.03 and -.01; Leading others into bad conduct, -.04 and -.05; Staying out late at night, -.04 and -.12; Popular, -.04 and -.09; Nailbiting, -.05 and -.07; Defiant, -.05 and -.01; Contrary, -.05 and .06; Grouped: swearing, etc., -.06 and .01; Lying, -.02; Smoking, -.06 (boys); Egocentric, -.06 and -.06; Temper tantrums, -.07 and -.00; Rude, -.07 and -.08; Fighting, -.07 and .12; Destructive, -.07 and -.00; Bad companions, -.07 and -.16; Grouped: fighting, etc., -.07 and .05; Overinterest in opposite sex, -.07 (girls); Grouped: disobedient, etc., -.08 and -.00; Quarrelsome, -.08 and .04; Violence, -.08 and .08; Truancy from home, -.08 and -.05; Unpopular, -.08 and -.02; Exclusion from school, -.09 and .01; Boastful, "show-off," -.10 and -.01; Sex delinquency (coitus), -.11 and -.15; Disturbing influence in school, -.11 and .04; Gang, -.11 (boys); Victim of sex abuse, -.11 (girls); Incorrigible, -.13 and -.08; Emotional instability, -.13 and -.16; Leader, -.17 and -.17
                Omitted—Slow, dull; Listless; Lack of initiative

or dull manner) for the simple reason that over three-quarters of the cases appearing in the broader grouping, dull or slow manner (including listlessness and lack of initiative, undifferentiated), were also placed under the specific group of slow or dull manner,[2]

[2] The reasons for this broader grouping were given in I, 44, and 86, Table 13, Item D.

and the material of the two tables (38 and 41) is, therefore,
largely identical. The marked similarity of the correlation coefficients in these two tables indicates that a separate consideration of the larger-category grouping was of little utility.

Relatively few correlations based upon the broader grouping in Table 41 were of statistically significant size of .20 or
above. Only three were of substantial size, ranging from .30 to
.34: absent-mindedness among boys and seclusiveness and inefficiency in work, play, etc., among girls, the corresponding coefficients for the other sex being of moderate size, ranging from .19
to .26. Three notations showed moderate correlations in the .20's
for both sexes: poor work in school, distractibility, and question
of hypophrenia. Three behavior traits among boys showed moderate
correlations in the .20's, with low positive coefficients below .20
for girls: laziness, queer behavior, and speech defect (other than
stuttering). Four notations among girls showed moderate correlations in the .20's, with low positive coefficients below .20 for
boys: repressed manner, preference for younger children as playmates, feeble-minded sibling, and retardation in school.

Two significant negative correlations were found, both
among girls, -.29 + .04 for "spoiled child" and -.22 + .05 for
overinterest in sex matters, the corresponding coefficients for
boys being negligible.

Among the six sex notations the only correlation of statistically significant size was the negative one of -.22 + .05
among girls for overinterest in sex matters. In general, it may be
noted that sex problems tended to be negatively or negligibly correlated with all three notations—slow or dull manner, listlessness,
and lack of initiative or ambition.

Among the seven physical or psychophysical notations only
one meaningful correlation was found—the moderate one of .21 + .03
with speech defect (other than stuttering) among boys. In general,
it may be concluded that these physical conditions tended to show
a low positive correlation with the three notations discussed in
this chapter.

Among our four home or familial conditions there were no
correlations of material size, all thirty-two coefficients presented in this chapter falling between -.17 and .14.

CHAPTER XXVII

OVERSUGGESTIBILITY; DISTRACTIBILITY;
PREFERENCE FOR YOUNGER CHILDREN
AS PLAYMATES

The three personality traits oversuggestibility, distractibility, and preference for younger children as playmates may be
conveniently considered together in this chapter as frequently
noted concomitants of mental deficiency. (In the data of this volume this relation for distractibility is obscured by the fact that
our 2,113 boys and 1,181 girls do not include the very young children below 6 years of age and below 50 in intelligence quotient,
among whom distractibility is especially frequent.) That these
three traits are not similar is shown by the non-significance of
their intercorrelations, which range from -.06 to .20.

The notation oversuggestibility ("patient too easily influenced by others") was found among 354 boys, or 16.8 per cent, and
among 174 girls, or 14.7 per cent, and was one of the more frequent
behavior notations among our clinic cases. It appeared to be of
negligible importance from a personality standpoint, probably of
moderate importance from the standpoint of conduct deviation, but
of substantial importance as an indicator of "juvenile delinquency,
especially among girls, for whom one notes the high tetrachoric correlation of .57 $\pm$ .03 with police arrest (Table 42).
Among both sexes the highest correlation was with bad companions, the coefficients being .43 $\pm$ .03 and .40 $\pm$ .04 for boys
and girls respectively. Stealing among boys also showed the substantial correlation of .38 $\pm$ .02 with a corresponding low coefficient of .13 among girls. Running with a gang (calculated for boys
only) also showed the substantial correlation of .31 $\pm$ .03. Sex
delinquency (coitus) among girls showed the substantial correlation
of .38 $\pm$ .04, with a corresponding low coefficient of .11 among
boys. Loitering or wandering among girls showed the similarly substantial correlation of .32 $\pm$ .06, with a corresponding moderate

256

TABLE 42

CORRELATIONS WITH "OVERSUGGESTIBLE"

	Boys	Girls
Personality-total.........................	.01 ± .02	.13 ± .03
Conduct-total.............................	.26 ± .02	.22 ± .03
Police arrest.............................	.36 ± .03	.57 ± .03
	Larger Correlations (Positive)	
Bad companions............................	.43 ± .03	.40 ± .04 (1)*
Stealing..................................	.38 ± .02	.13
Gang......................................	.31 ± .03	....
Follower..................................	.29 ± .04	.18
Truancy from school.......................	.28 ± .03	.09
Conduct prognosis bad.....................	.28 ± .05	.21 ± .07 (5-8)
Excuse-forming............................	.23 ± .03	.13
Lying.....................................	.21 ± .03	.12
Staying out late at night.................	.21 ± .03	.21 ± .05 (5-8)
Apprehensive..............................	.21 ± .03	.13
Loitering.................................	.20 ± .04	.32 ± .06 (3)
Unpopular.................................	.20 ± .04	.05
Sex delinquency (coitus)..................	.11	.38 ± .04 (2)
Queer.....................................	-.09	.27 ± .06 (4)
Violence..................................	.10	.21 ± .05 (5-8)
Absent-minded.............................	.05	.21 ± .06 (5-8)

*Rank order of girls' correlations.

Other Correlations (Positive to Negative)

Fantastical lying, .19 and .13; Teasing other children, .19 (boys);
Truancy from home, .19 and .17; Overinterest in opposite sex, .18 (girls); Masturbation, .16 and .11; Retardation in school, .16 and .04; Irregular attendance at school, .16 and -.09; Brother in penal detention, .16 and .06; Disturbing influence in school, .15 and .04; Refusal to attend school, .15 and -.07;
Exclusion from school, .15 and .14; Question of hypophrenia, .14 and .02; Incorrigible, .13 and .09; Swearing (general), .13 (boys); Lack of initiative, .13
and .17; Restless, .13 and .17; Poor work in school, .13 and .06; Grouped: disobedient, etc., .13 and .16; Enuresis, .12 and -.03; Leading others into bad
conduct, .12 and .05; Smoking, .12 (boys); Grouped: dull, slow, etc., .12 and
.15; Grouped: swearing, etc., .12 and .07; Boastful, "show-off," .11 and .15;
Destructive, .11 and .07; Changeable moods, .11 and .07; Slow, dull, .11 and
.10; Grouped: "nervous," etc., .11 and .10; Object of teasing, .10 and -.04;
Restless in sleep, .10 and .05; Spoiled child, .10 and .03; Stubborn, .09 and
.02; Speech defect, .09 and .16; Victim of sex abuse, .09 (girls); Fighting,
.08 and .03; Inefficient in work, play, etc., .08 and .13; Irresponsible, .08
and .18; Temper display, .08 and -.02; Bashful, .08 and .00; Complaining of bad
treatment by other children, .08 (boys); Lack of interest in school, .07 and
.08; Slovenly, .07 and .18; Irregular sleep habits, .07 and .14; Grouped: lack
of interest in school, etc., .07 and .04; Repressed, .06 and -.00; Neurological

TABLE 42—Continued

defect, .06 and .04; Sulky, .07 and .11; Overinterest in sex matters, .05 and
.17; Crying spells, .05 and .15; Daydreaming, .05 and .08; Listless, .05 and
.19; Inferiority feelings, .05 and .09; Emotional instability, .05 and .06;
Preference for younger children, .05 and .07; Stuttering, .05 (boys); Former
convulsions, .04 and .02; Discord between parents, .04 and .03; Grouped: temper, etc., .04 and -.04; Disobedient, .04 and .08; Nail-biting, .03 and .05;
Irritable, .03 and -.08; Grouped: fighting, etc., .03 and .12; Threatening
violence, .02 (boys); "Nervous," .02 and .03; Sex denied entirely, .02 and -.04;
Grouped: sensitive or worrisome, etc., .02 and .08; Temper tantrums, .01 and
.02; Sensitive (general), .01 and .10; Leader, .01 and -.09; Clean, .01 and
-.02; Headaches, .01 and -.10; Vicious home conditions, .01 and .11; Inattentive
in school, .00 and .02; Hatred or jealousy of sibling, .00 and -.06; Sensitive
over specific fact, .00 and .02; Popular, .00 and -.01; Selfish, -.00 and .12;
Mental conflict, -.00 and .02; Grouped: depressed, etc., -.00 and .13; Rude,
-.01 and -.03; Sullen, -.01 and -.00; Lues, -.01 and .03; Contrary, -.02 and
-.11; Depressed, -.02 and .08; Seclusive, -.02 and .17; Lazy, -.03 and .03; Unhappy, -.03 and .12; Attractive manner, -.03 and .06; Finicky food habits, -.04
and .12; Defiant, -.04 and .06; Underweight, -.04 and -.02; Worry over specific
fact, -.05 and .15; Quarrelsome, -.06 and .10; Distractible, -.06 and .11; Question of change of personality, -.08 and .16; Question of encephalitis, -.08 and
-.14; Feeble-minded sibling, -.08 and -.07; Bossy, -.09 and .11; Immoral home
conditions, -.09 and .11; Grouped: egocentric, etc., -.10 and .08; Psychoneurotic, -.13 and .19; Egocentric, -.14 and -.04; Vocational guidance, -.17 and
-.08

correlation of .20 ± .04 among boys.

Two notations—staying out late at night and staff notation
of unfavorable conduct prognosis—showed moderate correlations in
the .20's for both sexes. Six behavior traits showed moderate correlations ranging from .20 to .29 among boys but low positive correlations below .20 for girls: "follower," truancy from school,
excuse-forming attitude, apprehensiveness, lying, and unpopularity.
Three behavior notations among girls similarly showed moderate correlations in the .20's with negligible coefficients ranging from
-.09 to .10 among boys: queer behavior, absent-mindedness, and
violence.

Among the six sex notations all correlations with once exception were low or negligible, falling below .20. For sex delinquency (coitus) among girls, however, there was a substantial correlation of .38 ± .04 with oversuggestibility. Since sex misconduct and the fact of a juvenile-court arrest or commitment among
girls are so substantially correlated with the notation oversuggestibility, one wonders to what extent this relation represents
the true state of affairs and to what extent it may be due to an
overprotective attitude on the part of the parent or friend, who

desired to minimize a patient's conduct troubles by blaming them
upon other children. "She is a good girl around home but is too
easily influenced by other people."

Among the seven physical or psychophysical notations and
among the four home or familial notations there were found no correlation coefficients of significant size.

Distractibility or lack of concentration was noted among
264 boys, or 12.5 per cent, and among 116 girls, or 9.8 per cent.
It was especially characteristic of our youngest children.[1]

Among girls its bi-serial correlations with both the personality-total and the conduct-total were fairly high, .41 + .03
and .44 + .03 respectively, but among boys these coefficients were
of only moderate size in the .20's (Table 43). With the police-
arrest criterion of importance or "seriousness" its correlations
were very negligible.

Its highest correlations among girls were with restlessness, .56 + .04, and with disturbing influence in school, .46 +
.05. Among boys the two corresponding correlations were also meaningful, .39 + .03 and .24 + .03 respectively. Among girls question
or diagnosis of encephalitis yielded the very substantial correlation coefficient of .44 + .07, the corresponding coefficient for
boys being low, .17. Two behavior notations among girls each
yielded a correlation of .40—"nervousness" and violence—the corresponding coefficients for boys being .26 + .03 and .11. Among
boys the only correlation as large as .40 + .04 was with absent-
mindedness. Among boys inefficiency in work, play, etc., yielded
the substantial correlation of .36 + .05, with a similar correlation among girls of .29 + .06. Among girls two additional notations showed substantial correlations in the .30's, with corresponding moderate correlations in the .20's among boys: poor work
in school and bossy manner. There were thirteen notations among
girls showing substantial correlations in the .30's but low pos-
tive correlations below .20 for boys: question of change of personality, restlessness in sleep, queer behavior, worry over some
specific fact, boastful or "show-off" manner, object of teasing by
other children, quarrelsomeness, temper tantrums, stubbornness,

---

[1]See I, 204, Table 48.

TABLE 43

CORRELATIONS WITH "DISTRACTIBLE"

	Boys	Girls
Personality-total.........................	.25 ± .02	.41 + .03
Conduct-total.........................	.23 ± .02	.44 + .03
Police arrest.........................	-.05 ± .03	.07 + .05
		Larger Correlations (Positive)
Absent-minded.........................	.40 ± .04	.25 ± .07 (36-40)*
Restless.........................	.39 ± .03	.56 ± .04 (1)
Grouped: "nervous," etc.....................	.37 ± .03	.55 ± .03 (2)
Inefficient in work, play, etc..............	.36 ± .05	.29 ± .06 (24-26)
Poor work in school.....................	.28 ± .03	.34 ± .04 (10-13)
Grouped: dull, slow, etc.....................	.27 ± .03	.22 ± .04 (48-52)
"Nervous".........................	.26 ± .03	.40 ± .04 (5-6)
Disturbing influence in school................	.24 ± .03	.46 ± .05 (3)
Slow, dull.........................	.24 ± .03	.20 ± .05 (56-57)
Irresponsible.........................	.23 ± .05	.24 ± .06 (41-45)
Daydreaming.........................	.23 ± .05	.16
Bossy.........................	.22 ± .05	.32 ± .06 (17-19)
Lazy.........................	.22 ± .04	.06
Unpopular.........................	.22 ± .05	.26 ± .07 (34-35)
Listless.........................	.21 ± .04	.24 ± .06 (41-45)
Spoiled child.........................	.21 ± .04	.27 ± .06 (29-33)
Loitering.........................	.20 ± .04	.18
Teasing other children.....................	.20 ± .04	....
Question of encephalitis.....................	.17	.44 ± .07 (4)
Violence.........................	.11	.40 ± .06 (5-6)
Question of change of personality.............	.05	.39 ± .06 (7)
Grouped: lack of interest in school..........	.13	.38 ± .05 (8)
Exclusion from school.....................	.03	.36 ± .06 (9)
Grouped: fighting, etc.....................	.15	.34 ± .04 (10-13)
Inattentive in school.....................	.12	.34 ± .06 (10-13)
Worry over specific fact.....................	.04	.34 ± .07 (10-13)
Boastful, "show-off".....................	.18	.33 ± .06 (14-16)
Stubborn.........................	.07	.33 ± .05 (14-16)
Restless in sleep.........................	.14	.33 ± .05 (14-16)
Queer.........................	.15	.32 ± .06 (16-18)
Object of teasing.........................	.12	.31 ± .06 (19)
Temper tantrums.........................	.06	.30 ± .05 (20-23)
Depressed.........................	.04	.30 ± .06 (20-23)
Quarrelsome.........................	.18	.30 ± .05 (20-23)
Destructive.........................	.15	.30 ± .07 (20-23)
Fantastical lying.........................	.16	.29 ± .06 (24-26)
Neurological defect.........................	.18	.29 ± .05 (24-26)
Grouped: temper, etc.....................	.19	.28 ± .04 (27-28)
Changeable moods.........................	.12	.28 ± .05 (27-28)
Lack of interest in school.....................	.12	.27 ± .06 (29-33)

*Rank order of girls' correlations.

TABLE 43—Continued

	Boys	Girls
Sullen..	.11	.27 ± .06 (29-33)
Conduct prognosis bad.............................	.19	.27 ± .07 (29-33)
Grouped: disobedient, etc........................	.15	.27 ± .04 (29-33)
Disobedient.......................................	.13	.26 ± .05 (34-35)
Egocentric..	-.00	.25 ± .05 (36-40)
Irregular sleep habits............................	.01	.25 ± .07 (36-40)
Emotional instability.............................	.16	.25 ± .06 (36-40)
Grouped: swearing, etc...........................	.13	.25 ± .06 (36-40)
Grouped: depressed, etc..........................	-.03	.24 ± .05 (41-45)
Grouped: egocentric, etc.........................	.14	.24 ± .05 (41-45)
Defiant...	-.05	.24 ± .06 (41-45)
Incorrigible......................................	.15	.23 ± .05 (46-47)
Overinterest in sex matters.......................	.06	.23 ± .06 (46-47)
Inferiority feelings..............................	.16	.22 ± .07 (48-52)
Crying spells.....................................	.08	.22 ± .04 (48-52)
Stealing..	.06	.22 ± .05 (48-52)
Fighting..	.01	.22 ± .04 (48-52)
Lying...	.12	.21 ± .04 (53-55)
Truancy from home.................................	.01	.21 ± .05 (53-55)
Excuse-forming....................................	.09	.21 ± .06 (53-55)
Preference for younger children...................	.15	.20 ± .06 (56-57)
	Larger Correlations (Negative)	
Vicious home conditions...........................	.07	-.21 ± .07

Other Correlations (Positive to Negative)

Contrary, .19 and .00; Overinterest in opposite sex, .19 (girls); Complaining of bad treatment by other children, .18 (boys); Selfish, .17 and .10; Seclusive, .17 and .16; Temper display, .15 and -.03; Irritable, .15 and .19; Leading others into bad conduct, .14 and .18; Swearing (general), .14 (boys); Question of hypophrenia, .14 and .18; Hatred or jealousy of sibling, .13 and .16; Lack of initiative, .13 and .04; Speech defect, .13 and .19; Slovenly, .12 and .16; Sulky, .12 and .14; Follower, .12 and .16; Headaches, .12 and .18; Discord between parents, .12 and -.10; Masturbation, .11 and .14; Finicky food habits, .10 and .13; Threatening violence, .10 (boys); Irregular attendance at school, .10 and -.13; Enuresis, .09 and .18; Smoking, .09 (boys); Underweight, .09 and .06; Grouped: sensitive or worrisome, etc., .09 and .16; Nail-biting, .08 and .19; Sensitive over specific fact, .08 and .05; Stuttering, .08 (boys); Refusal to attend school, .07 and .08; Bashful, .07 and -.04; Former convulsions, .07 and .01; Attractive manner, .07 and .08; Rude, .06 and .11; Gang, .06 (boys); Retardation in school, .05 and .14; Leader, .05 and .12; Victim of sex abuse, .05 (girls); Feeble-minded sibling, .03 and .01; Bad companions, .03 and .09; Sensitive (general), .01 and .14; Staying out late at night, -.01 and .12; Unhappy, -.02 and .12; Sex denied entirely, -.02 and .07; Popular, -.02 and .18; Truancy from school, -.03 and .07; Immoral home conditions, -.03 and .00; Sex delinquency (coitus), -.04 and .05; Lues, -.04 and .17; Brother in penal detention, -.04 and -.14; Mental conflict, -.05 and .09; Clean, -.05 and .09; Oversuggestible, -.06 and .11; Repressed, -.07 and .05; Apprehensive, -.08 and .18; Vocational guidance, -.08 and .00; Psychoneurotic, -.14 and .12

destructiveness, distractibility, inattentiveness in school, and
exclusion from school.

Five personality difficulties showing moderate correlations
in the .20's among both sexes with distractibility were slow or
dull manner, listlessness, irresponsibility, "spoiled child," and
unpopularity and also the notation teasing other children, which
was computed for boys only. Three behavior notations among boys
also showed moderate correlations in the .20's but low positive
correlations below .20 for the girls: daydreaming, laziness, and
loitering or wandering. A large group of twenty-one notations
showed moderate correlations in the .20's among girls but low correlations ranging from -.05 to .19 among boys: changeable moods
and attitudes, emotional instability, crying spells, irregular
sleep habits, inferiority feelings, excuse-forming attitude, egocentricity, sullenness, incorrigibility, disobedience, defiant attitude, fighting, swearing or bad language (undifferentiated), lying, fantastical lying, stealing, truancy from home, preference for
younger children as playmates, overinterest in sex matters, staff
notation of unfavorable conduct prognosis, and neurological defect
(unspecified).

One notation showed a negative correlation of moderate size
among girls, vicious home conditions, -.21 ± .07, with a negligible
coefficient of .07 among boys.

Among the six sex notations distractibility showed only
one coefficient of moderate size—.23 ± .06 for overinterest in sex
matters among girls, the boys' coefficient of .06 being negligible.

Among the seven physical or psychophysical notations there
were two correlations of statistical significance, both for girls,
the very substantial one of .44 ± .07 for question or diagnosis of
encephalitis and .29 ± .05 with neurological defect (unspecified),
the corresponding coefficients for boys being .17 and .18 respectively.

Among the four home or familial correlations there was only
one of significant size, the negative coefficient of -.21 ± .07 for
vicious home conditions among girls.

Preference for younger children as playmates in our data
appeared to be of little importance, since its correlations with
our three criteria of "seriousness" were low, ranging from -.14 to

.15 (Table 44). It was noted among only 7 or 8 per cent of the children discussed in this volume.

The three highest correlations, ranging from .32 to .36, were among girls, the corresponding coefficients among boys being low, falling between .13 and .18: "nervousness" or restlessness

TABLE 44

CORRELATIONS WITH "PREFERENCE FOR YOUNGER CHILDREN"

	Boys	Girls
Personality-total............................	.12 ± .03	.13 ± .04
Conduct-total................................	.10 ± .03	.15 ± .04
Police arrest................................	-.05 ± .04	-.14 ± .06
	Larger Correlations (Positive)	
Restless in sleep............................	.27 ± .04	.20 ± .06 (22-28)*
Overinterest in sex matters..................	.24 ± .06	.15
Speech defect................................	.22 ± .05	.15
Poor work in school..........................	.21 ± .03	.23 ± .05 (10-16)
Selfish......................................	.20 ± .05	.19
Object of teasing............................	.20 ± .04	.22 ± .07 (17-20)
Grouped: "nervous," etc.....................	.15	.36 ± .04 (1)
Mental conflict..............................	.13	.33 ± .08 (2)
Question of hypophrenia......................	.18	.32 ± .05 (3)
Inattentive in school........................	.12	.29 ± .07 (4)
Grouped: Lack of interest in school, etc.....	.15	.28 ± .06 (5)
Grouped: dull, slow, etc....................	.16	.27 ± .05 (6-8)
Restless.....................................	.16	.27 ± .05 (6-8)
Bossy..	.19	.27 ± .07 (6-8)
Absent-minded................................	.13	.24 ± .08 (9)
Destructive..................................	.06	.23 ± .07 (10-16)
Enuresis.....................................	.13	.23 ± .05 (10-16)
Fighting.....................................	-.03	.23 ± .04 (10-16)
Changeable moods.............................	.12	.23 ± .06 (10-16)
Slow, dull...................................	.13	.23 ± .05 (10-16)
Unpopular....................................	.06	.23 ± .08 (10-16)
Grouped: sensitive or worrisome, etc........	.01	.22 ± .05 (17-20)
Retardation in school........................	.18	.22 ± .05 (17-20)
Worry over specific fact.....................	-.24 ± .06	.22 ± .09 (17-20)
Grouped: temper, etc........................	.09	.21 ± .05 (21)
Exclusion from school........................	.05	.20 ± .07 (22-28)
Sensitive over specific fact.................	.02	.20 ± .06 (22-28)
Distractible.................................	.15	.20 ± .06 (22-28)
Listless.....................................	.09	.20 ± .07 (22-28)
Nail-biting..................................	.14	.20 ± .05 (22-28)
Lazy...	.19	.20 ± .07 (22-28)

*Rank order of girls' correlations.

TABLE 44—Continued

	Boys	Girls
	Larger Correlations (Negative)	
Feeble-minded sibling...................	-.27 ± .05	-.08
Contrary................................	.02	-.25 ± .08
Former convulsions......................	.16	-.20 ± .04

Other Correlations (Positive to Negative)

Neurological defect, .19 and .10; Question of encephalitis, .19 and .19; Daydreaming, .18 and .03; Bashful, .18 and .08; Lack of interest in school, .18 and .17; Irresponsible, .17 and .07; Lack of initiative, .17 and .10; Fantastical lying, .16 and .10; Inefficient in work, play, etc., .15 and .18; Temper tantrums, .15 and .15; Seclusive, .15 and -.04; Grouped: disobedient, etc., .15 and .09; Disobedient, .13 and .01; "Nervous," .13 and .19; Repressed, .12 and .00; Apprehensive, .12 and .04; Sulky, .12 and .08; Quarrelsome, .11 and .12; Slovenly, .11 and .06; Stubborn, .11 and -.04; Threatening violence, .11 (boys); Grouped: fighting, etc., .11 and .16; Crying spells, .10 and .16; Violence, .10 and .13; Question of change of personality, .09 and .14; Irritable, .09 and .19; Queer, .09 and -.09; Sensitive (general), .09 and .12; Follower, .08 and .09; Inferiority feelings, .08 and .05; Egocentric, .08 and .15; Sex delinquency (coitus), .08 and -.13; Stealing, .08 and .18; Leading others into bad conduct, .08 and -.11; Boastful, "show-off," .08 and -.06; Lying, .07 and .16; Teasing other children, .07 (boys); Masturbation, .07 and .16; Unhappy, .07 and -.01; Leader, .07 and .06; Grouped: depressed, etc., .06 and .05; Spoiled child, .06 and .08; Finicky food habits, .05 and .04; Depressed, .05 and -.05; Oversuggestible, .05 and .07; Stuttering, .05 (boys); Irregular attendance at school, .05 and .01; Grouped: swearing, etc., .04 and .12; Vicious home conditions, .04 and -.03; Headaches, .04 and .17; Irregular sleep habits, .04 and -.08; Disturbing influence in school, .04 and .16; Loitering, .03 and -.00; Grouped: egocentric, etc., .03 and .16; Bad companions, .02 and .12; Swearing (general), .01 (boys); Psychoneurotic, .01 and -.08; Conduct prognosis bad, .01 and .14; Complaining of bad treatment by other children, .01 (boys); Overinterest in opposite sex, .01 (girls); Truancy from home, .00 and -.01; Hatred or jealousy of sibling, -.00 and .01; Excuse-forming, -.01 and .02; Truancy from school, -.01 and .11; Rude, -.01 and .00; Refusal to attend school, -.01 and .07; Vocational guidance, -.03 and .07; Staying out late at night, -.03 and -.04; Smoking, -.04 (boys); Temper display, -.04 and .18; Popular, -.04 and -.06; Clean, -.04 and .07; Attractive manner, -.04 and .09; Incorrigible, -.05 and .14; Immoral home conditions, -.06 and -.13; Sex denied entirely, -.06 and .06; Sullen, -.06 and .10; Emotional instability, -.07 and .06; Lues, -.07 and -.15; Discord between parents, -.07 and -.06; Victim of sex abuse, -.08 (girls); Defiant, -.09 and .11; Underweight, -.09 and .13; Gang, -.12 (boys); Brother in penal detention, -.14 and -.03

(including irritable temperament and changeable moods or attitudes, undifferentiated), mental conflict, and question of hypophrenia.

Three notations showed moderate correlations in the .20's for both sexes: restlessness in sleep, object of teasing by other children, and poor work in school. Three additional notations yielded moderate correlations in the .20's for boys but low correlations below .20 for girls: selfishness, overinterest in sex matters, and speech defect (other than stuttering). A large list of eighteen miscellaneous problems among girls yielded moderate correlations in the .20's, with low corresponding coefficients ranging from -.03 to .19 among boys: inattentiveness in school, restlessness, absent-mindedness, slow or dull manner, distractibility, listlessness, laziness, changeable moods or attitudes, bossy manner, fighting, destructiveness, unpopularity, temper tantrums or display (undifferentiated), sensitiveness over specific fact, enuresis, nail-biting, retardation in school, and exclusion from school. Worry over some specific fact, curiously, yielded a moderate positive correlation of $.22 \pm .09$ among girls and a significant negative coefficient of $-.24 \pm .06$ among boys.

In addition to worry over some specific fact there were three negative coefficients of statistically significant size with preference for younger children as playmates: among boys $-.27 \pm .05$ for feeble-minded sibling, and among girls $-.25 \pm .08$ and $-.20 \pm .04$ for contrariness and former convulsions respectively.

Among the six sex notations the only considerable correlation with preference for younger children as playmates was for overinterest in sex matters among boys, $.24 \pm .06$, with the corresponding coefficient for girls of .15.

Among our seven physical or psychophysical notations there were two coefficients of unquestionably significant size, $.23 \pm .05$ for enuresis among girls and $.22 \pm .05$ for speech defect (other than stuttering) among boys. The correlation of .19 among both boys and girls for question or diagnosis of encephalitis is also suggestive but because of the paucity of cases was scarcely of statistical significance.

None of the four home or familial conditions showed meaningful correlations with preference for younger children as playmates, the coefficients ranging from -.14 to .04.

CHAPTER XXVIII

"NERVOUSNESS"; RESTLESSNESS; IRRITABILITY

The three personality problems—"nervousness," restlessness, and irritable temperament—were among the most frequent of
behavior traits noted in our case material. Occasionally they appeared to be the chief reason for the child's being referred to
the clinic of the Illinois Institute for Juvenile Research, but
more commonly they were elicited in the actual interview by the
psychiatric social worker with the parent, teacher, or other informant. Collectively they are of moderate to substantial importance clinically but of little moment as indicators of "juvenile
delinquency." Their very substantial intercorrelations, ranging
from .26 to .51, indicate their essential similarity.

"Nervousness" in our data was a poorly defined term of
vague meaning, hence our persistent use of quotation marks whenever it is mentioned in this study. It showed substantial bi-serial
correlations in the .30's with personality-total among both sexes
and moderate correlations of .19 ± .02 and .24 ± .04 with the conduct-total for boys and girls respectively (Table 45). With the
police-arrest criterion the correlation for both sexes was zero.
"Nervousness" was noted among 344, or 16.3 per cent, of our 2,113
White boys and 197, or 16.7 per cent, of our 1,181 White girls.

The highest correlations among both sexes were with restlessness, .42 ± .03 and .51 ± .03 among boys and girls respectively.
Among girls there were in addition three very substantial correlations ranging from .40 to .47, with substantial correlations among
boys ranging from .30 to .34: changeable moods or attitudes, restlessness in sleep, and neurological defect (unspecified). Question
or diagnosis of encephalitis and distractibility similarly yielded
fairly high correlations in the .40's among girls but lesser coefficients of .14 and .26 ± .03 respectively among boys.

Four behavior notations yielded substantial correlations
in the .30's for both sexes: psychoneurotic trends, queer behavior,

TABLE 45

CORRELATIONS WITH "NERVOUS"

	Boys	Girls
Personality-total............................	.37 ± .02	.35 ± .03
Conduct-total................................	.19 ± .02	.24 ± .04
Police arrest................................	.00 ± .03	-.00 ± .04
	Larger Correlations (Positive)	
Restless.....................................	.42 ± .03	.51 ± .03 (1)*
Changeable moods.............................	.34 ± .03	.40 ± .04 (4-6)
Psychoneurotic...............................	.33 ± .05	.35 ± .06 (10-13)
Irritable....................................	.33 ± .03	.36 ± .04 (8-9)
Queer..	.32 ± .04	.35 ± .05 (10-13)
Neurological defect..........................	.31 ± .04	.44 ± .04 (3)
Restless in sleep............................	.30 ± .03	.47 ± .04 (2)
Grouped: temper, etc........................	.30 ± .03	.34 ± .04 (14)
Worry over specific fact.....................	.29 ± .04	.15
Depressed....................................	.28 ± .04	.09
Nail-biting..................................	.26 ± .03	.29 ± .04 (21)
Distractible.................................	.26 ± .03	.40 ± .04 (4-6)
Spoiled child................................	.26 ± .03	.35 ± .05 (10-13)
Bossy..	.25 ± .04	.24 ± .05 (27-30)
Unpopular....................................	.25 ± .04	.14
Grouped: sensitive or worrisome, etc........	.25 ± .03	.28 ± .04 (22)
Grouped: depressed, etc.....................	.24 ± .04	.16
Crying spells................................	.23 ± .03	.37 ± .04 (7)
Daydreaming..................................	.23 ± .04	.22 ± .05 (33)
Complaining of bad treatment by other children	.23 ± .04	....
Finicky food habits..........................	.23 ± .04	.31 ± .05 (19-20)
Absent-minded................................	.22 ± .02	.35 ± .06 (10-13)
Apprehensive.................................	.22 ± .05	.36 ± .04 (8-9)
Question of change of personality............	.21 ± .04	.32 ± .06 (15-18)
Object of teasing............................	.21 ± .03	.15
Sensitive (general)..........................	.21 ± .04	.25 ± .04 (24-26)
Emotional instability........................	.21 ± .05	.25 ± .04 (24-26)
Fantastical lying............................	.20 ± .03	.18
Teasing other children.......................	.20 ± .04	....
Irregular sleep habits.......................	.20 ± .04	.24 ± .06 (27-30)
Question of encephalitis.....................	.14	.40 ± .06 (4-6)
Disturbing influence in school...............	.10	.32 ± .05 (15-18)
Temper tantrums..............................	.11	.32 ± .05 (15-18)
Inferiority feelings.........................	.17	.32 ± .06 (15-18)
Fighting.....................................	.07	.31 ± .04 (19-20)
Violence.....................................	.19	.26 ± .05 (23)
Destructive..................................	.15	.25 ± .06 (24-26)
Grouped: fighting, etc......................	.14	.24 ± .04 (27-30)
Exclusion from school........................	.08	.24 ± .06 (27-30)
Hatred or jealousy of sibling................	.18	.23 ± .06 (31-32)

*Rank order of girls' correlations.

TABLE 45—Continued

	Boys	Girls
Headaches...	.19	.23 ± .05 (31-32)
Quarrelsome.......................................	.14	.21 ± .04 (34-35)
Former convulsions.............................	.19	.21 ± .06 (34-35)
Sensitive over specific fact..................	.15	.20 ± .05 (36)
	Larger Correlations (Negative)	
Feeble-minded sibling..........................	-.28 ± .04	-.15
Brother in penal detention....................	-.20 ± .04	-.30 ± .05
Sex delinquency (coitus)......................	-.03	-.24 ± .04
Vocational guidance............................	-.03	-.21 ± .04

Other Correlations (Positive to Negative)

Masturbation, .19 and .19; Underweight, .19 and .13; Contrary, .18 and .17; Temper display, .18 and .03; Swearing (general), .18 (boys); Boastful, "show-off," .16 and .15; Stubborn, .16 and .13; Rude, .15 and .05; Mental conflict, .15 and .13; Clean, .15 and .01; Selfish, .14 and .12; Leader, .14 and .12; Preference for younger children, .13 and .19; Grouped: disobedient, etc., .13 and .17; Disobedient, .12 and .19; Lack of interest in school, .12 and .12; Seclusive, .12 and .05; Conduct prognosis bad, .12 and -.01; Stuttering, .12 (boys); Grouped: lack of interest in school, etc., .12 and .15; Enuresis, .11 and .19; Bashful, .11 and .10; Speech defect, .11 and .17; Grouped: swearing, etc., .11 and .07; Inefficient in work, play, etc., .10 and .18; Sulky, .10 and -.04; Unhappy, .10 and .18; Excuse-forming, .09 and .05; Listless, .09 and -.04; Smoking, .08 (girls); Incorrigible, .07 and .14; Grouped: egocentric, etc., .07 and .14; Inattentive in school, .06 and .19; Irresponsible, .06 and .14; Lying, .06 and .19; Egocentric, .06 and .15; Bad companions, .06 and -.02; Refusal to attend school, .05 and -.10; Poor work in school, .05 and .14; Overinterest in sex matters, .04 and .07; Follower, .04 and .02; Loitering, .03 and -.04; Sullen, .03 and .04; Lack of initiative, .03 and -.05; Attractive manner, .03 and .07; Leading others into bad conduct, .02 and .10; Stealing, .02 and .07; Oversuggestible, .02 and .03; Question of hypophrenia, .02 and .01; Popular, .02 and .06; Victim of sex abuse, .02 (girls); Gang, .01 (boys); Truancy from school, .01 and .04; Repressed, .01 and .15; Vicious home conditions, .00 and -.15; Discord between parents, -.00 and -.11; Defiant, -.01 and .15; Slovenly, -.01 and .00; Grouped: dull, slow, etc., -.01 and -.02; Threatening violence, -.01 (boys); Overinterest in opposite sex, -.01 (girls); Lazy, -.02 and -.01; Truancy from home, -.02 and .12; Sex denied entirely, -.02 and .14; Irregular attendance at school, -.02 and -.08; Staying out late at night, -.03 and .06; Slow, dull, -.03 and -.01; Lues, -.04 and .04; Retardation in school, -.07 and -.14; Immoral home conditions, -.14 and .12
        Omitted—Grouped: "nervous," etc.

irritable temperament, and temper tantrums or display (undifferentiated). Six behavior notations yielded substantial correlations in the .30's among girls and moderate coefficients in the .20's for boys: crying spells, apprehensiveness, question of change of per-

sonality, "spoiled child," absent-mindedness, and finicky food
habits. Four behavior difficulties among girls similarly yielded
substantial correlations in the .30's but low positive correlations
below .20 for boys: temper tantrums, fighting, disturbing influence in school, and inferiority feelings.

Six personality and conduct problems showed moderate correlations in the .20's among both sexes: emotional instability,
irregular sleep habits, nail-biting, bossy manner, sensitivenss in
general, daydreaming; and also two which were calculated for boys
only, teasing other children and complaining of bad treatment by
other children. Among boys there were five behavior notations
showing moderate correlations in the .20's but low positive correlations below .20 for girls: worry over some specific fact, depressed spells, unpopularity, object of teasing by other children,
and fantastical lying. Among girls there were eight notations
showing moderate coefficients in the .20's, the corresponding correlations for the boys ranging from .08 to .19: violence, destructiveness, quarrelsomeness, exclusion from school, sensitiveness
over some specific fact, hatred or jealousy of sibling, headaches,
and former convulsions.

There were several negative coefficients of significant
magnitude with "nervousness." Brother in penal detention yielded
tetrachoric correlations of -.20 $\pm$ .04 and -.30 $\pm$ .05 among boys
and girls respectively. Among boys feeble-minded sibling yielded
the correlation of -.28 $\pm$ .04. Among girls sex delinquency (coitus) and the notation "request for vocational guidance" showed
negative correlations of moderate size in the -.20's.

Among sex notations we have noted the significant negative
correlation of -.24 $\pm$ .04 for sex delinquency (coitus) among girls,
the corresponding boys' coefficient being negligible. Among both
sexes masturbation showed a correlation of .19, which, though suggestive, is not of marked significance. The other sex notations—
overinterest in sex matters, sex misbehavior denied entirely, and
(calculated for girls only) overinterest in opposite sex and victim of sex abuse—showed negligible correlations with "nervousness."

Among the physical or psychophysical notations neurological
defect (unspecified) showed the meaningful coefficients of .31 $\pm$
.04 and .44 $\pm$ .04 among boys and girls respectively. Question or

diagnosis of encephalitis among girls similarly yielded the fairly
high correlation of .40 + .06, with a corresponding low correlation among boys of .14. Among the other five notations in this
field—underweight condition, enuresis, lues, speech defect, and
stuttering—the coefficients were low, ranging from -.04 to .19.

Brother in penal detention, as we have noted, showed the
curious negative correlations of -.20 + .04 and -.30 + .05 among
boys and girls respectively. The other three notations concerning
home or familial conditions—discord between parents and vicious
or immoral home conditions—showed low correlations ranging from
-.15 to .12.

Restlessness, overactivity, hyperkinesis, "patient has too
much energy," showed moderate to substantial correlations ranging
from .25 to .43 with the personality-total and the conduct-total
but negligible relations with police arrest. It was noted among
559, or 26.5 per cent, of our boys and among 258, or 21.8 per cent,
of our girls and is one of the most frequently noted behavior problems among our children. Its highest correlations among both sexes
were for "nervousness" and distractibility, with coefficients among
girls of .51 + .03 and .56 + .04 respectively and among boys of
.43 + .03 and .39 + .03 respectively (Table 46). Changeable moods,

TABLE 46

CORRELATIONS WITH "RESTLESS"

	Boys	Girls
Personality-total..............................	.25 ± .02	.34 ± .03
Conduct-total..................................	.34 ± .02	.43 ± .02
Police arrest..................................	.06 ± .03	.09 ± .04
	Larger Correlations (Positive)	
"Nervous"......................................	.43 ± .03	.51 ± .03 (2)*
Distractible...................................	.39 ± .03	.56 ± .04 (1)
Disturbing influence in school.................	.37 ± .03	.27 ± .05 (32-35)
Changeable moods...............................	.30 ± .03	.43 ± .04 (7)
Rude...	.30 ± .03	.22 ± .04 (48-51)
Absent-minded..................................	.29 ± .04	.10

*Rank order of girls' correlations.

TABLE 46—Continued

	Boys	Girls
Boastful, "show-off"...........................	.28 ± .03	.33 ± .05 (15-18)
Inattentive in school.........................	.28 ± .02	.37 ± .05 (13)
Restless in sleep.............................	.28 ± .03	.36 ± .04 (14)
Teasing other children........................	.27 ± .03	....
Question of encephalitis......................	.27 ± .05	.45 ± .06 (4-5)
Grouped: disobedient, etc....................	.27 ± .02	.31 ± .03 (20-23)
Grouped: temper, etc.........................	.27 ± .00	.40 ± .03 (9)
Grouped: lack of interest in school, etc.....	.27 ± .03	.38 ± .04 (12)
Grouped: depressed, etc......................	.27 ± .03	.19
Disobedient...................................	.26 ± .03	.23 ± .04 (43-47)
Irritable.....................................	.26 ± .03	.32 ± .04 (19)
Incorrigible..................................	.25 ± .03	.31 ± .04 (20-23)
Nail-biting...................................	.25 ± .03	.27 ± .04 (32-35)
Bossy...	.24 ± .04	.26 ± .05 (36-39)
Destructive...................................	.24 ± .06	.29 ± .06 (25-27)
Depressed.....................................	.24 ± .04	.22 ± .06 (48-51)
Fantastical lying.............................	.23 ± .03	.26 ± .05 (36-39)
Slovenly......................................	.23 ± .03	.19
Conduct prognosis bad.........................	.23 ± .04	.28 ± .06 (28-31)
Contrary......................................	.22 ± .04	.11
Unhappy.......................................	.22 ± .04	.08
Selfish.......................................	.21 ± .04	.15
Question of change of personality.............	.21 ± .04	.27 ± .05 (32-35)
Emotional instability.........................	.21 ± .04	.41 ± .05 (8)
Grouped: egocentric, etc.....................	.21 ± .03	.24 ± .04 (40-42)
Finicky food habits...........................	.20 ± .03	.26 ± .05 (36-39)
Inefficient in work, play, etc................	.20 ± .04	.16
Neurological defect...........................	.20 ± .03	.28 ± .04 (28-31)
Grouped: swearing, etc.......................	.20 ± .03	....
Leader..	.20 ± .04	.23 ± .05 (43-47)
Grouped: fighting, etc.......................	.18	.46 ± .03 (3)
Violence......................................	.15	.45 ± .04 (4-5)
Fighting......................................	.15	.44 ± .03 (6)
Exclusion from school.........................	.18	.39 ± .05 (10-11)
Temper tantrums...............................	.16	.39 ± .04 (10-11)
Unpopular.....................................	.16	.33 ± .06 (15-18)
Excuse-forming................................	.17	.33 ± .05 (15-18)
Quarrelsome...................................	.13	.33 ± .04 (15-18)
Crying spells.................................	.16	.31 ± .03 (20-23)
Lack of interest in school....................	.17	.30 ± .05 (24)
Worry over specific fact......................	.15	.29 ± .06 (25-27)
Queer...	.07	.29 ± .05 (25-27)
Lying...	.17	.28 ± .03 (28-31)
Object of teasing.............................	-.05	.28 ± .05 (28-31)
Preference for younger children...............	.16	.27 ± .05 (32-35)
Egocentric....................................	.18	.26 ± .04 (36-39)
Leading others into bad conduct...............	.09	.24 ± .06 (40-42)
Inferiority feelings..........................	.16	.24 ± .06 (40-42)
Headaches.....................................	.14	.23 ± .05 (43-47)
Daydreaming...................................	.12	.23 ± .05 (43-47)
Defiant.......................................	.17	.23 ± .05 (43-47)
Mental conflict...............................	.15	.22 ± .06 (48-51)

TABLE 46—Continued

	Boys	Girls
Grouped: sensitive or worrisome, etc.........	.15	.22 ± .04 (48-51)
Psychoneurotic..................................	.14	.21 ± .05 (52-55)
Hatred or jealousy of sibling..................	.14	.21 ± .06 (52-55)
Masturbation...................................	.14	.21 ± .04 (52-55)
Enuresis.......................................	.07	.21 ± .04 (52-55)
Stubborn.......................................	.16	.20 ± .04 (56-58)
Sullen...	.11	.20 ± .05 (56-58)
Truancy from home.............................	.12	.20 ± .04 (56-58)

Other Correlations (Positive to Negative)

Spoiled child, .19 and .19; Loitering, .18 and .14; Threatening violence, .18 (boys); Irregular sleep habits, .18 and .19; Irresponsible, .17 and .16; Swearing (general), .17 (boys); Overinterest in opposite sex, .17 (girls); Stealing, .15 and .19; Sulky, .15 and .14; Smoking, .14 (boys); Temper display, .14 and .13; Victim of sex abuse, .14 (girls); Staying out late at night, .13 and .15; Listless, .13 and .17; Oversuggestible, .13 and .17; Follower, .13 and .13; Overinterest in sex matters, .12 and .18; Sensitive (general), .11 and .13; Sensitive over specific fact, .11 and .09; Poor work in school, .11 and .14; Underweight, .11 and .10; Bad companions, .10 and .17; Former convulsions, .10 and .11; Refusal to attend school, .09 and .02; Truancy from school, .06 and .17; Lazy, .08 and .08; Gang, .08 (boys); Seclusive, .08 and .17; Discord between parents, .08 and -.05; Complaining of bad treatment by other children, .07 (boys); Lack of initiative, .06 and .01; Attractive manner, .06 and .05; Popular, .05 and .03; Clean, .05 and .03; Irregular attendance at school, .05 and -.12; Speech defect, .05 and .15; Vocational guidance, .04 and .02; Slow, dull, .03 and .11; Sex denied entirely, .01 and .09; Apprehensive, -.00 and .14; Grouped: dull, slow, etc., -.00 and .11; Repressed, -.04 and -.00; Stuttering, -.04 (boys); Bashful, -.05 and -.05; Question of hypophrenia, -.05 and .05; Immoral home conditions, -.08 and -.01; Vicious home conditions, -.08 and -.10; Retardation in school, -.08 and -.02; Sex delinquency (coitus), -.09 and .09; Lues, -.10 and -.03; Brother in penal detention, -.11 and .18; Feeble-minded sibling, -.11 and -.13
Omitted—Grouped: "nervous," etc.

emotional instability, and question or diagnosis of encephalitis among girls yielded very substantial correlations in the .40's, and moderate coefficients ranging from .21 to .30 among boys. Among girls fighting and violence also yielded the fairly substantial correlations of .44 ± .03 and .45 ± .04 respectively, the boys' coefficients being low, .15 for each trait.

Disturbing influence in school and rudeness among boys yielded substantial correlations in the .30's and moderate coefficients in the .20's among girls. Five behavior traits among girls showed substantial correlations in the .30's with corresponding moderate coefficients in the .20's for boys: restlessness in sleep

irritable temperament, boastful or "show-off" manner, inattentiveness in school, and incorrigibility. Seven additional notations
yielded substantial correlations in the .30's for girls but low
positive coefficients below .20 for boys: temper tantrums, quarrelsomeness, crying spells, unpopularity, excuse-forming attitude,
lack of interest in school, and exclusion from school.

     Restlessness showed moderate correlations in the .20's for
both sexes with the following eleven notations: nail-biting, finicky food habits, disobedience, destructiveness, staff notation of
unfavorable conduct prognosis, question of change of personality,
depressed spells, fantastical lying, bossy manner, "leader," neurological defect (unspecified); and also two which were calculated
for boys only, teasing other children and swearing or bad language
(undifferentiated). Six behavior traits among boys showed moderate
correlations in the .20's but low positive coefficients below .20
for girls: absent-mindedness, slovenliness, inefficiency in work,
play, etc., unhappiness, selfishness, and contrariness. A large
list of twenty behavior and other notations showed moderate correlations in the .20's for girls but low coefficients ranging from
-.03 to .18 for boys: sensitiveness or worrisomeness (undifferentiated), worry over some specific fact, inferiority feelings, mental conflict, psychoneurotic trends, queer behavior, hatred or
jealousy of sibling, egocentricity, defiant attitude, stubbornness,
leading others into bad conduct, truancy from home, sullenness, lying, daydreaming, object of teasing by other children, preference
for younger children as playmates, masturbation, headaches, and enuresis.

     Among the six sex notations restlessness showed only one
coefficient of significant size, .21 + .04 for masturbation among
girls.

     Among the seven physical or psychophysical notations there
were several meaningful correlations. Question or diagnosis of encephalitis showed tetrachoric r's of .27 + .05 and .45 + .06 for
boys and girls respectively. Neurological defect (unspecified)
showed the respective moderate coefficients of .20 + .03 and .28
+ .04. Among girls enuresis showed a correlation of .21 + .04,
the corresponding boys' coefficient being negligible, .07.

     Among the four home or familial notations all correlations
were low, ranging from -.11 to .18.

Irritable temperament, "patient high-strung or impatient" was noted among 448, or 21.2 per cent, of our boys and among 175, or 14.8 per cent, of our girls. Its bi-serial correlations with our criteria of personality and conduct deviation generally were of moderate size, ranging from .27 to .30. With the police-arrest criterion the girls' correlation was .22 ± .04, but among boys the correlation was negligible, .04 ± .03 (Table 47).

TABLE 47

CORRELATIONS WITH "IRRITABLE"

	Boys	Girls
Personality-total..............................	.29 ± .02	.27 ± .03
Conduct-total.................................	.30 ± .02	.29 ± .03
Police arrest.................................	.04 ± .03	.22 ± .04
	Larger Correlations (Positive)	
Changeable moods..............................	.43 ± .03	.35 ± .04 (7-10)*
Threatening violence..........................	.34 ± .04	....
Violence......................................	.34 ± .03	.30 ± .05 (17-19)
Question of change of personality.............	.33 ± .04	.26 ± .06 (23-28)
"Nervous".....................................	.33 ± .03	.36 ± .04 (5-6)
Grouped: fighting, etc.......................	.32 ± .03	.44 ± .04 (1)
Crying spells.................................	.32 ± .03	.30 ± .04 (17-19)
Temper tantrums...............................	.32 ± .03	.43 ± .04 (2)
Question of encephalitis......................	.30 ± .05	.31 ± .07 (16)
Temper display...............................	.30 ± .03	.42 ± .05 (3-4)
Contrary......................................	.29 ± .04	.33 ± .06 (12-14)
Selfish.......................................	.29 ± .04	.35 ± .04 (7-10)
Grouped: swearing, etc......................	.28 ± .03	.23 ± .05 (33-35)
Grouped: disobedient, etc...................	.27 ± .02	.34 ± .04 (11)
Emotional instability.........................	.27 ± .04	.26 ± .05 (23-28)
Irregular sleep habits........................	.27 ± .04	.28 ± .06 (21)
Bossy...	.26 ± .04	.25 ± .05 (29-32)
Restless......................................	.26 ± .03	.32 ± .04 (15)
Grouped: egocentric, etc....................	.25 ± .03	.29 ± .04 (20)
Queer...	.25 ± .04	.09
Hatred or jealousy of sibling.................	.24 ± .04	.22 ± .06 (36-37)
Swearing (general)............................	.24 ± .04	....
Stubborn......................................	.24 ± .03	.19
Smoking.......................................	.24 ± .04	....
Fantastical lying.............................	.24 ± .03	.26 ± .06 (23-28)
Psychoneurotic................................	.23 ± .05	.11
Restless in sleep.............................	.22 ± .03	.33 ± .04 (12-14)
Quarrelsome...................................	.22 ± .03	.35 ± .04 (7-10)

*Rank order of girls' correlations.

TABLE 47—Continued

	Boys	Girls
Finicky food habits	.22 ± .03	.42 ± .05 (3-4)
Fighting	.21 ± .03	.35 ± .04 (7-10)
Rude	.21 ± .03	.33 ± .04 (12-14)
Spoiled child	.21 ± .03	.26 ± .05 (23-28)
Unpopular	.20 ± .04	.19
Sullen	.20 ± .03	.26 ± .05 (23-28)
Leader	.12	.36 ± .05 (5-6)
Incorrigible	.16	.30 ± .04 (17-19)
Enuresis	.05	.27 ± .04 (22)
Sensitive (general)	.19	.26 ± .05 (23-28)
Neurological defect	.12	.25 ± .05 (29-32)
Inferiority feelings	.12	.25 ± .06 (29-32)
Daydreaming	.16	.25 ± .05 (29-32)
Headaches	.18	.23 ± .05 (33-35)
Boastful, "show-off"	.10	.23 ± .06 (33-35)
Grouped: depressed, etc.	.18	.22 ± .05 (36-37)
Defiant	.17	.21 ± .04 (38)
Disobedient	.16	.20 ± .04 (39-41)
Egocentric	.19	.20 ± .05 (39-41)
Grouped: lack of interest in school, etc.	.08	.20 ± .05 (39-41)
	Larger Correlations (Negative)	
Immoral home conditions	-.19	-.26 ± .05
Vicious home conditions	.06	-.24 ± .06
Sex delinquency (coitus)	-.04	-.24 ± .04
Brother in penal detention	-.00	-.22 ± .05
Victim of sex abuse	....	-.20 ± .05

Other Correlations (Positive to Negative)

Irresponsible, .19 and .16; Sulky, .19 and .19; Depressed, .18 and .19; Absent-minded, .18 and .06; Excuse-forming, .17 and .10; Worry over specific fact, .17 and .17; Conduct prognosis bad, .17 and -.04; Grouped: sensitive or worrisome, etc., .16 and .13; Seclusive, .16 and .11; Bashful, .16 and .08; Lying, .16 and .11; Disturbing influence in school, .16 and .19; Destructive, .16 and .10; Teasing other children, .15 (boys); Listless, .15 and -.11; Distractible, .15 and .19; Refusal to attend school, .14 and .09; Inefficient in work, play, etc., .13 and .18; Lack of interest in school, .13 and .14; Overinterest in sex matters, .13 and .10; Lack of initiative, .13 and -.12; Mental conflict, .13 and .06; Complaining of bad treatment by other children, .13 (boys); Former convulsions, .13 and .07; Speech defect, .12 and -.04; Nail-biting, .12 and .16; Lazy, .11 and .11; Masturbation, .11 and -.01; Apprehensive, .11 and -.02; Overinterest in opposite sex, .11 (girls); Lues, .10 and -.05; Exclusion from school, .10 and .04; Truancy from home, .10 and -.11; Stealing, .10 and .01; Gang, .09 (boys); Slovenly, .09 and -.01; Preference for younger children, .09 and .19; Poor work in school, .09 and .06; Follower, .09 and -.00; Clean, .09 and .07; Loitering, .07 and .06; Sensitive over specific fact, .07 and .02; Popular, .07 and .13; Unhappy, .06 and .14; Object of teasing, .06 and .15; Truancy from school, .06 and .08; Leading others into bad conduct, .06 and .13; Discord between parents, .04 and .11; Bad companions, .03 and -.03; Oversuggest-

TABLE 47—Continued
_____

ible, .03 and -.08; Stuttering, .03 (boys); Grouped: dull, slow, etc., .02 and
-.04; Underweight, .02 and .17; Staying out late at night, .00 and .11; Inattentive in school, -.00 and .18; Vocational guidance, -.02 and .00; Attractive
manner, -.04 and .02; Question of hypophrenia, -.04 and -.04; Slow, dull, -.05
and -.01; Irregular attendance at school, -.06 and .04; Repressed, -.07 and .06;
Retardation in school, -.11 and -.11; Feeble-minded sibling, -.14 and -.08; Sex
denied entirely, -.17 and .08
        Omitted—Grouped: "nervous," etc.; Grouped: temper, etc.

    Its highest correlations, ranging from .30 to .44 among
both sexes, were for "nervousness," fighting or quarrelsomeness
(undifferentiated), violence, threatening violence (calculated for
boys only), temper tantrums, changeable moods or attitudes, crying
spells, temper display, and question or diagnosis of encephalitis.
Question of change of personality among boys also yielded the substantial correlation of .33 + .04 and among girls the moderate correlation of .26 + .06. Among girls there were nine behavior difficulties yielding similar substantial correlations, ranging from
.30 to .42, with corresponding moderate coefficients in the .20's
for boys: restlessness, restlessness in sleep, disobedience or
incorrigibility (undifferentiated), contrariness, fighting, quarrelsomeness, rudeness, selfishness, and finicky food habits. Incorrigibility and "leader" also yielded substantial correlations
in the .30's for girls but low coefficients below .20 for boys.
    Eight behavior problems showed moderate correlations in
the .20's among both sexes: emotional instability, irregular sleep
habits, bossy manner, hatred or jealousy of sibling, sullenness,
swearing or bad language (undifferentiated), "spoiled child," and
fantastical lying and also smoking (calculated for boys only).
Four others showed moderate correlations in the .20's for boys but
low positive coefficients below .20 for girls: stubbornness, queer
behavior, psychoneurotic trends, and unpopularity. Among girls
there were twelve additional notations with moderate correlations
in the .20's but low positive correlations below .20 for boys:
boastful or "show-off" manner, disobedience, defiant attitude, egocentricity, sensitiveness in general, inferiority feelings, daydreaming, depressed spells or unhappiness (undifferentiated), lack
of interest or inattentiveness in school studies or employment (undifferentiated), enuresis, headaches, and neurological defect (unspecified).

There were five significant negative correlations with irritable temperament, ranging from -.20 to -.26, all among girls:
sex delinquency (coitus), victim of sex abuse by older child or
person (calculated for girls only), immoral and vicious home conditions, and brother in penal detention.

Among the sex notations there were two coefficients of significant size, both of negative sign, sex delinquency (coitus)
among girls, -.24 + .04, and victim of sex abuse by older child or
person (calculated for girls only), -.20 + .05.

Among physical or psychophysical notations there were several correlations of significant size. Question or diagnosis of
encephalitis yielded the substantial correlations of .30 + .05 and
.31 + .07 for boys and girls respectively. Neurological defect
(unspecified) and enuresis among girls showed moderate correlations
in the .20's.

Among home or familial conditions irritable temperament
showed three correlations of moderate size in the .20's, all negative in sign and all among girls: vicious and immoral home conditions and brother in penal detention.

When the three personality problems, "nervousness," restlessness, and irritable temperament, together with changeable moods
or attitudes (Table 35, p. 231), are combined under one rubric, we
have the correlation coefficients shown in Table 48. Under this

TABLE 48

CORRELATIONS WITH "GROUPED: NERVOUS, ETC."

	Boys	Girls
Personality-total............................	.42 ± .02	.48 ± .02
Conduct-total.................................	.35 ± .02	.41 ± .02
Police arrest.................................	.02 ± .03	-.20 ± .04
	Larger Correlations (Positive)	
Grouped: temper, etc.........................	.38 ± .02	.47 ± .03 (7-8)*
Distractible.................................	.37 ± .03	.55 ± .03 (3)
Question of encephalitis.....................	.35 ± .04	.48 ± .05 (6)

*Rank order of girls' correlations.

TABLE 48--Continued

	Boys	Girls
Emotional instability	.35 ± .04	.32 ± .04 (31-34)
Restless in sleep	.34 ± .03	.56 ± .03 (1-2)
Grouped: fighting, etc.	.33 ± .02	.53 ± .03 (4)
Violence	.33 ± .03	.46 ± .04 (9)
Grouped: disobedient, etc.	.32 ± .02	.36 ± .03 (21-25)
Rude	.32 ± .03	.24 ± .04 (55-56)
Temper tantrums	.32 ± .03	.52 ± .03 (5)
Crying spells	.32 ± .02	.47 ± .03 (7-8)
Finicky food habits	.31 ± .03	.45 ± .04 (10)
Contrary	.30 ± .04	.25 ± .05 (53-54)
Disturbing influence in school	.29 ± .03	.39 ± .04 (18-20)
Teasing other children	.29 ± .03	....
Question of change of personality	.29 ± .03	.36 ± .05 (21-25)
Quarrelsome	.28 ± .03	.42 ± .03 (11)
Spoiled child	.28 ± .03	.31 ± .04 (35-36)
Grouped: lack of interest in school, etc.	.28 ± .02	.30 ± .04 (37-41)
Psychoneurotic	.27 ± .04	.38 ± .05 (14-17)
Bossy	.26 ± .04	.38 ± .04 (14-17)
Selfish	.26 ± .03	.35 ± .04 (26-27)
Queer	.26 ± .04	.38 ± .05 (18-20)
Grouped: swearing, etc.	.26 ± .03	.23 ± .04 (57-58)
Boastful, "show-off"	.25 ± .03	.38 ± .04 (14-17)
Incorrigible	.25 ± .02	.31 ± .03 (35-36)
Nail-biting	.25 ± .03	.37 ± .03 (18-20)
Temper display	.25 ± .03	.30 ± .04 (37-41)
Daydreaming	.25 ± .03	.28 ± .04 (43-46)
Depressed	.25 ± .05	.26 ± .04 (49-52)
Irregular sleep habits	.25 ± .04	.34 ± .05 (28)
Sensitive (general)	.25 ± .03	.36 ± .04 (21-25)
Neurological defect	.25 ± .03	.41 ± .04 (12)
Grouped: sensitive or worrisome, etc.	.25 ± .02	.32 ± .03 (31-34)
Fighting	.24 ± .03	.56 ± .04 (1-2)
Inattentive in school	.24 ± .02	.40 ± .04 (13)
Swearing (general)	.24 ± .03	....
Threatening violence	.24 ± .04	....
Worry over specific fact	.24 ± .04	.27 ± .06 (47-48)
Grouped: egocentric, etc.	.24 ± .03	.30 ± .03 (37-41)
Headaches	.23 ± .04	.26 ± .04 (49-52)
Unpopular	.23 ± .04	.38 ± .05 (14-17)
Stubborn	.23 ± .03	.30 ± .03 (37-41)
Disobedient	.22 ± .02	.28 ± .03 (43-46)
Hatred or jealousy of sibling	.22 ± .04	.27 ± .05 (47-48)
Absent-minded	.22 ± .03	.26 ± .05 (49-52)
Conduct prognosis bad	.22 ± .04	.01
Destructive	.21 ± .03	.36 ± .05 (21-25)
Lack of interest in school	.21 ± .03	.18
Masturbation	.21 ± .02	.22 ± .04 (59-61)
Egocentric	.21 ± .03	.24 ± .04 (55-56)
Complaining of bad treatment by other children	.20 ± .04	....
Listless	.20 ± .03	.02
Sulky	.20 ± .04	.30 ± .05 (37-41)
Slovenly	.20 ± .03	.10

TABLE 48—Continued

	Boys	Girls
Preference for younger children...............	.15	.36 ± .04 (21-25)
Exclusion from school.........................	.15	.35 ± .05 (26-27)
Object of teasing.............................	.13	.33 ± .04 (29-30)
Fantastical lying.............................	.04	.33 ± .07 (29-30)
Defiant.......................................	.16	.32 ± .04 (31-34)
Enuresis......................................	.11	.32 ± .03 (31-34)
Lying...	.17	.28 ± .03 (43-46)
Inferiority feelings..........................	.19	.28 ± .05 (43-46)
Leader..	.17	.28 ± .05 (43-46)
Sullen..	.14	.26 ± .04 (49-52)
Grouped: depressed, etc......................	.14	.25 ± .04 (53-54)
Leading others into bad conduct...............	.07	.23 ± .05 (57-58)
Speech defect.................................	.14	.22 ± .04 (59-61)
Excuse-forming................................	.18	.22 ± .04 (59-61)
Sensitive over specific fact..................	.12	.21 ± .04 (62-64)
Stealing......................................	.14	.21 ± .03 (62-64)
Inefficient in work, play, etc................	.18	.21 ± .05 (62-64)
Apprehensive..................................	.15	.20 ± .04 (65-66)
Seclusive.....................................	.13	.20 ± .04 (65-66)
	Larger Correlations (Negative)	
Feeble-minded sibling.........................	-.24 ± .04	-.11
Brother in penal detention....................	-.14	-.27 ± .04
Vocational guidance...........................	-.01	-.27 ± .04
Sex delinquency (coitus)......................	-.00	-.25 ± .03

Other Correlations (Positive to Negative)

Former convulsions, .18 and .09; Mental conflict, .17 and .19; Follower, .16 and .09; Lack of initiative, .16 and .00; Smoking, .16 (boys); Irresponsible, .16 and .19; Overinterest in opposite sex, .15 (girls); Unhappy, .14 and .16; Overinterest in sex matters, .13 and .17; Poor work in school, .12 and .11; Lazy, .12 and .09; Loitering, .11 and .11; Oversuggestible, .11 and .10; Clean, .10 and .08; Refusal to attend school, .10 and -.03; Underweight, .10 and .18; Gang, .09 (boys); Truancy from school, .09 and .10; Bashful, .09 and .08; Discord between parents, .08 and .02; Truancy from home, .08 and .11; Stuttering, .08 (boys); Bad companions, .07 and .09; Staying out late at night, .05 and .05; Grouped: dull, slow, etc., .04 and .01; Popular, .04 and .07; Attractive manner, .02 and .08; Repressed, .01 and .09; Lues, -.03 and -.03; Irregular attendance at school, -.03 and -.17; Slow, dull, -.03 and -.03; Question of hypophrenia, -.04 and .04; Vicious home conditions, -.05 and -.12; Victim of sex abuse, -.05 (girls); Sex denied entirely, -.08 and .14; Retardation in school, -.11 and -.16; Immoral home conditions, -.15 and -.10

Omitted—Changeable moods; Irritable; Restless; "Nervous"

broader grouping fall 987, or 46.7 per cent, of our boys and 488, or 41.3 per cent, of our girls. Almost a half of our clinic population thus manifests one or more of these personality problems.

This combined "broader grouping" showed very substantial correlations ranging from .35 to .48 with <u>personality-total</u> and <u>conduct-total</u> but only a minor relation to the <u>police-arrest</u> criterion of overt juvenile delinquency, unless one considers the negative tetrachoric correlation of -.20 ± .04 among girls as meaningful.

Three personality notations—<u>distractibility</u>, <u>restlessness in sleep</u>, and <u>temper tantrums</u>—among girls yielded high correlations in the .50's, with substantial correlations among boys in the .30's. <u>Fighting</u> among girls also yielded a high correlation of .56 ± .04, with a moderate coefficient among boys of .24 ± .03. Four notations among girls yielded very substantial correlations in the .40's and substantial coefficients in the .30's for boys: <u>question or diagnosis of encephalitis</u>, <u>violence</u>, <u>crying spells</u>, and <u>finicky food habits</u>. Three additional notations among girls yielded very substantial correlations in the .40's, with corresponding moderate coefficients in the .20's among boys: <u>quarrelsomeness</u>, <u>inattentiveness in school</u>, and <u>neurological defect (unspecified)</u>. Among both sexes substantial correlations in the .30's were found for <u>emotional instability</u> and <u>disobedience or incorrigibility</u> (undifferentiated). <u>Rudeness</u> and <u>contrariness</u> among boys also yielded substantial correlations in the .30's, with corresponding moderate correlations in the .20's among girls. Seventeen behavior difficulties among girls yielded substantial correlations in the .30's, with moderate coefficients in the .20's among boys: <u>question of change of personality</u>, <u>psychoneurotic trends</u>, "<u>spoiled child</u>," <u>queer behavior</u>, <u>irregular sleep habits</u>, <u>sensitiveness in general</u>, <u>unpopularity</u>, <u>bossy manner</u>, <u>stubbornness</u>, <u>incorrigibility</u>, <u>destructiveness</u>, <u>temper display</u>, <u>disturbing influence in school</u>, <u>selfishness</u>, <u>sulkiness</u>, <u>boastful or "show-off" manner</u>, and <u>nail-biting</u>. Six additional notations among girls also showed substantial correlations in the .30's but low positive correlations below .20 for boys: <u>defiant attitude</u>, <u>fantastical lying</u>, <u>exclusion from school</u>, <u>object of teasing by other children</u>, <u>preference for younger children as playmates</u>, and <u>enuresis</u>.

Ten miscellaneous notations showed moderate correlations in the .20's among both sexes with the larger grouping "<u>nervousness</u>" or restlessness (undifferentiated): <u>daydreaming</u>, <u>depressed spells</u>, <u>absent-mindedness</u>, <u>worry over some specific fact</u>, <u>egocentricity</u>, <u>hatred or jealousy of sibling</u>, <u>disobedience</u>, <u>swearing or</u>

bad language (undifferentiated), masturbation, headaches; and the
following three notations which were calculated for boys only:
threatening violence, teasing other children, and complaining of
bad treatment by other children. Four notations among boys showed
moderate correlations in the .20's, with low positive coefficients
below .20 among girls: listlessness, slovenliness, lack of interest in school, and staff notation of unfavorable conduct prognosis.
Among girls there were twelve behavior traits showing moderate correlations in the .20's, with low positive coefficients below .20
for the boys: apprehensiveness, inferiority feelings, sensitiveness over some specific fact, seclusiveness, sullenness, inefficiency in work, play, etc., excuse-forming attitude, stealing, lying, leading others into bad conduct, "leader," and speech defect.

There were four negative coefficients of moderate size in
the -.20's: among boys for feeble-minded sibling, and among girls
for sex delinquency (coitus), brother in penal detention, and "request for vocational guidance."

Regarding the sex notations, the physical and psychophysical notations, and the home and familial notations, we may summarize the data of Tables 45, 46, 47, 48, and Table 35 (changeable
moods or attitudes) considered in this chapter as follows. Among
girls sex delinquency (coitus) showed moderate negative correlations in the .20's with "nervousness" and irritable temperament,
the boys' correlations being negligible. Masturbation among both
sexes showed moderate or low positive correlations with "nervousness," restlessness, and changeable moods or attitudes. The remaining four sex notations showed only occasional moderate correlations in this field.

Question or diagnosis of encephalitis and neurological defect (unspecified) consistently showed substantial correlations,
several of which were in the .40's, with all five notations "nervousness," restlessness, irritable temperament, changeable moods
or attitudes, and the broader grouping of "nervousness" or restlessness (undifferentiated). Enuresis among girls showed moderate
correlations ranging from .19 to .27 with "nervousness," restlessness, and irritable temperament, the corresponding coefficients
among boys, ranging from .05 to .11, being low and positive. Speech
defect (other than stuttering) among girls showed the moderate
tetrachoric r of .22 $\pm$ .04 with the combined grouping "nervousness"

or restlessness (undifferentiated) as shown in Table 48, but all other correlations were below .20. Stuttering, underweight condition, and lues (diagnosed or questioned) showed only low or negligible correlations with all five personality traits discussed in this chapter.

Among the four home or familial notations, brother in penal detention showed generally negative correlations of moderate size ranging from .18 to -.30 among girls for all five notations considered in this chapter. Among girls irritable temperament showed moderate negative correlations of -.24 ± .06 and -.26 ± .05 with vicious and immoral home conditions respectively.

In brief, the trends appearing among the correlations discussed in this chapter for the interrelated personality notations "nervousness," restlessness, irritable temperament, together with changeable moods or attitudes (Table 35, p. 231) is summarized in this paragraph. The neuropsychiatric notations, question or diagnosis of encephalitis and neurological defect (unspecified), which in our data overlap to a considerable extent, showed very meaningful correlations. Behavior problems showing substantial to high relationships were distractibility, temper tantrums, and, to a lesser extent, temper display, crying spells or crying easily, fighting (especially among girls), violence, restlessness in sleep, queer behavior, and question of change of personality.

Additional personality and conduct difficulties showing consistent moderate correlations in this field were staff notation of emotional instability, staff notation of psychoneurotic trends, "spoiled child," boastful or "show-off" manner, fantastical lying, bossy manner, rudeness, unpopularity, inferiority feelings or attitudes (especially among girls), depressed moods or spells, sensitiveness in general, quarrelsomeness, disturbing influence in school, finicky food habits, and nail-biting.

Masturbation among both sexes showed several moderate positive correlations, while sex delinquency (coitus) among girls showed several negative correlations of moderate size.

Among girls, brother in penal detention showed moderate negative correlations in the -.20's.

CHAPTER XXIX

RESTLESSNESS IN SLEEP AND IRREGULAR
SLEEP HABITS

The two notations restlessness in sleep and irregular sleep
habits or insomnia could not always be readily distinguished in the
case records, but the difference is clear enough. Restlessness in
sleep implies tossing, grinding of teeth, crying out, or "night-
mares," after the child has fallen asleep, while irregular sleep
habits implies wakefulness at a time when children are normally
asleep, which may be due to insomnia, to faulty family training in
bedtime hours, or to "reversal of sleep" occasionally occurring as
a psychiatric symptom. Their intercorrelations were moderate to
substantial, the tetrachoric coefficients for boys and girls being
.28 + .04 and .37 + .06 respectively. Both showed moderate to substantial bi-serial r's, ranging from .23 to .42 with the personal-
ity- and conduct-totals. With the police-arrest criterion of juvenile delinquency the tetrachoric correlations with restlessness
in sleep were negligible, while those with irregular sleep habits
were of significant size though moderate, the coefficients being
.24 + .04 among boys and .31 + .06 among girls.

Restlessness in sleep was one of the most frequently noted
behavior traits in our data, appearing in 324 cases, or 15.3 per
cent, of our 2,113 boys and in 146 cases, or 12.4 per cent, of our
1,181 girls.

Its highest correlation (.56 + .03) was among girls for
the broader grouping "nervousness" or restlessness (including irritable temperament and changeable moods or attitudes, undifferentiated), the boys' correlation of .34 + .03 also being substantial
(Table 49). Among girls two other notations yielded fairly high
correlations in the .40's—"nervousness" and nail-biting—with corresponding meaningful coefficients of .30 + .03 and .27 + .03 among
boys. Headaches among boys yielded the fairly high correlation of
.42 + .04, the corresponding coefficient among girls being .28 + .06.

283

TABLE 49

CORRELATIONS WITH "RESTLESS IN SLEEP"

	Boys	Girls
Personality-total............................	.26 ± .02	.35 ± .03
Conduct-total................................	.25 ± .02	.39 ± .03
Police arrests...............................	.06 ± .03	-.07 ± .05
		Larger Correlations (Positive)
Headaches....................................	.42 ± .04	.28 ± .06 (26-29)*
Grouped: "nervous" etc......................	.34 ± .03	.56 ± .03 (1)
Finicky food habits.........................	.34 ± .03	.38 ± .05 (5)
"Nervous"....................................	.30 ± .03	.47 ± .04 (2)
Former convulsions...........................	.29 ± .04	.26 ± .07 (34-39)
Neurological defect..........................	.28 ± .04	.32 ± .05 (17-18)
Restless.....................................	.28 ± .03	.36 ± .04 (9-11)
Irregular sleep habits.......................	.28 ± .04	.37 ± .06 (6-8)
Nail-biting..................................	.27 ± .03	.40 ± .04 (3)
Preference for younger children..............	.27 ± .04	.20 ± .06 (46-48)
Enuresis.....................................	.26 ± .03	.31 ± .04 (19-22)
Changeable moods.............................	.25 ± .04	.33 ± .05 (14-16)
Question of change of personality...........	.24 ± .04	.36 ± .06 (9-11)
Sensitive (general).........................	.23 ± .04	.13
Grouped: temper, etc........................	.22 ± .03	.37 ± .04 (6-8)
Irritable...................................	.22 ± .03	.33 ± .04 (14-16)
Teasing other children......................	.21 ± .04	....
Daydreaming.................................	.21 ± .04	.26 ± .05 (34-39)
Psychoneurotic..............................	.21 ± .05	.19
Discord between parents.....................	.20 ± .03	-.04
Queer.......................................	.20 ± .04	.39 ± .06 (4)
Smoking.....................................	.20 ± .04	....
Grouped: fighting, etc.....................	.10	.37 ± .04 (6-8)
Question of encephalitis....................	.15	.36 ± .07 (9-11)
Violence....................................	.11	.35 ± .05 (12)
Fantastical lying...........................	.12	.34 ± .06 (13)
Distractible................................	.14	.33 ± .05 (14-16)
Disturbing influence in school..............	.07	.32 ± .05 (17-18)
Defiant.....................................	.06	.31 ± .05 (19-22)
Hatred or jealousy of sibling...............	.19	.31 ± .06 (19-22)
Absent-minded...............................	.13	.31 ± .06 (19-22)
Unpopular...................................	.18	.30 ± .06 (23-24)
Stealing....................................	.07	.30 ± .04 (23-24)
Lying.......................................	.15	.29 ± .04 (25)
Leader......................................	.10	.28 ± .06 (26-29)
Inferiority feelings........................	.07	.28 ± .06 (26-29)
Masturbation................................	.18	.28 ± .05 (26-29)
Bossy.......................................	.16	.27 ± .06 (30-33)
Quarrelsome.................................	.14	.27 ± .05 (30-33)
Temper tantrums.............................	.17	.27 ± .05 (30-33)

*Rank order of girls' correlations.

TABLE 49--Continued

	Boys	Girls
Depressed..	.17	.27 ± .06 (30-33)
Grouped: swearing, etc.......................	.12	.26 ± .06 (34-39)
Temper display..................................	.17	.26 ± .06 (34-39)
Inattentive in school.........................	.07	.26 ± .06 (34-39)
Fighting..	.03	.26 ± .04 (34-39)
Apprehensive...................................	.13	.25 ± .05 (40-41)
Crying spells..................................	.19	.25 ± .04 (40-41)
Destructive....................................	.13	.24 ± .07 (42)
Disobedient....................................	.13	.23 ± .04 (43-44)
Grouped: disobedient, etc....................	.11	.23 ± .04 (43-44)
Selfish..	.08	.22 ± .04 (45)
Grouped: sensitive or worrisome, etc.........	.15	.20 ± .04 (46-48)
Grouped: egocentric, etc.....................	.08	.20 ± .05 (46-48)
	Larger Correlations (Negative)	
Sex delinquency (coitus)......................	-.01	-.23 ± .04

Other Correlations (Positive to Negative)

Boastful, "show-off," .19 and .13; Sulky, .19 and .14; Worry over specific fact, .17 and .12; Stubborn, .15 and .19; Grouped: depressed, etc., .14 and .17; Listless, .14 and .06; Bashful, .14 and .08; Overinterest in sex matters, .14 and .16; Rude, .14 and .14; Inefficient in work, play, etc., .14 and .14; Contrary, .13 and .11; Threatening violence, .13 (boys); Spoiled child, .13 and .17; Follower, .13 and .06; Irregular attendance at school, .13 and -.04; Vicious home conditions, .13 and -.19; Popular, .12 and .03; Stuttering, .12 (boys); Swearing (general), .12 (boys); Leading others into bad conduct, .12 and .05; Object of teasing, .11 and .17; Emotional instability, .11 and -.02; Underweight, .11 and .04; Speech defect, .11 and .14; Complaining of bad treatment by other children, .10 (boys); Oversuggestible, .10 and .05; Egocentric, .09 and .18; Truancy from home, .08 and .16; Bad companions, .07 and .09; Irresponsible, .07 and .11; Gang, .07 (boys); Excuse-forming, .07 and .16; Repressed, .07 and .09; Exclusion from school, .07 and .16; Lies, .07 and -.02; Grouped: dull, slow, etc., .07 and .09; Grouped: lack of interest in school, etc., .07 and .17; Attractive manner, .06 and .03; Seclusive, .06 and .01; Lazy, .06 and .04; Incorrigible, .06 and -.00; Lack of interest in school, .05 and .08; Slovenly, .05 and .14; Sensitive over specific fact, .05 and .14; Poor work in school, .05 and .02; Clean, .05 and .08; Immoral home conditions, .04 and -.07; Question of hypophrenia, .04 and .02; Loitering, .04 and .18; Victim of sex abuse, .04 (girls); Refusal to attend school, .03 and .09; Sullen, .03 and .12; Slow, dull, .03 and .06; Sex denied entirely, .02 and .05; Unhappy, .02 and -.01; Overinterest in opposite sex, .02 (girls); Mental conflict, .01 and .19; Lack of initiative, .00 and .11; Truancy from school, -.00 and .10; Staying out late at night, -.02 and .18; Retardation in school, -.04 and -.11; Conduct prognosis bad, -.06 and .11; Brother in penal detention, -.14 and -.17; Feeble-minded sibling, -.14 and -.15; Vocational guidance, -.17 and -.10

Finicky food habits among both sexes yielded substantial correlations in the .30's. Nine notations among girls yielded substantial correlations with restlessness in sleep in the .30's and moderate coefficients in the .20's among boys: irregular sleep habits, restlessness, changeable moods or attitudes, irritable temperament, temper tantrums or display (undifferentiated), question of change of personality, queer behavior, neurological defect (unspecified), and enuresis. Ten additional notations also yielded substantial correlations in the .30's among girls but low positive coefficients below .20 for boys: distractibility, absent-mindedness, violence, defiant attitude, disturbing influence in school, hatred or jealousy of sibling, unpopularity, fantastical lying, stealing, and question or diagnosis of encephalitis.

Three notations—daydreaming, preference for younger children as playmates, and former convulsions—showed moderate correlations in the .20's for both sexes. Teasing other children and smoking among boys also showed moderate correlations in the .20's, the coefficients for girls not being computed because of the paucity of girls' cases. Three additional notations among boys showed moderate correlations in the .20's but low or negligible coefficients below .20 among girls: psychoneurotic trends, sensitiveness in general, and discord between parents. Eighteen personality and conduct traits among girls also showed moderate correlations in the .20's, the correlations for boys being low and positive (below .20): apprehensiveness, temper tantrums, temper display, fighting, quarrelsomeness, bossy manner, destructiveness, selfishness, lying, swearing or bad language (undifferentiated), disobedience, inattentiveness in school, inferiority feelings, sensitiveness or worrisomeness (undifferentiated), depressed moods or spells, crying spells, masturbation, and "leader."

The only negative correlation of significant size with restlessness in sleep was among girls for sex delinquency (coitus), $-.23 \pm .04$, the boys' coefficient being negligible ($-.01$).

Among the six sex notations masturbation among girls yielded a positive correlation of $.28 \pm .05$ and sex delinquency (coitus) among girls a negative coefficient of $-.23 \pm .04$, all other coefficients in this field being low or negligible.

Among the seven physical or psychophysical notations neurological defect (unspecified) showed substantial correlations of

.28 + .04 and .32 + .05 among boys and girls respectively. Question or diagnosis of encephalitis showed corresponding coefficients
of .15 and .36 + .07. Enuresis (continuing beyond third birthday)
showed moderate to substantial correlations of .26 + .03 and .31
+ .04 for boys and girls respectively. The correlations for underweight condition, lues, speech defect, and stuttering were low or
negligible.

Among the four home or familial notations the only correlation of significant size with restlessness in sleep was with discord between parents among boys, .20 + .03, all other correlations
in this field ranging between -.19 and .13.

Irregular sleep habits or insomnia was noted among 123
boys, or 5.8 per cent, and among 64 girls, or 5.4 per cent.

Its highest correlations were among girls with question or
diagnosis of encephalitis, .44 + .09, and with queer behavior, .40
+ .07, the corresponding coefficients for boys being .30 + .07 and
.16 (Table 50). Question of change of personality and finicky food
habits yielded substantial correlations in the .30's for both
sexes. Fantastical lying among boys yielded the substantial correlation of .30 + .06 but a negligible correlation (-.01) among
girls. Three behavior difficulties among girls showed substantial
correlations in the .30's, with moderate coefficients in the .20's
among boys: restlessness in sleep, "nervousness" or restless (undifferentiated), and swearing or bad language (undifferentiated).
Eight additional notations among girls also showed substantial correlations in the .30's, with low or negligible coefficients below
.20 among boys: changeable moods or attitudes, emotional instability, sensitiveness in general, crying spells, apprehensiveness,
staff notation of psychoneurotic trends (unspecified), irregular
attendance at school, and neurological defect (unspecified).

Twelve personality and conduct problems showed moderate
correlations with irregular sleep habits in the .20's for both
sexes: irritable temperament, "nervousness," temper tantrums,
boastful or "show-off" manner, violence, fighting or quarrelsomeness (undifferentiated), disobedience, incorrigibility, staying out
late at night, refusal to attend school, "spoiled child," and worry
over some specific fact. Four notations (which were not computed
for girls because of paucity of cases) also showed moderate

TABLE 50

CORRELATIONS WITH "IRREGULAR SLEEP HABITS"

	Boys	Girls
Personality-total..............................	.23 ± .03	.42 ± .04
Conduct-total.................................	.38 ± .03	.32 ± .04
Police arrest.................................	.24 ± .04	.31 ± .06
	Larger Correlations (Positive)	
Question of change of personality.............	.34 ± .05	.35 ± .08 (5-6)*
Grouped: disobedient.........................	.34 ± .03	.28 ± .05 (17-19)
Finicky food habits...........................	.33 ± .05	.30 ± .07 (13-15)
Fantastical lying.............................	.30 ± .06	-.01
Question of encephalitis......................	.30 ± .07	.44 ± .09 (1)
Smoking.......................................	.29 ± .05	....
Staying out late at night.....................	.29 ± .04	.24 ± .06 (28-36)
Vicious home conditions.......................	.29 ± .06	.13
Restless in sleep.............................	.28 ± .04	.37 ± .06 (3)
Refusal to attend school......................	.27 ± .05	.24 ± .09 (28-36)
Irritable....................................	.27 ± .04	.28 ± .06 (17-19)
Grouped: fighting, etc.......................	.27 ± .04	.21 ± .05 (42-44)
Disobedient...................................	.26 ± .04	.23 ± .06 (37-39)
Unpopular.....................................	.26 ± .06	.08
Incorrigible..................................	.25 ± .04	.22 ± .06 (40-41)
Threatening violence..........................	.25 ± .06	....
Truancy from home.............................	.25 ± .04	.02
Grouped: "nervous," etc......................	.25 ± .04	.34 ± .05 (7-8)
Grouped: swearing, etc.......................	.25 ± .04	.35 ± .07 (5-6)
Teasing other children........................	.24 ± .05	....
Rude..	.24 ± .04	.15
Stubborn......................................	.24 ± .04	.06
Fighting......................................	.22 ± .04	.11
Slovenly......................................	.22 ± .04	.13
Temper tantrums...............................	.22 ± .05	.24 ± .07 (28-36)
Worry over specific fact......................	.22 ± .06	.22 ± .09 (40-41)
Complaining of bad treatment by other children	.21 ± .06	....
Boastful, "show-off"..........................	.20 ± .05	.23 ± .08 (37-39)
Violence......................................	.20 ± .05	.26 ± .07 (21-22)
"Nervous".....................................	.20 ± .04	.24 ± .06 (28-36)
Spoiled child.................................	.20 ± .05	.25 ± .07 (23-27)
Grouped: temper, etc.........................	.20 ± .04	.25 ± .05 (23-27)
Queer...	.16	.40 ± .07 (2)
Neurological defect...........................	.15	.36 ± .06 (4)
Irregular attendance at school................	.14	.34 ± .07 (7-8)
Changeable moods..............................	.19	.33 ± .06 (9-10)
Crying spells.................................	-.02	.33 ± .05 (9-10)
Psychoneurotic................................	.12	.32 ± .08 (11)
Sensitive (general)..........................	.09	.31 ± .07 (12)
Emotional instability.........................	.17	.30 ± .07 (13-15)

*Rank order of girls' correlations.

TABLE 50—Continued

	Boys	Girls
Apprehensive.....................................	.01	.30 ± .06 (13-15)
Inferiority feelings.............................	.05	.29 ± .08 (16)
Sex denied entirely..............................	.13	.28 ± .06 (17-19)
Former convulsions...............................	.15	.27 ± .08 (20)
Lazy...	.10	.26 ± .07 (21-22)
Distractible.....................................	.01	.25 ± .07 (23-27)
Lack of initiative...............................	.00	.25 ± .08 (23-27)
Clean..	.01	.25 ± .06 (23-27)
Grouped: sensitive or worrisome, etc.........	.17	.24 ± .05 (28-36)
Selfish..	-.10	.24 ± .04 (28-36)
Quarrelsome......................................	.10	.24 ± .06 (28-36)
Inefficient in work, play, etc.................	.18	.24 ± .08 (28-36)
Defiant..	.11	.24 ± .07 (28-36)
Nail-biting......................................	-.05	.23 ± .06 (37-39)
Loitering..	.10	.21 ± .08 (42-44)
Daydreaming......................................	.10	.21 ± .07 (42-44)
Grouped: egocentric, etc....................	.01	.20 ± .06 (45-49)
Seclusive..	.15	.20 ± .07 (45-49)
Depressed..	.08	.20 ± .08 (45-49)
Truancy from school..............................	.17	.20 ± .06 (45-49)
Destructive......................................	.19	.20 ± .08 (45-49)
	Larger Correlations (Negative)	
Lues...	-.23 ± .06	.03
Bashful..	-.20 ± .04	.06
Sulky..	.02	-.27 ± .08
Brother in penal detention......................	.09	-.23 ± .07

Other Correlations (Positive to Negative)

Bad companions, .18 and .17; Sullen, .18 and -.07; Lying, .18 and .16; Restless, .18 and .19; Stealing, .17 and .11; Sensitive over specific fact, .17 and .17; Mental conflict, .17 and -.04; Swearing (general), .16 (boys); Headaches, .16 and .16; Discord between parents, .16 and .19; Grouped: depressed, etc., .16 and .15; Contrary, .15 and .16; Unhappy, .15 and .10; Leading others into bad conduct, .14 and .10; Conduct prognosis bad, .14 and -.05; Disturbing influence in school, .13 and .16; Irresponsible, .13 and .17; Popular, .13 and .15; Attractive manner, .13 and .07; Lack of interest in school, .12 and .17; Gang, .11 (boys); Object of teasing, .11 and .14; Masturbation, .10 and .03; Grouped: lack of interest in school, .10 and .17; Leader, .09 and -.01; Overinterest in sex matters, .08 and .03; Temper display, .07 and .05; Listless, .07 and -.04; Oversuggestible, .07 and .14; Stuttering, .06 (boys); Bossy, .05 and .02; Exclusion from school, .05 and .12; Overinterest in opposite sex, .05 (girls); Inattentive in school, .04 and .03; Sex delinquency (coitus), .04 and -.15; Preference for younger children, .04 and -.08; Poor work in school, .04 and .04; Grouped: dull, slow, etc., .04 and .07; Enuresis, .03 and .11; Excuseforming, .03 and .19; Underweight, .03 and .10; Hatred or jealousy of sibling, .02 and .06; Egocentric, .02 and .19; Follower, .01 and -.08; Repressed, .01 and .05; Speech defect, .00 and -.05; Slow, dull, -.00 and .09; Vocational guidance,

TABLE 50—Continued

-.00 and .10; Question of hypophrenia, -.02 and .06; Victim of sex abuse, -.03 (girls); Immoral home conditions, -.04 and .07; Feeble-minded sibling, -.05 and -.08; Absent-minded, -.06 and -.02; Retardation in school, -.12 and -.14

correlations in the .20's for boys: smoking, threatening violence, teasing other children, and complaining of bad treatment by other children. Seven notations among boys also showed moderate correlations in the .20's, with low coefficients below .20 for girls: truancy from home, fighting, stubbornness, rudeness, slovenliness, unpopularity, and vicious home conditions. A large list of eighteen miscellaneous notations among girls showed moderate correlations in the .20's, with corresponding low coefficients ranging from -.10 to .19 among boys: distractibility, inefficiency in work, play, etc., lack of initiative, laziness, loitering or wandering, nail-biting, destructiveness, quarrelsomeness, defiant attitude, truancy from school, selfishness, inferiority feelings, depressed mood or spells, daydreaming, seclusiveness, clean habits, former convulsions, and sex misbehavior denied entirely.

Four negative correlations of moderate size ranging from -.20 to -.27 were found with irregular sleep habits: among boys, bashfulness and lues and among girls sulkiness and brother in penal detention.

Among the six sex notations the only correlation of significant size with irregular sleep habits was for sex misbehavior denied entirely among girls, .28 + .06.

Among our seven physical or psychophysical notations there were the substantial correlations of .30 + .07 and .44 + .09 for boys and girls respectively with question or diagnosis of encephalitis. Among girls neurological defect (unspecified) also showed a substantial correlation, .36 + .06. Lues among boys showed the moderate negative correlation of -.23 + .06.

Among home or familial notations there were two correlations of moderate size with irregular sleep habits, the positive correlation of .29 + .06 among boys with vicious home conditions and the negative coefficient of -.23 + .07 among girls with brother in penal detention.

CHAPTER XXX

EGOCENTRICITY AND SELFISHNESS

Staff notation of egocentric or self-centered attitude in our data was a formal notation made by the clinic's staff, usually by the psychiatrist, after examination of the patient, while selfishness was an informal descriptive term used by the "lay" informant. Egocentricity is an appraisal of a deep-lying personality trait, while selfishness is a mere description of overt behavior. Their intercorrelation among boys was only moderate, .21 ± .04; but among girls it was represented by one of the highest coefficients found for both of these notations, .45 ± .05. The fact that among girls these "undesirable" traits showed moderate correlations in the .20's with intelligence quotient (IQ) is interesting, the corresponding boys' correlations being positive but low (Table 10, p. 130).

Staff notation of egocentric or self-centered attitude was noted among 287, or 13.6 per cent, of our 2,113 White boys and among 147, or 12.4 per cent, of our 1,181 White girls and was one of the most frequent of the formal staff notations employed in the clinic of the Illinois Institute for Juvenile Research during the years in which these children were examined. Its bi-serial correlations with the conduct-total were fairly high, .41 ± .02 for boys and .48 ± .03 for girls (Table 51). With the personality-total its correlation among girls was substantial, .30 ± .03, but low among boys, .11 ± .02. With the police-arrest criterion of juvenile delinquency its tetrachoric correlation among boys was only moderate, .20 ± .03, and among girls negligible, .09 ± .05.

Its highest correlations were found among girls. Boastful or "show-off" manner and excuse-forming attitude among girls yielded fairly high coefficients in the .40's with corresponding substantial coefficients among boys in the .30's. Selfishness, quarrelsomeness, and temper tantrums among girls also yielded large coefficients in the .40's, with moderate coefficients in the .20's among boys. Rudeness and bossy manner yielded substantial correlations in the .30's for both sexes, with a similar coefficient for

291

TABLE 51

CORRELATIONS WITH "EGOCENTRIC"

	Boys	Girls
Personality-total.............................	.11 ± .02	.30 ± .03
Conduct-total.................................	.41 ± .02	.48 ± .03
Police arrest.................................	.20 ± .03	.09 ± .05
	Larger Correlations (Positive)	
Boastful, "show-off".........................	.39 ± .03	.45 ± .05 (1-2)*
Grouped: disobedient, etc....................	.35 ± .03	.35 ± .04 (11-14)
Excuse-forming................................	.32 ± .04	.41 ± .05 (4)
Contrary......................................	.31 ± .05	.24 ± .07 (35-37)
Rude..	.31 ± .03	.37 ± .04 (10)
Threatening violence..........................	.31 ± .05	....
Bossy...	.30 ± .04	.35 ± .05 (11-14)
Grouped: fighting, etc.......................	.30 ± .03	.38 ± .04 (6-9)
Defiant.......................................	.29 ± .04	.38 ± .05 (6-9)
Disobedient...................................	.29 ± .03	.35 ± .04 (11-14)
Unpopular.....................................	.29 ± .05	.38 ± .06 (6-9)
Fighting......................................	.28 ± .03	.23 ± .04 (38)
Lying...	.27 ± .03	.31 ± .04 (17-19)
Grouped: temper, etc.........................	.27 ± .03	.31 ± .04 (17-19)
Staying out late at night.....................	.26 ± .03	.22 ± .05 (39-41)
Hatred or jealousy of sibling.................	.26 ± .05	.38 ± .06 (6-9)
Fantastical lying.............................	.25 ± .03	.30 ± .06 (20-22)
Incorrigible..................................	.25 ± .03	.32 ± .04 (15-16)
Disturbing influence in school................	.24 ± .03	.28 ± .06 (24-27)
Violence......................................	.24 ± .03	.35 ± .05 (11-14)
Quarrelsome...................................	.23 ± .03	.42 ± .04 (3)
Sullen..	.23 ± .04	.30 ± .05 (20-22)
Temper tantrums...............................	.23 ± .08	.40 ± .05 (5)
Grouped: swearing, etc.......................	.23 ± .04	.20 ± .06 (47-51)
Destructive...................................	.22 ± .04	.22 ± .07 (39-41)
Conduct prognosis bad.........................	.22 ± .05	.28 ± .07 (24-27)
Selfish.......................................	.21 ± .04	.45 ± .05 (1-2)
Truancy from school...........................	.21 ± .03	.15
Grouped: "nervous," etc......................	.21 ± .03	.24 ± .04 (35-37)
Leading others into bad conduct...............	.20 ± .04	.28 ± .07 (24-27)
Gang..	.20 ± .04	....
Grouped: lack of interest in school, etc.....	.20 ± .03	.11
Psychoneurotic................................	.17	.32 ± .06 (15-16)
Overinterest in sex matters...................	.14	.31 ± .06 (17-19)
Stubborn......................................	.14	.30 ± .04 (20-22)
Finicky food habits...........................	.12	.29 ± .05 (23)
Changeable moods..............................	.09	.28 ± .05 (24-27)
Restless......................................	.18	.26 ± .04 (28-29)
Leader..	.17	.26 ± .06 (28-29)
Spoiled child.................................	.04	.25 ± .05 (30-34)

*Rank order of girls' correlations.

TABLE 51—Continued

	Boys	Girls
Distractible	-.00	.25 ± .05 (30-34)
Overinterest in opposite sex	....	.25 ± .05 (30-34)
Sulky	.05	.25 ± .06 (30-34)
Stealing	.17	.25 ± .04 (30-34)
Emotional instability	.18	.24 ± .06 (35-37)
Daydreaming	.07	.22 ± .06 (39-41)
Grouped: sensitive or worrisome, etc.	.09	.21 ± .04 (42-46)
Question of encephalitis	-.11	.21 ± .08 (42-46)
Sensitive (general)	.12	.21 ± .06 (42-46)
Depressed	.07	.21 ± .06 (42-46)
Slovenly	.15	.21 ± .05 (42-46)
Bad companions	.15	.20 ± .05 (47-51)
Irritable	.19	.20 ± .05 (47-51)
Sensitive over specific fact	-.00	.20 ± .05 (47-51)

	Larger Correlations (Negative)	
Vicious home conditions	-.08	-.33 ± .05
Speech defect	-.14	-.26 ± .06
Question of hypophrenia	-.19	-.21 ± .04
Retardation in school	-.17	-.21 ± .04

Other Correlations (Positive to Negative)

Truancy from home, .19 and .13; Worry over specific fact, .19 and .18; Lack of interest in school, .18 and .06; Teasing other children, .18 (boys); Temper display, .18 and .07; Exclusion from school, .18 and .13; Loitering, .16 and -.02; Swearing (general), .16 (boys); Inferiority feelings, .16 and .18; Smoking, .15 (boys); Queer, .15 and .18; Complaining of bad treatment by other children, .15 (boys); Inattentive in school, .14 and .13; Nail-biting, .12 and .04; Mental conflict, .12 and .19; Refusal to attend school, .11 and .09; Unhappy, .11 and .17; Irresponsible, .10 and .15; Lues, .10 and .01; Masturbation, .09 and .14; Restless in sleep, .09 and .18; Inefficient in work, play, etc., .08 and .09; Sex delinquency (coitus), .08 and .07; Question of change of personality, .08 and .13; Preference for younger children, .08 and .15; Clean, .08 and .03; Grouped: depressed, etc., .08 and .19; Lazy, .06 and .05; "Nervous," .06 and .15; Crying spells, .05 and .19; Brother in penal detention, .05 and .08; Enuresis, .04 and .08; Listless, .04 and .03; Object of teasing, .04 and -.10; Former convulsions, .03 and .05; Victim of sex abuse, .03 (girls); Irregular sleep habits, .02 and .19; Seclusive, .02 and .09; Discord between parents, .00 and .01; Irregular attendance at school, -.00 and .01; Follower, -.01 and .06; Absent-minded, -.02 and .03; Bashful, -.02 and -.10; Repressed, -.02 and .13; Sex denied entirely, -.02 and .05; Neurological defect, -.03 and .16; Vocational guidance, -.05 and .02; Poor work in school, -.06 and .04; Stuttering, -.06 (boys); Popular, -.06 and .19; Grouped: dull, slow, -.06 and -.06; Lack of initiative, -.08 and .12; Slow, dull, -.09 and -.10; Attractive manner, -.09 and -.01; Immoral home conditions, -.09 and -.02; Apprehensive, -.10 and -.05; Feeble-minded sibling, -.10 and -.14; Headaches, -.11 and .07; Oversuggestible, -.14 and -.04; Underweight, -.14 and -.05.

Omitted—Grouped: egocentric, etc.

threatening violence, which was computed for boys only. Contrariness showed correlations of .31 + .05 for boys and .24 + .07 for
girls. Nine behavior difficulties among girls also yielded substantial correlations in the .30's, with moderate correlations in
the .20's among boys: disobedience, defiant manner, incorrigibility, violence, sullenness, lying, fantastical lying, hatred or
jealousy of sibling, and unpopularity. Three additional behavior
problems among girls yielded substantial correlations in the .30's
but low positive coefficients ranging from .14 to .17 among boys:
stubbornness, staff notation of psychoneurotic trends (unspecified),
and overinterest in sex matters.

     Seven conduct notations showed moderate correlations in the
.20's with egocentricity among both sexes: fighting, destructiveness, swearing or bad language (undifferentiated), disturbing influence in school, staying out late at night, leading others into
bad conduct, and staff notation of unfavorable conduct prognosis
and also with running with a gang which was calculated for boys
only. Truancy from school and lack of interest or inattentiveness
in school studies or employment (undifferentiated) also showed moderate correlations in the .20's among boys, but low correlations of
.15 and .11 respectively among girls. A large group of seventeen
miscellaneous notations among girls showed moderate coefficients
in the .20's, the boys' coefficients being low or negligible:
"leader," restlessness, irritable temperament, changeable moods or
attitudes, emotional instability, distractibility, "spoiled child,"
stealing, bad companions, slovenliness, sulkiness, sensitiveness in
general, sensitive over some specific fact, depressed mood or
spells, daydreaming, finicky food habits, and question or diagnosis
of encephalitis and also one calculated for girls only—overinterest in the opposite sex.

     Four notations showed negative correlations of moderate
size ranging from -.20 to -.33 with egocentricity, all among girls:
question of hypophrenia, retardation in school, speech defect
(other than stuttering), and vicious (not "immoral") home conditions, the boys' correlations being also negative but low, ranging
from -.08 to -.19.

     Among the six sex notations, overinterest in sex matters
among girls yielded the substantial correlation of .31 + .06, the
boys' correlation being low, .14. Overinterest in the opposite

sex, which was calculated for girls only because of the paucity of boys' cases, showed a moderate correlation of .25 ± .05. The correlations for sex delinquency (coitus), masturbation, sex misbehavior denied entirely, and (calculated for girls only) victim of sex abuse by older child or person showed low coefficients ranging from -.02 to .14.

Among the seven physical or psychophysical notations there were two significant correlations of moderate size in the .20's, both among girls: the positive coefficient of .21 ± .08 with question or diagnosis of encephalitis, and the negative coefficient of -.26 ± .06 with speech defect (other than stuttering).

Among the four home or familial notations egocentricity showed only one correlation of significant size, the negative one of -.33 ± .05 with vicious home conditions among girls.

Selfishness was noted among 130 boys and 73 girls, the incidence for each sex being 6.2 per cent. Among girls its correlations with personality-total and conduct-total were meaningful, .44 ± .03 and .35 ± .04 respectively (Table 52). Among boys the corresponding coefficients were moderate, .25 ± .03 and .21 ± .03 respectively. With police arrest ("juvenile delinquency") the respective correlations for boys and girls were low, -.12 ± .04 and .15 ± .06.

Its highest correlations were among girls: egocentricity, .45 ± .05; defiant attitude, .41 ± .06; fighting or quarrelsomeness (undifferentiated), .40 ± .05; and finicky food habits, .40 ± .06. The corresponding correlations for boys were .21 ± .04, .21 ± .05, .22 ± .04, and .13. Its correlation among boys with contrariness was .31 ± .06, the girls' coefficient being negligible, -.01. Irritable temperament and boastful or "show-off" manner among girls yielded substantial correlations in the .30's, with corresponding moderate coefficients in the .20's among boys. Seven behavior problems among girls also yielded substantial correlations in the .30's but low coefficients below .20 among boys: quarrelsomeness, temper tantrums, stubbornness, changeable moods or attitudes, "spoiled child," irresponsibility, and psychoneurotic trends. Selfishness among both sexes showed moderate correlations in the .20's with the five traits, bossy manner, temper display, disobedience, hatred or jealousy of sibling, and unpopularity.

TABLE 52

CORRELATIONS WITH "SELFISH"

	Boys	Girls
Personality-total..............................	.25 ± .03	.44 ± .03
Conduct-total..................................	.21 ± .03	.35 ± .04
Police arrest.................................	-.12 ± .04	.15 ± .06
		Larger Correlations (Positive)
Grouped: temper, etc.........................	.31 ± .03	.39 ± .05 (5-6)*
Contrary......................................	.31 ± .06	-.01
Hatred or jealousy of sibling.................	.29 ± .06	.27 ± .04 (22-24)
Irritable.....................................	.29 ± .04	.35 ± .04 (12-13)
Bossy...	.27 ± .06	.29 ± .07 (17-19)
Lazy..	.27 ± .05	-.05
Rude..	.27 ± .04	.11
Boastful, "show-off".........................	.26 ± .04	.32 ± .07 (15)
Grouped: "nervous," etc......................	.26 ± .03	.35 ± .04 (12-13)
Seclusive.....................................	.25 ± .05	.19
Grouped: disobedient, etc....................	.25 ± .03	.38 ± .04 (7-9)
Teasing other children........................	.23 ± .05	....
Temper display...............................	.23 ± .05	.28 ± .04 (20-21)
Lack of initiative...........................	.23 ± .06	.01
Unpopular.....................................	.23 ± .06	.25 ± .04 (25-26)
Grouped: fighting...........................	.22 ± .04	.40 ± .05 (3-4)
Disobedient...................................	.21 ± .04	.29 ± .05 (17-19)
Defiant.......................................	.21 ± .05	.41 ± .06 (2)
Egocentric....................................	.21 ± .04	.45 ± .05 (1)
Restless......................................	.21 ± .04	.15
Preference for younger children..............	.20 ± .05	.19
Conduct prognosis bad........................	.20 ± .07	.02
Finicky food habits..........................	.13	.40 ± .06 (3-4)
Quarrelsome...................................	.13	.39 ± .05 (5-6)
Stubborn......................................	.14	.38 ± .05 (7-9)
Temper tantrums...............................	.12	.38 ± .06 (7-9)
Changeable moods..............................	.12	.36 ± .04 (10-11)
Spoiled child................................	.13	.36 ± .04 (10-11)
Irresponsible.................................	.19	.33 ± .07 (14)
Psychoneurotic................................	.03	.31 ± .04 (16)
Depressed.....................................	.19	.29 ± .04 (17-19)
Violence......................................	.19	.28 ± .04 (20-21)
Fantastical lying............................	.17	.27 ± .07 (22-24)
Sensitive over specific fact.................	.11	.27 ± .04 (22-24)
Lying...	.19	.25 ± .05 (25-26)
Destructive...................................	.10	.24 ± .08 (27-32)
Inattentive in school........................	.19	.24 ± .07 (27-32)
Question of change of personality............	.16	.24 ± .04 (27-32)
Excuse-forming................................	.18	.24 ± .04 (27-32)
Irregular sleep habits.......................	-.10	.24 ± .04 (27-32)

*Rank order of girls' correlations.

TABLE 52—Continued

	Boys	Girls
Neurological defect...........................	.07	.24 ± .04 (27-32)
Leading others into bad conduct...............	-.05	.23 ± .08 (33)
Fighting......................................	.14	.22 ± .04 (34-35)
Restless in sleep............................	.08	.22 ± .04 (34-35)
Grouped: sensitive or worrisome, etc.........	.17	.21 ± .04 (36-38)
Grouped: swearing, etc......................	.11	.21 ± .04 (36-38)
Crying spells................................	.15	.21 ± .04 (36-38)
		Larger Correlations (Negative)
Gang...	-.20 ± .05	....
Irregular attendance at school...............	.02	-.26 ± .04
Feeble-minded sibling........................	-.13	-.26 ± .04
Question of hypophrenia......................	-.06	-.22 ± .04
Repressed....................................	.04	-.21 ± .04

Other Correlations (Positive to Negative)

Sullen, .19 and .16; Smoking, .18 (boys); Sulky, .18 and -.02; Sensitive (general), .18 and .17; Distractible, .17 and .10; Nail-biting, .16 and .17; Truancy from home, .15 and .02; Mental conflict, .15 and .02; Grouped: depressed, etc., .15 and .17; Inefficient in work, play, etc., .14 and .19; "Nervous," .14 and .12; Worry over specific fact, .14 and .12; Lack of interest in school, .14 and .14; Disturbing influence in school, .13 and .15; Incorrigible, .13 and .18; Slovenly, .13 and .06; Sex delinquency (coitus), .13 and -.13; Inferiority feelings, .13 and .17; Stealing, .12 and .11; Swearing (general), .12 (boys); Threatening violence, .12 (boys); Daydreaming, .12 and .09; Discord between parents, .12 and .11; Bashful, .11 and .11; Leader, .11 and .15; Attractive manner, .11 and .02; Masturbation, .09 and .18; Follower, .09 and .10; Lack of interest in school, .08 and .01; Refusal to attend school, .08 and .01; Absent-minded, .08 and .12; Queer, .08 and .19; Stuttering, .08 (boys); Clean, .08 and .12; Speech defect, .07 and .14; Truancy from school, .06 and .00; Victim of sex abuse, .06 (girls); Complaining of bad treatment by other children, .05 (boys); Poor work in school, .05 and -.02; Unhappy, .04 and -.15; Immoral home conditions, .04 and -.12; Grouped: dull, slow, etc., .04 and -.07; Overinterest in sex matters, .03 and .09; Headaches, .02 and .08; Lues, .02 and -.07; Overinterest in opposite sex, .02 (girls); Loitering, .01 and .01; Exclusion from school, .01 and .08; Listless, .00 and .11; Oversuggestible, -.00 and .12; Vicious home conditions, -.02 and -.17; Question of encephalitis, -.02 and .14; Object of teasing, -.02 and .06; Slow, -.02 and -.09; Bad companions, -.03 and .11; Underweight, -.04 and -.03; Vocational guidance, -.05 and .01; Former convulsions, -.05 and .04; Popular, -.05 and .07; Sex denied entirely, -.06 and .08; Enuresis, -.06 and .12; Staying out late at night, -.07 and .12; Apprehensive, -.09 and .09; Emotional instability, -.11 and .08; Retardation in school, -.13 and -.19; Brother in penal detention, -.13 and -.18

Teasing other children, which was calculated for boys only, showed a moderate correlation of .23 ± .05. Seven behavior notations among boys showed moderate correlations in the .20's but low positive correlations below .20 among girls: <u>rudeness</u>, <u>laziness</u>, <u>lack of initiative or ambition</u>, <u>restlessness</u>, <u>preference for younger children as playmates</u>, <u>seclusiveness</u>, and <u>staff notation of unfavorable conduct prognosis</u>. Seventeen notations among girls showed moderate correlations in the .20's but low or negligible correlations below .20 among boys: <u>violence</u>, <u>fighting</u>, <u>destructiveness</u>, <u>swearing or bad language</u> (undifferentiated), <u>leading others into bad conduct</u>, <u>excuse-forming attitude</u>, <u>lying</u>, <u>fantastical lying</u>, <u>restlessness in sleep</u>, <u>irregular sleep habits</u>, <u>inattentiveness in school</u>, <u>question of change of personality</u>, <u>sensitiveness or worrisomeness</u> (undifferentiated), <u>sensitiveness over some specific fact</u>, <u>depressed mood or spells</u>, <u>crying spells</u>, and <u>neurological defect (unspecified)</u>.

Among the six sex notations the only correlation of probable statistical significant size was with <u>masturbation</u> among girls, .18, all other coefficients being negligible and falling between -.13 and .13.

<u>Neurological defect (unspecified)</u> among girls showed the moderate correlation of .24 $\pm$ .04, all our other correlations in the physical or psychophysical field being low or negligible.

Among the home or familial notations all correlations with <u>selfishness</u> were low or negligible.

When children noted as either "egocentric" by the clinic staff or "selfish" by the "lay" informant and also a handful of children manifesting a <u>self-indulgent attitude</u>[1] were grouped under one rubric, <u>egocentricity or selfishness</u> (undifferentiated), the resulting frequencies were 405 boys, or 19.2 per cent, and 211 girls, or 17.9 per cent. The correlation coefficients tended to resemble those of <u>egocentricity</u> (Table 51) more closely than those of <u>selfishness</u> (Table 52)—probably because the children noted as egocentric were more than twice as numerous in the composite group as those noted as selfish—but tended to be slightly larger than the corresponding correlations for either of the component notations. This fact indicates that the "broader grouping" in this instance tended to enhance the homogeneity of the dichotomies and was a justifiable procedure.[2]

Since the coefficients in Table 53 add little new information

---

[1] I, 50, Item 70.   [2] I, 44, and this volume, pp. 38-44.

TABLE 53

CORRELATIONS WITH "GROUPED: EGOCENTRIC, ETC."

	Boys	Girls
Personality-total............................	.25 ± .02	.39 ± .03
Conduct-total................................	.42 ± .02	.47 ± .02
Police arrest................................	.14 ± .03	.07 ± .04
	Larger Correlations (Positive)	
Boastful, "show-off".........................	.38 ± .03	.44 ± .05 (2)*
Grouped: disobedient, etc...................	.36 ± .02	.40 ± .03 (4-6)
Contrary.....................................	.35 ± .04	.15
Rude...	.35 ± .03	.34 ± .04 (11-13)
Defiant......................................	.32 ± .04	.40 ± .05 (4-6)
Hatred or jealousy of sibling................	.32 ± .04	.32 ± .06 (16-19)
Excuse-forming...............................	.32 ± .03	.38 ± .05 (7)
Grouped: fighting, etc......................	.31 ± .03	.40 ± .04 (4-6)
Grouped: temper, etc........................	.30 ± .03	.36 ± .04 (8-10)
Disobedient..................................	.30 ± .03	.34 ± .04 (11-13)
Unpopular....................................	.30 ± .04	.33 ± .06 (14-15)
Threatening violence.........................	.29 ± .04	....
Lying.......................................	.29 ± .03	.33 ± .04 (14-15)
Fantastical lying............................	.28 ± .03	.29 ± .05 (24-25)
Sullen.......................................	.27 ± .03	.27 ± .06 (27-29)
Disturbing influence in school...............	.27 ± .03	.20 ± .05 (45-51)
Bossy..	.26 ± .04	.31 ± .05 (20-21)
Incorrigible.................................	.26 ± .03	.30 ± .04 (22-23)
Conduct prognosis bad........................	.25 ± .05	.24 ± .06 (33-37)
Irritable....................................	.25 ± .03	.29 ± .04 (24-25)
Fighting.....................................	.25 ± .03	.27 ± .04 (27-29)
Grouped: "nervous," etc.....................	.24 ± .03	.30 ± .03 (22-23)
Violence.....................................	.24 ± .03	.31 ± .05 (20-21)
Truancy from home............................	.23 ± .03	.14
Smoking......................................	.23 ± .04	
Teasing other children.......................	.23 ± .03	....
Grouped: lack of interest in school, etc.....	.23 ± .03	.18
Quarrelsome..................................	.22 ± .03	.45 ± .04 (1)
Restless.....................................	.21 ± .03	.24 ± .04 (33-37)
Irresponsible................................	.21 ± .04	.36 ± .05 (8-10)
Grouped: swearing, etc......................	.21 ± .03	.14
Inattentive in school........................	.20 ± .03	.18
Staying out late at night....................	.20 ± .03	.24 ± .04 (33-37)
Stealing.....................................	.20 ± .03	.26 ± .04 (30-31)
Temper display...............................	.20 ± .03	.19
Temper tantrums..............................	.19	.41 ± .04 (3)
Finicky food habits..........................	.12	.36 ± .04 (8-10)
Stubborn.....................................	.15	.34 ± .04 (11-13)
Changeable moods.............................	.13	.32 ± .04 (16-19)
Psychoneurotic...............................	.12	.32 ± .05 (16-19)

*Rank order of girls' correlations.

TABLE 53—Continued

	Boys	Girls
Spoiled child	.08	.32 ± .05 (16-19)
Overinterest in opposite sex	....	.28 ± .04 (26)
Leader	.19	.27 ± .05 (27-29)
Destructive	.19	.26 ± .06 (30-31)
Leading others into bad conduct	.18	.25 ± .06 (32)
Overinterest in sex matters	.15	.24 ± .05 (33-37)
Distractible	.14	.24 ± .05 (33-37)
Depressed	.18	.23 ± .05 (38-39)
Slovenly	.19	.23 ± .04 (38-39)
Grouped: sensitive or worrisome, etc.	.11	.22 ± .04 (40)
Sensitive over specific fact	.04	.21 ± .04 (41-44)
Sensitive (general)	.15	.21 ± .04 (41-44)
Daydreaming	.12	.21 ± .05 (41-44)
Question of change of personality	.09	.21 ± .06 (41-44)
Bad companions	.12	.20 ± .05 (45-51)
Inefficient in work, play, etc.	.09	.20 ± .05 (45-51)
Crying spells	.09	.20 ± .04 (45-51)
Irregular sleep habits	.01	.20 ± .06 (45-51)
Queer	.13	.20 ± .06 (45-51)
Restless in sleep	.08	.20 ± .05 (45-51)

Larger Correlations (Negative)		
Vicious home conditions	-.03	-.29 ± .05
Question of hypophrenia	-.17	-.28 ± .04
Retardation in school	-.14	-.24 ± .04
Feeble-minded sibling	-.07	-.20 ± .05

Other Correlations (Positive to Negative)

Truancy from school, .19 and .16; Worry over specific fact, .19 and .15; Exclusion from school, .18 and .09; Inferiority feelings, .18 and .11; Lack of interest in school, .18 and .12; Mental conflict, .16 and .08; Nail-biting, .16 and .10; Swearing (general), .16 (boys); Gang, .16 (boys); Lazy, .16 and .09; Complaining of bad treatment by other children, .14 (boys); Sex delinquency (coitus), .14 and .03; Loitering, .14 and .06; Grouped: depressed, etc., .14 and .18; Sulky, .13 and .19; Masturbation, .13 and .18; Unhappy, .13 and .10; Seclusive, .12 and .11; Refusal to attend school, .12 and .11; Emotional instability, .11 and .17; "Nervous," .07 and .14; Clean, .07 and .05; Irregular attendance at school, .06 and -.02; Discord between parents, .05 and .05; Follower, .04 and .09; Listless, .04 and .11; Former convulsions, .04 and -.02; Neurological defect, .03 and .14; Enuresis, .03 and .03; Absent-minded, .03 and .10; Object of teasing, .03 and -.10; Preference for younger children, .03 and .16; Victim of sex abuse, .03 (girls); Attractive manner, .02 and -.02; Brother in penal detention, .02 and .01; Bashful, .01 and -.03; Lack of initiative, .01 and -.07; Repressed, .01 and .05; Sex denied entirely, -.00 and .02; Poor work in school, -.01 and .02; Stuttering, -.02 (boys); Grouped: dull, slow, etc., -.02 and -.03; Question of encephalitis, -.03 and .18; Slow, dull, -.05 and -.06; Speech defect, -.05 and -.12; Vocational guidance, -.05 and .03; Immoral home conditions, -.06 and -.00; Popular, -.06 and .15; Lues, -.08 and -.06; Headaches, -.08 and .08; Underweight, -.10 and -.09; Apprehensive, -.10 and .01; Oversuggestible, -.10 and .08

Omitted—Selfish; Egocentric

beyond that afforded in Tables 51 and 52, a brief summary of the
trends will be sufficient. Consistent correlations of fairly substantial size among both sexes and with both egocentricity and
selfishness were found for boastful or "show-off" manner, bossy
manner, defiant attitude, disobedience, hatred or jealousy for sibling, and unpopularity. Among boys contrariness and rudeness
showed consistently substantial correlations, the girls' coefficients being variable or low. Among the girls, ten behavior difficulties showed consistent substantial correlations with both egocentricity and selfishness, the corresponding boys' coefficients
being variable: quarrelsomeness, stubbornness, temper tantrums,
excuse-forming attitude, lying, fantastical lying, "spoiled child,"
staff notation of psychoneurotic trends (unspecified), changeable
moods or attitudes, and finicky food habits. Among the seventeen
sex, physical, psychophysical, home, and familial notations considered in the present volume there were a few moderate correlations in the .20's with one of the two traits egocentricity and
selfishness; but none of these seventeen notations showed significant correlations of .20 or more with both egocentricity and selfishness.

CHAPTER XXXI

EXCUSE-FORMING ATTITUDE

Excuse-forming attitude ("patient always blames others for his difficulties") was noted among 237, or 11.2 per cent, of our 2,113 White boys and among 99, or 8.4 per cent, of our 1,181 White girls. It showed large correlations of .44 ± .02 and .53 ± .03 with conduct-total for boys and girls respectively (Table 54). With police arrest among both sexes and personality-total among girls the coefficients were of moderate size, ranging from .22 to .27, while among boys the correlation with personality-total was low, .13 ± .02.

Its highest correlations were among girls. Egocentricity and swearing or bad language (undifferentiated) among girls yielded large tetrachoric correlations in the .40's and substantial correlations in the .30's among boys. Fighting, quarrelsomeness, and disobedience or incorrigibility (undifferentiated) among girls also yielded large correlations in the .40's with corresponding moderate correlations in the .20's among boys.

Stealing and lying among both sexes yielded substantial correlations in the .30's. Threatening violence, which was calculated for boys only, also yielded a substantial correlation of .35 ± .05. Five behavior problems among girls yielded substantial correlations in the .30's with corresponding moderate correlations in the .20's among boys: boastful or "show-off" manner, temper tantrums or display (undifferentiated), incorrigibility, disturbing influence in school, and truancy from home. Six additional behavior problems also showed substantial correlations in the .30's among girls but low positive coefficients below .20 among boys: temper tantrums, restlessness, inattentiveness in school, inefficiency in work, play, etc., rudeness, and sulkiness.

Seven personality and conduct problems showed moderate correlations in the .20's among both boys and girls: violence, staying out late at night, bad companions, slovenliness, changeable moods or attitudes, unpopularity, and overinterest in sex matters.

302

TABLE 54

CORRELATIONS WITH "EXCUSE-FORMING"

	Boys	Girls
Personality-total...........................	.13 ± .02	.25 ± .03
Conduct-total...............................	.44 ± .02	.53 ± .03
Police arrest...............................	.27 ± .03	.22 ± .05
	Larger Correlations (Positive)	
Stealing....................................	.37 ± .03	.30 ± .05 (19-20)*
Threatening violence........................	.35 ± .05	....
Defiant.....................................	.32 ± .04	.24 ± .06 (33-36)
Egocentric..................................	.32 ± .04	.41 ± .05 (5-6)
Grouped: egocentric, etc...................	.32 ± .03	.38 ± .05 (7-8)
Destructive.................................	.30 ± .04	.27 ± .07 (27-30)
Lying.......................................	.30 ± .03	.36 ± .04 (11-12)
Grouped: swearing, etc.....................	.30 ± .04	.41 ± .06 (5-6)
Leading others into bad conduct.............	.29 ± .04	.10
Unpopular...................................	.29 ± .05	.24 ± .07 (33-36)
Grouped: fighting, etc.....................	.29 ± .03	.45 ± .04 (1)
Boastful, "show-off"........................	.28 ± .04	.33 ± .06 (13-15)
Hatred or jealousy of sibling...............	.28 ± .05	.15
Sullen......................................	.27 ± .04	.05
Swearing (general).........................	.26 ± .04	....
Follower....................................	.25 ± .04	-.02
Grouped: temper, etc......................	.25 ± .03	.30 ± .04 (19-20)
Disturbing influence in school..............	.24 ± .03	.32 ± .06 (16-17)
Quarrelsome.................................	.24 ± .04	.43 ± .05 (3-4)
Smoking.....................................	.24 ± .04	....
Violence....................................	.24 ± .04	.28 ± .06 (23-25)
Bad companions..............................	.23 ± .03	.26 ± .06 (31-32)
Fighting....................................	.23 ± .04	.43 ± .03 (3-4)
Teasing other children......................	.23 ± .04	....
Truancy from school.........................	.23 ± .03	.15
Changeable moods............................	.23 ± .04	.27 ± .05 (27-30)
Oversuggestible.............................	.23 ± .03	.13
Grouped: disobedient, etc.................	.23 ± .03	.44 ± .04 (2)
Fantastical lying...........................	.22 ± .03	.17
Incorrigible................................	.21 ± .03	.37 ± .05 (9-10)
Truancy from home...........................	.21 ± .03	.31 ± .05 (18)
Overinterest in sex matters.................	.21 ± .05	.29 ± .06 (21-22)
Slovenly....................................	.20 ± .04	.28 ± .05 (23-26)
Staying out late at night...................	.20 ± .04	.29 ± .05 (21-22)
Exclusion from school.......................	.20 ± .04	.16
Unhappy.....................................	.05	.28 ± .07 (23-26)
Temper tantrums.............................	.19	.38 ± .05 (7-8)
Rude..	.18	.37 ± .05 (9-10)
Inefficient in work, play, etc.............	.08	.36 ± .06 (11-12)
Restless....................................	.17	.33 ± .05 (13-15)

*Rank order of girls' correlations.

TABLE 54—Continued

	Boys	Girls
Inattentive in school........................	.18	.33 ± .06 (13-15)
Sulky..	.07	.32 ± .07 (16-17)
Disobedient..................................	.18	.28 ± .05 (23-26)
Grouped: lack of interest in school, etc.....	.17	.27 ± .05 (27-30)
Sensitive (general)..........................	.03	.27 ± .06 (27-30)
Stubborn.....................................	.11	.26 ± .05 (31-32)
Grouped: depressed, etc.....................	.05	.24 ± .06 (33-36)
Selfish.....................................	.18	.24 ± .04 (33-36)
Overinterest in opposite sex.................	....	.23 ± .05 (37)
Grouped: "nervous," etc.....................	.18	.22 ± .04 (38-41)
Emotional instability........................	.08	.22 ± .06 (38-41)
Daydreaming..................................	.07	.22 ± .06 (38-41)
Contrary....................................	.12	.22 ± .08 (38-41)
Bossy.......................................	.17	.21 ± .06 (42-45)
Temper display..............................	.12	.21 ± .06 (42-45)
Distractible................................	.09	.21 ± .06 (42-45)
Queer.......................................	-.05	.21 ± .07 (42-45)
Grouped: sensitive or worrisome, etc........	.02	.20 ± .05 (46)

	Larger Correlations (Negative)	
Feeble-minded sibling........................	-.02	-.20 ± .06

Other Correlations (Positive to Negative)

Irresponsible, .17 and .18; Irritable, .17 and .10; Brother in penal detention, .16 and .05; Apprehensive, .15 and .04; Complaining of bad treatment by other children, .15 (boys); Mental conflict, .14 and -.05; Spoiled child, .14 and -.01; Refusal to attend school, .12 and .05; Gang, .12 (boys); Conduct prognosis bad, .11 and .03; Enuresis, .10 and .13; Lack of interest in school, .10 and .17; Masturbation, .10 and .11; Worry over specific fact, .10 and .04; Attractive manner, .10 and .05; Vicious home conditions, .10 and .01; Loitering, .09 and .13; Nail-biting, .09 and .04; Crying spells, .09 and .19; "Nervous," .09 and .05; Inferiority feelings, .09 and .17; Discord between parents, .09 and .10; Lazy, .08 and .14; Leader, .08 and .18; Object of teasing, .07 and .16; Restless in sleep, .07 and .16; Absent-minded, .06 and -.12; Former convulsions, .06 and -.08; Question of change of personality, .05 and .15; Poor work in school, .05 and .16; Depressed, .04 and .13; Victim of sex abuse, .04 (girls); Irregular sleep habits, .03 and .19; Clean, .03 and .06; Neurological defect, .03 and .15; Irregular attendance at school, .03 and .05; Speech defect, .03 and -.05; Immoral home conditions, .03 and -.06; Grouped: dull, slow, etc., .03 and .02; Finicky food habits, .12 and .14; Seclusive, .02 and .04; Sex denied entirely, .02 and .00; Slow, dull, .01 and .00; Psychoneurotic, .01 and .03; Popular, .00 and .14; Repressed, -.00 and .09; Listless, -.00 and -.03; Sensitive over specific fact, -.01 and -.14; Preference for younger children, -.01 and .02; Vocational guidance, -.01 and .04; Bashful, -.02 and -.07; Sex delinquency (coitus), -.04 and .09; Question of encephalitis, -.04 and .19; Lack of initiative, -.05 and -.01; Retardation in school, -.05 and -.10; Lues, -.05 and -.05; Underweight, -.06 and -.10; Stuttering, -.07 (boys); Headaches, -.08 and .07; Question of hypophrenia, -.11 and -.05

Smoking and teasing other children, which were calculated for boys
only, and overinterest in the opposite sex, for which only the
girls' correlations were computed, also showed moderate correlations in the .20's. Eight behavior traits among boys showed moderate correlations in the .20's but low positive correlations below .20 for girls: fantastical lying, oversuggestibility, "follower," sullenness, hatred or jealousy of sibling, truancy from
school, leading others into bad conduct, and exclusion from school.
Twelve behavior traits among girls showed moderate correlations in
the .20's but low coefficients below .20 for boys: disobedience,
stubbornness, contrariness, bossy manner, selfishness, temper display, emotional instability, distractibility, sensitiveness in
general, unhappiness, daydreaming, and queer behavior.

Only one notation yielded a negative correlation of probable statistical significance, feeble-minded sibling among girls,
$-.20 \pm .06$.

Among the six sex notations, moderate positive correlations
in the .20's were found for overinterest in sex matters among both
sexes and for overinterest in the opposite sex, which was calculated for girls only.

Among the seven physical or psychophysical notations and
the four home or familial notations all obtained coefficients were
low, falling between -.10 and .19.

CHAPTER XXXII

STAFF NOTATION OF "UNFAVORABLE CONDUCT
PROGNOSIS"

Staff notation of "unfavorable conduct prognosis" or similar notation by another clinic was a very important notation, since
it embodies a formal composite staff prognosis of the child's future conduct after the clinical examination is completed. (It
should be noted that no follow-up is involved in the present study
to ascertain whether these prognoses were correct.) It was not
frequently employed, appearing in only 78 cases, or 3.7 per cent,
of our 2,113 White boys and in only 47 cases, or 4.0 per cent, of
our 1,181 White girls. It was used to designate overt conduct difficulties rather than such "personality problems" as would not result in patent antisocial behavior. This notation was made typically among the older or adolescent children[1] and among children
of lower intelligence (IQ).[2] Its correlations with IQ for boys and
girls were -.18 and -.12 respectively (Table 10, p. 130).

With conduct-total its correlations for both boys and girls
were large, the bi-serial correlations being .40 ± .03 and .46 ±
.04 respectively (Table 55). With the police-arrest criterion of
"juvenile delinquency" its tetrachoric correlation among girls,
.47 ± .06, was large, but among boys the corresponding coefficient
was moderate, .29 ± .05. With personality-total the correlations
were quite moderate, .19 ± .03 and .22 ± .05.

Among four behavior notations fairly large coefficients
were found. The highest was for sex delinquency (coitus) among
girls, .48 ± .05, the boys' coefficient also being substantial,
.32 ± .08. Overinterest in the opposite sex among girls similarly
yielded the large correlation of .43 ± .05; a corresponding coefficient for the boys was not computed because of the paucity of cases.
Among boys the largest coefficients were .40 for both emotional

[1] I, 207, Fig. 48.
[2] I, 195, Table 40; 199, Table 48; 211, Fig. 50; 214, Fig. 51, and 238.

TABLE 55

CORRELATIONS WITH "CONDUCT PROGNOSIS BAD"

	Boys	Girls
Personality-total.........................	.19 ± .03	.22 ± .05
Conduct-total.............................	.40 ± .03	.46 ± .04
Police arrest.............................	.29 ± .05	.47 ± .06
Larger Correlations (Positive)		
Incorrigible..............................	.40 ± .04	.20 ± .06 (33-35)*
Emotional instability.....................	.40 ± .06	.32 ± .08 (7-8)
Violence..................................	.33 ± .05	.25 ± .08 (17-22)
Overinterest in sex matters..............	.33 ± .07	.15
Sex delinquency (coitus).................	.32 ± .08	.48 ± .05 (1)
Exclusion from school....................	.30 ± .06	.35 ± .08 (4-5)
Grouped: disobedient, etc...............	.30 ± .04	.17
Loitering................................	.29 ± .06	.11
Stealing.................................	.28 ± .04	.22 ± .06 (27)
Threatening violence.....................	.28 ± .07	....
Oversuggestible..........................	.28 ± .05	.21 ± .07 (28-32)
Stuttering...............................	.28 ± .07	....
Gang.....................................	.27 ± .05	....
Question of hypophrenia..................	.26 ± .05	.04
Grouped: swearing, etc..................	.26 ± .05	.31 ± .08 (9)
Grouped: fighting, etc..................	.25 ± .04	.32 ± .06 (7-8)
Grouped: egocentric, etc...............	.25 ± .05	.24 ± .06 (23-24)
Staying out late at night...............	.24 ± .05	.23 ± .07 (25-26)
Sullen...................................	.23 ± .05	.34 ± .07 (6)
Restless.................................	.23 ± .04	.28 ± .06 (10-12)
Fighting.................................	.22 ± .05	.17
Egocentric...............................	.22 ± .05	.28 ± .07 (10-12)
Grouped: "nervous," etc................	.22 ± .04	.01
Bad companions...........................	.21 ± .05	.17
Teasing other children...................	.21 ± .06	....
Contrary.................................	.20 ± .07	-.02
Lying....................................	.20 ± .04	.24 ± .06 (23-24)
Selfish..................................	.20 ± .07	.02
Former convulsions.......................	.20 ± .06	.02
Overinterest in opposite sex.............	....	.43 ± .05 (2)
Leading others into bad conduct..........	.08	.38 ± .09 (3)
Question of encephalitis.................	.13	.35 ± .10 (4-5)
Question of change of personality........	.07	.28 ± .09 (10-12)
Distractible.............................	.19	.27 ± .07 (13-14)
Temper tantrums..........................	.14	.27 ± .07 (13-14)
Destructive..............................	.14	.26 ± .08 (15-16)
Unpopular................................	.16	.26 ± .09 (15-16)
Changeable moods.........................	.12	.25 ± .07 (17-22)
Quarrelsome..............................	.14	.25 ± .07 (17-22)
Irresponsible............................	.12	.25 ± .06 (17-22)

*Rank order of girls' correlations.

TABLE 55—Continued

	Boys	Girls
Inefficient in work, play, etc...............	.08	.25 ± .08 (17-22)
Disturbing influence in school...............	.17	.25 ± .08 (17-22)
Crying spells................................	.09	.23 ± .06 (25-26)
Victim of sex abuse..........................	....	.21 ± .08 (28-32)
Listless....................................	.07	.21 ± .08 (28-32)
Fantastical lying............................	.14	.21 ± .08 (28-32)
Boastful, "show-off".........................	.19	.21 ± .08 (28-32)
Finicky food habits..........................	-.02	.20 ± .08 (33-35)
Disobedient.................................	.13	.20 ± .06 (33-35)
	Larger Correlations (Negative)	
Popular......................................	-.09	-.27 + .08
Inattentive in school........................	-.04	-.21 ± .08
Refusal to attend school.....................	.02	-.20 ± .10
Lack of initiative...........................	-.09	-.20 ± .09
	Not Calculable	
Sex denied entirely..........................	(n.c.)	.11
Mental conflict..............................	.02	(n.c.)
Repressed....................................	-.09	(n.c.)

Other Correlations (Positive to Negative)

Swearing (general), .18 (boys); Irritable, .17 and -.04; Headaches, .17 and .11; Masturbation, .16 and .17; Neurological defect, .16 and .11; Grouped: temper, etc., .16 and .10; Rude, .14 and .13; Irregular sleep habits, .14 and -.05; Inferiority feelings, .14 and -.07; Complaining of bad treatment by other children, .14 (boys); Enuresis, .13 and .00; Sulky, .13 and .01; Temper display, .13 and -.05; Truancy from school, .13 and .12; Feeble-minded sibling, .13 and .15; "Nervous," .12 and -.01; Stubborn, .11 and .10; Truancy from home, .11 and .16; Excuse-forming, .11 and .03; Poor work in school, .11 and .01; Object of teasing, .10 and .08; Sensitive over specific fact, .10 and -.08; Absent-minded, .09 and .11; Apprehensive, .09 and -.02; Hatred or jealousy of sibling, .08 and -.05; Spoiled child, .07 and .12; Lues, .07 and .05; Speech defect, .07 and -.08; Nail-biting, .06 and .06; Queer, .06 and .09; Unhappy, .06 and -.02; Defiant, .05 and .16; Slovenly, .05 and .09; Bashful, .05 and -.07; Daydreaming, .05 and .11; Psychoneurotic, .05 and .18; Grouped: sensitive or worrisome, etc., .05 and -.07; Grouped: depressed, etc., .05 and .03; Retardation in school, .04 and .06; Brother in penal detention, .04 and .19; Underweight, .04 and -.15; Discord between parents, .04 and .05; Vicious home conditions, .03 and -.06; Leader, .02 and -.06; Depressed, .01 and .12; Preference for younger children, .01 and .14; Bossy, .00 and .02; Lack of interest in school, .00 and .16; Grouped: dull, slow, etc., -.00 and .16; Slow, dull, -.01 and .06; Seclusive, -.01 and .06; Grouped: lack of interest in school, etc., -.01 and .08; Lazy, -.02 and .01; Worry over specific fact, -.03 and -.00; Clean, -.03 and -.04; Attractive manner, -.04 and -.10; Irregular attendance at school, -.04 and -.03; Follower, -.05 and .05; Restless in sleep, -.06 and .11; Smoking, -.08 (boys); Vocational guidance, -.08 and -.17; Sensitive (general), -.10 and -.17; Immoral home conditions, -.11 and .01

instability and incorrigibility, the corresponding coefficients for
girls being .32 + .08 and .20 + .06 respectively.

Exclusion from school among both sexes yielded substantial
correlations in the .30's. Among boys violence and overinterest
in sex matters likewise yielded substantial correlations in the
.30's, with lesser corresponding correlations of .25 + .08 and .15
among girls. Among girls three conduct notations yielded substantial correlations in the .30's, with corresponding moderate coefficients in the .20's among boys: sullenness, fighting or quarrelsomeness (including violence, undifferentiated), and swearing or
bad language (undifferentiated). Leading others into bad conduct
and question or diagnosis of encephalitis also yielded substantial
correlations in the .30's among girls but low positive correlations
of .08 and .13 respectively among boys.

Six conduct and personality problems showed moderate correlations in the .20's for both sexes: stealing, staying out late at
night, lying, egocentricity, restlessness, and oversuggestibility.
Victim of sex attack or abuse by older child or person among girls
showed the moderate correlation of .21 + .08, the corresponding coefficient for boys not being calculated because of paucity of boys'
cases. Four similar moderate correlations in the .20's were found
among boys for threatening violence, teasing other children, running with a gang, and stuttering, the coefficients for girls not
being computed because of a paucity of girls' cases. Seven additional case-record notations among boys showed moderate correlations in the .20's but low correlations below .20 among girls: bad
companions, loitering or wandering, fighting, contrariness, selfishness, question of hypophrenia, and former convulsions. Sixteen
notations among girls showed moderate correlations in the .20's but
low correlations below .20 among boys: disturbing influence in
school, quarrelsomeness, temper tantrums, destructiveness, disobedience, fantastical lying, boastful or "show-off" manner, inefficiency in work, play, etc., irresponsibility, distractibility,
listlessness, unpopularity, question of change of personality,
changeable moods or attitudes, crying spells, and finicky food
habits.

Four negative correlations of moderate size in the -.20's
were found among girls, the boys' coefficients being negligible:
lack of initiative or ambition, inattentiveness in school, refusal

to attend school, and popularity. In three notations the tetrachoric r's were not calculable because there were no instances in
which both notations were made: sex misbehavior denied entirely
among boys and mental conflict and repressed manner among girls.
The corresponding coefficients for the other sex were low or negligible.

Among the six sex notations there were several coefficients
of substantial or large size. Among girls we have noted that the
highest correlation in Table 55 was with sex delinquency (coitus),
.48 ± .05, with the corresponding coefficient of .32 ± .08 among
boys. For overinterest in the opposite sex, which was calculated
for girls only, we noted the large correlation of .43 ± .05. With
overinterest in sex matters the boys' correlation of .33 ± .07 was
substantial, the girls' coefficient being low, .15. With victim
of sex abuse by older child or person, which was calculated for
girls only, we noted the moderate correlation of .21 ± .08.

Among the seven physical or psychophysical notations, question or diagnosis of encephalitis among girls yielded the substantial correlation of .35 ± .10, the boys' coefficient being low,
.13. For stuttering, which was calculated for boys only, there
was an interesting correlation of moderate size, .28 ± .07.

Among the four home or familial notations (discord between
parents, brother in penal detention, and vicious and immoral home
conditions) the correlations with staff notation of unfavorable
conduct prognosis were all low, ranging from -.11 to .19.

CHAPTER XXXIII

STEALING

Stealing was the most frequent of overt conduct difficulties noted among our cases, its incidence being 815, or 38.6 per
cent, of our 2,113 White boys and 271, or 22.9 per cent, of our
1,181 White girls. Among boys its tetrachoric correlation with
police arrest ("juvenile delinquency") was high, .63 ± .02, its
correlation among girls also being substantial, .37 ± .04 (Table
56). Among both sexes its bi-serial correlations of .55 ± .01 and
.51 ± .02 with conduct-total were also high. With personality-
total its correlations were low to moderate, the coefficients for
girls and boys being .19 ± .02 and .29 ± .03 respectively. As an
indicator of conduct deviation the importance of stealing is unquestioned, but its relation to personality problems appears to be
relatively minor.

Lying among both sexes yielded very high tetrachoric correlations in the .60's. Among boys truancy from home and truancy
from school also yielded very high correlations in the .60's, the
corresponding coefficients for girls also being large or high,
.54 ± .03 and .39 ± .04.

Among boys, staying out late at night, associating with
bad companions, and running with a gang yielded high correlations
in the .50's. Among girls the coefficients for staying out late
at night and bad companions were .39 ± .04 and .25 ± .04 respectively. For running with a gang the coefficients for girls were
not calculated because of the paucity of cases. Defiant attitude
among girls also yielded a high correlation of .51 ± .04, the boys'
coefficient being substantial, .32 ± .03.

Incorrigibility and destructiveness among boys yielded
large correlations in the .40's, with corresponding substantial coefficients in the .30's among girls. Smoking (calculated for boys
only) yielded the large correlation of .43 ± .03. Leading others
into bad conduct among boys yielded the large coefficient of .46
± .03 but among girls the low coefficient of .16. Among girls

311

TABLE 56

CORRELATIONS WITH "STEALING"

	Boys	Girls
Personality-total.........................	.19 ± .02	.29 ± .03
Conduct-total.............................	.55 ± .01	.51 ± .02
Police arrest.............................	.63 ± .02	.37 ± .04
	Larger Correlations (Positive)	
Truancy from home.........................	.64 ± .02	.54 ± .03 (2)*
Truancy from school.......................	.62 ± .02	.39 ± .04 (8-11)
Lying.....................................	.61 ± .02	.68 ± .02 (1)
Bad companions............................	.57 ± .02	.25 ± .04 (33-35)
Gang......................................	.54 ± .02	....
Staying out late at night.................	.50 ± .02	.39 ± .04 (8-11)
Leading others into bad conduct...........	.46 ± .03	.16
Smoking...................................	.43 ± .03	....
Destructive..............................	.41 ± .03	.35 ± .05 (16-17)
Grouped: disobedient, etc.................	.41 ± .02	.44 ± .03 (4-6)
Incorrigible.............................	.40 ± .02	.39 ± .04 (8-11)
Loitering................................	.39 ± .03	.35 ± .05 (16-17)
Oversuggestible..........................	.38 ± .02	.13
Excuse-forming...........................	.37 ± .03	.30 ± .05 (21-23)
Grouped: swearing, etc...................	.33 ± .03	.44 ± .04 (4-6)
Swearing (general).......................	.33 ± .03	....
Fantastical lying........................	.33 ± .04	.37 ± .05 (13-15)
Defiant..................................	.32 ± .03	.51 ± .04 (3)
Masturbation.............................	.32 ± .02	.44 ± .04 (4-6)
Boastful, "show-off".....................	.30 ± .03	.24 ± .05 (36-40)
Grouped: fighting, etc...................	.29 ± .02	.38 ± .03 (12)
Brother in penal detention...............	.28 ± .03	.02
Conduct prognosis bad....................	.28 ± .04	.22 ± .06 (43-44)
Fighting.................................	.28 ± .03	.40 ± .03 (7)
Exclusion from school....................	.27 ± .03	.37 ± .05 (13-15)
Violence.................................	.26 ± .03	.39 ± .05 (8-11)
Sullen...................................	.26 ± .03	.30 ± .05 (21-23)
Slovenly.................................	.26 ± .03	.31 ± .04 (19-20)
Disobedient..............................	.26 ± .02	.26 ± .04 (28-32)
Disturbing influence in school...........	.25 ± .03	.28 ± .05 (25-26)
Irresponsible............................	.25 ± .04	.24 ± .05 (36-40)
Threatening violence.....................	.24 ± .04	....
Refusal to attend school.................	.24 ± .03	.13
Rude.....................................	.23 ± .03	.29 ± .04 (24)
Grouped: temper, etc.....................	.21 ± .02	.12
Grouped: lack of interest in school, etc.....	.21 ± .03	.24 ± .04 (36-40)
Grouped: egocentric, etc.................	.20 ± .03	.26 ± .04 (28-32)
Unpopular................................	.18	.37 ± .05 (13-15)
Queer....................................	.11	.34 ± .05 (18)
Overinterest in opposite sex.............	....	.31 ± .04 (19-20)

*Rank order of girls' correlations.

TABLE 56—Continued

	Boys	Girls
Restless in sleep	.07	.30 ± .04 (21-23)
Overinterest in sex matters	.13	.28 ± .05 (25-26)
Contrary	.19	.27 ± .06 (27)
Question of encephalitis	.08	.26 ± .06 (28-32)
Stubborn	.11	.26 ± .04 (28-32)
Nail-biting	.16	.26 ± .04 (28-32)
Bossy manner	.14	.25 ± .05 (33-35)
Egocentric	.17	.25 ± .04 (33-35)
Vicious home conditions	.17	.24 ± .05 (36-40)
Sex delinquency (coitus)	.16	.24 ± .04 (36-40)
Quarrelsome	.15	.23 ± .04 (41-42)
Sensitive over specific fact	.11	.23 ± .04 (41-42)
Distractible	.06	.22 ± .05 (43-44)
Inattentive in school	.18	.21 ± .05 (45-52)
Inefficient in work, play, etc.	.14	.21 ± .05 (45-52)
Temper tantrums	.17	.21 ± .04 (45-52)
Question of change of personality	.11	.21 ± .05 (45-52)
Daydreaming	.12	.21 ± .05 (45-52)
Leader	.12	.21 ± .05 (45-52)
Grouped: "nervous," etc.	.14	.21 ± .03 (45-52)
Lack of interest in school	.17	.21 ± .05 (45-52)
Mental conflict	.17	.20 ± .10 (53)
	Larger Correlations (Negative)	
Vocational guidance	-.22 ± .02	-.31 ± .04

Other Correlations (Positive to Negative)

Discord between parents, .18 and .12; Emotional instability, .18 and .09; Enuresis, .18 and .19; Victim of sex abuse, .18 (girls); Teasing other children, .17 (boys); Irregular sleep habits, .17 and .11; Complaining of bad treatment by other children, .17 (boys); Crying spells, .16 and .15; Restless, .15 and .19; Irregular attendance at school, .14 and -.04; Spoiled child, .13 and .05; Unhappy, .13 and .06; Changeable moods, .12 and .18; Hatred or jealousy of sibling, .12 and .10; Temper display, .12 and .13; Selfish, .12 and .11; Popular, .11 and -.01; Follower, .11 and -.03; Sex denied entirely, .10 and .10; Inferiority feelings, .10 and .07; Irritable, .10 and .01; Sulky, .10 and .14; Bashful, .09 and -.13; Repressed, .09 and .03; Preference for younger children, .08 and .18; Depressed, .07 and .18; Grouped: sensitive or worrisome, etc., .06 and .11; Clean, .06 and -.11; Absent-minded, .05 and .13; Grouped: depressed, etc., .02 and .12; Immoral home conditions, .02 and .11; Former convulsions, .02 and -.06; Object of teasing, .02 and .19; "Nervous," .02 and .07; Lazy, .01 and .11; Lues, .00 and -.02; Attractive manner, .00 and -.01; Listless, .00 and .08; Poor work in school, -.01 and -.05; Retardation in school, -.01 and -.04; Sensitive (general), -.02 and .06; Seclusive, -.02 and -.06; Slow, dull, -.02 and -.11; Apprehensive, -.02 and .13; Worry over specific fact, -.03 and .10; Headaches, -.03 and .10; Feeble-minded sibling, -.03 and -.10; Grouped: dull, slow, etc., -.03 and -.02; Neurological defect, -.04 and -.09; Finicky food habits, -.04 and .06; Question of hypophrenia, -.08 and -.08; Psychoneurotic, -.09 and .03; Speech defect, -.09 and -.05; Stuttering, -.10 (boys); Underweight, -.10 and -.02; Lack of initiative, -.12 and -.01

swearing or bad language (undifferentiated) and masturbation yielded
large correlations in the .40's, with corresponding substantial
correlations in the .30's for boys. Fighting among girls also
yielded the large correlation of .40 ± .03, the boys' coefficient
being of moderate size, .28 ± .03.

Three conduct difficulties yielded substantial correlations
in the .30's for both sexes: loitering or wandering, excuse-forming attitude, and fantastical lying. Overinterest in the opposite
sex among girls similarly yielded the substantial correlation of
.31 ± .04, the boys' coefficient not being computed because of a
paucity of cases. Boastful or "show-off" manner and oversuggestibility among boys yielded substantial correlations in the .30's,
the girls' correlations being somewhat lower, .24 ± .05 and .13 respectively. Four additional notations among girls also yielded
substantial correlations in the .30's, with moderate coefficients
in the .20's among boys: violence, sullenness, slovenliness, and
exclusion from school. Three personality problems among girls
yielded similarly substantial correlations in the .30's but low
positive correlations below .20 among boys: restlessness in sleep,
queer behavior, and unpopularity.

Five notations showed moderate correlations in the .20's
with stealing among both sexes: disobedience, disturbing influence
in school, rudeness, irresponsibility, and staff notation of unfavorable conduct prognosis. Among boys threatening violence also
showed a moderate correlation of .24 ± .04, the girls' coefficient
not being computed because of the fewness of cases. Three notations among boys similarly showed moderate correlations in the
.20's, with low positive coefficients below .20 among girls: temper tantrums or display (undifferentiated), refusal to attend
school, and brother in penal detention. Among girls there was a
large list of twenty miscellaneous case notations showing moderate correlations in the .20's but low positive correlations below
.20 among boys: contrariness, stubbornness, egocentricity, quarrelsomeness, bossy manner, temper tantrums, "nervousness" or restlessness (including irritable temperament and changeable moods or
attitudes, undifferentiated), nail-biting, distractibility, daydreaming, sensitiveness over some specific fact, question of change
of personality, inattentiveness in school, lack of interest in
school, inefficiency in work, play, etc., sex delinquency (coitus),

overinterest in sex matters, "leader," question or diagnosis of
encephalitis, and vicious home conditions. (The coefficient of
.20 + .10 among girls for mental conflict is of doubtful reliability because of its large probable error.)

The only significant negative correlations were found with
the notation "request for vocational guidance," -.22 + .02 and
-.31 + .04 among boys and girls respectively.

Among the six sex notations several positive correlations
of moderate and substantial size with stealing were found. Masturbation showed the considerable coefficients of .32 + .02 and
.44 + .04 for boys and girls respectively. Among girls there were
moderate correlations in the .20's for sex delinquency (coitus)
and overinterest in sex matters. The substantial correlation of
.31 + .04 with overinterest in the opposite sex was found among
girls, the boys' correlation not being computed because of paucity
of cases.

Among the seven physical or psychophysical notations the
only statistically significant correlation was .26 + .06 with question or diagnosis of encephalitis among girls. The correlations
of .18 and .19 with enuresis may also be considered as suggestive.

Among the four home or familial notations there were two
correlations of moderate size with stealing: among boys for
brother in penal detention, .28 + .03, and among girls for vicious
home conditions, .24 + .05.

CHAPTER XXXIV

TRUANCY FROM HOME AND STAYING OUT
LATE AT NIGHT

The fact that truancy from home and staying out late at
night are very similar notations is shown by the fact of their
high intercorrelation, the tetrachoric coefficients being .62 ± .02
and .53 ± .04 for boys and girls respectively (Table 57), and by
the general similarity of their "outside correlations" with numerous other notations. From the standpoint both of juvenile delinquency and of undesirable conduct manifestation they are of grave
importance, the bi-serial and tetrachoric r's ranging from .42 to
.68. With personality deviations as measured by personality-total
their importance is relatively minor, the bi-serial coefficients
ranging from .16 to .24.

Truancy from home was noted among 503 cases, or 23.8 per
cent, of our 2,113 White boys and among 189, or 16.0 per cent, of
our 1,181 White girls. It was one of the most frequently occurring conduct problems in our data.

Its highest correlations among both sexes were with stealing and staying out late at night, the boys' correlations being
.64 ± .02 and .62 ± .02 respectively and the girls' correlations
being .54 ± .03 and .53 ± .04 respectively. Truancy from school
among boys also yielded the very high correlation of .61 ± .02,
the girls' coefficient also being large, .48 ± .04. Loitering or
wandering among boys yielded the high correlation of .53 ± .03,
with a moderate correlation of .25 ± .06 among girls. Lying and
incorrigibility among both sexes yielded fairly high correlations
in the .40's. Smoking yielded a large correlation of .42 ± .03
among boys, the coefficients for the girls not being computed because of fewness of cases. Bad companions among boys yielded a
similarly large correlation of .47 ± .02, the girls' coefficient
being moderate, .21 ± .05. Fantastical lying yielded very substantial correlations of .38 ± .04 and .40 ± .05 for boys and girls

316

TABLE 57

CORRELATIONS WITH "TRUANCY FROM HOME"

	Boys	Girls
Personality-total	.17 ± .02	.19 ± .03
Conduct-total	.56 ± .02	.42 ± .03
Police arrest	.68 ± .02	.67 ± .03
	Larger Correlations (Positive)	
Stealing	.64 ± .02	.54 ± .03 (1)*
Staying out late at night	.62 ± .02	.53 ± .04 (2)
Truancy from school	.61 ± .02	.48 ± .04 (3-5)
Loitering	.53 ± .03	.25 ± .06 (18-19)
Bad companions	.47 ± .02	.21 ± .05 (22-28)
Lying	.46 ± .02	.48 ± .03 (3-5)
Incorrigible	.45 ± .02	.44 ± .04 (6)
Smoking	.42 ± .03	....
Grouped: disobedient, etc.	.42 ± .02	.42 ± .03 (7)
Fantastical lying	.38 ± .04	.40 ± .05 (8)
Gang	.37 ± .03	....
Disobedient	.32 ± .03	.19
Destructive	.31 ± .03	-.16
Leading others into bad conduct	.31 ± .04	.21 ± .06 (22-28)
Swearing (general)	.29 ± .04	....
Refusal to attend school	.28 ± .04	.31 ± .06 (13-15)
Grouped: fighting, etc.	.27 ± .03	.16
Exclusion from school	.26 ± .03	.25 ± .06 (18-19)
Contrary	.25 ± .04	.02
Violence	.25 ± .03	.24 ± .05 (20-21)
Irregular sleep habits	.25 ± .04	.02
Complaining of bad treatment by other children	.24 ± .04	....
Defiant	.23 ± .03	.27 ± .05 (17)
Fighting	.23 ± .03	.31 ± .04 (13-15)
Irresponsible	.23 ± .04	.16
Slovenly	.23 ± .03	.21 ± .04 (22-28)
Brother in penal detention	.23 ± .04	.07
Grouped: egocentric, etc.	.23 ± .03	.14
Grouped: swearing, etc.	.23 ± .03	.33 ± .05 (11-12)
Unhappy	.22 ± .04	.13
Disturbing influence in school	.21 ± .03	.10
Excuse-forming	.21 ± .03	.31 ± .05 (13-15)
Rude	.20 ± .03	.20 ± .04 (29-31)
Sullen	.20 ± .03	.11
Sex delinquency (coitus)	.16	.48 ± .04 (3-5)
Masturbation	.19	.35 ± .04 (9)
Question of change of personality	.13	.34 ± .04 (10)
Overinterest in opposite sex	....	.33 ± .04 (11-12)
Victim of sex abuse	....	.28 ± .05 (16)
Question of encephalitis	.02	.24 ± .07 (20-21)

*Rank order of girls' correlations.

TABLE 57—Continued

	Boys	Girls
Vicious home conditions........................	.18	.21 ± .06 (22-28)
Distractible....................................	.01	.21 ± .05 (22-28)
Stubborn..	.16	.21 ± .04 (22-28)
Boastful, "show-off"..........................	.17	.21 ± .06 (22-28)
Temper display.................................	.10	.20 ± .05 (29-31)
Restless.......................................	.12	.20 ± .04 (29-31)
		Larger Correlations (Negative)
Vocational guidance............................	-.16	-.29 ± .04
Sensitive (general)............................	-.03	-.25 ± .04
Sex denied entirely.....	.09	-.24 ± .06

Other Correlations (Positive to Negative)

Oversuggestible, .19 and .17; Egocentric, .19 and .13; Irregular attendance at school, .18 and -.13; Temper tantrums, .17 and .16; Grouped: temper, etc., .17 and .11; Queer, .16 and .19; Lack of interest in school, .15 and .11; Selfish, .15 and .02; Sulky, .15 and .14; Threatening violence, .15 (boys); Grouped: lack of interest in school, .15 and .11; Nail-biting, .14 and .16; Mental conflict, .14 and -.05; Discord between parents, .14 and .10; Enuresis, .13 and -.00; Unpopular, .13 and .16; Feeble-minded sibling, .13 and -.12; Teasing other children, .12 (boys); Quarrelsome, .12 and .08; Hatred or jealousy of sibling, .12 and .09; Leader, .12 and -.07; Conduct prognosis bad, .11 and .16; Former convulsions, .11 and -.07; Bossy, .10 and .05; Inattentive in school, .10 and .07; Irritable, .10 and -.11; Inefficient in work, play, etc., .09 and .13; Emotional instability, .09 and .18; Popular, .09 and .03; Restless in sleep, .08 and .16; Lazy, .08 and -.05; Seclusive, .08 and .01; Crying spells, .08 and .03; Grouped: "nervous," etc., .08 and .11; Spoiled child, .07 and .07; Headaches, .07 and .11; Grouped: depressed, etc., .06 and .10; Absent-minded, .04 and .06; Daydreaming, .04 and .15; Overinterest in sex matters, .04 and .10; Sensitive over specific fact, .04 and .05; Finicky food habits, .03 and .02; Changeable moods, .03 and .17; Inferiority feelings, .03 and .02; Attractive manner, .01 and -.08; Repressed, .01 and -.01; Preference for younger children, .00 and -.01; Poor work in school, -.00 and -.09; Follower, -.01 and -.01; "Nervous," -.02 and .12; Clean, -.02 and -.16; Underweight, -.02 and -.06; Object of teasing, -.03 and .15; Question of hypophrenia, -.03 and -.05; Retardation in school -.03 and -.05; Grouped: sensitive or worrisome, etc., -.04 and -.02; Apprehensive, -.05 and .14; Listless, -.05 and -.10; Neurological defect, -.05 and .01; Lues, -.05 and .16; Lack of initiative, -.06 and -.03; Speech defect, -.06 and -.14; Immoral home conditions, -.07 and .11; Psychoneurotic, -.08 and .05; Grouped: dull, slow, etc., -.08 and -.05; Slow, dull, -.09 and .04; Stuttering, -.09 (boys); Worry over specific fact, -.10 and -.02; Depressed, -.11 and .07; Bashful, -.13 and -.19

respectively. Sex delinquency (coitus) among girls likewise yield the important correlation of .48 ± .04 with truancy from home, but among boys this relationship was low, .16.

Running with a gang, which was computed for boys only, and overinterest in the opposite sex, which was computed for girls only, yielded substantial correlations in the .30's. Leading others into bad conduct and disobedience among boys similarly yielded substantial correlations in the .30's, with only moderate correlations of .21 ± .06 and .19 respectively among girls. Destructiveness showed an interesting divergence in its correlations, the boys' correlation being .31 ± .03, while the corresponding girls' coefficient was negative, -.16. Four conduct problems among girls yielded substantial correlations in the .30's, with moderate coefficients in the .20's among boys: refusal to attend school, excuse-forming attitude, fighting, and swearing or bad language (undifferentiated).

Five notations showed moderate correlations in the .20's for both sexes: defiant attitude, violence, rudeness, slovenliness, and exclusion from school. Complaining of bad treatment by other children, which was calculated for boys only, and victim of sex abuse by older child or person, which was calculated for girls only, showed moderate correlations in the .20's. Eight notations among boys showed moderate correlations in the .20's but low positive correlations below .20 among girls: irregular sleep habits, contrariness, sullenness, irresponsibility, disturbing influence in school, egocentricity or selfishness (undifferentiated), unhappiness, and brother in penal detention. Seven miscellaneous notations among girls showed moderate correlations in the .20's but low positive correlations below .20 among boys: stubbornness, temper display, boastful or "show-off" manner, distractibility, restlessness, question or diagnosis of encephalitis, and vicious home conditions.

With truancy from home there were three negative correlations of moderate size in the -.20's, all among girls: sensitiveness in general, sex misbehavior denied entirely, and "request for vocational guidance."

Among the six sex notations there were several correlations of significant size, all among girls, the corresponding boys' coefficients ranging from .04 to .19: for sex delinquency (coitus) the large correlation of .48 ± .04, for masturbation the substantial correlation of .35 ± .04, for overinterest in the opposite sex and victim of sex abuse by older child or person the very substantial

coefficients of .33 ± .04 and .28 ± .05 respectively, the corresponding coefficients for boys being omitted because of paucity
of cases, and for sex misbehavior denied entirely the negative coefficient of -.24 ± .06.

The correlations for the seven physical or psychophysical
notations were all low or negligible, except for question or diagnosis of encephalitis among girls, which showed a moderate correlation of .24 ± .07.

Among the four home or familial notations there were two
coefficients of moderate size, brother in penal detention among
boys, .23 ± .04, and vicious home conditions among girls, .21 ± .06

Staying out late at night was noted among 319, or 15.1 per
cent, of our boys and among 140, or 11.9 per cent, of our girls.

Its highest correlation was with truancy from home among
boys, .62 ± .02, with a similarly high correlation among girls,
.53 ± .04 (Table 58). Truancy from school also showed high coefficients in the .50's for both sexes. Overinterest in the opposite sex, which was computed for girls only, likewise yielded the
high correlation of .50 ± .04. Bad companions among girls yielded
the high correlation of .59 ± .04, with a corresponding large coefficient of .44 ± .03 among boys. Stealing among boys yielded
the high correlation of .50 ± .02, with a corresponding substantial coefficient of .39 ± .04 among girls.

Incorrigibility and loitering or wandering among both sexes
yielded large correlations ranging from .46 to .49. Swearing or
bad language (undifferentiated) yielded substantial or large correlations of .31 ± .03 and .48 ± .05 for boys and girls respectively. Among girls sex delinquency (coitus) and vicious home
conditions likewise yielded high correlations in the .40's but low
coefficients of .10 and .14 respectively among boys.

Substantial correlations in the .30's among both sexes
were found for disobedience, leading others into bad conduct, and
lying and also for two conduct difficulties which were computed
only for boys, running with a gang and smoking. Irresponsibility
among boys yielded the substantial correlation of .33 ± .04 but a
low correlation of .13 among girls. Defiant attitude yielded the
moderate or substantial correlations of .27 ± .04 and .35 ± .05
among boys and girls respectively. Among girls three behavior

TABLE 58

CORRELATIONS WITH "STAYING OUT LATE AT NIGHT"

	Boys	Girls
Personality-total...........................	.16 ± .02	.24 ± .03
Conduct-total...............................	.48 ± .02	.51 ± .03
Police arrest...............................	.52 ± .03	.49 ± .04
	Larger Correlations (Positive)	
Truancy from home...........................	.62 ± .02	.53 ± .04 (3)*
Stealing....................................	.50 ± .02	.39 ± .04 (11-12)
Truancy from school........................	.50 ± .02	.54 ± .04 (2)
Incorrigible...............................	.47 ± .03	.46 ± .04 (7)
Grouped: disobedient, etc..................	.47 ± .03	.44 ± .04 (8-9)
Loitering..................................	.46 ± .03	.49 ± .06 (5)
Bad companions.............................	.44 ± .03	.59 ± .04 (1)
Gang.......................................	.35 ± .03	....
Disobedient................................	.34 ± .03	.37 ± .04 (13-14)
Leading others into bad conduct............	.34 ± .04	.39 ± .06 (11-12)
Smoking....................................	.34 ± .04	....
Irresponsible..............................	.33 ± .04	.13
Lying......................................	.31 ± .03	.31 ± .04 (17)
Grouped: swearing, etc....................	.31 ± .03	.48 ± .05 (6)
Irregular sleep habits.....................	.29 ± .04	.24 ± .06 (24-28)
Emotional instability......................	.28 ± .05	.12
Defiant....................................	.27 ± .04	.35 ± .05 (15)
Rude.......................................	.27 ± .03	.28 ± .05 (21-22)
Egocentric.................................	.26 ± .03	.22 ± .05 (32)
Fantastical lying..........................	.25 ± .03	.24 ± .06 (24-28)
Threatening violence.......................	.25 ± .05	....
Refusal to attend school...................	.24 ± .04	.28 ± .07 (21-22)
Slovenly...................................	.24 ± .03	.14
Conduct prognosis bad......................	.24 ± .05	.23 ± .07 (29-31)
Swearing (general).........................	.23 ± .04	....
Boastful, "show-off".......................	.22 ± .04	.04
Destructive................................	.21 ± .04	.23 ± .07 (29-31)
Oversuggestible............................	.21 ± .03	.21 ± .05 (33-34)
Unhappy....................................	.21 ± .05	.11
Leader.....................................	.20 ± .04	.03
Fighting...................................	.20 ± .03	.14
Grouped: egocentric, etc..................	.20 ± .03	.24 ± .04 (24-28)
Excuse-forming.............................	.20 ± .04	.29 ± .05 (19-20)
Unpopular..................................	.20 ± .05	.20 ± .07 (35-37)
Overinterest in opposite sex...............	....	.50 ± .04 (4)
Sex delinquency (coitus)...................	.10	.44 ± .04 (8-9)
Vicious home conditions....................	.14	.41 ± .06 (10)
Violence...................................	.18	.37 ± .05 (13-14)
Poor work in school........................	.07	.34 ± .04 (16)
Question of change of personality..........	.03	.30 ± .06 (18)
Grouped: fighting, etc....................	.19	.29 ± .04 (19-20)
Lack of interest in school.................	.11	.25 ± .05 (23)

*Rank order of girls' correlations.

TABLE 58—Continued

	Boys	Girls
Grouped: lack of interest in school, etc.....	.15	.24 ± .05 (24-28)
Stubborn..	.13	.24 ± .04 (24-28)
Temper tantrums.................................	.16	.23 ± .05 (29-31)
Question of encephalitis......................	.02	.21 ± .08 (33-34)
Temper display.................................	.05	.20 ± .06 (35-37)
Grouped: temper, etc..........................	.10	.20 ± .04 (35-37)
	Larger Correlations (Negative)	
Vocational guidance...........................	-.08	-.23 ± .04

Other Correlations (Positive to Negative)

Inefficient in work, play, etc., .19 and .08; Complaining of bad treatment by other children, .18 (boys); Disturbing influence in school, .17 and .06; Popular, .17 and .04; Exclusion from school, .16 and .08; Sullen, .15 and .13; Sex denied entirely, .15 and .02; Teasing other children, .14 (boys); Sulky, .14 and .03; Masturbation, .14 and .11; Contrary, .13 and .11; Queer, .13 and .19; Restless, .13 and .15; Sensitive over specific fact, .13 and .03; Discord between parents, .13 and .16; Inattentive in school, .12 and .18; Daydreaming, .12 and .18; Brother in penal detention, .12 and -.05; Quarrelsome, .11 and .15; Hatred or jealousy of sibling, .11 and .08; Spoiled child, .11 and .19; Victim of sex abuse, .11 (girls); Overinterest in sex matters, .08 and .01; Apprehensive, .08 and .17; Crying spells, .08 and .11; Bossy, .07 and .11; Finicky food habits, .07 and .13; Enuresis, .07 and .15; Object of teasing, .07 and .14; Irregular attendance at school, .07 and .05; Nail-biting, .06 and .07; Absentminded, .06 and -.18; Psychoneurotic, .06 and -.03; Inferiority feelings, .06 and .12; Grouped: depressed, etc., .06 and .13; Grouped: "nervous," etc., .05 and .05; Lack of initiative, .04 and -.06; Former convulsions, .04 and .01; Speech defect, .04 and -.17; Immoral home conditions, .04 and .14; Lazy, .02 and .05; Seclusive, .02 and -.03; Attractive manner, .02 and .02; Mental conflict, .01 and .13; Retardation in school, .01 and -.09; Stuttering, .01 (boys); Follower, .01 and .01; Grouped: sensitive or worrisome, etc., .01 and .01; Irritable, .00 and .11; Underweight, .00 and .02; Clean, -.01 and -.07; Question of hypophrenia, -.01 and -.04; Distractible, -.01 and .12; Changeable moods, -.01 and .17; Restless in sleep, -.02 and .18; Listless, -.02 and -.09; Preference for younger children, -.03 and -.04; "Nervous," -.03 and .06; Slow, dull, -.04 and .13; Grouped: dull, slow, etc., -.04 and .12; Headaches, -.05 and -.05; Feeble-minded sibling, -.06 and -.11; Selfish, -.07 and .12; Repressed, -.08 and -.19; Lues, -.08 and .09; Neurological defect, -.09 and .09; Bashful, -.10 and -.13; Depressed, -.11 and .09; Sensitive (general), -.15 and -.05; Worry over specific fact, -.16 and .02

problems similarly yielded substantial correlations in the .30's but low coefficients below .20 among boys: violence, question of change of personality, and poor work in school.

Ten behavior problems showed moderate correlations in the .20's with staying out late at night among both sexes: irregular

sleep habits, refusal to attend school, oversuggestibility, excuse-
forming attitude, fantastical lying, egocentricity, rudeness, destructiveness, unpopularity, and staff notation of unfavorable conduct prognosis. Threatening violence (calculated only for boys)
also showed the moderate correlation of .25 ± .05. Six behavior
traits among boys showed moderate correlations in the .20's but
low coefficients below .20 among girls: fighting, boastful or
"show-off" manner, unhappiness, emotional instability, slovenliness, and "leader." Among girls five notations showed moderate
correlations in the .20's, the coefficients for boys being below
.20: lack of interest in school, stubbornness, temper tantrums,
temper display, and question or diagnosis of encephalitis.

     The notation "request for vocational guidance" showed the
moderate negative correlation of -.23 ± .04 among girls with staying out late at night.

     Among the six sex notations two very significant correla-
tions, both among girls, were with sex delinquency (coitus), .44
± .04, and overinterest in the opposite sex, .50 ± .04 (calculated
for girls only). The remaining coefficients in this field were
positive but low, ranging from .02 to .15.

     Among the seven physical or psychophysical notations, the
only statistically significant coefficient was the moderate one
of .21 ± .08 with question or diagnosis of encephalitis among girls.

     Among the four home or familial notations the only signif-
icant correlation with staying out late at night was the very substantial one of .41 ± .06 with vicious home conditions among girls.

     (Since the correlations discussed in this chapter tended
to be similar to those for truancy from school and refusal to attend school, a further summary will be found at the end of the next
chapter.)

CHAPTER XXXV

TRUANCY FROM SCHOOL AND REFUSAL
TO ATTEND SCHOOL

Truancy from school was so highly intercorrelated with truancy from home and staying out late at night (the tetrachoric r's
ranging from .48 to .61) and other "outside correlations" with
other notations were so similar that all three conduct problems
must be considered to be closely interrelated (Table 59). It was
a grave indicator of conduct disorder, its correlations with conduct-total and police arrest ranging from .42 to .57, but of minor
importance as to personality deviation. It was one of the most
frequent of the conduct problems among our clinic cases, occurring
among 675 (or 31.9 per cent) of our 2,113 White boys and among 143
(or 12.1 per cent) of our 1,181 White girls.

The highest correlations for truancy from school were among
boys, the tetrachoric r's with stealing and truancy from home being .62 ± .02 and .61 ± .02 respectively. Among girls the corresponding coefficients of .39 ± .04 and .48 ± .04 were also very
substantial. For girls the highest correlations were with staying
out late at night (.54 ± .04) and refusal to attend school (.54 ±
.06), the corresponding coefficients of .50 ± .02 and .44 ± .03 for
boys also being large or high.

Bad companions and lying yielded large correlations in the
.40's among both sexes. Running with a gang and smoking, which
were computed only for boys, and overinterest in the opposite sex,
which was computed only for girls, also yielded large correlations
in the .40's. Two additional conduct problems yielded correlations
almost as large: loitering or wandering, with its coefficients of
.49 ± .03 and .39 ± .06 for boys and girls respectively, and incorrigibility, with corresponding correlations of .37 ± .02 and .42
± .04.

Four conduct traits among boys yielded substantial correlations in the .30's, the girls' coefficients being of moderate
size in the .20's: irregular attendance at school, leading others

TABLE 59

CORRELATIONS WITH "TRUANCY FROM SCHOOL"

	Boys	Girls
Personality-total..........................	.11 ± .02	.22 ± .03
Conduct-total..............................	.45 ± .02	.44 ± .03
Police arrest..............................	.57 ± .02	.42 ± .04
	Larger Correlations (Positive)	
Stealing...................................	.62 ± .02	.39 ± .04 (8-9)*
Truancy from home..........................	.61 ± .02	.48 ± .04 (3-4)
Staying out late at night..................	.50 ± .02	.54 ± .04 (1-2)
Loitering..................................	.49 ± .03	.39 ± .06 (8-9)
Bad companions.............................	.48 ± .02	.43 ± .05 (5)
Gang.......................................	.46 ± .03	....
Refusal to attend school...................	.44 ± .03	.54 ± .06 (1-2)
Lying......................................	.42 ± .02	.48 ± .04 (3-4)
Smoking....................................	.40 ± .03	....
Grouped: disobedient, etc..................	.38 ± .02	.36 ± .04 (11-12)
Incorrigible...............................	.37 ± .02	.42 ± .04 (6-7)
Irregular attendance at school.............	.35 ± .03	.26 ± .05 (26)
Leading others into bad conduct............	.35 ± .03	.29 ± .07 (17-18)
Brother in penal detention.................	.32 ± .03	.18
Disobedient................................	.31 ± .03	.28 ± .04 (19-20)
Fighting...................................	.31 ± .03	.27 ± .04 (21-25)
Grouped: lack of interest in school, etc...	.30 ± .03	.27 ± .05 (21-25)
Lack of interest in school.................	.29 ± .03	.28 ± .05 (19-20)
Fantastical lying..........................	.29 ± .04	.33 ± .06 (14)
Oversuggestible............................	.28 ± .03	.09
Slovenly...................................	.26 ± .03	.27 ± .04 (21-25)
Grouped: swearing, etc.....................	.26 ± .03	.34 ± .05 (13)
Destructive................................	.25 ± .03	.25 ± .07 (27-29)
Excuse-forming.............................	.23 ± .03	.15
Swearing (general).........................	.22 ± .04	....
Sullen.....................................	.22 ± .03	.27 ± .05 (21-25)
Boastful, "show-off".......................	.21 ± .03	.24 ± .06 (30)
Rude.......................................	.21 ± .03	.25 ± .05 (27-29)
Egocentric.................................	.21 ± .03	.15
Sex denied entirely........................	.21 ± .04	.01
Exclusion from school......................	.21 ± .03	.22 ± .06 (31-32)
Defiant....................................	.20 ± .03	.38 ± .05 (10)
Overinterest in opposite sex...............	....	.42 ± .04 (6-7)
Sex delinquency (coitus)...................	.03	.36 ± .04 (11-12)
Disturbing influence in school.............	.19	.32 ± .05 (15-16)
Vicious home conditions....................	.18	.32 ± .06 (15-16)
Violence...................................	.13	.29 ± .06 (17-18)
Worry over specific fact...................	-.13	.27 ± .07 (21-25)
Temper tantrums............................	.08	.25 ± .05 (27-29)
Question of change of personality..........	.16	.22 ± .06 (31-32)

*Rank order of girls' correlations.

TABLE 59—Continued

	Boys	Girls
Daydreaming.....................................	.06	.21 ± .06 (33)
Irregular sleep habits.........................	.17	.20 ± .06 (34-36)
Immoral home conditions........................	.05	.20 ± .06 (34-36)
Grouped: sensitive or worrisome, etc..........	-.05	.20 ± .04 (34-36)
	Larger Correlations (Negative)	
Vocational guidance............................	.02	-.25 ± .05

Other Correlations (Positive to Negative)

Contrary, .19 and -.01; Complaining of bad treatment by other children, .19 (boys); Grouped: fighting, etc., .19 and .18; Grouped: egocentric, etc., .19 and .16; Inattentive in school, .18 and .16; Nail-biting, .17 and .17; Threatening violence, .17 (boys); Hatred or jealousy of sibling, .17 and .04; Enuresis, .15 and .12; Irresponsible, .14 and .04; Leader, .14 and .14; Discord between parents, .13 and .10; Conduct prognosis bad, .13 and .12; Masturbation, .13 and .19; Inefficient in work, play, etc.; .12 and .02; Sulky, .12 and .15; Unpopular, .12 and .17; Grouped: temper, etc., .11 and .15; Temper display, .11 and .09; Stubborn, .11 and .18; Victim of sex abuse, .11 (girls); Crying spells, .10 and .07; Retardation in school, .10 and -.03; Follower, .10 and -.01; Grouped: "nervous," etc., .09 and .10; Former convulsions, .09 and -.06; Spoiled child, .09 and .16; Lazy, .09 and .06; Bossy, .06 and .14; Selfish, .06 and .00; Restless, .06 and .17; Absent-minded, .06 and .03; Irritable, .06 and .08; Question of encephalitis, .06 and .09; Headaches, .05 and .05; Popular, .05 and -.12; Poor work in school, .05 and .06; Unhappy, .05 and .08; Emotional instability, .05 and .13; Apprehensive, .05 and .19; Quarrelsome, .04 and .01; Lues, .03 and .10; Clean, .03 and -.16; Mental conflict, .03 and .12; Object of teasing, .03 and .17; Queer, .02 and .13; Seclusive, .02 and .05; Attractive manner, .02 and .12; Sensitive over specific fact, .01 and .16; "Nervous," .01 and .04; Slow, dull, .01 and -.13; Overinterest in sex matters, .01 and .19; Teasing other children, .01 (boys); Finicky food habits, .00 and .11; Repressed, .00 and .09; Grouped: dull, slow, etc., .00 and -.09; Restless in sleep, -.00 and .10; Preference for younger children, -.01 and .11; Grouped: depressed, etc., -.01 and .03; Lack of initiative, -.02 and -.11; Speech defect, -.02 and -.05; Underweight, -.02 and -.00; Inferiority feelings, -.02 and .06; Changeable moods, -.02 and -.01; Distractible, -.03 and .07; Question of hypophrenia, -.03 and -.06; Feeble-minded sibling, -.06 and .01; Depressed, -.08 and .02; Sensitive (general), -.08 and .05; Stuttering, -.10 (boys); Listless, -.10 and -.09; Psychoneurotic, -.11 and -.03; Neurological defect, -.13 and -.04; Bashful, -.14 and -.04

into bad conduct, disobedience, and fighting. Brother in penal detention among boys yielded likewise a substantial correlation of .32 ± .03, the girls' coefficient being comparatively low, .18. Among girls defiant attitude, swearing or bad language (undifferentiated), and fantastical lying yielded substantial correlations

in the .30's with moderate coefficients in the .20's among boys.
Among girls sex delinquency (coitus), disturbing influence in
school, and vicious home conditions also yielded substantial correlations in the .30's but low positive coefficients below .20 for
boys.

Seven notations showed moderate correlations in the .20's
with truancy from school among both sexes: exclusion from school,
lack of interest in school, sullenness, rudeness, boastful or
"show-off" manner, slovenliness, and destructiveness. Four notations among boys showed moderate correlations in the .20's but low
coefficients below .20 among girls: egocentricity, excuse-forming
attitude, oversuggestibility, and sex misbehavior denied entirely.
Eight miscellaneous notations among girls similarly showed moderate correlations in the .20's but low coefficients below .20 among
boys: violence, temper tantrums, question of change of personality, daydreaming, sensitiveness or worrisomeness (undifferentiated),
worry over some specific fact, irregular sleep habits, and immoral
home conditions.

The only negative correlation of moderate size was for
"request for vocational guidance" among girls, -.25 ± .05.

Among the six sex notations substantial correlations with
truancy from school were found among girls for sex delinquency
(coitus), .36 ± .04, and for overinterest in the opposite sex, .42
± .04. Among boys sex misbehavior denied entirely showed the moderate correlation of .21 ± .04. All other correlations in this
field were positive but low, ranging from .01 to .19.

All correlations in the physical or psychophysical field
were low or negligible, ranging from -.13 to .15.

Among the four home or familial notations, truancy from
school yielded substantial correlations in the .30's for brother
in penal detention among boys and vicious home conditions among
girls and a moderate coefficient of .20 ± .06 for immoral home conditions among girls. All other correlations in this field were
positive and low, ranging from .05 to .18.

Refusal or marked unwillingness to attend school was fairly
highly correlated with truancy from school, the tetrachoric r's for
boys and girls being .44 ± .03 and .54 ± .06 respectively (Table
60). It was noted among 145 boys, or 6.9 per cent, and among 46

TABLE 60

CORRELATIONS WITH "REFUSAL TO ATTEND SCHOOL"

	Boys	Girls
Personality-total............................	.17 ± .03	.08 ± .04
Conduct-total................................	.30 ± .03	.22 ± .04
Police arrest................................	.30 ± .04	.07 ± .07
	Larger Correlations (Positive)	
Truancy from school..........................	.44 ± .03	.54 ± .06 (1)*
Loitering....................................	.36 ± .05	.13
Irregular attendance at school...............	.34 ± .05	.32 ± .07 (2)
Truancy from home............................	.28 ± .04	.31 ± .06 (3-4)
Queer..	.28 ± .05	.11
Irregular sleep habits.......................	.27 ± .05	.24 ± .09 (10-12)
Incorrigible.................................	.25 ± .04	.21 ± .06 (15-16)
Leading others into bad conduct..............	.25 ± .05	.17
Grouped: disobedient, etc....................	.25 ± .03	.27 ± .05 (8)
Staying out late at night....................	.24 ± .04	.28 ± .07 (7)
Stealing.....................................	.24 ± .03	.13
Swearing (general)..........................	.24 ± .05	....
Fighting.....................................	.23 ± .04	.19
Gang...	.23 ± .05	....
Violence.....................................	.23 ± .04	.18
Smoking......................................	.22 ± .05	....
Stubborn.....................................	.22 ± .04	.19
Exclusion from school........................	.21 ± .05	.03
Contrary.....................................	.21 ± .06	.18
Question of change of personality............	.20 ± .05	.23 ± .09 (13-14)
Finicky food habits..........................	.10	.31 ± .07 (3-4)
Defiant......................................	.19	.30 ± .08 (5-6)
Lack of interest in school...................	.18	.30 ± .07 (5-6)
Sullen.......................................	.18	.25 ± .08 (9)
Grouped: swearing, etc.......................	.17	.24 ± .08 (10-12)
Spoiled child................................	.17	.24 ± .08 (10-12)
Grouped: lack of interest in school, etc.....	.16	.23 ± .07 (13-14)
Overinterest in opposite sex.................	....	.21 ± .07 (15-16)
Clean..	.13	.20 ± .07 (17-18)
Vocational guidance..........................	.03	.20 ± .07 (17-18)
	Larger Correlations (Negative)	
Feeble-minded sibling........................	-.28 ± .06	-.06
Grouped: depressed, etc......................	.09	-.25 ± .07
Unhappy......................................	.17	-.22 ± .09
Conduct prognosis bad........................	.02	-.20 ± .10

*Rank order of girls' correlations.

TABLE 60—Continued

Other Correlations (Positive to Negative)

Disturbing influence in school, .19 and .08; Temper tantrums, .19 and .17; Complaining of bad treatment by other children, .17 (boys); Grouped: fighting, etc., .19 and .06; Irresponsible, .18 and -.01; Destructive, .17 and .13; Disobedient, .17 and .12; Sulky, .17 and .10; Emotional instability, .17 and .04; Temper display, .16 and .05; Apprehensive, .16 and .19; Daydreaming, .16 and .12; Popular, .16 and .18; Brother in penal detention, .16 and .16; Rude, .15 and .13; Threatening violence, .15 (boys); Oversuggestible, .15 and -.07; Grouped: temper, etc., .15 and .08; Bad companions, .14 and .14; Overinterest in sex matters, .14 and .14; Hatred or jealousy of sibling, .14 and .14; Depressed, .14 and -.13; Listless, .14 and -.06; Psychoneurotic, .14 and .04; Irritable, .14 and .09; Seclusive, .14 and .18; Unpopular, .14 and -.00; Poor work in school, .14 and .16; Inefficient in work, play, etc., .13 and -.03; Crying spells, .13 and .00; Follower, .13 and .00; Lying, .12 and .16; Teasing other children, .12 (boys); Absent-minded, .12 and .16; Excuse-forming, .12 and .05; Grouped: egocentric, etc., .12 and .11; Changeable moods, .11 and -.03; Egocentric, .11 and .09; Object of teasing, .11 and -.01; Worry over specific fact, .10 and .03; Repressed, .10 and -.08; Question of encephalitis, .10 and .19; Discord between parents, .10 and .06; Grouped: "nervous," etc., .10 and -.03; Slovenly, .09 and -.07; Restless, .09 and .02; Sensitive (general), .09 and .13; Leader, .09 and .15; Headaches, .09 and .14; Boastful, "show-off," .08 and .00; Inattentive in school, .08 and -.08; Selfish, .08 and .01; Former convulsions, .08 and .01; Fantastical lying, .07 and .14; Distractible, .07 and .08; Mental conflict, .07 and .13; Masturbation, .06 and .02; Sensitive over specific fact, .06 and .19; Sex denied entirely, .06 and .19; Lazy, .05 and .04; Nail-biting, .05 and -.06; Lack of initiative, .05 and -.18; "Nervous," etc., .05 and -.10; Grouped: dull, slow, etc., .05 and -.12; Sex delinquency (coitus), .05 and -.01; Grouped: sensitive or worrisome, etc., .04 and .15; Restless in sleep, .03 and .09; Lues, .03 and .10; Immoral home conditions, .03 and .00; Inferiority feelings, .02 and .18; Stuttering, .02 (boys); Attractive manner, .02 and -.11; Neurological defect, .02 and -.18; Quarrelsome, .02 and .03; Slow, dull, .01 and -.07; Bashful, .00 and .00; Question of hypophrenia, -.00 and -.07; Preference for younger children, -.01 and .07; Victim of sex abuse, -.02 (girls); Vicious home conditions, -.02 and -.06; Retardation in school, -.03 and -.09; Speech defect, -.04 and -.10; Bossy, -.06 and -.09; Enuresis, -.07 and .12; Underweight, -.08 and .11

girls, or 3.9 per cent. In contrast with truancy from home or from school, its importance as an indicator either of conduct disorder or of overt juvenile delinquency was only moderate, the correlations ranging from .07 to .30. As a correlate of personality deviation its importance was very minor, the bi-serial r's for boys and girls being only .17 + .03 and .08 + .04.

Its highest correlations were with truancy from school, with coefficients of .44 + .03 and .54 + .06 for boys and girls respectively. Irregular attendance at school yielded substantial correlations in the .30's for both sexes. Loitering or wandering yielded the substantial correlation of .36 + .05 among boys but a low coefficient of .13 among girls. Truancy from home among girls

yielded the substantial correlation of .31 ± .06, the corresponding coefficient among boys being practically as large, .28 ± .04.
Three behavior problems among girls—lack of interest in school,
defiant attitude, and finicky food habits—similarly yielded substantial correlations in the .30's but low coefficients below .20
for boys.

Among both sexes refusal to attend school showed moderate
correlations in the .20's with four behavior difficulties: staying out late at night, incorrigibility, irregular sleep habits, and
question of change of personality. Three conduct problems, for
which only the boys' correlations were computed because of the paucity of girls' cases: running with a gang, swearing in general,
and smoking, and one computed only for girls, overinterest in the
opposite sex, also showed moderate correlations in the .20's.
Eight notations among boys showed moderate correlations in the
.20's but low positive coefficients below .20 among girls: exclusion from school, stealing, fighting, stubbornness, contrariness,
violence, leading others into bad conduct, and queer behavior.
Five notations among girls similarly showed moderate correlations
in the .20's but low positive coefficients below .20 among boys:
sullenness, swearing or bad language (undifferentiated), "spoiled
child," clean habits, and "request for vocational guidance."
Negative correlations of moderate size in the -.20's were
found among boys for feeble-minded sibling and among girls for unhappiness and staff notation of unfavorable conduct prognosis.

Among the six sex notations in our data the only coefficient with a claim to statistical significance was for overinterest in the opposite sex (calculated for girls only), .21 ± .07.

Among the seven physical or psychophysical notations and
among the four home or familial notations all twenty-two correlations with refusal to attend school were low or negligible, ranging from -.18 to .19.

Since the four conduct traits discussed in chapters xxxiv
and xxxv—truancy from home, staying out late at night, truancy
from school, and refusal to attend school—appear to form a fairly
closely interrelated group, we may summarize certain trends among
the correlations. The following six behavior traits showed, in
the main, substantial to high correlations with all four notations,

ranging from the .20's to the .60's, among both sexes: stealing, loitering or wandering, incorrigibility, and swearing or bad language (undifferentiated) and also running with a gang and smoking, for which only the boys' correlations were computed. The four conduct problems, leading others into bad conduct, fighting, violence, and defiant attitude, tended to yield moderate to substantial correlations in the .20's and .30's for all four notations among both sexes and among boys also sullenness and irregular sleep habits.

With the three notations, truancy from home and from school, and staying out late at night, two conduct problems, associating with bad companions and lying, tended to yield substantial to large correlations, ranging from the .20's to the .50's. Disobedience, fantastical lying, and excuse-forming attitude similarly tended to yield moderate to substantial correlations in the .20's and .30's with these three notations. Among girls, sex delinquency (coitus) and overinterest in the opposite sex (computed only for girls) yielded substantial to large correlations ranging from .33 to .50 with all three notations. With these three notations vicious home conditions among girls yielded moderate to substantial correlations ranging from .21 to .41. Vicious home conditions among boys and immoral home conditions among both sexes tended to show low or negligible correlations ranging from -.07 to .20.

CHAPTER XXXVI

DISOBEDIENCE; INCORRIGIBILITY; DEFIANCE;
STUBBORNNESS; AND CONTRARINESS

That the five conduct problems discussed in this chapter
—disobedience, incorrigibility, defiant attitude, stubbornness,
and contrariness—are closely interrelated is indicated by the
fact of their generally large intercorrelation and also by the
fact of the similarity of their "outside correlations" with other
traits. The first three of these traits—disobedience, incorrigibility, and defiant attitude—are especially closely intercorrelated, the tetrachoric r's ranging from .41 to .52. Stubbornness
and contrariness are less closely intercorrelated with the other
three traits, their coefficients ranging from .16 to .44. In
view of their frequency of occurrence and their relatively high
importance as indicators of behavior deviation, it seemed advisable to consider each of the five notations separately as well as
under one rubric, disobedience or incorrigibility (undifferentiated).

All five notations were notably important as indicators
of conduct difficulties, their bi-serial r's with conduct-total
ranging from .25 to .68. As indicators of overt juvenile delinquency or of undesirable personality traits their importance is
not so great, their correlations with police arrest and personality-total ranging from .08 to .53.

Disobedience was noted among 459 of our 2,113 White boys
(21.7 per cent) and among 207 of our 1,181 White girls (17.5 per
cent).

Its highest correlations among both sexes were with incorrigibility, rudeness, defiant attitude, disturbing influence in
school, and fighting or quarrelsomeness (including violence, undifferentiated), the boys' coefficients ranging from .36 to .48
and the girls' from .44 to .52 (Table 61). Lying, destructiveness,
and violence among girls also yielded large correlations in the

332

TABLE 61

CORRELATIONS WITH "DISOBEDIENT"

	Boys	Girls
Personality-total............................	.24 ± .02	.31 ± .03
Conduct-total................................	.43 ± .02	.49 ± .02
Police arrest................................	.21 ± .03	.18 ± .04
	Larger Correlations (Positive)	
Incorrigible.................................	.48 ± .02	.52 ± .03 (1-2)*
Rude...	.46 ± .03	.52 ± .04 (1-2)
Defiant......................................	.41 ± .03	.47 ± .04 (3)
Disturbing influence in school..............	.36 ± .03	.45 ± .05 (4)
Grouped: fighting, etc......................	.36 ± .02	.44 ± .03 (5)
Staying out late at night...................	.34 ± .04	.37 ± .04 (10-11)
Grouped: swearing, etc......................	.34 ± .03	.36 ± .05 (12-14)
Truancy from home...........................	.32 ± .03	.19
Smoking......................................	.31 ± .03	....
Truancy from school.........................	.31 ± .03	.28 ± .04 (31-32)
Grouped: lack of interest in school, etc......	.31 ± .03	.29 ± .04 (26-30)
Lying..	.31 ± .03	.43 ± .03 (6)
Boastful, "show-off".........................	.30 ± .03	.20 ± .05 (47-51)
Stubborn.....................................	.30 ± .03	.37 ± .04 (10-11)
Grouped: egocentric, etc....................	.30 ± .03	.34 ± .04 (18)
Destructive..................................	.29 ± .03	.41 ± .05 (7-8)
Fighting.....................................	.29 ± .03	.35 ± .05 (15-17)
Inattentive in school.......................	.29 ± .03	.30 ± .05 (23-25)
Leading others into bad conduct.............	.29 ± .04	.30 ± .06 (23-25)
Violence.....................................	.29 ± .03	.41 ± .05 (7-8)
Egocentric...................................	.29 ± .03	.35 ± .04 (15-17)
Quarrelsome..................................	.28 ± .03	.38 ± .04 (9)
Exclusion from school.......................	.28 ± .03	.36 ± .05 (12-14)
Contrary.....................................	.27 ± .04	.16
Stealing.....................................	.26 ± .02	.26 ± .04 (34-36)
Sullen.......................................	.26 ± .03	.32 ± .05 (19-22)
Swearing (general)..........................	.26 ± .04	....
Irregular sleep habits......................	.26 ± .04	.23 ± .06 (40-43)
Restless.....................................	.26 ± .04	.23 ± .04 (40-43)
Unpopular....................................	.26 ± .04	.36 ± .06 (12-14)
Teasing other children......................	.25 ± .03	....
Grouped: temper, etc........................	.25 ± .03	.32 ± .04 (19-22)
Fantastical lying...........................	.25 ± .04	.24 ± .05 (38-39)
Question of change of personality............	.24 ± .04	.32 ± .05 (19-22)
Loitering....................................	.23 ± .04	.07
Temper tantrums.............................	.23 ± .03	.35 ± .04 (15-17)
Irresponsible...............................	.22 ± .04	.25 ± .06 (37)
Gang...	.22 ± .03	....
Sulky..	.22 ± .04	.18
Complaining of bad treatment by other children	.22 ± .04	....

*Rank order of girls' correlations.

TABLE 61—Continued

	Boys	Girls
Grouped: "nervous," etc.	.22 ± .02	.29 ± .03 (26-30)
Lack of interest in school	.21 ± .03	.20 ± .05 (47-51)
Selfish	.21 ± .04	.29 ± .05 (26-30)
Lazy	.20 ± .04	.09
Threatening violence	.20 ± .04	
Overinterest in opposite sex	....	.32 ± .04 (19-22)
Overinterest in sex matters	.09	.30 ± .05 (23-25)
Bossy	.11	.29 ± .05 (26-30)
Question of encephalitis	.15	.29 ± .07 (26-30)
Excuse-forming	.18	.28 ± .05 (31-32)
Spoiled child	.16	.27 ± .05 (33)
Finicky food habits	.11	.26 ± .05 (34-36)
Distractible	.13	.26 ± .05 (34-36)
Sex delinquency (coitus)	-.03	.24 ± .04 (38-39)
Restless in sleep	.13	.23 ± .04 (40-43)
Queer	.07	.23 ± .06 (40-43)
Slovenly	.16	.22 ± .04 (44-45)
Masturbation	.06	.22 ± .04 (44-45)
Mental conflict	.05	.21 ± .06 (46)
Bad companions	.19	.20 ± .05 (47-51)
Irritable	.16	.20 ± .04 (47-51)
Conduct prognosis bad	.13	.20 ± .06 (47-51)

Other Correlations (Positive to Negative)

Temper display, .19 and .19; Leader, .18 and .15; Refusal to attend school, .17 and .12; Unhappy, .17 and .17; Hatred or jealousy of sibling, .15 and .11; Psychoneurotic, .15 and .16; Grouped: depressed, etc., .15 and .11; Inefficient in work, play, etc., .14 and .13; Crying spells, .14 and .13; Depressed, .14 and -.03; Changeable moods, .13 and .12; Preference for younger children, .13 and .01; Victim of sex abuse, .12 (girls); "Nervous," .12 and .19; Brother in penal detention, .12 and -.02; Enuresis, .11 and .12; Absent-minded, .11 and .05; Object of teasing, .11 and .17; Sensitive (general), .11 and .02; Former convulsions, .11 and .02; Inferiority feelings, .10 and .04; Poor work in school, .10 and .16; Nail-biting, .09 and .07; Discord between parents, .09 and .19; Emotional instability, .08 and .19; Grouped: dull, slow, etc., .08 and -.14; Grouped: sensitive or worrisome, .08 and .06; Sensitive over specific fact, .07 and .04; Sex denied entirely, .07 and -.05; Popular, .07 and .05; Attractive manner, .07 and .04; Seclusive, .06 and -.08; Oversuggestible, .04 and .08; Retardation in school, .04 and -.06; Neurological defect, .04 and -.03; Worry over specific fact, .03 and .13; Follower, .03 and .00; Daydreaming, .02 and .13; Stuttering, .02 (boys); Underweight, .02 and .03; Question of hypophrenia, .01 and .04; Headaches, .00 and .10; Irregular attendance at school, -.01 and .16; Immoral home conditions, -.03 and -.02; Speech defect, -.03 and -.07; Repressed, -.03 and .04; Vocational guidance, -.05 and -.15; Clean, -.05 and -.06; Slow, dull, -.06 and -.13; Listless, -.07 and .03; Vicious home conditions, -.08 and .13; Apprehensive, -.08 and .06; Lack of initiative, -.10 and -.06; Bashful, -.13 and -.06; Lues, -.14 and .02; Feeble-minded sibling, -.18 and -.14

Omitted—Grouped: disobedient, etc.

.40's, with substantial coefficients among boys ranging from .29 to .31.

Three conduct problems—stubbornness, staying out late at night, and swearing or bad language (undifferentiated)—yielded substantial correlations in the .30's for both sexes. Smoking, for which only the boys' correlation was calculated, and overinterest in the opposite sex, for which only the girls' coefficient was computed, also yielded substantial correlations in the .30's. Among boys boastful or "show-off" manner and truancy from home yielded substantial correlations in the .30's and lesser coefficients of .20 $\pm$ .05 and .19 respectively among girls. Among girls ten notations yielded substantial correlations in the .30's, with corresponding moderate coefficients in the .20's among boys: sullenness, temper tantrums, leading others into bad conduct, fighting, quarrelsomeness, egocentricity, question of change of personality, inattentiveness in school, exclusion from school, and unpopularity. Overinterest in sex matters among girls also yielded the substantial correlation of .30 $\pm$ .05 but a corresponding low correlation of .09 among boys.

Disobedience showed moderate correlations in the .20's among both sexes for seven behavior traits: stealing, selfishness, irresponsibility, fantastical lying, restlessness, irregular sleep habits, and lack of interest in school. Five behavior problems, for which only the boys' correlations were calculated, also showed moderate correlations in the .20's: swearing in general, running with a gang, threatening violence, teasing other children, and complaining of bad treatment by other children. Four conduct notations among boys similarly showed moderate correlations in the .20's but low positive correlations below .20 among girls: contrariness, laziness, loitering or wandering, and sulkiness. Among girls a large list of fifteen miscellaneous notations showed moderate correlations in the .20's, but low or negligible correlations ranging from -.03 to .19 among boys: sex delinquency (coitus), masturbation, excuse-forming attitude, bad companions, "spoiled child," irritable temperament, bossy manner, distractibility, slovenliness, restlessness in sleep, finicky food habits, mental conflict, queer behavior, question or diagnosis of encephalitis, and staff notation of unfavorable conduct prognosis.

No negative correlations of statistically significant size

were found with disobedience.

Among the six sex notations moderate to substantial correlations in the .20's to .30's were found among girls for sex delinquency (coitus), overinterest in sex matters, masturbation, and
overinterest in the opposite sex (calculated for girls only). All
the boys' correlations in this field were low or negligible.

Among the seven physical or psychophysical notations the
only significant correlation was with question or diagnosis of encephalitis among girls, .29 ± .07, all the other coefficients in
this field being low or negligible.

Among the four home or familial notations (discord between
parents, vicious or immoral home conditions, and brother in penal
detention) all coefficients were low or negligible, ranging from
-.08 to .19.

Incorrigibility was noted among 501, or 23.7 per cent, of
our boys and among 212, or 18.0 per cent, of our girls. In compar
ison with the other five conduct problems in this chapter, its cor
relations with conduct-total were unusually high, the coefficients
for boys and girls respectively being .52 ± .02 and .59 ± .02 (Table 62). With the personality-total and police-arrest criteria
its correlations were moderate or substantial, ranging from .23
to .38.

Its highest correlations were in the .50's among girls for
disobedience and swearing or bad language (undifferentiated), the
corresponding boys' coefficients in the .40's also being large.
The six conduct disorders—defiant attitude, rudeness, truancy
from home, staying out late at night, fighting, and stealing—
yielded large correlations ranging from .39 to .49 among both
sexes. Overinterest in the opposite sex (computed for girls only)
also yielded the large correlation of .42 ± .04. Destructiveness
and staff notation of unfavorable conduct prognosis among boys
yielded similarly large correlations in the .40's, the girls' coefficients being lower, .33 ± .06 and .20 ± .06 respectively.
Among girls, five conduct problems similarly yielded large correlations in the 40's with corresponding substantial coefficients
in the .30's among boys: disturbing influence in school, truancy
from school, violence, quarrelsomeness, and temper tantrums.

Six notations consistently yielded substantial correlation

TABLE 62

CORRELATIONS WITH "INCORRIGIBLE"

	Boys	Girls
Personality-total..........................	.23 ± .02	.35 ± .03
Conduct-total.............................	.52 ± .02	.59 ± .02
Police arrest.............................	.38 ± .03	.28 ± .04
	Larger Correlations (Positive)	
Defiant...................................	.48 ± .03	.49 ± .04 (4)*
Disobedient...............................	.48 ± .02	.52 ± .03 (1-2)
Staying out late at night.................	.47 ± .03	.46 ± .04 (8-9)
Truancy from home.........................	.45 ± .02	.44 ± .04 (11)
Rude......................................	.44 ± .03	.47 ± .04 (5-7)
Grouped: fighting, etc...................	.43 ± .02	.51 ± .02 (3)
Destructive...............................	.41 ± .03	.33 ± .06 (25-26)
Fighting..................................	.40 ± .03	.46 ± .03 (8-9)
Conduct prognosis bad.....................	.40 ± .04	.20 ± .06 (52-54)
Stealing..................................	.40 ± .02	.39 ± .04 (16-18)
Grouped: swearing, etc..................	.40 ± .03	.52 ± .04 (1-2)
Contrary..................................	.39 ± .04	.21 ± .06 (50-51)
Violence..................................	.39 ± .03	.47 ± .05 (5-7)
Disturbing influence in school............	.37 ± .03	.40 ± .05 (15)
Truancy from school.......................	.37 ± .02	.42 ± .04 (12-14)
Swearing (general)........................	.36 ± .04	....
Threatening violence......................	.36 ± .04	....
Leading others into bad conduct...........	.34 ± .04	.34 ± .06 (22-24)
Gang......................................	.34 ± .03	....
Quarrelsome...............................	.34 ± .03	.42 ± .04 (12-14)
Lying.....................................	.32 ± .02	.37 ± .03 (19-21)
Exclusion from school.....................	.32 ± .03	.39 ± .05 (16-18)
Bad companions............................	.30 ± .03	.26 ± .05 (40)
Temper tantrums...........................	.30 ± .03	.47 ± .04 (5-7)
Smoking...................................	.29 ± .03	....
Loitering.................................	.28 ± .03	.34 ± .05 (22-24)
Slovenly..................................	.28 ± .03	.27 ± .04 (37-39)
Sullen....................................	.28 ± .03	.27 ± .05 (37-39)
Boastful, "show-off"......................	.27 ± .03	.30 ± .05 (31-33)
Grouped: temper, etc....................	.27 ± .02	.45 ± .03 (10)
Fantastical lying.........................	.26 ± .03	.27 ± .05 (37-39)
Grouped: egocentric, etc................	.26 ± .03	.30 ± .04 (31-33)
Refusal to attend school..................	.25 ± .04	.21 ± .06 (50-51)
Egocentric................................	.25 ± .03	.32 ± .04 (27)
Irregular sleep habits....................	.25 ± .04	.22 ± .06 (46-49)
Restless..................................	.25 ± .03	.31 ± .04 (28-30)
Grouped: "nervous," etc.................	.25 ± .02	.31 ± .03 (28-30)
Teasing other children....................	.23 ± .03	....
Emotional instability.....................	.23 ± .04	.39 ± .05 (34-35)
Unhappy...................................	.23 ± .04	.22 ± .06 (46-49)

*Rank order of girls' correlations.

TABLE 62—Continued

	Boys	Girls
Stubborn..	.21 ± .03	.34 ± .04 (22-24)
Excuse-forming....................................	.21 ± .03	.37 ± .05 (19-21)
Complaining of bad treatment by other children	.21 ± .04	
Overinterest in opposite sex.....................	....	.42 ± .04 (12-14)
Unpopular...	.19	.39 ± .06 (16-18)
Question of change of personality.............	.18	.37 ± .05 (19-21)
Temper display..................................	.16	.33 ± .05 (25-26)
Question of encephalitis.......................	.10	.31 ± .07 (28-30)
Irritable..	.16	.30 ± .04 (31-33)
Finicky food habits.............................	.05	.29 ± .05 (34-35)
Queer...	.15	.28 ± .06 (36)
Irresponsible....................................	.17	.24 ± .06 (41-42)
Daydreaming......................................	.05	.24 ± .05 (41-42)
Masturbation.....................................	.14	.23 ± .04 (43-45)
Changeable moods.................................	.11	.23 ± .04 (43-45)
Distractible....................................	.15	.23 ± .05 (43-45)
Sex delinquency (coitus)........................	.09	.22 ± .04 (46-49)
Grouped: lack of interest in school, etc.....	.19	.22 ± .04 (46-49)
Object of teasing...............................	.00	.20 ± .05 (52-54)
Grouped: depressed, etc.......................	.17	.20 ± .05 (52-54)
	Larger Correlations (Negative)	
Vocational guidance.............................	-.17	-.21 ± .04

Other Correlations (Positive to Negative)

Inattentive in school, .19 and .19; Discord between parents, .18 and .03; Spoiled child, .17 and .19; Selfish, .13 and .18; Oversuggestible, .13 and .09; Lack of interest in school, .12 and .14; Overinterest in sex matters, .12 and .12; Enuresis, .11 and .17; Nail-biting, .11 and .18; Sulky, .11 and .14; Crying spells, .11 and .10; Depressed, .10 and .15; Bossy, .09 and .19; Inefficient in work, play, etc., .09 and .14; Inferiority feelings, .09 and .06; Popular, .09 and .05; Brother in penal detention, .09 and -.07; Hatred or jealousy of sibling, .08 and -.01; Sex denied entirely, .08 and -.06; Irregular attendance at school, .08 and -.12; Victim of sex abuse, .08 (girls); "Nervous," .07 and .14; Mental conflict, .07 and -.00; Question of hypophrenia, .07 and .07; Restless in sleep, .06 and -.00; Poor work in school, .06 and .08; Leader, .06 and .17; Former convulsions, .05 and .04; Lazy, .04 and .08; Absent-minded, .04 and .12; Sensitive over specific fact, .04 and .09; Retardation in school, .04 and -.01; Headaches, .04 and .14; Attractive manner, .04 and -.04; Seclusive, .03 and .02; Clean, -.00 and -.07; Grouped: sensitive or worrisome, etc., -.01 and .01; Vicious home conditions, -.01 and .07; Psychoneurotic, -.01 and .02; Apprehensive, -.02 and .08; Worry over specific fact, -.04 and .03; Repressed, -.04 and -.00; Neurological defect, -.05 and -.03; Preference for younger children, -.05 and .14; Follower, -.06 and -.08; Sensitive (general), -.06 and -.06; Stuttering, -.07 (boys); Speech defect, -.08 and -.10; Underweight, -.08 and .03; Listless, -.08 and -.03; Lack of initiative, -.09 and -.14; Bashful, -.10 and -.17; Immoral home conditions, -.11 and -.01; Slow, dull, -.12 and -.10; Feeble-minded sibling, -.13 and -.15; Grouped: dull, slow, etc., -.13 and -.08; Lues, -.15 and .14

Omitted—Grouped: disobedient, etc.

in the .30's: leading others into bad conduct, lying, exclusion
from school, and the three for which only the boys' coefficients
were calculated—running with a gang, threatening violence, and
swearing in general. Contrariness and bad companions among boys
similarly yielded substantial coefficients in the .30's, with moderate coefficients in the .20's among girls. Seven conduct and
personality difficulties among girls similarly yielded substantial
correlations in the .30's, with moderate coefficients in the .20's
among boys: stubbornness, egocentricity, boastful or "show-off"
manner, excuse-forming attitude, loitering or wandering, restlessness, and emotional instability. An additional five notations
also yielded substantial correlations in the .30's among girls but
low coefficients below .20 among boys: temper display, irritable
temperament, question of change of personality, unpopularity, and
question or diagnosis of encephalitis.

      Nine behavior traits uniformly showed moderate correla-
tions with incorrigibility in the .20's: sullenness, refusal to
attend school, fantastical lying, irregular sleep habits, slovenliness, unhappiness, and the three behavior problems for which
only the boys' coefficients were calculated—smoking, teasing other
children, and complaining of bad treatment by other children. Ten
personality and conduct problems among girls showed moderate correlations in the .20's but low positive coefficients below .20
among boys: sex delinquency (coitus), masturbation, irresponsibility, distractibility, changeable moods or attitudes, lack of
interest or inattentiveness in school studies or employment (undifferentiated), daydreaming, queer behavior, finicky food habits,
and object of teasing by other children.

      The only negative correlation of significant size was with
the routine notation "request for vocational guidance" among girls,
$-.21 \pm .04$.

      Among the six sex notations there were three statistically
significant correlations with incorrigibility, all among girls:
the large tetrachoric r of $.42 \pm .04$ with overinterest in the opposite sex (calculated for girls only), and the moderate coefficients of $.22 \pm .04$ with sex delinquency (coitus) and $.23 \pm .04$
with masturbation. All other correlations in this field were low
or negligible.

      Among the seven physical or psychophysical notations the

only meaningful correlation was the substantial coefficient of
.31 + .07 with question or diagnosis of encephalitis among girls,
all other coefficients in this field being low or negligible.

Among the four home or familial conditions all correlations
were low or negligible, ranging from -.11 to .18.

Defiant attitude toward parents, teachers, etc. was noted
among 178, or 8.4 per cent, of the boys and among 95, or 8.0 per
cent, of the girls. Its bi-serial correlations with the conduct-
total, .43 + .02 and .68 + .03 for boys and girls respectively,
and also with the personality-total for girls, .53 + .03, were
high, while its tetrachoric correlations with police arrest and
the boys' bi-serial correlation with the personality-total were
only moderate or low, ranging from .14 to .20 (Table 63). Its correlations with disobedience, incorrigibility, and stubbornness were
large, ranging from .41 to .49, and its correlation with contrariness substantial, the coefficients being .33 and .34.

Its highest correlations were with rudeness, the coefficients being .49 + .03 and .54 + .04 for boys and girls respectively. Stealing and temper tantrums among girls also yielded
high coefficients in the .50's, with substantial correlations in
the .30's among boys. Its correlations with sullenness were also
large, .41 + .04 and .44 + .06 for boys and girls respectively.
Violence and egocentricity or selfishness (undifferentiated) among
girls yielded large correlations in the .40's with substantial coefficients in the .30's among boys. Four undesirable behavior
traits similarly yielded large correlations in the .40's for girls
and moderate correlations in the .20's for boys: disturbing influence in school, fighting, lying, and selfishness.

Four conduct problems yielded substantial correlations in
the .30's for both sexes: contrariness, quarrelsomeness, destructiveness, and swearing or bad language (undifferentiated). Excuse-
forming attitude and exclusion from school among boys similarly
yielded substantial correlations in the .30's, with moderate correlations in the .20's among girls. Among girls there were five
undesirable behavior traits showing substantial correlations in
the .30's and moderate correlations in the .20's among boys: leading others into bad conduct, staying out late at night, truancy
from school, egocentricity, and boastful or "show-off" manner.

TABLE 63

CORRELATIONS WITH "DEFIANT"

	Boys	Girls
Personality-total..............................	.20 ± .03	.53 ± .03
Conduct-total.................................	.43 ± .02	.68 ± .03
Police arrest.................................	.20 ± .04	.14 ± .05
	Larger Correlations (Positive)	
Rude..	.49 ± .03	.54 ± .04 (1)*
Incorrigible..................................	.48 ± .03	.49 ± .04 (4)
Stubborn......................................	.42 ± .03	.44 ± .04 (10-13)
Disobedient...................................	.41 ± .03	.47 ± .04 (6-7)
Sullen..	.41 ± .04	.44 ± .06 (10-13)
Grouped: swearing, etc......................	.36 ± .04	.34 ± .06 (24-25)
Grouped: fighting, etc......................	.35 ± .03	.48 ± .04 (5)
Contrary......................................	.33 ± .05	.34 ± .07 (24-25)
Grouped: temper, etc.......................	.33 ± .03	.44 ± .04 (10-13)
Stealing......................................	.32 ± .03	.51 ± .04 (3)
Temper tantrums...............................	.32 ± .04	.52 ± .05 (2)
Excuse-forming................................	.32 ± .04	.24 ± .06 (49-52)
Grouped: egocentric, etc...................	.32 ± .04	.40 ± .05 (15)
Destructive...................................	.31 ± .04	.31 ± .07 (33-34)
Violence......................................	.31 ± .04	.47 ± .06 (6-7)
Quarrelsome...................................	.30 ± .04	.36 ± .05 (19-21)
Exclusion from school.........................	.30 ± .04	.21 ± .07 (60-63)
Boastful, "show-off"..........................	.29 ± .04	.32 ± .06 (29-32)
Swearing (general)............................	.29 ± .05	....
Egocentric....................................	.29 ± .04	.38 ± .05 (17-18)
Disturbing influence in school...............	.28 ± .04	.46 ± .06 (8)
Lying...	.28 ± .03	.44 ± .04 (10-13)
Staying out late at night.....................	.27 ± .04	.35 ± .05 (22-23)
Gang..	.26 ± .04	....
Sulky...	.26 ± .05	.28 ± .07 (39-41)
Grouped: lack of interest in school, etc.....	.26 ± .04	.26 ± .05 (44-46)
Fighting......................................	.25 ± .04	.45 ± .06 (9)
Threatening violence..........................	.25 ± .05	....
Inattentive in school........................	.24 ± .04	.17
Truancy from home............................	.23 ± .04	.27 ± .05 (42-43)
Overinterest in opposite sex.................	....	.23 ± .05 (53-54)
Smoking.......................................	.22 ± .04	....
Leading others into bad conduct..............	.21 ± .05	.32 ± .07 (29-32)
Selfish......................................	.21 ± .05	.41 ± .06 (14)
Hatred or jealousy of sibling................	.21 ± .06	.16
Truancy from school..........................	.20 ± .03	.38 ± .05 (17-18)
Queer..	.00	.39 ± .06 (16)
Depressed....................................	.13	.36 ± .06 (19-21)
Finicky food habits..........................	.09	.36 ± .06 (19-21)
Inefficient in work, play, etc..............	-.06	.35 ± .06 (22-23)

*Rank order of girls' correlations.

TABLE 63—Continued

	Boys	Girls
Daydreaming	.08	.33 ± .06 (26-28)
Spoiled child	.17	.33 ± .06 (26-28)
Grouped: depressed, etc.	.14	.33 ± .06 (26-28)
Question of change of personality	.19	.32 ± .07 (29-32)
Grouped: "nervous," etc.	.16	.32 ± .04 (29-32)
Restless in sleep	.06	.31 ± .05 (33-34)
Refusal to attend school	.19	.30 ± .08 (35)
Temper display	.17	.29 ± .06 (36-38)
Masturbation	.00	.29 ± .05 (36-38)
Unpopular	-.01	.29 ± .07 (36-38)
Bad companions	.09	.28 ± .06 (39-41)
Leader	.18	.28 ± .07 (39-41)
Changeable moods	.16	.27 ± .05 (42-43)
Slovenly	.16	.26 ± .05 (44-46)
Object of teasing	.04	.26 ± .06 (44-46)
Inferiority feelings	.10	.25 ± .07 (47-48)
Question of encephalitis	.15	.25 ± .08 (47-48)
Irresponsible	.12	.24 ± .07 (49-52)
Irregular sleep habits	.11	.24 ± .07 (49-52)
Distractible	-.05	.24 ± .06 (49-52)
Restless	.17	.23 ± .05 (53-54)
Fantastical lying	.11	.22 ± .07 (55-59)
Loitering	.10	.22 ± .07 (55-59)
Sensitive over specific fact	.01	.22 ± .05 (55-59)
Worry over specific fact	-.04	.22 ± .08 (55-59)
Grouped: sensitive or worrisome, etc.	.04	.22 ± .05 (55-59)
Lack of interest in school	.17	.21 ± .06 (60-63)
Irritable	.17	.21 ± .05 (60-63)
Unhappy	.16	.21 ± .06 (60-63)
Lazy	.13	.20 ± .07 (64)
	Larger Correlations (Negative)	
Feeble-minded sibling	-.19	-.32 ± .06
Follower	-.12	-.25 ± .06

Other Correlations (Positive to Negative)

Nail-biting, .18 and .15; Teasing other children, .17 (boys); Popular, .17 and .12; Bossy, .16 and .19; Former convulsions, .15 and .08; Emotional instability, .14 and .18; Seclusive, .13 and .19; Complaining of bad treatment by other children, .12 (boys); Victim of sex abuse, .12 (girls); Attractive manner, .11 and .07; Crying spells, .10 and .19; Discord between parents, .07 and .06; Clean, .06 and -.02; Conduct prognosis bad, .05 and .16; Listless, .04 and .11; Enuresis, .03 and .16; Overinterest in sex matters, .03 and .16; Psychoneurotic, .03 and .09; Sensitive (general), .03 and .13; Sex delinquency (coitus), .01 and .07; Mental conflict, .01 and .14; Repressed, .01 and .04; Sex denied entirely, .00 and .07; Poor work in school, -.00 and -.01; "Nervous," -.01 and .15; Vocational guidance, -.02 and .01; Immoral home conditions, -.03 and -.04; Apprehensive, -.03 and .19; Brother in penal detention, -.04 and -.09; Oversuggestible, -.04 and .06; Slow, dull, -.04 and -.06; Grouped: dull, slow, etc., -.05 and

TABLE 63—Continued

-.01; Lack of initiative, -.05 and .05; Lues, -.06 and .04; Neurological defect, -.06 and .08; Absent-minded, -.06 and .01; Stuttering, -.08 (boys); Vicious home conditions, -.09 and .11; Speech defect, -.09 and .04; Irregular attendance at school, -.09 and -.13; Headaches, -.09 and .11; Preference for younger children, -.09 and .11; Bashful, -.09 and .06; Underweight, -.13 and -.01; Question of hypophrenia, -.14 and -.11; Retardation in school, -.17 and -.17
    Omitted—Grouped: disobedient, etc.

Nine additional behavior problems among girls yielded substantial correlations in the .30's, but low correlations below .20 among boys: refusal to attend school, "spoiled child," finicky food habits, inefficiency in work, play, etc., restlessness in sleep, question of change of personality, depressed mood or spells, daydreaming, and queer behavior.

    Sulkiness, truancy from home, and lack of interest or inattentiveness in school studies or employment (undifferentiated) showed moderate correlations in the .20's among both sexes with defiant attitude. Three behavior problems, for which only the boys' correlations were calculated, also showed only moderate correlations in the .20's: running with a gang, threatening violence, and smoking. Overinterest in the opposite sex (calculated for girls only) similarly showed the moderate correlation of .23 ± .05. Hatred or jealousy of sibling among boys showed the moderate correlation of .21 ± .06 but a corresponding low coefficient of .16 among girls. A large list of twenty-three miscellaneous notations among girls showed moderate correlations in the .20's but low coefficients ranging from -.05 to .19 among boys: bad companions, temper display, irritable temperament, loitering or wandering, fantastical lying, laziness, slovenliness, lack of interest in school, irresponsibility, restlessness, distractibility, irregular sleep habits, changeable moods or attitudes, sensitiveness or worrisomeness (undifferentiated), sensitiveness over some specific fact, worry over some specific fact, inferiority feelings, unhappiness, unpopularity, object of teasing by other children, masturbation, "leader," and question or diagnosis of encephalitis.

    Two notations showed negative correlations among both sexes, -.32 ± .06 for feeble-minded sibling and -.25 ± .06 for "follower" among girls, the corresponding boys' coefficients being low, -.19 and -.12 respectively.

Among the six sex notations <u>defiant attitude</u> showed moderate correlations among the girls with <u>masturbation</u>, .29 + .05, and with <u>overinterest in the opposite sex</u>, .23 + .05 (calculated for girls only). All other correlations in this field were neglibible.

Among the seven physical or psychophysical notations the only significant correlation was the moderate one of .25 + .08 with <u>question or diagnosis of encephalitis</u> among girls. All other correlations in this field were low or negligible.

Among the four home or familial notations all correlations were negligible, ranging from -.09 to .11.

<u>Stubbornness</u> was noted among 420 boys, or 19.9 per cent, and among 220 girls, or 18.6 per cent. Its bi-serial correlations with <u>conduct-total</u> and <u>personality-total</u> were generally substantial, the coefficients ranging from .25 to .43 (Table 64). Its correlations of .08 and .09 with the <u>police-arrest</u> criterion of "juvenile delinquency" were quite negligible. Its correlations with <u>defiant attitude</u> were fairly large, .42 + .03 and .44 + .04, while its correlations with <u>disobedience</u>, <u>incorrigibility</u>, and <u>contrariness</u> were only moderate or substantial, ranging from .21 to .37.

Its largest correlations among both sexes thus were with <u>defiant attitude</u>. Among girls large correlations in the .40's were found for <u>temper tantrums</u> and <u>depressed mood or spells</u>, the corresponding boys' coefficients being definitely lower, .23 + .03 and .14 respectively.

The three conduct problems—<u>disobedience</u>, <u>sullenness</u>, and (calculated for boys only) <u>smoking</u>—yielded substantial correlations in the .30 s. <u>Contrariness</u> among boys yielded the substantial correlation of .33 + .04, with a corresponding moderate correlation of .22 + .06 among girls. Six conduct problems among girls yielded substantial correlations in the .30's, with moderate correlations in the .20's among boys: <u>incorrigibility</u>, <u>disturbing influence in school</u>, <u>violence</u>, <u>temper display</u>, <u>rudeness</u>, and "<u>nervousness</u>" or restlessness (including <u>irritable temperament</u> and <u>changeable moods or attitudes</u>, undifferentiated). In addition, five undesirable behavior traits among girls yielded substantial correlations in the .30's but low positive correlations below .20 among boys: <u>selfishness</u>, <u>egocentricity</u>, <u>lying</u>, <u>hatred or jealousy</u>

TABLE 64

CORRELATIONS WITH "STUBBORN"

	Boys	Girls
Personality-total............................	.29 ± .02	.36 ± .03
Conduct-total................................	.25 ± .02	.43 ± .02
Police arrest................................	.08 ± .03	.09 ± .04
	Larger Correlations (Positive)	
Defiant......................................	.42 ± .03	.44 ± .04 (1)*
Sullen.......................................	.35 ± .03	.31 ± .05 (15-17)
Smoking......................................	.34 ± .03	....
Grouped: temper, etc.......................	.34 ± .03	.40 ± .03 (4)
Contrary.....................................	.33 ± .04	.22 ± .06 (47-49)
Disobedient..................................	.30 ± .03	.37 ± .04 (6)
Grouped: fighting, etc.....................	.29 ± .03	.32 ± .04 (14)
Rude...	.26 ± .03	.34 ± .04 (8-11)
Queer..	.26 ± .04	.25 ± .06 (32-36)
Temper display..............................	.25 ± .03	.34 ± .05 (8-11)
Quarrelsome..................................	.24 ± .03	.27 ± .04 (24-27)
Bossy..	.24 ± .04	.25 ± .05 (32-36)
Sulky..	.24 ± .04	.24 ± .06 (37-40)
Irregular sleep habits......................	.24 ± .04	.06
Irritable...................................	.24 ± .03	.19
Grouped: "nervous," etc...................	.23 ± .03	.30 ± .03 (18-20)
Spoiled child...............................	.23 ± .03	.20 ± .05 (52-53)
Violence.....................................	.23 ± .03	.36 ± .05 (7)
Temper tantrums.............................	.23 ± .03	.43 ± .04 (2-3)
Refusal to attend school....................	.22 ± .04	.19
Grouped: swearing, etc....................	.21 ± .03	.25 ± .05 (32-36)
Incorrigible................................	.21 ± .03	.34 ± .04 (8-11)
Inefficient in work, play, etc.............	.21 ± .04	.23 ± .05 (41-46)
Fighting.....................................	.21 ± .03	.29 ± .04 (21-22)
Disturbing influence in school.............	.20 ± .03	.31 ± .05 (15-17)
Swearing (general)..........................	.20 ± .04	....
Daydreaming.................................	.20 ± .04	.23 ± .05 (41-46)
Depressed...................................	.14	.43 ± .05 (2-3)
Selfish.....................................	.14	.38 ± .05 (5)
Grouped: egocentric, etc.................	.15	.34 ± .04 (8-11)
Lying.......................................	.18	.33 ± .03 (12-13)
Distractible................................	.07	.33 ± .05 (12-13)
Hatred or jealousy of sibling..............	.16	.31 ± .06 (15-17)
Grouped: depressed, etc..................	.15	.30 ± .04 (18-20)
Egocentric..................................	.14	.30 ± .04 (18-20)
Overinterest in opposite sex...............	....	.29 ± .04 (21-22)
Inattentive in school......................	.16	.28 ± .05 (23)
Unpopular...................................	.16	.27 ± .06 (24-27)
Worry over specific fact...................	-.04	.27 ± .06 (24-27)
Exclusion from school......................	.10	.27 ± .05 (24-27)

*Rank order of girls' correlations.

TABLE 64—Continued

	Boys	Girls
Excuse-forming	.11	.26 ± .05 (28-31)
Masturbation	.08	.26 ± .04 (28-31)
Stealing	.11	.26 ± .04 (28-31)
Leading others into bad conduct	.08	.26 ± .06 (28-31)
Lazy	.18	.25 ± .06 (32-36)
Changeable moods	.15	.25 ± .04 (32-36)
Grouped: lack of interest in school, etc.	.14	.24 ± .04 (37-40)
Staying out late at night	.13	.24 ± .04 (37-40)
Fantastical lying	.13	.24 ± .05 (37-40)
Boastful, "show-off"	.19	.23 ± .05 (41-46)
Finicky food habits	.14	.23 ± .05 (41-46)
Destructive	.13	.23 ± .06 (41-46)
Enuresis	.10	.23 ± .04 (41-46)
Mental conflict	-.00	.22 ± .06 (47-49)
Question of change of personality	.16	.22 ± .06 (47-49)
Truancy from home	.16	.21 ± .04 (50-51)
Sensitive over specific fact	.17	.21 ± .04 (50-51)
Restless	.16	.20 ± .04 (52-53)
	Larger Correlations (Negative)	
Feeble-minded sibling	-.15	-.24 ± .05

Other Correlations (Positive to Negative)

Absent-minded, .19 and .09; Threatening violence, .18 (boys); Teasing other children, .17 (boys); Seclusive, .17 and .17; "Nervous," .16 and .13; Leader, .15 and .12; Grouped: sensitive or worrisome, etc., .15 and .19; Restless in sleep, .15 and .19; Victim of sex abuse, .15 (girls); Slovenly, .14 and .17; Complaining of bad treatment by other children, .13 (boys); Unhappy, .13 and .07; Headaches, .13 and .01; Discord between parents, .12 and .08; Crying spells, .12 and .15; Bashful, .12 and -.03; Truancy from school, .11 and .18; Lack of initiative, .11 and -.02; Object of teasing, .11 and .12; Conduct prognosis bad, .11 and .10; Preference for younger children, .11 and -.04; Question of encephalitis, .10 and .13; Former convulsions, .10 and -.06; Emotional instability, .10 and .15; Inferiority feelings, .10 and .07; Nail-biting, .10 and .09; Attractive manner, .09 and -.09; Loitering, .09 and .02; Oversuggestible, .09 and .02; Neurological defect, .08 and .09; Lack of interest in school, .08 and .16; Gang, .07 (boys); Sensitive (general), .07 and .17; Popular, .07 and .02; Grouped: dull, slow, etc., .07 and -.02; Vocational guidance, .06 and .11; Repressed, .06 and .02; Bad companions, .05 and .18; Irresponsible, .05 and .12; Slow, dull, .05 and -.04; Clean, .04 and .12; Follower, .04 and -.11; Immoral home conditions, .03 and .10; Apprehensive, .01 and -.01; Sex denied entirely, .01 and .11; Poor work in school, .01 and -.06; Psychoneurotic, -.00 and .16; Listless, -.01 and .17; Speech defect, -.02 and -.06; Brother in penal detention, -.03 and -.18; Lues, -.07 and -.00; Underweight, -.07 and -.01; Stuttering, -.07 (boys); Question of hypophrenia, -.07 and -.08; Overinterest in sex matters, -.07 and .19; Irregular attendance at school, -.08 and -.08; Sex delinquency (coitus), -.09 and .12; Retardation in school, -.11 and -.06; Vicious home conditions, -.11 and .11

Omitted—Grouped: disobedient, etc.

of sibling, and distractibility.

Nine behavior traits showed correlations in the .20's with stubbornness among both sexes: fighting, quarrelsomeness, swearing or bad language (undifferentiated), bossy manner, sulkiness, "spoiled child," queer behavior, inefficiency in work, play, etc., and daydreaming. Overinterest in the opposite sex, which was calculated for girls only, also showed a moderate correlation of .29 ± .04. Three additional traits—refusal to attend school, irritable temperament, and irregular sleep habits—among boys yielded moderate correlations in the .20's but low positive correlations below .20 for girls. A large list of twenty-one miscellaneous notations among girls showed moderate correlations in the .20's but low correlations below .20 for the boys: stealing, truancy from home, staying out late at night, leading others into bad conduct, excuse-forming attitude, fantastical lying, boastful or "show-off" manner, destructiveness, laziness, restlessness, mental conflict, question of change of personality, changeable moods or attitudes, sensitiveness over some specific fact, worry over some specific fact, unpopularity, inattentiveness in school, exclusion from school, masturbation, finicky food habits, and enuresis.

Feeble-minded sibling showed low or moderate negative correlations of -.15 and -.24 ± .05 among boys and girls respectively.

Among the six sex notations there were two coefficients of moderate size, both among girls: masturbation, .26 ± .04, and (calculated for girls only) overinterest in the opposite sex, .29 ± .04, the other coefficients in this field being low or negligible.

Among the seven physical or psychophysical notations there was one coefficient of moderate size, enuresis among girls, .23 ± .04, the remaining coefficients in this field being negligible, ranging from -.07 to .13.

The four home or familial notations showed only low or negligible correlations with stubbornness.

The notation contrariness, negativism, resistiveness, antagonistic attitude, etc., was noted among 4.2 per cent of our boys and among 4.3 per cent of our girls. Its correlations with the personality-total and conduct-total were large (especially among boys), its bi-serial correlations ranging from .34 to .48 (Table 65).

TABLE 65

CORRELATIONS WITH "CONTRARY"

	Boys	Girls
Personality-total...........................	.45 ± .03	.38 ± .04
Conduct-total...............................	.48 ± .03	.34 ± .04
Police arrest...............................	.27 ± .04	-.02 ± .07
	Larger Correlations (Positive)	
Rude..	.42 ± .04	.32 ± .06 (13-14)*
Incorrigible...............................	.39 ± .04	.21 ± .06 (32-35)
Sullen.....................................	.38 ± .05	.33 ± .07 (10-12)
Destructive................................	.37 ± .04	.46 ± .08 (1)
Hatred or jealousy of sibling..............	.37 ± .06	.04
Grouped: swearing, etc....................	.37 ± .05	.32 ± .07 (13-14)
Grouped: fighting, etc...................	.35 ± .04	.29 ± .06 (16-19)
Defiant....................................	.33 ± .05	.34 ± .07 (8-9)
Stubborn...................................	.33 ± .04	.22 ± .06 (29-31)
Question of change of personality..........	.32 ± .06	.15
Grouped: temper, etc.....................	.32 ± .04	.38 ± .05 (3)
Disturbing influence in school.............	.31 ± .05	.19
Selfish....................................	.31 ± .06	-.01
Egocentric.................................	.31 ± .05	.24 ± .07 (25-27)
Grouped: "nervous," etc..................	.30 ± .04	.25 ± .05 (23-24)
Boastful, "show-off".......................	.29 ± .05	.29 ± .08 (16-19)
Fighting...................................	.29 ± .05	.23 ± .08 (28)
Irritable..................................	.29 ± .04	.33 ± .06 (10-12)
Queer......................................	.29 ± .06	.29 ± .08 (16-19)
Question of encephalitis...................	.29 ± .07	-.09
Fantastical lying..........................	.28 ± .07	.11
Violence...................................	.28 ± .04	.33 ± .08 (10-12)
Disobedient................................	.27 ± .04	.16
Unpopular..................................	.27 ± .06	.13
Exclusion from school......................	.27 ± .05	.13
Slovenly...................................	.26 ± .05	.14
Smoking....................................	.26 ± .06	....
Seclusive..................................	.26 ± .05	.28 ± .07 (20)
Temper display.............................	.25 ± .05	.24 ± .08 (25-27)
Temper tantrums............................	.25 ± .05	.29 ± .07 (16-19)
Truancy from home..........................	.25 ± .04	.02
Changeable moods...........................	.25 ± .05	.36 ± .06 (4-6)
Complaining of bad treatment by other children	.24 ± .06	....
Gang.......................................	.23 ± .05	....
Inferiority feelings.......................	.23 ± .05	(n.c.)
Spoiled child..............................	.23 ± .05	.15
Threatening violence.......................	.23 ± .07	....
Restless...................................	.22 ± .04	.11
Refusal to attend school...................	.21 ± .06	.18
Quarrelsome................................	.21 ± .05	.17

*Rank order of girls' correlations.

TABLE 65—Continued

	Boys	Girls
Absent-minded............................	.21 ± .06	-.06
Overinterest in opposite sex............	....	.21 ± .06 (32-35)
Sulky....................................	.20 ± .07	.36 ± .08 (4-6)
Swearing (general)......................	.20 ± .06	....
Daydreaming.............................	.20 ± .06	.20 ± .08 (36-37)
Conduct prognosis bad...................	.20 ± .07	-.02
Leading others into bad conduct.........	.08	.41 ± .09 (2)
Listless................................	.08	.36 ± .07 (4-6)
Grouped: depressed, etc.................	.13	.35 ± .07 (7)
Unhappy..................................	.18	.34 ± .08 (8-9)
Repressed...............................	.18	.30 ± .09 (15)
Stealing................................	.19	.27 ± .06 (21-22)
Depressed...............................	.09	.27 ± .06 (21-22)
Finicky food habits.....................	.08	.25 ± .07 (23-24)
Lack of interest in school..............	.19	.24 ± .07 (25-27)
Excuse-forming..........................	.12	.22 ± .08 (29-31)
Grouped: lack of interest in school, etc.....	.18	.22 ± .06 (29-31)
Object of teasing.......................	.16	.21 ± .08 (32-35)
Sensitive (general).....................	.10	.21 ± .08 (32-35)
Lazy....................................	.04	.20 ± .08 (36-37)
	Larger Correlations (Negative)	
Speech defect...........................	-.22 ± .06	.06
Preference for younger children.........	.02	-.25 ± .08

Other Correlations (Positive to Negative)

Lying, .19 and .11; Truancy from school, .19 and -.01; Distractible, .19 and .00; Inefficient in work, play, etc., .18 and .05; "Nervous," .18 and .17; Nail-biting, .17 and -.09; Irresponsible, .16 and .13; Emotional instability, .16 and .08; Irregular attendance at school, .16 and -.02; Neurological defect, .16 and .09; Overinterest in sex matters, .15 and -.13; Apprehensive, .15 and .08; Irregular sleep habits, .15 and .16; Bossy, .14 and .18; Staying out late at night, .13 and .11; Restless in sleep, .13 and .11; Attractive manner, .13 and .04; Masturbation, .12 and .10; Crying spells, .12 and .12; Mental conflict, .12 and .01; Teasing other children, .11 (boys); Enuresis, .10 and -.03; Inattentive in school, .09 and .03; Worry over specific fact, .09 and .03; Poor work in school, .09 and .01; Leader, .09 and .04; Sex denied entirely, .08 and .09; Headaches, .08 and .08; Discord between parents, .08 and -.07; Loitering, .06 and .10; Grouped: sensitive or worrisome, etc., .06 and .12; Sensitive over specific fact, .05 and .01; Clean, .04 and .10; Underweight, .03 and -.09; Bad companions, .03 and .01; Psychoneurotic, .02 and .09; Vicious home conditions, .02 and .00; Sex delinquency (coitus), .00 and .07; Former convulsions, -.02 and -.03; Question of hypophrenia, -.02 and -.01; Oversuggestible, -.02 and -.11; Lack of initiative, -.02 and .03; Brother in penal detention, -.03 and -.09; Grouped: dull, slow, etc., -.05 and .06; Follower, -.05 and -.18; Bashful, -.05 and -.09; Vocational guidance, -.07 and -.04; Popular, -.07 and .11; Slow, dull, -.10 and -.07; Stuttering, -.11 (boys); Retardation in school, -.13 and -.13; Lues, -.16 and .13; Victim of sex abuse, -.18 (girls); Immoral home conditions, -.18 and -.02; Feeble-minded sibling, -.18 and -.09

Omitted—Grouped: disobedient, etc.

Its tetrachoric correlations with police arrest among boys was moderate, .27 + .04, but negligible among girls. Its correlations with the other four similar traits—disobedience, incorrigibility, defiant attitude, and stubbornness—were generally substantial, ranging from .16 to .39.

The highest correlations were in the .40's. Rudeness yielded correlations of .42 + .04 and .32 + .06 for boys and girls respectively. Destructiveness yielded corresponding correlations of .37 + .04 and .46 + .08. Leading others into bad conduct among girls yielded the large correlation of .41 + .09 but a corresponding low coefficient of .08 among boys.

Four conduct problems yielded substantial correlations in the .30's for both sexes: sullenness, swearing or bad language (undifferentiated), defiant attitude, and temper tantrums or display (undifferentiated). Four undesirable behavior traits among boys yielded substantial correlations in the .30's, with corresponding moderate coefficients in the .20's among girls: stubbornness, egocentricity, incorrigibility, and "nervousness" or restlessness (including irritable temperament and changeable moods or attitudes, undifferentiated). Four additional behavior traits among boys similarly yielded substantial correlations in the .30's but low coefficients below .20 among girls: selfishness, disturbing influence in school, hatred or jealousy of sibling, and question of change of personality. Among girls four behavior traits yielded substantial correlations in the .30's, with moderate coefficients in the .20's among boys: sulkiness, changeable moods or attitudes, irritable temperament, and violence. Three additional behavior traits among girls yielded substantial correlations in the .30's but low positive coefficients below .20 among boys: unhappiness, listlessness, and repressed manner.

Seven conduct and personality traits showed moderate correlations in the .20's with contrariness among both sexes: temper tantrums, temper display, fighting, boastful or "show-off" manner, queer behavior, seclusiveness, and daydreaming. Five behavior traits, for which only the boys' correlations were computed because of the paucity of girls' cases, also showed moderate correlations in the .20's: running with a gang, threatening violence, swearing in general, smoking, and complaining of bad treatment by other children. Overinterest in the opposite sex (calculated for girls

only) likewise showed the moderate correlation of .21 ± .06. Thirteen miscellaneous notations among boys showed moderate correlations in the .20's but low coefficients below .20 among girls:
disobedience, refusal to attend school, "spoiled child," truancy
from home, quarrelsomeness, fantastical lying, exclusion from
school, unpopularity, restlessness, slovenliness, absent-mindedness,
staff notation of unfavorable conduct prognosis, and question or
diagnosis of encephalitis. Eight behavior problems among girls
showed moderate correlations in the .20's but low positive coefficients below .20 among boys: stealing, laziness, excuse-forming
attitude, lack of interest in school, finicky food habits, sensitiveness in general, depressed mood or spells, and object of teasing by other children.

        Contrariness showed two negative correlations of moderate
size in the -.20's: speech defect among boys and preference for
younger children as playmates among girls, the other two coefficients being quite negligible in size.

        Among the six sex notations the only coefficient of moder-
ate size was with overinterest in the opposite sex, .21 ± .06 among
girls, the boys' coefficient not being computed because of paucity
of cases.

        Among the seven physical or psychophysical notations there
were two correlations of moderate size both among boys: .29 ± .07
with question or diagnosis of encephalitis and the negative coefficient of -.22 ± .06 with speech defect (other than stuttering).

        Among the four home or familial notations all correlations
with contrariness were low or negligible.

        When the cases falling under the five rubrics, disobedi-
ence, incorrigibility, defiant attitude, stubbornness, and contrariness, were combined into one broad grouping,[1] there were 992 such
cases, or 46.9 per cent, among our 2,113 White boys and 482 cases,
or 40.8 per cent, of our 1,181 White girls. These conduct problems thus provided the most frequently appearing behavior notations among our clinic cases The resulting correlation coefficients (Table 66) were so similar to those for the five component

_____

        [1]The reasons for this broader grouping were given in I, 44; see 86,
Table 13, Item B.

TABLE 66

CORRELATIONS WITH "GROUPED: DISOBEDIENT, ETC."

	Boys	Girls
Personality-total...............................	.31 ± .02	.40 ± .02
Conduct-total..................................	.56 ± .01	.64 ± .02
Police arrest..................................	.33 ± .02	.27 ± .04
	Larger Correlations (Positive)	
Rude...	.54 ± .02	.60 ± .03 (1)*
Staying out late at night......................	.47 ± .02	.44 ± .04 (11-13)
Grouped: fighting, etc........................	.45 ± .02	.52 ± .03 (5-6)
Sullen...	.44 ± .03	.41 ± .04 (16)
Violence.......................................	.42 ± .03	.56 ± .04 (2)
Truancy from home.............................	.42 ± .02	.42 ± .03 (15)
Stealing......................................	.41 ± .02	.44 ± .03 (11-13)
Disturbing influence in school................	.41 ± .02	.45 ± .04 (9-10)
Grouped: swearing, etc.......................	.41 ± .03	.46 ± .04 (8)
Fighting......................................	.39 ± .03	.43 ± .03 (14)
Destructive...................................	.38 ± .03	.35 ± .05 (29-30)
Leading others into bad conduct...............	.38 ± .03	.40 ± .05 (17-20)
Truancy from school...........................	.38 ± .02	.36 ± .04 (25-28)
Exclusion from school.........................	.37 ± 03	.37 ± .04 (22-24)
Grouped: egocentric, etc.....................	.36 ± .02	.40 ± .03 (17-20)
Grouped: temper, etc.........................	.36 ± .02	.53 ± .03 (3-4)
Threatening violence..........................	.36 ± .04	....
Lying...	.36 ± .02	.53 ± .03 (3-4)
Boastful, "show-off"..........................	.36 ± .03	.34 ± .04 (31-32)
Quarrelsome...................................	.35 ± .03	.45 ± .03 (9-10)
Smoking.......................................	.35 ± .03	....
Sulky...	.35 ± .03	.33 ± .05 (33-34)
Egocentric....................................	.35 ± .03	.35 ± .04 (29-30)
Irregular sleep habits........................	.34 ± .03	.28 ± .05 (43-44)
Swearing (general)............................	.34 ± .03	....
Grouped: "nervous," etc......................	.32 ± .02	.36 ± .03 (25-28)
Temper tantrums...............................	.32 ± .03	.52 ± .03 (5-6)
Gang..	.32 ± .03	....
Inattentive in school.........................	.30 ± .03	.33 ± .04 (33-34)
Unpopular.....................................	.30 ± .04	.37 ± .05 (22-24)
Conduct prognosis bad.........................	.30 ± .04	.17
Bad companions................................	.28 ± .03	.29 ± .04 (41-42)
Fantastical lying.............................	.28 ± .04	.32 ± .04 (35)
Slovenly......................................	.28 ± .03	.31 ± .03 (36-38)
Temper display................................	.28 ± .03	.49 ± .04 (7)
Spoiled child.................................	.27 ± .03	.28 ± .04 (43-44)
Restless......................................	.27 ± .02	.31 ± .03 (36-38)
Irritable.....................................	.27 ± .02	.34 ± .04 (31-32)
Teasing other children........................	.27 ± .03	....
Loitering.....................................	.26 ± .03	.36 ± .05 (25-28)

*Rank order of girls' correlations.

TABLE 66—Continued

	Boys	Girls
Refusal to attend school......................	.25 ± .03	.27 ± .05 (45-48)
Selfish.......................................	.25 ± .03	.38 ± .04 (21)
Complaining of bad treatment by other children	.25 ± .04	....
Hatred or jealousy of sibling.................	.23 ± .04	.20 ± .05 (58-62)
Excuse-forming................................	.23 ± .03	.44 ± .04 (11-13)
Question of change of personality.............	.22 ± .04	.37 ± .05 (22-24)
Changeable moods..............................	.21 ± .03	.23 ± .04 (53-57)
Emotional instability.........................	.20 ± .04	.17
Queer...	.18	.40 ± .04 (17-20)
Overinterest in opposite sex..................	....	.40 ± .03 (17-20)
Irresponsible.................................	.18	.36 ± .05 (25-28)
Depressed.....................................	.13	.31 ± .06 (36-38)
Lazy..	.19	.30 ± .04 (39-40)
Grouped: lack of interest in school, etc.....	.15	.30 ± .04 (39-40)
Finicky food habits...........................	.14	.29 ± .04 (41-42)
Sex delinquency (coitus)......................	.10	.27 ± .03 (45-48)
Daydreaming...................................	.14	.27 ± .04 (45-48)
Distractible..................................	.15	.27 ± .04 (45-48)
Masturbation..................................	.14	.26 ± .04 (49)
Unhappy.......................................	.19	.25 ± .05 (50)
Inefficient in work, play, etc...............	.18	.24 ± .05 (51-52)
Question of encephalitis......................	.14	.24 ± .06 (51-52)
Bossy...	.17	.23 ± .04 (53-57)
Overinterest in sex matters..................	.10	.23 ± .05 (53-57)
Object of teasing.............................	.09	.23 ± .04 (53-57)
Restless in sleep.............................	.11	.23 ± .04 (53-57)
Enuresis......................................	.14	.20 ± .03 (58-62)
Mental conflict...............................	.03	.20 ± .06 (58-62)
Lack of interest in school...................	.19	.20 ± .04 (58-62)
Grouped: depressed, etc......................	.16	.20 ± .04 (58-62)
	Larger Correlations (Negative)	
Feeble-minded sibling.........................	-.20 ± .04	-.27 ± .04

Other Correlations (Positive to Negative)

Leader, .19 and .14; Preference for younger children, .15 and .09; Absent-minded, .15 and .06; Victim of sex abuse, .15 (girls); Crying spells, .14 and .16; Former convulsions, .13 and -.03; Sensitive over specific fact, .13 and .13; Oversuggestible, .13 and .16; "Nervous," .13 and .17; Nail-biting, .13 and .11; Inferiority feelings, .12 and .08; Poor work in school, .12 and .07; Discord between parents, .11 and .12; Grouped: sensitive or worrisome, etc., .11 and .10; Seclusive, .11 and .08; Psychoneurotic, .10 and .12; Popular, .08 and .07; Sensitive (general), .06 and .10; Headaches, .06 and .06; Brother in penal detention, .06 and -.07; Attractive manner, .05 and -.05; Apprehensive, .04 and .11; Follower, .03 and .08; Clean, .01 and .00; Speech defect, .01 and -.05; Irregular attendance at school, -.00 and -.11; Lack of initiative, -.01 and -.03; Neurological defect, -.03 and .05; Worry over specific fact, -.03 and .10; Sex denied entirely, -.03 and -.03; Stuttering, -.04 (boys); Repressed, -.04 and .04; Bashful, -.04 and -.08; Vicious home conditions, -.05 and .15; Retardation

TABLE 66—Continued
_____

in school, -.05 and -.03; Question of hypophrenia, -.06 and -.01; Slow, dull,
-.07 and -.03; Listless, -.08 and .16; Grouped: dull, slow, etc., -.08 and
-.00; Vocational guidance, -.09 and -.15; Immoral home conditions, -.11 and .05;
Underweight, -.15 and -.03; Lues, -.18 and .04
          Omitted—Contrary; Defiant; Disobedient; Stubborn; Incorrigible

notations, though generally slightly larger, that only a brief summary is necessary.

The following nine conduct problems consistently yielded
large or high correlations with the larger grouping disobedience
or incorrigibility (including defiant attitude, stubbornness, and
contrariness, undifferentiated), ranging from the .40's to the
.60's: rudeness, violence, staying out late at night, sullenness,
disturbing influence in school, swearing or bad language (undifferentiated), truancy from home, stealing, and (calculated for
girls only) overinterest in the opposite sex. Seven additional
conduct notations among girls yielded large correlations ranging
from .40 to .53, with moderate to substantial coefficients ranging from .23 to .39 for boys: lying, fighting, quarrelsomeness,
temper tantrums, temper display, leading others into bad conduct,
and excuse-forming attitude. A large list of twenty-five behavior
notations showed moderate to substantial correlations ranging from
.17 to .40 among both sexes: bad companions, running with a gang
(calculated for boys only), refusal to attend school, threatening
violence (calculated for boys only), destructiveness, boastful or
"show-off" manner, truancy from school, exclusion from school,
smoking (calculated for boys only), "spoiled child," hatred or
jealousy of sibling, egocentricity, selfishness, irritable temperament, sulkiness, loitering or wandering, irresponsibility, inefficiency in work, play, etc., restlessness, queer behavior, changeable moods or attitudes, question of change of personality, unpopularity, unhappiness, and staff notation of unfavorable conduct
prognosis.

Among the six sex notations the following four showed coefficients of significant size, all among girls: overinterest in
the opposite sex (calculated for girls only), .40 $\pm$ .03, sex delinquency (coitus), .27 $\pm$ .03, overinterest in sex matters, .23 $\pm$
.05, and masturbation, .26 $\pm$ .04.

Among the seven physical or psychophysical notations there

were two correlations of moderate size in the .20's, both among
girls: enuresis and question or diagnosis of encephalitis.

Among the home or familial notations all correlations were
low, ranging from -.11 to .15.

We may summarize the more interesting correlations for all
five notations, disobedience, incorrigibility, defiant attitude,
stubbornness, and contrariness (Tables 61-65, inclusive), as follows. The largest correlations, ranging from .20's to the .50's,
were found for the following thirteen behavior notations: rudeness, sullenness, violence, disturbing influence in school, fighting, swearing or bad language (undifferentiated), threatening violence (calculated for boys only), stealing, overinterest in the
opposite sex (calculated for girls only), temper tantrums, smoking
(calculated for boys only), egocentricity, and boastful or "show-
off" manner. Another group of fifteen notations showed many substantial or large correlations but not uniformly for all five
traits or for both sexes: staying out late at night, leading
others into bad conduct, running with a gang (calculated for boys
only), truancy from home, quarrelsomeness, irritable temperament,
lying, selfishness, "spoiled child," finicky food habits, queer behavior, question of change of personality, unpopularity, exclusion
from school, and question or diagnosis of encephalitis.

Among the six sex notations all five traits considered in
this chapter showed moderate or substantial correlations, ranging
from .21 to .42, with overinterest in the opposite sex, for which
only the girls' correlations were calculated. Masturbation among
girls showed moderate correlations in the .20's for all these notations except contrariness. Sex delinquency (coitus) among girls
showed moderate correlations in the .20's with disobedience and incorrigibility. The remaining correlations for girls and all coefficients for boys in the sex sphere were low or negligible.

Among the seven physical or psychophysical notations question or diagnosis of encephalitis among girls showed moderate correlations, ranging from .25 to .31, with disobedience, incorrigibility, and defiant attitude and among boys with contrariness.
Among boys enuresis showed moderate correlations of .23 ± .04 with
stubbornness. Speech defect (other than stuttering) among boys
showed the moderate negative coefficient of -.22 ± .06 with contra-

riness. The remaining coefficients in this field were low or negligible.

Among the four home or familial notations all the forty
correlation coefficients were low or negligible.

CHAPTER XXXVII

LYING, PROTECTIVE AND FANTASTICAL

Lying or marked untruthfulness[1] (generally "protective" in
purpose) was noted among 637 cases, or 30.1 per cent, of our 2,113
White boys and among 340 cases, or 28.8 per cent, of our 1,181
White girls and was thus one of the most frequently occurring conduct problems in our data. Its bi-serial correlations of .48 ± .02
and .56 ± .02 with the conduct-total among boys and girls respectively indicates a high relationship with behavior problems in the
conduct sphere (Table 67). With police arrest and personality-
total its correlations were of substantial size in the .30's among
girls and of moderate size in the .20's among boys. Its correlations with intelligence quotient (IQ) in the data of the present
volume were negligible (Table 10, p. 130) but among younger or pre-
adolescent children its correlations with IQ were of moderate size,
.24 ± .02 and .27 ± .03 for boys and girls respectively.[2]

Among both sexes its highest correlations were with stealing and fantastical lying, the tetrachoric correlations ranging
from .56 to .68. Among girls the two notations, unpopularity and
disobedience or incorrigibility (undifferentiated), also yielded
large coefficients in the .50's, with corresponding coefficients
among boys of substantial size in the .30's.

Four conduct problems yielded large correlations in the
.40's: truancy from home and truancy from school, among both
sexes, and smoking (calculated for boys only) and overinterest in

---

[1]In the original indexing of 5,000 cases, separate categories were included for question of making false accusations (I, 61, Table 3, Item 222); question of pathological lying, i.e., derogatory to self (ibid., Item 252); lying
to police or school official, etc., re identity, address, etc., or assuming
false name, address, disguise, etc. (ibid., Item 264); question of pathological
accusation, i.e., inculpating self (ibid., Item 289); and lying concerning age
to person with whom patient was sexually delinquent or to whom patient was engaged (ibid., Item 300); but these interesting notations were of too infrequent
incidence to warrant separate correlational analysis.

[2]I, 175-77.

TABLE 67

CORRELATIONS WITH "LYING"

	Boys	Girls
Personality-total............................	.24 ± .02	.35 ± .02
Conduct-total................................	.48 ± .02	.56 ± .02
Police arrest................................	.25 ± .03	.31 ± .04
	Larger Correlations (Positive)	
Stealing.....................................	.61 ± .02	.68 ± .02 (1)*
Fantastical lying............................	.56 ± .03	.61 ± .04 (2)
Truancy from home............................	.46 ± .02	.48 ± .03 (5-6)
Truancy from school..........................	.42 ± .02	.48 ± .04 (5-6)
Smoking......................................	.40 ± .03	....
Swearing (general)..........................	.37 ± .03	....
Grouped: disobedient, etc...................	.36 ± .02	.53 ± .03 (3)
Bad companions..............................	.35 ± .03	.32 ± .04 (30)
Masturbation................................	.35 ± .02	.39 ± .04 (18)
Unpopular...................................	.34 ± .04	.50 ± .05 (4)
Boastful, "show-off"........................	.33 ± .03	.31 ± .07 (31-35)
Destructive.................................	.33 ± .03	.35 ± .05 (23-24)
Incorrigible................................	.32 ± .02	.37 ± .03 (19)
Leading others into bad conduct.............	.32 ± .03	.31 ± .05 (31-35)
Loitering...................................	.32 ± .03	.35 ± .05 (23-24)
Disobedient.................................	.31 ± .03	.43 ± .03 (10-11)
Fighting....................................	.31 ± .03	.42 ± .03 (12-13)
Staying out late at night...................	.31 ± .03	.31 ± .04 (31-35)
Grouped: swearing, etc.....................	.31 ± .03	.41 ± .04 (14-15)
Disturbing influence in school..............	.30 ± .03	.40 ± .04 (16-17)
Excuse-forming..............................	.30 ± .03	.36 ± .04 (20-22)
Rude..	.29 ± .03	.36 ± .04 (20-22)
Grouped: egocentric, etc...................	.29 ± .03	.33 ± .04 (27-29)
Defiant.....................................	.28 ± .03	.44 ± .04 (9)
Egocentric..................................	.27 ± .03	.31 ± .04 (31-35)
Grouped: fighting, etc....................	.26 ± .02	.46 ± .03 (7-8)
Teasing other children......................	.25 ± .03	....
Gang..	.25 ± .03	....
Overinterest in sex matters.................	.24 ± .04	.43 ± .04 (10-11)
Complaining of bad treatment by other children	.24 ± .04	
Exclusion from school.......................	.24 ± .03	.42 ± .05 (12-13)
Grouped: temper, etc.......................	.24 ± .02	.27 ± .03 (42-46)
Sullen......................................	.22 ± .03	.23 ± .05 (57)
Inattentive in school.......................	.21 ± .02	.24 ± .05 (51-56)
Irresponsible...............................	.21 ± .04	.46 ± .04 (7-8)
Threatening violence........................	.21 ± .04	
Temper tantrums.............................	.21 ± .03	.24 ± .04 (51-56)
Violence....................................	.21 ± .03	.41 ± .04 (14-15)
Oversuggestible.............................	.21 ± .03	.12
Mental conflict.............................	.21 ± .04	.27 ± .06 (42-46)

*Rank order of girls' correlations.

TABLE 67—Continued

	Boys	Girls
Bossy..	.20 ± .04	.27 ± .05 (42-46)
Slovenly......................................	.20 ± .03	.25 ± .04 (48-50)
Inferiority feelings..........................	.20 ± .03	.20 ± .05 (59)
Conduct prognosis bad.........................	.20 ± .04	.24 ± .06 (51-56)
Grouped: lack of interest in school, etc.....	.20 ± .03	.29 ± .04 (36-38)
Overinterest in opposite sex..................	....	.40 ± .04 (16-17)
Quarrelsome...................................	.18	.36 ± .04 (20-22)
Inefficient in work, play, etc...............	.15	.34 ± .05 (25-26)
Queer...	.10	.31 ± .05 (25-26)
Stubborn......................................	.18	.33 ± .03 (27-29)
Sex delinquency (coitus)......................	.15	.33 ± .03 (27-29)
Daydreaming...................................	.12	.31 ± .04 (31-35)
Victim of sex abuse...........................	....	.29 ± .04 (36-38)
Restless in sleep............................	.15	.29 ± .04 (36-38)
Lack of interest in school...................	.12	.28 ± .04 (39-41)
Restless......................................	.17	.28 ± .03 (39-41)
Grouped: "nervous," etc......................	.17	.28 ± .03 (39-41)
Temper display...............................	.18	.27 ± .05 (42-46)
Question of encephalitis......................	-.10	.27 ± .06 (42-46)
Sensitive over specific fact.................	.10	.26 ± .04 (47)
Selfish.......................................	.19	.25 ± .05 (48-50)
Question of change of personality............	.04	.25 ± .05 (48-50)
Sulky...	.13	.24 ± .05 (51-56)
Emotional instability........................	.13	.24 ± .05 (51-56)
Leader..	.19	.24 ± .05 (51-56)
Distractible.................................	.12	.21 ± .04 (58)
	Larger Correlations (Negative)	
Vocational guidance..........................	-.13	-.31 ± .04

Other Correlations (Positive to Negative)

Contrary, .19 and .11; Nail-biting, .19 and .18; Unhappy, .19 and .15; Lazy, .18 and .13; Irregular sleep habits, .18 and .16; Spoiled child, .18 and .17; Irregular attendance at school, .18 and .07; Hatred or jealousy of sibling, .17 and .15; Irritable, .16 and .11; Former convulsions, .15 and -.08; Vicious home conditions, .14 and .17; Enuresis, .13 and .19; Repressed, .13 and .05; Brother in penal detention, .13 and -.03; Discord between parents, .13 and .19; Grouped: depressed, etc., .13 and .16; Refusal to attend school, .12 and .16; Follower, .11 and .08; Grouped: sensitive or worrisome, etc., .10 and .18; Crying spells, .09 and .16; Object of teasing, .09 and .18; Popular, .08 and .02; Absent-minded, .07 and .14; Depressed, .07 and .14; Preference for younger children, .07 and .16; Attractive manner, .07 and .13; "Nervous," .06 and .19; Headaches, .06 and .19; Immoral home conditions, .06 and .13; Finicky good habits, .05 and .12; Seclusive, .05 and .05; Sensitive (general), .05 and .01; Worry over specific fact, .05 and .12; Poor work in school, .04 and .04; Sex denied entirely, .02 and .07; Clean, -.00 and -.00; Apprehensive, -.01 and .12; Lues, -.02 and .02; Speech defect, -.03 and -.10; Slow, dull, -.03 and -.05; Neurological defect, -.04 and .09; Grouped: dull, slow, etc., -.06 and -.02; Under-

TABLE 67—Continued

weight, -.06 and -.02; Stuttering, -.06 (boys); Question of hypophrenia, -.06
and -.08; Lack of initiative, -.06 and -.02; Bashful, -.06 and -.09; Listless,
-.07 and .02; Retardation in school, -.08 and -.11; Psychoneurotic, -.08 and
.04; Changeable moods, -.12 and .18; Feeble-minded sibling, -.18 and -.11

the opposite sex (calculated for girls only). Among girls four
conduct problems similarly yielded large correlations in the .40's,
with substantial coefficients of .30 or .31 among boys: disobedience, disturbing influence in school, fighting, and swearing or
bad language (undifferentiated). Five additional behavior notations among girls similarly yielded large correlations in the
.40's but moderate coefficients in the .20's among boys: defiant
attitude, violence, irresponsibility, exclusion from school, and
overinterest in sex matters.

Eleven undesirable behavior manifestations yielded substantial correlations, ranging from .27 to .39, among both sexes:
boastful or "show-off" manner, excuse-forming attitude, egocentricity, rudeness, incorrigibility, staying out late at night, loitering or wandering, bad companions, leading others into bad conduct,
destructiveness, and masturbation. Among girls six additional
traits yielded substantial correlations in the .30's but low positive coefficients below .20 among boys: stubbornness, quarrelsomeness, inefficiency in work, play, etc., queer behavior, daydreaming, and sex delinquency (coitus).

Lying yielded moderate correlations in the .20's with thirteen behavior problems: sullenness, bossy manner, temper tantrums,
slovenliness, inattentiveness in school, mental conflict, inferiority feelings, staff notation of unfavorable conduct prognosis,
and the four notations for which only the boys' correlations were
computed—running with a gang, threatening violence, teasing other
children, complaining of bad treatment by other children, and victim of sex abuse by older child or person, which was computed for
girls only. Oversuggestibility similarly showed the moderate correlation of .21 ± .03 among boys but a low correlation of .12 among
girls. Twelve behavior problems among girls showed moderate correlations in the .20's but low coefficients below .20 among boys:
selfishness, sulkiness, temper display, restlessness, restlessness
in sleep, distractibility, staff notation of emotional instability,

lack of interest in school, sensitiveness over some specific fact,
question of change of personality, "leader," and question or diagnosis of encephalitis.

    The only negative correlation of significant size was with
"request for vocational guidance" among girls, -.31 + .04.

    Among the six sex problems there was a tendency toward
substantial correlations with lying among both sexes. Masturbation
yielded coefficients of .35 + .02 and .39 + .04 for boys and girls
respectively. Overinterest in sex matters among girls yielded the
fairly large correlation of .43 + .04, with a moderate correlation
of .24 + .04 among boys. Sex delinquency (coitus) among girls
yielded the substantial correlation of .33 + .03 and a low positive
coefficient of .15 among boys. Among girls overinterest in the opposite sex and victim of sex abuse by older child or person yielded
the substantial correlations of .40 + .04 and .29 + .04 respectively, the boys' coefficients not being computed because of paucity
of cases. Sex misbehavior denied entirely showed the negligible
coefficients of .02 and .07.

    Among the seven physical or psychophysical notations all
correlations were low or negligible, except two coefficients among
girls, .27 + .06 with question or diagnosis of encephalitis and
.19 with enuresis (continued beyond third birthday).

    Among the four home or familial notations all correlations
with lying tended to be positive but low, ranging from -.03 to .19.

    Fantastical lying in our data was rigidly defined as the
telling of imaginative false stories for the purpose of either
glorifying the narrator or of attracting the favorable attention
of the listener. It did not include "pathological lying and accusation," which in our data was defined to include only cases in
which the apparent purpose of the child's false assertions seemed
to be derogatory to himself. Fantastical lying was noted among
104, or 4.9 per cent, of our boys and among 75, or 6.4 per cent,
of our girls. Its large bi-serial correlations in the .40's with
the conduct-total indicate its meaningful relation with conduct
disorders (Table 68), and its almost equally large correlations
with the personality-total suggests that fantastical lying is a
greater indicator of personality deviation than "protective" lying,
in which we have previously noted that the correlations were only

TABLE 68

CORRELATIONS WITH "FANTASTICAL LYING"

	Boys	Girls
Personality-total.............................	.41 ± .03	.41 ± .03
Conduct-total.................................	.46 ± .03	.49 ± .03
Police arrest.................................	.31 ± .04	.22 ± .06
	Larger Correlations (Positive)	
Lying...	.56 ± .03	.61 ± .04 (1)*
Boastful, "show-off"..........................	.52 ± .03	.37 ± .07 (6-7)
Loitering.....................................	.38 ± .05	.21 ± .08 (52-57)
Truancy from home.............................	.38 ± .04	.40 ± .05 (3-4)
Stealing......................................	.33 ± .04	.37 ± .05 (6-7)
Daydreaming...................................	.32 ± .05	.30 ± .07 (23-25)
Unpopular.....................................	.32 ± .06	.38 ± .07 (5)
Destructive...................................	.31 ± .05	.24 ± .08 (43-47)
Spoiled child.................................	.31 ± .05	.30 ± .06 (23-25)
Disturbing influence in school................	.30 ± .04	.32 ± .07 (17-19)
Irregular sleep habits........................	.30 ± .06	-.01
Truancy from school...........................	.29 ± .04	.33 ± .06 (13-16)
Overinterest in sex matters...................	.29 ± .07	.35 ± .07 (8-9)
Contrary......................................	.28 ± .07	.11
Grouped: disobedient, etc....................	.28 ± .04	.32 ± .07 (17-19)
Grouped: egocentric..........................	.28 ± .03	.29 ± .05 (26-29)
Incorrigible..................................	.26 ± .05	.27 ± .05 (34-35)
Disobedient...................................	.25 ± .03	.24 ± .05 (43-47)
Staying out late at night.....................	.25 ± .03	.24 ± .06 (43-47)
Masturbation..................................	.25 ± .03	.15
Egocentric....................................	.25 ± .03	.30 ± .06 (23-25)
Irritable.....................................	.24 ± .03	.26 ± .06 (36-39)
Complaining of bad treatment by other children	.24 ± .03	....
Bossy...	.23 ± .06	.28 ± .07 (30-33)
Irresponsible.................................	.23 ± .03	.21 ± .07 (52-57)
Leading others into bad conduct...............	.23 ± .03	.34 ± .08 (10-12)
Rude..	.23 ± .03	.29 ± .06 (26-29)
Restless......................................	.23 ± .03	.26 ± .05 (36-39)
Grouped: temper, etc.........................	.23 ± .03	.28 ± .05 (30-33)
Changeable moods..............................	.22 ± .03	.42 ± .05 (2)
Excuse-forming................................	.22 ± .03	.17
Nail-biting...................................	.21 ± .03	.16
Sullen..	.21 ± .03	.21 ± .07 (52-57)
Emotional instability.........................	.21 ± .03	.31 ± .07 (20-22)
Grouped: swearing, etc.......................	.21 ± .03	.32 ± .07 (17-19)
Fighting......................................	.20 ± .03	.24 ± .07 (43-47)
Gang..	.20 ± .03	....
Smoking.......................................	.20 ± .03	....
"Nervous".....................................	.20 ± .03	.18
Hatred or jealousy of sibling.................	.16	.40 ± .07 (3-4)

*Rank order of girls' correlations.

TABLE 68—Continued

	Boys	Girls
Queer....................................	.18	.35 ± .07 (8-9)
Overinterest in opposite sex.................	....	.34 ± .05 (10-12)
Restless in sleep...........................	.12	.34 ± .06 (10-12)
Violence..................................	.16	.33 ± .07 (13-16)
Question of change of personality............	.06	.33 ± .07 (13-16)
Grouped: "nervous," etc.....................	.04	.33 ± .07 (13-16)
Crying spells...............................	.05	.31 ± .05 (20-22)
Leader...................................	.18	.31 ± .07 (20-22)
Inefficient in work, play, etc...............	.14	.29 ± .07 (26-29)
Distractible...............................	.16	.29 ± .06 (26-29)
Quarrelsome...............................	.15	.28 ± .05 (30-33)
Grouped: fighting, etc.....................	.19	.28 ± .05 (30-33)
Selfish...................................	.17	.27 ± .07 (34-35)
Bad companions............................	.18	.26 ± .06 (36-39)
Slovenly..................................	.17	.26 ± .05 (36-39)
Sulky....................................	.16	.25 ± .07 (40-42)
Mental conflict............................	.18	.25 ± .08 (40-42)
Grouped: lack of interest in school, etc.....	.15	.25 ± .06 (40-42)
Stubborn..................................	.13	.24 ± .05 (43-47)
Inattentive in school.......................	.17	.23 ± .07 (48)
Defiant...................................	.11	.22 ± .07 (49-51)
Temper display............................	.06	.22 ± .07 (49-51)
Headaches.................................	-.02	.22 ± .07 (49-51)
Temper tantrums...........................	.17	.21 ± .06 (52-57)
Depressed.................................	.17	.21 ± .07 (52-57)
Conduct prognosis bad......................	.14	.21 ± .08 (52-57)
Object of teasing..........................	.12	.20 ± .07 (58-60)
Sensitive (general).........................	.16	.20 ± .07 (58-60)
Exclusion from school......................	.17	.20 ± .07 (58-60)
	Larger Correlations (Negative)	
Vocational guidance........................	-.17	-.44 ± .05
Feeble-minded sibling.......................	.11	-.27 ± .06

Other Correlations (Positive to Negative)

Teasing other children, .19 (boys); Threatening violence, .19 (boys); Oversuggestible, .19 and .13; Worry over specific fact, .19 and .11; Inferiority feelings, .19 and .00; Discord between parents, .19 and .04; Victim of sex abuse, .19 (girls); Clean, .18 and .06; Immoral home conditions, .18 and .06; Vicious home conditions, .18 and -.02; Grouped: depressed, etc., .17 and .10; Swearing (general), .16 (boys); Attractive manner, .16 and .12; Preference for younger children, .16 and .10; Unhappy, .15 and -.16; Former convulsions, .15 and .04; Lack of interest in school, .14 and .15; Irregular attendance at school, .13 and .10; Sex delinquency (coitus), .12 and .01; Enuresis, .11 and .15; Absent-minded, .11 and .16; Poor work in school, .11 and .11; Repressed, .10 and -.08; Grouped: sensitive or worrisome, .10 and .18; Lazy, .08 and .09; Seclusive, .08 and -.03; Refusal to attend school, .07 and .14; Neurological defect, .07 and .11; Stuttering, .06 (boys); Speech defect, .06 and -.10; Question of hypophrenia, .05 and -.02; Question of encephalitis, .04 and .14; Popular, .03 and .01; Finicky food

TABLE 68—Continued

habits, .01 and .19; Brother in penal detention, .01 and -.13; Sensitive over specific fact, -.01 and .12; Psychoneurotic, -.01 and .19; Listless, -.01 and .02; Apprehensive, -.02 and .08; Grouped: dull, slow, etc., -.03 and -.01; Bashful, -.03 and -.03; Slow, dull, -.04 and -.03; Underweight, -.07 and .02; Follower, -.09 and -.03; Lack of initiative, -.09 and .11; Retardation in school, -.09 and -.10; Lues, -.13 and .07; Sex denied entirely, -.19 and -.00

moderate to substantial. Its moderate tetrachoric correlations of .31 ± .04 and .22 ± .06 among boys and girls respectively with police arrest were of about the same magnitude as those for "protective" lying. In general, lying and fantastical lying showed similar correlations with other notations with, however, a few exceptions.

The highest correlations for fantastical lying were with (protective) lying, the coefficients being .56 ± .03 and .61 ± .04. Among boys boastful or "show-off" manner yielded the high correlation of .52 ± .03, with a substantial coefficient of .37 ± .07 among girls. Truancy from home yielded large correlations of .38 ± .04 among boys and .40 ± .05 among girls. Among girls changeable moods or attitudes and hatred or jealousy of sibling also yielded large correlations in the .40's, with moderate or low coefficients of .22 ± .03 and .16 respectively for the boys.

Seven conduct and personality difficulties yielded substantial correlations ranging from .29 to .39 with fantastical lying among both sexes: daydreaming, "spoiled child," unpopularity, stealing, truancy from school, disturbing influence in school, overinterest in sex matters, and also one calculated for girls only, overinterest in the opposite sex. Among boys loitering or wandering and irregular sleep habits also yielded substantial correlations in the .30's, with lesser coefficients of .21 ± .08 and -.01 among girls. Among girls six behavior problems yielded substantial correlations in the .30's, with corresponding moderate coefficients in the .20's among boys: egocentricity, emtoional instability, swearing or bad language (undifferentiated), truancy from school, leading others into bad conduct, and overinterest in sex matters. An additional six traits among girls also yielded substantial correlations in the .30's but low positive correlations below .20 among boys: queer behavior, question of change of personality, crying spells, restlessness in sleep, violence, and "leader."

With _fantastical lying_ there were fourteen behavior problems showing moderate correlations in the .20's: _bossy manner_, _irritable temperament_, _temper tantrums or display_ (undifferentiated), _fighting_, _sullenness_, _restlessness_, _rudeness_, _irresponsibility_, _disobedience_, _incorrigibility_, _staying out late at night_, and the three behavior problems for which only the boys' correlations were calculated—_running with a gang_, _smoking_, and _complaining of bad treatment by other children_. Among boys five behavior problems showed moderate correlations in the .20's but low positive coefficients below .20 among girls: _excuse-forming attitude_, _contrariness_, "_nervousness_," _nail-biting_, and _masturbation_. A large list of nineteen miscellaneous notations among girls showed moderate correlations in the .20's but low coefficients below .20 for boys: _selfishness_, _defiant attitude_, _stubbornness_, _sulkiness_, _slovenliness_, _distractibility_, _inefficiency in work, play, etc._, _inattentiveness in school_, _exclusion from school_, _quarrelsomeness_, _temper display_, _temper tantrums_, _bad companions_, _mental conflict_, _sensitiveness in general_, _depressed moods or spells_, _object of teasing by other children_, _staff notation of unfavorable conduct prognosis_, and _headaches_.

Two negative correlations of significant size were found, both among girls: -.27 ± .06 with _feeble-minded sibling_ and -.44 ± .05 with "_request for vocational guidance_."

Among the six sex notations moderate to substantial correlations ranging from .25 to .35 were found for _overinterest in sex matters_ among boys and girls, _masturbation_ among boys, and _overinterest in the opposite sex_ (calculated only for girls).

In the fields of physical disabilities and home or familial handicaps all correlations with _fantastical lying_ were low or negligible.

CHAPTER XXXVIII

FIGHTING; QUARRELSOMENESS; VIOLENCE; THREATENING

The four similar conduct problems—fighting, quarrelsomeness, violence, and threatening violence—in our data were distinguished briefly as follows. Fighting implies physical combat with
one or more adversaries of similar or equal prowess. Quarrelsomeness implies verbal rather than physical conflict. Violence includes striking, kicking, or otherwise injuring another person
without regard for any ethical formalities which more or less sur-
round fighting. That these three are closely related is shown by
the fact that their intercorrelations tend to be higher than their
correlations with other traits, the boys' intercorrelations ranging
from .41 to .45 and the girls' intercorrelations from .49 to .61.
Their bi-serial correlations with conduct-total, ranging from .34
to .54 among boys and from .46 to .79 among girls, shows their importance as indicators of conduct disorder. With overt juvenile
delinquency their importance was only moderate, the tetrachoric
correlations with police arrest ranging from .08 to .29. Among
girls their correlations with personality-total were large or high,
the bi-serial r's ranging from .43 to .64; but among boys this relation was moderate, the coefficients ranging from .18 to .31.

Fighting was noted among 291 of our 2,113 White boys, or
13.8 per cent, and among 89 of our 1,181 White girls, or 7.5 per
cent. It was more rarely noted among girls, but its presence among
girls indicated a more serious extent of deviation in both the conduct and the personality fields.

Its largest correlations were with violence, the tetrachoric r's for boys and girls being .43 ± .03 and .61 ± .05 respectively (Table 69). Among girls swearing or bad language (undifferentiated) and "nervousness" or restlessness (including irritable
temperament and changeable moods, undifferentiated) yielded high
correlations of .54 ± .03 and .56 ± .04 respectively, with the
considerable coefficients among boys of .35 ± .03 and .24 ± .03.

TABLE 69

CORRELATIONS WITH "FIGHTING"

	Boys	Girls
Personality-total..........................	.18 ± .02	.43 ± .03
Conduct-total.............................	.43 ± .02	.55 ± .03
Police arrest.............................	.20 ± .03	.22 ± .05
	Larger Correlations (Positive)	
Violence..................................	.43 ± .03	.61 ± .05 (1)*
Quarrelsome...............................	.41 ± .03	.49 ± .03 (4)
Incorrigible..............................	.40 ± .03	.46 ± .03 (6)
Unpopular.................................	.39 ± .04	.28 ± .04 (34)
Grouped: disobedient, etc................	.39 ± .03	.43 ± .03 (13-16)
Disturbing influence in school...........	.38 ± .03	.43 ± .06 (13-16)
Grouped: temper, etc....................	.36 ± .03	.48 ± .03 (5)
Grouped: swearing, etc..................	.35 ± .03	.54 ± .03 (3)
Destructive..............................	.34 ± .04	.45 ± .07 (7-9)
Temper display...........................	.34 ± .03	.30 ± .04 (29-31)
Swearing (general).......................	.32 ± .04	....
Lying....................................	.31 ± .03	.42 ± .03 (17)
Rude.....................................	.31 ± .03	.44 ± .03 (10-12)
Temper tantrums..........................	.31 ± .04	.45 ± .03 (7-9)
Truancy from school......................	.31 ± .03	.27 ± .04 (35-38)
Boastful, "show-off"....................	.30 ± .03	.23 ± .07 (44-48)
Contrary.................................	.29 ± .05	.23 ± .08 (44-48)
Disobedient..............................	.29 ± .05	.35 ± .05 (22-24)
Threatening violence.....................	.29 ± .05	....
Stealing.................................	.28 ± .03	.40 ± .03 (18)
Egocentric...............................	.28 ± .03	.23 ± .04 (44-48)
Exclusion from school....................	.28 ± .04	.44 ± .03 (10-12)
Smoking..................................	.27 ± .04	....
Gang.....................................	.26 ± .04	....
Defiant..................................	.25 ± .04	.45 ± .06 (7-9)
Grouped: egocentric, etc...............	.25 ± .03	.27 ± .04 (35-38)
Complaining of bad treatment by other children	.24 ± .04	....
Grouped: "nervous," etc................	.24 ± .03	.56 ± .04 (2)
Refusal to attend school.................	.23 ± .04	.19
Teasing other children...................	.23 ± .05	....
Truancy from home........................	.23 ± .03	.31 ± .04 (27-28)
Excuse-forming...........................	.23 ± .04	.43 ± .03 (13-16)
Irregular sleep habits...................	.22 ± .04	.11
Emotional instability....................	.22 ± .05	.25 ± .04 (40-42)
Conduct prognosis bad....................	.22 ± .05	.17
Bossy....................................	.21 ± .05	.38 ± .06 (19-20)
Inattentive in school....................	.21 ± .04	.19
Loitering................................	.21 ± .04	.02
Stubborn.................................	.21 ± .03	.29 ± .04 (32-33)
Irritable................................	.21 ± .03	.35 ± .04 (22-24)

*Rank order of girls' correlations.

TABLE 69—Continued

	Boys	Girls
Fantastical lying	.20 ± .03	.24 ± .07 (43)
Leading others into bad conduct	.20 ± .04	.36 ± .04 (21)
Staying out late at night	.20 ± .03	.14
Object of teasing	.20 ± .03	.43 ± .03 (13-16)
Grouped: lack of interest in school, etc.	.20 ± .03	.33 ± .04 (26)
Restless	.15	.44 ± .03 (10-12)
Lack of interest in school	.10	.38 ± .04 (19-20)
Queer	.13	.35 ± .04 (22-24)
Irresponsible	-.06	.34 ± .04 (25)
"Nervous"	.07	.31 ± .04 (27-28)
Changeable moods	.16	.30 ± .04 (29-31)
Question of change of personality	.05	.30 ± .04 (29-31)
Inferiority feelings	.11	.29 ± .04 (32-33)
Masturbation	.16	.27 ± .04 (35-38)
Question of encephalitis	.09	.27 ± .04 (35-38)
Restless in sleep	.03	.26 ± .04 (39)
Finicky food habits	.04	.24 ± .06 (40-42)
Sullen	.17	.25 ± .04 (40-42)
Repressed	-.02	.23 ± .04 (44-48)
Preference for younger children	-.03	.23 ± .04 (44-48)
Selfish	.14	.22 ± .04 (49-51)
Overinterest in opposite sex	....	.22 ± .04 (49-51)
Distractible	.01	.22 ± .04 (49-51)
Mental conflict	.16	.21 ± .04 (52-53)
Speech defect	-.02	.21 ± .04 (52-53)
Nail-biting	.06	.20 ± .04 (54)

Other Correlations (Positive to Negative)

Bad companions, .19 and .17; Slovenly, .18 and .17; Sulky, .17 and .09; Enuresis, .13 and .19; Leader, .13 and -.07; Discord between parents, .13 and .09; Crying spells, .12 and .13; Former convulsions, .12 and .04; Hatred or jealousy of sibling, .11 and .18; Popular, .11 and .12; Lazy, .10 and .09; Depressed, .09 and .12; Sex delinquency (coitus), .08 and .09; Brother in penal detention, .08 and -.03; Absent-minded, .08 and .17; Oversuggestible, .08 and .03; Spoiled child, .08 and .18; Grouped: depressed, etc., .08 and .18; Overinterest in sex matters, .07 and .14; Inefficient in work, play, etc., .06 and .09; Poor work in school, .06 and .06; Headaches, .05 and .09; Sex denied entirely, .04 and .09; Listless, .03 and .16; Daydreaming, .02 and .16; Sensitive (general), .02 and .09; Retardation in school, .01 and -.05; Psychoneurotic, .00 and -.04; Feeble-minded sibling, -.00 and -.09; Follower, -.00 and -.07; Victim of sex abuse, -.01 (girls); Worry over specific fact, -.01 and .10; Unhappy, -.01 and .19; Apprehensive, -.01 and .06; Neurological defect, -.02 and .04; Question of hypophrenia, -.02 and -.06; Grouped: sensitive or worrisome, etc., -.03 and .15; Stuttering, -.05 (boys); Sensitive over specific fact, -.05 and .11; Lack of initiative, -.05 and .02; Vocational guidance, -.06 and -.04; Lues, -.06 and .10; Grouped: dull, slow, etc., -.07 and .12; Attractive manner, -.07 and .02; Seclusive, -.07 and -.11; Underweight, -.08 and -.03; Clean, -.08 and .12; Slow, dull, -.08 and .05; Irregular attendance at school, -.09 and .03; Bashful, -.12 and -.11; Vicious home conditions, -.13 and -.01; Immoral home conditions, -.17 and .12

Omitted—Grouped: fighting, etc.

Quarrelsomeness and incorrigibility yielded large correlations in the .40's among both sexes. Five conduct problems among girls yielded large correlations in the .40's, with corresponding substantial coefficients in the .30's among boys: temper tantrums, destructiveness, disturbing influence in school, rudeness, and lying. Six additional notations among girls yielded large correlations in the .40's, the boys' coefficients being moderate, ranging from .15 to .28: defiant attitude, object of teasing by other children, excuse-forming attitude, restlessness, stealing, and exclusion from school.

Temper display yielded the substantial correlations of .34 + .03 and .30 + .04 with fighting among boys and girls respectively. Three behavior problems—boastful or "show-off" manner, truancy from school, and unpopularity—among boys yielded substantial correlations in the .30's, with moderate coefficients in the .20's among girls. Five undesirable behavior traits among girls yielded substantial correlations in the .30's, with corresponding moderate coefficients in the .20's among boys: irritable temperament, bossy manner, leading others into bad conduct, disobedience, and truancy from home. Six behavior difficulties among girls yielded substantial correlations in the .30's but low coefficients below .20 among boys: "nervousness," changeable moods or attitudes, question of change of personality, irresponsibility, queer behavior, and lack of interest in school.

Fighting showed moderate correlations in the .20's for five behavior traits—egocentricity, contrariness, stubbornness, fantastical lying, and emotional instability—among both sexes and also for the five conduct problems for which only the boys' correlations were computed: threatening violence, running with a gang, smoking, teasing other children, and complaining of bad treatment by other children and also for overinterest in the opposite sex, for which only the girls' correlations were computed. Six undesirable traits among boys showed moderate correlations in the .20's but low positive correlations below .20 among girls: refusal to attend school, staying out late at night, loitering or wandering, inattentiveness in school, staff notation of unfavorable conduct prognosis, and irregular sleep habits. Thirteen miscellaneous notations among girls showed moderate correlations in the .20's but low correlations below .20 among boys: sullenness, repressed manner, mental conflict,

inferiority feelings, restlessness in sleep, nail-biting, finicky
food habits, distractibility, selfishness, preference for younger
children as playmates, masturbation, question or diagnosis of encephalitis, and speech defect (other than stuttering).

    Among the six sex notations two moderate correlations in
the .20's were found: masturbation among girls and overinterest
in the opposite sex (calculated only for girls).

    Among the seven physical or psychophysical notations there
were two correlations of moderate size in the .20's, both among
girls, question or diagnosis of encephalitis and speech defect
(other than stuttering).

    Among the four home or familial notations all correlations
with fighting were low, ranging from -.17 to .13.

    Quarrelsomeness was noted among 292, or 13.8 per cent, of
the boys and among 186, or 15.7 per cent, of the girls. Its highest correlations among both sexes were with violence, the respective correlations for boys and girls being .45 $\pm$ .03 and .50 $\pm$ .04
(Table 70). Its next highest correlation was among girls for unpopularity with a correlation of .52 $\pm$ .05, the boys' coefficient
also being substantial, .36 $\pm$ .04. Fighting yielded large correlations in the .40's for both sexes. Boastful or "show-off" manner among boys yielded a large correlation of .41 $\pm$ .03, the girls'
coefficient being moderate, .27 $\pm$ .05. Among girls six undesirable
behavior traits also yielded large correlations in the .40's, with
moderate or substantial coefficients ranging from .22 to .34 among
boys: incorrigibility, egocentricity, rudeness, excuse-forming attitude, swearing or bad language (undifferentiated), and "nervousness" or restlessness (including irritable temperament and changeable moods, undifferentiated).

    Four conduct problems yielded substantial correlations in
the .30's with quarrelsomeness among both sexes: bossy manner,
temper tantrums, disturbing influence in school, defiant attitude,
and also one calculated for boys only, teasing other children.
Among girls seven undesirable behavior traits yielded substantial
correlations in the .30's, with moderate correlations in the .20's
among boys: temper display, irritable temperament, sullenness,
disobedience, destructiveness, hatred or jealousy of sibling, and
queer behavior. Among girls an additional five behavior difficul-

TABLE 70

CORRELATIONS WITH "QUARRELSOME"

	Boys	Girls
Personality-total.............................	.27 ± .02	.44 ± .02
Conduct-total.................................	.34 ± .02	.46 ± .03
Police arrest.................................	.11 ± .03	.08 ± .05
	Larger Correlations (Positive)	
Violence......................................	.45 ± .03	.54 ± .04 (1)*
Boastful, "show-off"..........................	.41 ± .03	.27 ± .05 (34-37)
Fighting......................................	.41 ± .03	.49 ± .03 (3)
Unpopular.....................................	.36 ± .04	.52 ± .05 (2)
Grouped: disobedient, etc....................	.35 ± .03	.45 ± .03 (6-7)
Incorrigible..................................	.34 ± .03	.42 ± .04 (10-12)
Bossy...	.33 ± .04	.37 ± .05 (16)
Teasing other children.......................	.33 ± .04	....
Grouped: swearing, etc.......................	.33 ± .03	.43 ± .05 (8-9)
Grouped: temper, etc.........................	.32 ± .03	.48 ± .03 (4)
Temper tantrums...............................	.31 ± .04	.38 ± .04 (14-15)
Disturbing influence in school...............	.31 ± .03	.36 ± .05 (17-19)
Defiant.......................................	.30 ± .04	.36 ± .05 (17-19)
Disobedient...................................	.28 ± .03	.38 ± .04 (14-15)
Grouped: "nervous," etc......................	.28 ± .03	.42 ± .03 (10-12)
Temper display................................	.26 ± .04	.31 ± .05 (25)
Threatening violence..........................	.26 ± .02	....
Exclusion from school.........................	.26 ± .04	.29 ± .06 (29-31)
Swearing (general)............................	.25 ± .04	....
Stubborn......................................	.24 ± .03	.27 ± .04 (34-37)
Excuse-forming................................	.24 ± .04	.43 ± .05 (8-9)
Queer...	.24 ± .04	.33 ± .06 (21-23)
Emotional instability.........................	.24 ± .05	.27 ± .05 (34-37)
Sullen..	.23 ± .04	.30 ± .05 (26-28)
Egocentric....................................	.23 ± .04	.42 ± .04 (10-12)
Complaining of bad treatment by other children	.23 ± .04	....
Destructive...................................	.22 ± .04	.30 ± .06 (26-28)
Rude..	.22 ± .03	.47 ± .04 (5)
Irritable.....................................	.22 ± .03	.35 ± .04 (20)
Grouped: egocentric, etc.....................	.22 ± .04	.45 ± .04 (6-7)
Contrary......................................	.21 ± .05	.17
Hatred or jealousy of sibling.................	.21 ± .05	.33 ± .06 (21-23)
Inefficient in work, play, etc...............	.20 ± .05	.23 ± .06 (46-47)
Changeable moods..............................	.20 ± .04	.25 ± .05 (38-41)
Inferiority feelings.........................	.20 ± .04	.21 ± .06 (49-51)
Selfish.......................................	.13	.39 ± .05 (13)
Lying...	.18	.36 ± .04 (17-19)
Restless......................................	.13	.33 ± .04 (21-23)
Crying spells.................................	.18	.32 ± .04 (24)
Distractible..................................	.18	.30 ± .05 (26-28)

*Rank order of girls' correlations.

TABLE 70—Continued

	Boys	Girls
Finicky food habits	.12	.29 ± .05 (29-31)
Irresponsible	.10	.29 ± .06 (29-31)
Fantastical lying	.15	.28 ± .05 (32-33)
Slovenly	.14	.28 ± .04 (32-33)
Restless in sleep	.14	.27 ± .05 (34-37)
Conduct prognosis bad	.14	.25 ± .07 (38-41)
Daydreaming	.10	.25 ± .05 (38-41)
Inattentive in school	.18	.25 ± .05 (38-41)
Leading others into bad conduct	.16	.24 ± .06 (42-45)
Irregular sleep habits	.10	.24 ± .06 (42-45)
Grouped: lack of interest in school, etc.	.19	.24 ± .04 (42-45)
Grouped: depressed, etc.	.07	.24 ± .05 (42-45)
Stealing	.15	.23 ± .04 (46-47)
Enuresis	.18	.22 ± .04 (48)
Sulky	.07	.21 ± .06 (49-51)
"Nervous"	.14	.21 ± .04 (49-51)

Other Correlations (Positive to Negative)

Question of encephalitis, .19 and .14; Bad companions, .18 and .09; Lazy, .17 and .14; Overinterest in sex matters, .17 and .15; Question of change of personality, .17 and .16; Lack of interest in school, .16 and .14; Loitering, .16 and .07; Mental conflict, .15 and .18; Seclusive, .14 and .03; Overinterest in opposite sex, .13 (girls); Smoking, .12 (boys); Truancy from home, .12 and .08; Neurological defect, .12 and .00; Victim of sex abuse, .12 (girls); Staying out late at night, .11 and .15; Masturbation, .11 and .18; Psychoneurotic, .11 and .14; Preference for younger children, .11 and .12; Unhappy, .11 and .19; Vocational guidance, .11 and -.08; Object of teasing, .10 and .13; Sensitive (general), .10 and .18; Spoiled child, .10 and .12; Worry over specific fact, .09 and -.01; Leader, .09 and .05; Grouped: sensitive or worrisome, etc., .09 and .17; Nail-biting, .08 and .16; Poor work in school, .08 and .05; Depressed, .07 and .18; Discord between parents, .07 and .15; Repressed, .05 and .08; Speech defect, .05 and -.01; Truancy from school, .04 and .01; Sensitive over specific fact, .04 and .16; Gang, .03 (boys); Listless, .03 and .01; Refusal to attend school, .02 and .03; Sex denied entirely, .02 and .16; Popular, .01 and -.09; Vicious home conditions, .01 and -.02; Bashful, .00 and -.03; Headaches, -.01 and .04; Attractive manner, -.01 and -.08; Absent-minded, -.01 and -.09; Immoral home conditions, -.02 and -.02; Irregular attendance at school, -.02 and -.07; Former convulsions, -.02 and .11; Question of hypophrenia, -.03 and .06; Sex delinquency (coitus), -.03 and -.01; Clean, -.04 and -.03; Underweight, -.05 and .04; Oversuggestible, -.06 and .10; Lack of initiative, -.06 and -.06; Slow, dull, -.07 and .03; Grouped: dull, slow, etc., -.08 and .04; Retardation in school, -.08 and -.09; Apprehensive, -.08 and .08; Feeble-minded sibling, -.09 and -.07; Follower, -.09 and .06; Stuttering, -.09 (boys); Lues, -.11 and .01; Brother in penal detention, -.11 and .14
        Omitted—Grouped: fighting, etc.

ties yielded substantial correlations in the .30's but low positive correlations ranging from .13 to .18 among boys: <u>selfishness</u>, <u>lying</u>, <u>crying spells</u>, <u>restlessness</u>, and <u>distractibility</u>.

Six behavior difficulties showed moderate correlations in the .20's with quarrelsomeness among both sexes: stubbornness, emotional instability, inferiority feelings, changeable moods or attitudes, inefficiency in work, play, etc., exclusion from school, and the three notations for which only the boys' correlations were calculated—threatening violence, swearing in general, and complaining of bad treatment by other children. Contrariness showed the low or moderate correlations of .21 + .05 and .17 for boys and girls respectively. Fifteen behavior traits among girls showed moderate correlations in the .20's but low positive correlations below .20 among boys: sulkiness, stealing, leading others into bad conduct, fantastical lying, slovenliness, irresponsibility, inattentiveness in school, daydreaming, "nervousness," restlessness in sleep, irregular sleep habits, finicky food habits, depressed spells or unhappiness (undifferentiated), enuresis, and staff notation of unfavorable conduct prognosis.

Among the sex notations, the physical or psychophysical disabilities, and the home or familial notations, the only statistically significant coefficient was for enuresis among girls, .22 + .04.

Violence (actual or attempted) was noted among 281, or 13.3 per cent, of our boys and among 87, or 7.4 per cent, of our girls. Among girls violence was a very grave indicator of behavior maladjustment in both the personality and the conduct categories. Its bi-serial correlation of .79 + .02 was the largest but one of all the correlations with conduct-total (Table 7, p. 98), while its correlation of .64 + .03 with personality-total was the largest of all correlations found among girls with personality-total (Table 6, p. 89). Among boys the correlation with conduct-total was high, .54 + .02, and with the personality-total somewhat substantial, .31 + .02 (Table 71). Its tetrachoric correlations with the police-arrest criterion of "juvenile delinquency" was only moderate, the respective coefficients for boys and girls being .29 + .03 and .18 + .05.

Among girls the three notations, swearing or bad language (undifferentiated), temper tantrums, and fighting, yielded very high correlations ranging from .61 to .64 with violence, the corresponding coefficients among boys being almost as large, .44 + .03,

TABLE 71

CORRELATIONS WITH "VIOLENCE"

	Boys	Girls
Personality-total..............................	.31 ± .02	.64 ± .03
Conduct-total.................................	.54 ± .02	.79 ± .02
Police arrest.................................	.29 ± .03	.18 ± .05
	Larger Correlations (Positive)	
Temper tantrums...............................	.54 ± .03	.61 ± .04 (2-3)*
Threatening violence..........................	.54 ± .04	....
Grouped: temper, etc.........................	.52 ± .02	.57 ± .04 (4)
Quarrelsome...................................	.45 ± .03	.54 ± .04 (6)
Grouped: swearing, etc......................	.44 ± .03	.64 ± .05 (1)
Destructive...................................	.44 ± .03	.44 ± .07 (15-16)
Fighting......................................	.43 ± .03	.61 ± .05 (2-3)
Grouped: disobedient, etc...................	.42 ± .03	.56 ± .04 (5)
Swearing (general)............................	.40 ± .04	....
Incorrigible..................................	.39 ± .03	.47 ± .05 (8-10)
Temper display................................	.39 ± .03	.26 ± .06 (54-57)
Teasing other children........................	.38 ± .04	
Disturbing influence in school................	.36 ± .03	.47 ± .06 (8-10)
Rude..	.36 ± .03	.39 ± .05 (23-24)
Exclusion from school.........................	.36 ± .04	.49 ± .06 (7)
Irritable.....................................	.34 ± .03	.30 ± .05 (44-45)
Conduct prognosis bad.........................	.33 ± .05	.25 ± .08 (58-61)
Grouped: "nervous," etc.....................	.33 ± .03	.46 ± .04 (11-13)
Emotional instability.........................	.32 ± .05	.30 ± .06 (44-45)
Defiant.......................................	.31 ± .04	.47 ± .06 (8-10)
Disobedient...................................	.29 ± .03	.41 ± .05 (18-19)
Unpopular.....................................	.29 ± .05	.40 ± .07 (20-22)
Contrary......................................	.28 ± .04	.33 ± .08 (34-36)
Stealing......................................	.26 ± .03	.39 ± .05 (23-24)
Sullen..	.25 ± .04	.27 ± .06 (52-53)
Truancy from home.............................	.25 ± .03	.24 ± .05 (62-64)
Hatred or jealousy of sibling.................	.25 ± .05	.14
Grouped: egocentric, etc....................	.24 ± .03	.31 ± .05 (37-43)
Egocentric....................................	.24 ± .03	.36 ± .05 (27-29)
Excuse-forming................................	.24 ± .04	.28 ± .06 (48-51)
Refusal to attend school......................	.23 ± .04	.18
Stubborn......................................	.23 ± .03	.36 ± .05 (27-29)
Changeable moods..............................	.23 ± .04	.31 ± .06 (37-43)
Complaining of bad treatment by other children	.23 ± .05	....
Boastful, "show-off"..........................	.22 ± .04	.40 ± .06 (20-22)
Lying...	.21 ± .03	.41 ± .04 (18-19)
Sulky...	.21 ± .05	.17
Object of teasing.............................	.21 ± .03	.36 ± .06 (27-29)
Irregular sleep habits........................	.20 ± .05	.26 ± .07 (54-57)
Queer...	.20 ± .05	.46 ± .06 (11-13)

*Rank order of girls' correlations.

TABLE 71—Continued

	Boys	Girls
Bossy	.19	.46 ± .06 (11-13)
Restless	.15	.45 ± .04 (14)
Leading others into bad conduct	.08	.44 ± .07 (15-16)
Spoiled child	.16	.42 ± .06 (17)
Distractible	.11	.40 ± .06 (20-22)
Daydreaming	.03	.38 ± .06 (25)
Staying out late at night	.18	.37 ± .05 (26)
Restless in sleep	.11	.35 ± .05 (30-32)
Question of change of personality	.09	.35 ± .07 (30-32)
Finicky food habits	.14	.35 ± .06 (30-32)
Overinterest in opposite sex	....	.34 ± .05 (33)
Mental conflict	.07	.33 ± .08 (34-36)
Fantastical lying	.16	.33 ± .07 (34-36)
Grouped: depressed, etc.	.08	.31 ± .06 (37-43)
Headaches	.11	.31 ± .06 (37-43)
Overinterest in sex matters	.18	.31 ± .07 (37-43)
Slovenly	.17	.31 ± .05 (37-43)
Depressed	.09	.29 ± .07 (46-47)
Truancy from school	.13	.29 ± .06 (46-47)
Enuresis	.10	.28 ± .05 (48-51)
Selfish	.19	.28 ± .04 (48-51)
Masturbation	.13	.28 ± .06 (48-51)
Question of encephalitis	.17	.27 ± .09 (52-53)
"Nervous"	.19	.26 ± .05 (54-57)
Neurological defect	.09	.26 ± .06 (54-57)
Grouped: lack of interest in school, etc.	.16	.25 ± .05 (58-61)
Listless	.04	.25 ± .07 (58-61)
Lack of interest in school	.14	.25 ± .06 (58-61)
Loitering	.18	.24 ± .07 (62-64)
Crying spells	.12	.24 ± .05 (62-64)
Inefficient in work, play, etc.	.14	.23 ± .07 (65)
Unhappy	.07	.21 ± .07 (66-69)
Inferiority feelings	.12	.21 ± .07 (66-69)
Worry over specific fact	.04	.21 ± .09 (66-69)
Oversuggestible	.10	.21 ± .05 (66-69)
Nail-biting	.15	.20 ± .05 (70-71)
Lues	-.00	.20 ± .07 (70-71)

Other Correlations (Positive to Negative)

Former convulsions, .17 and -.00; Smoking, .16 (boys); Apprehensive, .14 and .13; Gang, .14 (boys); Sex delinquency (coitus), .13 and .14; Question of hypophrenia, .13 and .11; Seclusive, .11 and .15; Lazy, .11 and .12; Bad companions, .11 and .09; Preference for younger children, .10 and .13; Lack of initiative, .09 and -.18; Inattentive in school, .09 and .18; Retardation in school, .08 and -.02; Discord between parents, .07 and .14; Absent-minded, .07 and .01; Irresponsible, .06 and .19; Psychoneurotic, .06 and .19; Repressed, .05 and -.04; Leader, .04 and .12; Irregular attendance at school, .04 and .06; Speech defect, .04 and .17; Popular, .03 and .11; Stuttering, .03 (boys); Sensitive over specific fact, .02 and .14; Grouped: sensitive or worrisome, etc., .02 and .14; Victim of sex abuse, .02 (girls); Poor work in school, .01 and .01; Clean, .01 and .06; Vicious home conditions, -.02 and .09; Sensitive (general),

TABLE 71—Continued
_____

-.03 and .05; Underweight, -.03 and .03; Follower, -.04 and -.11; Immoral home
conditions, -.05 and -.16; Brother in penal detention, -.06 and -.02; Sex denied entirely, -.08 and .09; Attractive manner, -.08 and .09; Grouped: dull,
slow, etc., -.08 and .08; Bashful, -.11 and .01; Slow, dull, -.11 and .09; Vocational guidance, -.12 and -.13; Feeble-minded sibling, -.12 and .12
        Omitted—Grouped: fighting, etc.

.54 ± .03, and .43 ± .03 respectively. Threatening violence among
boys yielded a similarly high correlation of .54 ± .04, the corresponding coefficient for the girls not being calculated because
of the paucity of cases. With quarrelsomeness and the larger
grouping disobedience or incorrigibility (including defiant attitude, stubbornness, and contrariness, undifferentiated), the girls'
correlations in the .50's also were high, with the boys' coefficients in the .40's almost as large.

Destructiveness yielded large correlations of .44 among
both sexes. Among girls five behavior problems yielded large correlations in the .40's, with substantial corresponding correlations
in the .30's among boys: incorrigibility, defiant attitude, disturbing influence in school, exclusion from school, and the larger
grouping, "nervousness" or restlessness (including irritable temperament and changeable moods, undifferentiated). Five undesirable conduct and personality traits among girls yielded similarly
large correlations in the .40's, with moderate coefficients in the
.20's among boys: disobedience, boastful or "show-off" manner,
lying, unpopularity, and queer behavior. Five additional behavior
problems among girls yielded large correlations in the .40's, but
low positive coefficients below .20 among boys: bossy manner,
leading others into bad conduct, "spoiled child," restlessness,
and distractibility.

Three behavior problems—irritable temperament, rudeness,
and emotional instability—together with teasing other children
(calculated for boys only) and overinterest in the opposite sex
(calculated for girls only) yielded uniformly substantial correlations in the .30's with violence. Among boys temper display and
staff notation of unfavorable conduct prognosis yielded substantial correlations in the .30's, with moderate coefficients in the
.20's among girls. Among girls six behavior problems yielded substantial correlations in the .30's, with moderate coefficients in

the .20's among boys: <u>object of teasing by other children</u>, <u>stubbornness</u>, <u>contrariness</u>, <u>egocentricity</u>, <u>changeable moods and attitudes</u>, and <u>stealing</u>. Ten additional miscellaneous notations among girls yielded substantial correlations in the .30's, but low positive correlations below .20 among boys: <u>staying out late at night</u>, <u>fantastical lying</u>, <u>restlessness in sleep</u>, <u>question of change of personality</u>, <u>finicky food habits</u>, <u>mental conflict</u>, <u>daydreaming</u>, <u>slovenliness</u>, <u>overinterest in sex matters</u>, and <u>headaches</u>.

Four behavior problems—<u>sullenness</u>, <u>truancy from home</u>, <u>excuse-forming attitude</u>, and <u>irregular sleep habits</u>—together with <u>complaining of bad treatment by other children</u> (calculated for boys only), showed moderate correlations in the .20's with <u>violence</u>. Three additional conduct problems—<u>hatred or jealousy of sibling</u>, <u>refusal to attend school</u>, and <u>sulkiness</u>—among boys showed moderate correlations in the .20's, with low positive correlations below .20 among girls. A large list of nineteen miscellaneous notations among girls similarly showed moderate correlations in the .20's but low positive coefficients below .20 among boys: <u>selfishness</u>, <u>truancy from school</u>, "<u>nervousness</u>," <u>depressed mood or spells</u>, <u>unhappiness</u>, <u>crying spells</u>, <u>inferiority feelings</u>, <u>worry over some specific fact</u>, <u>listlessness</u>, <u>lack of interest in school</u>, <u>inefficiency in work, play</u>, etc., <u>loitering or wandering</u>, <u>oversuggestibility</u>, <u>enuresis</u>, <u>nail-biting</u>, <u>masturbation</u>, <u>question or diagnosis of encephalitis</u>, <u>neurological defect (unspecified)</u>, and <u>lues</u>.

Among the six sex notations there were three coefficients of moderate or substantial size ranging from .28 to .34, all among girls: <u>masturbation</u>, <u>overinterest in sex matters</u>, and (calculated for girls only) <u>overinterest in the opposite sex</u>.

Among the seven physical or psychophysical disabilities there were three moderate correlations in the .20's, all among girls: <u>question or diagnosis of encephalitis</u>, <u>neurological defect (unspecified)</u>, and <u>enuresis</u>.

Among the four home or familial notations all coefficients were low or negligible, ranging from -.16 to .14.

<u>Threatening violence or to kill someone</u> was noted among 102, or 4.8 per cent, of our White boys. It occurred so rarely among girls that correlation coefficients were not practicable because of the paucity of girls' cases, and all the coefficients reported in

Table 72 were among boys only. Its bi-serial correlation with the
conduct-total was high, .52 ± .03. With the personality-total its
bi-serial r was substantial, .34 ± .03. With police arrest its
tetrachoric r was moderate, .26 ± .04.

High correlations in the .50's were found for violence and
temper tantrums and large correlations in the .40's for swearing
or bad language (undifferentiated) and destructiveness.

Substantial correlations in the .30's were found for the
six behavior traits incorrigibility, irritable temperament, egocentricity, sullenness, swearing in general, and excuse-forming
attitude.

Moderate correlations in the .20's were found for a large
list of twenty-eight miscellaneous notations: fighting, quarrelsomeness, temper display, teasing other children, boastful or
"show-off" manner, bossy manner, disobedience, defiant attitude,
contrariness, disturbing influence in school, exclusion from
school, complaining of bad treatment by other children, unpopularity, hatred or jealousy of sibling, rudeness, leading others into
bad conduct, stealing, staying out late at night, irregular sleep
habits, lying, lack of interest in school, "nervousness" or restlessness (undifferentiated), changeable moods or attitudes, queer
behavior, daydreaming, question or diagnosis of encephalitis, headaches, and staff notation of unfavorable conduct prognosis.

The only negative correlation of probable statistical significance was with underweight condition, -.20 ± .05.

Among the sex notations, the physical or psychophysical
disabilities, and the home or familial notations the only correlations of probable statistical significance were with question or
diagnosis of encephalitis, .22 ± .07, and the negative correlation
with underweight condition, -.20 ± .05. All the other twelve coefficients in these fields were low or negligible, ranging from -.07
to .13.

When the cases falling under the four rubrics, fighting,
quarrelsomeness, violence, and threatening violence were combined
into a broad grouping,[1] there were 644 such cases, or 30.5 per

---

[1] The reasons for this broader grouping were given in I, 44; see 86,
Table 13, Item E.

TABLE 72

CORRELATIONS WITH "THREATENING VIOLENCE"
(Boys Only)

Personality-total	.34 ± .03
Conduct-total	.52 ± .03
Police arrest	.26 ± .04

Larger Correlations (Positive)

Grouped: temper, etc.	.57 ± .03
Violence	.54 ± .04
Temper tantrums	.53 ± .04
Grouped: swearing, etc.	.43 ± .04
Destructive	.42 ± .05
Incorrigible	.36 ± .04
Grouped: disobedient, etc.	.36 ± .04
Excuse-forming	.35 ± .05
Irritable	.34 ± .04
Sullen	.32 ± .05
Swearing (general)	.32 ± .06
Egocentric	.31 ± .05
Fighting	.29 ± .05
Unpopular	.29 ± .06
Grouped: egocentric, etc.	.29 ± .04
Temper display	.28 ± .05
Conduct prognosis bad	.28 ± .07
Changeable moods	.27 ± .05
Quarrelsome	.26 ± .02
Queer	.26 ± .06
Boastful, "show-off"	.25 ± .05
Defiant	.25 ± .05
Rude	.25 ± .05
Staying out late at night	.25 ± .05
Irregular sleep habits	.25 ± .06
Leading others into bad conduct	.24 ± .06
Exclusion from school	.24 ± .05
Grouped: "nervous," etc.	.24 ± .04
Stealing	.24 ± .04
Contrary	.23 ± .07
Disturbing influence in school	.22 ± .05
Teasing other children	.22 ± .05
Question of encephalitis	.22 ± .07
Lying	.21 ± .04
Hatred or jealousy of sibling	.21 ± .07
Headaches	.21 ± .06
Bossy	.20 ± .06
Disobedient	.20 ± .04
Lack of interest in school	.20 ± .05
Daydreaming	.20 ± .05
Complaining of bad treatment by other children	.20 ± .06

Larger Correlations (Negative)

Underweight	-.20 ± .05

TABLE 72—Continued

Other Correlations (Positive to Negative)

Fantastical lying, .19; Smoking, .19; Stubborn, .18; Restless, .18; Unhappy, .18; Truancy from school, .17; Object of teasing, .16; Refusal to attend school, .15; Truancy from home, .15; Spoiled child, .15; Grouped: depressed, etc., .15; Sulky, .14; Masturbation, .14; Question of hypophrenia, .14; Nail-biting, .13; Overinterest in sex matters, .13; Question of change of personality, .13; Restless in sleep, .13; Inferiority feelings, .13; Selfish, .12; Depressed, .11; Seclusive, .11; Preference for younger children, .11; Grouped: lack of interest in school, etc., .11; Stuttering, .10; Distractible, .10; Irresponsible, .09; Enuresis, .09; Mental conflict, .09; Finicky food habits, .08; Sex delinquency (coitus), .08; Crying spells, .08; Emotional instability, .08; Lues, .08; Bad companions, .07; Inefficient in work, play, etc., .07; Discord between parents, .06; Sensitive over specific fact, .05; Retardation in school, .05; Speech defect, .05; Listless, .04; Grouped: dull, slow, etc., .03; Slovenly, .02; Oversuggestible, .02; Poor work in school, .02; Leader, .02; Former convulsions, .02; Neurological defect, .01; Attractive manner, .01; Brother in penal detention, .01; Grouped: sensitive or worrisome, etc., .01; Slow, dull, .00; Lack of initiative, -.00; Worry over specific fact, -.00; Feeble-minded sibling, -.00; Immoral home conditions, -.00; Loitering, -.01; Psychoneurotic, -.01; "Nervous," -.01; Lazy, -.02; Apprehensive, -.03; Sensitive (general), -.03; Clean, -.03; Gang, -.04; Inattentive in school, -.05; Bashful, -.05; Repressed, -.06; Vicious home conditions, -.06; Sex denied entirely, -.07; Popular, -.07; Vocational guidance, -.07; Follower, -.08; Absent-minded, -.11; Irregular attendance at school, -.11
Omitted—Grouped: fighting, etc.

cent, of the 2,113 White boys and 273, or 23.1 per cent, of the 1,181 White girls. These afforded some of the most numerous of the behavior difficulties or reasons for referring children for examination to the clinic in which this study was made. The fact that the resulting correlations as shown in Table 73 are generally similar to those of the four component notations but somewhat larger indicates the general similarity of these conduct notations.

Large or high coefficients in the .40's to .60's among both sexes were found for temper tantrums, swearing or bad language (undifferentiated), incorrigibility, and destructiveness. Additional behavior notations yielding substantial to high correlations from the .30's to the 50's among both sexes were temper display, unpopularity, disturbing influence in school, disobedience, defiant attitude, rudeness, exclusion from school, "nervousness" or restlessness

TABLE 73

CORRELATIONS WITH "GROUPED: FIGHTING, ETC."

	Boys	Girls
Personality-total.......................	.30 ± .02	.48 ± .02
Conduct-total...........................	.53 ± .02	.65 ± .02
Police arrest...........................	.23 ± .03	.08 ± .04

	Larger Correlations (Positive)	
Grouped: temper, etc...................	.50 ± .02	.58 ± .03 (2)*
Temper tantrums........................	.49 ± .03	.54 ± .04 (3)
Grouped: swearing, etc................	.47 ± .03	.60 ± .04 (1)
Incorrigible..........................	.43 ± .02	.51 ± .03 (7)
Temper display........................	.42 ± .03	.35 ± .05 (27)
Destructive...........................	.41 ± .03	.47 ± .05 (10)
Swearing (general)....................	.41 ± .03	....
Disturbing influence in school........	.39 ± .03	.44 ± .04 (14-16)
Unpopular.............................	.37 ± .08	.53 ± .05 (4-5)
Teasing other children................	.36 ± .03	....
Disobedient...........................	.36 ± .02	.44 ± .03 (14-16)
Contrary..............................	.35 ± .04	.29 ± .06 (37-43)
Defiant...............................	.35 ± .04	.48 ± .04 (9)
Rude..................................	.35 ± .03	.49 ± .03 (8)
Exclusion from school.................	.34 ± .03	.38 ± .05 (21-24)
Grouped: "nervous," etc..............	.33 ± .02	.53 ± .03 (4-5)
Bossy.................................	.32 ± .04	.43 ± .04 (17)
Irritable.............................	.32 ± .03	.44 ± .04 (14-16)
Grouped: egocentric, etc.............	.31 ± .03	.40 ± .04 (18-20)
Egocentric............................	.30 ± .03	.38 ± .04 (21-24)
Stealing..............................	.29 ± .02	.38 ± .03 (21-24)
Stubborn..............................	.29 ± .03	.32 ± .04 (30-33)
Excuse-forming........................	.29 ± .03	.45 ± .04 (13)
Sullen................................	.28 ± .03	.34 ± .05 (28-29)
Boastful, "show-off"..................	.28 ± .03	.29 ± .05 (37-43)
Truancy from home.....................	.27 ± .03	.16
Changeable moods......................	.27 ± .03	.28 ± .04 (44-47)
Irregular sleep habits................	.27 ± .04	.21 ± .05 (60-61)
Lying.................................	.26 ± .02	.46 ± .03 (11-12)
Smoking...............................	.25 ± .03	....
Conduct prognosis bad.................	.25 ± .04	.32 ± .06 (30-33)
Queer.................................	.24 ± .04	.36 ± .05 (26)
Question of encephalitis..............	.23 ± .05	.29 ± .06 (37-43)
Complaining of bad treatment by other children	.22 ± .06	....
Hatred or jealousy of sibling.........	.22 ± .04	.30 ± .05 (34-36)
Selfish...............................	.22 ± .04	.40 ± .05 (18-20)
Grouped: lack of interest in school, etc.....	.22 ± .03	.32 ± .04 (30-33)
Crying spells.........................	.21 ± .03	.29 ± .04 (37-43)
Emotional instability.................	.21 ± .06	.24 ± .05 (56-57)
Restless..............................	.18	.46 ± .03 (11-12)

*Rank order of girls' correlations.

TABLE 73—Continued

	Boys	Girls
Leading others into bad conduct...............	.16	.40 ± .05 (18-20)
Finicky food habits...........................	.16	.38 ± .04 (21-24)
Restless in sleep.............................	.10	.37 ± .04 (25)
Distractible..................................	.15	.34 ± .04 (28-29)
Irresponsible.................................	.07	.32 ± .05 (30-33)
Object of teasing.............................	.14	.30 ± .05 (34-36)
Nail-biting...................................	.13	.30 ± .04 (34-36)
Grouped: depressed, etc.......................	.15	.29 ± .04 (37-43)
Inattentive in school.........................	.18	.29 ± .05 (37-43)
Staying out late at night.....................	.19	.29 ± .04 (37-43)
Daydreaming...................................	.05	.28 ± .05 (44-47)
Fantastical lying.............................	.19	.28 ± .05 (44-47)
Enuresis......................................	.13	.28 ± .04 (44-47)
Slovenly......................................	.17	.27 ± .04 (48-50)
Sulky...	.17	.27 ± .05 (48-50)
Masturbation..................................	.15	.27 ± .04 (48-50)
Unhappy.......................................	.10	.26 ± .05 (51-52)
Question of change of personality.............	.15	.26 ± .05 (51-52)
Lack of interest in school....................	.18	.25 ± .05 (53-55)
Inferiority feelings..........................	.17	.25 ± .05 (53-55)
Mental conflict...............................	.18	.25 ± .06 (53-55)
"Nervous".....................................	.14	.24 ± .04 (56-57)
Loitering.....................................	.19	.23 ± .05 (58-59)
Sensitive over specific fact..................	.03	.23 ± .04 (58-59)
Spoiled child.................................	.14	.21 ± .05 (60-61)
Grouped: sensitive or worrisome, etc.........	.03	.20 ± .04 (62)

Other Correlations (Positive to Negative)

Refusal to attend school, .19 and .06; Truancy from school, .19 and .18; Lazy, .18 and .09; Overinterest in opposite sex, .18 (girls); Sex delinquency (coitus), .17 and .09; Overinterest in sex matters, .17 and .18; Gang, .17 (boys); Inefficient in work, play, etc., .17 and .13; Bad companions, .16 and .12; Depressed, .16 and .19; Psychoneurotic, .14 and .08; Leader, .11 and .10; Neurological defect, .11 and .11; Preference for younger children, .11 and .16; Seclusive, .10 and .03; Former convulsions, .09 and .09; Discord between parents, .08 and .16; Sensitive (general), .05 and .14; Poor work in school, .05 and -.01; Popular, .04 and .03; Listless, .04 and .05; Worry over specific fact, .04 and .07; Apprehensive, .04 and .10; Headaches, .03 and .11; Oversuggestible, .03 and .12; Question of hypophrenia, .03 and .02; Repressed, .02 and .11; Victim of sex abuse, .01 (girls); Retardation in school, -.02 and -.07; Brother in penal detention, -.02 and .12; Absent-minded, -.04 and .01; Attractive manner, -.04 and -.02; Clean, -.04 and .05; Speech defect, -.05 and .09; Stuttering, -.05 (boys); Follower, -.06 and .04; Lues, -.06 and .04; Underweight, -.06 and .07; Grouped: dull, slow, etc., -.07 and .05; Vicious home conditions, -.07 and .09; Irregular attendance at school, -.07 and -.03; Lack of initiative, -.07 and -.07; Sex denied entirely, -.07 and .09; Slow, dull, -.08 and .03; Feeble-minded sibling, -.08 and -.07; Vocational guidance, -.08 and -.16; Immoral home conditions, -.10 and .03; Bashful, -.10 and -.07
Omitted—Fighting; Quarrelsome; Threatening violence; Violence

(undifferentiated), irritable temperament, bossy manner, egocentricity, and (computed for boys only) teasing other children.

The following additional nineteen notations yielded moderate to large correlations from the .20's to the .40's among both sex sexes: contrariness, stubbornness, boastful or "show-off" manner, stealing, excuse-forming attitude, sullenness, lying, hatred or jealousy of sibling, selfishness, lack of interest or inattentiveness in school studies or employment (undifferentiated), queer behavior, emotional instability, changeable moods or attitudes, crying spells, complaining of bad treatment by other children (calculated for boys only), irregular sleep habits, smoking (calculated for boys only), question or diagnosis of encephalitis, and staff notation of unfavorable conduct prognosis. Among girls the following eight behavior difficulties yielded substantial or large correlations ranging from .30 to .46 but low positive coefficients below .20 among boys: leading others into bad conduct, object of teasing by other children, restlessness, restlessness in sleep, distractibility, irresponsibility, finicky food habits, and nailbiting.

Truancy from home among boys showed the moderate correlation of .27 ± .03 but a low coefficient of .16 among girls. The following fifteen personality and conduct problems among girls yielded moderate correlations in the .20's but low positive correlations below .20 among boys: staying out late at night, depressed spells or unhappiness (undifferentiated), fantastical lying, sulkiness, slovenliness, loitering or wandering, "spoiled child," mental conflict, inferiority feelings, daydreaming, question of change of personality, sensitiveness or worrisomeness (undifferentiated), sensitiveness over some specific fact, masturbation, and enuresis.

Among the six sex notations the larger grouping, fighting or quarrelsomeness (undifferentiated), showed only one statistically significant correlation, .27 ± .04, with masturbation among girls.

Among the seven physical or psychophysical notations, moderate correlations in the .20's were found for question or diagnosis of encephalitis among both sexes and for enuresis among girls.

Among the home or familial notations all correlations were low or negligible.

CHAPTER XXXIX

DESTRUCTIVENESS.

Destructiveness (breaking toys, windows, etc., or tearing
books, clothing, etc.) was noted among 227, or 10.7 per cent, of
our 2,113 White boys and among 55, or 4.7 per cent, of our 1,181
White girls. It appeared more frequently among the younger children, especially among the girls' cases.[1] Its bi-serial correlations in the .50's with conduct-total indicated its seriousness as
a symptom of conduct deviation (Table 74). With the personality-
total its correlations of .30 ± .02 among boys and .40 ± .04 among
girls were substantial but not large. With the police-arrest criterion of "juvenile delinquency" its tetrachoric correlation among
boys, .30 ± .03, was similarly substantial but not large, while
among girls the correlation was low, .15 ± .06.

Its highest correlations were in the .40's among both sexes
temper tantrums, violence, swearing or bad language (undifferentiated), and (calculated for boys only) threatening violence. Incorrigibility and stealing among boys yielded large correlations
in the .40's with moderate correlations in the .30's among girls.
Among girls five notations similarly yielded large correlations in
the .40's, with substantial coefficients ranging from .29 to .39
among boys: contrariness, fighting, disobedience, leading others
into bad conduct, and exclusion from school.

Three behavior problems yielded substantial correlations in the .30's among both sexes: disturbing influence in
school, defiant attitude, and lying. Teasing other children
(calculated for boys only) and overinterest in the opposite sex
(calculated for girls only) also yielded substantial correlations
in the .30's. Among boys four undesirable behavior traits yielded
substantial correlations in the .30's with moderate correlations
in the .20's among girls: rudeness, hatred or jealousy of
sibling, fantastical lying, and excuse-forming attitude. Truancy

---

[1]See I, 216, Fig. 52.

TABLE 74

CORRELATIONS WITH "DESTRUCTIVE"

	Boys	Girls
Personality-total	.30 ± .02	.40 ± .04
Conduct-total	.59 ± .02	.54 ± .04
Police arrest	.30 ± .03	.15 ± .06
	Larger Correlations (Positive)	
Temper tantrums	.46 ± .04	.45 ± .06 (4-5)*
Violence	.44 ± .03	.44 ± .07 (6-7)
Grouped: swearing, etc	.43 ± .03	.44 ± .07 (6-7)
Threatening violence	.42 ± .05	....
Incorrigible	.41 ± .03	.33 ± .06 (16-19)
Stealing	.41 ± .03	.35 ± .05 (13-15)
Grouped: fighting, etc	.41 ± .03	.47 ± .05 (1-2)
Grouped: disobedient, etc	.38 ± .03	.35 ± .05 (13-15)
Rude	.38 ± .03	.22 ± .06 (45-47)
Contrary	.37 ± .04	.46 ± .08 (3)
Disturbing influence in school	.36 ± .03	.32 ± .07 (20-21)
Hatred or jealousy of sibling	.35 ± .05	.29 ± .08 (27-30)
Fighting	.34 ± .04	.45 ± .07 (4-5)
Teasing other children	.34 ± .04	....
Exclusion from school	.34 ± .04	.40 ± .07 (9)
Grouped: temper, etc	.34 ± .03	.36 ± .05 (10-12)
Lying	.33 ± .03	.35 ± .05 (13-15)
Defiant	.31 ± .04	.31 ± .07 (22-23)
Fantastical lying	.31 ± .05	.24 ± .08 (36-38)
Leading others into bad conduct	.31 ± .04	.47 ± .08 (1-2)
Truancy from home	.31 ± .03	-.16
Excuse-forming	.30 ± .04	.27 ± .07 (31)
Disobedient	.29 ± .03	.41 ± .05 (8)
Masturbation	.29 ± .03	.29 ± .06 (27-30)
Unpopular	.27 ± .05	.17
Bossy	.26 ± .05	.12
Swearing (general)	.26 ± .05	....
Truancy from school	.25 ± .03	.25 ± .07 (34-35)
Inattentive in school	.25 ± .04	.23 ± .07 (39-44)
Boastful, "show-off"	.25 ± .04	.19
Restless	.24 ± .03	.29 ± .06 (27-30)
Slovenly	.23 ± .04	.17
Quarrelsome	.22 ± .04	.30 ± .06 (24-26)
Egocentric	.22 ± .04	.22 ± .07 (45-47)
Irresponsible	.22 ± .05	.10
Sullen	.22 ± .04	-.07
Gang	.22 ± .04	....
Grouped: "nervous," etc	.21 ± .03	.36 ± .05 (10-12)
Grouped: lack of interest in school, etc	.21 ± .03	.23 ± .06 (39-44)
Staying out late at night	.21 ± .04	.23 ± .07 (39-44)

*Rank order of girls' correlations.

TABLE 74—Continued

	Boys	Girls
Spoiled child	.21 ± .04	.10
Complaining of bad treatment by other children	.20 ± .05	....
Queer	.19	.36 ± .08 (10-12)
Mental conflict	.12	.33 ± .09 (16-19)
Question of change of personality	.11	.33 ± .08 (16-19)
Question of encephalitis	.05	.33 ± .10 (16-19)
Overinterest in opposite sex	....	.32 ± .06 (20-21)
Emotional instability	.05	.31 ± .07 (22-23)
Distractible	.15	.30 ± .07 (24-26)
Worry over specific fact	-.11	.30 ± .10 (24-26)
Changeable moods	.18	.29 ± .06 (27-30)
Grouped: egocentric, etc.	.19	.26 ± .06 (32-33)
Conduct prognosis bad	.14	.26 ± .08 (32-33)
"Nervous"	.15	.25 ± .06 (34-35)
Restless in sleep	.13	.24 ± .07 (36-38)
Selfish	.10	.24 ± .08 (36-38)
Temper display	.19	.23 ± .07 (39-44)
Stubborn	.13	.23 ± .06 (39-44)
Preference for younger children	.06	.23 ± .07 (39-44)
Bad companions	.17	.22 ± .07 (45-47)
Irregular sleep habits	.19	.20 ± .08 (48-51)
Nail-biting	.14	.20 ± .06 (48-51)
Discord between parents	.12	.20 ± .06 (48-51)
Repressed	.02	.20 ± .08 (48-51)
	Larger Correlations (Negative)	
Feeble-minded sibling	-.24 ± .05	-.14
Victim of sex abuse	....	-.29 ± .07
Vicious home conditions	.10	-.26 ± .08
Lazy	.06	-.24 ± .07
	Not Calculable	
Lack of initiative	-.15	(n.c.)

Other Correlations (Positive to Negative)

Enuresis, .19 and .09; Loitering, .18 and .16; Unhappy, .18 and .11; Finicky food habits, .17 and .12; Refusal to attend school, .17 and .13; Overinterest in sex matters, .17 and .05; Sulky, .16 and .18; Irritable, .16 and .10; Object of teasing, .16 and .06; Inferiority feelings, .13 and .17; Lack of interest in school, .12 and .12; Crying spells, .12 and .13; Oversuggestible, .11 and .07; Grouped: depressed, etc., .10 and .19; Absent-minded, .09 and .17; Daydreaming, .09 and .11; Popular, .09 and -.02; Apprehensive, .08 and .09; Inefficient in work, play, etc., .08 and .19; Smoking, .08 (boys); Headaches, .07 and .15; Neurological defect, .06 and .12; Leader, .05 and -.01; Attractive manner, .05 and -.06; Clean, .04 and -.04; Irregular attendance at school, .03 and .03; Seclusive, .02 and .03; Psychoneurotic, .02 and .08; Follower, .02 and .06; Lues, .02 and .11; Sensitive over specific fact, .01 and .11; Poor work in school,

TABLE 74—Continued

.01 and .00; Underweight, .01 and .01; Brother in penal detention, .01 and .01;
Listless, .00 and .09; Question of hypophrenia, .00 and .11; Immoral home conditions, -.00 and -.04; Retardation in school, -.01 and -.05; Grouped: sensitive
or worrisome, etc., -.03 and .16; Depressed, -.02 and .17; Speech defect, -.03
and .18; Former convulsions, -.03 and .02; Sensitive (general), -.03 and -.08;
Bashful, -.04 and -.04; Sex denied entirely, -.05 and -.02; Sex delinquency (coitus), -.06 and .02; Grouped: dull, slow, etc., -.07 and -.00; Slow, dull, -.07
and .00; Vocational guidance, -.09 and -.13; Stuttering, -.10 (boys)

from home among boys similarly yielded the substantial correlation
of .31 ± .03 but a negative coefficient of -.16 among girls. Among
girls eight additional notations yielded substantial correlations
in the .30's but low or negligible coefficients ranging between
-.11 to .22 among boys: quarrelsomeness, emotional instability,
distractibility, question of change of personality, queer behavior,
mental conflict, worry over some specific fact, and question or
diagnosis of encephalitis.

Six behavior problems showed moderate correlations in the
.20's with destructiveness among both sexes: restlessness, egocentricity, truancy from school, inattentiveness in school, staying out late at night, and masturbation, and the three notations
for which only the boys' correlations were computed—swearing in
general, running with a gang, and complaining of bad treatment by
other children. Seven undesirable behavior traits among boys
showed moderate correlations in the .20's but low coefficients below .20 among girls: bossy manner, boastful or "show-off" manner,
sullenness, slovenliness, irresponsibility, "spoiled child," and
unpopularity. Among girls thirteen miscellaneous notations showed
moderate correlations in the .20's but low positive coefficients
below .20 among boys: temper display, selfishness, stubbornness,
bad companions, preference for younger children as playmates, "nervousness," nail-biting, restlessness in sleep, irregular sleep
habits, changeable moods or attitudes, repressed manner, staff notation of unfavorable conduct prognosis, and discord between parents.

There were four negative correlations with destructiveness,
all of moderate size in the -.20's: laziness and vicious home conditions among girls, victim of sex abuse by older child or person
(calculated for girls only), and feeble-minded sibling among boys.

Among girls the correlation of destructiveness with lack of

initiative could not be calculated because there were no instances
in which the same girls were noted as manifesting both problems.

Among the six sex notations there were several correlations
of statistically significant size: overinterest in the opposite
sex (calculated for girls only), .32 $\pm$ .06; masturbation, .29 $\pm$ .03
among boys and .29 $\pm$ .06 among girls; and victim of sex abuse by
older child or person, -.29 $\pm$ .07 (computed for girls only). The
other correlations in this field were low or negligible.

Among the seven physical or psychophysical notations the
only noteworthy correlation was the substantial coefficient of
.33 $\pm$ .10 for question or diagnosis of encephalitis among girls.

Among the four home or familial notations there were two
correlations of moderate size with destructiveness, both among
girls: .20 $\pm$ .06 with discord between parents and the curious negative correlation of -.26 $\pm$ .08 with vicious home conditions.

CHAPTER XL

TEASING OR "PICKING ON" OTHER CHILDREN

Teasing or "picking on" other children in our data ranged all the way from bullying or cruelty down to merely annoying or "pestering" other children. It was noted among 210 of 2,113 White boys, or 9.9 per cent. It was noted so seldom among the girls' cases that reliable correlation coefficients could not be computed for them.

Its bi-serial correlations with the personality-total and and conduct-total, .35 ± .02 and .41 ± .02 respectively, were substantial, but its tetrachoric correlation with police arrest was low, .14 ± .03 (Table 75).

TABLE 75

CORRELATIONS WITH "TEASING OTHER CHILDREN"
(Boys Only)

Personality-total . . . . .35 ± .02
Conduct-total . . . . .41 ± .02
Police arrest . . . . .14 ± .03

Larger Correlations (Positive)

Disturbing influence in school . . . . .45 ± .03
Violence . . . . .38 ± .04
Grouped: fighting, etc. . . . . .36 ± .03
Unpopular . . . . .35 ± .05
Boastful, "show-off" . . . . .34 ± .04
Destructive . . . . .34 ± .04
Quarrelsome . . . . .33 ± .04
Rude . . . . .30 ± .04
Grouped: "nervous," etc. . . . . .29 ± .03
Grouped: lack of interest in school, etc. . . . .28 ± .03
Restless . . . . .27 ± .03
Grouped: disobedient, etc. . . . . .27 ± .03
Grouped: swearing, etc. . . . . .27 ± .04
Bossy . . . . .26 ± .05
Inattentive in school . . . . .26 ± .03
Swearing (general) . . . . .26 ± .05
Spoiled child . . . . .26 ± .04
Disobedient . . . . .25 ± .03
Lying . . . . .25 ± .03
Worry over specific fact . . . . .25 ± .05

TABLE 75—Continued

Exclusion from school	.25 ± .04
Irregular sleep habits	.24 ± .05
Incorrigible	.23 ± .03
Fighting	.23 ± .05
Selfish	.23 ± .05
Excuse-forming	.23 ± .04
Grouped: temper, etc.	.23 ± .03
Grouped: egocentric, etc.	.23 ± .03
Leading others into bad conduct	.22 ± .05
Threatening violence	.22 ± .05
Smoking	.21 ± .04
Temper tantrums	.21 ± .04
Masturbation	.21 ± .03
Apprehensive	.21 ± .04
Restless in sleep	.21 ± .04
Conduct prognosis bad	.21 ± .06
Slovenly	.20 ± .04
Distractible	.20 ± .04
"Nervous"	.20 ± .04

Other Correlations (Positive to Negative)

Fantastical lying, .19; Overinterest in sex matters, .19; Question of change of personality, .19; Hatred or jealousy of sibling, .18; Absent-minded, .18; Egocentric, .18; Oversuggestible, .18; Complaining of bad treatment by other children, .18; Former convulsions, .18; Defiant, .17; Enuresis, .17; Inefficient in work, play, etc., .17; Stealing, .17; Stubborn, .17; Daydreaming, .17; Poor work in school, .17; Lack of interest in school, .16; Nail-biting, .16; Changeable moods, .16; Bad companions, .15; Irresponsible, .15; Lazy, .15; Sulky, .15; Temper display, .15; Irritable, .15; Vicious home conditions, .15; Staying out late at night, .14; Bashful, .14; Loitering, .13; Sullen, .13; Refusal to attend school, .12; Truancy from home, .12; Depressed, .12; Listless, .12; Sensitive over specific fact, .12; Inferiority feelings, .12; Popular, .12; Attractive manner, .12; Neurological defect, .12; Contrary, .11; Queer, .11; Headaches, .11; Discord between parents, .11; Grouped: sensitive or worrisome, etc., .11; Finicky food habits, .10; Grouped: depressed, etc., .10; Object of teasing, .09; Repressed, .09; Clean, .09; Preference for younger children, .07; Follower, .07; Leader, .07; Seclusive, .06; Sex denied entirely, .06; Crying spells, .05; Mental conflict, .05; Underweight, .05; Vocational guidance, .05; Unhappy, .04; Stuttering, .03; Grouped: dull, slow, etc., .03; Question of hypophrenia, .02; Truancy from school, .01; Sex delinquency (coitus), .01; Irregular attendance at school, -.00; Speech defect, -.01; Slow, dull, -.01; Sensitive (general), -.02; Psychoneurotic, -.02; Brother in penal detention, -.04; Question of encephalitis, -.04; Feeble-minded sibling, -.05; Lack of initiative, -.05; Immoral home conditions, -.07; Gang, -.08; Retardation in school, -.09; Emotional instability, -.13; Lues, -.14

Its highest correlation was with <u>disturbing influence in school</u>, .45 + .03. Six correlations of substantial size in the .30's were found for <u>violence</u>, <u>destructiveness</u>, <u>unpopularity</u>, <u>boastful or "show-off" manner</u>, <u>quarrelsomeness</u>, and <u>rudeness</u>. A large list of twenty-five notations showed moderate correlations in the .20's: <u>fighting</u>, <u>threatening violence</u>, <u>bossy manner</u>, <u>swearing in general</u>, <u>selfishness</u>, <u>incorrigibility</u>, <u>disobedience</u>, <u>temper tantrums</u>, <u>"spoiled child,"</u> <u>restlessness</u>, <u>restlessness in sleep</u>, <u>"nervousness,"</u> <u>irregular sleep habits</u>, <u>distractibility</u>, <u>apprehensiveness</u>, <u>leading others into bad conduct</u>, <u>smoking</u>, <u>excuse-forming attitude</u>, <u>exclusion from school</u>, <u>lying</u>, <u>worry over some specific fact</u>, <u>inattentiveness in school</u>, <u>slovenliness</u>, <u>masturbation</u>, and <u>staff notation of unfavorable conduct prognosis</u>.

Among the four sex notations for which boys' correlations were calculated there were only two coefficients worthy of note, for <u>masturbation</u>, .21 + .03, and for <u>overinterest in sex matters</u>, .19.

Among the seven physical or psychophysical notations and the four home or familial notations, all coefficients were low or negligible, ranging from -.14 to .15.

CHAPTER XLI

TEMPER TANTRUMS AND TEMPER DISPLAY

Since the rubric temper tantrums automatically includes temper display, it was not legitimate to calculate their intercorrelations. "Tantrums" characteristically applies to such bizarre behavior as throwing one's self on the floor, striking or biting one's self, or pounding one's head against the wall or floor. A comparison of their correlations with "outside" traits, as shown in the two tables in this chapter, indicates a considerable extent of similarity, but not enough to render unnecessary the separate statistical treatment of the two rubrics.

Both notations appeared with almost equal frequency among our cases. Of the two, temper tantrums appeared to be of greater "seriousness" or "ominousness."

Temper tantrums was noted among 221, or 10.5 per cent, of our 2,113 White boys and among 127, or 10.8 per cent, of our 1,181 White girls. Among girls its bi-serial correlations with the personality-total and conduct-total were both high, .54 $\pm$ .03 and .57 $\pm$ .03 respectively, while among boys these coefficients were substantial, the respective coefficients being .29 $\pm$ .02 and .38 $\pm$ .02 (Table 76). Its tetrachoric correlations with police arrest, however, were quite negligible.

Its highest correlations were with violence, the respective coefficients for boys and girls being .54 $\pm$ .03 and .61 $\pm$ .04, and with threatening violence, with a coefficient of .53 $\pm$ .04 among boys, the girls' correlation being omitted because of paucity of cases. Among girls defiant attitude and "nervousness" or restlessness (undifferentiated) also yielded high correlations in the .50's, with substantial coefficients in the .30's among boys.

Destructiveness and swearing or bad language (undifferentiated) yielded large correlations in the .40's for both sexes. Among girls four notations yielded large correlations in the .40's, with substantial coefficients in the .30's among boys: irritable

TABLE 76

CORRELATIONS WITH "TEMPER TANTRUMS"

	Boys	Girls
Personality-total.............................	.29 ± .02	.54 ± .03
Conduct-total.................................	.38 ± .02	.57 ± .03
Police arrest.................................	.08 ± .03	.03 ± .05
	Larger Correlations (Positive)	
Violence......................................	.54 ± .03	.61 ± .04 (1)*
Threatening violence..........................	.53 ± .04	....
Grouped: fighting, etc.......................	.49 ± .03	.54 ± .04 (2)
Destructive...................................	.46 ± .04	.45 ± .06 (7-8)
Grouped: swearing, etc.......................	.43 ± .03	.42 ± .05 (11)
Swearing (general)............................	.42 ± .04	....
Grouped: "nervous," etc......................	.32 ± .03	.52 ± .03 (3-5)
Grouped: disobedient, etc....................	.32 ± .03	.52 ± .03 (3-5)
Irritable.....................................	.32 ± .03	.43 ± .04 (9-10)
Defiant.......................................	.32 ± .04	.52 ± .03 (3-5)
Quarrelsome...................................	.31 ± .04	.38 ± .04 (22-24)
Fighting......................................	.31 ± .04	.45 ± .03 (7-8)
Incorrigible..................................	.30 ± .03	.47 ± .04 (6)
Rude..	.30 ± .04	.40 ± .04 (14-19)
Exclusion from school.........................	.26 ± .04	.37 ± .06 (25-26)
Unpopular.....................................	.26 ± .05	.35 ± .07 (28-29)
Contrary......................................	.25 ± .05	.29 ± .07 (40)
Bossy...	.25 ± .05	.24 ± .06 (48-50)
Changeable moods..............................	.24 ± .04	.29 ± .05 (20-21)
Stubborn......................................	.23 ± .03	.43 ± .04 (9-10)
Headaches.....................................	.23 ± .05	.16
Disobedient...................................	.23 ± .03	.35 ± .04 (28-29)
Egocentric....................................	.23 ± .08	.40 ± .05 (14-19)
Finicky food habits...........................	.22 ± .04	.31 ± .05 (35-36)
Irregular sleep habits........................	.22 ± .05	.24 ± .07 (48-50)
Lying...	.21 ± .03	.24 ± .04 (48-50)
Teasing other children........................	.21 ± .04	....
Emotional instability.........................	.21 ± .05	.34 ± .06 (30-33)
Boastful, "show-off"..........................	.20 ± .04	.40 ± .06 (14-19)
Enuresis......................................	.20 ± .03	.27 ± .04 (42-45)
Spoiled child.................................	.20 ± .04	.34 ± .05 (30-33)
Complaining of bad treatment by other children	.20 ± .05	....
Grouped: egocentric, etc.....................	.19	.41 ± .04 (12-13)
Disturbing influence in school................	.19	.41 ± .05 (12-13)
Leading others into bad conduct...............	.12	.40 ± .07 (14-19)
Question of change of personality.............	.19	.40 ± .06 (14-19)
Question of encephalitis......................	.04	.40 ± .07 (14-19)
Restless......................................	.16	.39 ± .04 (20-21)
Selfish.......................................	.12	.38 ± .06 (22-24)
Excuse-forming................................	.19	.38 ± .05 (22-24)

*Rank order of girls' correlations.

TABLE 76—Continued

	Boys	Girls
Queer	.19	.37 ± .06 (25-26)
Sulky	.15	.36 ± .06 (27)
Sullen	.09	.34 ± .05 (30-33)
Crying spells	.17	.34 ± .04 (30-33)
"Nervous"	.11	.32 ± .05 (34)
Depressed	.01	.31 ± .06 (35-36)
Overinterest in opposite sex	....	.30 ± .05 (37-39)
Distractible	.06	.30 ± .05 (37-39)
Mental conflict	.12	.30 ± .07 (37-39)
Masturbation	.16	.28 ± .05 (41)
Conduct prognosis bad	.14	.27 ± .07 (42-45)
Restless in sleep	.17	.27 ± .05 (42-45)
Psychoneurotic	.13	.27 ± .06 (42-45)
Grouped: lack of interest in school, etc.	.08	.26 ± .05 (46)
Truancy from school	.08	.25 ± .05 (47)
Grouped: depressed, etc.	.02	.23 ± .05 (51-52)
Staying out late at night	.16	.23 ± .05 (51-52)
Inattentive in school	.03	.22 ± .06 (53)
Neurological defect	.03	.21 ± .05 (54-59)
Stealing	.17	.21 ± .04 (54-59)
Slovenly	.08	.21 ± .05 (54-59)
Lack of interest in school	.09	.21 ± .06 (54-59)
Irresponsible	.01	.21 ± .06 (54-59)
Fantastical lying	.17	.21 ± .06 (54-59)

	Larger Correlations (Negative)	
Feeble-minded sibling	-.27 ± .05	-.14
Brother in penal detention	-.26 ± .05	-.17
Immoral home conditions	-.22 ± .05	-.03

Other Correlations (Positive to Negative)

Refusal to attend school, .19 and .17; Truancy from home, .17 and .16; Sensitive (general), .17 and .15; Former convulsions, .17 and -.09; Preference for younger children, .15 and .15; Nail-biting, .13 and .13; Loitering, .12 and .09; Smoking, .12 (boys); Daydreaming, .11 and .19; Grouped: sensitive or worrisome, etc., .10 and .17; Overinterest in sex matters, .10 and .10; Hatred or jealousy of sibling, .09 and .15; Object of teasing, .09 and .05; Sensitive over specific fact, .09 and .16; Inferiority feelings, .09 and .17; Popular, .07 and .16; Inefficient in work, play, etc., .06 and .18; Repressed, .06 and .18; Gang, .06 (boys); Lack of initiative, .05 and -.13; Leader, .05 and .10; Bad companions, .04 and .09; Lazy, .04 and .00; Speech defect, .04 and .01; Discord between parents, .04 and .03; Apprehensive, .03 and .17; Oversuggestible, .01 and .02; Seclusive, .01 and -.00; Unhappy, .01 and .14; Absent-minded, .00 and .04; Question of hypophrenia, .00 and .02; Clean, -.00 and .10; Victim of sex abuse, -.02 (girls); Underweight, -.02 and -.09; Vocational guidance, -.03 and .02; Lues, -.03 and .05; Attractive manner, -.03 and -.07; Bashful, -.03 and -.12; Irregular attendance at school, -.04 and .02; Listless, -.04 and .07; Stuttering, -.05 (boys); Retardation in school, -.06 and -.03; Sex delinquency (coitus), -.06 and .08; Grouped: dull, slow, etc., -.07 and -.00; Follower, -.07 and -.17;

TABLE 76—Continued

Worry over specific fact, -.07 and .11; Vicious home conditions, -.08 and .13;
Sex denied entirely, -.08 and .13; Poor work in school, -.09 and .05; Slow,
dull, -.14 and .05
        Omitted—Grouped: temper, etc.; Temper display

temperament, fighting, incorrigibility, and rudeness. Among girls
three additional notations yielded large correlations in the .40's,
with moderate correlations in the .20's among boys: stubbornness,
egocentricity, and boastful or "show-off" manner. Four additional
notations among girls similarly yielded large correlations in the
.40's but low positive coefficients below .20 among boys: disturbing influence in school, leading others into bad conduct, question
of change of personality, and question or diagnosis of encephalitis.
     Temper tantrums yielded substantial correlations in the
.30's with quarrelsomeness among both sexes and with overinterest
in the opposite sex, for which only the girls' correlation was calculated. Seven notations yielded substantial correlations in the
.30's among girls with moderate coefficients in the .20's among
boys: changeable moods or attitudes, emotional instability,
"spoiled child," disobedience, finicky food habits, unpopularity,
and exclusion from school. Among girls an additional eleven personality and conduct problems yielded substantial correlations in
the .30's but low positive coefficients below .20 among boys:
restlessness, "nervousness," distractibility, crying spells, mental conflict, selfishness, excuse-forming attitude, sulkiness,
sullenness, queer behavior, and depressed mood or spells.
     Five behavior problems showed moderate correlations in the
.20's with temper tantrums among both sexes: bossy manner, contrariness, lying, irregular sleep habits, and enuresis and also two
conduct problems for which only the boys' coefficients were calculated, teasing other children and complaining of bad treatment by
other children. Headaches among boys showed the moderate correlation of .23 ± .05 but a low positive coefficient of .16 among girls.
Among girls thirteen additional miscellaneous notations showed moderate correlations in the .20's but low positive coefficients below
.20 among boys: restlessness in sleep, psychoneurotic trends, fantastical lying, irresponsibility, inattentiveness in school, lack
of interest in school, slovenliness, truancy from school, stealing,

staying out late at night, masturbation, staff notation of unfavorable conduct prognosis, and neurological defect (unspecified).

Three negative correlations of moderate size in the -.20's
were found among the boys: feeble-minded sibling, brother in penal
detention, and immoral home conditions.

Among the six sex notations temper tantrums showed moderate
correlations of .28 + .05 with masturbation among girls and .30 +
.05 with overinterest in the opposite sex (calculated for girls
only).

Among the seven physical or psychophysical disabilities,
question or diagnosis of encephalitis among girls yielded the large
correlation of .40 + .07 and neurological defect (unspecified)
among girls the moderate correlation of .21 + .05. Enuresis showed
moderate correlations of .20 + .03 and .27 + .04 among boys and
girls respectively.

Among the four home or familial notations there were negative coefficients of moderate size in the -.20's among boys for
immoral home conditions and brother in penal detention.

Temper display (not "tantrums") was noted among 250, or
11.8 per cent, of our boys and among 93, or 7.9 per cent, of our
girls. Among boys its bi-serial correlation with the personality-
total, was of moderate size, .25 + .02, but all other correlations
among both sexes with the personality-total, conduct-total, and
police arrest were low, ranging from .06 to .19 (Table 77). One
may conclude that temper display is of minor importance as an indicator of behavior difficulties.

Its highest correlations (in the .40's) were found among
girls for disobedience or incorrigibility (including defiant attitude, stubbornness, and contrariness, undifferentiated), and irritable temperament, the boys' coefficients also being substantial,
.28 + .03 and .30 + .03 respectively.

Fighting yielded substantial correlations in the .30's
among both sexes. Violence yielded the substantial correlation of
.39 + .03 among boys, and a moderate coefficient of .26 + .06 among
girls. Among girls four conduct problems yielded substantial correlations in the .30's, with moderate coefficients in the .20's
among boys: quarrelsomeness, stubbornness, bossy manner, and
swearing or bad language (undifferentiated). Among girls an

TABLE 77

CORRELATIONS WITH "TEMPER DISPLAY"

	Boys	Girls
Personality-total............................	.25 ± .02	.16 ± .04
Conduct-total................................	.19 ± .02	.08 ± .04
Police arrest................................	.06 ± .03	.06 ± .05
	Larger Correlations (Positive)	
Grouped: fighting, etc.......................	.42 ± .03	.35 ± .05 (5-6)*
Violence.....................................	.39 ± .03	.26 ± .06 (20-21)
Fighting.....................................	.34 ± .03	.30 ± .04 (11-13)
Irritable....................................	.30 ± .03	.42 ± .05 (2)
Threatening violence.........................	.28 ± .05	....
Grouped: disobedient, etc....................	.28 ± .03	.49 ± .04 (1)
Changeable moods.............................	.27 ± .04	.27 ± .06 (18-19)
Quarrelsome..................................	.26 ± .04	.31 ± .05 (10)
Grouped: "nervous," etc......................	.25 ± .03	.30 ± .04 (11-13)
Stubborn.....................................	.25 ± .03	.34 ± .05 (7)
Contrary.....................................	.25 ± .05	.24 ± .08 (22)
Emotional instability........................	.23 ± .04	.00
Selfish......................................	.23 ± .05	.28 ± .04 (17)
Grouped: swearing, etc.......................	.22 ± .04	.37 ± .06 (4)
Bossy..	.22 ± .05	.30 ± .06 (11-13)
Object of teasing............................	.21 ± .04	.19
Grouped: egocentric, etc.....................	.20 ± .03	.19
Former convulsions...........................	.20 ± .04	.10
Unhappy......................................	.20 ± .05	.02
Inferiority feelings.........................	.20 ± .04	.09
Swearing (general)..........................	.20 ± .05	....
Sulky..	.20 ± .05	.29 ± .07 (14-16)
Hatred or jealousy of sibling................	.15	.39 ± .07 (3)
Lazy...	.11	.35 ± .06 (5-6)
Rude...	.17	.33 ± .05 (8-9)
Incorrigible.................................	.16	.33 ± .05 (8-9)
Defiant......................................	.17	.29 ± .06 (14-16)
Irresponsible................................	-.02	.29 ± .07 (14-16)
Lying..	.18	.27 ± .05 (18-19)
Restless in sleep............................	.17	.26 ± .06 (20-21)
Finicky food habits..........................	.18	.23 ± .06 (23-24)
Destructive..................................	.19	.23 ± .07 (23-24)
Fantastical lying............................	.06	.22 ± .07 (25)
Sullen.......................................	.15	.21 ± .06 (26-27)
Excuse-forming...............................	.12	.21 ± .06 (26-27)
Truancy from home............................	.10	.20 ± .05 (28-29)
Staying out late at night....................	.05	.20 ± .06 (28-29)
	Larger Correlations (Negative)	
Feeble-minded sibling........................	.02	-.31 ± .06

*Rank order of girls' correlations.

TABLE 77—Continued

	Boys	Girls
Mental conflict................................	.00	-.26 ± .08
Repressed......................................	-.11	-.24 ± .08
Vocational guidance............................	-.06	-.22 ± .05
Question of encephalitis.......................	.14	-.21 ± .09
Victim of sex abuse...........................	....	-.21 ± .06
		Not Calculable
Vicious home conditions.......................	.05	(n.c.)

Other Correlations (Positive to Negative)

Disobedient, .19 and .19; Absent-minded, .19 and -.09; Queer, .18 and -.14; "Nervous," .18 and .03; Egocentric, .18 and .07; Boastful, "show-off," .17 and .08; Disturbing influence in school, .17 and .12; Refusal to attend school, .16 and .05; Crying spells, .16 and .15; Unpopular, .16 and .10; Headaches, .15 and .02; Distractible, .15 and -.03; Question of change of personality, .15 and .09; Teasing other children, .15 (boys); Enuresis, .15 and .10; Restless, .14 and .13; Conduct prognosis bad, .13 and -.05; Nail-biting, .12 and .11; Stealing, .12 and .13; Grouped: depressed, etc., .12 and .14; Truancy from school, .11 and .09; Slovenly, .10 and .04; Smoking, .10 (boys); Sensitive over specific fact, .10 and .07; Worry over specific fact, .10 and .03; Discord between parents, .10 and .11; Leader, .10 and .14; Exclusion from school, .10 and .03; Complaining of bad treatment by other children, .09 (boys); Depressed, .09 and .17; Inattentive in school, .09 and .01; Oversuggestible, .08 and -.02; Seclusive, .08 and -.07; Clean, .08 and .06; Speech defect, .07 and .02; Neurological defect, .07 and .04; Question of hypophrenia, .07 and -.06; Spoiled child, .07 and .09; Irregular sleep habits, .07 and .05; Loitering, .07 and .15; Bad companions, .06 and .03; Masturbation, .06 and -.07; Apprehensive, .06 and .02; Daydreaming, .06 and .14; Poor work in school, .06 and -.04; Lues, .06 and -.08; Brother in penal detention, .06 and -.08; Grouped: sensitive or worrisome, etc. .06 and .10; Grouped: dull, slow, etc., .05 and .03; Under weight, .05 and -.05; Retardation in school, .04 and -.04; Immoral home conditions, .03 and -.08; Irregular attendance at school, .03 and .09; Grouped: lack of interest in school, etc., .03 and .01; Follower, .03 and .10; Psychoneurotic, .02 and -.00; Stuttering, .02 (boys); Attractive manner, .01 and .02; Gang, .01 (boys); Bashful, -.00 and .04; Sex delinquency (coitus), -.00 and -.09; Overinterest in opposite sex, -.01 (girls); Lack of interest in school, -.01 and .00; Listless, -.01 and -.07; Lack of initiative, -.02 and -.12; Overinterest in sex matters, -.03 and -.11; Popular, -.04 and -.06; Preference for younger children, -.04 and .19; Sensitive (general), -.04 and .05; Inefficient in work, play, etc., -.04 and .17; Sex denied entirely, -.05 and -.14; Slow, dull, -.06 and .07; Leading others into bad conduct, -.13 and .10
        Omitted—Grouped: temper, etc.; Temper tantrums

additional four conduct problems similarly yielded substantial cor relations in the .30's but low positive coefficients below .20 among boys: incorrigibility, hatred or jealousy of sibling, lazi ness, and rudeness.

Five behavior difficulties showed consistently moderate
correlations in the .20's with temper display: changeable moods
or attitudes, contrariness, selfishness, sulkiness, and (calculated for boys only) threatening violence. Among boys five miscellaneous notations showed moderate correlations in the .20's
but low positive coefficients below .20 among girls: emotional
instability, unhappiness, inferiority feelings, object of teasing
by other children, and former convulsions. Eleven behavior problems among girls showed moderate correlations in the .20's but
low coefficients below .20 among boys: destructiveness, defiant
attitude, restlessness in sleep, sullenness, excuse-forming attitude, lying, fantastical lying, truancy from home, staying out
late at night, finicky food habits, and irresponsibility.

There were six negative correlations of moderate size,
ranging from -.31 down to -.21, all among girls: feeble-minded
sibling, mental conflict, repressed manner, "request for vocational guidance," question or diagnosis of encephalitis, and
(calculated for girls only) victim of sex abuse by older child or
person.

Among the six sex notations there was only one correlation of statistically significant size, -.21 ± .06 with victim
of sex abuse by older child or person (calculated for girls
only).

Among the seven physical or psychophysical notations all
correlations were low or negligible, except the doubtfully significant negative coefficient of -.21 ± .09 with question or diagnosis of encephalitis among girls.

Among the four home or familial notations all correlations
were low or negligible.

A "larger grouping" was made of the three similar notations, temper tantrums (Table 76), temper display (Table 77), and
irritable temperament (Table 47, p. 274).[1] The resulting populations were 736, or 34.8 per cent, of our 2,113 White boys and 312,
or 26.4 per cent, of our 1,181 White girls. This broader grouping

---

[1]The reasons for this broader grouping were given in I, 44; see 86,
Table 13, Item C.

thus comprises one of the most frequent of behavior problems reported among our cases. The resulting coefficients (Table 78) were usually larger than those computed upon the more restricted rubrics.

It will suffice to summarize the coefficients for this larger grouping, temper tantrums or display (including irritable temperament, undifferentiated), briefly.

Four notations consistently yielded large or high coefficients ranging from .43 to .57: violence, swearing or bad language (undifferentiated), and the two notations for which only the boys' coefficients were calculated, threatening violence and swearing in general.

Thirteen notations yielded substantial or large correlations in the .30's and .40's among both sexes: fighting, quarrelsomeness, destructiveness, stubbornness, defiant attitude, contrariness, bossy manner, selfishness, question of change of personality, changeable moods or attitudes, "nervousness," crying spells and question or diagnosis of encephalitis.

Twenty behavior problems among both sexes yielded moderate to high correlations ranging from the .20's to the .40's: incorrigibility, disobedience, disturbing influence in school, exclusion from school, lying, fantastical lying, egocentricity, rudeness, sullenness, sulkiness, "spoiled child," hatred or jealousy of sibling, excuse-forming attitude, restlessness, restlessness in sleep, irregular sleep habits, finicky food habits, staff notation of emotional instability, queer behavior, and unpopularity and the two notations for which only the boys' correlations were computed—teasing other children and smoking.

Among the six sex notations there was one correlation of significant size, .20 $\pm$ .04 with overinterest in the opposite sex among girls, the boys' coefficient not being calculated because of paucity of cases.

Among the seven physical or psychophysical disabilities, question or diagnosis of encephalitis yielded the substantial coefficients of .31 $\pm$ .04 and .33 $\pm$ .06 for boys and girls respectively. Enuresis among girls yielded the substantial correlation of .31 $\pm$ .03. Neurological defect (unspecified) among girls showe the moderate correlation of .24 $\pm$ .04.

Among the four home or familial notations the only

TABLE 78

CORRELATIONS WITH "GROUPED: TEMPER, ETC."

	Boys	Girls
Personality-total...........................	.36 ± .02	.42 ± .02
Conduct-total...............................	.39 ± .02	.50 ± .02
Police arrest...............................	.09 ± .03	-.06 ± .04
	Larger Correlations (Positive)	
Threatening violence........................	.57 ± .03	....
Violence....................................	.52 ± .02	.57 ± .04 (2)*
Grouped: fighting, etc.....................	.50 ± .02	.58 ± .03 (1)
Swearing (general)..........................	.43 ± .03	....
Grouped: swearing, etc.....................	.43 ± .03	.43 ± .04 (10-11)
Changeable moods............................	.39 ± .03	.43 ± .04 (10-11)
Grouped: "nervous," etc....................	.38 ± .02	.47 ± .03 (6)
Grouped: disobedient, etc.................	.36 ± .02	.53 ± .03 (3)
Fighting....................................	.36 ± .03	.48 ± .03 (4-5)
Emotional instability.......................	.36 ± .04	.28 ± .05 (39-41)
Destructive.................................	.34 ± .03	.36 ± .05 (23-26)
Stubborn....................................	.34 ± .03	.40 ± .03 (13-15)
Defiant.....................................	.33 ± .03	.44 ± .04 (8-9)
Question of change of personality...........	.33 ± .04	.38 ± .07 (17-21)
Contrary....................................	.32 ± .04	.38 ± .05 (17-21)
Quarrelsome.................................	.32 ± .03	.48 ± .03 (4-5)
Bossy.......................................	.31 ± .04	.36 ± .04 (23-26)
Selfish.....................................	.31 ± .03	.39 ± .05 (16)
Question of encephalitis....................	.31 ± .04	.33 ± .06 (29-30)
Grouped: egocentric, etc..................	.30 ± .03	.36 ± .04 (23-26)
Crying spells...............................	.30 ± .04	.38 ± .03 (17-21)
"Nervous"...................................	.30 ± .03	.34 ± .04 (27-28)
Incorrigible................................	.27 ± .02	.45 ± .03 (7)
Rude..	.27 ± .03	.44 ± .03 (8-9)
Egocentric..................................	.27 ± .03	.31 ± .04 (33-34)
Restless....................................	.27 ± .03	.40 ± .03 (13-15)
Queer.......................................	.26 ± .04	.21 ± .05 (50-52)
Finicky food habits.........................	.26 ± .03	.42 ± .04 (12)
Disobedient.................................	.25 ± .03	.32 ± .04 (31-32)
Excuse-forming..............................	.25 ± .03	.30 ± .04 (35-37)
Unpopular...................................	.25 ± .04	.38 ± .05 (17-21)
Lying.......................................	.24 ± .02	.27 ± .03 (42-43)
Disturbing influence in school..............	.24 ± .03	.40 ± .04 (13-15)
Fantastical lying...........................	.23 ± .03	.28 ± .05 (39-41)
Teasing other children......................	.23 ± .03	....
Sulky.......................................	.23 ± .04	.36 ± .05 (23-26)
Exclusion from school.......................	.22 ± .03	.20 ± .05 (53-57)
Restless in sleep...........................	.22 ± .03	.37 ± .04 (22)
Smoking.....................................	.22 ± .03	....
Stealing....................................	.21 ± .02	.12

*Rank order of girls' correlations.

TABLE 78—Continued

	Boys	Girls
Hatred or jealousy of sibling................	.21 ± .04	.33 ± .05 (29-30)
Spoiled child................................	.21 ± .03	.27 ± .04 (42-43)
Irregular sleep habits......................	.20 ± .04	.25 ± .05 (44)
Absent-minded...............................	.20 ± .04	.02
Sullen......................................	.20 ± .03	.34 ± .04 (27-28)
Former convulsions..........................	.20 ± .03	.02
Boastful, "show-off"........................	.16	.38 ± .04 (17-21)
Leading others into bad conduct.............	.06	.32 ± .05 (31-32)
Enuresis....................................	.16	.31 ± .03 (33-34)
Depressed...................................	.12	.30 ± .06 (35-37)
Irresponsible...............................	.12	.30 ± .05 (35-37)
Leader......................................	.12	.29 ± .05 (38)
Distractible................................	.19	.28 ± .04 (39-41)
Neurological defect.........................	.10	.24 ± .04 (45)
Inefficient in work, play, etc.............	.09	.23 ± .05 (46)
Inferiority feelings.......................	.18	.22 ± .05 (47-49)
Lazy..	.12	.22 ± .05 (47-49)
Grouped: depressed, etc....................	.15	.22 ± .04 (47-49)
Daydreaming.................................	.12	.21 ± .05 (50-52)
Preference for younger children............	.09	.21 ± .05 (50-52)
Psychoneurotic..............................	.18	.20 ± .05 (53-57)
Overinterest in opposite sex...............	....	.20 ± .05 (53-57)
Staying out late at night..................	.10	.20 ± .04 (53-57)
Grouped: lack of interest in school, etc..	.10	.20 ± .04 (53-57)
	Larger Correlations (Negative)	
Brother in penal detention.................	-.08	-.22 ± .05
Lack of initiative.........................	.09	-.20 ± .05

Other Correlations (Positive to Negative)

Headaches, .19 and .19; Nail-biting, .17 and .19; Truancy from home, .17 and .11; Complaining of bad treatment by other children, .17 (boys); Conduct prognosis bad, .16 and .10; Refusal to attend school, .15 and .08; Grouped: sensitive or worrisome, etc., .14 and .18; Masturbation, .14 and .11; Object of teasing, .14 and .18; Sensitive (general), .14 and .18; Unhappy, .14 and .07; Loitering, .13 and .11; Worry over specific fact, .12 and .17; Mental conflict, .11 and .09; Truancy from school, .11 and .15; Slovenly, .11 and .11; Lack of interest in school, .11 and .17; Listless, .10 and -.00; Seclusive, .09 and .02; Apprehensive, .09 and .08; Speech defect, .09 and .03; Discord between parents, .08 and .08; Gang, .08 (boys); Sensitive over specific fact, .08 and .09; Lues, .06 and .03; Bad companions, .06 and .02; Inattentive in school, .06 and .14; Overinterest in sex matters, .06 and .05; Bashful, .06 and .00; Popular, .06 and .12; Follower, .06 and -.02; Clean, .05 and .12; Oversuggestible, .04 and -.04; Question of hypophrenia, .02 and .02; Poor work in school, .01 and .04; Underweight, .01 and .00; Grouped: dull, slow, etc., -.01 and -.00; Sex delinquency (coitus), -.01 and -.09; Vicious home conditions, -.03 and -.13; Retardation in school, -.03 and -.05; Vocational guidance, -.06 and .10; Attractive manner, -.06 and -.02; Stuttering, -.06 (boys); Repressed, -.07 and .07; Slow, dull, -.07 and .06; Irregular attendance at school, -.08 and -.01; Feeble-

TABLE 78—Continued

minded sibling, -.11 and -.17; Victim of sex abuse, -.15 (girls); Immoral home
conditions, -.16 and -.16; Sex denied entirely, -.16 and .04
          Omitted—Temper display; Temper tantrums; Irritable

significant coefficient was the negative correlation of -.22 $\pm$ .05
with brother in penal detention among girls.

CHAPTER XLII

SWEARING AND BAD LANGUAGE

In the original indexing of the behavior problems and
"reasons for referral" among the children examined consecutively
in the behavior clinic at the Illinois Institute for Juvenile Research during the years 1923-27,[1] separate categories were set up
for swearing or cursing in general; obscene, indecent, or suggestive language; profane, bad, or vile language (not including obscene language); and swearing at mother, stepmother, teacher, matron, etc., or "calling them names";[2] but these items were noted
so infrequently that in spite of their clinical importance it was
possible to calculate coefficients for only two categories—swearing in general among boys and swearing or bad language (including
the four categories undifferentiated) among both sexes. These notations were important as indicators of conduct deviation, the
girls' correlations being especially high, and, to a lesser extent,
of personality deviation. As indicators of "juvenile delinquency,"
as measured by the correlations with police arrest, their significance was only moderate or low.

Swearing in general was noted among 137 of our 2,113 White
boys, or 6.5 per cent. Among our 1,181 White girls it was noted
in only 37 instances, too few to justify correlational treatment.
With the conduct-total its bi-serial r was high, .51 $\pm$ .02. With
the personality-total its correlation was substantial, .30 $\pm$ .03.
With police arrest its tetrachoric r was low, .17 $\pm$ .04 (Table 79).
Swearing in general yielded large correlations in the .40's
with the three notations temper tantrums, smoking, and violence.
With six conduct problems it yielded substantial correlations in
the .30's: incorrigibility, fighting, threatening violence,

_____

[1] Vol. I, chap. 1.
[2] Ibid., pp. 57-68, Table 3, Items 179, 195, 200, and 223.

TABLE 79

CORRELATIONS WITH "SWEARING (GENERAL)"
(Boys Only)

Personality-total . . . . .30 ± .03
Conduct-total . . . . .51 ± .02
Police arrest . . . . .17 ± .04

Larger Correlations (Positive)

Grouped: temper, etc. . . . . .43 ± .03
Temper tantrums . . . . .42 ± .04
Grouped: fighting, etc. . . . . .41 ± .03
Smoking .41 ± .04
Violence .40 ± .04
Rude . . . . .38 ± .04
Lying . . . . .37 ± .03
Incorrigible . . . . .36 ± .04
Grouped: disobedient, etc. . . . . .34 ± .03
Stealing .33 ± .03
Fighting .32 ± .04
Threatening violence . . . . .32 ± .06
Defiant . . . . .29 ± .05
Leading others into bad conduct . . . . .29 ± .05
Truancy from home . . . . .29 ± .04
Exclusion from school . . . . .29 ± .05
Disturbing influence in school . . . . .27 ± .04
Destructive . . . . .26 ± .05
Disobedient . . . . .26 ± .04
Teasing other children . . . . .26 ± .05
Excuse-forming . . . . .26 ± .04
Unpopular .26 ± .06
Quarrelsome . . . . .25 ± .04
Grouped: "nervous," etc. . . . . .24 ± .03
Queer . . . . .24 ± .06
Irritable .24 ± .04
Masturbation . . . . .24 ± .04
Refusal to attend school. . . . . .24 ± .05
Staying out late at night . . . . .23 ± .04
Truancy from school . . . . .22 ± .04
Overinterest in sex matters . . . . .21 ± .06
Sullen . . . . .21 ± .05
Inferiority feelings . . . . .20 ± .05
Temper display . . . . .20 ± .05
Stubborn . . . . .20 ± .04
Enuresis . . . . .20 ± .04
Contrary . . . . .20 ± .06

Larger Correlations (Negative)

Lack of initiative . . . . -.29 ± .03

Other Correlations (Positive to Negative)

Bad companions, .19; "Nervous," .18; Conduct prognosis bad, .18; Nail-biting, .18; Loitering, .18; Restless, .17; Mental conflict, .17; Grouped: depressed, etc., .16;

TABLE 79—Continued

Former convulsions, .16; Unhappy, .16; Grouped: egocentric, etc., .16; Complaining of bad treatment by other children, .16; Irregular sleep habits, .16; Egocentric, .16; Hatred or jealousy of sibling, .16; Fantastical lying, .16; Question of encephalitis, .15; Boastful, "show-off," .14; Bossy, .14; Gang, .14; Sulky, .14; Changeable moods, .14; Question of change of personality, .14; Crying spells, .14; Distractible, .14; Object of teasing, .14; Discord between parents, .14; Neurological defect, .13; Oversuggestible, .13; Lazy, .13; Finicky food habits, .13; Selfish, .12; Restless in sleep, .12; Depressed, .11; Slovenly, .10; Leader, .10; Question of hypophrenia, .09; Absent-minded, .09; Spoiled child, .08; Emotional instability, .08; Lack of interest in school, .08; Sex delinquency (coitus), .07; Daydreaming, .07; Grouped: lack of interest in school, etc., .07; Vicious home conditions, .06; Apprehensive, .06; Retardation in school, .05; Inefficient in work, play, etc., .04; Follower, .04; Headaches, .04; Brother in penal detention, .03; Popular, .03; Sensitive over specific fact, .03; Poor work in school, .02; Attractive manner, .02; Vocational guidance, .02; Preference for younger children, .01; Psychoneurotic, .01; Slow, dull, .01; Irresponsible, .01; Inattentive in school, .01; Lues, .00; Grouped: dull, slow, etc., -.01; Grouped: sensitive or worrisome, etc., -.01; Listless, -.02; Sensitive (general), -.02; Repressed, -.03; Seclusive, -.03; Clean, -.06; Speech defect, -.07; Underweight, - 07; Stuttering, -.07; Bashful, -.08; Feeble-minded sibling, -.08; Irregular attendance at school, -.10; Sex denied entirely, -.10; Worry over specific fact, -.11; Immoral home conditions, -.12
Omitted—Grouped: swearing, etc.

rudeness, lying, and stealing. A large list of twenty-four conduct and personality problems showed moderate correlations in the .20's: defiant attitude, disobedience, stubbornness, contrariness, quarrelsomeness, teasing other children, temper display, irritable temperament, destructiveness, truancy from home, staying out late at night, truancy from school, refusal to attend school, disturbing influence in school, exclusion from school, leading others into bad conduct, sullenness, excuse-forming attitude, unpopularity, inferiority feelings, queer behavior, masturbation, overinterest in sex matters, and enuresis.

The only negative correlation with swearing in general was for lack of initiative, -.29 ± .03.

Among the four sex notations for which the boys' correlations were computed moderate correlations in the .20's were found for masturbation and overinterest in sex matters.

Among the seven physical or psychophysical disabilities the

only statistically significant correlation was with <u>enuresis</u>, .20
± .04.

   With the four home or familial notations the correlations
with <u>swearing in general</u> were low or negligible.

   The broader grouping, <u>swearing or bad language</u> (undifferentiated), was made up of the four categories described above: <u>swear-
ing or cursing in general</u>; <u>obscene, indecent, or suggestive lan-
guage</u>; <u>profane, bad, or vile language</u> (not including <u>obscene lan-
guage</u>); and <u>swearing at mother, stepmother, teacher, matron, etc.,
or "calling them names."</u> It was noted among 278, or 13.2 per cent,
of our 2,113 White boys and among 90, or 7.6 per cent, of our 1,181
White girls.

   Among girls its unusually high bi-serial correlation of .76
± .02 was one of the three highest of the girls' correlations found
with <u>conduct-total</u> (Table 7, p. 98), and among boys its very high
coefficient of .61 ± .02 was the highest of all the boys' correlations found with <u>conduct-total</u>. Its correlation with <u>personality-
total</u> among girls was large, .43 ± .03, and among boys also substantial, .33 ± .02. With <u>police arrest</u> its respective tetrachoric
<u>r</u>'s for boys and girls were moderate or low, .23 ± .03 and .18 ±
.05 (Table 80).

TABLE 80

CORRELATIONS WITH "GROUPED: SWEARING, ETC."

	Boys	Girls
Personality-total.............................	.33 ± .02	.43 ± .03
Conduct-total.................................	.61 ± .02	.76 ± .02
Police arrest.................................	.23 ± .03	.18 ± .05
	Larger Correlations (Positive)	
Grouped: fighting, etc.......................	.47 ± .03	.60 ± .04 (2)*
Rude..	.45 ± .03	.50 ± .05 (5)
Violence......................................	.44 ± .03	.64 ± .05 (1)
Grouped: temper, etc.........................	.43 ± .03	.43 ± .04 (10-12)
Destructive...................................	.43 ± .03	.44 ± .07 (8-9)
Temper tantrums...............................	.43 ± .03	.42 ± .05 (13-14)

*Rank order of girls' correlations.

TABLE 80—Continued

	Boys	Girls
Threatening violence	.43 ± .04	....
Grouped: disobedient, etc.	.41 ± .03	.46 ± .04 (7)
Incorrigible	.40 ± .03	.52 ± .04 (4)
Contrary	.37 ± .05	.32 ± .07 (33-37)
Smoking	.37 ± .04	
Defiant	.36 ± .04	.34 ± .06 (28-30)
Fighting	.35 ± .03	.54 ± .03 (3)
Disobedient	.34 ± .03	.36 ± .05 (25)
Sullen	.34 ± .04	.19
Quarrelsome	.33 ± .03	.43 ± .05 (10-12)
Stealing	.33 ± .03	.44 ± .04 (8-9)
Disturbing influence in school	.32 ± .03	.41 ± .06 (15-17)
Overinterest in sex matters	.32 ± .05	.32 ± .06 (33-37)
Unpopular	.31 ± .05	.42 ± .07 (13-14)
Staying out late at night	.31 ± .03	.48 ± .05 (6)
Lying	.31 ± .03	.41 ± .04 (15-17)
Excuse-forming	.30 ± .04	.41 ± .06 (15-17)
Exclusion from school	.29 ± .04	.39 ± .06 (18-20)
Irritable	.28 ± .03	.23 ± .05 (59-62)
Teasing other children	.27 ± .04	....
Hatred or jealousy of sibling	.27 ± .07	.25 ± .07 (52-56)
Conduct prognosis bad	.26 ± .05	.31 ± .08 (38-40)
Truancy from school	.26 ± .03	.34 ± .05 (28-30)
Grouped: "nervous," etc.	.26 ± .03	.23 ± .04 (59-62)
Irregular sleep habits	.25 ± .04	.35 ± .07 (26-27)
Loitering	.24 ± .04	.30 ± .07 (41-42)
Leading others into bad conduct	.24 ± .04	.43 ± .07 (10-12)
Truancy from home	.23 ± .03	.33 ± .05 (31-32)
Complaining of bad treatment by other children	.23 ± .05	....
Egocentric	.23 ± .04	.20 ± .06 (65-67)
Temper display	.22 ± .04	.37 ± .06 (22-24)
Queer	.21 ± .05	.33 ± .07 (31-32)
Stubborn	.21 ± .03	.25 ± .05 (52-56)
Grouped: egocentric, etc.	.21 ± .03	.16
Lazy	.21 ± .04	.14
Fantastical lying	.21 ± .03	.32 ± .07 (33-37)
Boastful, "show-off"	.21 ± .04	.31 ± .07 (38-40)
Bad companions	.21 ± .03	.27 ± .06 (45-46)
Bossy	.20 ± .05	.34 ± .06 (28-30)
Slovenly	.20 ± .03	.23 ± .05 (59-62)
Masturbation	.20 ± .03	.26 ± .06 (47-51)
Restless	.20 ± .03	.31 ± .05 (38-40)
Unhappy	.20 ± .05	.32 ± .07 (33-37)
Grouped: lack of interest in school, etc.	.07	.39 ± .05 (18-20)
Question of encephalitis	.10	.39 ± .08 (18-20)
Changeable moods	.16	.38 ± .05 (21)
Question of change of personality	.19	.37 ± .07 (22-24)
Lack of interest in school	.10	.37 ± .06 (22-24)
Vicious home conditions	.05	.35 ± .07 (26-27)
Overinterest in opposite sex	....	.32 ± .05 (33-37)
Headaches	.06	.30 ± .06 (41-42)
Inattentive in school	.02	.29 ± .07 (43)
Enuresis	.15	.28 ± .05 (44)

TABLE 80—Continued

	Boys	Girls
Victim of sex abuse	....	.27 ± .06 (45-46)
Finicky food habits	.09	.26 ± .06 (47-51)
Restless in sleep	.12	.26 ± .06 (47-51)
Object of teasing	.17	.26 ± .06 (47-51)
Emotional instability	.11	.26 ± .07 (47-51)
Mental conflict	.11	.25 ± .08 (52-56)
Distractible	.13	.25 ± .06 (52-56)
Irregular attendance at school	.08	.25 ± .06 (52-56)
Refusal to attend school	.17	.24 ± .08 (57-58)
Crying spells	.08	.24 ± .05 (57-58)
Grouped: depressed, etc.	.17	.23 ± .06 (59-62)
Daydreaming	.09	.22 ± .06 (63)
Selfish	.11	.21 ± .04 (64)
Sex delinquency (coitus)	.05	.20 ± .05 (65-67)
Apprehensive	.01	.20 ± .06 (64-67)
	Larger Correlations (Negative)	
Lack of initiative	-.13	-.29 ± .07

Other Correlations (Positive to Negative)

Inferiority feelings, .17 and -.04; Gang, .16 (boys); Irresponsible, .16 and .08; Discord between parents, .16 and .15; Nail-biting, .15 and .16; Sulky, .15 and .06; Spoiled child, .13 and .02; Oversuggestible, .12 and .07; Depressed, .12 and .07; Inefficient in work, play, etc., .12 and .10; Neurological defect, .11 and .12; "Nervous," .11 and .07; Worry over specific fact, .10 and .19; Former convulsions, .08 and -.00; Sensitive over specific fact, .07 and .15; Seclusive, .06 and .10; Leader, .06 and .09; Absent-minded, .06 and .04; Preference for younger children, .04 and .12; Attractive manner, .04 and .09; Immoral home conditions, .04 and .14; Grouped: sensitive or worrisome, etc., .03 and .09; Repressed, .03 and .10; Clean, .02 and -.03; Sensitive (general), .01 and -.04; Stuttering, .00 (boys); Poor work in school, .00 and .03; Popular, -.00 and .01; Underweight, -.00 and .01; Question of hypophrenia, -.01 and .03; Psychoneurotic, -.01 and .10; Brother in penal detention, -.02 and .08; Listless, -.02 and .05; Retardation in school, -.03 and .06; Follower, -.04 and -.03; Sex denied entirely, -.05 and .03; Vocational guidance, -.05 and -.19; Grouped: dull, slow, etc., -.06 and .01; Slow, dull, -.06 and .03; Bashful, -.07 and -.11; Lues, -.09 and .13; Feeble-minded sibling, -.16 and .01; Speech defect, -.16 and -.04
Omitted—Swearing in general

Its highest correlation was with <u>violence</u>, among girls, .64 ± .05, the corresponding coefficient for boys also being large, .44 ± .03. <u>Fighting</u> among girls yielded the high correlation of .54 ± .03, the boys' coefficient, .35 ± .03, also being substantial. Five conduct problems yielded large correlations ranging

from .40 to .52 among both sexes: temper tantrums, incorrigibility, rudeness, destructiveness, and (calculated for boys only)
threatening violence. Among girls seven undesirable behavior
traits yielded large correlations in the .40's with corresponding
substantial coefficients in the .30's among boys: quarrelsomeness,
disturbing influence in school, stealing, staying out late at
night, lying, excuse-forming attitude, and unpopularity. Leading
others into bad conduct also yielded the high correlation of .43
± .07 among girls but a moderate coefficient of .24 ± .04 among
boys.

Four behavior difficulties yielded substantial correlations
in the .30's among both sexes: disobedience, defiant attitude,
contrariness, and overinterest in sex matters. Two traits, smoking (calculated for boys only) and overinterest in the opposite
sex (calculated for girls only), also yielded substantial correlations in the .30's. Sullenness among boys yielded a substantial
correlation of .34 ± .04 but a low coefficient of .19 among girls.
Among girls thirteen conduct and personality traits yielded substantial correlations in the .30's with moderate corresponding coefficients in the .20's for boys: temper display, boastful or
"show-off" manner, bossy manner, restlessness, irregular sleep
habits, truancy from home, truancy from school, exclusion from
school, loitering or wandering, fantastical lying, queer behavior,
unhappiness, and staff notation of unfavorable conduct prognosis.
Six notations among girls similarly yielded substantial correlations in the .30's but low positive correlations below .20 among
boys: changeable moods or attitudes, question of change of personality, lack of interest in school, question or diagnosis of encephalitis, headaches, and vicious (not "immoral") home conditions.
Seven undesirable behavior problems showed moderate correlations in the .20's with swearing or bad language (undifferentiated) among both sexes: irritable temperament, stubbornness, egocentricity, hatred or jealousy of sibling, bad companions, slovenliness, and masturbation. Similar moderate correlations were found
for two traits for which only the boys' coefficients were calculated—teasing other children and complaining of bad treatment by
other children—and (calculated for girls only) victim of sex abuse
by older child or person. Among girls sixteen notations showed
moderate correlations in the .20's but corresponding low coeffi-

cients below .20 among boys: restlessness in sleep, emotional instability, distractibility, refusal to attend school, irregular
attendance at school, inattentiveness in school, selfishness, mental conflict, daydreaming, crying spells, depressed spells or unhappiness (undifferentiated), apprehensiveness, object of teasing
by other children, finicky food habits, sex delinquency (coitus),
and enuresis.

Only one negative correlation was found, the moderate coefficient of -.29 + .07, with lack of initiative among girls.

Swearing or bad language (undifferentiated) tended to be
significantly correlated with sex misbehavior among both sexes.
Overinterest in sex matters among both sexes and overinterest in
the opposite sex, for which only the girls' coefficients were calculated, all yielded substantial correlations of .32. Masturbation
among both sexes and victim of sex abuse by older child or person,
for which only the girls' correlations were calculated, showed moderate coefficients ranging from .20 to .27. Sex delinquency (coitus) among girls showed the moderate coefficient of .20 + .05, the
corresponding coefficient for the boys being .05. For sex misbehavior denied entirely the two coefficients were negligible.

Among the six physical or psychophysical defects there
were two correlations of statistically significant size, both
among girls: question or diagnosis of encephalitis, .39 + .08,
and enuresis, .28 + .05.

Among the four home or familial notations vicious (not
"immoral") home conditions among girls yielded the substantial coefficient of .35 + .07, all other coefficients in this field being
low or negligible.

CHAPTER XLIII

SMOKING

Smoking was noted among 190, or 9.0 per cent, of our 2,113 White boys. Among girls it was noted so infrequently (at least during the years 1923-27, during which period our cases were examined) that a correlational analysis among girls was not feasible. Among boys it was a fairly substantial indicator of conduct deviation and delinquency, but only a moderate index of personality disorder. It was a considerable indicator of conduct deviation and "juvenile delinquency," its correlations with conduct-total and police arrest being .49 ± .02 and .35 ± .03 respectively. With personality-total its bi-serial r of .21 ± .03 was of only moderate size.

Seven conduct problems yielded large tetrachoric correlations in the .40's (Table 81): leading others into bad conduct,

TABLE 81

CORRELATIONS WITH "SMOKING"
(Boys Only)

Personality-total	.21 ± .03
Conduct-total	.49 ± .02
Police arrest	.35 ± .03

Larger Correlations (Positive)

Leading others into bad conduct	.48 ± .04
Gang	.46 ± .04
Stealing	.43 ± .03
Truancy from home	.42 ± .03
Swearing (general)	.41 ± .04
Lying	.40 ± .03
Truancy from school	.40 ± .03
Grouped: swearing, etc.	.37 ± .04
Grouped: disobedient, etc.	.35 ± .03
Bad companions	.35 ± .03
Staying out late at night	.34 ± .04
Stubborn	.34 ± .03
Boastful, "show-off"	.32 ± .04
Disobedient	.31 ± .03
Incorrigible	.29 ± .03

TABLE 81—Continued

Irregular sleep habits	.29 ± .05
Loitering	.28 ± .04
Fighting	.27 ± .04
Sullen	.27 ± .04
Unpopular	.27 ± .05
Contrary	.26 ± .06
Disturbing influence in school	.26 ± .04
Rude	.25 ± .04
Grouped: fighting, etc.	.25 ± .03
Slovenly	.24 ± .04
Question of change of personality	.24 ± .05
Excuse-forming	.24 ± .04
Irritable	.24 ± .04
Grouped: egocentric, etc.	.23 ± .04
Defiant	.22 ± .04
Refusal to attend school	.22 ± .05
Grouped: temper, etc.	.22 ± .03
Teasing other children	.21 ± .04
Fantastical lying	.20 ± .03
Restless in sleep	.20 ± .04

Larger Correlations (Negative)

Headaches	-.20 ± .05

Other Correlations (Positive to Negative)

Lack of interest in school, .19; Threatening violence, .19; Grouped: lack of interest in school, etc., .18; Selfish, .18; Masturbation, .17; Popular, .17; Leader, .17; Grouped: "nervous," etc., .16; Nail-biting, .16; Sulky, .16; Violence, .16; Changeable moods, .16; Grouped: depressed, etc., .15; Egocentric, .15; Exclusion from school, .15; Sex delinquency (coitus), .14; Restless, .14; Depressed, .13; Follower, .13; Quarrelsome, .12; Temper tantrums, .12; Over-suggestible, .12; Irregular attendance at school, .12; Enuresis, .11; Inattentive in school, .10; Temper display, .10; Sensitive (general), .10; Unhappy, .10; Inefficient in work, play, etc., .09; Hatred or jealousy of sibling, .09; Distractible, .09; Conduct prognosis bad, .09; Clean, .09; Attractive manner, .09; Destructive, .08; Irresponsible, .08; Listless, .08; "Nervous," .08; Spoiled child, .08; Question of encephalitis, .08; Finicky food habits, .07; Daydreaming, .07; Worry over specific fact, .07; Inferiority feelings, .07; Complaining of bad treatment by other children, .07; Discord between parents, .07; Crying spells, .06; Sensitive over specific fact, .06; Grouped: sensitive or worrisome, etc., .05; Queer, .05; Poor work in school, .05; Bossy, .04; Stuttering, .04; Brother in penal detention, .04; Lazy, .02; Emotional instability, .02; Former convulsions, .02; Overinterest in sex matters, .01; Apprehensive, .01; Seclusive, .01; Repressed, .01; Object of teasing, -.00; Feeble-minded sibling, -.01; Underweight, -.01; Sex denied entirely, -.01; Mental conflict, -.01; Lues, -.03; Preference for younger children, -.04; Slow, dull, -.05; Grouped: dull, slow, etc., -.06; Psychoneurotic, -.06; Speech defect, -.08; Retardation

TABLE 81—Continued
_____

in school, -.09; Neurological defect, -.09; Immoral home conditions, -.09; Vicious home conditions, -.10;   sent-minded,
-.10; Question of hypophrenia, -.13; Vocations guidance, -.14;
Lack of initiative, -.14; Bashful, -.18

running with a gang, stealing, truancy from home, truancy from
home, truancy from school, swearing in general, and lying. Five
conduct problems yielded substantial correlations in the .30's:
bad companions, staying out late at night, boastful or "show-off"
manner, disobedience, and stubbornness.

A large list of twenty undesirable conduct or personality
traits showed moderate correlations in the .20's: incorrigibility,
contrariness, defiant attitude, refusal to attend school, fighting,
disturbing influence in school, temper tantrums or display (undifferentiated), teasing other children, rudeness, irritable temperament, egocentricity or selfishness (undifferentiated), sullenness,
loitering or wandering, slovenliness, irregular sleep habits, restlessness in sleep, excuse-forming attitude, fantastical lying,
question of change of personality, and unpopularity.

One statistically significant negative correlation was
found with smoking, the moderate coefficient of -.20 ± .05 with
headaches.

Among the four sex notations, the seven physical or psychophysical defects, and the four home or familial notations for
which the boys coefficients were calculated, the correlations were
low or negligible, ranging from -.10 to .17.

CHAPTER XLIV

ASSOCIATING WITH BAD COMPANIONS; RUNNING WITH
A GANG; AND LEADING OTHERS INTO BAD CONDUCT

Three notations—associating with bad companions, running
with a gang, and leading others into bad conduct—were of considerable importance as indicators of conduct deviation and juvenile
delinquency but of lesser importance as indicators of personality
difficulties.

Bad companions was noted among 370, or 17.5 per cent, of
our 2,113 White boys and among 132, or 11.2 per cent, of our 1,181
White girls. With the police-arrest criterion of "juvenile delinquency" its tetrachoric correlation among boys was high, .59 ± .02,
and also fairly meaningful among girls, .40 ± .04 (Table 82). With

TABLE 82

CORRELATIONS WITH "BAD COMPANIONS"

	Boys	Girls
Personality-total............................	.14 ± .02	.22 ± .03
Conduct-total................................	.40 ± .02	.35 ± .03
Police arrest................................	.59 ± .02	.40 ± .04
	Larger Correlations (Positive)	
Stealing.....................................	.57 ± .02	.25 ± .04 (18)*
Truancy from school..........................	.48 ± .02	.43 ± .05 (2)
Truancy from home............................	.47 ± .02	.21 ± .05 (22-25)
Staying out late at night....................	.44 ± .03	.59 ± .04 (1)
Oversuggestible..............................	.43 ± .03	.40 ± .04 (4)
Gang...	.41 ± .03	....
Leading others into bad conduct..............	.37 ± .04	.05
Lying..	.35 ± .03	.32 ± .04 (6-7)
Smoking......................................	.35 ± .03	....
Loitering....................................	.31 ± .04	.27 ± .06 (12-14)

*Rank order of girls' correlations.

415

TABLE 82—Continued

	Boys	Girls
Incorrigible	.30 ± .03	.26 ± .05 (15-17)
Grouped: disobedient, etc.	.28 ± .03	.29 ± .04 (9)
Vicious home conditions	.26 ± .05	.28 ± .06 (10-11)
Brother in penal detention	.25 ± .04	.07
Boastful, "show-off"	.24 ± .03	.18
Lack of interest in school	.24 ± .03	.17
Overinterest in sex matters	.24 ± .05	.32 ± .06 (6-7)
Unhappy	.24 ± .05	.07
Excuse-forming	.23 ± .03	.26 ± .06 (15-17)
Follower	.23 ± .04	.07
Masturbation	.22 ± .03	.20 ± .05 (26-31)
Conduct prognosis bad	.21 ± .05	.17
Grouped: swearing, etc.	.21 ± .03	.27 ± .06 (12-14)
Rude	.20 ± .03	.17
Grouped: lack of interest in school, etc.	.20 ± .03	.20 ± .05 (26-31)
Overinterest in opposite sex	....	.41 ± .04 (3)
Sex delinquency (coitus)	.14	.37 ± .04 (5)
Worry over specific fact	-.01	.30 ± .07 (8)
Defiant	.09	.28 ± .06 (10-11)
Fantastical lying	.18	.26 ± .06 (15-17)
Irresponsible	.14	.24 ± .06 (19)
Destructive	.17	.22 ± .07 (20-21)
Victim of sex abuse	....	.22 ± .06 (20-21)
Disturbing influence in school	.19	.21 ± .06 (22-25)
Inattentive in school	.08	.21 ± .06 (22-25)
Queer	-.00	.21 ± .06 (22-25)
Bossy	.09	.20 ± .06 (26-31)
Disobedient	.19	.20 ± .05 (26-31)
Egocentric	.15	.20 ± .05 (26-31)
Grouped: egocentric, etc.	.12	.20 ± .05 (26-31)
	Larger Correlations (Negative)	
Stuttering	-.27 ± .05	....
Feeble-minded sibling	.02	-.26 ± .06
Retardation in school	-.05	-.26 ± .04

Other Correlations (Positive to Negative)

Fighting, .19 and .17; Swearing (general), .19 (boys); Sex denied entirely, .19 and -.14; Quarrelsome, .18 and .09; Irregular sleep habits, .18 and .17; Discord between parents, .18 and .17; Slovenly, .17 and .13; Hatred or jealousy of sibling, .17 and .17; Sulky, .16 and .17; Sullen, .16 and .09; Grouped: fighting, etc., .16 and .12; Teasing other children, .15 (boys); Emotional instability, .15 and .17; Leader, .15 and .13; Irregular attendance at school, .15 and .05; Refusal to attend school, .14 and .14; Exclusion from school, .14 and .02; Spoiled child, .13 and .13; Attractive manner, .13 and -.01; Nail-biting, .11 and .04; Violence, .11 and .09; Apprehensive, .11 and .13; Mental conflict, .11 and .06; Enuresis, .10 and .00; Lazy, .10 and .11; Restless, .10 and .17; Complaining of bad treatment by other children, .10 (boys); Daydreaming, .09 and .05; Headaches, .09 and .10; Former convulsions,

TABLE 82—Continued

.09 and .02; Vocational guidance, .09 and -.07; Finicky food habits, .08 and
.11; Grouped: depressed, etc., .08 and .09; Threatening violence, .07 (boys);
Crying spells, .07 and .12; Restless in sleep, .07 and .09; Repressed, .07 and
-.03; Popular, .07 and .10; Grouped: "nervous," etc., .07 and .09; "Nervous,"
.06 and -.02; Temper display, .06 and .03; Grouped: temper, etc., .06 and .02;
Sensitive over specific fact, .06 and .11; Clean, .06 and -.06; Inefficient in
work, play, etc., .05 and .14; Stubborn, .05 and .18; Temper tantrums, .04 and
.09; Unpopular, .04 and .10; Inferiority feelings, .04 and -.01; Poor work in
school, .04 and -.10; Immoral home conditions, .04 and .15; Contrary, .03 and
.01; Irritable, .03 and -.03; Distractible, .03 and .09; Question of change of
personality, .02 and .19; Object of teasing, .02 and .14; Preference for younger
children, .02 and .12; Underweight, .01 and -.01; Grouped: sensitive or worrisome, etc., .00 and .16; Seclusive, -.01 and .00; Changeable moods, -.01 and
.07; Selfish, -.03 and .11; Depressed, -.04 and .07; Listless, -.04 and -.13;
Psychoneurotic, -.05 and .03; Neurological defect, -.06 and .06; Bashful, -.07
and -.11; Question of hypophrenia, -.07 and -.16; Grouped: dull, slow, etc.,
-.07 and -.16; Slow, dull, -.08 and -.15; Absent-minded, -.08 and -.00; Sensitive (general), -.10 and .04; Lack of initiative, -.10 and -.15; Speech defect,
-.11 and -.07; Question of encephalitis, -.13 and .07; Lues, -.15 and .16

the conduct-total criterion of conduct disorders, not necessarily
amounting to "juvenile delinquency," its correlations were substantial, its respective bi-serial r's for boys and girls being
.40 ± .02 and .35 ± .03. With the personality-total criterion of
personality difficulties its relationships were low or moderate,
the respective correlations for boys and girls being .14 ± .02 and
.22 ± .03. It is probable that the high correlation with bad companions may illustrate the enhancing effect of what on pages 34-35
has been designated as "prejudicial" factors in case-record information when it is obtained in so large a degree from parents of
the children. Parents are wont to excuse or explain the troubles
of their own child by saying that other people's children have led
him into bad conduct.

The highest correlations among boys were with stealing,
the tetrachoric r being .57 ± .02, while the corresponding girls'
correlation was of only moderate size, .25 ± .04. Among girls the
highest correlation was with staying out late at night, .59 ± .04,
the corresponding boys' coefficient also being large, .44 ± .03.
Two conduct difficulties—truancy from school and oversuggestibility—yielded large correlations in the .40's among both sexes.
Running with a gang, for which only the boys' correlation was calculated, and overinterest in the opposite sex, for which only the
girls' correlation was calculated, similarly yielded large corre-

lations in the .40's. Truancy from home yielded correlations of
.47 + .02 and .21 + .05 among boys and girls respectively.

Lying among both sexes and smoking (calculated for boys
only) yielded substantial correlations in the .30's. Incorrigibility and loitering or wandering among boys similarly yielded substantial correlations in the .30's with moderate correlations in
the .20's among girls. Leading others into bad conduct among boys
yielded the substantial correlation of .37 + .04 but a negligible
coefficient of .05 among girls. Among girls overinterest in sex
matters yielded a substantial correlation of .32 + .06, the corresponding coefficient among boys being somewhat lower, .24 + .05.
Sex delinquency (coitus) and worry over some specific fact among
girls similarly yielded substantial correlations in the .30's but
low respective coefficients of .14 and -.01 among boys.

Four notations—masturbation, swearing or bad language (undifferentiated), excuse-forming attitude, and vicious home conditions—showed moderate correlations in the .20's with bad companions among both sexes. Victim of sex abuse by older child or person, which was calculated for girls only, also showed the moderate
correlation of .22 + .06. Among boys seven miscellaneous notations
showed moderate correlations in the .20's but low coefficients below .20 among girls: brother in penal detention, "follower," lack
of interest in school, rudeness, boastful or "show-off" manner, unhappiness, and staff notation of unfavorable conduct prognosis.
Among girls ten notations similarly showed moderate correlations
in the .20's but low coefficients below .20 among boys: disobedience, defiant attitude, egocentricity, bossy manner, irresponsibility, inattentiveness in school, disturbing influence in school,
destructiveness, fantastical lying, and queer behavior.

Bad companions showed three negative correlations of moderate size in the -.20's: stuttering (calculated for boys only)
and retardation in school and feeble-minded sibling among girls.

Among sex-misbehavior notations there was a tendency toward
positive correlation. Overinterest in the opposite sex (calculated
for girls only) yielded the large correlation of .41 + .04. Sex
delinquency (coitus) and overinterest in sex matters among girls
yielded substantial correlations in the .30's with corresponding
positive correlations of .14 and .24 + .05 among boys. Masturbation among both sexes and victim of sex abuse by older child or

<u>person</u> (calculated for girls only) showed moderate correlations in
the .20's. <u>Sex misbehavior denied entirely</u> showed low correlations
of .19 and -.14 among boys and girls respectively.

Among the seven physical or psychophysical notations the
only statistically significant correlation was the negative one of
-.27 ± .05 with <u>stuttering</u> (calculated for boys only), all other
coefficients being low or negligible, ranging from -.15 to .16.

Among the four home or familial notations there were three
coefficients of moderate size in the .20's: <u>vicious home condi-
tions</u> among both boys and girls and <u>brother in penal detention</u>
among boys.

<u>Running with a gang</u> was noted among 219, or 10.4 per cent,
of our 2,113 White boys. Among girls it occurred so infrequently
that the calculation of correlation coefficients was not feasible.
Among boys its correlations resembled those of <u>bad companions</u>, as
one might suppose, but in general were slightly smaller. Its tetrachoric correlation with <u>police arrest</u> was large, .45 ± .03, its
bi-serial correlation with the <u>conduct-total</u> was substantial, .35
± .02, but with <u>personality-total</u> the relationship was negligible,
.09 ± .02.

Its largest correlation was with <u>stealing</u>, .54 ± .02 (Table 83). Large correlations in the .40's were found for three

TABLE 83

CORRELATIONS WITH "GANG"
(Boys Only)

Personality-total . . . . .09 ± .02
Conduct-total . . . . .35 ± .02
Police arrest . . . . .45 ± .03

Larger Correlations (Positive)

Stealing . . . . .54 ± .02
Smoking . . . . .46 ± .04
Truancy from school . . . . .46 ± .03
Bad companions . . . . .41 ± .03
Truancy from home . . . . .37 ± .03
Loitering . . . . .36 ± .04
Staying out late at night . . . . .35 ± .03
Incorrigible . . . . .34 ± .03
Grouped: disobedient, etc. . . . . .32 ± .03
Oversuggestible . . . . .31 ± .03
Leading others into bad conduct . . . . .27 ± .05

TABLE 83—Continued

```
Conduct prognosis bad . . . . . . . . . . . . .   .27 ± .05
Defiant . . . . . . . . . . . . . . . . . . . .   .26 ± .04
Fighting . . . . . . . . . . . . . . . . . . .    .26 ± .04
Slovenly . . . . . . . . . . . . . . . . . . .    .26 ± .04
Leader . . . . . . . . . . . . . . . . . . . .    .26 ± .04
Lying . . . . . . . . . . . . . . . . . . . . .   .25 ± .03
Sullen . . . . . . . . . . . . . . . . . . . .    .24 ± .04
Rude . . . . . . . . . . . . . . . . . . . . .    .24 ± .04
Sex denied entirely . . . . . . . . . . . . .     .24 ± .05
Contrary . . . . . . . . . . . . . . . . . . .    .23 ± .05
Refusal to attend school . . . . . . . . . . .    .23 ± .05
Destructive . . . . . . . . . . . . . . . . . .   .22 ± .04
Disobedient . . . . . . . . . . . . . . . . . .   .22 ± .03
Follower . . . . . . . . . . . . . . . . . . .    .21 ± .04
Boastful, "show-off" . . . . . . . . . . . . .    .20 ± .04
Fantastical lying . . . . . . . . . . . . . .     .20 ± .03
Egocentric . . . . . . . . . . . . . . . . . .    .20 ± .04
Brother in penal detention . . . . . . . . . .    .20 ± .05
```

Larger Correlations (Negative)

```
Stuttering . . . . . . . . . . . . . . . . . .    -.24 ± .05
Vocational guidance . . . . . . . . . . . . . .   -.21 ± .04
Selfish . . . . . . . . . . . . . . . . . . . .   -.20 ± .05
```

Other Correlations (Positive to Negative)

Lack of interest in school, .17; Grouped: fighting, etc., .17; Grouped: lack of interest in school, etc., .17; Disturbing influence in school, .16; Grouped: egocentric, etc., .16; Grouped: swearing, etc., .16; Mental conflict, .16; Spoiled child, .15; Swearing (general), .14; Violence, .14; Exclusion from school, .13; Sulky, .12; Masturbation, .12; Question of change of personality, .12; Excuseforming, .12; Irregular attendance at school, .12; Irregular sleep habits, .11; Emotional instability, .10; Sex delinquency (coitus), .09; Hatred or jealousy of sibling, .09; Irritable, .09; Queer, .09; Grouped: "nervous," etc., .09; Restless, .08; Sensitive over specific fact, .08; Grouped: temper, etc., .08; Inattentive in school, .07; Stubborn, .07; Restless in sleep, .07; Popular, .07; Irresponsible, .06; Temper tantrums, .06; Changeable moods, .06; Distractible, .06; Feeble-minded sibling, .05; Poor work in school, .04; Former convulsions, .04; Vicious home conditions, .04; Nail-biting, .03; Quarrelsome, .03; Apprehensive, .03; Seclusive, .03; Repressed, .03; Clean, .02; Grouped: sensitive or worrisome, etc., .02; Temper display, .01; "Nervous," .01; Unhappy, .01; Overinterest in sex matters, .00; Sensitive (general), .00; Complaining of bad treatment by other children, .00; Lues, .00; Immoral home conditions, -.00; Crying spells, -.01; Retardation in school, -.02; Lazy, -.02; Enuresis, -.02; Finicky food habits, -.02; Discord between parents, -.03; Attractive manner, -.03; Absent-minded, -.04; Threatening violence, -.04; Daydreaming, -.05; Bossy, -.05; Grouped: depressed, etc., -.06; Question of encephalitis, -.07; Neurological defect, -.07; Question of hypophrenia, -.07; Infer-

TABLE 83—Continued

---

iority feelings, -.07; Inefficient in work, play, etc., -.07;
Worry over specific fact, -.08; Object of teasing, -.08; Teasing other children, -.08; Listless, -.09; Depressed, -.09;
Speech defect, -.10; Psychoneurotic, -.10; Grouped: dull,
slow, etc., -.11; Unpopular, -.11; Lack of initiative, -.11;
Preference for younger children, -.12; Slow, dull, -.12; Bashful, -.12; Underweight, -.13; Headaches, -.16

conduct problems: bad companions, truancy from school, and smoking. Substantial correlations in the .30's were found for truancy
from home, staying out late at night, loitering or wandering, oversuggestibility, and incorrigibility.

Running with a gang showed moderate correlations in the
.20's with a large list of nineteen miscellaneous notations: leading others into bad conduct, "leader," "follower," disobedience,
defiant attitude, contrariness, refusal to attend school, egocentricity, boastful or "show-off" manner, sullenness, rudeness, destructiveness, fighting, lying, fantastical lying, slovenliness,
staff notation of unfavorable conduct prognosis, sex misbehavior
denied entirely, and brother in penal detention.

There were three negative correlations of moderate size
in the -.20's: selfishness, stuttering, and "request for vocational guidance."

Among the four sex notations for which the boys' correlations were calculated the only significant correlation with running
with a gang was the moderate one of .24 ± .05 with sex misbehavior
denied entirely.

Among the seven physical or psychophysical disabilities
the only significant coefficient was the negative one of -.24 ± .05
with stuttering.

Among the four home or familial notations the only significant correlation was with brother in penal detention, .20 ± .05.

Leading others into bad conduct was noted among 138 boys,
or 6.5 per cent, and among 50 girls, or 4.2 per cent. With the
conduct-total its correlations were definitely high, the respective
bi-serial r's for boys and girls being .51 ± .02 and .65 ± .03 (Table 84). With the personality-total among girls its correlation
was large, .45 ± .04, but among boys only moderate, .20 ± .03.

TABLE 84

CORRELATIONS WITH "LEADING OTHERS INTO BAD CONDUCT"

	Boys	Girls
Personality-total..............................	.20 ± .03	.45 ± .04
Conduct-total.................................	.51 ± .02	.65 ± .03
Police arrest.................................	.40 ± .04	.27 ± .06
		Larger Correlations (Positive)
Smoking..	.48 ± .04	....
Stealing.......................................	.46 ± .03	.16
Grouped: disobedient, etc....................	.38 ± .03	.40 ± .05 (10-14)*
Bad companions................................	.37 ± .04	.05
Truancy from school...........................	.35 ± .03	.29 ± .07 (33-35)
Incorrigible..................................	.34 ± .04	.34 ± .06 (23-29)
Staying out late at night.....................	.34 ± .04	.39 ± .06 (15)
Lying...	.32 ± .03	.31 ± .05 (28-29)
Leader..	.32 ± .05	.18
Destructive...................................	.31 ± .04	.47 ± .08 (1-2)
Truancy from home.............................	.31 ± .04	.21 ± .06 (56-58)
Disturbing influence in school................	.31 ± .04	.21 ± .08 (56-58)
Exclusion from school.........................	.31 ± .05	.47 ± .07 (1-2)
Boastful, "show-off"..........................	.30 ± .04	.37 ± .08 (18-19)
Disobedient...................................	.29 ± .04	.30 ± .06 (30-32)
Swearing (general)............................	.29 ± .05	....
Excuse-forming................................	.29 ± .04	.10
Gang..	.27 ± .05	....
Brother in penal detention....................	.27 ± .05	.22 ± .08 (52-55)
Slovenly......................................	.26 ± .04	.23 ± .06 (47-51)
Refusal to attend school......................	.25 ± .05	.17
Masturbation..................................	.25 ± .04	.36 ± .06 (20-22)
Rude..	.24 ± .04	.40 ± .06 (10-14)
Threatening violence..........................	.24 ± .06	....
Grouped: swearing, etc......................	.24 ± .04	.43 ± .07 (5-6)
Fantastical lying.............................	.23 ± .03	.34 ± .08 (23-24)
Loitering.....................................	.22 ± .03	.11
Teasing other children........................	.22 ± .05	....
Unpopular.....................................	.22 ± .06	.43 ± .08 (5-6)
Inefficient in work, play, etc................	.21 ± .06	.16
Defiant.......................................	.21 ± .05	.32 ± .07 (26-27)
Sullen..	.21 ± .05	.40 ± .07 (10-14)
Overinterest in sex matters...................	.21 ± .06	.42 ± .07 (7)
Fighting......................................	.20 ± .04	.36 ± .04 (20-22)
Egocentric....................................	.20 ± .04	.28 ± .07 (36)
Sex delinquency (coitus)......................	.11	.45 ± .05 (3)
Violence......................................	.08	.44 ± .07 (4)
Contrary......................................	.08	.41 ± .09 (8-9)
Queer...	-.02	.41 ± .08 (8-9)
Temper tantrums...............................	.12	.40 ± .07 (10-14)

*Rank order of girls' correlations.

TABLE 84—Continued

	Boys	Girls
Grouped: fighting, etc......................	.16	.40 ± .05 (10-14)
Question of change of personality.............	.03	.38 ± .08 (16-17)
Conduct prognosis bad.......................	.08	.38 ± .08 (18-19)
Overinterest in opposite sex..................	....	.37 ± .06 (18-19)
Mental conflict...............................	.05	.36 ± .09 (20-22)
Irresponsible................................	.17	.33 ± .08 (25)
Grouped: temper, etc........................	.06	.32 ± .05 (26-27)
Emotional instability........................	.11	.31 ± .08 (28-29)
Listless......................................	.07	.30 ± .08 (30-32)
Grouped: depressed, etc.....................	.14	.30 ± .07 (30-32)
Bossy..	.02	.29 ± .08 (33-35)
Changeable moods............................	.07	.29 ± .07 (33-35)
Spoiled child.................................	.07	.27 ± .07 (37-38)
Unhappy.....................................	.18	.27 ± .09 (37-38)
Stubborn.....................................	.08	.26 ± .06 (39)
Sulky..	.11	.25 ± .08 (40-43)
Hatred or jealousy of sibling.................	.16	.25 ± .09 (40-43)
Vicious home conditions......................	.13	.25 ± .08 (40-43)
Grouped: egocentric, etc.....................	.18	.25 ± .06 (40-43)
Quarrelsome..................................	.16	.24 ± .06 (44-46)
Crying spells.................................	.00	.24 ± .06 (44-46)
Restless......................................	.09	.24 ± .06 (44-46)
Selfish.......................................	-.05	.23 ± .08 (47-51)
Sensitive over specific fact..................	.05	.23 ± .07 (47-51)
Grouped: "nervous," etc.....................	.07	.23 ± .05 (47-51)
Grouped: sensitive or worrisome, etc.........	-.02	.23 ± .06 (47-51)
Depressed....................................	.06	.22 ± .08 (52-55)
Psychoneurotic...............................	-.08	.22 ± .09 (52-55)
Worry over specific fact......................	.05	.22 ± .10 (52-55)
Lack of interest in school....................	.17	.21 ± .07 (56-58)
Lazy...	.17	.20 ± .08 (59)
	Larger Correlations (Negative)	
Stuttering....................................	-.20 ± .06	....
Speech defect................................	-.13	-.27 ± .08
	Not Calculable	
Absent-minded................................	.04	(n.c.)

Other Correlations (Positive to Negative)

Discord between parents, .16 and .03; Grouped: lack of interest in school, etc., .16 and .10; Enuresis, .14 and .10; Irregular sleep habits, .14 and .10; Distractible, .14 and .18; Temper display, .13 and .10; Inferiority feelings, .13 and .17; Victim of sex abuse, .13 (girls); Oversuggestible, .12 and .05; Restless in sleep, .12 and .05; Complaining of bad treatment by other children, .12 (boys); Sex denied entirely, .12 and -.13; Lues, .10 and -.05; Inattentive in school, .10 and -.12; Attractive manner, .09 and -.09; Preference

TABLE 84—Continued

for younger children, .08 and .11; Poor work in school, .08 and .10; Irregular
attendance at school, .08 and -.02; Object of teasing, .07 and .08; Retardation
in school, .07 and .08; Former convulsions, .07 and .13; Irritable, .06 and .13;
Feeble-minded sibling, .06 and -.02; Clean, .05 and .07; Nail-biting, .04 and
.08; Daydreaming, .03 and .16; Question of hypophrenia, .03 and .14; Underweight,
.03 and .13; "Nervous," .02 and .10; Follower, .02 and .09; Seclusive, .01 and
.03; Repressed, .00 and .12; Immoral home conditions, -.00 and .18; Bashful,
-.01 and .04; Popular, -.03 and .17; Finicky food habits, -.03 and .19; Grouped:
dull, slow, etc., -.04 and -.05; Slow, dull, -.04 and -.04; Neurological defect,
-.06 and .10; Apprehensive, -.06 and .14; Question of encephalitis, -.09 and
.16; Lack of initiative, -.09 and -.06; Vocational guidance, -.12 and -.01; Sensitive (general), -.14 and .01; Headaches, -.15 and .03

With police arrest its tetrachoric r among boys was definitely substantial, .40 ± .04, but only moderate among girls, .27 ± .06.

Among boys its largest correlations were with smoking (calculated for boys only), .48 ± .04. Among boys stealing also yielded
the large correlation of .46 ± .03, the corresponding coefficient
for girls being low, .16. Among girls exclusion from school and
destructiveness yielded its largest correlations, .47 ± .07 and
.47 ± .08 respectively, the corresponding coefficients for boys
being substantial, .31 ± .05 and .31 ± .04. Five undesirable behavior traits among girls similarly yielded large correlations in
the .40's with moderate coefficients in the .20's among boys:
overinterest in sex matters, swearing or bad language (undifferentiated), rudeness, sullenness, and unpopularity. An additional
five behavior problems among girls yielded large coefficients in
the .40's but low coefficients ranging from -.02 to .12 among boys:
sex delinquency (coitus), violence, temper tantrums, contrariness,
and queer behavior.

Leading others into bad conduct yielded consistently substantial correlations in the .30's for the five notations: incorrigibility, staying out late at night, lying, boastful or "show-
off" manner, and (calculated for girls only) overinterest in the
opposite sex. Three notations—truancy from school, disturbing
influence in school, and truancy from home—among boys yielded substantial correlations in the .30's with moderate coefficients in
the .20's among girls. Bad companions and "leader" among boys
yielded substantial correlations in the .30's but low coefficients
below .20 among girls. Among girls five conduct problems yielded
substantial correlations in the .30's with moderate coefficients

in the .20's among boys: disobedience, defiant attitude, fighting, fantastical lying, and masturbation. Among girls an additional six behavior notations yielded substantial correlations in the .30's but low coefficients below .20 among boys: mental conflict, question of change of personality, emotional instability, listlessness, irresponsibility, and staff notation of unfavorable conduct prognosis.

Six notations consistently showed moderate correlations in the .20's: egocentricity, slovenliness, brother in penal detention, and the three traits for which only the boys' correlations were computed—running with a gang, threatening violence, and teasing other children. Four undesirable traits among boys showed moderate correlations in the .20's but low positive coefficients below .20 among girls: refusal to attend school, excuse-forming attitude, loitering or wandering, and inefficiency in work, play, etc. Among girls a large list of eighteen miscellaneous notations showed moderate correlations in the .20's but low coefficients below .20 among boys: bossy manner, selfishness, stubbornness, "spoiled child," sulkiness, hatred or jealousy of sibling, quarrelsomeness, restlessness, lack of interest in school, laziness, changeable moods or attitudes, crying spells, depressed mood or spells, unhappiness, sensitiveness over some specific fact, worry over some specific fact, psychoneurotic trends, and vicious home conditions.

Leading others into bad conduct showed negative moderate correlations in the -.20's with speech defect among girls and with stuttering (calculated for boys only).

With sex misbehavior leading others into bad conduct tended to be significantly associated. Sex delinquency (coitus) and overinterest in sex matters among girls yielded large correlations in the .40's, the respective boys' coefficients of .11 and .21 ± .06 being low or moderate. Overinterest in the opposite sex (calculated for girls only) yielded the substantial correlation of .37 ± .06. With masturbation the respective coefficients for girls and boys were .36 ± .06 and .25 ± .04. For sex misbehavior denied entirely and victim of sex abuse by older child or person (calculated for girls only) the coefficients were low or negligible.

Among the seven physical or psychophysical disabilities the only significant correlations found were the moderate negative

ones of -.27 ± .08 for <u>speech defect</u> (other than <u>stuttering</u>) among
girls and -.20 ± .06 for <u>stuttering</u> (calculated for boys only).

Among the four home or familial notations moderate positive correlations in the .20's were found for <u>brother in penal de-
tention</u> among both boys and girls and for vicious (not "immoral")
<u>home conditions</u> among girls.

CHAPTER XLV

LOITERING; LAZINESS; INEFFICIENCY;
IRRESPONSIBILITY

The four behavior notations, loitering or wandering, laziness, inefficiency in work, play, etc., and irresponsibility, are
grouped together in the present chapter only as a matter of convenience. They are not greatly similar to each other as far as
may be inferred either from their intercorrelations or from their
"outside" correlations with other traits.

Loitering or wandering, loafing or bumming on the street
or in pool halls, dance halls, and the like, was noted among 174,
or 8.2 per cent, of our 2,113 White boys and 61, or 5.2 per cent,
of our 1,181 White girls. Among boys its correlations with the
conduct-total and police-arrest criteria of seriousness were of
fairly large size in the .40's but of only moderate size, .23 ±
.03, with the personality-total criterion (Table 85). Among girls

TABLE 85

CORRELATIONS WITH "LOITERING"

	Boys	Girls
Personality-total.............................	.23 ± .03	.06 ± .04
Conduct-total.................................	.43 ± .02	.27 ± .04
Police arrest.................................	.41 ± .03	.23 ± .06
	Larger Correlations (Positive)	
Truancy from home.............................	.53 ± .03	.25 ± .06 (13-14)*
Truancy from school...........................	.49 ± .03	.39 ± .06 (2)
Staying out late at night.....................	.46 ± .03	.49 ± .06 (1)
Stealing......................................	.39 ± .03	.35 ± .05 (4-5)
Fantastical lying.............................	.38 ± .05	.21 ± .08 (18-19)
Refusal to attend school......................	.36 ± .05	.13

*Rank order of girls' correlations.

TABLE 85—Continued

	Boys	Girls
Gang..	.36 ± .04	....
Irresponsible..................................	.34 ± .05	.08
Slovenly.......................................	.33 ± .05	.07
Lying..	.32 ± .03	.35 ± .05 (4-5)
Bad companions.................................	.31 ± .04	.27 ± .06 (12)
Conduct prognosis bad..........................	.29 ± .06	.11
Incorrigible...................................	.28 ± .03	.34 ± .05 (6)
Smoking..	.28 ± .04	....
Irregular attendance at school.................	.27 ± .05	.16
Disturbing influence in school.................	.26 ± .04	.13
Grouped: disobedient, etc......................	.26 ± .03	.36 ± .05 (3)
Inefficient in work, play, etc.................	.25 ± .05	.00
Unpopular......................................	.25 ± .05	.09
Emotional instability..........................	.25 ± .05	.08
Grouped: swearing, etc.........................	.24 ± .04	.30 ± .07 (10)
Disobedient....................................	.23 ± .04	.07
Lack of interest in school.....................	.23 ± .04	.06
Leading others into bad conduct................	.22 ± .05	.11
Fighting.......................................	.21 ± .04	.02
Distractible...................................	.20 ± .04	.18
Oversuggestible................................	.20 ± .04	.32 ± .06 (8-9)
Spoiled child..................................	.20 ± .04	.01
Exclusion from school..........................	.20 ± .04	.18
Sex delinquency (coitus).......................	.16	.33 ± .05 (7)
Overinterest in opposite sex...................	....	.32 ± .06 (8-9)
Question of change of personality..............	.18	.29 ± .08 (11)
Question of encephalitis.......................	.12	.25 ± .10 (13-14)
Violence.......................................	.18	.24 ± .07 (15)
Grouped: fighting, etc.........................	.19	.23 ± .05 (16)
Defiant..	.10	.22 ± .07 (17)
Irregular sleep habits.........................	.10	.21 ± .08 (18-19)
Queer..	.13	.20 ± .08 (20)

Larger Correlations (Negative)		
Vocational guidance............................	.11	-.34 ± .06
Speech defect..................................	.02	-.31 ± .07
Unhappy..	.12	-.25 ± .08
Inferiority feelings...........................	.01	-.24 ± .08
Sullen...	.06	-.21 ± .07
Clean..	-.07	-.21 ± .06

Not Calculable		
Popular..	.13	(n.c.)
Repressed......................................	-.01	(n.c.)

TABLE 85—Continued

Other Correlations (Positive to Negative)

Vicious home conditions, .19 and .14; Boastful, "show-off," .18 and .16; Destructive, .18 and .16; Swearing (general), .18 (boys); Restless, .18 and .14; Grouped: lack of interest in school, etc., .18 and .10; Absent-minded, .17 and -.10; Quarrelsome, .16 and .07; Masturbation, .16 and .00; Egocentric, .16 and -.02; Seclusive, .16 and -.03; Grouped: egocentric, etc., .14 and .06; Lazy, .13 and .15; Nail-biting, .13 and .06; Teasing other children, .13 (boys); Leader, .13 and .11; Headaches, .13 and .13; Grouped: temper, etc., .13 and .11; Bossy, .12 and -.03; Sulky, .12 and .09; Temper tantrums, .12 and .09; Overinterest in sex matters, .12 and .14; Hatred or jealousy of sibling, .12 and -.09; Discord between parents, .12 and .08; Rude, .11 and .02; Poor work in school, .11 and .08; Attractive manner, .11 and .01; Former convulsions, .11 and -.06; Grouped: "nervous," etc., .11 and .11; Complaining of bad treatment by other children, .10 (boys); Question of hypophrenia, .10 and .15; Stubborn, .09 and .02; Excuse-forming, .09 and .13; Crying spells, .08 and -.01; Grouped: depressed, etc., .07 and -.07; Temper display, .07 and .15; Daydreaming, .07 and -.06; Irritable, .07 and .06; Sex denied entirely, .07 and -.18; Underweight, .07 and -.07; Contrary, .06 and .10; Bashful, .06 and -.18; Object of teasing, .06 and -.04; Follower, .06 and -.02; Neurological defect, .06 and -.06; Brother in penal detention, .06 and -.02; Listless, .05 and .02; Lack of initiative, .05 and -.11; Inattentive in school, .04 and .14; Restless in sleep, .04 and .18; Lues, .04 and .13; Enuresis, .03 and .12; "Nervous," .03 and -.04; Preference for younger children, .03 and - 00; Apprehensive, .02 and .06; Immoral home conditions, .02 and .08; Selfish, .01 and .01; Depressed, .01 and .01; Sensitive over specific fact, .01 and -.13; Grouped: dull, slow, etc., .01 and .00; Grouped: sensitive or worrisome, etc., -.10 and -.04; Slow, dull, -.00 and .01; Worry over specific fact, -.01 and .16; Threatening violence, -.01 (boys); Changeable moods, -.02 and .09; Finicky food habits, -.02 and .15; Victim of sex abuse, -.02 (girls); Stuttering, -.03 (boys); Sensitive (general), -.03 and -.05; Feeble-minded sibling, -.04 and -.07; Psychoneurotic, -.08 and -.02; Retardation in school, -.08 and .04; Mental conflict, -.17 and -.17

the correlations with <u>conduct-total</u> and <u>police arrest</u> were of only moderate size, in the .20's, and its correlation with <u>personality-total</u> negligible.

The highest correlation with <u>loitering or wandering</u> was with <u>truancy from home</u>, .53 ± .03, the corresponding correlation among girls being moderate, .25 ± .06. <u>Staying out late at night</u> and <u>truancy from school</u> among boys yielded the large correlations of .46 ± .03 and .49 ± .03, the corresponding coefficients among girls being almost as large, .49 ± .06 and .39 ± .06 respectively.

Four notations consistently yielded substantial correlations in the .30's: <u>stealing</u>, <u>lying</u>, and (calculated for boys only) <u>running with a gang</u>, and (calculated for girls only) <u>overinterest in the opposite sex</u>. <u>Fantastical lying</u> and <u>bad companions</u> among boys yielded substantial correlations in the .30's with moderate correlations in the .20's among girls. Three notations—

irresponsibility, slovenliness, and refusal to attend school—among
boys yielded substantial correlations in the .30's but low coefficients below .20 among girls. Among girls incorrigibility yielded
the substantial correlation of .34 $\pm$ .05, with a moderate correlation of .28 $\pm$ .03 among boys. Sex delinquency (coitus) among girls
also yielded the substantial correlation of .33 $\pm$ .05 but a low coefficient of .16 among boys.

Smoking among boys showed the moderate correlation of .28
$\pm$ .04 with loitering or wandering, the girls' coefficient not being
calculated because of paucity of cases. Among boys the following
thirteen behavior notations showed moderate correlations in the
.20's but low coefficients below .20 among girls: inefficiency in
work, play, etc., irregular attendance at school, lack of interest
in school, disturbing influence in school, exclusion from school,
leading others into bad conduct, distractibility, fighting, disobedience, "spoiled child," unpopularity, emotional instability,
and staff notation of unfavorable conduct prognosis. Among girls
six notations showed moderate correlations in the .20's but low
positive coefficients below .20 among boys: irregular sleep habits
defiant attitude, violence, question of change of personality,
queer behavior, and question or diagnosis of encephalitis.

With loitering or wandering there were six statistically
significant negative correlations, ranging from -.21 to -.34, all
among girls, the corresponding boys' coefficients being negligible:
unhappiness, inferiority feelings, sullenness, clean habits, speech
defect (other than stuttering), and "request for vocational guidance."

For two notations, repressed manner and popularity, the
tetrachoric coefficients among girls could not be calculated because there were no instances in which girls with either of these
notations also were noted as given to loitering or wandering.

Among the six sex notations there were two correlations of
substantial size in the .30's, both among girls: sex delinquency
(coitus) and (calculated for girls only) overinterest in the opposite sex.

Among the seven physical or psychophysical disabilities
speech defect (other than stuttering) yielded the substantial negative coefficient of -.31 $\pm$ .07 among girls. Question or diagnosis
of encephalitis among girls showed the doubtfully significant coefficient of .25 $\pm$ .10.

Among the four home or familial notations all correlations with <u>loitering or wandering</u> were low or negligible.

<u>Laziness</u> was noted among 182 boys, or in 8.6 per cent of our cases, and among 79 girls, or 6.7 per cent. With the <u>person-ality-total</u> and <u>conduct-total</u> its correlations among boys were moderate, the bi-serial <u>r</u>'s being .29 $\pm$ .02 and .22 $\pm$ .03 respectively (Table 86), and low among girls, the coefficients in both instances being .17 $\pm$ .04. With <u>police arrest</u> the girls' tetrachoric <u>r</u> of .30 $\pm$ .05 was perhaps substantial, but the boys' coefficient of -.05 $\pm$ .04 was quite negligible. <u>Laziness</u> may, therefore, be considered to be of minor importance or seriousness from the standpoint of personality or conduct deviation.

Its largest correlation, .41 $\pm$ .06, was among girls for <u>in-efficiency in work, play, etc.</u>, the corresponding coefficient for boys, .34 $\pm$ .05, being also substantial. Among boys <u>listlessness</u> and <u>poor work in school</u> yielded substantial correlations in the .30's, with moderate coefficients in the .20's among girls. <u>Irre-sponsibility</u> and <u>slovenliness</u> among girls yielded substantial correlations in the .30's, with moderate coefficients in the .20's among boys. <u>Temper display</u> among girls similarly yielded the substantial correlation of .35 $\pm$ .06, but a low coefficient of .11 among boys.

Six behavior problems showed moderate correlations in the .20's with <u>laziness</u> among both sexes: <u>lack of initiative or ambi-tion</u>, <u>inattentiveness in school</u>, <u>lack of interest in school</u>, <u>boast-ful or "show-off" manner</u>, <u>rudeness</u>, and <u>unpopularity</u>. Nine undesirable behavior traits among boys showed moderate correlations in the .20's, but low or negligible coefficients below .20 among girls: <u>absent-mindedness</u>, <u>distractibility</u>, <u>selfishness</u>, <u>disobedience</u>, <u>swearing or bad language</u> (undifferentiated), <u>disturbing influence in school</u>, <u>inferiority feelings</u>, <u>unhappiness</u>, and <u>masturbation</u>. Eleven notations among girls showed moderate correlations in the .20's but low positive coefficients below .20 among boys: <u>stub-bornness</u>, <u>contrariness</u>, <u>defiant attitude</u>, <u>bossy manner</u>, <u>leading others into bad conduct</u>, <u>preference for younger children as play-mates</u>, <u>seclusiveness</u>, <u>depressed mood or spells</u>, <u>irregular sleep habits</u>, <u>enuresis</u>, and <u>"request for vocational guidance."</u>

<u>Laziness</u> showed three negative correlations of moderate

TABLE 86

CORRELATIONS WITH "LAZY"

	Boys	Girls
Personality-total................................	.29 ± .02	.17 ± .04
Conduct-total....................................	.22 ± .03	.17 ± .04
Police arrest...................................	-.05 ± .04	.30 ± .05
	Larger Correlations (Positive)	
Listless..	.36 ± .04	.24 ± .07 (12-14)*
Inefficient in work, play, etc.................	.34 ± .05	.41 ± .06 (1)
Grouped: lack of interest in school, etc.....	.31 ± .03	.23 ± .05 (15-16)
Poor work in school............................	.30 ± .03	.21 ± .05 (20-23)
Irresponsible...................................	.28 ± .05	.36 ± .07 (2-3)
Grouped: dull, slow, etc......................	.28 ± .03	.18
Selfish...	.27 ± .05	-.05
Inferiority feelings...........................	.27 ± .04	.04
Boastful, "show-off"............................	.26 ± .04	.25 ± .07 (10-11)
Inattentive in school..........................	.26 ± .03	.22 ± .06 (17-19)
Disturbing influence in school.................	.25 ± .04	.14
Lack of interest in school.....................	.25 ± .04	.24 ± .06 (12-14)
Slovenly..	.25 ± .04	.36 ± .05 (2-3)
Rude..	.24 ± .04	.23 ± .06 (15-16)
Lack of initiative.............................	.23 ± .05	.27 ± .04 (7)
Absent-minded...................................	.22 ± .05	-.04
Distractible....................................	.22 ± .04	.06
Unpopular.......................................	.21 ± .05	.29 ± .08 (6)
Grouped: swearing, etc........................	.21 ± .04	.16
Disobedient.....................................	.20 ± .04	.09
Masturbation....................................	.20 ± .03	-.05
Unhappy...	.20 ± .06	.16
Temper display.................................	.11	.35 ± .06 (4)
Grouped: disobedient, etc.....................	.19	.30 ± .04 (5)
Irregular sleep habits.........................	.10	.26 ± .07 (8-9)
Enuresis..	.06	.26 ± .05 (8-9)
Stubborn..	.18	.25 ± .06 (10-11)
Seclusive.......................................	.19	.24 ± .06 (12-14)
Grouped: temper, etc..........................	.12	.22 ± .05 (17-19)
Grouped: depressed, etc.......................	.15	.22 ± .06 (17-19)
Vocational guidance............................	.11	.21 ± .06 (20-23)
Bossy...	.05	.21 ± .07 (20-23)
Depressed.......................................	.14	.21 ± .07 (20-23)
Contrary..	.04	.20 ± .08 (24-27)
Defiant...	.13	.20 ± .07 (24-27)
Leading others into bad conduct................	.17	.20 ± .08 (24-27)
Preference for younger children................	.19	.20 ± .07 (24-27)
	Larger Correlations (Negative)	
Sex delinquency (coitus).......................	-.28 + .06	-.11

*Rank order of girls' correlations.

TABLE 86—Continued

	Boys	Girls
Destructive..	.06	-.24 ± .05
Retardation in school..........................	-.19	-.20 ± .05
		Not Calculable
Sex denied entirely...........................	.16	(n.c.)
Question of encephalitis.....................	-.06	(n.c.)

Other Correlations (Positive to Negative)

Daydreaming, .19 and .09; Attractive manner, .19 and .05; Lying, .18 and .13; Slow, dull, .18 and .14; Grouped: fighting, etc., .18 and .09; Quarrelsome, .17 and .14; Sullen, .17 and -.00; Hatred or jealousy of sibling, .17 and .17; Bashful, .16 and -.07; Sensitive over specific fact, .16 and -.01; Queer, .16 and .17; Mental conflict, .16 and -.00; Spoiled child, .16 and .11; Grouped: egocentric, etc., .16 and .09; Teasing other children, .15 (boys); Repressed, .15 and .10; Grouped: sensitive or worrisome, etc., .15 and .01; Overinterest in opposite sex, .15 (girls); Clean, .14 and .04; Loitering, .13 and .15; Sulky, .13 and .12; Swearing (general), .13 (boys); Sensitive (general), .13 and .10; Complaining of bad treatment by other children, .13 (boys); Object of teasing, .12 and .07; Grouped: "nervous," etc., .12 and .09; Violence, .12 and .12; Overinterest in sex matters, .11 and -.01; Irritable, .11 and .11; Follower, .11 and -.04; Bad companions, .10 and .11; Fighting, .10 and .09; Nail-biting, .10 and .01; Headaches, .09 and .11; Truancy from school, .09 and .06; Finicky food habits, .08 and .06; Fantastical lying, .08 and .09; Truancy from home, .08 and -.05; Excuse-forming, .08 and .14; Restless, .08 and .08; Exclusion from school, .07 and .13; Discord between parents, .07 and .06; Crying spells, .06 and .03; Egocentric, .06 and .05; Restless in sleep, .06 and .04; Stuttering, .06 (boys); Former convulsions, .06 and -.02; Refusal to attend school, .05 and -.04; Popular, .05 and -.02; Immoral home conditions, .05 and .12; Incorrigible, .04 and .08; Temper tantrums, .04 and .00; Apprehensive, .04 and -.02; Changeable moods, .03 and .01; Emotional instability, .03 and .09; Lues, .03 and .01; Smoking, .02 (boys); Staying out late at night, .02 and .05; Question of change of personality, .02 and .09; Leader, .02 and -.11; Stealing, .01 and .11; Neurological defect, .01 and -.06; Speech defect, .01 and -.14; Brother in penal detention, -.02 and -.04; Conduct prognosis bad, -.02 and .01; Victim of sex abuse, -.02 (girls); "Nervous," -.02 and -.01; Psychoneurotic, -.02 and -.02; Threatening violence, -.02 (boys); Gang, -.02 (boys); Oversuggestible, -.03 and .03; Irregular attendance at school, -.04 and .14; Underweight, -.05 and .02; Vicious home conditions, -.07 and .02; Worry over specific fact, -.08 and -.00; Question of hypophrenia, -.10 and .06; Feeble-minded sibling, -.18 and -.13

size in the -.20's: sex delinquency (coitus) among boys and destructiveness and retardation in school among girls.

Among the six sex notations there were two correlations of moderate size with laziness, both among boys, the interesting negative one of -.28 ± .06 with sex delinquency (coitus) and the positive one of .20 ± .03 with masturbation.

Among the seven physical or psychophysical defects the
only statistically significant correlation was .26 ± .05 with enuresis among girls.

Among the four home or familial notations all coefficients
were negligible, ranging from -.07 to .12.

The notation inefficiency or carelessness in work, studies,
play, etc., forgetting errands, etc., was found among 106 boys, or
5.0 per cent of our cases, and among 75 girls, or 6.4 per cent.
Its bi-serial correlations with the personality-total were large,
.42 ± .03 and .50 ± .03 for boys and girls respectively (Table 87).
With the conduct-total its correlation among boys was moderate,
.24 ± .03, and among girls substantial, .35 ± .04. With police
arrest its tetrachoric correlations were negligible.

Its largest correlations among both sexes were with absent-
mindedness, with coefficients in the .40's. Irresponsibility among
boys also yielded the large correlation of .47 ± .05, with a substantial coefficient among girls of .35 ± .07. Laziness among
girls yielded the large correlation of .41 ± .06, with a substantial coefficient of .34 ± .05 among boys. Daydreaming and depressed mood or spells among girls similarly yielded large correlations in the .40's with moderate coefficients in the .20's among
boys.

Distractibility and queer behavior yielded substantial correlations ranging from .29 to .36 among both sexes. Among girls
three behavior problems, slovenliness, emotional instability, and
changeable moods or attitudes, yielded substantial correlations in
the .30's with moderate coefficients in the .20's among boys.
Among girls four additional conduct problems yielded substantial
correlations in the .30's but low coefficients below .20 among boys:
boys: excuse-forming attitude, lying, defiant attitude, and boastful or "show-off" manner.

Seven behavior traits showed consistent moderate correlations with inefficiency in work, play, etc., in the .20's: listlessness, lack of interest in school, poor work in school, sensitiveness in general, crying spells, stubbornness, and quarrelsomeness, and also one calculated for girls only, overinterest in the
opposite sex. Nine notations among boys showed moderate correlations in the .20's but low coefficients below .20 among girls:

TABLE 87

CORRELATIONS WITH "INEFFICIENT IN WORK, PLAY, ETC."

	Boys	Girls
Personality-total...........................	.42 ± .03	.50 ± .03
Conduct-total...............................	.24 ± .03	.35 ± .04
Police arrest...............................	.08 ± .04	.00 ± .06
	Larger Correlations (Positive)	
Irresponsible...............................	.47 ± .05	.35 ± .07 (7-8)*
Absent-minded...............................	.47 ± .05	.42 ± .07 (1-2)
Distractible................................	.36 ± .05	.29 ± .06 (15-19)
Lazy..	.34 ± .05	.41 ± .06 (3-4)
Unpopular...................................	.31 ± .06	.33 ± .08 (10)
Queer.......................................	.30 ± .06	.29 ± .07 (15-18)
Poor work in school.........................	.29 ± .04	.22 ± .05 (37-38)
Listless....................................	.28 ± .05	.28 ± .07 (19-20)
Grouped: lack of interest in school, etc.....	.28 ± .04	.20 ± .06 (42-46)
Lack of interest in school..................	.27 ± .05	.23 ± .06 (29-36)
Daydreaming.................................	.26 ± .05	.42 ± .06 (1-2)
Lack of initiative..........................	.26 ± .06	.11
Grouped: dull, slow, etc....................	.26 ± .04	.30 ± .05 (14)
Loitering...................................	.25 ± .05	.00
Grouped: depressed, etc....................	.25 ± .05	.29 ± .06 (15-18)
Sensitive (general).........................	.24 ± .05	.26 ± .07 (22-23)
Inattentive in school.......................	.23 ± .03	.11
Changeable moods............................	.23 ± .05	.31 ± .06 (12-13)
Depressed...................................	.23 ± .06	.41 ± .07 (3-4)
Crying spells...............................	.22 ± .04	.23 ± .05 (29-36)
Seclusive...................................	.22 ± .05	.17
Unhappy.....................................	.22 ± .07	.13
Leading others into bad conduct.............	.21 ± .06	.16
Slovenly....................................	.21 ± .05	.31 ± .05 (12-13)
Stubborn....................................	.21 ± .04	.23 ± .05 (29-36)
Emotional instability.......................	.21 ± .06	.36 ± .07 (5-6)
Grouped: sensitive or worrisome, etc........	.21 ± .04	.21 ± .05 (39-41)
Quarrelsome.................................	.20 ± .05	.23 ± .06 (29-36)
Restless....................................	.20 ± .04	.16
Spoiled child...............................	.20 ± .05	.18
Question of encephalitis....................	.20 ± .07	-.03
Excuse-forming..............................	.08	.36 ± .06 (5-6)
Defiant.....................................	-.06	.35 ± .06 (7-8)
Lying.......................................	.15	.34 ± .05 (9)
Boastful, "show-off"........................	.09	.32 ± .07 (11)
Fantastical lying...........................	.14	.29 ± .07 (15-18)
Rude..	.16	.28 ± .06 (19-20)
Question of change of personality...........	.08	.27 ± .07 (21)
Disturbing influence in school..............	.15	.26 ± .07 (22-23)
Sulky.......................................	.09	.25 ± .07 (24-25)

*Rank order of girls' correlations.

TABLE 87—Continued

	Boys	Girls
Conduct prognosis bad............................	.08	.25 ± .08 (24-25)
Irregular sleep habits............................	.18	.24 ± .08 (26-28)
Inferiority feelings............................	.08	.24 ± .08 (26-28)
Grouped: disobedient, etc....................	.18	.24 ± .05 (26-28)
Violence..	.14	.23 ± .07 (29-36)
Slow, dull......................................	.18	.23 ± .05 (29-36)
Immoral home conditions.......................	-.11	.23 ± .07 (29-36)
Grouped: temper, etc..........................	.09	.23 ± .05 (29-36)
Exclusion from school.........................	.01	.22 ± .07 (37-38)
Stealing..	.14	.21 ± .05 (39-41)
Grouped: "nervous," etc......................	.18	.21 ± .05 (39-41)
Overinterest in opposite sex..................	....	.20 ± .06 (42-46)
Mental conflict................................	.16	.20 ± .09 (42-46)
Headaches.......................................	.19	.20 ± .07 (42-46)
Grouped: egocentric, etc.....................	.09	.20 ± .05 (42-46)
Larger Correlations (Negative)		
Speech defect..................................	.09	-.33 ± .07
Irregular attendance at school................	-.07	-.20 ± .07

Other Correlations (Positive to Negative)

Staying out late at night, .19 and .08; Contrary, .18 and .05; Lues, .18 and .11; Teasing other children, .17 (boys); Complaining of bad treatment by other children, .17 (boys); Grouped: fighting, etc., .17 and .13; Stuttering, .16 (boys); Preference for younger children, .15 and .18; Neurological defect, .15 and .16; Discord between parents, .15 and .06; Disobedient, .14 and .13; Selfish, .14 and .19; Restless in sleep, .14 and .14; Sensitive over specific fact, .14 and .17; Worry over specific fact, .14 and .16; Refusal to attend school, .13 and -.03; Irritable, .13 and .18; Object of teasing, .13 and .08; Truancy from school, .12 and .02; Grouped: swearing, etc., .12 and .10; Sullen, .11 and .16; Masturbation, .11 and .08; "Nervous," .10 and .18; Former convulsions, .10 and -.01; Bossy, .09 and .10; Incorrigible, .09 and .14; Nail-biting, .09 and -.02; Smoking, .09 (boys); Truancy from home, .09 and .13; Attractive manner, .09 and .06; Vocational guidance, .09 and -.17; Destructive, .08 and .19; Overinterest in sex matters, .08 and .14; Bashful, .08 and .02; Egocentric, .08 and .09; Oversuggestible, .08 and .12; Popular, .08 and -.00; Threatening violence, .07 (boys); Hatred or jealousy of sibling, .07 and .18; Fighting, .06 and .09; Temper tantrums, .06 and .18; Sex delinquency (coitus), .06 and .01; Bad companions, .05 and .14; Finicky food habits, .05 and -.06; Apprehensive, .05 and .12; Follower, .05 and .06; Enuresis, .04 and .19; Swearing (general), .04 (boys); Feeble-minded sibling, .04 and -.12; Repressed, .01 and .11; Victim of sex abuse, -.00 (girls); Underweight, -.00 and .04; Question of hypophrenia, -.00 and .04; Clean, -.02 and .06; Leader, -.02 and -.11; Psychoneurotic, -.02 and .10; Sex denied entirely, -.04 and .13; Temper display, -.04 and .17; Retardation in school, -.07 and -.02; Gang, -.07 (boys); Brother in penal detention, -.12 and -.19; Vicious home conditions, -.13 and .09

lack of initiative or ambition, inattentiveness in school, loitering or wandering, "spoiled child," restlessness, unhappiness, seclusiveness, leading others into bad conduct, and question or diagnosis of encephalitis. Among girls nineteen miscellaneous notations showed moderate correlations in the .20's but low or negligible coefficients below .20 among boys: slow or dull manner,
fantastical lying, mental conflict, inferiority feelings, question
of change of personality, egocentricity or selfishness (undifferentiated), rudeness, sulkiness, "nervousness" or restlessness (including irritable temperament and changeable moods, undifferentiated), irregular sleep habits, disobedience or incorrigibility
(including defiant attitude, stubbornness, and contrariness, undifferentiated), violence, temper tantrums or display (including
irritable temperament, undifferentiated), disturbing influence in
school, exclusion from school, stealing, staff notation of unfavorable conduct prognosis, immoral home conditions, and headaches.

There were two negative correlations of statistically significant size with inefficiency in work, play, etc., both among
girls: speech defect (other than stuttering), -.33 + .07, and irregular attendance at school, -.20 + .07.

Among the six sex notations the only significant correlation was .20 + .06 for overinterest in the opposite sex, for which
only the girls' correlations were calculated.

Among the seven physical or psychophysical disabilities
there were two statistically significant correlations, the positive
one of .20 + .07 with question or diagnosis of encephalitis among
boys and the curious negative one of -.33 + .07 with speech defect
(other than stuttering) among girls.

Among the four home or familial notations the only correlation of statistically significant size was with immoral home conditions among girls, .23 + .07.

Irresponsibility was noted among 118 of our boys, or 5.6
per cent, and among 70 of our girls, or 5.9 per cent. With the
personality-total and conduct-total its correlations were moderate,
ranging from .24 to .32 (Table 88). With police arrest its correlations were negligible.

Its largest correlation among boys was .47 + .05 with inefficiency in work, play, etc., the corresponding coefficient for

TABLE 88

CORRELATIONS WITH "IRRESPONSIBLE"

	Boys	Girls
Personality-total............................	.24 ± .03	.29 ± .04
Conduct-total................................	.27 ± .03	.32 ± .04
Police arrest................................	.10 ± .04	.08 ± .06
	Larger Correlations (Positive)	
Inefficient in work, play, etc..............	.47 ± .05	.35 ± .07 (5)*
Loitering....................................	.34 ± .05	.08
Staying out late at night....................	.33 ± .04	.13
Absent-minded................................	.30 ± .05	.17
Lazy...	.28 ± .05	.36 ± .07 (2-4)
Daydreaming..................................	.26 ± .05	.09
Lack of interest in school..................	.25 ± .05	.26 ± .07 (17-18)
Stealing....................................	.25 ± .04	.24 ± .05 (21-26)
Fantastical lying...........................	.23 ± .03	.21 ± .07 (29-32)
Truancy from home...........................	.23 ± .04	.16
Distractible................................	.23 ± .05	.24 ± .06 (21-26)
Immoral home conditions.....................	.23 ± .06	-.05
Grouped: lack of interest in school, etc.....	.23 ± .04	.21 ± .06 (29-32)
Destructive.................................	.22 ± .05	.10
Disobedient.................................	.22 ± .04	.25 ± .06 (19-20)
Unpopular....................................	.22 ± .06	.13
Lying.......................................	.21 ± .04	.46 ± .04 (1)
Slovenly....................................	.21 ± .04	.20 ± .06 (33-35)
Grouped: egocentric, etc....................	.21 ± .04	.36 ± .05 (2-4)
Listless....................................	.20 ± .05	-.16
Grouped: disobedient, etc..................	.18	.36 ± .05 (2-4)
Fighting....................................	-.06	.34 ± .04 (6-7)
Unhappy.....................................	.17	.34 ± .07 (6-7)
Leading others into bad conduct.............	.17	.33 ± .08 (8-9)
Selfish....................................	.19	.33 ± .07 (8-9)
Grouped: fighting, etc.....................	.07	.32 ± .05 (10)
Grouped: depressed, etc....................	.12	.31 ± .06 (11)
Grouped: temper, etc......................	.12	.30 ± .05 (12)
Disturbing influence in school.............	.18	.29 ± .07 (13-15)
Quarrelsome.................................	.10	.29 ± .06 (13-15)
Temper display..............................	-.02	.29 ± .07 (13-15)
Emotional instability.......................	.05	.28 ± .07 (16)
Nail-biting................................	.18	.26 ± .05 (17-18)
Conduct prognosis bad.......................	.12	.25 ± .09 (19-20)
Bad companions.............................	.14	.24 ± .06 (21-26)
Defiant....................................	.12	.24 ± .07 (21-26)
Incorrigible...............................	.17	.24 ± .06 (21-26)
Spoiled child..............................	.13	.24 ± .07 (21-26)
Crying spells..............................	.05	.22 ± .05 (27-28)
Sensitive over specific fact..............	-.04	.22 ± .06 (27-28)

*Rank order of girls' correlations.

TABLE 88—Continued

	Boys	Girls
Temper tantrums..............................	-.01	.21 ± .06 (29-32)
Question of change of personality...	.16	.21 ± .08 (29-32)
Overinterest in opposite sex..................	....	.20 ± .06 (33-35)
Queer...	.14	.20 ± .08 (33-35)
	Larger Correlations (Negative)	
Feeble-minded sibling.........................	-.23 ± .06	(n.c.)
Vicious home conditions.......................	.11	-.27 ± .08
Retardation in school.........................	.07	-.24 ± .05
	Not Calculable	
Worry over specific fact......................	.01	(n.c.)
Headaches.....................................	(n.c.)	-.03
Question of encephalitis......................	.10	(n.c.)

Other Correlations (Positive to Negative)

Irritable, .19 and .16; Lack of initiative, .19 and .08; Poor work in school, .19 and .09; Boastful, "show-off," .18 and .16; Bossy, .18 and .17; Refusal to attend school, .18 and -.01; Mental conflict, .18 and .03; Excuse-forming, .17 and .18; Restless, .17 and .16; Preference for younger children, .17 and .07; Contrary, .16 and .13; Changeable moods, .16 and .08; Seclusive, .16 and .01; Grouped: "nervous," etc., .16 and .19; Grouped: swearing, etc., .16 and .08; Teasing other children, .15 (boys); Rude, .15 and .15; Popular, .15 and .02; Grouped: dull, slow, etc., .15 and -.03; Truancy from school, .14 and .04; Exclusion from school, .14 and .16; Inattentive in school, .13 and .09; Overinterest in sex matters, .13 and .03; Irregular sleep habits, .13 and .17; Masturbation, .12 and .05; Leader, .12 and .19; Neurological defect, .12 and -.03; Object of teasing, .11 and .15; Complaining of bad treatment by other children, .11 (boys); Egocentric, .10 and .15; Threatening violence, .09 (boys); Smoking, .08 (boys); Oversuggestible, .08 and .18; Attractive manner, .08 and .12; Discord between parents, .08 and .11; Hatred or jealousy of sibling, .07 and .10; Slow, dull, .07 and -.03; Restless in sleep, .07 and .11; Irregular attendance at school, .07 and -.06; Brother in penal detention, .07 and -.05; Gang, .06 (boys); Violence, .06 and .19; "Nervous," .06 and .14; Follower, .06 and.08; Vocational guidance, .06 and -.08; Stubborn, .05 and .12; Apprehensive, .05 and .05; Inferiority feelings, .04 and .13; Repressed, .04 and -.17; Underweight, .04 and .04; Sulky, .03 and .06; Depressed, .02 and .18; Stuttering, .02 (boys); Bashful, .01 and -.03; Former convulsions, .01 and -.17; Sensitive (general), .00 and .06; Swearing (general), -.01 (boys); Sullen, -.01 and -.01; Finicky food habits, -.01 and .06; Enuresis, -.02 and .07; Victim of sex abuse, -.03 (girls); Lues, -.04 and -.06; Psychoneurotic, -.04 and .13; Grouped: sensitive or worrisome, etc., -.05 and .13; Speech defect, -.05 and .06; Clean, -.07 and .06; Question of hypophrenia, -.10 and .01; Sex denied entirely, -.11 and .02; Sex delinquency (coitus), -.14 and .11

girls being substantial, .35 + .07. Among girls its largest correlation was .46 + .04 with lying, the corresponding coefficient
for boys being only moderate, .21 + .04.

Three behavior problems—loitering or wandering, absent-
mindedness, and staying out late at night—among boys yielded substantial correlations in the .30's but low coefficients below .20
among girls. Laziness among girls yielded the substantial correlation of .36 + .07 and among boys the moderate coefficient of
.28 + .05. Five behavior traits among girls yielded substantial
correlations in the .30's but low coefficients below .20 among
boys: disobedience or incorrigibility (undifferentiated), selfishness, fighting, leading others into bad conduct, and unhappiness.

Irresponsibility showed consistent moderate correlations
in the .20's with the following six undesirable behavior traits:
lack of interest in school, slovenliness, distractibility, fantastical lying, disobedience, and stealing and also one calculated
for girls only, overinterest in the opposite sex. Among boys six
notations showed moderate correlations in the .20's but low coefficients below .20 among girls: listlessness, daydreaming, destructiveness, truancy from home, unpopularity, and immoral home
conditions. Among girls fifteen personality and conduct difficulties showed moderate correlations in the .20's but low coefficients
below .20 among boys: disturbing influence in school, incorrigibility, defiant attitude, emotional instability, temper tantrums,
temper display, quarrelsomeness, "spoiled child," crying spells,
sensitiveness over some specific fact, question of change of personality, queer behavior, nail-biting, bad companions, and staff
notation of unfavorable conduct prognosis.

There were three negative correlations with irresponsibility of moderate size in the -.20's: among boys for feeble-minded
sibling and among girls for retardation in school and vicious home
conditions.

Among the six sex notations the only correlation of significant size with irresponsibility was for overinterest in the opposite sex, .20 + .06 (calculated for girls only).

Among the seven physical or psychophysical disabilities
the correlations with irresponsibility were very low or negligible.

Among the four home or familial notations there were two

moderate correlations in the .20's, the <u>positive</u> one of .23 $\pm$ .06
with <u>immoral home conditions</u> among boys and the <u>negative</u> one of
-.27 $\pm$ .08 with <u>vicious home conditions</u> among girls.

CHAPTER XLVI

SLOVENLINESS AND CLEANLINESS

Slovenliness or marked lack of cleanliness or neatness in dress or appearance was noted among 337 of our 2,113 White boys (15.9 per cent) and among 205 of our 1,181 White girls (17.4 per cent). It was of only moderate importance or seriousness, its biserial correlations with the personality-total and conduct-total ranging from .22 to .30 (Table 89). With police arrest its tetrachoric r's for boys and girls respectively were only .19 ± .03 and -.02 ± .04.

TABLE 89

CORRELATIONS WITH "SLOVENLY"

	Boys	Girls
Personality-total	.22 ± .02	.25 ± .03
Conduct-total	.30 ± .02	.30 ± .03
Police arrest	.19 ± .03	-.02 ± .04
	Larger Correlations (Positive)	
Loitering	.33 ± .05	.07
Nail-biting	.31 ± .03	.12
Disturbing influence in school	.28 ± .03	.22 ± .05 (22-30)*
Incorrigible	.28 ± .03	.27 ± .04 (9-12)
Grouped: disobedient, etc.	.28 ± .03	.31 ± .03 (2-5)
Contrary	.26 ± .05	.14
Leading others into bad conduct	.26 ± .04	.23 ± .06 (18-21)
Gang	.26 ± .04	....
Stealing	.26 ± .03	.31 ± .04 (2-5)
Truancy from school	.26 ± .03	.27 ± .04 (9-12)
Lazy	.25 ± .04	.36 ± .05 (1)
Smoking	.24 ± .04	....
Staying out late at night	.24 ± .03	.14
Destructive	.23 ± .04	.17
Rude	.23 ± .03	.26 ± .04 (13-16)
Truancy from home	.23 ± .03	.21 ± .04 (31-34)

*Rank order of girls' correlations.

	Boys	Girls
Restless....................................	.23 ± .03	.19
Irregular sleep habits......................	.22 ± .04	.13
Complaining of bad treatment by other children	.22 ± .04	....
Inefficient in work, play, etc...............	.21 ± .05	.31 ± .05 (2-5)
Irresponsible...............................	.21 ± .04	.20 ± .06 (35-36)
Lying.......................................	.20 ± .03	.25 ± .04 (17)
Teasing other children......................	.20 ± .04	....
Excuse-forming..............................	.20 ± .04	.28 ± .05 (6-8)
Irregular attendance at school..............	.20 ± .04	.09
Grouped: "nervous," etc.....................	.20 ± .03	.10
Grouped: swearing, etc......................	.20 ± .03	.23 ± .05 (18-21)
Violence....................................	.17	.31 ± .05 (2-5)
Quarrelsome.................................	.14	.28 ± .04 (6-8)
Overinterest in sex matters.................	-.02	.28 ± .05 (6-8)
Queer.......................................	.07	.27 ± .06 (9-12)
Grouped: fighting, etc......................	.17	.27 ± .04 (9-12)
Defiant.....................................	.16	.26 ± .05 (13-16)
Fantastical lying...........................	.17	.26 ± .05 (13-16)
Masturbation................................	.13	.26 ± .04 (13-16)
Depressed...................................	.15	.23 ± .06 (18-21)
Grouped: egocentric, etc....................	.19	.23 ± .04 (18-21)
Boastful, "show-off"........................	.19	.22 ± .05 (22-30)
Disobedient.................................	.16	.22 ± .04 (22-30)
Lack of interest in school..................	.13	.22 ± .05 (22-30)
Overinterest in opposite sex................	....	.22 ± .04 (22-30)
Hatred or jealousy of sibling...............	.13	.22 ± .06 (22-30)
Listless....................................	.13	.22 ± .05 (22-30)
Vicious home conditions.....................	.10	.22 ± .06 (22-30)
Grouped: depressed, etc.....................	.16	.22 ± .05 (22-30)
Temper tantrums.............................	.08	.21 ± .05 (31-34)
Daydreaming.................................	.05	.21 ± .05 (31-34)
Egocentric..................................	.15	.21 ± .05 (31-34)
Grouped: lack of interest in school, etc.....	.14	.20 ± .04 (35-36)

Other Correlations (Positive to Negative)

Absent-minded, .19 and -.03; Fighting, .18 and .17; Bad companions, .17 and .13; Unhappy, .17 and .09; Changeable moods, .16 and .08; Enuresis, .15 and .13; Emotional instability, .15 and .07; Sex denied entirely, .15 and .10; Stubborn, .14 and .17; Mental conflict, .14 and .15; Bossy, .13 and .16; Selfish, .13 and .06; Sullen, .13 and .03; Unpopular, .13 and .15; Discord between parents, .13 and .17; Follower, .13 and -.06; Grouped: dull, slow, etc., .13 and .15; Sulky, .12 and .13; Lack of initiative, .12 and .12; Distractible, .12 and .16; Leader, .12 and -.06; Seclusive, .11 and .09; Spoiled child, .11 and -.03; Preference for younger children as playmates, .11 and .06; Grouped: temper, etc., .11 and .11; Swearing (general), .10 (boys); Temper display, .10 and .04; Question of change of personality, .10 and .15; Inattentive in school, .09 and .13; Refusal to attend school, .09 and -.07; Crying spells, .09 and .11; Irritable, .09 and -.01; Slow, dull, .09 and .08; Object of teasing, .09 and .09; Popular, .09 and -.01; Exclusion from school, .08 and .13; Poor work in school, .08 and .12; Attractive manner, .08 and -.04; Question of encephalitis, .08 and -.03; Sex delinquency (coitus), .07 and .06; Oversuggestible, .07 and .18;

TABLE 89—Continued

Feeble-minded sibling, .07 and .07; Repressed, .06 and -.01; Victim of sex abuse, .06 (girls); Apprehensive, .05 and .08; Restless in sleep, .05 and .14; Conduct prognosis bad, .05 and .09; Retardation in school, .05 and -.01; Former convulsions, .05 and .03; Brother in penal detention, .05 and .17; Inferiority feelings, .04 and .07; Stuttering, .03 (boys); Neurological defect, .04 and .07; Underweight, .04 and -.01; Grouped: sensitive or worrisome, etc., .02 and .07; Threatening violence, .02 (boys); Psychoneurotic, .02 and .05; Headaches, .02 and .14; Finicky food habits, .01 and .03; Bashful, .01 and .03; Question of hypophrenia, .01 and .08; Sensitive over specific fact, .01 and .06; Lues, .00 and -.05; Speech defect, -.01 and -.16; Sensitive (general), -.01 and .04; "Nervous," -.01 and .00; Worry over specific fact, -.05 and .02; Immoral home conditions, -.07 and .03; Vocational guidance, -.07 and -.14
        Omitted—Clean

Among boys its highest correlations, in the .30's, were with nail-biting and loitering or wandering, the corresponding correlation for girls being low, .12 and .07 respectively. Among girls four notations yielded substantial correlations in the .30's, the corresponding correlations for boys being moderate, ranging from .17 to .26: laziness, inefficiency in work, play, etc., stealing, and violence.

Slovenliness showed consistent moderate correlations in the .20's with fourteen conduct and personality problems: irresponsibility, excuse-forming attitude, incorrigibility, disturbing influence in school, leading others into bad conduct, rudeness, truancy from home, truancy from school, lying, swearing or bad language (undifferentiated), and the four notations for which only the boys' coefficients were calculated, running with a gang, smoking, teasing other children, and complaining of bad treatment by other children. Among boys six notations showed moderate correlations in the .20's but low coefficients below .20 among girls: contrariness, staying out late at night, destructiveness, restlessness, irregular sleep habits, and irregular attendance at school. Among girls sixteen notations showed moderate correlations in the .20's but low coefficients below .20 among boys: listlessness, lack of interest in school, daydreaming, depressed mood or spells, queer behavior, fantastical lying, boastful or "show-off" manner, egocentricity, quarrelsomeness, hatred or jealousy of sibling, disobedience, defiant attitude, temper tantrums, masturbation, overinterest in sex matters, and vicious home conditions.

Among the six sex notations there were three correlations

of moderate size in the .20's, all among girls: masturbation, overinterest in sex matters, and (calculated for girls only) overinterest in the opposite sex.

Among the seven physical or psychophysical notations all correlations were low or negligible.

Among the four home or familial notations the only correlation of moderate size with slovenliness was with vicious (not "immoral") home conditions, among girls, .22 + .06.

Clean, neat habits or appearance was one of the few "desirable" behavior traits which were noted frequently enough in our data to justify correlational treatment. It was noted among 318, or 15.0 per cent of our boys and among 171, or 14.5 per cent, of our girls. Its correlations with our three criteria of seriousness or "ominousness" were all low or negligible.

Attractive manner yielded substantial correlations in the .30's among both sexes (Table 90). Worry over some specific fact among girls also yielded the substantial correlation of .34 + .07 with a moderate coefficient of .24 + .05 among boys.

Sensitiveness or worrisomeness (undifferentiated) and sensitiveness in general showed moderate correlations in the .20's among both sexes. Three notations—boastful or "show-off" manner, sensitiveness over some specific fact, and daydreaming—among boys showed moderate correlations in the .20's but among girls low coefficients below .20. Six notations among girls showed moderate correlations in the .20's but low positive coefficients below .20 among boys: popularity, sex misbehavior denied entirely, repressed manner, changeable moods or attitudes, irregular sleep habits, and refusal to attend school.

Clean habits showed negative correlations of moderate size in the -.20's with three notations: among boys with retardation in school and among girls with feeble-minded sibling and loitering or wandering.

Among the six sex notations the seven physical or psychophysical disabilities and the four home or familial notations the only significant correlation with clean habits was with sex misbehavior denied entirely among girls, .25 + .07. All other correlations in these fields were low or negligible, ranging from -.16 to .18.

TABLE 90

CORRELATIONS WITH "CLEAN"

	Boys	Girls
Personality-total.............................	.15 ± .02	.14 ± .03
Conduct-total.................................	.06 ± .02	.04 ± .03
Police arrest.................................	.10 ± .03	-.03 ± .05
Larger Correlations (Positive)		
Attractive manner.............................	.32 ± .03	.30 ± .04 (2)*
Boastful, "show-off"..........................	.25 ± .03	-.03
Grouped: sensitive or worrisome, etc.........	.24 ± .03	.22 ± .04 (7)
Worry over specific fact......................	.24 ± .05	.34 ± .07 (1)
Sensitive over specific fact.................	.22 ± .03	.12
Daydreaming...................................	.20 ± .04	.01
Sensitive (general)..........................	.20 ± .04	.29 ± .05 (3)
Irregular sleep habits.......................	.01	.25 ± .06 (4-6)
Sex denied entirely..........................	.13	.25 ± .07 (4-6)
Popular.......................................	.17	.25 ± .06 (4-6)
Repressed.....................................	.10	.21 ± .07 (8-9)
Changeable moods..............................	.07	.21 ± .05 (8-9)
Refusal to attend school.....................	.13	.20 ± .07 (10)
Larger Correlations (Negative)		
Retardation in school........................	-.24 ± .03	-.15 / -.15
Feeble-minded sibling........................	-.18	-.26 ± .05
Loitering.....................................	-.07	-.21 ± .06

*Rank order of girls' correlations.

Other Correlations (Positive to Negative)

Fantastical lying, .18 and .06; Sex delinquency (coitus), .18 and -.06; Lack of initiative, .18 and .06; "Nervous," .15 and .01; Irregular attendance at school, .15 and .12; Bashful, .15 and .03; Inferiority feelings, .14 and .10; Lazy, .14 and .04; Hatred or jealousy of sibling, .13 and -.01; Complaining of bad treatment by other children, .12 (boys); Unpopular, .12 and -.08; Masturbation, .12 and .08; Bossy, .11 and .18; Finicky food habits, .11 and .18; Mental conflict, .11 and .10; Grouped: depressed, etc., .10 and .13; Grouped: "nervous," etc., .10 and .08; Seclusive, .10 and .08; Depressed, .10 and .14; Inattentive in school, .10 and -.08; Teasing other children, .09 (boys); Smoking, .09 (boys); Irritable, .09 and .07; Unhappy, .09 and .09; Leader, .09 and .07; Speech defect, .08 and .04; Headaches, .08 and -.01; Egocentric, .08 and .03; Temper display, .08 and .06; Sullen, .08 and -.03; Selfish, .08 and .12; Rude, .07 and .09; Immoral home conditions, .07 and -.02; Discord between parents, .07 and .02; Grouped: egocentric, etc., .07 and .05; Grouped: lack of interest in school, etc., .07 and .05; Victim of sex abuse, .07 (girls); Exclusion from school, .06 and -.01; Spoiled child, .06 and .06; Apprehensive, .06 and .11; Bad companions, .06 and -.06; Sulky, .06 and .14; Stealing, .06 and

TABLE 90—Continued

-.11; Defiant, .06 and -.02; Lack of interest in school, .05 and -.04; Leading others into bad conduct, .05 and .07; Question of change of personality, .05 and .02; Restless, .05 and .03; Restless in sleep, .05 and .08; Former convulsions, .05 and .01; Grouped: temper, etc., .05 and .12; Poor work in school, .04 and -.06; Vocational guidance, .04 and .19; Psychoneurotic, .04 and .06; Overinterest in sex matters, .04 and .00; Stubborn, .04 and .12; Destructive, .04 and -.04; Contrary, .04 and .10; Truancy from school, .03 and -.16; Crying spells, .03 and .06; Excuse-forming, .03 and .06; Neurological defect, .03 and .11; Lues, .03 and .06; Grouped: swearing, etc., .02 and -.03; Absent-minded, .02 and .16; Gang, .02 (boys); Disturbing influence in school, .01 and -.02; Violence, .01 and .06; Oversuggestible, .01 and -.02; Grouped: disobedient, etc., .01 and .00; Incorrigible, -.00 and -.07; Lying, -.00 and -.00; Temper tantrums, -.00 and .10; Vicious home conditions, -.01 and .00; Staying out late at night, -.01 and -.07; Nail-biting, -.01 and .04; Enuresis, -.01 and .12; Inefficient in work, play, etc., -.02 and .06; Truancy from home, -.02 and .16; Listless, -.02 and .13; Object of teasing, -.02 and -.09; Grouped: dull, slow, etc., -.03 and .07; Follower, -.03 and .07; Conduct prognosis bad, -.03 and -.04; Threatening violence, -.03 (boys); Quarrelsome, -.04 and -.03; Stuttering, -.04 (boys); Preference for younger children, -.04 and .07; Grouped: fighting, etc., -.04 and .05; Question of encephalitis, -.05 and .17; Distractible, -.05 and .09; Disobedient, -.05 and -.06; Swearing (general), -.06 (boys); Irresponsible, -.07 and .06; Overinterest in opposite sex, -.07 (girls); Fighting, -.08 and .12; Brother in penal detention, -.08 and -.16; Queer, -.09 and .07; Emotional instability, -.10 and .07; Slow, dull, -.11 and .06; Question of hypophrenia, -.12 and -.17; Underweight, -.15 and .13
Omitted—Slovenly

In general it may be said that clean habits showed almost no association with undesirable conduct manifestations but did show a few moderate correlations with personality difficulties. It appeared to be positively associated with such desirable traits as attractive manner and popularity.

A comparison of the corresponding correlations for the presumably antithetical notations slovenliness (Table 89) and clean habits (Table 90) shows again the curious statistical phenomenon that many of the coefficients for these antithetical pairs of traits were not of opposite sign and of similar magnitude, as would be expected if strictly objectively measurable traits were being used, but were often of the same sign (though of different magnitude). Among the 119 pairs of corresponding coefficients for the boys in Table 89 (slovenliness) and Table 90 (clean habits) there were 78 pairs of like sign and only 41 of unlike sign. Among 114 pairs of girls' coefficients there were 71 pairs of like sign and only 43 of unlike sign. The intercolumnar correlations (Pearson's product-moment) were $-.11 \pm .06$ for boys and $-.27 \pm .06$ for girls.

(A discussion and attempted explanation of this phenomenon may be
found in I, 134-35 and 249-50, and in this volume, p. 45, and in
the concluding paragraphs of chaps. xx, xxv, and liii.)

CHAPTER XLVII

LACK OF INTEREST OR INATTENTIVENESS IN SCHOOL STUDIES, EMPLOYMENT, ETC.

To distinguish between the notations <u>lack of interest in school or inattentiveness in school studies, employment, etc.</u>, and the similar notation <u>inattentiveness in school</u> was frequently not easy in the perusal of the actual case records, and it is probable that these rubrics have been inadequately differentiated in our original indexing of the data. "<u>Lack of interest</u>" was intended to denote a more fundamental attitude in the patient, while "<u>inattentiveness</u>" was intended to designate a more superficial overt behavior in the classroom. The bi-serial correlations for each rubric with the <u>personality-total</u> and <u>conduct-total</u> were only moderate, ranging from .18 to .32. Their tetrachoric correlations with <u>police arrest</u> were low with the exception of the moderate coefficient of .26 ± .05 among girls for <u>inattentiveness in school</u>.

Lack of interest in school was noted among 279 of our 2,113 White boys (13.2 per cent) and among 107 of our 1,181 White girls (9.1 per cent). Among both sexes its largest correlations were with <u>poor work in school</u>, the respective coefficients for boys and girls being 32. ± .03 and .42 ± .04 (Table 91). <u>Disturbing influence in school</u> yielded the substantial correlations of .31 ± .03 and .29 ± .06 among boys and girls respectively. Six behavior traits among girls also yielded substantial correlations in the .30's but low positive coefficients ranging from .10 to .21 among boys: <u>refusal to attend school</u>, <u>restlessness</u>, <u>question of change of personality</u>, <u>sullenness</u>, <u>fighting</u>, and <u>swearing or bad language</u> (undifferentiated).

Lack of interest in school showed consistent moderate correlations in the .20's with eight behavior difficulties: <u>irresponsibility</u>, <u>laziness</u>, <u>inefficiency in work, play, etc.</u>, <u>truancy from school</u>, <u>disobedience</u>, <u>rudeness</u>, and (calculated for boys only) <u>threatening violence</u> and (calculated for girls only) <u>overinterest in the opposite sex</u>. Nine behavior notations among boys showed

449

TABLE 91

CORRELATIONS WITH "LACK OF INTEREST IN SCHOOL"

	Boys	Girls
Personality-total............................	.26 ± .02	.32 ± .03
Conduct-total................................	.20 ± .02	.28 ± .03
Police arrest................................	.15 ± .03	.08 ± .06
		Larger Correlations (Positive)
Poor work in school..........................	.32 ± .03	.42 ± .04 (1)*
Disturbing influence in school...............	.31 ± .03	.29 ± .06 (8-9)
Truancy from school..........................	.29 ± .03	.28 ± .05 (10-12)
Inefficient in work, play, etc..............	.27 ± .05	.23 ± .06 (21-22)
Hatred or jealousy of sibling................	.27 ± .05	.16
Rude...	.26 ± .03	.29 ± .05 (8-9)
Irresponsible................................	.25 ± .05	.26 ± .07 (14)
Lazy...	.25 ± .04	.24 ± .06 (19-20)
Bad companions...............................	.24 ± .03	.17
Loitering....................................	.23 ± .04	.06
Disobedient..................................	.21 ± .03	.20 ± .06 (31-33)
Sullen.......................................	.21 ± .04	.30 ± .06 (5-7)
Unpopular....................................	.21 ± .05	.14
Leader.......................................	.21 ± .04	-.00
Boastful, "show-off".........................	.21 ± .04	.14
Grouped: "nervous," etc.....................	.21 ± .03	.18
Threatening violence.........................	.20 ± .05	....
Mental conflict..............................	.20 ± .05	.11
Unhappy......................................	.20 ± .05	.17
Question of change of personality...........	.17	.39 ± .06 (2)
Fighting.....................................	.10	.38 ± .04 (3)
Grouped: swearing, etc......................	.10	.37 ± .06 (4)
Refusal to attend school.....................	.18	.30 ± .07 (5-7)
Restless.....................................	.17	.30 ± .05 (5-7)
Inattentive in school........................	.06	.28 ± .06 (10-12)
Lying..	.12	.28 ± .04 (10-12)
Distractible.................................	.12	.27 ± .06 (13)
Staying out late at night....................	.11	.25 ± .05 (15-18)
Stealing.....................................	.17	.25 ± .05 (15-18)
Violence.....................................	.14	.25 ± .06 (15-18)
Grouped: fighting, etc.....................	.18	.25 ± .05 (15-18)
Contrary.....................................	.19	.24 ± .07 (19-20)
Exclusion from school........................	.18	.23 ± .07 (21-22)
Slovenly.....................................	.13	.22 ± .05 (23-25)
Overinterest in opposite sex.................	....	.22 ± .05 (23-25)
Object of teasing............................	.08	.22 ± .06 (23-25)
Defiant......................................	.17	.21 ± .06 (26-30)
Leading others into bad conduct..............	.17	.21 ± .07 (26-30)
Temper tantrums..............................	.09	.21 ± .06 (26-30)
Apprehensive.................................	-.00	.21 ± .05 (26-30)

*Rank order of girls' correlations.

	Boys	Girls
Sensitive over specific fact..................	.16	.21 ± .05 (26-30)
Changeable moods.............................	.02	.20 ± .05 (31-33)
Grouped: disobedient, etc...................	.19	.20 ± .04 (31-33)

Other Correlations (Positive to Negative)

Smoking, .19 (boys); Daydreaming, .19 and .19; Complaining of bad treatment by other children, .19 (boys); Egocentric, .18 and .06; Inferiority feelings, .18 and .11; Preference for younger children, .18 and .17; Grouped: egocentric, etc., .18 and .12; Gang, .17 (boys); Lack of initiative, .17 and .06; Sensitive (general), .17 and .02; Grouped: sensitive or worrisome, etc., .17 and .16; Teasing other children, .16 (boys); Quarrelsome, .16 and .14; Seclusive, .16 and .12; Grouped: depressed, etc., .16 and .13; Truancy from home, .15 and .11; Fantastical lying, .14 and .15; Listless, .14 and .16; Sulky, .13 and .03; Irritable, .13 and .14; Follower, .13 and .14; Destructive, .12 and .12; Incorrigible, .12 and .14; Crying spells, .12 and .10; Depressed, .12 and .07; Irregular sleep habits, .12 and .17; "Nervous," .12 and .12; Spoiled child, .11 and .13; Sex denied entirely, .11 and .04; Grouped: temper, etc., .11 and .17; Excuse-forming, .10 and .17; Queer, .10 and .18; Headaches, .10 and -.05; Bashful, .09 and .05; Grouped: dull, slow, etc., .09 and .17; Bossy, .08 and .18; Nail-biting, .08 and .08; Selfish, .08 and .01; Stubborn, .08 and .16; Swearing (general), .08 (boys); Worry over specific fact, .08 and .01; Question of encephalitis, .08 and .11; Discord between parents, .08 and -.03; Oversuggestible, .07 and .08; Vocational guidance, .07 and .01; Irregular attendance at school, .07 and .19; Masturbation, .06 and .10; Enuresis, .05 and .04; Restless in sleep, .05 and .08; Emotional instability, .05 and .08; Clean, .05 and -.04; Underweight, .03 and -.03; Absent-minded, .02 and .08; Victim of sex abuse, .02 (girls); Attractive manner, .02 and .15; Vicious home conditions, .01 and .18; Repressed, .01 and .12; Conduct prognosis bad, .00 and .16; Speech defect, .00 and .13; Neurological defect, -.00 and .12; Popular, -.01 and -.04; Psychoneurotic, -.01 and .05; Temper display, -.01 and .00; Finicky food habits, -.01 and .09; Brother in penal detention, -.02 and -.08; Question of hypophrenia, -.02 and .04; Slow, dull, -.02 and .13; Former convulsions, -.04 and .01; Retardation in school, -.06 and -.04; Lues, -.07 and .11; Feeble-minded sibling, -.09 and -.08; Overinterest in sex matters, -.09 and .12; Immoral home conditions, -.11 and .08; Stuttering, -.12 (boys); Sex delinquency (coitus), -.13 and .10

Omitted—Grouped: lack of interest in school, etc.

moderate correlations in the .20's but low coefficients below .20 among girls: loitering or wandering, bad companions, hatred or jealousy of sibling, boastful or "show-off" manner, "nervousness" or restlessness (undifferentiated), unpopularity, mental conflict, unhappiness, and "leader." Sixteen undesirable notations among girls showed moderate correlations in the .20's but low coefficients below .20 among boys: inattentiveness in school, distractibility, slovenliness, changeable moods or attitudes, contrariness,

defiant attitude, temper tantrums, violence, stealing, staying out
late at night, lying, leading others into bad conduct, exclusion
from school, object of teasing by other children, apprehensiveness,
and sensitiveness over some specific fact.

Among the six sex notations the only one of moderate size
was with overinterest in the opposite sex among girls, .22 ± .05,
the corresponding boys' coefficient being omitted because of the
paucity of boys' cases. All other correlations in the sphere of
sex, as well as for the seven physical notations and the four familial notations, were low or negligible, ranging from -.12 to .18.

Inattentiveness in school was noted among 223 boys (10.6
per cent) and among 81 girls (6.9 per cent).

Its more considerable correlations were as follows. Disturbing influence in school yielded substantial correlations in
the .30's among both sexes (Table 92). Lack of initiative among
boys yielded the substantial coefficient of .39 ± .04, but the negligible one of .09 among girls. Victim of sex abuse by older child
or person among girls also yielded the substantial correlation of
.30 ± .06, the boys' correlations being omitted because of paucity
of boys' cases. Disobedience and restlessness among girls yielded
substantial correlations in the .30's with moderate coefficients
in the .20's among boys. Excuse-forming attitude, distractibility,
and overinterest in sex matters among girls similarly yielded substantial correlations in the .30's but low coefficients below .20
among boys.

Inattentiveness in school showed consistent moderate correlations in the .20's with the following eight undesirable notations: poor work in school, laziness, lying, destructiveness, unpopularity, masturbation, exclusion from school, and (calculated
for boys only) teasing other children. Six personality and conduct problems among boys showed moderate correlations in the .20's
but among girls low positive coefficients below .20: daydreaming,
inefficiency in work, play, etc., rudeness, boastful or "show-off"
manner, defiant attitude, and fighting. Among girls a list of
seventeen miscellaneous behavior traits showed moderate correlations in the .20's but low positive coefficients below .20 among
boys: lack of interest in school, listlessness, "spoiled child,"
finicky food habits, stubbornness, quarrelsomeness, selfishness,

TABLE 92

CORRELATIONS WITH "INATTENTIVE IN SCHOOL"

	Boys	Girls
Personality-total...........................	.18 ± .02	.25 ± .04
Conduct-total...............................	.22 ± .02	.24 ± .04
Police arrest...............................	.06 ± .03	.26 ± .05
	Larger Correlations (Positive)	
Lack of initiative..........................	.39 ± .04	.09
Disturbing influence in school..............	.35 ± .03	.38 ± .06 (2)*
Grouped: disobedient, etc..................	.30 ± .03	.33 ± .04 (5-6)
Disobedient.................................	.29 ± .03	.30 ± .05 (7-9)
Restless....................................	.28 ± .02	.37 ± .05 (3)
Lazy..	.26 ± .03	.22 ± .07 (27-31)
Teasing other children.....................	.26 ± .03	....
Destructive................................	.25 ± .04	.23 ± .07 (24-26)
Defiant.....................................	.24 ± .04	.17
Daydreaming.................................	.24 ± .03	.03
Poor work in school........................	.24 ± .03	.26 ± .05 (17-18)
Grouped: "nervous," etc...................	.24 ± .02	.40 ± .04 (1)
Inefficient in work, play, etc.............	.23 ± .03	.11
Unpopular...................................	.22 ± .03	.22 ± .08 (27-31)
Boastful, "show-off"........................	.21 ± .04	.16
Fighting....................................	.21 ± .04	.19
Lying.......................................	.21 ± .02	.24 ± .05 (21-23)
Rude..	.21 ± .03	.11
Masturbation................................	.20 ± .02	.22 ± .06 (27-31)
Grouped: egocentric, etc..................	.20 ± .03	.18
Exclusion from school......................	.20 ± .03	.25 ± .07 (19-20)
Distractible...............................	.12	.34 ± .06 (4)
Excuse-forming.............................	.18	.33 ± .06 (5-6)
Overinterest in sex matters................	.08	.30 ± .07 (7-9)
Victim of sex abuse........................	....	.30 ± .06 (7-9)
Preference for younger children............	.12	.29 ± .07 (10-12)
Grouped: fighting, etc....................	.18	.29 ± .05 (10-12)
Grouped: swearing, etc....................	.02	.29 ± .07 (10-12)
Lack of interest in school.................	.06	.28 ± .06 (13-16)
Stubborn....................................	.16	.28 ± .05 (13-16)
Object of teasing..........................	.06	.28 ± .07 (13-16)
Mental conflict............................	.12	.28 ± .08 (13-16)
Restless in sleep..........................	.07	.26 ± .06 (17-18)
Quarrelsome................................	.18	.25 ± .05 (19-20)
Selfish....................................	.19	.24 ± .07 (21-23)
Listless...................................	.18	.24 ± .07 (21-23)
Finicky food habits........................	.06	.23 ± .06 (24-26)
Fantastical lying..........................	.17	.23 ± .07 (24-26)
Temper tantrums............................	.03	.22 ± .06 (27-31)
Spoiled child..............................	.19	.22 ± .06 (27-31)

*Rank order of girls' correlations.

TABLE 92—Continued

	Boys	Girls
Bad companions.................................	.08	.21 ± .06 (32-34)
Stealing...	.18	.21 ± .05 (32-34)
Leader..	.12	.21 ± .07 (32-34)
	Larger Correlations (Negative)	
Feeble-minded sibling.........................	-.28 ± .05	-.22 ± .06
Sex denied entirely...........................	-.09	-.24 ± .08
Conduct prognosis bad.........................	-.04	-.21 ± .08

Other Correlations (Positive to Negative)

Incorrigible, .19 and .19; Truancy from school, .18 and .16; Hatred or jealousy of sibling, .18 and .11; Complaining of bad treatment by other children, .17 (boys); Overinterest in opposite sex, .16 (girls); Changeable moods, .15 and .09; Queer, .15 and -.04; Egocentric, .14 and .13; Attractive manner, .14 and .02; Bossy, .13 and .17; Irresponsible, .13 and .09; Absent-minded, .13 and .17; Worry over specific fact, .13 and .18; Staying out late at night, .12 and .18; Seclusive, .12 and .11; Nail-biting, .11 and .11; Leading others into bad conduct, .10 and -.12; Smoking, .10 (boys); Truancy from home, .10 and .07; Clean, .10 and -.08; Contrary, .09 and .03; Slovenly, .09 and .13; Sulky, .09 and .01; Temper display, .09 and .01; Violence, .09 and .18; Headaches, .09 and .15; Refusal to attend school, .08 and -.08; Inferiority feelings, .08 and .15; Popular, .08 and .05; Gang, .07 (boys); Crying spells, .07 and -.01; Question of hypophrenia, .07 and -.15; Grouped: dull, slow, etc., .07 and .03; Sullen, .06 and .07; "Nervous," .06 and .19; Irregular attendance at school, .06 and -.03; Discord between parents, .06 and .01; Vicious home conditions, .06 and -.11; Grouped: temper, etc., .06 and .14; Enuresis, .05 and .09; Former convulsions, .05 and -.05; Loitering, .04 and .14; Irregular sleep habits, .04 and .03; Neurological defect, .04 and -.03; Grouped: sensitive or worrisome, etc., .04 and .06; Apprehensive, .03 and .13; Repressed, .03 and .16; Bashful, .02 and -.02; Psychoneurotic, .02 and -.02; Swearing (general), .01 (boys); Sex delinquency (coitus), .01 and -.04; Question of change of personality, .01 and .08; Slow, dull, .01 and -.08; Sensitive (general), .01 and .04; Underweight, .01 and .02; Vocational guidance, .01 and .06; Oversuggestible, .00 and .02; Sensitive over specific fact, -.00 and .09; Irritable, -.00 and .18; Depressed, -.02 and .08; Brother in penal detention, -.03 and -.00; Emotional instability, -.03 and -.04; Follower, -.04 and .11; Grouped: depressed, etc., -.05 and .04; Immoral home conditions, -.05 and -.09; Threatening violence, -.05 (boys); Lues, -.06 and -.17; Stuttering, -.06 (boys); Retardation in school, -.08 and -.10; Question of encephalitis, -.09 and .18; Unhappy, -.10 and -.00; Speech defect, -.11 and .00

Omitted—Grouped: lack of interest in school, etc.

temper tantrums, swearing or bad language (undifferentiated), restlessness in sleep, stealing, bad companions, fantastical lying, mental conflict, object of teasing by other children, preference for younger children as playmates, and "leader."

Three notations showed moderate negative correlations ranging from -.21 to -.28: feeble-minded sibling among both sexes, and sex misbehavior denied entirely and staff notation of unfavorable conduct prognosis among girls.

Among the six sex notations there were several correlation coefficients of statistically significant size in the .20's and .30's: masturbation among both sexes, overinterest in sex matters among girls, and victim of sex abuse by older child or person (calculated for girls only). Sex misbehavior denied entirely among girls showed the negative correlation of -.24 + .08.

Among the seven physical or psychophysical disabilities and among the four home or familial notations, all correlations with inattentiveness in school were low or negligible, ranging from -.17 to .18.

When the cases falling under the rubrics lack of interest in school or school studies, employment, etc., and inattentiveness in school were combined into a broad grouping,[1] there were 467 such cases, or 22.1 per cent, among our 2,113 White boys and 172 cases, or 14.6 per cent, among our 1,181 White girls. An examination of the resulting correlation coefficients as shown in Table 93 with the corresponding correlations in the two preceding chapters shows that the effect of combining these notations was in general to increase the size of the resulting coefficients. The fact of this increase in the resulting correlations indicates a close similarity between the two rubrics and suggests the likelihood that the two component notations overlapped to such a degree that one should not have attempted to set up more than one category in the original indexing of this material. We may, therefore, summarize the correlations in Table 93 in the following brief manner.

The highest correlations, ranging from .32 to .41 with the broader grouping lack of interest or inattentiveness in school studies or employment (undifferentiated), were with the two notations disturbing influence in school and poor work in school.

Fifteen undesirable notations yielded moderate to substantial correlations in the .20's and .30's among both sexes: lazi-

---

[1] The reasons for this broader grouping were given in I, 44; see p. 86, Table 13, Item H.

TABLE 93

CORRELATIONS WITH "GROUPED: LACK OF INTEREST IN SCHOOL, ETC."

	Boys	Girls
Personality-total............................	.26 ± .02	.33 ± .03
Conduct-total................................	.32 ± .02	.36 ± .03
Police arrest................................	.14 ± .03	-.01 ± .05
	Larger Correlations (Positive)	
Disturbing influence in school...............	.41 ± .03	.39 ± .05 (1-2)*
Poor work in school..........................	.32 ± .03	.38 ± .04 (3-5)
Lazy...	.31 ± .03	.23 ± .05 (30-33)
Disobedient..................................	.31 ± .03	.29 ± .04 (12-17)
Truancy from school..........................	.30 ± .03	.27 ± .05 (16-17)
Rude...	.29 ± .03	.25 ± .05 (21-25)
Grouped: "nervous," etc.....................	.28 ± .02	.30 ± .04 (10-11)
Inefficient in work, play, etc..............	.28 ± .04	.20 ± .06 (41-48)
Teasing other children......................	.28 ± .03	....
Hatred or jealousy of sibling...............	.28 ± .04	.15
Restless.....................................	.27 ± .03	.38 ± .04 (3-5)
Defiant......................................	.26 ± .04	.26 ± .05 (18-20)
Unpopular....................................	.26 ± .04	.23 ± .06 (30-33)
Daydreaming..................................	.26 ± .03	.16
Boastful, "show-off"........................	.25 ± .03	.17
Grouped: egocentric, etc...................	.23 ± .03	.18
Irresponsible...............................	.23 ± .04	.21 ± .06 (38-40)
Exclusion from school.......................	.22 ± .03	.31 ± .06 (9)
Grouped: fighting, etc.....................	.22 ± .03	.32 ± .04 (8)
Destructive.................................	.21 ± .03	.23 ± .06 (30-33)
Stealing....................................	.21 ± .03	.24 ± .04 (26-29)
Egocentric..................................	.20 ± .03	.11
Lying.......................................	.20 ± .03	.29 ± .04 (12-14)
Fighting....................................	.20 ± .03	.33 ± .04 (7)
Bad companions..............................	.20 ± .03	.20 ± .05 (41-48)
Grouped: swearing, etc.....................	.07	.39 ± .05 (1-2)
Distractible................................	.13	.38 ± .05 (3-5)
Question of change of personality..........	.13	.37 ± .06 (6)
Grouped: disobedient, etc..................	.15	.30 ± .04 (10-11)
Object of teasing...........................	.09	.29 ± .05 (12-14)
Preference for younger children............	.15	.28 ± .06 (15)
Excuse-forming..............................	.17	.27 ± .05 (16-17)
Temper tantrums.............................	.08	.26 ± .05 (18-20)
Overinterest in sex matters................	.02	.26 ± .06 (18-20)
Fantastical lying...........................	.15	.25 ± .06 (21-25)
Sullen......................................	.16	.25 ± .05 (21-25)
Violence....................................	.16	.25 ± .05 (21-25)
Overinterest in opposite sex................	....	.25 ± .04 (21-25)
Staying out late at night..................	.15	.24 ± .05 (26-29)
Stubborn....................................	.14	.24 ± .04 (26-29)

*Rank order of girls' correlations.

TABLE 93—Continued

	Boys	Girls
Quarrelsome	.19	.24 ± .04 (26-29)
Refusal to attend school	.16	.23 ± .07 (30-33)
Victim of sex abuse	....	.22 ± .05 (34-37)
Apprehensive	.01	.22 ± .05 (34-37)
Incorrigible	.19	.22 ± .04 (34-37)
Contrary	.18	.22 ± .06 (34-37)
Masturbation	.10	.21 ± .05 (38-40)
Listless	.17	.21 ± .05 (38-40)
Mental conflict	.19	.20 ± .07 (41-48)
Irritable	.08	.20 ± .05 (41-48)
Slovenly	.14	.20 ± .06 (41-48)
Bossy	.14	.20 ± .06 (41-48)
Grouped: temper, etc.	.10	.20 ± .04 (41-48)
Question of encephalitis	.03	.20 ± .07 (41-48)

Other Correlations (Positive to Negative)

Complaining of bad treatment by other children, .19 (boys); Leader, .18 and .15; Smoking, .18 (boys); Loitering, .18 and .10; Gang, .17 (boys); Spoiled child, .17 and .19; Leading others into bad conduct, .16 and .10; Sulky, .15 and .03; Truancy from home, .15 and .11; Queer, .15 and .15; Inferiority feelings, .14 and .13; Worry over specific fact, .14 and .10; Seclusive, .14 and .15; Selfish, .14 and .14; Grouped: sensitive or worrisome, etc., .14 and .12; Crying spells, .13 and .09; Lack of initiative, .13 and .03; Sensitive over specific fact, .12 and .18; "Nervous," .12 and .15; Threatening violence, .11 (boys); Sensitive (general), .11 and .04; Unhappy, .11 and .14; Irregular sleep habits, .10 and .17; Depressed, .10 and .09; Absent-minded, .10 and .15; Grouped: dull, slow, etc., .10 and .10; Grouped: depressed, etc., .10 and .13; Headaches, .10 and .04; Irregular attendance at school, .10 and .09; Changeable moods, .09 and .18; Follower, .08 and .11; Discord between parents, .08 and -.02; Vocational guidance, .08 and .02; Attractive manner, .08 and .09; Swearing (general), .07 (boys); Oversuggestible, .07 and .04; Restless in sleep, .07 and .17; Clean, .07 and .05; Popular, .06 and .03; Bashful, .06 and .04; Finicky food habits, .05 and .18; Nail-biting, .04 and .08; Enuresis, .04 and .09; Vicious home conditions, .04 and .09; Sex denied entirely, .03 and -.04; Underweight, .03 and -.00; Emotional instability, .03 and .07; Neurological defect, .03 and .09; Temper display, .03 and .01; Repressed, .02 and .17; Psychoneurotic, .02 and .02; Slow, dull, .00 and .03; Former convulsions, -.00 and .01; Conduct prognosis bad, -.01 and .08; Brother in penal detention, -.02 and -.05; Lues, -.05 and .04; Question of hypophrenia, -.05 and -.03; Retardation in school, -.05 and -.07; Sex delinquency (coitus), -.09 and .06; Speech defect, -.09 and .01; Immoral home conditions, -.09 and .03; Stuttering, -.11 (boys); Feebleminded sibling, -.17 and -.13

Omitted—Inattentive in school; Lack of interest in school

ness, inefficiency in work, play, etc., irresponsibility, truancy from school, bad companions, exclusion from school, disobedience, stealing, defiant attitude, destructiveness, fighting, rudeness, restlessness, lying, and unpopularity and (calculated for boys only) <u>teasing other children</u> and (calculated for girls only) <u>over-interest in opposite sex</u> and <u>victim of sex abuse by older child or person</u>. Among boys <u>daydreaming</u>, <u>boastful or "show-off" manner</u>, <u>egocentricity</u>, and <u>hatred or jealousy of sibling</u> showed moderate correlations in the .20's but low positive coefficients below .20 among girls. Twenty-five personality and conduct problems among girls showed moderate to substantial correlations in the .20's and .30's but low positive correlations below .20 among boys: <u>refusal to attend school</u>, <u>stubbornness</u>, <u>incorrigibility</u>, <u>contrariness</u>, <u>violence</u>, <u>quarrelsomeness</u>, <u>staying out late at night</u>, <u>distractibility</u>, <u>listlessness</u>, <u>slovenliness</u>, <u>question of change of personality</u>, <u>mental conflict</u>, <u>apprehensiveness</u>, <u>excuse-forming attitude</u>, <u>temper tantrums</u>, <u>irritable temperament</u>, <u>swearing or bad language</u> (undifferentiated), <u>fantastical lying</u>, <u>sullenness</u>, <u>bossy manner</u>, <u>object of teasing by other children</u>, <u>preference for younger children as playmates</u>, <u>masturbation</u>, <u>overinterest in sex matters</u>, and <u>question or diagnosis of encephalitis</u>.

Among the six sex notations there were four positive coefficients of moderate size in the .20's, all among girls: <u>overinterest in sex matters</u>, <u>masturbation</u>, and two for which only the girls' correlations were calculated—<u>overinterest in the opposite sex</u> and <u>victim of sex abuse by older child or person</u>.

Among the seven physical or psychophysical notations the only correlation of moderate size was the statistically questionable one of .20 $\pm$ .07 with <u>question or diagnosis of encephalitis</u> among girls.

Among the four home or familial notations all correlations in this chapter were low or negligible.

CHAPTER XLVIII

DISTURBING INFLUENCE IN SCHOOL

<u>Disturbing influence or marked mischievousness in school</u> was noted among 348, or 16.5 per cent, of our 2,113 White boys and among 89, or 7.5 per cent, of our 1,181 White girls. It is a matter of common observation that girls adjust their conduct better in school routine than do the boys. With the factor of chronological age, its bi-serial correlation among girls was negative and of moderate size, -.24 ± .04, and among boys negligible, -.06 (Table 9, p. 128). With intelligence quotient (IQ) its bi-serial correlations were negligible, -.01 and .04 (Table 10, p. 130).

Its bi-serial correlations with the <u>conduct-total</u> among both sexes and with <u>personality-total</u> among girls were large, ranging from .46 to .52 (Table 94). Among boys the correlation

TABLE 94

CORRELATION WITH "DISTURBING INFLUENCE IN SCHOOL"

	Boys	Girls
Personality-total............................	.26 ± .02	.52 ± .03
Conduct-total...............................	.46 ± .02	.48 ± .03
Police arrest................................	.23 ± .03	.04 ± .07
	Larger Correlations (Positive)	
Exclusion from school.......................	.51 ± .03	.51 ± .06 (1)*
Boastful, "show-off".........................	.51 ± .03	.44 ± .06 (9-10)
Teasing other children.......................	.45 ± .03	....
Unpopular....................................	.42 ± .04	.49 ± .07 (2)
Grouped: disobedient, etc...................	.41 ± .02	.45 ± .04 (6-8)
Grouped: lack of interest in school, etc.....	.41 ± .03	.39 ± .05 (17)
Rude...	.40 ± .03	.35 ± .05 (21-22)
Grouped: fighting, etc......................	.39 ± .03	.44 ± .04 (9-10)
Fighting.....................................	.38 ± .03	.43 ± .06 (11)
Incorrigible.................................	.37 ± .03	.40 ± .05 (14-16)

*Rank order of girls' correlations.

459

TABLE 94—Continued

	Boys	Girls
Restless	.37 ± .03	.27 ± .05 (38)
Disobedient	.36 ± .03	.45 ± .05 (6-8)
Destructive	.36 ± .03	.32 ± .07 (25-31)
Violence	.36 ± .03	.47 ± .06 (3)
Inattentive in school	.35 ± .03	.38 ± .06 (18)
Grouped: swearing, etc	.32 ± .03	.41 ± .06 (12-13)
Lack of interest in school	.31 ± .03	.29 ± .06 (34-35)
Contrary	.31 ± .05	.19
Leading others into bad conduct	.31 ± .04	.21 ± .08 (45-47)
Quarrelsome	.31 ± .03	.36 ± .05 (20)
Fantastical lying	.30 ± .04	.32 ± .07 (25-31)
Lying	.30 ± .03	.40 ± .04 (14-16)
Grouped: "nervous," etc	.29 ± .03	.37 ± .04 (19)
Defiant	.28 ± .04	.46 ± .06 (4-5)
Slovenly	.28 ± .03	.22 ± .05 (44)
Swearing (general)	.27 ± .04	....
Grouped: egocentric, etc	.27 ± .03	.20 ± .05 (48-55)
Loitering	.26 ± .04	.13
Smoking	.26 ± .04	....
Lazy	.25 ± .04	.14
Stealing	.25 ± .03	.28 ± .05 (36-37)
Complaining of bad treatment by other children	.25 ± .04	....
Bossy	.24 ± .04	.23 ± .07 (43)
Excuse-forming	.24 ± .03	.32 ± .06 (25-31)
Egocentric	.24 ± .03	.28 ± .06 (36-37)
Distractible	.24 ± .03	.46 ± .05 (4-5)
Grouped: temper, etc	.24 ± .03	.40 ± .04 (14-16)
Poor work in school	.23 ± .03	.32 ± .05 (25-31)
Sulky	.22 ± .04	.18
Threatening violence	.22 ± .05	....
Truancy from home	.21 ± .03	.10
Stubborn	.20 ± .03	.31 ± .05 (32-33)
Spoiled child	.20 ± .03	.26 ± .06 (39-40)
Object of teasing	.18	.45 ± .06 (6-8)
Temper tantrums	.19	.41 ± .05 (12-13)
Queer	.13	.35 ± .07 (21-22)
Question of change of personality	.08	.33 ± .07 (23-24)
Daydreaming	.00	.33 ± .06 (23-24)
Truancy from school	.19	.32 ± .05 (25-31)
"Nervous"	.10	.32 ± .05 (25-31)
Restless in sleep	.07	.32 ± .05 (25-31)
Question of encephalitis	.18	.31 ± .08 (32-33)
Irresponsible	.18	.29 ± .07 (34-35)
Inefficient in work, play, etc	.15	.26 ± .07 (39-40)
Conduct prognosis bad	.17	.25 ± .08 (41-42)
Emotional instability	.13	.25 ± .07 (41-42)
Bad companions	.19	.21 ± .06 (45-47)
Crying spells	.09	.21 ± .05 (45-47)
Enuresis	.10	.20 ± .05 (48-55)
Nail-biting	.17	.20 ± .05 (48-55)
Overinterest in sex matters	.13	.20 ± .07 (48-55)
Changeable moods	.16	.20 ± .06 (48-55)

TABLE 94—Continued

	Boys	Girls
Neurological defect	-.01	.20 ± .06 (48-55)
Lues	-.05	.20 ± .07 (48-55)
Speech defect	-.07	.20 ± .07 (48-55)
		Larger Correlations (Negative)
Lack of initiative	-.25 ± .04	-.04
Feeble-minded sibling	-.23 ± .04	-.09

Other Correlations (Positive to Negative)

Refusal to attend school, .19 and .08; Sullen, .19 and .17; Inferiority feelings, .19 and .18; Overinterest in opposite sex, .19 (girls); Staying out late at night, .17 and .06; Temper display, .17 and .12; Leader, .17 and .18; Gang, .16 (boys); Irritable, .16 and .19; Oversuggestible, .15 and .04; Mental conflict, .14 and .10; Selfish, .13 and .12; Irregular sleep habits, .13 and .16; Masturbation, .12 and .12; Former convulsions, .12 and .08; Vicious home conditions, .11 and .13; Depressed, .10 and .13; Unhappy, .10 and .10; Finicky food habits, .09 and .08; Grouped: depressed, etc., .09 and .13; Attractive manner, .08 and .09; Sex denied entirely, .07 and .03; Victim of sex abuse, .07 (girls); Hatred or jealousy of sibling, .06 and -.02; Headaches, .06 and .14; Retardation in school, .05 and -.02; Irregular attendance at school, .05 and -.00; Discord between parents, .05 and -.01; Preference for younger children, .04 and .16; Absent-minded, .03 and .08; Sensitive (general), .03 and .06; Follower, .03 and .01; Popular, .02 and .12; Clean, .01 and -.02; Grouped: sensitive or worrisome, etc., .01 and .17; Worry over specific fact, -.00 and .17; Sensitive over specific fact, -.00 and .10; Question of hypophrenia, -.01 and .12; Listless, -.02 and .10; Apprehensive, -.02 and .19; Underweight, -.03 and .01; Seclusive, -.03 and -.01; Brother in penal detention, -.04 and .06; Immoral home conditions, -.06 and -.12; Vocational guidance, -.08 and .03; Repressed, -.08 and .01; Stuttering, -.09 (boys); Sex delinquency (coitus), -.09 and .02; Grouped: dull, slow, etc., -.11 and .04; Slow, -.11 and .05; Bashful, -.12 and -.06; Psychoneurotic, -.16 and -.04

with personality-total was only moderate, .26 ± .02. With the police-arrest criterion of seriousness, the boys' tetrachoric correlation was only moderate, .23 ± .03, and the girls' coefficient negligible, .04 ± .07.

Its largest correlations were for exclusion from school with the coefficients of .51 among both sexes. Boastful or "show-off" manner also yielded large coefficients of .51 ± .03 and .44 ± .06 for boys and girls respectively. Unpopularity and (calculated for boys only) teasing other children yielded large correlations in the .40's. Rudeness yielded respective coefficients of .40 ± .03 and .35 ± .05 among boys and girls. The following six

conduct difficulties among girls yielded large correlations in the
.40's and among boys substantial coefficients in the .30's: <u>fight-
ing</u>, <u>violence</u>, <u>incorrigibility</u>, <u>disobedience</u>, <u>swearing or bad lan-
guage</u> (undifferentiated), and <u>lying</u>. Four behavior traits among gi▮
girls similarly yielded large correlations in the .40's and moderate coefficients ranging from .18 to .28 among boys: <u>defiant at-
titude</u>, <u>temper tantrums</u>, <u>distractibility</u>, and <u>object of teasing by
other children</u>.

Four conduct problems yielded substantial correlations in
the .30's among both sexes: <u>inattentiveness in school</u>, <u>quarrel-
someness</u>, <u>destructiveness</u>, and <u>fantastical lying</u>. Four undesirable
behavior traits among boys yielded substantial correlations in the
.30's and moderate coefficients ranging from .19 to .29 among
girls: <u>lack of interest in school</u>, <u>leading others into bad con-
duct</u>, <u>contrariness</u>, and <u>restlessness</u>. Three notations among girls
yielded substantial correlations in the .30's and among boys moderate correlations in the .20's: <u>poor work in school</u>, <u>stubborn-
ness</u>, and <u>excuse-forming attitude</u>. An additional seven miscellaneous conduct and personality problems among girls yielded substantial correlations in the .30's but low positive coefficients below
.20 among boys: <u>truancy from school</u>, <u>daydreaming</u>, <u>question of
change of personality</u>, <u>queer behavior</u>, <u>"nervousness,"</u> <u>restlessness
in sleep</u>, and <u>question or diagnosis of encephalitis</u>.

Nine conduct and personality difficulties showed consistently moderate correlations in the .20's: <u>bossy manner</u>, <u>egocen-
tricity</u>, <u>"spoiled child,"</u> <u>slovenliness</u>, <u>stealing</u>, and the four
conduct problems for which only the boys' coefficients were calculated: <u>swearing in general</u>, <u>smoking</u>, <u>threatening violence</u>, and
<u>complaining of bad treatment</u> by other children. Four conduct dif-
ficulties among boys showed moderate coefficients in the .20's but
low coefficients ranging from .10 to .18 among girls: <u>truancy from
home</u>, <u>sulkiness</u>, <u>laziness</u>, and <u>loitering or wandering</u>. Among girls
thirteen miscellaneous case-record notations showed moderate correlations in the .20's but low or negligible coefficients below
.20 among boys: <u>emotional instability</u>, <u>changeable moods or atti-
tudes</u>, <u>crying spells</u>, <u>irresponsibility</u>, <u>inefficiency in work, play</u>,
etc., <u>bad companions</u>, <u>overinterest in sex matters</u>, <u>enuresis</u>, <u>nail-
biting</u>, <u>neurological defect (unspecified)</u>, <u>lues</u>, <u>speech defect</u>
(other than <u>stuttering</u>), and <u>staff notation of unfavorable conduct
prognosis</u>.

Two notations showed moderate negative correlations in the
-.20's with disturbing influence in school, both among boys: lack
of initiative and feeble-minded sibling.

Among the six sex notations all correlations were low except the doubtfully significant one of .20 $\pm$ .07 with overinterest
in sex matters among girls.

Among the seven physical or psychophysical notations there
were five coefficients of moderate size ranging from .20 to .31,
all among girls: question of diagnosis of encephalitis, neurological defect (unspecified), lues, enuresis, and speech defect (other
than stuttering).

Among the four home or familial notations all correlations
with disturbing influence in school were low or negligible.

CHAPTER XLIX

RUDENESS

<u>Rudeness, impertinence, impudence, etc., toward adults</u> was a fairly frequently appearing notation among our cases, the incidence being about 15 per cent of both boys and girls in this study. Its bi-serial correlations with the <u>conduct-total</u> were large, .48 ± .02 and .55 ± .02 among boys and girls respectively (Table 95).

TABLE 95

CORRELATIONS WITH "RUDE"

	Boys	Girls
Personality-total............................	.32 ± .02	.39 ± .03
Conduct-total................................	.48 ± .02	.55 ± .02
Police arrest................................	.19 ± .03	.20 ± .04
	Larger Correlations (Positive)	
Grouped: disobedient, etc....................	.54 ± .02	.60 ± .03 (1)*
Defiant......................................	.49 ± .03	.54 ± .04 (2)
Disobedient..................................	.46 ± .03	.52 ± .04 (3)
Grouped: swearing, etc......................	.45 ± .03	.50 ± .05 (4)
Incorrigible.................................	.44 ± .03	.47 ± .04 (6-7)
Contrary.....................................	.42 ± .04	.32 ± .06 (26-27)
Disturbing influence in school..............	.40 ± .03	.35 ± .05 (19)
Destructive..................................	.38 ± .03	.22 ± .06 (51-53)
Swearing (general)..........................	.38 ± .04	....
Violence.....................................	.36 ± .03	.39 ± .05 (14)
Grouped: fighting, etc......................	.35 ± .03	.49 ± .03 (5)
Grouped: egocentric, etc....................	.35 ± .03	.34 ± .04 (20-22)
Hatred or jealousy of sibling...............	.34 ± .04	.29 ± .06 (31-37)
Exclusion from school.......................	.34 ± .04	.31 ± .06 (28)
Grouped: "nervous," etc....................	.32 ± .03	.24 ± .04 (46-48)
Boastful, "show-off"........................	.31 ± .03	.40 ± .05 (11-13)
Fighting.....................................	.31 ± .03	.44 ± .03 (8-9)
Egocentric...................................	.31 ± .03	.37 ± .04 (15-17)
Teasing other children......................	.30 ± .04	....
Temper tantrums.............................	.30 ± .04	.40 ± .04 (11-13)
Restless.....................................	.30 ± .03	.22 ± .04 (51-53)

*Rank order of girls' correlations.

464

TABLE 95—Continued

	Boys	Girls
Lying....................................	.29 ± .03	.36 ± .04 (18)
Grouped: lack of interest in school, etc.....	.29 ± .03	.25 ± .04 (44-45)
Selfish.................................	.27 ± .04	.11
Staying out late at night....................	.27 ± .03	.28 ± .05 (38-39)
Sullen..................................	.27 ± .03	.42 ± .05 (10)
Changeable moods.........................	.27 ± .04	.34 ± .04 (20-22)
Grouped: temper, etc.....................	.27 ± .03	.44 ± .03 (8-9)
Bossy...................................	.26 ± .04	.16
Lack of interest in school.................	.26 ± .04	.29 ± .05 (31-37)
Stubborn................................	.26 ± .03	.34 ± .04 (20-22)
Smoking.................................	.25 ± .04	....
Threatening violence......................	.25 ± .05	....
Spoiled child...........................	.25 ± .04	.27 ± .05 (40-41)
Lazy....................................	.24 ± .04	.23 ± .06 (49-50)
Leading others into bad conduct.............	.24 ± .04	.40 ± .06 (11-13)
Gang....................................	.24 ± .04	....
Irregular sleep habits.....................	.24 ± .04	.15
Fantastical lying........................	.23 ± .03	.29 ± .06 (31-37)
Slovenly................................	.23 ± .03	.26 ± .04 (42-43)
Stealing................................	.23 ± .03	.29 ± .04 (31-37)
Inferiority feelings.......................	.23 ± .04	.17
Quarrelsome.............................	.22 ± .03	.47 ± .04 (6-7)
Depressed...............................	.22 ± .04	.17
Unpopular...............................	.22 ± .05	.30 ± .06 (29-30)
Inattentive in school.....................	.21 ± .03	.11
Sulky...................................	.21 ± .05	.29 ± .06 (31-37)
Truancy from school.......................	.21 ± .03	.25 ± .05 (44-45)
Irritable...............................	.21 ± .03	.33 ± .04 (23-25)
Bad companions...........................	.20 ± .03	.17
Truancy from home........................	.20 ± .03	.20 ± .04 (54)
Complaining of bad treatment by other children	.20 ± .04	....
Daydreaming.............................	.02	.37 ± .05 (15-17)
Excuse-forming...........................	.18	.37 ± .05 (15-17)
Temper display...........................	.17	.33 ± .05 (23-25)
Overinterest in opposite sex................	....	.33 ± .04 (23-25)
Queer...................................	.19	.32 ± .06 (26-27)
Overinterest in sex matters................	.18	.30 ± .05 (29-30)
Finicky food habits.......................	.07	.29 ± .05 (31-37)
Masturbation............................	.14	.29 ± .04 (31-37)
Inefficient in work, play, etc.............	.16	.28 ± .05 (38-39)
Question of change of personality...........	.10	.27 ± .06 (40-41)
Emotional instability.....................	.06	.26 ± .05 (42-43)
Question of encephalitis...................	-.02	.24 ± .07 (46-48)
Unhappy.................................	.16	.24 ± .06 (46-48)
Grouped: depressed, etc..................	.19	.23 ± .05 (49-50)
Crying spells............................	.02	.22 ± .04 (51-53)
	Larger Correlations (Negative)	
Speech defect............................	-.14	-.26 ± .05
Bashful.................................	-.05	-.20 ± .04

TABLE 95—Continued

Other Correlations (Positive to Negative)

Nail-biting, .17 and .12; Irresponsible, .15 and .15; Refusal to attend school, .15 and .13; "Nervous," .15 and .05; Restless in sleep, .14 and .14; Conduct prognosis bad, .14 and .13; Sensitive over specific fact, .13 and .01; Discord between parents, .13 and .15; Sex denied entirely, .12 and -.09; Loitering, .11 and .02; Sex delinquency (coitus), .11 and .06; Mental conflict, .11 and .12; Poor work in school, .11 and .09; Vicious home conditions, .11 and .13; Leader, .10 and .07; Enuresis, .09 and .07; Repressed, .09 and .03; Attractive manner, .09 and .06; Grouped: sensitive or worrisome, etc., .08 and .10; Clean, .07 and .09; Immoral home conditions, .07 and .10; Psychoneurotic, .06 and .13; Distractible, .06 and .11; Seclusive, .06 and .05; Irregular attendance at school, .06 and .01; Apprehensive, .05 and .14; Object of teasing, .05 and .10; Worry over specific fact, .05 and .07; Headaches, .05 and .18; Former convulsions, .05 and .04; Victim of sex abuse, .05 (girls); Brother in penal detention, .05 and .11; Popular, .04 and .04; Absent-minded, .03 and .08; Follower, .03 and -.09; Listless, .02 and .05; Neurological defect, .02 and .01; Sensitive (general), .00 and .16; Lues, .00 and -.00; Vocational guidance, .00 and -.06; Underweight, -.01 and .04; Preference for younger children, -.01 and .00; Oversuggestible, -.01 and -.03; Grouped: dull, slow, etc., -.07 and -.08; Question of hypophrenia, -.07 and -.12; Lack of initiative, -.07 and -.13; Slow, dull, -.09 and -.12; Retardation in school, -.11 and -.11; Feeble-minded sibling, -.12 and .17; Stuttering, -.19 (boys)

Its corresponding correlations with the personality-total were substantial, .32 ± .02 and .39 ± .03. With the police-arrest criterion of "juvenile delinquency" its tetrachoric correlations were only moderate, .19 ± .03 and .20 ± .04.

Its highest correlations among both sexes ranged from .44 to .54 for the four conduct problems, defiant attitude, disobedience, incorrigibility, and swearing or bad language (undifferentiated). Contrariness and disturbing influence in school among boys yielded correlations in the .40's and among girls in the .30's. Three conduct problems among girls similarly yielded large correlations in the .40's with similar substantial coefficients in the .30's among boys: boastful or "show-off" manner, fighting, and temper tantrums. An additional three conduct difficulties among girls yielded large correlations in the .40's but moderate coefficients in the .20's among boys: sullenness, quarrelsomeness, and leading others into bad conduct.

Six unfavorable notations consistently yielded substantial correlations in the .30's: violence, egocentricity, exclusion from school, and the two notations for which only the boys' coefficients were calculated—teasing other children and swearing in general—and (calculated for girls only) overinterest in the opposite sex.

Three conduct and personality difficulties among boys yielded substantial correlations in the .30's with moderate correlations in
the .20's among girls: destructiveness, hatred or jealousy of
sibling, and restlessness. Among girls five behavior traits
yielded substantial correlations in the .30's with moderate coefficients in the .20's among boys: stubbornness, irritable temperament, changeable moods or attitudes, lying, and unpopularity.
Five additional behavior traits among girls yielded substantial
correlations in the .30's but low positive coefficients below .20
among boys: temper display, excuse-forming attitude, daydreaming,
queer behavior and (calculated for girls only) overinterest in sex
matters.

Rudeness showed consistent moderate correlations in the
.20's with fourteen undesirable conduct and personality manifestations: "spoiled child," sulkiness, laziness, slovenliness, truancy from school, staying out late at night, lack of interest in
school, stealing, fantastical lying, and the four traits for which
only the boys' coefficients were calculated—threatening violence,
running with a gang, smoking, and complaining of bad treatment by
other children. Seven personality and conduct difficulties showed
moderate correlations in the .20's among boys but low positive coefficients below .20 among girls: bossy manner, selfishness, bad
companions, inattentiveness in school, depressed mood or spells,
inferiority feelings, and irregular sleep habits. Among girls
eight miscellaneous notations showed moderate correlations in the
.20's but low coefficients below .20 among boys: emotional instability, question of change of personality, unhappiness, crying
spells, inefficiency in work, play, etc., finicky food habits, masturbation, and question or diagnosis of encephalitis.

Rudeness among girls showed negative correlations of moderate size in the -.20's with bashfulness and speech defect (other
than stuttering).

Among the six sex notations there were three moderate or
substantial correlations ranging from .29 to .33, all among girls:
masturbation, overinterest in sex matters, and (calculated for
girls only) overinterest in the opposite sex.

Among the seven physical or psychophysical disabilities
there were two correlations of moderate size, both among girls:
the positive coefficient of .24 $\pm$ .07 with question or diagnosis

of <u>encephalitis</u> and the negative one of -.26 ± .05 with <u>speech defect</u>.

Among the four home or familial notations all correlations were low or negligible, ranging from .05 to .15.

CHAPTER L

SEX NOTATIONS

A miscellaneous group of six sex notations which appeared with sufficient frequency in our case-record material to justify correlational treatment is discussed in this chapter. Although in the original indexing of our total 5,000 cases there were a large variety of sex items (as listed in I, 56, Table 2; 69-71, Table 4; and 72, Table 5), most of these items occurred so seldom that adequate statistical treatment was not feasible. In addition to the six notations to be discussed in Tables 96-101, there were another six categories (sex attack on person of opposite sex, "annoying" girls, mutual masturbation with child of the same sex, homosexual practices with child of same age, passive pederasty, and exhibitionism or "indecent exposure") for which correlations could be calculated among boys, but only with the personality-total, conduct-total, police arrest, chronological age, and intelligence quotient (this volume, Tables 6-10 inclusive).

Sex delinquency, which in our study has been rigidly defined as "coitus or copulation with a person of the opposite sex," was noted among only 70 of our 2,113 White boys, or 3.3 per cent, but among 218 of our 1,181 White girls, or 18.5 per cent. Among girls its tetrachoric correlation of .76 $\pm$ .02 with the police-arrest criterion of "juvenile delinquency" was unusually high, in fact, conspicuously the largest correlation with police arrest found among all our correlations (Table 96). All other correlations among both sexes with our three criteria of seriousness or "ominousness" were consistently low, the coefficients ranging from .08 to .18.

Its largest correlations among both sexes were in the .40's with the two sex notations, overinterest in sex matters and masturbation. Victim of sex abuse by older child or person among girls yielded the large correlation of .44 $\pm$ .04, the boys' coefficient not being calculated because of the paucity of boys' cases. Staff

469

TABLE 96

CORRELATIONS WITH "SEX DELINQUENCY (COITUS)"

	Boys	Girls
Personality-total..............................	.08 ± .04	.08 ± .03
Conduct-total.................................	.17 ± .04	.16 ± .03
Police arrest.................................	.18 ± .05	.76 ± .02
	Larger Correlations (Positive)	
Overinterest in sex matters...................	.48 ± .07	.47 ± .05 (3)*
Masturbation..................................	.43 ± .04	.41 ± .04 (7)
Conduct prognosis bad.........................	.32 ± .08	.48 ± .05 (1-2)
Daydreaming...................................	.22 ± .06	-.01
Sulky...	.20 ± .07	-.08
Mental conflict...............................	.20 ± .07	.23 ± .06 (19-21)
Truancy from home.............................	.16	.48 ± .04 (1-2)
Leading others into bad conduct...............	.11	.45 ± .05 (4)
Staying out late at night.....................	.10	.44 ± .04 (5-6)
Victim of sex abuse...........................	....	.44 ± .04 (5-6)
Oversuggestible...............................	.11	.38 ± .04 (8-9)
Overinterest in opposite sex..................	....	.38 ± .04 (8-9)
Bad companions................................	.14	.37 ± .04 (10)
Truancy from school...........................	.03	.36 ± .04 (11)
Loitering.....................................	.16	.33 ± .05 (12-13)
Lying...	.15	.33 ± .03 (12-13)
Bashful.......................................	-.09	.30 ± .04 (14)
Immoral home conditions.......................	.13	.29 ± .03 (15)
Grouped: disobedient, etc.....................	.10	.27 ± .03 (16)
Stealing......................................	.16	.24 ± .04 (17-18)
Disobedient...................................	-.03	.24 ± .04 (17-18)
Underweight...................................	-.12	.23 ± .04 (19-21)
Lues..	.04	.23 ± .05 (19-21)
Incorrigible..................................	.09	.22 ± .04 (22)
Grouped: swearing, etc........................	.05	.20 ± .05 (23)
	Larger Correlations (Negative)	
Vocational guidance...........................	-.39 ± .05	-.41 ± .04
Lazy..	-.28 ± .06	-.11
Irregular attendance at school................	-.21 ± .06	-.14
Lack of initiative............................	-.20 ± .07	-.03
Stuttering....................................	-.20 ± .08	....
Grouped: "nervous," etc.......................	-.00	-.25 ± .03
Irritable.....................................	.04	-.24 ± .04
"Nervous".....................................	-.03	-.24 ± .04
Restless in sleep.............................	-.01	-.23 ± .04
Neurological defect...........................	.01	-.21 ± .05
Question of encephalitis......................	-.06	-.21 ± .07

*Rank order of girls' correlations.

TABLE 96—Continued

Other Correlations (Positive to Negative)

Popular, .18 and -.01; Clean, .18 and -.06; Worry over specific fact, .18 and .15; Psychoneurotic, .17 and -.05; Grouped: fighting, etc., .17 and .09; Depressed, .16 and .01; Inferiority feelings, .15 and -.09; Smoking, .14 (boys); Grouped: egocentric, etc., .14 and .03; Selfish, .13 and -.13; Violence, .13 and .14; Sensitive over specific fact, .13 and .01; Grouped: depressed, etc., .13 and .03; Fantastical lying, .12 and .01; Rude, .11 and .06; Grouped: sensitive or worrisome, etc., .11 and -.01; Gang, .09 (boys); Fighting, .08 and .09; Threatening violence, .08 (boys); Preference for younger children, .08 and -.13; Unhappy, .08 and .01; Follower, .08 and .17; Egocentric, .08 and .07; Nail-biting, .07 and .03; Slovenly, .07 and .06; Sullen, .07 and .09; Swearing (general), .07 (boys); Exclusion from school, .07 and .18; Former convulsions, .07 and -.14; Brother in penal detention, .07 and .10; Inefficient in work, play, etc., .06 and .01; Discord between parents, .06 and .06; Vicious home conditions, .06 and .19; Crying spells, .05 and -.05; Repressed, .05 and -.08; Leader, .05 and -.04; Refusal to attend school, .04 and -.01; Irregular sleep habits, .04 and -.15; Queer, .04 and .17; Emotional instability, .04 and .17; Question of change of personality, .03 and .13; Boastful, "show-off," .02 and .10; Listless, .02 and .01; Defiant, .01 and .07; Inattentive in school, .01 and -.04; Teasing other children, .01 (boys); Contrary, .00 and .07; Temper display, -.00 and -.09; Feeble-minded sibling, -.00 and .11; Changeable moods, -.00 and .03; Object of teasing, -.01 and -.08; Question of hypophrenia, -.01 and -.08; Grouped: temper, etc., -.01 and -.09; Enuresis, -.01 and .05; Sensitive (general), -.02 and -.18; Headaches, -.02 and -.08; Finicky food habits, -.03 and -.04; Quarrelsome, -.03 and -.01; Complaining of bad treatment by other children, -.03 (boys); Excuse-forming, -.04 and .09; Distractible, -.04 and .05; Apprehensive, -.05 and -.00; Destructive, -.06 and .02; Temper tantrums, -.06 and .08; Spoiled child, - 06 and -.08; Hatred or jealousy of sibling, -.07 and -.09; Disturbing influence in school, -.09 and .02; Stubborn, -.09 and .12; Slow, dull, -.09 and .01; Restless, -.09 and .09; Seclusive, -.09 and -.04; Unpopular, -.09 and .18; Grouped: lack of interest in school, -.09 and .06; Speech defect, -.10 and -.09; Poor work in school, -.11 and -.19; Retardation in school, -.11 and -.02; Grouped: dull, slow, etc., -.11 and -.15; Lack of interest in school, -.13 and .10; Bossy, -.14 and .01; Irresponsible, -.14 and .11; Attractive manner, -.14 and -.13; Absent-minded, -.16 and .03

Omitted—Sex denied entirely

notation of unfavorable conduct prognosis among girls yielded the large correlation of .48 + .05, and a substantial coefficient of .32 + .08 among boys. Three additional notations among girls yielded large correlations in the .40's but low positive coefficients ranging from .10 to .16 among boys: truancy from home, staying out late at night, and leading others into bad conduct.

Overinterest in the opposite sex among girls yielded the substantial correlation of .38 + .04, the boys' coefficient not being calculated because of fewness of boys' cases. Six additional conduct and personality difficulties among girls yielded substantial correlations in the .30's but low coefficients below .20 among boys: <u>oversuggestibility</u>, <u>bad companions</u>, <u>loitering or wandering</u>, <u>truancy from school</u>, <u>lying</u>, and <u>bashfulness</u>.

<u>Mental conflict</u> showed moderate correlations in the .20's with <u>sex delinquency (coitus</u>) among both sexes. <u>Daydreaming</u> and <u>sulkiness</u> among boys showed moderate correlations in the .20's but negligible coefficients of negative sign among girls. Seven miscellaneous notations among girls showed moderate correlations in the .20's but low coefficients below .20 among boys: <u>immoral home conditions</u>, <u>incorrigibility</u>, <u>disobedience</u>, <u>swearing or bad language</u> (undifferentiated), <u>stealing</u>, <u>lues</u>, and <u>underweight condition</u>.

<u>Sex delinquency (coitus</u>) showed many negative correlations of moderate size in the -.20's: among boys for the four notations, <u>laziness</u>, <u>lack of initiative</u>, <u>irregular attendance at school</u>, and <u>stuttering</u> and among girls for the five notations, "<u>nervousness</u>," <u>irritable temperament</u>, <u>restlessness in sleep</u>, <u>question or diagnosis of encephalitis</u>, and <u>neurological defect (unspecified</u>). "<u>Request for vocational guidance</u>" yielded the substantial negative correlations of -.39 $\pm$ .05 and -.41 $\pm$ .04 among boys and girls respectively.

<u>Sex delinquency (coitus</u>) yielded substantial or large correlations ranging from .38 to .48 with four other sex notations—<u>masturbation</u> and <u>overinterest in sex matters</u>—among both sexes and the two notations for which only the girls' coefficients were calculated, <u>overinterest in the opposite sex</u> and <u>victim of sex abuse by older child or person</u>.

Among the seven physical or psychophysical disabilities, two showed moderate positive correlations in the .20's among girls, <u>lues</u> and <u>underweight condition</u>. Two showed moderate <u>negative</u> correlations in the -.20's among girls, <u>question or diagnosis of encephalitis</u> and <u>neurological defect (unspecified</u>). <u>Stuttering</u> among boys showed the doubtfully significant negative correlation of -.20 $\pm$ .08, the girls' coefficient being omitted because of paucity of girls' cases.

Among the four home or familial notations the only statistically significant correlation with <u>sex delinquency (coitus</u>) was the moderate positive one of .29 $\pm$ .03 with <u>immoral home conditions</u> among girls.

Masturbation in our data was one of the most frequently appearing behavior notations, especially among boys. It was noted among 599, or 28.3 per cent, of our 2,113 White boys, and among 154, or 13.0 per cent, of our 1,181 White girls. With the personality-total and conduct-total criteria of seriousness or "ominousness" its bi-serial correlations ranging from .30 to .41 may be considered substantial but not large (Table 97). With the police-arrest criterion of overt juvenile delinquency its tetrachoric correlations of .20 $\pm$ .03 and .21 $\pm$ .05 were only moderate.

Its largest correlations were with overinterest in sex matters, the respective coefficients for boys and girls being .54 $\pm$ .03 and .46 $\pm$ .04. Sex delinquency (coitus) yielded large correlations in the .40's among both sexes. Stealing among girls yielded a large correlation of .44 $\pm$ .04, and a substantial coefficient of .32 $\pm$ .02 among boys.

Lying yielded substantial correlations in the .30's among both sexes. Daydreaming among boys yielded the substantial correlations of .37 $\pm$ .03, but a moderate correlation among girls of .25 $\pm$ .05. Among girls three notations—truancy from home, leading others into bad conduct, and worry over some specific fact—yielded substantial correlations in the .30's and among boys moderate coefficients ranging from .19 to .28.

Eleven personality and conduct problems showed moderate coefficients in the .20's with masturbation among both sexes: sensitiveness or worrisomeness (undifferentiated), sensitiveness over some specific fact, mental conflict, changeable moods or attitudes, "nervousness" or restlessness (including irritable temperament and changeable moods, undifferentiated), nail-biting, inattentiveness in school, bad companions, destructiveness, swearing or bad language (undifferentiated), and exclusion from school. Two conduct problems for which only the boys' coefficients were calculated—swearing in general and teasing other children—and two notations for which only the girls' coefficients were calculated—overinterest in the opposite sex and victim of sex abuse by older child or person—also showed moderate correlations in the .20's. Six notations among boys showed moderate correlations in the .20's but low coefficients below .20 among girls: enuresis, inferiority feelings, boastful or "show-off" manner, fantastical lying, object of teasing by other children, and laziness. A large list of eighteen

CHILDREN'S BEHAVIOR PROBLEMS

TABLE 97

CORRELATIONS WITH "MASTURBATION"

	Boys	Girls
Personality-total............................	.32 ± .02	.30 ± .03
Conduct-total................................	.32 ± .02	.41 ± .03
Police arrest................................	.20 ± .03	.21 ± .05
	Larger Correlations (Positive)	
Overinterest in sex matters...................	.54 ± .03	.46 ± .04 (1)*
Sex delinquency (coitus)......................	.43 ± .04	.41 ± .04 (3)
Daydreaming...................................	.37 ± .03	.25 ± .05 (30)
Lying...	.35 ± .02	.39 ± .04 (4)
Stealing......................................	.32 ± .02	.44 ± .04 (2)
Destructive...................................	.29 ± .03	.29 ± .06 (8-12)
Objective of teasing..........................	.29 ± .03	.09
Worry over specific fact......................	.28 ± .04	.33 ± .07 (7)
Grouped: sensitive or worrisome, etc.........	.27 ± .03	.28 ± .04 (13-17)
Fantastical lying.............................	.25 ± .03	.15
Leading others into bad conduct..............	.25 ± .04	.36 ± .06 (5)
Enuresis......................................	.24 ± .03	.19
Swearing (general)............................	.24 ± .04	....
Inferiority feelings..........................	.24 ± .03	.11
Mental conflict...............................	.24 ± .04	.27 ± .07 (18-23)
Sensitive over specific fact.................	.23 ± .03	.27 ± .05 (18-23)
Bad companions................................	.22 ± .03	.20 ± .05 (41-43)
Boastful, "show-off"..........................	.22 ± .03	.17
Changeable moods..............................	.22 ± .03	.20 ± .05 (41-43)
Nail-biting...................................	.21 ± .03	.26 ± .04 (24-29)
Teasing other children........................	.21 ± .03	....
Grouped: "nervous," etc......................	.21 ± .02	.22 ± .04 (34-37)
Inattentive in school.........................	.20 ± .02	.22 ± .06 (34-37)
Lazy..	.20 ± .04	-.05
Exclusion from school.........................	.20 ± .03	.29 ± .06 (8-12)
Grouped: swearing, etc.......................	.20 ± .03	.26 ± .06 (24-29)
Truancy from home.............................	.19	.35 ± .04 (6)
Defiant.......................................	.00	.29 ± .05 (8-12)
Rude..	.14	.29 ± .04 (8-12)
Victim of sex abuse...........................	....	.29 ± .05 (8-12)
Question of encephalitis......................	.18	.28 ± .07 (13-17)
Restless in sleep.............................	.18	.28 ± .05 (13-17)
Temper tantrums...............................	.16	.28 ± .05 (13-17)
Violence......................................	.13	.28 ± .06 (13-17)
Fighting......................................	.16	.27 ± .04 (18-23)
Overinterest in opposite sex..................	....	.27 ± .05 (18-23)
Grouped: fighting, etc.......................	.15	.27 ± .04 (18-23)
Grouped: depressed, etc......................	.16	.27 ± .05 (18-23)
Queer...	.19	.26 ± .06 (24-29)
Grouped: disobedient, etc....................	.14	.26 ± .04 (24-29)

*
Rank order of girls' correlations.

TABLE 97—Continued

	Boys	Girls
Stubborn....................................	.08	.26 ± .04 (24-29)
Slovenly....................................	.13	.26 ± .04 (24-29)
Bossy.......................................	.10	.24 ± .06 (31)
Incorrigible................................	.14	.23 ± .04 (32-33)
Psychoneurotic..............................	.15	.23 ± .06 (32-33)
Depressed...................................	.13	.22 ± .06 (34-37)
Disobedient.................................	.06	.22 ± .04 (34-37)
Sullen......................................	.07	.21 ± .05 (38-40)
Restless....................................	.14	.21 ± .04 (38-40)
Grouped: lack of interest in school, etc.....	.10	.21 ± .05 (38-40)
Unhappy.....................................	.15	.20 ± .06 (41-43)
	Larger Correlations (Negative)	
Vocational guidance.........................	-.10	-.37 + .04

Other Correlations (Positive to Negative)

"Nervous," .19 and .19; Repressed, .19 and .04; Complaining of bad treatment by other children, .19 (boys); Smoking, .17 (boys); Hatred or jealousy of sibling, .17 and .15; Question of change of personality, .17 and .17; Unpopular, .17 and .18; Loitering, .16 and .00; Oversuggestible, .16 and .11; Conduct prognosis bad, .16 and .17; Spoiled child, .15 and .01; Neurological defect, .15 and .16; Staying out late at night, .11 and .11; Threatening violence, .14 (boys); Emotional instability, .14 and .16; Grouped: temper, etc., .14 and .11; Truancy from school, .13 and .19; Crying spells, .13 and .15; Popular, .13 and .01; Discord between parents, .13 and .11; Grouped: egocentric, etc., .13 and .18; Contrary, .12 and .10; Disturbing influence in school, .12 and .12; Irresponsible, .12 and .05; Gang, .12 (boys); Absent-minded, .12 and .15; Clean, .12 and .08; Attractive manner, .12 and .05; Inefficient in work, play, etc., .11 and .08; Quarrelsome, .11 and .18; Listless, .11 and .00; Irritable, .11 and -.01; Distractible, .11 and .14; Excuse-forming, .10 and .11; Irregular sleep habits, .10 and .03; Selfish, .09 and .18; Apprehensive, .09 and .10; Egocentric, .09 and .14; Vicious home conditions, .09 and .07; Sulky, .08 and .18; Bashful, .08 and -.07; Sensitive (general), .08 and .06; Finicky food habits, .07 and .13; Preference for younger children, .07 and .16; Headaches, .07 and .14; Lack of interest in school, .06 and .10; Refusal to attend school, .06 and .02; Temper display, .06 and -.07; Leader, .06 and .15; Seclusive, .05 and .12; Underweight, .04 and .00; Speech defect, .04 and .08; Immoral home conditions, .04 and .11; Former convulsions, .02 and -.04; Poor work in school, .01 and -.09; Follower, .01 and -.09; Lack of initiative, .00 and -.13; Irregular attendance at school, -.01 and - 03; Grouped: dull, slow, etc., -.01 and -.12; Brother in penal detention, -.02 and -.01; Question of hypophrenia, -.03 and .00; Slow, dull, -.04 and -.05; Lues, -.04 and .06; Stuttering, -.06 (boys); Feeble-minded sibling, -.08 and -.10; Retardation in school, -.14 and -.15

Omitted—Sex denied entirely

miscellaneous case-record notations among girls showed moderate correlations in the .20's but low positive coefficients below .20 among boys: incorrigibility, disobedience, defiant attitude, stubbornness, fighting, violence, temper tantrums, rudeness, bossy manner, sullenness, slovenliness, restlessness, restlessness in sleep, queer behavior, psychoneurotic trends, depressed mood or spells, unhappiness, and question or diagnosis of encephalitis.

The only negative correlation of significant size was with the routine item "request for vocational guidance," -.37 ± .04 among girls.

Among the six sex notations the intercorrelations of masturbation with the two sex traits sex delinquency (coitus) and overinterest in sex matters were large, as we have noted, ranging from .41 to .54 among both sexes. With two notations for which only the girls' correlations were computed—overinterest in the opposite sex and victim of sex abuse by older child or person—the coefficients were of moderate size in the .20's.

Among the seven physical or psychophysical disabilities moderate correlations in the .20's were found for enuresis among boys and question or diagnosis of encephalitis among girls.

With the four home or familial notations all correlations with masturbation were low or negligible, ranging from -.02 to .13.

Manifesting precocious interest or overinterest in the opposite sex was noted among 175 of our 1,181 White girls (14.8 per cent). Its incidence among our boys was so small that satisfactory correlation coefficients could not be computed. Its bi-serial correlation with conduct-total was fairly large, .47 ± .03, and with the personality-total probably substantial, .31 ± .03 (Table 98). Its correlation with police arrest was low, .18 ± .04.

Its largest correlation, .50 ± .04, was with staying out late at night. Five conduct problems also yielded large correlations in the .40's: bad companions, truancy from school, incorrigibility, lying, and staff notation of unfavorable conduct prognosis.

Overinterest in the opposite sex yielded substantial correlations in the .30's with the following seventeen conduct and personality notations: sex delinquency (coitus), overinterest in sex matters, leading others into bad conduct, truancy from home,

TABLE 98

CORRELATIONS WITH "OVERINTEREST IN OPPOSITE SEX"
(Girls Only)

```
Personality-total . . . . . . . . . . . . . . .      .31 + .03
Conduct-total . . . . . . . . . . . . . . . .        .47 + .03
Police arrest . . . . . . . . . . . . . . . .        .18 + .04
```

Larger Correlations (Positive)

```
Staying out late at night . . . . . . . . . .        .50 + .04
Conduct prognosis bad . . . . . . . . . . . .        .43 + .05
Truancy from school . . . . . . . . . . . . .        .43 + .04
Incorrigible . . . . . . . . . . . . . . . . .       .42 + .04
Bad companions . . . . . . . . . . . . . . .         .41 + .04
Lying . . . . . . . . . . . . . . . . . . . .        .40 + .04
Grouped: disobedient, etc. . . . . . . . . . .       .40 + .03
Sex delinquency (coitus) . . . . . . . . . . .       .38 + .05
Leading others into bad conduct . . . . . . .        .37 + .06
Queer . . . . . . . . . . . . . . . . . . . .        .37 + .06
Unpopular . . . . . . . . . . . . . . . . . .        .34 + .06
Violence . . . . . . . . . . . . . . . . . . .       .34 + .05
Fantastical lying . . . . . . . . . . . . . .        .34 + .05
Boastful, "show-off" . . . . . . . . . . . . .       .33 + .05
Rude . . . . . . . . . . . . . . . . . . . . .       .33 + .04
Truancy from home . . . . . . . . . . . . . .        .33 + .04
Exclusion . . . . . . . . . . . . . . . . . .        .33 + .06
Grouped: swearing, etc. . . . . . . . . . . .        .32 + .05
Loitering . . . . . . . . . . . . . . . . . .        .32 + .06
Disobedient . . . . . . . . . . . . . . . . .        .32 + .04
Destructive . . . . . . . . . . . . . . . . .        .32 + .06
Stealing . . . . . . . . . . . . . . . . . . .       .31 + .04
Overinterest in sex matters . . . . . . . . .        .30 + .05
Temper tantrums . . . . . . . . . . . . . . .        .30 + .05
Stubborn . . . . . . . . . . . . . . . . . . .       .29 + .04
Grouped: egocentric, etc. . . . . . . . . . .        .28 + .04
Changeable moods . . . . . . . . . . . . . . .       .28 + .05
Masturbation . . . . . . . . . . . . . . . . .       .27 + .05
Sullen . . . . . . . . . . . . . . . . . . . .       .25 + .05
Egocentric . . . . . . . . . . . . . . . . . .       .25 + .05
Grouped: lack of interest in school, etc. . .        .25 + .04
Defiant . . . . . . . . . . . . . . . . . . .        .23 + .05
Question of change of personality . . . . . .        .23 + .06
Excuse-forming . . . . . . . . . . . . . . . .       .23 + .05
Emotional instability . . . . . . . . . . . .        .23 + .05
Victim of sex abuse . . . . . . . . . . . . .        .22 + .05
Slovenly . . . . . . . . . . . . . . . . . . .       .22 + .04
Lack of interest in school . . . . . . . . . .       .22 + .05
Fighting . . . . . . . . . . . . . . . . . . .       .22 + .04
Contrary . . . . . . . . . . . . . . . . . . .       .21 + .06
Refusal to attend school . . . . . . . . . . .       .21 + .07
Lues . . . . . . . . . . . . . . . . . . . . .       .21 + .05
Grouped: temper, etc. . . . . . . . . . . . .        .20 + .04
Unhappy . . . . . . . . . . . . . . . . . . .        .20 + .06
Irresponsible . . . . . . . . . . . . . . . .        .20 + .06
Inefficient in work, play, etc. . . . . . . .        .20 + .06
```

TABLE 98—Continued

Larger Correlations (Negative)

Lack of initiative . . . . -.23 ± .06

Other Correlations (Positive to Negative)

Disturbing influence in school, .19; Psychoneurotic,
.19; Distractible, .19; Grouped: depressed, etc., .18;
Grouped: fighting, etc., .18; Oversuggestible, .18; Depressed, .17; Restless, .17; Poor work in school, .17; Inattentive in school, .16; Lazy, .15; Grouped: "nervous,"
etc., .15; Daydreaming, .14; Nail-biting, .14; Quarrelsome,
.14; Headaches, .13; Listless, .11; Irritable, .11; Leader,
.11; Question of encephalitis, .10; Mental conflict, .10;
Absent-minded, .09; Object of teasing, .09; Worry over specific fact, .09; Immoral home conditions, .08; Hatred or
jealousy of sibling, .08; Finicky food habits, .07; Discord
between parents, .07; Grouped: sensitive or worrisome, etc.,
.06; Sulky, .06; Bossy, .06; Irregular sleep habits, .05;
Sensitive over specific fact, .05; Vicious home conditions,
.05; Brother in penal detention, .04; Neurological defect,
.04; Enuresis, .04; Crying spells, .03; Feeble-minded sibling, .02; Irregular attendance at school, .02; Spoiled
child, .02; Repressed, .02; Restless in sleep, .02; Selfish, .02; Preference for younger children, .01; Former
convulsions, -.00; Apprehensive, - 00; Underweight, -.01;
"Nervous," -.01; Temper display, -.01; Question of hypophrenia, -.03; Popular, -.03; Attractive manner, -.03; Sex
denied entirely, -.04; Apprehensive, -.05; Follower, -.05;
Sensitive (general), -.06; Clean, -.07; Grouped: dull, slow,
etc., -.07; Bashful, -.09; Slow, dull, -.11; Inferiority
feelings, -.11; Vocational guidance, -.11; Seclusive, -.13;
Speech defect, -.15

loitering or wandering, disobedience, violence, temper tantrums,
destructiveness, stealing, rudeness, boastful or "show-off" manner, fantastical lying, swearing or bad language (undifferentiated), queer behavior, unpopularity, and exclusion from school.

Moderate correlations in the .20's were found for nineteen
notations: masturbation, victim of sex abuse by older child or
person, stubbornness, defiant attitude, contrariness, sullenness,
refusal to attend school, lack of interest in school, inefficiency
in work, play, etc., slovenliness, irresponsibility, egocentricity,
fighting, excuse-forming attitude, emotional instability, changeable moods or attitudes, question of change of personality, unhappiness, and lues.

Only one negative correlation of significant size was found
—lack of initiative—with a coefficient of -.23 ± .06.

Among its intercorrelations with five other sex notations, <u>overinterest in the opposite sex</u> yielded substantial correlations in the .30's with <u>sex delinquency (coitus)</u> and <u>overinterest in sex matters</u>, and moderate coefficients in the .20's with <u>masturbation</u> and <u>victim of sex attack or abuse by older child or person</u>.

Among the six physical or psychophysical disabilities considered in Table 98, the only correlation of moderate size was with <u>lues</u>, .21 ± .05.

Among the four home or familial notations all correlations were negligible, ranging from .04 to .08.

<u>Manifesting precocious interest or overinterest in sex matters</u> was noted among 86 of our 2,113 White boys, or 4.1 per cent, and among 81 of our 1,181 White girls, or 6.9 per cent. With <u>personality-total</u> and <u>conduct-total</u> its bi-serial correlations were substantial, ranging from .31 to .42 (Table 99). With <u>police arrest</u> its tetrachoric correlations were of moderate size in the

TABLE 99

CORRELATIONS WITH "OVERINTEREST IN SEX MATTERS"

	Boys	Girls
Personality-total..........................	.31 ± .03	.35 ± .04
Conduct-total.............................	.34 ± .03	.42 ± .03
Police arrest..............................	.27 ± .04	.28 ± .05
	Larger Correlations (Positive)	
Masturbation..............................	.54 ± .03	.46 ± .04 (2)*
Sex delinquency (coitus)..................	.48 ± .07	.47 ± .05 (1)
Conduct prognosis bad.....................	.33 ± .07	.15
Grouped: swearing, etc...................	.32 ± .05	.32 ± .06 (12-13)
Immoral home conditions..................	.30 ± .07	.17
Fantastical lying.........................	.29 ± .07	.35 ± .07 (9)
Grouped: sensitive or worrisome, etc....	.27 ± .04	.29 ± .05 (21-22)
Worry over specific fact.................	.27 ± .07	.40 ± .08 (7)
Exclusion from school....................	.26 ± .05	.25 ± .07 (29)
Preference for younger children..........	.24 ± .06	.15
Lying.....................................	.24 ± .04	.43 ± .04 (4)
Bad companions...........................	.24 ± .05	.32 ± .06 (12-13)
Boastful, "show-off".....................	.23 ± .05	.34 ± .07 (10-11)

*Rank order of girls' correlations.

TABLE 99—Continued

	Boys	Girls
Leading others into bad conduct..................	.21 ± .06	.42 ± .07 (5-6)
Swearing (general)............................	.21 ± .06	....
Excuse-forming................................	.21 ± .05	.29 ± .06 (21-22)
Psychoneurotic................................	.21 ± .07	.08
Sensitive over specific fact..................	.21 ± .05	.21 ± .06 (35)
Mental conflict...............................	.20 ± .07	.42 ± .08 (5-6)
Victim of sex abuse...........................	....	.44 ± .05 (3)
Bossy...	.14	.38 ± .06 (8)
Hatred or jealousy of sibling.................	.10	.34 ± .07 (10-11)
Violence......................................	.18	.31 ± .07 (14-15)
Egocentric....................................	.14	.31 ± .06 (14-15)
Headaches.....................................	-.04	.30 ± .07 (16-20)
Overinterest in opposite sex..................	....	.30 ± .05 (16-20)
Rude..	.18	.30 ± .05 (16-20)
Inattentive in school........................	.08	.30 ± .07 (16-20)
Disobedient...................................	.09	.30 ± .05 (16-20)
Stealing......................................	.13	.28 ± .05 (23-24)
Slovenly......................................	-.02	.28 ± .05 (23-24)
Unhappy.......................................	.18	.27 ± .07 (25)
Grouped: depressed, etc......................	.15	.26 ± .06 (26-28)
Grouped: lack of interest in school, etc.....	.02	.26 ± .06 (26-28)
Daydreaming...................................	.19	.26 ± .07 (26-28)
Grouped: egocentric, etc.....................	.15	.24 ± .05 (30)
Distractible..................................	.06	.23 ± .06 (31-32)
Grouped: disobedient, etc....................	.10	.23 ± .05 (31-32)
Leader..	-.05	.22 ± .07 (33-34)
Inferiority feelings..........................	.15	.22 ± .08 (33-34)
Queer...	.19	.20 ± .07 (36-38)
Sullen..	.03	.20 ± .07 (36-38)
Disturbing influence in school...............	.13	.20 ± .07 (36-38)
	Larger Correlations (Negative)	
Question of hypophrenia.......................	-.01	-.22 ± .05
Grouped: dull, slow, etc....................	-.06	-.22 ± .05
Feeble-minded sibling.........................	-.03	-.21 ± .06
Former convulsions............................	.15	-.21 ± .08
	Not Calculable	
Sex denied entirely...........................	-.14	(n.c.)

Other Correlations (Positive to Negative)

Teasing other children, .19 (boys); Crying spells, .19 and .12; Sulky, .18 and .11; Unpopular, .18 and .18; Grouped: fighting, etc., .17 and .18; Quarrelsome, .17 and .15; Destructive, .17 and .05; Apprehensive, .16 and .03; Discord between parents, .15 and .07; Changeable moods, .15 and .03; Contrary, .15 and -.13; Refusal to attend school, .14 and .14; Restless in sleep, .14 and .16; Sensitive (general), .14 and .11; Grouped: "nervous," etc., .13 and .17;

TABLE 99—Continued

Vicious home conditions, .13 and -.04; Irritable, .13 and .10; Threatening violence, .13 (boys); Irresponsible, .13 and .03; Incorrigible, .12 and .12; Loitering, .12 and .14; Restless, .12 and .18; Emotional instability, .12 and .13;
Complaining of bad treatment by other children, .12 (boys); Popular, .12 and
.04; Neurological defect, .12 and -.02; Lazy, .11 and -.01; Finicky food habits,
.11 and -.06; Temper tantrums, .10 and .10; Repressed, .09 and .06; Seclusive,
.09 and .14; Inefficient in work, play, etc., .08 and .14; Staying out late at
night, .08 and .01; Irregular sleep habits, .08 and .03; Attractive manner, .08
and .19; Question of encephalitis, .07 and .04; Depressed, .07 and .16; Fighting, .07 and .14; Absent-minded, .06 and .13; Grouped: temper, etc., .06 and
.05; Brother in penal detention, .05 and .11; Oversuggestible, .05 and .17; Truancy from home, .04 and .10; "Nervous," .04 and .07; Follower, .04 and -.05;
Clean, .04 and .00; Speech defect, .03 and -.14; Lues, .03 and -.05; Object of
teasing, .03 and .03; Listless, .03 and -.10; Selfish, .03 and .09; Defiant,
.03 and .16; Enuresis, .02 and .14; Spoiled child, .02 and .17; Irregular attendance at school, .01 and -.04; Truancy from school, .01 and .19; Smoking,
.01 (boys); Gang, .00 (boys); Question of change of personality, -.00 and .13;
Nail-biting, -.01 and .09; Retardation in school, -.03 and -.15; Temper display,
-.03 and -.11; Poor work in school, -.05 and .04; Bashful, -.05 and .07; Slow,
dull, -.06 and -.14; Stubborn, -.07 and .19; Lack of initiative, -.07 and -.17;
Underweight, -.08 and .02; Lack of interest in school, -.09 and .12; Stuttering, -.10 (boys); Vocational guidance, -.11 and .03

.20's. Its highest correlations, ranging from .46 to .54 among
both sexes, were with masturbation and sex delinquency (coitus).
Victim of sex abuse by older child or person (calculated only for
girls) also yielded a large correlation of .44 ± .05. Four undesirable behavior traits among girls similarly yielded large correlations in the .40's but moderate coefficients in the .20's among
boys: mental conflict, worry over some specific fact, leading
others into bad conduct, and lying.

Overinterest in sex matters yielded substantial correlations in the .30's among both sexes with swearing or bad language
(undifferentiated) and among girls with overinterest in the opposite sex, the boys' coefficient not being calculated because of
paucity of cases. Immoral home conditions and staff notation of
unfavorable conduct prognosis among boys yielded substantial correlations in the .30's but low coefficients of .17 and .15 respectively among girls. Three conduct problems yielded substantial
correlations in the .30's among girls, and moderate coefficients
in the .20's among boys: bad companions, boastful or "show-off"
manner, and fantastical lying. An additional eight miscellaneous
notations among girls yielded substantial correlations in the .30's
but low coefficients below .20 among boys: disobedience, violence,

egocentricity, bossy manner, rudeness, hatred or jealousy of sibling, inattentiveness in school, and headaches.

Overinterest in sex matters among both sexes showed moderate correlations in the .20's with four undesirable notations: sensitiveness or worrisomeness (undifferentiated), sensitiveness over some specific fact, excuse-forming attitude, and exclusion from school. Among boys psychoneurotic trends and preference for younger children as playmates showed moderate correlations in the .20's but low coefficients below .20 among girls. Ten behavior traits among girls showed moderate correlations in the .20's but low coefficients below .20 among boys: daydreaming, distractibility, inferiority feelings, unhappiness, queer behavior, sullenness, slovenliness, disturbing influence in school, stealing, and "leader."

There were four negative correlations of moderate size in the -.20's with overinterest in sex matters, all among girls: question of hypophrenia, dull or slow manner (including listlessness and lack of initiative, undifferentiated), former convulsions, and feeble-minded sibling.

Among the five intercorrelations of overinterest in sex matters with the other sex notations, consistently large coefficients ranging from .44 to .54 were found for the three traits, sex delinquency (coitus), masturbation, and (calculated for girls only) victim of sex abuse by older child or person. A fairly substantial correlation of .30 ± .05 was found for overinterest in the opposite sex, for which only the girls' correlations were calculated.

Among the seven physical or psychophysical disabilities all correlations were low or negligible, ranging from -.14 to .14.

Among the four home or familial notations the only correlation of significant size with overinterest in sex matters was .30 ± .07 with immoral home conditions among boys.

The case-record notation, victim of actual or attempted rape or sex abuse by adult person (not a relative) or by older child, was noted among 104 of our 1,181 White girls, or 8.8 per cent. Among boys it occurred so seldom that correlations were not feasible in our data. As an indicator of behavior disorder it appears to be of little meaning. With the conduct-total its correlation was only moderate, .21 ± .03, while with the personality-total and police arrest its correlations were low, .11 ± .03 and

.19 $\pm$ .05 (Table 100). Its largest correlations, .44 $\pm$ .04 and
.44 $\pm$ .05, were with <u>sex delinquency (coitus)</u> and <u>overinterest in</u>
<u>sex matters</u> respectively. Substantial correlations in the .30's

TABLE 100

CORRELATIONS WITH "VICTIM OF SEX ABUSE"
(Girls Only)

Personality-total	.11 $\pm$ .03
Conduct-total	.21 $\pm$ .03
Police arrest	.19 $\pm$ .05

Larger Correlations (Positive)

Sex delinquency (coitus)	.44 $\pm$ .04
Overinterest in sex matters	.44 $\pm$ .05
Vicious home conditions	.33 $\pm$ .06
Inattentive in school	.30 $\pm$ .06
Masturbation	.29 $\pm$ .05
Lying	.29 $\pm$ .04
Truancy from home	.28 $\pm$ .05
Grouped: swearing, etc.	.27 $\pm$ .06
Apprehensive	.25 $\pm$ .05
Unhappy	.23 $\pm$ .07
Grouped: depressed, etc.	.22 $\pm$ .06
Grouped: lack of interest in school, etc. . . .	.22 $\pm$ .05
Overinterest in opposite sex	.22 $\pm$ .05
Bad companions	.22 $\pm$ .06
Mental conflict	.21 $\pm$ .08
Conduct prognosis bad	.21 $\pm$ .08
Discord between parents	.20 $\pm$ .05

Larger Correlations (Negative)

Destructive	-.29 $\pm$ .07
Sex denied entirely	-.28 $\pm$ .07
Temper display	-.21 $\pm$ .06
Irritable	-.20 $\pm$ .05

Other Correlations (Positive to Negative)

Fantastical lying, .19; Queer, .19; Exclusion from
school, .19; Immoral home conditions, .18; Sensitive over
specific fact, .18; Stealing, .18; Bossy, .17; Brother in
penal detention, .17; Boastful, "show-off," .15; Stubborn,
.15; Grouped: disobedient, etc., .15; Restless, .14; Question of change of personality, .14; Leading others into bad
conduct, .13; Worry over specific fact, .13; Quarrelsome,
.12; Disobedient, .12; Defiant, .12; Enuresis, .11; Staying
out late at night, .11; Truancy from school, .11; Depressed,
.11; Grouped: sensitive or worrisome, etc., .10; Absent-
minded, .09; Daydreaming, .09; Oversuggestible, .09; Follower, .09; Repressed, .08; Incorrigible, .08; Disturbing
influence in school, .07; Seclusive, .07; Clean, .07; Headaches, .07; Psychoneurotic, .06; Slovenly, .06; Selfish, .06;

TABLE 100—Continued

Nail-biting, .06; Rude, .05; Distractible, .05; Poor work in
school, .05; Attractive manner, .05; Feeble-minded sibling,
.04; Restless in sleep, .04; Excuse-forming, .04; Changeable
moods, .03; Egocentric, .03; Grouped: egocentric, etc., .03;
Neurological defect, .02; Leader, .02; "Nervous," .02; Violence, .02; Lack of interest in school, .02; Spoiled child,
.01; Grouped: fighting, etc., .01; Inefficient in work,
play, etc., -.00; Sulky, -.00; Hatred or jealousy of sibling,
-.00; Listless, -.00; Fighting, -.01; Lazy, -.02; Refusal to
attend school, -.02; Temper tantrums, -.02; Underweight, -.02;
Lues, -.02; Loitering, -.02; Emotional instability, -.03;
Lack of initiative, -.03; Irregular sleep habits, -.03; Sullen, -.03; Irresponsible, -.03; Bashful, -.05; Unpopular,
-.05; Grouped: "nervous," etc., -.05; Crying spells, -.06;
Object of teasing, -.07; Preference for younger children,
-.08; Popular, -.08; Former convulsions, -.08; Question of
hypophrenia, -.09; Grouped: dull, slow, etc., -.11; Speech
defect, -.11; Question of encephalitis, -.11; Slow, dull,
-.11; Finicky food habits, -.11; Retardation in school, -.12;
Vocational guidance, -.12; Irregular attendance at school,
-.12; Sensitive (general), -.14; Inferiority feelings, -.15;
Grouped: temper, etc., -.16; Contrary, -.18

were yielded by <u>vicious home conditions</u> and <u>inattentiveness in
school</u>.

   <u>Victim of sex abuse by older child or person</u> showed moderate correlations in the .20's with the following eleven miscellaneous notations: <u>overinterest in the opposite sex</u>, <u>masturbation</u>,
<u>bad companions</u>, <u>truancy from home</u>, <u>lying</u>, <u>swearing or bad language</u>
(undifferentiated), <u>apprehensiveness</u>, <u>unhappiness</u>, <u>mental conflict</u>,
<u>discord between parents</u>, and <u>staff notation of unfavorable conduct
prognosis</u>.

   Negative correlations of moderate size in the -.20's were
found for the following four notations: <u>sex misbehavior denied
entirely</u>, <u>irritable temperament</u>, <u>temper display</u>, and <u>destructive-
ness</u>.

   Among the five intercorrelations between <u>victim of sex
abuse by older child or person</u> and the other sex notations, large
correlations in the .40's were found for <u>sex delinquency (coitus)</u>
and <u>overinterest in sex matters</u> and moderate coefficients in the
.20's with <u>masturbation</u> and <u>overinterest in the opposite sex</u>. With
<u>sex misbehavior denied entirely</u> the correlation was negative and
of moderate size, -.28 + .07.

   With the six physical or psychophysical disabilities considered in Table 100, all coefficients were low or negligible, ranging from -.11 to .11.

Among the four home or familial notations, <u>vicious home conditions</u> yielded the substantial correlation of .33 ± .06, <u>discord between parents</u> the moderate correlation of .20 ± .05, and <u>immoral home conditions</u> and <u>brother in penal detention</u> the low positive coefficients of .18 and .17 respectively with <u>victim of sex abuse by older child or person</u>.

The notation <u>sex misbehavior denied entirely</u> (i.e., <u>patient denies masturbation, sex delinquency, homosexual practices, etc.</u>) was employed when there was no information contradicting the child's own denials. It was noted among 142 boys, or 6.7 per cent, and among 47 girls, or 4.0 per cent. The data in this instance are of course very incomplete, because in the clinical examinations it was not always considered advisable to investigate exhaustively the child's sex misbehavior beyond what was objectively verifiable. Its correlations with our three criteria of seriousness were all low or negligible, ranging from -.16 to .17 (Table 101).

TABLE 101

CORRELATIONS WITH "SEX DENIED ENTIRELY"

	Boys	Girls
Personality-total	.04 ± .03	.17 ± .04
Conduct-total	.02 ± .03	-.00 ± .04
Police arrest	.07 ± .04	-.16 ± .06
	Larger Correlations (Positive)	
Attractive manner	.25 ± .04	.13
Gang	.24 ± .05	....
Crying spells	.24 ± .04	.15
Truancy from school	.21 ± .04	.01
Hatred or jealousy of sibling	.20 ± .06	.14
Irregular sleep habits	.13	.28 ± .09 (1)*
Depressed	-.02	.25 ± .08 (2-3)
Clean	.13	.25 ± .07 (2-3)
Underweight	-.12	.21 ± .06 (3-4)
Changeable moods	-.13	.21 ± .07 (3-4)

*Rank order of girls' correlations.

TABLE 101—Continued

	Boys	Girls
	Larger Correlations (Negative)	
Victim of sex abuse............................	....	-.28 ± .07
Inattentive in school.........................	-.09	-.24 ± .08
Truancy from home.............................	.09	-.24 ± .06
Vicious home conditions.......................	.07	-.20 ± .09
	Not Calculable	
Lazy..	.16	(n.c.)
Lack of initiative...........................	.05	(n.c.)
Conduct prognosis bad.........................	(n.c.)	.11
Overinterest in sex matters..................	-.14	(n.c.)

Other Correlations (Positive to Negative)

Bad companions, .19 and -.14; Follower, .16 and -.08; Immoral home conditions, .16 and .16; Slovenly, .15 and .10; Staying out late at night, .15 and
.02; Enuresis, .13 and .12; Mental conflict, .13 and -.11; Leading others into
bad conduct, .12 and -.13; Rude, .12 and -.01; Spoiled child, .12 and .17; Lack
of interest in school, .11 and .04; Leader, .11 and .12; Stealing, .10 and .10;
Sullen, .10 and .07; Apprehensive, .10 and -.10; Brother in penal detention,
.10 and .06; Discord between parents, .10 and .16; Seclusive, .09 and .14; Unhappy, .09 and .11; Headaches, .09 and .04; Lues, .09 and .04; Speech defect,
.09 and -.15; Contrary, .08 and .09; Incorrigible, .08 and -.06; Loitering, .08
and -.18; Nail-biting, .08 and .13; Sulky, .08 and -.07; Psychoneurotic, .08
and -.05; Disobedient, .07 and -.05; Disturbing influence in school, .07 and
.03; Sensitive over specific fact, .07 and .11; Repressed, .07 and .12; Poor
work in school, .07 and .01; Irregular attendance at school, .07 and .11; Teasing other children, .06 (boys); Refusal to attend school, .06 and .19; Slow,
dull, .06 and -.19; Queer, .06 and .10; Complaining of bad treatment by other
children, .06 (boys); Grouped: dull, slow, etc., .06 and -.07; Grouped: sensitive or worrisome, etc., .06 and .06; Sensitive (general), .05 and .18; Fighting, .04 and .09; Popular, .04 and .13; Boastful, "show-off," .04 and .18; Question of change of personality, .03 and .17; Unpopular, .03 and .08; Neurological defect, .03 and .11; Grouped: lack of interest in school, etc., .03 and
-.04; Lying, .02 and .07; Quarrelsome, .02 and .16; Excuse-forming, .02 and .00;
Object of teasing, .02 and -.13; Oversuggestible, .02 and -.04; Restless in
sleep, .02 and .05; Stubborn, .01 and .11; Restless, .01 and .09; Grouped: depressed, etc., .01 and .18; Defiant, .00 and .07; Vocation guidance, .00 and
.01; Absent-minded, .00 and -.18; Feeble-minded sibling, -.00 and -.01; Grouped:
egocentric, etc., -.00 and .02; Smoking, -.01 (boys); Former convulsions, -.01
and -.12; Egocentric, -.02 and .05; Distractible, -.02 and .07; "Nervous," -.02
and .14; Grouped: disobedient, etc., -.03 and -.03; Inefficient in work, play,
etc., -.04 and .13; Worry over specific fact, -.04 and -.09; Inferiority feelings, -.04 and .05; Question of encephalitis, -.04 and .17; Overinterest in
opposite sex, -.04 (girls); Destructive, -.05 and -.02; Temper display, -.05
and -.14; Listless, -.05 and .15; Grouped: swearing, etc., -.05 and .03; Selfish, -.06 and .08; Preference for younger children, -.06 and .06; Threatening
violence, -.07 (boys); Violence, -.07 and .09; Stuttering, -.07 (boys); Grouped:
fighting, etc., -.07 and .09; Finicky food habits, -.08 and .10; Temper tantrums,

TABLE 101—Continued

-.08 and .13; Grouped: "nervous," etc., -.08 and .14; Retardation in school,
-.09 and .03; Swearing (general), -.10 (boys); Irresponsible, -.11 and .02;
Question of hypophrenia, -.11 and -.01; Exclusion from school, - 11 and -.08;
Bossy, -.12 and .10; Bashful, -.13 and -.07; Daydreaming, -.16 and .13; Grouped:
temper, etc., -.16 and .04; Irritable, -.17 and .08; Emotional instability, -.18
and -.03; Fantastical lying, -.19 and -.00
          Omitted—Sex delinquency (coitus), Masturbation

          Its highest correlations were only of moderate size in the
.20's. Among boys five behavior traits showed correlations ranging from .20 to .25: attractive manner, truancy from school, hatred or jealousy of sibling, crying spells, and (calculated for
boys only) running with a gang. The corresponding girls' coefficients were low, ranging from .01 to .15. Among girls five notations showed moderate correlations in the .20's but low coefficients among boys ranging from -.13 to .13: clean habits, depressed
mood or spells, changeable moods or attitudes, irregular sleep
habits, and underweight condition.
          Sex misbehavior denied entirely among girls showed four
negative correlations of moderate size in the -.20's: truancy from
home, inattentiveness in school, vicious home conditions, and (computed for girls only) victim of sex abuse by older child or person.
          Among the three sex notations for which tetrachoric corre-
lations with sex misbehavior denied entirely were calculated, the
only one of significant size was the moderate negative coefficient
of -.28 + .07 with victim of sex abuse by older child or person
(computed for girls only).
          Among the seven physical or psychophysical disabilities
the only coefficient of probable significant size was the moderate
one of .21 + .06 with underweight condition among girls.
          Among the four home or familial notations all correlations
with sex misbehavior denied entirely were low or negligible with
the exception of the very doubtfully significant negative coefficient of -.20 + .09 with vicious home conditions among girls.

          A few words summarizing the trends in the six tables dis-
cussed in this chapter may be appropriate in view of the considerable prominence given to sex behavior in children's behavior
clinics. Among both boys and girls, sex problems appear to be

conspicuously intercorrelated with one another. Among girls, sex
notations are frequently associated to a considerable extent with
conduct and personality disorders of nonsexual character, but among
boys such correlations appear to be of relatively minor degree.
Among girls the highest correlation was between sex delinquency
(coitus) and the fact of police arrest or detention, .76 $\pm$ .02.
With physical defects the correlations were largely low or negligible. With immoral home conditions and vicious home conditions
there were occasionally correlations of moderate or substantial
size. With discord between parents there appeared to be almost no
relationship with sex notations.

CHAPTER LI

ENURESIS; NAIL-BITING; AND FINICKY FOOD HABITS

The three "nervous habits"—enuresis, nail-biting, and finicky food habits—showed only minor correlations either among themselves or with the other notations considered in this study. So far as our correlational results indicate, all three appear to be of little importance clinically, with the possible exception of the correlation of finicky food habits with the personality-total among girls with the fairly high bi-serial coefficient of .41 ± .03.

Enuresis or bed-wetting (present or former) was considered a conduct problem in our present study if it continued beyond the third birthday into the third year of age. (The appropriateness of our including enuresis in our conduct-total is admittedly open to question, and the writer in retrospect now feels that it should not have been so included. The effect upon our correlational results, however, is probably of little importance.) It was noted as having occurred among 576, or 27.3 per cent, of our 2,113 White boys and among 250, or 21.2 per cent, of our 1,181 White girls and is thus a frequently noted item, though only seldom did it appear to be a principal reason for referring the child to the clinic for examination. Its bi-serial correlations with the personality-total and conduct-total were low, ranging from .16 to .20 (Table 102). With police arrest its tetrachoric correlations for boys and girls respectively were .07 ± .03 and -.25 ± .04. Its largest correlations with specific behavior problems were only .32 among girls and .26 among boys.

Its highest correlation, .32 ± .03, was found among girls for the "broader grouping" of "nervousness" or restlessness (including irritable temperament and changeable moods, undifferentiated), the corresponding coefficient among boys being low, .11. Restlessness in sleep showed the moderate correlations of .26 ± .03 and .31 ± .04 among boys and girls respectively. Mental conflict

TABLE 102

CORRELATIONS WITH "ENURESIS"

	Boys	Girls
Personality-total............................	.17 ± .02	.20 ± .03
Conduct-total................................	.16 ± .02	.18 ± .03
Police arrest................................	.07 ± .03	-.25 ± .04
		Larger Correlations (Positive)
Restless in sleep............................	.26 ± .03	.31 ± .04 (2-4)*
Masturbation.................................	.24 ± .03	.19
Sensitive over specific fact.................	.22 ± .03	.09
Swearing (general)...........................	.20 ± .04	....
Temper tantrums..............................	.20 ± .03	.27 ± .04 (8-9)
Grouped: "nervous," etc.....................	.11	.32 ± .03 (1)
Mental conflict	.03	.31 ± .06 (2-4)
Grouped: temper, etc........................	.16	.31 ± .03 (2-4)
Violence.....................................	.10	.28 ± .05 (5-7)
Grouped: fighting, etc......................	.13	.28 ± .04 (5-7)
Grouped: swearing, etc......................	.15	.28 ± .05 (5-7)
Irritable....................................	.05	.27 ± .04 (8-9)
Lazy...	.06	.26 ± .05 (10)
Nail-biting..................................	.18	.24 ± .04 (11)
Stubborn.....................................	.10	.23 ± .04 (12-14)
Daydreaming..................................	.13	.23 ± .05 (12-14)
Preference for younger children..............	.13	.23 ± .05 (12-14)
Quarrelsome..................................	.18	.22 ± .04 (15-18)
Unpopular....................................	.08	.22 ± .06 (15-18)
Question of encephalitis.....................	.08	.22 ± .07 (15-18)
Speech defect................................	.14	.22 ± .05 (15-18)
Restless.....................................	.07	.21 ± .04 (19)
Disturbing influence in school...............	.10	.20 ± .05 (20-21)
Grouped: disobedient, etc...................	.14	.20 ± .03 (20-21)

*Rank order of girls' correlations.

Other Correlations (Positive to Negative)

Destructive, .19 and .09; Grouped: sensitive or worrisome, etc., .19 and .13; Stealing, .18 and .19; Teasing other children, .17 (boys); Sulky, .16 and .09; Exclusion from school, .16 and .17; Former convulsions, .16 and .13; Slovenly, .15 and .13; Temper display, .15 and .10; Truancy from school, .15 and .12; Inferiority feelings, .15 and .10; Leading others into bad conduct, .14 and .10; Crying spells, .14 and .17; Fighting, .13 and .19; Lying, .13 and .19; Truancy from home, .13 and -.00; Conduct prognosis bad, .13 and .00; Spoiled child, .13 and .10; Sex denied entirely, .13 and .12; Boastful, "show-off," .12 and .08; Oversuggestible, .12 and -.03; Discord between parents, .12 and -.00; Finicky food habits, .11 and .19; Disobedient, .11 and .12; Fantastical lying, .11 and .15; Incorrigible, .11 and .17; Smoking, .11 (boys); Changeable mood, .11 and .01; Listless, .11 and .18; "Nervous," .11 and .19; Vicious

TABLE 102—Continued

home conditions, .11 and .01; Victim of sex abuse, .11 (girls); Bad companions, .10 and .00; Bossy, .10 and .17; Contrary, .10 and -.03; Excuse-forming, .10 and .13; Headaches, .10 and .09; Threatening violence, .09 (boys); Rude, .09 and .07; Distractible, .09 and .18; Sensitive (general), .09 and .14; Worry over specific fact, .09 and .09; Follower, .09 and .06; Lack of initiative, .08 and .05; Object of teasing, .08 and .14; Staying out late at night, .07 and .15; Psychoneurotic, .07 and -.07; Repressed, .07 and .12; Grouped: dull, slow, etc., .07 and .04; Apprehensive, .06 and .07; Underweight, .06 and .11; Grouped: depressed, etc., .06 and .13; Inattentive in school, .05 and .09; Lack of interest in school, .05 and .04; Bashful, .05 and .02; Queer, .05 and .08; Question of hypophrenia, .05 and .16; Inefficient in work, play, etc., .04 and .19; Absent-minded, .04 and .14; Egocentric, .04 and .08; Unhappy, .04 and -.01; Grouped: lack of interest in school, etc., .04 and .09; Overinterest in opposite sex, .04 (girls); Defiant, .03 and .16; Loitering, .03 and .12; Hatred or jealousy of sibling, .03 and .09; Depressed, .03 and .18; Slow, dull, .03 and .05; Irregular sleep habits, .03 and .11; Seclusive, .03 and .05; Complaining of bad treatment by other children, .03 (boys); Neurological defect, .03 and .06; Grouped: egocentric, etc., .03 and .03; Emotional instability, .02 and .08; Popular, .02 and -.03; Lues, .02 and .15; Overinterest in sex matters, .02 and .14; Irregular attendance at school, .02 and .01; Brother in penal detention, .02 and -.11; Retardation in school, -.00 and .04; Sullen, -.00 and -.07; Immoral home conditions, - 01 and .03; Attractive manner, -.01 and -.02; Clean, -.01 and .12; Poor work in school, -.01 and -.13; Sex delinquency (coitus), -.01 and .05; Gang, -.02 (boys); Irresponsible, -.02 and .07; Stuttering, -.03 (boys); Question of change of personality, -.04 and .07; Leader, -.06 and .18; Selfish, -.06 and .12; Refusal to attend school, -.07 and .12; Vocational guidance, -.10 and -.18; Feeble-minded sibling, -.17 and .01

and temper tantrums or display (including irritable temperament, undifferentiated) also yielded moderate or possibly substantial coefficients of .31 each among the girls, and low coefficients of .03 and .16 respectively among boys.

Enuresis showed moderate correlations in the .20's among both sexes with temper tantrums and also with swearing in general, for which only the boys' coefficients were computed. Sensitiveness over some specific fact and masturbation among boys showed moderate correlations in the .20's but low positive coefficients below .20 among girls. Fourteen miscellaneous notations among girls showed moderate correlations in the .20's but low positive coefficients below .20 among boys: nail-biting, restlessness, irritable temperament, quarrelsomeness, violence, stubbornness, swearing or bad language (undifferentiated), disturbing influence in school, laziness, preference for younger children as playmates, daydreaming, unpopularity, speech defect (other than stuttering), and question or diagnosis of encephalitis.

The only negative correlation of moderate size was the interesting one with police arrest among girls, -.25 ± .04.

Among the six sex notations the only correlations of meaningful size were with <u>masturbation</u>, the respective coefficients for boys and girls being .24 ± .03 and .19.

Among the six physical or psychophysical disabilities, for which correlations with <u>enuresis</u> were calculated, there were two of moderate size, both among girls: <u>question or diagnosis of encephalitis</u>, .22 ± .07, and <u>speech defec</u>t (other than <u>stuttering</u>), .22 ± .05.

Among the four home or familial notations, all correlations were low or negligible, ranging from -.11 to .12.

<u>Enuresis</u> in our data, therefore, appears to have little meaning other than as an annoyance in itself.

<u>Nail-biting</u> was noted among 300 of our boys, or in 14.2 per cent, and among 246 of our girls, or in 20.8 per cent. Its incidence thus appears to be definitely greater among girls. With the <u>personality-total</u> its bi-serial correlations among both sexes were of moderate size in the .20's. With the <u>conduct-total</u> its correlations were low, .19 ± .02 and .17 ± .03 for boys and girls respectively. With <u>police arrest</u> its corresponding tetrachoric correlations of .10 ± .03 and .06 ± .04 respectively were negligible (Table 103).

TABLE 103

CORRELATIONS WITH "NAIL-BITING"

	Boys	Girls
Personality-total.............................	.28 ± .02	.24 ± .03
Conduct-total.................................	.19 ± .02	.17 ± .03
Police arrest.................................	.10 ± .03	.06 ± .04
	Larger Correlations (Positive)	
Slovenly......................................	.31 ± .03	.12
Restless in sleep.............................	.27 ± .03	.40 ± .04 (1)*
"Nervous"....................................	.26 ± .03	.29 ± .04 (5)
Restless......................................	.25 ± .03	.27 ± .06 (7)
Unhappy.......................................	.25 ± .05	.07
Grouped: "nervous," etc......................	.25 ± .03	.37 ± .03 (2)

*Rank order of girls' correlations.

TABLE 103—Continued

	Boys	Girls
Fantastical lying	.21 ± .03	.16
Masturbation	.21 ± .03	.26 ± .04 (8-12)
Changeable moods	.21 ± .04	.26 ± .04 (8-12)
Bossy	.20 ± .05	.23 ± .05 (14-15)
Crying spells	.20 ± .03	.21 ± .04 (16)
Finicky food habits	.18	.30 ± .05 (3-4)
Grouped: fighting, etc.	.13	.30 ± .04 (3-4)
Unpopular	.18	.28 ± .06 (6)
Irresponsible	.18	.26 ± .05 (8-12)
Stealing	.16	.26 ± .04 (8-12)
Neurological defect	.11	.26 ± .05 (8-12)
Enuresis	.18	.24 ± .04 (13)
Irregular sleep habits	-.05	.23 ± .06 (14-15)
Destructive	.14	.20 ± .06 (17-22)
Disturbing influence in school	.17	.20 ± .05 (17-22)
Fighting	.06	.20 ± .04 (17-22)
Preference for younger children	.14	.20 ± .05 (17-22)
Violence	.15	.20 ± .05 (17-22)
Hatred or jealousy of sibling	.16	.20 ± .06 (17-22)

Other Correlations (Positive to Negative)

Lying, .19 and .18; Grouped: depressed, etc., .19 and .15; Inferiority feelings, .18 and .13; Defiant, .18 and .15; Swearing (general), .18 (boys); Contrary, .17 and -.09; Rude, .17 and .12; Truancy from school, .17 and .17; Daydreaming, .17 and .08; Grouped: temper, etc., .17 and .19; Teasing other children, .16 (boys); Selfish, .16 and .17; Smoking, .16 (boys); Depressed, .16 and .17; Grouped: egocentric, etc., .16 and .10; Exclusion from school, .15 and .18; Grouped: swearing, etc., .15 and .16; Truancy from home, .14 and .16; Queer, .14 and .18; Overinterest in opposite sex, .14 (girls); Headaches, .14 and .18; Loitering, .13 and .06; Temper tantrums, .13 and .13; Threatening violence, .13 (boys); Complaining of bad treatment by other children, .13 (boys); Grouped: disobedient, etc., .13 and .11; Grouped: sensitive, etc., .13 and .19; Temper display, .12 and .11; Question of change of personality, .12 and .13; Egocentric, .12 and .04; Irritable, .12 and .16; Spoiled child, .12 and .13; Bad companions, .11 and .04; Inattentive in school, .11 and .11; Incorrigible, .11 and .18; Worry over specific fact, .11 and .16; Former convulsions, .11 and .05; Boastful, "show-off," .10 and .17; Lazy, .10 and .01; Stubborn, .10 and .09; Psychoneurotic, .10 and -.01; Sensitive over specific fact, .10 and .17; Follower, .10 and .13; Disobedient, .09 and .07; Inefficient in work, play, etc., .09 and -.02; Apprehensive, .09 and .15; Excuse-forming, .09 and .04; Seclusive, .09 and -.04; Sensitive (general), .09 and .11; Attractive manner, .09 and .06; Irregular attendance at school, .09 and .03; Discord between parents, .09 and .12; Lack of interest in school, .08 and .08; Quarrelsome, .08 and .16; Absent-minded, .08 and .08; Distractible, .08 and .19; Sex denied entirely, .08 and .13; Question of encephalitis, .08 and .13; Sex delinquency (coitus), .07 and .03; Object of teasing, .07 and .19; Vicious home conditions, .07 and -.01; Staying out late at night, .06 and .07; Conduct prognosis bad, .06 and .06; Leader, .06 and .06; Vocational guidance, .06 and -.05; Victim of sex abuse, .06 (girls); Refusal to attend school, .05 and -.06; Sullen, .05 and .09; Mental conflict, .05 and .06; Speech defect, .05 and .18; Leading others into bad conduct, .04 and .08; Sulky, .04 and .02; Bashful, .04 and .01; List-

TABLE 103—Continued

less, .04 and -.17; Repressed, .04 and .06; Popular, .04 and -.07; Grouped:
lack of interest in school, etc., .04 and .08; Gang, .03 (boys); Oversuggestible,
.03 and .05; Lack of initiative, .02 and .03; Overinterest in sex matters, .01
and .09; Stuttering, .01 (boys); Lies, .00 and .04; Clean, -.01 and .04; Underweight, - 02 and .07; Poor work in school, -.02 and -.10; Feeble-minded sibling,
-.03 and -.15; Question of hypophrenia, -.03 and .06; Retardation in school,
-.04 and -.05; Grouped: dull, slow, etc., -.05 and -.07; Emotional instability,
-.06 and .13; Slow, dull, -.07 and -.08; Immoral home conditions, -.12 and .12;
Brother in penal detention, -.14 and -.11

Its largest correlations of .40 + .04 and .37 + .03 were
found among girls for restlessness in sleep and "nervousness" or
restlessness (including irritable temperament and changeable moods,
undifferentiated) respectively, the corresponding coefficients
among boys being of moderate size in the .20's.

Nail-biting showed moderate correlations in the .20's with
sex personality and conduct problems: "nervousness," restlessness,
changeable moods or attitudes, crying spells, bossy manner, and
masturbation. The three behavior notations slovenliness, unhappiness, and fantastical lying among boys showed moderate correlations
ranging from .21 to .31 but low coefficients below .20 among girls.
Thirteen miscellaneous notations among girls showed moderate coefficients ranging from .20 to .30 but low coefficients below .20
among boys: enuresis, finicky food habits, fighting, violence,
hatred or jealousy of sibling, destructiveness, disturbing influence in school, irregular sleep habits, stealing, irresponsibility,
unpopularity, preference for younger children as playmates, and
neurological defect (unspecified).

Among the six sex notations, nail-biting showed moderate
correlations in the .20's with masturbation among both sexes.

Among the seven physical or psychophysical disabilities,
enuresis and neurological defect (unspecified) showed moderate correlations in the .20's among girls.

Among the four home or familial notations all correlations
were low or negligible.

"Finicky" food habits or capricious or irregular appetite
was noted among 236 boys, or 11.2 per cent, and among 105 girls,
or 8.9 per cent. Among girls it appeared to be of some significance as an indicator of personality deviation, its correlation

with <u>personality-total</u> being .41 ± .03 (Table 104). Among girls
its correlations with <u>conduct-total</u> and <u>police arrest</u> were of moderate size in the .20's. Among boys it showed a moderate correlation of .26 ± .02 with <u>personality-total</u>, but low or negligible
correlations with <u>conduct-total</u> and <u>police arrest</u>.

TABLE 104

CORRELATIONS WITH "FINICKY FOOD HABITS"

	Boys	Girls
Personality-total..........................	.26 ± .02	.41 ± .03
Conduct-total.............................	.10 ± .02	.28 ± .03
Police arrest.............................	.01 ± .03	.26 ± .05
	Larger Correlations (Positive)	
Restless in sleep.........................	.34 ± .03	.38 ± .05 (5-6)*
Irregular sleep habits....................	.33 ± .05	.30 ± .07 (15-17)
Grouped: "nervous," etc..................	.31 ± .03	.45 ± .04 (1)
Sensitive (general).......................	.31 ± .04	.33 ± .06 (11)
Headaches.................................	.29 ± .05	.27 ± .06 (24-25)
Spoiled child.............................	.27 ± .04	.27 ± .06 (24-25)
Grouped: temper, etc.....................	.26 ± .03	.42 ± .04 (2-3)
Popular...................................	.25 ± .05	.02
Changeable moods..........................	.24 ± .04	.12
"Nervous".................................	.23 ± .04	.31 ± .05 (12-14)
Temper tantrums...........................	.22 ± .04	.31 ± .05 (12-14)
Question of change of personality.........	.22 ± .05	.09
Irritable.................................	.22 ± .03	.42 ± .05 (2-3)
Grouped: sensitive or worrisome, etc.....	.22 ± .03	.19
Restless..................................	.20 ± .03	.26 ± .05 (26-29)
Selfish...................................	.13	.40 ± .06 (4)
Grouped: fighting, etc...................	.16	.38 ± .04 (5-6)
Defiant...................................	.09	.36 ± .06 (7-8)
Grouped: egocentric, etc.................	.12	.36 ± .04 (7-8)
Violence..................................	.14	.35 ± .06 (9-10)
Question of encephalitis..................	.12	.35 ± .08 (9-10)
Refusal to attend school..................	.10	.31 ± .07 (12-14)
Nail-biting...............................	.18	.30 ± .05 (15-17)
Former convulsions........................	.06	.30 ± .07 (15-17)
Incorrigible..............................	.05	.29 ± .05 (18-22)
Quarrelsome...............................	.12	.29 ± .05 (18-22)
Rude......................................	.07	.29 ± .05 (18-22)
Egocentric................................	.12	.29 ± .05 (18-22)
Grouped: disobedient, etc................	.14	.29 ± .04 (18-22)
Daydreaming...............................	.15	.28 ± .06 (23)
Disobedient...............................	.11	.26 ± .05 (26-29)
Sullen....................................	-.08	.26 ± .06 (26-29)
Grouped: swearing, etc...................	.09	.26 ± .06 (26-29)

*Rank order of girls' correlations.

TABLE 104—Continued

	Boys	Girls
Contrary..	.08	.25 ± .07 (30-31)
Fighting...	.04	.25 ± .06 (30-31)
Inattentive in school...........................	.06	.23 ± .06 (32-35)
Stubborn...	.14	.23 ± .05 (32-35)
Temper display....................................	.18	.23 ± .06 (32-35)
Irregular attendance at school...............	-.08	.23 ± .06 (32-35)
Psychoneurotic....................................	.13	.21 ± .07 (36-38)
Worry over specific fact.......................	.05	.21 ± .08 (36-38)
Discord between parents.......................	.06	.21 ± .05 (36-38)
Crying spells.......................................	.13	.20 ± .05 (39-43)
Seclusive..	.02	.20 ± .06 (39-43)
Inferiority feelings..............................	.11	.20 ± .07 (39-43)
Conduct prognosis bad.........................	-.02	.20 ± .08 (39-43)
Neurological defect..............................	.05	.20 ± .06 (39-43)

Other Correlations (Positive to Negative)

Boastful, "show-off," .17 and .18; Destructive, .17 and .12; Underweight, .16 and .18; Bossy, .15 and .03; Follower, .14 and .12; Grouped: depressed, etc., .14 and .13; Sulky, .13 and .15; Swearing (general), .13 (boys);
Depressed, .13 and .17; Queer, .13 and .04; Listless, .12 and .10; Enuresis,
.11 and .19; Overinterest in sex matters, .11 and -.06; Sensitive over specific
fact, .11 and .05; Clean, .11 and .18; Teasing other children, .10 (boys); Distractible, .10 and .13; Emotional instability, .10 and .06; Unhappy, .10 and
.12; Disturbing influence in school, .09 and .08; Apprehensive, .09 and .11;
Attractive manner, .09 and .14; Bad companions, .08 and .11; Lazy, .08 and .06;
Threatening violence, .08 (boys); Absent-minded, .08 and -.04; Lack of initiative, .08 and .11; Smoking, .07 (boys); Staying out late at night, .07 and .13;
Masturbation, .07 and .13; Bashful, .07 and .14; Repressed, .07 and .15; Overinterest in opposite sex, .07 (girls); Inefficient in work, play, etc., .05 and
-.06; Lying, .05 and .12; Object of teasing, .05 and .14; Preference for younger
children, .05 and .04; Stuttering, .05 (boys); Grouped: lack of interest in
school, etc., .05 and .18; Poor work in school, .04 and -.02; Vicious home conditions, .04 and -.17; Truancy from home, .03 and .02; Hatred or jealousy of
sibling, .03 and .02; Complaining of bad treatment by other children, .03
(boys); Unpopular, .02 and .11; Mental conflict, .02 and -.07; Grouped: dull,
slow, etc., .02 and -.02; Excuse-forming, .02 and .14; Fantastical lying, .01
and .19; Slovenly, .01 and .03; Truancy from school, .00 and .11; Exclusion
from school, .00 and .14; Speech defect, -.00 and -.11; Leader, -.00 and .17;
Vocational guidance, -.01 and .02; Lack of interest in school, -.01 and .09;
Irresponsible, -.01 and .06; Lues, -.02 and .05; Gang, -.02 (boys); Loitering,
-.02 and .15; Sex delinquency (coitus), -.03 and -.04; Leading others into bad
conduct, -.03 and .19; Oversuggestible, -.04 and .12; Stealing, -.04 and .06;
Feeble-minded sibling, -.06 and -.13; Question of hypophrenia, -.06 and -.15;
Sex denied entirely, -.08 and .10; Brother in penal detention, -.09 and .06;
Slow, dull, -.09 and -.12; Victim of sex abuse, -.11 (girls); Immoral home con-
ditions, -.14 and -.16; Retardation in school, -.15 and -.11

Among girls its largest correlations ranging from .42 to
.45 were with "nervousness" or restlessness (including irritable

temperament and changeable moods, undifferentiated), temper tantrums or display (including irritable temperament, undifferentiated), and irritable temperament, the corresponding coefficients for boys being of moderate size ranging from .22 to .31. Selfishness among girls similarly yielded the fairly large correlation of .40 ± .06 but a low coefficient of .13 among boys.

Three notations—restlessness in sleep, irregular sleep habits, and sensitiveness in general—yielded substantial correlations in the .30's among both sexes. Six notations among girls yielded substantial correlations in the .30's but low positive coefficients below .20 among boys: nail-biting, violence, defiant attitude, refusal to attend school, question or diagnosis of encephalitis, and former convulsions.

Finicky food habits showed moderate correlations in the .20's among both sexes for the three notations, "spoiled child," restlessness, and headaches. Four traits among boys showed moderate correlations in the .20's but low coefficients below .20 among girls: question of change of personality, changeable moods or attitudes, sensitiveness or worrisomeness (undifferentiated), and popularity. A large list of twenty-two miscellaneous case-record notations among girls showed moderate correlations in the .20's but low or negligible coefficients below .20 among boys: incorrigibility, disobedience, contrariness, stubbornness, fighting, quarrelsomeness, temper display, rudeness, egocentricity, sullenness, swearing or bad language (undifferentiated), inattentiveness in school, daydreaming, seclusiveness, inferiority feelings, worry over some specific fact, psychoneurotic trends, crying spells, irregular attendance at school, discord between parents, neurological defect (unspecified), and staff notation of unfavorable conduct prognosis.

Among the six sex notations all correlations with finicky food habits were low or negligible, ranging from -.11 to .11.

Among the seven physical or psychophysical disabilities there were two correlations of statistically significant size, both among girls: question or diagnosis of encephalitis, .35 ± .08, and neurological defect (unspecified), .20 ± .06.

Among the four home or familial notations, the only coefficient of moderate size was with discord between parents among girls, .21 ± .05.

CHAPTER LII

BOASTFUL OR "SHOW-OFF" MANNER

From the standpoint of clinical importance, <u>boastful or "show-off" manner</u> appeared in our data to be of considerable importance, especially among girls. With both the <u>personality-total</u> and the <u>conduct-total</u> the bi-serial correlations among girls were in the .50's and the corresponding correlations among boys in the .40's (Table 105). With the <u>police-arrest</u> criterion of juvenile

TABLE 105

CORRELATIONS WITH "BOASTFUL, SHOW-OFF"

	Boys	Girls
Personality-total...........................	.42 ± .02	.56 ± .03
Conduct-total...............................	.48 ± .02	.52 ± .03
Police arrest...............................	.29 ± .03	.10 ± .06
	Larger Correlations (Positive)	
Fantastical lying...........................	.52 ± .03	.37 ± .07 (15-16)*
Disturbing influence in school..............	.51 ± .03	.44 ± .06 (4-5)
Quarrelsome.................................	.41 ± .03	.27 ± .05 (38-41)
Egocentric..................................	.39 ± .03	.45 ± .05 (3)
Grouped: egocentric, etc...................	.38 ± .03	.44 ± .05 (4-5)
Grouped: disobedient, etc..................	.36 ± .03	.34 ± .04 (18-19)
Teasing other children......................	.34 ± .04	....
Bossy.......................................	.33 ± .05	.47 ± .06 (2)
Lying.......................................	.33 ± .03	.31 ± .05 (28-30)
Unpopular...................................	.33 ± .05	.49 ± .07 (1)
Smoking.....................................	.32 ± .04	....
Spoiled child..............................	.32 ± .04	.38 ± .06 (12-14)
Rude..	.31 ± .03	.40 ± .05 (8-11)
Disobedient................................	.30 ± .03	.20 ± .05 (54-55)
Fighting...................................	.30 ± .03	.23 ± .07 (47-50)
Leading others into bad conduct............	.30 ± .04	.37 ± .08 (15-16)
Stealing...................................	.30 ± .03	.24 ± .05 (45-46)
Contrary...................................	.29 ± .05	.29 ± .08 (33-35)
Defiant....................................	.29 ± .04	.32 ± .06 (25-27)

*Rank order of girls' correlations.

	Boys	Girls
Excuse-forming	.28 ± .04	.33 ± .06 (20-24)
Restless	.28 ± .03	.33 ± .05 (20-24)
Inferiority feelings	.28 ± .04	.28 ± .08 (36-37)
Exclusion from school	.28 ± .04	.16
Grouped: fighting, etc.	.28 ± .03	.29 ± .05 (33-35)
Incorrigible	.27 ± .03	.30 ± .05 (31-32)
Lazy	.26 ± .04	.25 ± .07 (43-44)
Selfish	.26 ± .04	.32 ± .07 (25-27)
Hatred or jealousy of sibling	.26 ± .05	.26 ± .08 (42)
Destructive	.25 ± .04	.19
Threatening violence	.25 ± .05	....
Clean	.25 ± .03	-.03
Grouped: "nervous," etc.	.25 ± .03	.38 ± .04 (12-14)
Grouped: lack of interest in school, etc.	.25 ± .03	.17
Bad companions	.24 ± .03	.18
Overinterest in sex matters	.23 ± .05	.34 ± .07 (18-19)
Leader	.23 ± .04	.27 ± .07 (38-41)
Staying out late at night	.22 ± .04	.04
Violence	.22 ± .04	.40 ± .06 (8-11)
Masturbation	.22 ± .03	.19
Mental conflict	.22 ± .05	.01
Inattentive in school	.21 ± .04	.16
Lack of interest in school	.21 ± .04	.14
Sulky	.21 ± .05	.25 ± .07 (43-44)
Truancy from school	.21 ± .03	.24 ± .06 (45-46)
Grouped: swearing, etc.	.21 ± .04	.31 ± .07 (28-30)
Gang	.20 ± .04	....
Temper tantrums	.20 ± .04	.40 ± .06 (8-11)
Irregular sleep habits	.20 ± .05	.23 ± .08 (47-50)
Changeable moods	.15	.42 ± .05 (6-7)
Daydreaming	.18	.42 ± .06 (6-7)
Queer	.16	.40 ± .07 (8-11)
Grouped: temper, etc.	.16	.38 ± .04 (12-14)
Emotional instability	.18	.36 ± .07 (17)
Overinterest in opposite sex	....	.33 ± .05 (20-24)
Distractible	.18	.33 ± .06 (20-24)
Headaches	.08	.33 ± .07 (20-24)
Inefficient in work, play, etc.	.09	.32 ± .07 (25-27)
Sensitive (general)	.16	.31 ± .07 (28-30)
Psychoneurotic	.04	.30 ± .07 (31-32)
Repressed	.05	.29 ± .08 (33-35)
Depressed	.18	.28 ± .07 (36-37)
Unhappy	.07	.27 ± .07 (38-41)
Grouped: depressed, etc.	.14	.27 ± .06 (38-41)
Stubborn	.19	.23 ± .05 (47-50)
Irritable	.10	.23 ± .06 (47-50)
Slovenly	.19	.22 ± .05 (51)
Truancy from home	.19	.21 ± .06 (52-53)
Conduct prognosis bad	.19	.21 ± .08 (52-53)
Question of encephalitis	.02	.20 ± .09 (54-55)

TABLE 105—Continued

	Boys	Girls
	Larger Correlations (Negative)	
Feeble-minded sibling..........................	.05	-.38 ± .06
Follower.......................................	.00	-.28 ± .06
	Not Calculable	
Lack of initiative............................	-.05	(n.c.)

Other Correlations (Positive to Negative)

Restless in sleep, .19 and .13; Attractive manner, .19 and .09; Irresponsible, .18 and .16; Loitering, .18 and .16; Complaining of bad treatment by other children, .18 (boys); Finicky food habits, .17 and .18; Sullen, .17 and .14; Temper display, .17 and .08; "Nervous," .16 and .15; Object of teasing, .16 and .13; Popular, .16 and .18; Worry over specific fact, .15 and .11; Victim of sex abuse, .15 (girls); Swearing (general), .14 (boys); Grouped: sensitive or worrisome, etc., .14 and .19; Sensitive over specific fact, .13 and .11; Enuresis, .12 and .08; Absent-minded, .12 and .16; Poor work in school, .12 and .14; Discord between parents, .12 and .03; Oversuggestible, .11 and .15; Nail-biting, .10 and .17; Former convulsions, .10 and -.03; Refusal to attend school, .08 and .00; Question of change of personality, .08 and .14; Preference for younger children, .08 and -.06; Brother in penal detention, .08 and -.19; Seclusive, .06 and .08; Vicious home conditions, .06 and .03; Neurological defect, .05 and -.07; Sex denied entirely, .04 and .18; Crying spells, .03 and .17; Irregular attendance at school, .03 and .02; Sex delinquency (coitus), .02 and .09; Apprehensive, .02 and .18; Vocational guidance, .01 and .06; Immoral home conditions, .00 and -.03; Stuttering, -.02 (boys); Listless, -.03 and .14; Bashful, -.03 and .11; Speech defect, -.07 and -.05; Question of hypophrenia, -.08 and - 05; Grouped: dull, slow, etc., -.10 and -.01; Underweight, -.11 and -.01; Lues, -.15 and .10; Retardation in school, -.17 and -.08; Slow, dull, -.17 and -.03

delinquency its tetrachoric correlation of .29 ± .03 among boys was of moderate size, while the corresponding coefficient for girls was low, .10 ± .06. It was noted among 251, or 11.9 per cent, of our 2,113 White boys and among 77, or 6.5 per cent, of our 1,181 White girls. It yielded high correlations in the .50's with fantastical lying and disturbing influence in school among boys and meaningful coefficients of .37 ± .07 and .44 ± .06 among girls. Quarrelsomeness among boys yielded the large correlation of .41 ± .03 and a moderate coefficient of .27 ± .05 among girls. Four undesirable behavior traits among girls yielded large correlations in the .40's and substnatial coefficients in the .30's among boys: egocentricity, bossy manner, rudeness, and unpopularity. Violence

and temper tantrums among girls also yielded substantial correlations in the .40's but moderate correlations in the .20's among
boys. Three personality difficulties among girls similarly yielded
large correlations in the .40's but low coefficients below .20
among boys: changeable moods or attitudes, daydreaming, and queer
behavior.

Boastful or "show-off" manner yielded substantial correlations in the .30's among both sexes with the four behavior problems, "spoiled child," disobedience or incorrigibility (including
defiant attitude, stubbornness, and contrariness, undifferentiated), lying, and leading others into bad conduct. The two conduct
problems for which only the boys' coefficients were calculated—
teasing other children and smoking—and also overinterest in the
opposite sex, for which only the girls' coefficient was computed,
also yielded substantial coefficients in the .30's. Three conduct
problems yielded substantial correlations in the .30's among boys
and moderate correlations in the .20's among girls: fighting, disobedience, and stealing. Seven conduct and personality problems
among girls yielded substantial correlations in the .30's and moderate coefficients in the .20's among boys: defiant attitude, incorrigibility, swearing or bad language (undifferentiated), selfishness, restlessness, excuse-forming attitude, and overinterest
in sex matters. Six notations among girls yielded substantial correlations in the .30's and low positive coefficients below .20
among boys: emotional instability, psychoneurotic trends, distractibility, inefficiency in work, play, etc., sensitiveness in general,
and headaches.

Boastful or "show-off" manner showed moderate correlations
in the .20's with eight behavior traits among both sexes: inferiority feelings, "leader," contrariness, laziness, sulkiness, truancy from school, irregular sleep habits, and hatred or jealousy
of sibling. Two conduct problems for which only the boys' correlations were computed also showed moderate correlations in the
.20's: threatening violence and running with a gang. Nine notations showed moderate correlations in the .20's among boys but low
coefficients below .20 among girls: inattentiveness in school,
lack of interest in school, exclusion from school, bad companions,
staying out late at night, destructiveness, mental conflict, masturbation, and clean habits. Nine case-record notations among
girls showed moderate correlations in the .20's but low positive

coefficients below .20 among boys: <u>irritable temperament</u>, <u>stub-</u>
<u>bornness</u>, <u>slovenliness</u>, <u>depressed mood or spells</u>, <u>unhappiness</u>, <u>re-</u>
<u>pressed manner</u>, <u>truancy from home</u>, <u>question or diagnosis of en-</u>
<u>cephalitis</u>, and <u>staff notation of unfavorable conduct prognosis</u>.

    Two negative correlations of significant size were found,
both among girls: "<u>follower</u>," -.28 + .06, and <u>feeble-minded sib-</u>
<u>ling</u>, -.38 + .06.

    With the six sex notations <u>boastful or "show-off" manner</u>
showed several meaningful correlations. With <u>overinterest in sex</u>
<u>matters</u> the respective correlations among boys and girls were .23
+ .05 and .34 + .07. With <u>masturbation</u> the coefficients for boys
and girls respectively were .22 + .03 and .19. With <u>overinterest</u>
<u>in the opposite sex</u>, for which only the girls' coefficient was com-
puted, the substantial correlation of .33 + .05 was found. With
<u>sex delinquency (coitus)</u>, however, both coefficients were negli-
gible.

    Among the seven physical or psychophysical notations, all
correlations were low or negligible, except possibly the coefficient of very questionable statistical significance, .20 + .09,
with <u>question or diagnosis of encephalitis</u> among girls.

    With the four home or familial notations all correlations
were low or negligible.

CHAPTER LIII

"BOSSY"; "LEADER"; AND "FOLLOWER"

In our data <u>bossy manner</u> was considered as an undesirable conduct problem. The notations "<u>leader</u>" and "<u>follower</u>" were included in the original indexing as behavior traits to be considered neither as personality nor as conduct problems but as a "neutral" trait included for comparative purposes.

<u>Bossy manner toward playmates</u> was noted among 112, or 5.3 per cent, of our 2,113 White boys and among 86, or 7.3 per cent, of our 1,181 White girls. Among girls it appeared to be of considerable clinical importance, its bi-serial correlations with the <u>personality-total</u> and <u>conduct-total</u> being .50 ± .03 and .43 ± .03 respectively (Table 106). Among boys the corresponding correlations of .32 ± .03 and .28 ± .03 were of moderate size. With the

TABLE 106

CORRELATIONS WITH "BOSSY"

	Boys	Girls
Personality-total.............................	.32 ± .03	.50 ± .03
Conduct-total.................................	.28 ± .03	.43 ± .03
Police arrest.................................	.02 ± .04	-.08 ± .06
	Larger Correlations (Positive)	
Unpopular.....................................	.36 ± .06	.54 ± .06 (1)*
Boastful, "show-off"..........................	.33 ± .05	.47 ± .06 (2)
Quarrelsome...................................	.33 ± .04	.37 ± .05 (9-10)
Grouped: fighting, etc.......................	.32 ± .04	.43 ± .04 (4)
Grouped: temper, etc.........................	.31 ± .04	.36 ± .04 (11)
Egocentric....................................	.30 ± .04	.35 ± .05 (12-14)
Hatred or jealousy of sibling.................	.29 ± .06	.37 ± .07 (9-10)
Mental conflict...............................	.28 ± .06	.30 ± .08 (22-24)
Selfish.......................................	.27 ± .06	.29 ± .07 (25-28)

*Rank order of girls' correlations.

TABLE 106—Continued

	Boys	Girls
Spoiled child...............................	.27 ± .05	.38 ± .06 (5-8)
Destructive................................	.26 ± .05	.12
Teasing other children.....................	.26 ± .05	....
Rude.......................................	.26 ± .04	.16
Irritable..................................	.26 ± .04	.25 ± .05 (37-39)
Grouped: "nervous," etc....................	.26 ± .04	.38 ± .04 (5-8)
Grouped: egocentric, etc..................	.26 ± .04	.31 ± .05 (20-21)
Temper tantrums............................	.25 ± .05	.24 ± .06 (40-42)
"Nervous"..................................	.25 ± .04	.24 ± .05 (40-42)
Sensitive (general)........................	.25 ± .05	.20 ± .07 (54-57)
Inferiority feelings.......................	.25 ± .05	.09
Disturbing influence in school.............	.24 ± .04	.23 ± .07 (43-47)
Stubborn...................................	.24 ± .04	.25 ± .05 (37-39)
Restless...................................	.24 ± .04	.26 ± .05 (34-36)
Fantastical lying..........................	.23 ± .06	.28 ± .07 (29-30)
Crying spells..............................	.23 ± .04	.17
Temper display.............................	.22 ± .05	.30 ± .06 (22-24)
Distractible...............................	.22 ± .05	.32 ± .06 (17-19)
Fighting...................................	.21 ± .05	.38 + .06 (5-8)
Lying......................................	.20 ± .04	.27 ± .05 (31-33)
Nail-biting................................	.20 ± .05	.23 ± .05 (43-47)
Threatening violence.......................	.20 ± .06	....
Grouped: swearing, etc....................	.20 ± .05	.34 ± .06 (15-16)
Violence...................................	.19	.46 + .06 (3)
Overinterest in sex matters...............	.14	.38 ± .06 (5-8)
Changeable moods...........................	.10	.35 ± .05 (12-14)
Grouped: depressed, etc...................	.12	.35 ± .06 (12-14)
Object of teasing..........................	.10	.34 ± .06 (15-16)
Worry over specific fact...................	.14	.32 ± .08 (17-19)
Grouped: sensitive or worrisome, etc........	.19	.32 ± .05 (17-19)
Depressed..................................	-.02	.31 ± .07 (20-21)
Sensitive over specific fact...............	.16	.30 ± .05 (22-24)
Disobedient................................	.11	.29 ± .05 (25-28)
Leading others into bad conduct............	.02	.29 ± .08 (25-28)
Sulky......................................	-.09	.29 ± .07 (25-28)
Restless in sleep..........................	.16	.27 ± .06 (31-33)
Preference for younger children............	.19	.27 ± .07 (31-33)
Queer......................................	.06	.26 ± .07 (34-36)
Unhappy....................................	.16	.26 ± .07 (34-36)
Stealing...................................	.14	.25 ± .05 (37-39)
Masturbation...............................	.10	.24 ± .06 (40-42)
Psychoneurotic.............................	.02	.23 ± .07 (43-47)
Exclusion from school......................	.07	.23 ± .07 (43-47)
Grouped: disobedient, etc.................	.17	.23 ± .04 (43-47)
Sullen.....................................	.10	.22 ± .06 (48-51)
Leader.....................................	.18	.22 ± .07 (48-51)
Emotional instability......................	.07	.22 ± .07 (48-51)
Lazy.......................................	.05	.21 + .07 (52-53)
Excuse-forming.............................	.17	.21 ± .06 (52-53)
Bad companions.............................	.09	.20 ± .06 (54-57)
Apprehensive...............................	.05	.20 ± .06 (54-57)
Grouped: lack of interest in school, etc.....	.14	.20 ± .06 (54-57)

TABLE 106—Continued

	Boys	Girls
	Larger Correlations (Negative)	
Question of encephalitis......................	-.27 ± .07	.22 ± .09 (48-51)
Vocational guidance..........................	.01	-.25 ± .05
Lack of initiative...........................	.09	-.22 ± .07
	Not Calculable	
Feeble-minded sibling........................	(n.c.)	-.17

Other Correlations (Positive to Negative)

Irresponsible, .18 and .17; Victim of sex abuse, .17 (girls); Defiant, .16 and .19; Neurological defect, .16 and .11; Finicky food habits, .15 and .03; Complaining of bad treatment by other children, .15 (boys); Attractive manner, .15 and .06; Contrary, .14 and .18; Swearing (general), .14 (boys); Inattentive in school, .13 and .17; Slovenly, .13 and .16; Daydreaming, .13 and .16; Loitering, .12 and -.03; Clean, .11 and .18; Former convulsions, .11 and -.01; Enuresis, .10 and .17; Truancy from home, .10 and .05; Inefficient in work, play, etc., .09 and .10; Incorrigible, .09 and .19; Lack of interest in school, .08 and .18; Stuttering, .08 (boys); Staying out late at night, .07 and .11; Truancy from school, .06 and .14; Lues, .06 and -.01; Speech defect, .06 and .10; Overinterest in opposite sex, .06 (girls); Irregular sleep habits, .05 and .02; Smoking, .04 (boys); Bashful, .04 and -.04; Question of change of personality, .04 and .19; Absent-minded, .03 and -.13; Seclusive, .03 and .10; Repressed, .03 and .15; Headaches, .03 and -.09; Discord between parents, .03 and .06; Poor work in school, .02 and .05; Underweight, .01 and .05; Irregular attendance at school, .01 and -.05; Conduct prognosis bad, .00 and .02; Grouped: dull, slow, etc., -.02 and -.01; Slow, dull, -.04 and .01; Gang, -.05 (boys); Refusal to attend school, -.06 and -.09; Vicious home conditions, -.07 and .05; Immoral home conditions, -.08 and -.16; Follower, -.08 and -.16; Brother in penal detention, -.09 and -.06; Oversuggestible, -.09 and .11; Question of hypophrenia, -.11 and -.05; Sex denied entirely, -.12 and -.10; Popular, -.14 and .12; Sex delinquency (coitus), -.14 and .01; Listless, -.16 and -.10; Retardation in school, -.17 and -.08

police-arrest criterion of overt juvenile delinquency its tetrachoric correlations of .02 and -.08 among both sexes were negligible.

Its largest correlations were with unpopularity, the respective coefficients for boys and girls being .36 ± .06 and .54 ± .06. The second highest correlations among both sexes were with boastful or "show-off" manner, the corresponding coefficients being .33 ± .05 and .47 ± .06. Violence among girls also yielded the large correlation of .46 ± .06 but a low positive correlation among boys of .19.

Three conduct problems yielded substantial correlations in the .30's with <u>bossy manner</u> among both sexes: <u>egocentricity</u>, <u>quarrelsomeness</u>, and <u>temper tantrums or display</u> (undifferentiated). Among girls eight conduct and personality problems yielded substantial correlations in the .30's, the corresponding coefficients among boys being of moderate size in the .20's: "<u>spoiled child</u>," <u>temper display</u>, "<u>nervousness</u>" or restlessness (including <u>irritable temperament</u> and <u>changeable moods</u>, undifferentiated), <u>distractibility</u>, <u>fighting</u>, <u>swearing or bad language</u> (undifferentiated), <u>hatred or jealousy of sibling</u>, and <u>mental conflict</u>. Among girls an additional six personality and conduct problems yielded substantial correlations in the .30's but low coefficients below .20 among boys: <u>object of teasing by other children</u>, <u>sensitiveness over some specific fact</u>, <u>worry over some specific fact</u>, <u>depressed mood or spells</u>, <u>changeable moods or attitudes</u>, and <u>overinterest in sex matters</u>.

<u>Bossy manner</u> showed moderate correlations in the .20's among both sexes for the following eleven undesirable behavior manifestations: <u>selfishness</u>, <u>irritable temperament</u>, "<u>nervousness</u>," <u>restlessness</u>, <u>nail-biting</u>, <u>stubbornness</u>, <u>temper tantrums</u>, <u>disturbing influence in school</u>, <u>lying</u>, <u>fantastical lying</u>, and <u>sensitiveness in general</u>. Two conduct problems for which only the boys' correlations were computed also showed moderate correlations in the .20's: <u>threatening violence</u> and <u>teasing other children</u>. Four personality and conduct problems showed moderate correlations in the .20's among boys but low coefficients below .20 among girls: <u>rudeness</u>, <u>destructiveness</u>, <u>crying spells</u>, and <u>inferiority feelings</u>. A large list of nineteen miscellaneous case-record notations showed correlations in the .20's among girls but low coefficients below .20 among boys: "<u>leader</u>," <u>leading others into bad conduct</u>, <u>preference for younger children as playmates</u>, <u>disobedience</u>, <u>bad companions</u>, <u>stealing</u>, <u>excuse-forming attitude</u>, <u>sullenness</u>, <u>sulkiness</u>, <u>laziness</u>, <u>lack of interest or inattentiveness in school studies or employment</u> (undifferentiated), <u>emotional instability</u>, <u>psychoneurotic trends</u>, <u>unhappiness</u>, <u>apprehensiveness</u>, <u>queer behavior</u>, <u>restlessness in sleep</u>, <u>masturbation</u>, and <u>exclusion from school</u>.

<u>Question or diagnosis of encephalitis</u> showed a curious divergence of relationship among the two sexes, its correlation among boys being <u>negative</u>, $-.27 \pm .07$, while its correlation among girls

was of <u>positive</u> sign, .22 ± .09, though the latter coefficient is of very doubtful statistical significance since it is less than three times its probable error. <u>Lack of initiative</u> and "<u>request for vocational guidance</u>" among girls showed negative correlations of moderate size in the -.20's.

Among the six sex notations there were two correlations of significant size with <u>bossy manner</u> among girls, .38 ± .06 with <u>overinterest in sex matters</u> and .24 ± .06 with <u>masturbation</u>, the corresponding correlations for boys being low, .14 and .10.

Among the seven physical or psychophysical disabilities the only meaningful correlations were with <u>question or diagnosis of encephalitis</u>, as noted above.

Among the four home or familial notations all correlations were low or negligible.

The notation <u>patient a leader in group of same age</u> was noted among 152 of our boys, or 7.2 per cent, and among 78 or our girls, or 6.6 per cent. Its correlations with all three criteria of seriousness were low but positive, ranging from .05 to .21 (Table 107).

TABLE 107
CORRELATIONS WITH "LEADER"

	Boys	Girls
Personality-total	.05 ± .03	.16 ± .04
Conduct-total	.21 ± .03	.19 ± .04
Police arrest	.13 ± .04	.07 ± .06
	Larger Correlations (Positive)	
Popular	.32 ± .05	.40 ± .07 (1)*
Leading others into bad conduct	.32 ± .05	.18
Gang	.26 ± .04	....
Boastful, "show-off"	.23 ± .04	.27 ± .07 (8-10)
Lack of interest in school	.21 ± .04	-.00
Attractive manner	.21 ± .04	.23 ± .06 (13-15)
Staying out late at night	.20 ± .03	.03
Restless	.20 ± .04	.23 ± .05 (13-15)
Irritable	.12	.36 ± .05 (2)

*Rank order of girls' correlations.

TABLE 107—Continued

	Boys	Girls
Fantastical lying.............................	.18	.31 ± .07 (3)
Grouped: temper, etc.........................	.12	.29 ± .05 (4)
Grouped: "nervous," etc......................	.17	.28 ± .05 (5-7)
Restless in sleep............................	.10	.28 ± .06 (5-7)
Defiant......................................	.18	.28 ± .07 (5-7)
Unpopular....................................	.12	.27 ± .08 (8-10)
Grouped: egocentric, etc.....................	.19	.27 ± .05 (8-10)
Egocentric...................................	.17	.26 ± .06 (11)
Lying..	.19	.24 ± .05 (12)
Changeable moods.............................	.12	.23 ± .06 (13-15)
Daydreaming..................................	-.02	.22 ± .07 (16-18)
Overinterest in sex matters.................	-.05	.22 ± .07 (16-18)
Bossy..	.18	.22 ± .07 (16-18)
Inattentive in school.......................	.12	.21 ± .07 (19-20)
Stealing.....................................	.12	.21 ± .05 (19-20)
	Larger Correlations (Negative)	
Queer..	-.29 ± .05	.03
Neurological defect..........................	-.24 ± .05	.12
Retardation in school.......................	-.12	-.32 ± .04
Repressed....................................	-.02	-.24 ± .08
Feeble-minded sibling........................	-.11	-.21 ± .07
Seclusive....................................	-.19	-.20 ± .07
Immoral home conditions......................	.04	-.20 ± .07

Other Correlations (Positive to Negative)

Grouped: disobedient, etc., .19 and .14; Grouped: lack of interest in school, etc., .18 and .15; Disobedient, .18 and .15; Hatred or jealousy of sibling, .18 and .07; Disturbing influence in school, .18 and .18; Smoking, .17 (boys); Bad companions, .15 and .13; Stubborn, .15 and .12; "Nervous," .14 and .12; Truancy from school, .14 and .14; Fighting, .13 and -.07; Loitering, .13 and .11; Truancy from home, .12 and -.07; Sullen, .12 and .12; Slovenly, .12 and -.06; Irresponsible, .12 and .19; Selfish, .11 and .15; Sensitive over specific fact, .11 and .11; Spoiled child, .11 and .12; Sex denied entirely, .11 and .12; Grouped: fighting, etc., .11 and .10; Overinterest in opposite sex, .11 (girls); Temper display, .10 and .14; Swearing (general), .10 (boys); Rude, .10 and .07; Contrary, .09 and .04; Refusal to attend school, .09 and .15; Quarrelsome, .09 and .05; Irregular sleep habits, .09 and -.01; Worry over specific fact, .09 and .05; Clean, .09 and .07; Emotional instability, .08 and .11; Excuse-forming, .08 and .18; Teasing other children, .07 (boys); Preference for younger children, .07 and -.06; Grouped: sensitive or worrisome, etc., .07 and .10; Nail-biting, .06 and .06; Grouped: swearing, etc., .06 and .09; Masturbation, .06 and .15; Incorrigible, .06 and .17; Exclusion from school, .06 and -.11; Destructive, .05 and -.01; Temper tantrums, .05 and .10; Sex delinquency (coitus), .05 and -.04; Distractible, .05 and .12; Mental conflict, .05 and .08; Discord between parents, .05 and -.02; Complaining of bad treatment by other children, .04 (boys); Crying spells, .04 and .19; Violence, .04 and .12; Bashful, .03 and -.08; Irregular attendance at school, .03 and -.03; Conduct prognosis bad, .02 and -.06; Threatening violence, .02 (boys); Lazy, .02 and -.11;

TABLE 107—Continued

Victim of sex abuse, .02 (girls); Absent-minded, .01 and -.09; Oversuggestible,
.01 and -.09; Vocational guidance, .00 and -.01; Finicky food habits, -.00 and
.17; Question of encephalitis, -.00 and -.05; Poor work in school, -.01 and
-.00; Inferiority feelings, -.01 and .06; Lack of initiative, -.01 and -.11;
Inefficient in work, play, etc., -.02 and -.11; Lues, -.02 and -.09; Brother in
penal detention, -.02 and -.03; Unhappy, -.03 and .06; Sulky, -.04 and .08; Vicious home conditions, -.05 and -.03; Psychoneurotic, -.05 and -.01; Enuresis,
-.06 and .18; Grouped: depressed, etc., -.06 and .12; Speech defect, -.07 and
-.19; Sensitive (general), -.07 and .05; Depressed, -.08 and .09; Headaches,
-.09 and .15; Stuttering, -.09 (boys); Object of teasing, -.09 and -.19; Question of change of personality, -.09 and .07; Underweight, -.11 and -.06; Question of hypophrenia, -.11 and .19; Apprehensive, -.11 and -.02; Former convulsions, -.12 and -.04; Listless, -.15 and -.14; Slow, dull, -.17 and .14;
Grouped: dull, slow, etc., -.17 and -.17
        Omitted—Follower

Its largest correlations were with popularity, the respective coefficients for boys and girls being .32 ± .05 and .40 ± .07.
Leading others into bad conduct among boys yielded the substantial
correlation of .32 ± .05 but among girls a low coefficient of .18.
Irritable temperament and fantastical lying among girls yielded
substantial correlations in the .30's but low positive coefficients
below .20 among boys.

"Leader" showed moderate correlations in the .20's among
both sexes with the three traits boastful or "show-off" manner,
restlessness, and attractive manner and also with running with a
gang (calculated for boys only). Two conduct problems among boys—
staying out late at night and lack of interest in school—showed
moderate correlations in the .20's but negligible coefficients below .20 among girls. Among the girls twelve undesirable manifestations showed moderate correlations in the .20's but among boys low
coefficients below .20: bossy manner, egocentricity, changeable
moods or attitudes, temper tantrums or display (including irritable
temperament, undifferentiated), restlessness in sleep, daydreaming,
inattentiveness in school, stealing, lying, defiant attitude, overinterest in sex matters, and unpopularity.

It may seem curious that the notation "leader" shows positive correlations with both of the apparently antithetical traits
popularity and unpopularity. This problem was discussed in earlier pages (p. 45 and in the concluding paragraphs of chaps. xx,
xxv, and xlvi). These apparently contradictory correlations may,
of course, be due to a general inaccuracy in case-record material

of the kind utilized in this study. But the explanation may also
be made on a curvilinearity of regression of "leader" with the
trait popularity-unpopularity. It may be that a child who tends
to be a leader among other children is likely to be both popular
and unpopular among his associates, according to the specific relation of a "leader" to another individual child affected by his
"leadership." It is interesting to note that the correlations of
"follower" with both popularity and unpopularity are very low or
negligible, as will be found in Table 108 (p. 511).

    "Leader" among boys showed negative correlations of moder-
ate size ranging from -.20 to -.32 with queer behavior and neurological defect (unspecified) and among girls with repressed manner,
seclusiveness, retardation in school, feeble-minded sibling, and
immoral home conditions.

    Among the six sex notations the only correlation of moder-
ate size was with overinterest in sex matters among girls, .22 +
.07. All other correlations in this field were low or negligible,
ranging from -.05 to .15.

    Among the seven physical or psychophysical disabilities the
only correlation of moderate size was the negative one of -.24 +
.05 with neurological defect (unspecified) among boys.

    Among the four home or familial notations the largest cor-
relation with "leader" was the negative one, -.20 + .07, with immoral home conditions among girls, which is of doubtful statistical
significance, since it is less than the conventionally accepted
"three times its probable error."

    Patient a "follower" in group of similar age was noted
among 202 cases, or 9.6 per cent, of our 2,113 White boys and among
103 cases, or 8.7 per cent, of our 1,181 White girls. Its correlations with our three criteria of seriousness or "ominousness"
were low or negligible, ranging from -.03 to .12 (Table 108).
Since almost all its correlation coefficients with other separate
case notations were of negligible size (only nine showing coefficients as high as the .20's) it may be concluded that "follower"
is of very minor importance from clinical considerations.

    The largest positive correlation was the moderate one of .2
.29 + .04 with oversuggestibility among boys, the corresponding
coefficient among girls being .18. Bashfulness showed moderate

TABLE 108

CORRELATIONS WITH "FOLLOWER"

	Boys	Girls
Personality-total............................	.12 ± .03	.07 ± .04
Conduct-total................................	.07 ± .03	-.03 ± .04
Police arrest................................	.08 ± .04	.05 ± .05
	Larger Correlations (Positive)	
Oversuggestible..............................	.29 ± .04	.18
Excuse-forming...............................	.25 ± .04	-.02
Bad companions...............................	.23 ± .04	.07
Bashful......................................	.22 ± .04	.23 ± .05 (2)*
Gang...	.21 ± .04	....
Speech defect................................	.21 ± .04	.10
Crying spells................................	.20 ± .03	.19
Lack of initiative...........................	.16	.25 ± .07 (1)
Lues...	.09	.21 ± .06 (3)
	Larger Correlations (Negative)	
Question of change of personality............	-.21 ± .05	.06
Repressed....................................	.04	-.29 ± .08
Boastful, "show-off".........................	.00	-.28 ± .06
Defiant......................................	-.12	-.25 ± .06

*Rank order of girls' correlations.

Other Correlations (Positive to Negative)

Absent-minded, .18 and .03; Changeable moods, .17 and .04; Grouped: "nervous," etc., .16 and .09; Sex denied entirely, .16 and -.08; Poor work in school, .14 and .13; Finicky food habits, .14 and .12; Lack of interest in school, .13 and .14; Refusal to attend school, .13 and .00; Slovenly, .13 and -.06; Smoking, .13 (boys); Restless, .13 and .13; Restless in sleep, .13 and .06; Grouped: dull, slow, etc., .12 and .15; Distractible, .12 and .16; Lazy, .11 and -.04; Lying, .11 and .08; Stealing, .11 and -.03; Apprehensive, .11 and .12; Slow, dull, .11 and .12; Truancy from school, .10 and -.01; Nail-biting, .10 and .13; Enuresis, .09 and .06; Selfish, .09 and .10; Irritable, .09 and -.00; Retardation in school, .09 and .01; Victim of sex abuse, .09 (girls); Grouped: lack of interest in school, etc., .08 and .11; Preference for younger children, .08 and .09; Mental conflict, .08 and .12; Sex delinquency (coitus), .08 and .17; Teasing other children, .07 (boys); Worry over specific fact, .07 and -.04; Complaining of bad treatment by other children, .07 (boys); Unhappy, .07 and -.04; Grouped: sensitive or worrisome, etc., .07 and .03; Grouped: temper, etc., .06 and -.02; Immoral home conditions, .06 and -.11; Vicious home conditions, .06 and -.10; Sullen, .06 and -.02; Loitering, .06 and -.02; Irresponsible, .06 and .08; Inefficient in work, play, etc., .05 and .06; Question of hypophrenia, .05 and .09; Grouped: egocentric, etc., .04 and .09; Brother

TABLE 108—Continued

in penal detention, .04 and .00; "Nervous," .04 and .02; Overinterest in sex matters, .04 and -.05; Daydreaming, .04 and -.01; Swearing (general), .04 (boys); Stubborn, .04 and -.11; Disobedient, .03 and .00; Disturbing influence in school, .03 and .01; Rude, .03 and -.09; Sulky, .03 and -.05; Temper display, .03 and .10; Emotional instability, .03 and -.06; Grouped: disobedient, etc., .03 and .08; Exclusion from school, .02 and .04; Leading others into bad conduct, .02 and .09; Fighting, -.00 and -.07; Listless, -.00 and .05; Object of teasing, -.00 and .13; Grouped: depressed, etc., -.00 and -.09; Egocentric, -.01 and .06; Truancy from home, -.01 and -.01; Inferiority feelings, -.02 and .08; Former convulsions, -.02 and -.15; Discord between parents, -.03 and -.12; Destructive, .02 and .06; Hatred or jealousy of sibling, .02 and .09; Staying out late at night, .01 and .01; Masturbation, .01 and -.09; Depressed, .01 and -.19; Irregular sleep habits, .01 and -.08; Sensitive over specific fact, .01 and .06; Unpopular, .01 and -.11; Spoiled child, .01 and .01; Neurological defect, .01 and -.16; Vocational guidance, .01 and -.05; Stuttering, .00 (boys); Underweight, -.03 and -.06; Clean, -.03 and .07; Sensitive (general), -.03 and .03; Inattentive in school, -.04 and .11; Violence, -.04 and -.11; Headaches, -.04 and .02; Grouped: swearing, etc., -.04 and -.03; Conduct prognosis bad, -.05 and .05; Contrary, -.05 and -.18; Overinterest in opposite sex, -.05 (girls); Incorrigible, -.06 and -.07; Queer, -.06 and -.10; Seclusive, -.06 and -.01; Grouped: fighting, etc., -.06 and .04; Temper tantrums, -.07 and -.17; Bossy, -.08 and -.16; Threatening violence, -.08 (boys); Popular, -.08 and .10; Quarrelsome, -.09 and .06; Fantastical lying, -.09 and -.03; Attractive manner, -.10 and .01; Irregular attendance at school, -.10 and -.07; Psychoneurotic, -.12 and -.08; Feeble-minded sibling, -.14 and .07; Question of encephalitis, -.18 and -.11
          Omitted—Leader

correlations in the .20's among both sexes. Running with a gang among boys similarly showed the moderate correlation of .21 ± .04, the corresponding coefficient for girls not being calculated because of the paucity of girls' cases. Four additional notations among boys showed moderate correlations in the .20's, but low coefficients below .20 among girls: bad companions, excuse-forming attitude, crying spells, and speech defect (other than stuttering). Two notations among girls showed moderate correlations in the .20's but low positive coefficients below .20 among boys: lack of initiative and lues.

"Follower" showed four negative correlations of moderate size ranging from -.21 to -.29: among boys for question of change of personality and among girls for repressed manner, boastful or "show-off" manner, and defiant attitude.

Among the six sex notations all correlations with "follower" were low or negligible, ranging from -.09 to .17.

Among the seven physical or psychophysical disabilities there were two coefficients of moderate size in the .20's, speech defect (other than stuttering) among boys and lues among girls.

Among the four home or familial notations all correlations were low or negligible, ranging from -.12 to .06.

A comparison of the corresponding correlations for the presumably antithetical notations "<u>leader</u>" (Table 107) and "<u>follower</u>" (Table 108) shows again the curious statistical phenomenon that many of the coefficients for these antithetical pairs of traits were not of opposite sign and of similar magnitude, as would be supposed if strictly objectively measurable traits were being used but were often of the same sign (though of different magnitude). Among the 118 pairs of corresponding coefficients for the boys in Table 107 ("<u>leader</u>") and Table 108 ("<u>follower</u>") there were 75 pairs of like sign and only 43 of unlike sign. Among 113 pairs of girls' coefficients there were 58 pairs of like sign and 55 of unlike sign. The intercolumnar correlations (Pearson's product-moment) were .10 $\pm$ .06 for boys and -.10 $\pm$ .06 for girls. (A discussion and attempted explanation of this phenomenon may be found in I, 134-35 and 249-50, and in this volume, p. 45, and in the concluding paragraphs of chaps. xx, xxv, and xlvi.)

CHAPTER LIV

SULLENNESS AND SULKINESS

Sullenness and sulkiness appeared to be of little more
than moderate importance so far as its correlations with our three
criteria of seriousness or "ominousness" are concerned.

Sullenness was noted among 243 of our 2,113 White boys
(11.5 per cent) and among 97 of our 1,181 White girls (8.2 per
cent). With personality-total and conduct-total the correlations
were of only moderate or scarcely substantial size, ranging from
.29 to .35 (Table 109). With police arrest its tetrachoric r among
boys was moderate, .23 ± .03, and among girls negligible, .08 ±
.05.

TABLE 109

CORRELATIONS WITH "SULLEN"

	Boys	Girls
Personality-total.............................	.29 ± .02	.34 ± .03
Conduct-total.................................	.35 ± .02	.33 ± .03
Police arrest.................................	.23 ± .03	.08 ± .05
	Larger Correlations (Positive)	
Grouped: disobedient, etc....................	.44 ± .03	.41 ± .04 (3)*
Defiant.......................................	.41 ± .04	.44 ± .06 (1)
Contrary......................................	.38 ± .05	.33 ± .07 (9)
Stubborn......................................	.35 ± .03	.31 ± .05 (11-13)
Grouped: swearing, etc......................	.34 ± .04	.19
Threatening violence..........................	.32 ± .05	....
Incorrigible..................................	.28 ± .03	.27 ± .05 (21-27)
Grouped: fighting, etc......................	.28 ± .03	.34 ± .05 (5-8)
Grouped: egocentric, etc....................	.27 ± .03	.27 ± .06 (21-27)
Excuse-forming................................	.27 ± .04	.05
Smoking.......................................	.27 ± .04	....
Rude..	.27 ± .03	.42 ± .05 (2)

*Rank order of girls' correlations.

TABLE 109—Continued

	Boys	Girls
Disobedient..................................	.26 ± .03	.32 ± .05 (10)
Stealing.....................................	.26 ± .03	.30 ± .05 (14-18)
Sulky.......................................	.26 ± .05	.30 ± .07 (14-18)
Hatred or jealousy of sibling................	.26 ± .05	.15
Violence....................................	.25 ± .04	.27 ± .06 (21-27)
Unhappy.....................................	.24 ± .05	.31 ± .07 (11-13)
Gang..	.24 ± .04	....
Quarrelsome.................................	.23 ± .04	.30 ± .05 (14-18)
Egocentric..................................	.23 ± .04	.30 ± .05 (14-18)
Unpopular...................................	.23 ± .05	.14
Conduct prognosis bad.......................	.23 ± .05	.34 ± .07 (5-8)
Exclusion from school.......................	.22 ± .04	.27 ± .07 (21-27)
Truancy from school.........................	.22 ± .04	.27 ± .05 (21-27)
Destructive.................................	.22 ± .04	-.07
Fantastical lying...........................	.21 ± .03	.21 ± .07 (39-42)
Lack of interest in school..................	.21 ± .04	.30 ± .06 (14-18)
Leading others into bad conduct.............	.21 ± .05	.40 ± .07 (4)
Lying.......................................	.21 ± .03	.23 ± .05 (36)
Swearing (general)..........................	.21 ± .05	....
Repressed...................................	.21 ± .05	.20 ± .08 (43-49)
Grouped: temper, etc........................	.20 ± .03	.34 ± .04 (5-8)
Irritable...................................	.20 ± .03	.26 ± .05 (28-30)
Truancy from home...........................	.20 ± .03	.11
Temper tantrums.............................	.09	.34 ± .05 (5-8)
Spoiled child...............................	.16	.31 ± .06 (11-13)
Depressed...................................	.07	.29 ± .07 (19)
Changeable moods............................	.05	.28 ± .05 (20)
Distractible................................	.11	.27 ± .06 (21-27)
Grouped: depressed, etc.....................	.17	.27 ± .06 (21-27)
Grouped: "nervous," etc.....................	.14	.26 ± .04 (28-30)
Finicky food habits.........................	-.08	.26 ± .06 (28-30)
Fighting....................................	.17	.25 ± .04 (31-35)
Refusal to attend school....................	.18	.25 ± .08 (31-35)
Overinterest in opposite sex................	....	.25 ± .05 (31-35)
Grouped: lack of interest in school, etc.....	.16	.25 ± .05 (31-35)
Grouped: sensitive or worrisome, etc.........	.09	.25 ± .05 (31-35)
Seclusive...................................	.18	.22 ± .06 (37-38)
Bossy.......................................	.10	.22 ± .06 (37-38)
Temper display..............................	.15	.21 ± .06 (39-42)
Masturbation................................	.07	.21 ± .05 (39-42)
Sensitive (general).........................	.11	.21 ± .06 (39-42)
Restless....................................	.11	.20 ± .05 (43-49)
Object of teasing...........................	.08	.20 ± .06 (43-49)
Daydreaming.................................	.14	.20 ± .06 (43-49)
Crying spells...............................	.11	.20 ± .05 (43-49)
Absent-minded...............................	.01	.20 ± .07 (43-49)
Overinterest in sex matters.................	.03	.20 ± .07 (43-49)
	Larger Correlations (Negative)	
Loitering...................................	.06	-.21 ± .07
Irregular attendance at school..............	.07	-.20 ± .06

TABLE 109—Continued

Other Correlations (Positive to Negative)

Disturbing influence in school, .19 and .17; Selfish, .19 and .16; Irregular sleep habits, .18 and -.07; Boastful, "show-off," .17 and .14; Question of change of personality, .17 and .19; Lazy, .16 and -.00; Bad companions, .16 and .09; Staying out late at night, .15 and .13; Vicious home conditions, .14 and .14; Teasing other children, .13 (boys); Slovenly, .13 and .03; Leader, .12 and .12; Mental conflict, .12 and .13; Inefficient in work, play, etc., .11 and .16; Queer, .11 and .18; Brother in penal detention, .11 and .11; Sex denied entirely, .10 and .07; Sensitive over specific fact, .09 and .17; Inferiority feelings, .09 and -.13; Complaining of bad treatment by other children, .09 (boys); Discord between parents, .08 and .01; Immoral home conditions, .08 and .06; Clean, .08 and -.03; Poor work in school, .08 and .02; Inattentive in school, .07 and .07; Sex delinquency (coitus), .07 and .09; Slow, dull, .07 and .08; Listless, .07 and .15; Emotional instability, .07 and .17; Follower, .06 and -.02; Nail-biting, .05 and .09; Popular, .05 and .03; Grouped: dull, slow, etc., .04 and .07; Apprehensive, .04 and .10; Bashful, .03 and -.05; "Nervous," .03 and .04; Restless in sleep, .03 and .12; Retardation in school, .02 and -.02; Vocational guidance, .00 and -.04; Enuresis, -.00 and -.07; Question of hypophrenia, -.00 and .05; Lues, -.00 and .07; Feeble-minded sibling, -.00 and -.05; Headaches, -.01 and .06; Attractive manner, -.01 and -.06; Oversuggestible, -.01 and -.00; Irresponsible, -.01 and -.01; Lack of initiative, -.02 and -.13; Victim of sex abuse, -.03 (girls); Worry over specific fact, -.03 and -.04; Stuttering, -.04 (boys); Question of encephalitis, -.05 and .08; Former convulsions, -.05 and -.08; Psychoneurotic, -.06 and .08; Preference for younger children, -.06 and .10; Neurological defect, -.08 and .11; Underweight, -.09 and .10; Speech defect, -.12 and -.09

Among both sexes, its largest correlations were with defiant attitude, the respective coefficients for boys and girls being .41 ± .04 and .44 ± .06. Rudeness and leading others into bad conduct among girls yielded large correlations in the .40's but among boys only moderate coefficients in the .20's.

Contrariness and stubbornness among both sexes yielded substantial correlations in the .30's. Threatening violence, for which only the boys' coefficient was computed, also yielded the substantial correlation of .32 ± .05. Swearing or bad language (undifferentiated) among boys yielded the substantial correlation of .34 ± .04 but among girls a low coefficient of .19. Nine undesirable behavior notations among girls yielded substantial correlations in the .30's with corresponding moderate coefficients in the .20's among boys: sulkiness, disobedience, egocentricity, lack of interest in school, quarrelsomeness, temper tantrums or display (undifferentiated), unhappiness, stealing, and staff notation of unfavorable conduct prognosis. Two additional behavior problems among girls yielded substantial correlations in the .30's but low

positive coefficients below .20 among boys: "spoiled child" and
temper tantrums.

Eight notations showed moderate correlations in the .20's
among both sexes: incorrigibility, violence, irritable temperament, lying, fantastical lying, truancy from school, exclusion
from school, and repressed manner. Three notations for which only
boys' correlations were computed—running with a gang, smoking,
and swearing in general—and the notation overinterest in the opposite sex, for which only the girls' coefficient was computed,
also showed moderate coefficients in the .20's. Five undesirable
behavior traits showed moderate correlations in the .20's among
boys but low coefficients below .20 among girls: hatred or jealousy of sibling, truancy from home, destructiveness, excuse-forming
attitude, and unpopularity. Seventeen personality and conduct
problems among girls showed moderate correlations in the .20's but
low coefficients below .20 among boys: refusal to attend school,
fighting, temper display, bossy manner, seclusiveness, absent-
mindedness, distractibility, restlessness, depressed mood or spells,
daydreaming, changeable moods or attitudes, sensitiveness in general, object of teasing by other children, crying spells, finicky
food habits, masturbation, and overinterest in sex matters.

Sullenness among girls showed negative correlations of moderate size in the -.20's with loitering or wandering and irregular
attendance at school.

Among the six sex notations there were three correlations
of moderate size in the .20's among girls: masturbation, overinterest in sex matters, and (calculated for girls only) overinterest in the opposite sex.

Among the seven physical or psychophysical notations and
the four home or familial notations, all correlations were low or
negligible, ranging from -.12 to .14.

Sulkiness or pouting was noted among 112, or 5.3 per cent,
of our boys and among 68, or 5.8 per cent, of our girls. With personality-total and conduct-total its bi-serial correlations were of
moderate size in the .20's (Table 110). With police arrest its
tetrachoric correlations for both sexes were low, .16 and .07 for
boys and girls respectively.

The only notation among both sexes yielding substantial

TABLE 110

CORRELATIONS WITH "SULKY"

	Boys	Girls
Personality-total.............................	.21 ± .03	.29 ± .04
Conduct-total.................................	.24 ± .03	.27 ± .04
Police arrest.................................	.16 ± .04	.07 ± .06
	Larger Correlations (Positive)	
Grouped:　disobedient, etc....................	.35 ± .03	.33 ± .05 (5-6)*
Defiant.......................................	.26 ± .05	.28 ± .07 (18)
Sullen..	.26 ± .05	.30 ± .07 (10-13)
Apprehensive..................................	.26 ± .04	-.06
Stubborn......................................	.24 ± .04	.24 ± .06 (25-26)
Grouped:　temper, etc.........................	.23 ± .04	.36 ± .05 (2-4)
Crying spells.................................	.23 ± .04	.20 ± .05 (29-31)
Disobedient...................................	.22 ± .04	.18
Disturbing influence in school................	.22 ± .04	.18
Boastful, "show-off"..........................	.21 ± .05	.25 ± .07 (20-24)
Rude..	.21 ± .05	.29 ± .06 (14-17)
Violence......................................	.21 ± .05	.17
Grouped:　"nervous," etc......................	.20 ± .04	.30 ± .05 (10-13)
Sex delinquency (coitus)......................	.20 ± .07	-.08
Temper display...............................	.20 ± .05	.29 ± .07 (14-17)
Contrary......................................	.20 ± .07	.36 ± .08 (2-4)
Sensitive (general)..........................	.12	.37 ± .07 (1)
Temper tantrums...............................	.15	.36 ± .06 (2-4)
Unhappy.......................................	.04	.33 ± .08 (5-6)
Excuse-forming................................	.07	.32 ± .07 (7-9)
Queer...	-.01	.32 ± .07 (7-9)
Grouped:　depressed, etc......................	.08	.32 ± .06 (7-9)
Changeable moods..............................	.17	.30 ± .06 (10-13)
Grouped:　sensitive or worrisome, etc.........	.16	.30 ± .05 (10-13)
Depressed.....................................	.06	.29 ± .07 (14-17)
Bossy...	-.09	.29 ± .07 (14-17)
Grouped:　fighting, etc.......................	.17	.27 ± .05 (19)
Egocentric....................................	.05	.25 ± .06 (20-24)
Leading others into bad conduct..............	.11	.25 ± .08 (20-24)
Inefficient in work, play, etc...............	.09	.25 ± .07 (20-24)
Fantastical lying............................	.16	.25 ± .07 (20-24)
Lying...	.13	.24 ± .05 (25-26)
Unpopular.....................................	.05	.22 ± .08 (27)
Quarrelsome...................................	.07	.21 ± .06 (28)
Object of teasing............................	.10	.20 ± .07 (29-31)
Worry over specific fact.....................	.14	.20 ± .09 (29-31)
	Larger Correlations (Negative)	
Feeble-minded sibling........................	-.22 ± .06	-.25 ± .07
Irregular sleep habits.......................	.02	-.27 ± .08

*Rank order of girls' correlations.

TABLE 110—Continued

Other Correlations (Positive to Negative)

Irritable, .19 and .19; Restless in sleep, .19 and .14; Selfish, .18 and -.02; Overinterest in sex matters, .18 and .11; Spoiled child, .17 and .10; Absent-minded, .17 and .14; Refusal to attend school, .17 and .10; Fighting, .17 and .09; Bad companions, .16 and .17; Destructive, .16 and .18; Enuresis, .16 and .09; Smoking, .16 (boys); Sensitive over specific fact, .16 and .15; Popular, .16 and .17; Restless, .15 and .14; Grouped: swearing, etc., .15 and .06; Grouped: lack of interest in school, etc., .15 and .03; Vicious home conditions, .15 and -.07; Complaining of bad treatment by other children, .15 (boys); Truancy from home, .15 and .14; Teasing other children, .15 (boys); Staying out late at night, .14 and .03; Swearing (general), .14 (boys); Threatening violence, .14 (boys); Repressed, .14 and .11; Grouped: egocentric, etc., .13 and .19; Conduct prognosis bad, .13 and .01; Lazy, .13 and .12; Lack of interest in school, .13 and .03; Finicky food habits, .13 and .15; Loitering, .12 and .09; Gang, .12 (boys); Slovenly, .12 and .13; Truancy from school, .12 and .15; Question of change of personality, .12 and .17; Distractible, .12 and .14; Preference for younger children, .12 and .08; Seclusive, .11 and .08; Incorrigible, .11 and .14; Stealing, .10 and .14; "Nervous," .10 and .04; Emotional instability, .10 and .14; Exclusion from school, .10 and .19; Attractive manner, .09 and .10; Inattentive in school, .09 and .01; Masturbation, .08 and .18; Hatred or jealousy of sibling, .08 and .04; Sex denied entirely, .08 and -.07; Discord between parents, .07 and .01; Mental conflict, .07 and .17; Listless, .07 and .09; Daydreaming, .07 and .18; Bashful, .06 and .06; Clean, .06 and .14; Overinterest in opposite sex, .06 (girls); Former convulsions, .05 and -.01; Inferiority feelings, .05 and .09; Oversuggestible, .05 and .11; Nail-biting, .04 and .02; Question of hypophrenia, .04 and .01; Headaches, .03 and .05; Follower, .03 and -.05; Stuttering, .03 (boys); Irresponsible, .03 and .06; Slow, dull, .02 and .03; Poor work in school, .02 and .12; Grouped: dull, slow, etc., .02 and .06; Speech defect, .01 and -.07; Retardation in school, .01 and .03; Lack of initiative, .01 and -.04; Victim of sex abuse, -.00 (girls); Vocational guidance, -.01 and -.14; Irregular attendance at school, -.02 and .05; Immoral home conditions, -.03 and .00; Neurological defect, -.03 and .04; Psychoneurotic, -.03 and .08; Leader, -.04 and .08; Question of encephalitis, -.12 and .09; Lues, -.13 and -.06; Underweight, -.17 and -.07; Brother in penal detention, -.19 and .09

correlations in the .30's was the "larger grouping," disobedience or incorrigibility (including defiant attitude, stubbornness, and contrariness, undifferentiated). Among girls three behavior problems yielded substantial correlations in the .30's and moderate coefficients in the .20's among boys: sullenness, contrariness, and "nervousness" or restlessness (including irritable temperament and changeable moods, undifferentiated). Six additional undesirable behavior problems yielded substantial correlations in the .30's among girls but low coefficients below .20 among boys: sensitiveness in general, changeable moods or attitudes, unhappiness, queer behavior, temper tantrums, and excuse-forming attitude.

Sulkiness showed moderate correlations in the .20's among

both sexes with six conduct and personality problems: <u>rudeness</u>, <u>stubbornness</u>, <u>defiant attitude</u>, <u>temper display</u>, <u>boastful or "show-off" manner</u>, and <u>crying spells</u>. Five conduct and personality problems among boys showed moderate correlations in the .20's, but low coefficients below .20 among girls: <u>disobedience</u>, <u>violence</u>, <u>disturbing influence in school</u>, <u>apprehensiveness</u>, and <u>sex delinquency</u> (<u>coitus</u>). Among girls eleven undesirable behavior traits showed moderate correlations in the .20's but low coefficients below .20 among boys: <u>quarrelsomeness</u>, <u>egocentricity</u>, <u>bossy manner</u>, <u>leading others into bad conduct</u>, <u>depressed mood or spells</u>, <u>inefficiency in work, play, etc.</u>, <u>object of teasing by other children</u>, <u>worry over some specific fact</u>, <u>lying</u>, <u>fantastical lying</u>, and <u>unpopularity</u>.

Two case-record notations showed <u>negative</u> correlations of moderate size in the -.20's, <u>irregular sleep habits among girls</u> and <u>feeble-minded sibling</u> among both sexes.

Among the six sex notations the only correlation of meaningful size with <u>sulkiness</u> was the statistically questionable coefficient of .20 ± .07 with sex delinquency (<u>coitus</u>) among boys.

Among the seven physical or psychophysical disabilities and the four home or familial notations all correlations were low or negligible.

CHAPTER LV

HATRED OR JEALOUSY FOR SIBLING

Hatred or jealousy for sibling, step-sibling, foster-sibling, etc., was noted among 95 of our 2,113 White boys, or 4.5 per cent, and among 58 of our 1,181 White girls, or 4.9 per cent. Its bi-serial correlations (in the .40's) with the personality-total were fairly large and also substantial (in the .30's) with conduct-total (Table 111). Its tetrachoric correlations with the police-arrest criterion of overt juvenile delinquency, however, were low.

TABLE 111

CORRELATIONS WITH "HATRED OR JEALOUSY OF SIBLING"

	Boys	Girls
Personality-total............................	.43 ± .03	.45 ± .04
Conduct-total................................	.32 ± .03	.33 ± .04
Police arrest................................	.10 ± .04	-.11 ± .06
	Larger Correlations (Positive)	
Contrary.....................................	.37 ± .06	.04
Inferiority feelings.........................	.36 ± .05	.43 ± .08 (1)*
Destructive..................................	.35 ± .05	.29 ± .08 (17-18)
Rude...	.34 ± .04	.29 ± .06 (17-18)
Grouped: egocentric, etc....................	.32 ± .04	.32 ± .06 (11)
Queer..	.30 ± .06	.21 ± .08 (32-34)
Daydreaming..................................	.30 ± .05	.07
Bossy..	.29 ± .06	.37 ± .07 (5)
Selfish......................................	.29 ± .06	.27 ± .04 (20-22)
Grouped: lack of interest in school, etc.....	.28 ± .04	.15
Spoiled child................................	.28 ± .05	.19
Excuse-forming...............................	.28 ± .05	.15
Lack of interest in school..................	.27 ± .05	.16
Grouped: swearing, etc.....................	.27 ± .07	.25 ± .07 (25-27)
Egocentric...................................	.26 ± .05	.38 ± .06 (4)
Sullen.......................................	.26 ± .05	.15

*Rank order of girls' correlations.

521

TABLE 111—Continued

	Boys	Girls
Boastful, "show-off"	.26 ± .05	.26 ± .08 (23-24)
Violence	.25 ± .05	.14
Grouped: depressed, etc.	.25 ± .05	.25 ± .07 (25-27)
Irritable	.24 ± .04	.22 ± .06 (30-31)
Depressed	.24 ± .06	.31 ± .08 (12-15)
Sensitive over specific fact	.23 ± .05	.31 ± .06 (12-15)
Attractive manner	.23 ± .05	.10
Grouped: disobedient, etc.	.23 ± .04	.20 ± .05 (35-38)
Grouped: fighting, etc.	.22 ± .04	.30 ± .05 (16)
Grouped: "nervous," etc.	.22 ± .04	.27 ± .05 (20-22)
Unhappy	.22 ± .07	.18
Defiant	.21 ± .06	.16
Quarrelsome	.21 ± .05	.33 ± .06 (9-10)
Threatening violence	.21 ± .07	....
Seclusive	.21 ± .05	.13
Mental conflict	.21 ± .07	.27 ± .09 (20-22)
Grouped: temper, etc.	.21 ± .04	.33 ± .05 (9-10)
Grouped: sensitive or worrisome, etc.	.20 ± .04	.34 ± .05 (6-8)
Sex denied entirely	.20 ± .06	.14
Fantastical lying	.16	.40 ± .07 (2)
Temper display	.15	.39 ± .07 (3)
Sensitive (general)	.19	.34 ± .07 (6-8)
Overinterest in sex matters	.10	.34 ± .07 (6-8)
Restless in sleep	.19	.31 ± .06 (12-15)
Stubborn	.16	.31 ± .06 (12-15)
Crying spells	.16	.28 ± .05 (19)
Headaches	.11	.26 ± .07 (23-24)
Leading others into bad conduct	.16	.25 ± .09 (25-27)
Worry over specific fact	.05	.24 ± .10 (28)
"Nervous"	.18	.23 ± .06 (29)
Slovenly	.13	.22 ± .06 (30-31)
Repressed	.18	.21 ± .09 (32-34)
Restless	.14	.21 ± .06 (32-34)
Nail-biting	.16	.20 ± .06 (35-38)
Changeable moods	.06	.20 ± .07 (35-38)
Former convulsions	.15	.20 ± .09 (35-38)
	Larger Correlations (Negative)	
Brother in penal detention	.10	-.32 ± .07
Vicious home conditions	.18	-.25 ± .08
Question of hypophrenia	-.10	-.21 ± .06
Retardation in school	-.15	-.20 ± .05
	Not Calculable	
Vocational guidance	(n.c.)	-.12
Feeble-minded sibling	(n.c.)	-.32 ± .07

TABLE 111—Continued

Other Correlations (Positive to Negative)

Complaining of bad treatment by other children, .19 (boys); Discord between parents, .19 and -.05; Leader, .18 and .07; Object of teasing, .18 and .13; Psychoneurotic, .18 and .18; Teasing other children, .18 (boys); Inattentive in school, .18 and .11; Bad companions, .17 and .17; Lazy, .17 and .17; Lying, .17 and .15; Truancy from school, .17 and .04; Masturbation, .17 and .15; Exclusion from school, .17 and .04; Swearing (general), .16 (boys); Disobedient, .15 and .12; Bashful, .15 and .04; Refusal to attend school, .14 and .14; Apprehensive, .14 and .16; Clean, .13 and -.01; Distractible, .13 and .15; Loitering, .12 and -.09; Stealing, .12 and .10; Truancy from home, .12 and .09; Neurological defect, .12 and .09; Staying out late at night, .11 and .08; Fighting, .11 and .18; Poor work in school, .10 and .04; Temper tantrums, .09 and .15; Smoking, .09 (boys); Gang, .09 (boys); Incorrigible, .08 and -.01; Sulky, .08 and .04; Conduct prognosis bad, .08 and -.05; Immoral home conditions, .08 and .00; Overinterest in opposite sex, .08 (girls); Irresponsible, .07 and .10; Inefficient in work, play, etc., .07 and .18; Disturbing influence in school, .06 and -.02; Lues, .06 and -.08; Popular, .05 and .08; Underweight, .04 and .02; Speech defect, .04 and -.10; Slow, dull, .03 and .18; Enuresis, .03 and .09; Finicky food habits, .03 and .17; Irregular sleep habits, .02 and .06; Lack of initiative, .02 and .13; Stuttering, .02 (boys); Follower, .02 and .09; Oversuggestible, .00 and -.06; Preference for younger children, -.00 and .01; Victim of sex abuse, -.00 (girls); Unpopular, -.01 and .16; Grouped: dull, slow, etc., -.01 and -.09; Listless, -.03 and .04; Absent-minded, -.04 and .19; Emotional instability, -.04 and .15; Irregular attendance at school, -.05 and -.12; Question of change of personality, -.06 and .12; Sex delinquency (coitus), -.07 and -.09; Question of encephalitis, -.08 and -.11

Among both boys and girls its largest correlations were with inferiority feelings, the respective coefficients being .36 ± .05 and .43 ± .08. Fantastical lying among girls also yielded a large correlation of .40 ± .07 but a low coefficient of .16 among boys.

Three conduct and personality problems—rudeness, destructiveness, and queer behavior—also yielded substantial correlations in the .30's among boys and moderate correlations in the .20's among girls. Contrariness and daydreaming among boys similarly yielded substantial correlations in the .30's but negligible coefficients among girls. Six personality and conduct problems among girls yielded substantial correlations in the .30's with corresponding moderate coefficients in the .20's among boys: egocentricity, bossy manner, quarrelsomeness, temper tantrums or display (undifferentiated), sensitiveness over some specific fact, and depressed mood or spells. Among girls five additional personality and conduct difficulties yielded substantial correlations in the .30's but low positive coefficients below .20 among boys: stubbornness, temper display, sensitiveness in general, restlessness in sleep, and overinterest in sex matters.

Six personality and conduct problems consistently showed moderate correlations in the .20's: selfishness, boastful or "show-off" manner, irritable temperament, swearing or bad language (undifferentiated), mental conflict, and (calculated for boys only) threatening violence. Ten personality problems among boys showed moderate correlations in the .20's but low positive coefficients below .20 among girls: "spoiled child," sullenness, defiant attitude, violence, excuse-forming attitude, lack of interest in school, seclusiveness, unhappiness, attractive manner, and sex misbehavior denied entirely. Eleven miscellaneous notations among girls showed moderate correlations in the .20's but low positive coefficients below .20 among boys: leading others into bad conduct, slovenliness, repressed manner, "nervousness," restlessness, changeable moods or attitudes, crying spells, worry over some specific fact, nail-biting, former convulsions, and headaches.

Hatred or jealousy of sibling showed negative correlations of moderate size ranging from -.20 to -.32 with four notations, all among girls: question of hypophrenia, retardation in school, vicious home conditions, and brother in penal detention.

Among the six sex notations there were two correlations of significant size, overinterest in sex matters among girls, .34 ± .07, and sex misbehavior denied entirely among boys, .20 ± .06.

Among the seven physical or psychophysical notations all correlations were negligible, ranging from -.11 to .12.

Among the four home or familial notations there were two negative correlations of moderate size, both among girls: vicious home conditions, -.25 ± .08, and brother in penal detention, -.32 ± .07.

CHAPTER LVI

SCHOOL NOTATIONS: POOR WORK, RETARDATION,
EXCLUSION

The three frequently appearing school notations considered
in this chapter were not counted as either personality or conduct
problems. Poor work in school and retardation in school showed
only minor correlations with our three criteria of seriousness,
but exclusion from school appeared to be of considerable importance with respect to conduct deviation.

Poor work in school was noted among 632 cases, or 29.9 per
cent, of our 2,113 White boys and among 319 cases, or 27.0 per cent,
of our 1,181 White girls. With the personality-total its bi-serial
correlations of .21 + .02 and .18 + .03 among boys and girls respectively indicate a palpable relationship (Table 112). Its bi-
serial correlations with the conduct-total among both sexes and its

TABLE 112

CORRELATIONS WITH "POOR WORK IN SCHOOL"

	Boys	Girls
Personality-total............................	.21 + .02	.18 + .03
Conduct-total................................	.11 + .02	.08 + .03
Police arrest................................	-.04 + .03	-.26 + .04
	Larger Correlations (Positive)	
Lack of interest in school...................	.32 + .03	.42 + .04 (1)*
Grouped: lack of interest in school, etc.....	.32 + .03	.38 + .04 (2)
Lazy...	.30 + .03	.21 + .05 (14-16)
Inefficient in work, play, etc...............	.29 + .04	.22 + .05 (12-13)
Grouped: dull, slow, etc....................	.29 + .02	.21 + .03 (14-16)
Distractible.................................	.28 + .03	.34 + .04 (3-4)
Absent-minded................................	.27 + .04	.21 + .05 (14-16)

*Rank order of girls' correlations.

TABLE 112—Continued

	Boys	Girls
Slow, dull...............................	.26 ± .03	.11
Inattentive in school....................	.24 ± .03	.26 ± .05 (6)
Disturbing influence in school..........	.23 ± .03	.32 ± .05 (5)
Lack of initiative.......................	.23 ± .04	.22 ± .05 (12-13)
Listless.................................	.21 ± .03	.24 ± .05 (7)
Preference for younger children.........	.21 ± .03	.23 ± .05 (8-11)
Question of hypophrenia..................	.20 ± .06	.23 ± .03 (8-11)
Irregular attendance at school..........	.20 ± .03	.03
Staying out late at night...............	.07	.34 ± .04 (3-4)
Exclusion from school....................	.07	.23 ± .05 (8-11)
Inferiority feelings.....................	.17	.23 ± .05 (8-11)
Unpopular................................	.19	.20 ± .06 (17)
	Larger Correlations (Negative)	
Immoral home conditions..................	-.12	-.26 ± .04

Other Correlations (Positive to Negative)

Irresponsible, .19 and .09; Object of teasing, .19 and .14; Daydreaming, .18 and .06; Teasing other children, .17 (boys); Overinterest in opposite sex, .17 (girls); Seclusive, .16 and .19; Spoiled child, .16 and .10; Refusal to attend school, .14 and .16; Complaining of bad treatment by other children, .14 (boys); Unhappy, .14 and .09; Follower, .14 and .13; Oversuggestible, .13 and .06; Attractive manner, .13 and .08; Speech defect, .13 and .12; Boastful, "show-off," .12 and .14; Grouped: "nervous," etc., .12 and .11; Grouped: disobedient, etc., .12 and .07; Fantastical lying, .11 and .11; Loitering, .11 and .08; Rude, .11 and .09; Bashful, .11 and .06; Listless, .11 and .14; Mental conflict, .11 and .06; Conduct prognosis bad, .11 and .01; Crying spells, .10 and .08; Disobedient, .10 and .16; Hatred or jealousy of sibling, .10 and .04; Contrary, .09 and .01; Question of change of personality, .09 and .06; Irritable, .09 and .06; Sensitive (general), .09 and .09; Vocational guidance, .09 and .11; Leading others into bad conduct, .08 and .10; Quarrelsome, .08 and .05; Slovenly, .08 and .12; Sullen, .08 and .02; Headaches, .08 and .13; Apprehensive, .07 and .12; Sensitive over specific fact, .07 and .07; Worry over specific fact, .07 and -.03; Sex denied entirely, .07 and .01; Grouped: sensitive or worrisome, etc., .07 and .10; Grouped: depressed, etc., .07 and .08; Fighting, .06 and .06; Incorrigible, .06 and .08; Temper display, .06 and -.04; Queer, .06 and .08; Selfish, .05 and -.02; Smoking, .05 (boys); Truancy from school, .05 and .06; Excuse-forming, .05 and .16; "Nervous," .05 and .14; Restless in sleep, .05 and .02; Grouped: fighting, etc., .05 and -.01; Victim of sex abuse, .05 (girls); Finicky food habits, .04 and -.02; Lying, .04 and .04; Gang, .04 (boys); Irregular sleep habits, .04 and .04; Clean, .04 and -.06; Former convulsions, .04 and -.01; Bad companions, .04 and -.10; Underweight, .04 and .01; Changeable moods, .03 and .04; Depressed, .03 and .05; Bossy, .02 and .05; Sulky, .02 and .12; Swearing (general), .02 (boys); Threatening violence, .02 (boys); Repressed, .02 and .09; Popular, .02 and -.01; Question of encephalitis, .02 and -.07; Vicious home conditions, .02 and -.03; Destructive, .01 and .00; Stubborn, .01 and -.06; Violence, .01 and .01; Masturbation, .01 and -.09; Brother in penal detention, .01 and -.08; Discord between parents, .01 and -.11; Grouped: temper, etc., .01 and .04; Grouped: swearing, etc., .00 and .03;

TABLE 112—Continued

Truancy from home, -.00 and -.09; Defiant, -.00 and -.01; Enuresis, -.01 and
-.13; Stealing, -.01 and -.05; Emotional instability, -.01 and -.02; Retardation in school, -.01 and .06; Leader, -.01 and -.00; Grouped: egocentric, etc.,
-.01 and .02; Nail-biting, -.02 and -.10; Neurological defect, -.03 and .06;
Overinterest in sex matters, -.05 and .04; Egocentric, -.06 and .04; Lues, -.06
and .13; Feeble-minded sibling, -.07 and .04; Temper tantrums, -.08 and .05;
Psychoneurotic, -.08 and -.01; Stuttering, -.08 (boys); Sex delinquency (coitus),
-.11 and -.19

tetrachoric r with police arrest among boys were low or negligible,
ranging from -.04 and .11, but among girls it showed a curious negative correlation, -.26 $\pm$ .04, with police arrest.

Its highest correlations were with lack of interest in
school, with respective coefficients of .32 $\pm$ .03 and .42 $\pm$ .04
among boys and girls. With two behavior problems it yielded substantial correlations in the .30's for girls and moderate coefficients in the .20's for boys: distractibility and disturbing influence in school. Staying out late at night yielded divergent
coefficients of .07 and .34 $\pm$ .04.

Nine miscellaneous behavior notations showed moderate correlations ranging from .20 to .30 for both sexes: inattentiveness
in school, inefficiency in work, play, etc., listlessness, lack of
initiative, laziness, absent-mindedness, dull or slow manner (including listlessness and lack of initiative, undifferentiated),
question of hypophrenia, and preference for younger children as
playmates. Irregular attendance at school among boys showed the
moderate correlation of .20 $\pm$ .03 but the negligible coefficient
of .03 among girls. Three miscellaneous notations among girls
showed moderate correlations in the .20's but low positive coefficients below .20 among boys: exclusion from school, inferiority
feelings, and unpopularity.

The only significant negative correlation with poor work
in school was with immoral home conditions among girls, -.26 $\pm$ .04.

Among the six sex notations and the seven physical or psychophysical disabilities all correlations were low or negligible,
ranging from -.19 to .17.

Among the four home or familial notations the only significant negative correlation was with immoral home conditions among
girls, -.26 $\pm$ .04, as noted above.

Retardation in school (which presumably will amount to two years or more at the age of 16) was found among 878, or 41.6 per cent, of our White boys and among 474, or 40.1 per cent, of our White girls and was one of the most frequent case-record notations in our data. Its negligible relationship with poor work in school, the tetrachoric correlations being only -.01 and .06, is curious and unexpected. It appears from our data to be of almost negligible importance as an indicator of personality or conduct deviation, the correlations with our three criteria of seriousness or "ominousness" ranging from -.14 to .13 (Table 113).

TABLE 113

CORRELATIONS WITH "RETARDATION IN SCHOOL"

	Boys	Girls
Personality-total.............................	-.12 ± .02	.13 ± .02
Conduct-total.................................	-.08 ± .02	-.14 ± .02
Police arrest.................................	-.03 ± .03	-.05 ± .04
	Larger Correlations (Positive)	
Question of hypophrenia.......................	.55 ± .02	.48 ± .03 (1)*
Feeble-minded sibling.........................	.25 ± .04	.34 ± .04 (2)
Slow, dull....................................	.24 ± .03	.30 ± .03 (3)
Grouped: dull, slow, etc.....................	.17	.24 ± .03 (4)
Irregular attendance at school...............	.17	.23 ± .04 (5)
Preference for younger children..............	.18	.22 ± .05 (6)
Vicious home conditions......................	-.04	.21 ± .05 (7)
	Larger Correlations (Negative)	
Worry over specific fact......................	-.36 ± .04	-.34 ± .05
Vocational guidance...........................	-.31 ± .03	-.32 ± .04
Attractive manner.............................	-.26 ± .03	-.16
Psychoneurotic................................	-.25 ± .04	-.26 ± .05
Clean...	-.24 ± .03	-.15
Daydreaming...................................	-.21 ± .03	-.21 ± .05
Mental conflict...............................	-.09	-.36 ± .05
Leader..	-.12	-.32 ± .04
Sensitive over specific fact.................	-.14	-.28 ± .04
Grouped: sensitive or worrisome, etc.........	-.17	-.28 ± .03
Depressed.....................................	-.14	-.26 ± .06
Bad companions................................	-.05	-.26 ± .04
Grouped: egocentric, etc.....................	-.14	-.24 ± .04

* Rank order of girls' correlations.

TABLE 113—Continued

	Boys	Girls
Spoiled child..................................	-.14	-.24 ± .04
Irresponsible.................................	.07	-.24 ± .05
Grouped: depressed, etc......................	-.14	-.22 ± .04
Egocentric....................................	-.17	-.21 ± .04
Inferiority feelings..........................	-.11	-.21 ± .05
Lazy..	-.19	-.20 ± .05
Hatred or jealousy of sibling.................	-.15	-.20 ± .05

Other Correlations (Positive to Negative)

Oversuggestible, .16 and .04; Lues, .12 and .11; Truancy from school, .10 and -.08; Underweight, .09 and .16; Follower, .09 and .01; Violence, .08 and -.02; Speech defect, .08 and .12; Brother in penal detention, .07 and .09; Leading others into bad conduct, .07 and .08; Former convulsions, .05 and -.00; Distractible, .05 and .14; Threatening violence, .05 (boys); Swearing (general), .05 (boys); Slovenly, .05 and -.01; Disturbing influence in school, .05 and -.02; Disobedient, .04 and -.06; Incorrigible, .04 and -.01; Temper display, .04 and -.04; Apprehensive, .04 and -.04; Conduct prognosis bad, .04 and .06; Sullen, .02 and -.02; Exclusion from school, .02 and .05; Headaches, .02 and -.07; Object of teasing, .01 and .05; Sulky, .01 and .03; Staying out late at night, .01 and -.09; Fighting, .01 and -.05; Complaining of bad treatment by other children, .00 (boys); Enuresis, -.00 and .04; Destructive, -.01 and -.05; Stealing, -.01 and -.04; Crying spells, -.01 and -.09; Poor work in school, -.01 and .06; Question of encephalitis, -.01 and .09; Grouped: fighting, etc., -.02 and -.07; Stuttering, -.02 (boys); Listless, -.02 and -.01; Gang, -.02 (boys); Refusal to attend school, -.03 and -.09; Truancy from home, -.03 and -.05; Overinterest in sex matters, -.03 and -.15; Grouped: temper, etc., -.03 and -.05; Grouped: swearing, etc., -.03 and .06; Restless in sleep, -.04 and -.11; Nail-biting, -.04 and -.05; Bashful, -.05 and -.05; Excuse-forming, -.05 and -.10; Neurological defect, -.05 and -.06; Grouped: disobedient, etc., -.05 and -.03; Grouped: lack of interest in school, etc., -.05 and -.07; Overinterest in opposite sex, -.05 (girls); Seclusive, -.06 and -.07; Lack of initiative, -.06 and -.06; Temper tantrums, -.06 and -.03; Lack of interest in school, -.06 and -.04; Inefficient in work, play, etc., -.07 and -.02; "Nervous," -.07 and -.14; Restless, -.08 and -.02; Queer, -.08 and -.18; Quarrelsome, -.08 and -.09; Lying, -.08 and -.11; Loitering, -.08 and .03; Inattentive in school, -.08 and -.10; Fantastical lying, -.09 and -.10; Teasing other children, -.09 (boys); Smoking, -.09 (boys); Absent-minded, -.09 and .08; Sex denied entirely, -.09 and .03; Emotional instability, -.10 and -.17; Repressed, -.10 and -.13; Unpopular, -.10 and -.05; Rude, -.11 and -.11; Stubborn, -.11 and -.06; Sex delinquency (coitus), -.11 and -.02; Irritable, -.11 and -.11; Unhappy, -.11 and -.12; Grouped: "nervous," etc., -.11 and -.15; Sensitive (general), -.12 and -.14; Irregular sleep habits, -.12 and -.14; Victim of sex abuse, -.12 (girls); Contrary, -.13 and -.13; Selfish, -.13 and -.18; Changeable moods, -.13 and -.13; Immoral home conditions, -.13 and .11; Discord between parents, -.13 and -.05; Masturbation, -.14 and -.15; Finicky food habits, -.14 and -.11; Question of change of personality, -.15 and -.10; Boastful, "show-off," -.17 and -.08; Bossy, -.17 and -.08; Defiant, -.17 and -.17; Popular, -.18 and -.12

Its largest correlations were with question of hypophrenia, the respective coefficients for boys and girls being .55 + .02 and .48 + .03. Positive correlations of substantial size in the .30's were found among girls for slow or dull manner and feeble-minded sibling, the corresponding coefficients for boys being of moderate size in the .20's. Three additional notations showed moderate positive correlations in the .20's among girls but low coefficients below .20 among boys: irregular attendance at school, preference for younger children as playmates, and vicious home conditions.

Retardation in school showed a relatively large number of negative correlations of statistically significant magnitude. Worry over some specific fact and "request for vocational guidance" yielded substantial negative correlations in the -.30's among both sexes. Mental conflict and "leader" among girls yielded substantial negative correlations in the -.30's but low negative coefficients less than -.20 among boys.

Psychoneurotic trends and daydreaming showed moderate negative correlations in the -.20's among both sexes. The two "desirable" traits, attractive manner and clean habits, showed moderate negative correlations in the -.20's among boys but low coefficients less than -.20 among girls. Ten notations, chiefly personality problems, among girls showed negative correlations in the -.20's but low negative or negligible coefficients less than + .20 among boys: egocentricity, "spoiled child," hatred or jealousy of sibling, laziness, irresponsibility, inferiority feelings, depressed mood or spells, sensitiveness or worrisomeness (undifferentiated), sensitiveness over some specific fact, and bad companions. It is curious that laziness shows negative correlations of -.19 and -.20 + .05 with retardation in school, in view of the fact that it was correlated positively to a statistically significant degree with poor work in school, as noted above, those correlations being .30 + .03 and .21 + .05 among boys and girls respectively.

Among the six sex notations and among the seven physical or psychophysical disabilities all correlations with retardation in school were low or negligible, ranging from -.15 to .16.

Among the four home or familial notations, the only correlation of significant size was the moderate positive one of .21 + .05 with vicious home conditions among girls.

Exclusion, expulsion, or suspension from school was noted among 204, or 9.7 per cent, of our 2,113 White boys and among 71, or 6.0 per cent, of our 1,181 White girls. In contrast with the two school notations previously discussed in this chapter, exclusion from school appears to be of definite clinical significance as an indicator of conduct deviation, its bi-serial correlations with the conduct-total being .49 ± .02 and .56 ± .03 for boys and girls respectively (Table 114). Among boys its correlations with

TABLE 114

CORRELATIONS WITH "EXCLUSION FROM SCHOOL"

	Boys	Girls
Personality-total............................	.32 ± .02	.16 ± .04
Conduct-total................................	.49 ± .02	.56 ± .03
Police arrest................................	.33 ± .03	.22 ± .06
	Larger Correlations (Positive)	
Disturbing influence in school...............	.51 ± .03	.51 ± .03 (1)*
Grouped: disobedient, etc...................	.37 ± .03	.37 ± .04 (14-17)
Violence.....................................	.36 ± .04	.49 ± .06 (2)
Destructive..................................	.34 ± .04	.40 ± .07 (7)
Rude...	.34 ± .04	.31 ± .06 (25-26)
Grouped: fighting, etc.....................	.34 ± .03	.38 ± .05 (11-13)
Incorrigible.................................	.32 ± .03	.39 ± .05 (8-10)
Leading others into bad conduct..............	.31 ± .05	.47 ± .07 (4)
Defiant......................................	.30 ± .04	.21 ± .07 (46)
Conduct prognosis bad........................	.30 ± .06	.35 ± .08 (20-22)
Swearing (general)...........................	.29 ± .05	....
Grouped: swearing, etc.....................	.29 ± .04	.39 ± .06 (8-10)
Boastful, "show-off".........................	.28 ± .04	.16
Disobedient..................................	.28 ± .03	.36 ± .05 (18-19)
Fighting.....................................	.28 ± .04	.44 ± .03 (5)
Contrary.....................................	.27 ± .05	.13
Stealing.....................................	.27 ± .03	.37 ± .05 (14-17)
Quarrelsome..................................	.26 ± .04	.29 ± .06 (28-30)
Temper tantrums..............................	.26 ± .04	.37 ± .06 (14-17)
Truancy from home............................	.26 ± .03	.25 ± .06 (36-38)
Overinterest in sex matters..................	.26 ± .05	.25 ± .07 (36-38)
Teasing other children.......................	.25 ± .04	....
Complaining of bad treatment by other children	.25 ± .05	....
Lying..	.24 ± .03	.42 ± .05 (6)
Threatening violence.........................	.24 ± .05	....
Question of encephalitis.....................	.24 ± .06	.48 ± .08 (3)
Sullen.......................................	.22 ± .04	.27 ± .07 (32-33)

*Rank order of girls' correlations.

TABLE 114—Continued

	Boys	Girls
Grouped: temper, etc.	.22 ± .03	.20 ± .05 (47-50)
Grouped: lack of interest in school, etc.	.22 ± .03	.31 ± .06 (25-26)
Refusal to attend school.	.21 ± .05	.03
Truancy from school.	.21 ± .03	.22 ± .06 (43-45)
Inattentive in school.	.20 ± .03	.25 ± .07 (36-38)
Loitering.	.20 ± .04	.18
Masturbation.	.20 ± .03	.29 ± .06 (28-30)
Excuse-forming.	.20 ± .04	.16
Emotional instability.	.20 ± .05	.38 ± .07 (11-13)
Restless.	.18	.39 ± .05 (8-10)
Question of change of personality.	.04	.38 ± .07 (11-13)
Unpopular.	.15	.37 ± .08 (14-17)
Distractible.	.03	.36 ± .06 (18-19)
Grouped: "nervous," etc.	.15	.35 ± .05 (20-22)
Mental conflict.	.03	.35 ± .08 (20-22)
Object of teasing.	.17	.34 ± .07 (23)
Overinterest in opposite sex.	....	.33 ± .06 (24)
Neurological defect.	.08	.30 ± .06 (27)
Changeable moods.	.07	.29 ± .06 (28-30)
Queer.	.18	.28 ± .07 (31)
Stubborn.	.10	.27 ± .05 (32-33)
Worry over specific fact.	-.12	.26 ± .09 (34-35)
Question of hypophrenia.	.15	.26 ± .05 (34-35)
"Nervous".	.08	.24 ± .06 (39)
Poor work in school.	.07	.23 ± .05 (40-42)
Lack of interest in school.	.18	.23 ± .07 (40-42)
Bossy.	.07	.23 ± .07 (40-42)
Inefficient in work, play, etc.	.01	.22 ± .07 (43-45)
Absent-minded.	.00	.22 ± .08 (43-45)
Fantastical lying.	.17	.20 ± .07 (47-50)
Preference for younger children.	.05	.20 ± .07 (47-50)
Headaches.	.03	.20 ± .07 (47-50)
	Larger Correlations (Negative)	
Bashful.	-.20 ± .04	-.13

Other Correlations (Positive to Negative)

Victim of sex abuse, .19 (girls); Egocentric, .18 and .13; Grouped: egocentric, etc., .18 and .09; Hatred or jealousy of sibling, .17 and .04; Enuresis, .16 and .17; Staying out late at night, .16 and .08; Nail-biting, .15 and .18; Smoking, .15 (boys); Oversuggestible, .15 and .14; Bad companions, .14 and .02; Irresponsible, .14 and .16; Gang, .13 (boys); Former convulsions, .11 and .10; Sulky, .10 and .19; Temper display, .10 and .03; Irritable, .10 and .04; Inferiority feelings, .10 and .08; Popular, .09 and .03; Slovenly, .08 and .13; Daydreaming, .08 and .17; Irregular attendance at school, .08 and .08; Speech defect, .08 and -.04; Lazy, .07 and .13; Sex delinquency (coitus), .07 and .18; Depressed, .07 and .10; Restless in sleep, .07 and .16; Leader, .07 and -.11; Clean, .06 and -.01; Underweight, .06 and .14; Irregular sleep habits, .05 and .12; Brother in penal detention, .05 and -.06; Crying spells, .04 and

TABLE 114—Continued

.15; Grouped: depressed, etc., .04 and .11; Spoiled child, .03 and .09; Psychoneurotic, .02 and .12; Retardation in school, .02 and .05; Follower, .02 and .04; Discord between parents, .02 and -.02; Selfish, .01 and .08; Apprehensive, .01 and .05; Finicky food habits, .00 and .14; Vicious home conditions, .00 and .10; Seclusive, -.00 and .15; Sensitive over specific fact, -.01 and .11; Attractive manner, -.01 and .09; Vocational guidance, -.01 and -.13; Listless, -.02 and .05; Sensitive (general), -.04 and .02; Lues, -.04 and .09; Grouped: sensitive or worrisome, etc., -.06 and .13; Repressed, -.07 and .03; Slow, dull, -.08 and -.06; Unhappy, -.08 and .08; Grouped: dull, slow, etc., -.09 and .01; Immoral home conditions, -.10 and .12; Sex denied entirely, -.11 and -.08; Lack of initiative, -.16 and .07; Stuttering, -.16 (boys); Feeble-minded sibling, -.17 and -.06

personality-total and police arrest may be considered as substantial, the respective coefficients being .32 + .02 and .33 + .03. Among girls the corresponding correlations, .16 + .04 and .22 + .06, were less meaningful. The children in our study comprising the group falling under the rubric exclusion from school are not of homogeneous character. While the principal cause for this exclusion among our cases appeared to be for reasons of conduct disturbing to school routine, in many cases exclusion was due to an inability to learn and in some instances because of some physical disability rendering the child unable to be adequately cared for in the public schools.

Its highest correlations were with disturbing influence in school, the coefficient being .51 + .03 for both boys and girls. Three conduct problems among girls yielded large correlations in the .40's and moderate coefficients in the .30's among boys: violence, destructiveness, and leading others into bad conduct. Among girls an additional three notations similarly yielded large correlations in the .40's but only moderate coefficients in the .20's among boys: fighting, lying, and question or diagnosis of encephalitis.

Four conduct notations yielded uniformly substantial correlations in the .30's: incorrigibility, rudeness, staff notation of unfavorable conduct prognosis, and (calculated for girls only) overinterest in the opposite sex. Five conduct and personality problems yielded substantial correlations in the .30's among girls and moderate coefficients in the .20's among boys: disobedience, stealing, swearing or bad language (undifferentiated), temper tantrums, and emotional instability. Seven notations among girls

yielded substantial correlations in the .30's but low positive coefficients below .20 among boys: <u>restlessness</u>, <u>distractibility</u>,
<u>question of change of personality</u>, <u>mental conflict</u>, <u>object of teas-
ing by other children</u>, <u>unpopularity</u>, and <u>neurological defect (un-
specified</u>).

        Eight conduct problems showed moderate correlations ranging
from .20 to .30 with <u>exclusion from school</u> among both sexes: <u>de-
fiant attitude</u>, <u>sullenness</u>, <u>quarrelsomeness</u>, <u>truancy from school</u>,
<u>truancy from home</u>, <u>inattentiveness in school</u>, <u>overinterest in sex
matters</u>, and <u>masturbation</u>. Four behavior problems for which only
the boys' correlations were computed also showed moderate correlations in the .20's: <u>swearing in general</u>, <u>teasing other children</u>,
<u>complaining of bad treatment by other children</u>, and <u>threatening
violence</u>. Five undesirable behavior manifestations among boys
showed moderate correlations in the .20's but low positive coefficients below .20 among girls: <u>refusal to attend school</u>, <u>contrari-
ness</u>, <u>loitering or wandering</u>, <u>boastful or "show-off" manner</u>, and
<u>excuse-forming attitude</u>. Among girls fourteen miscellaneous no-
tations showed moderate correlations in the .20's but low coefficients below .20 among boys: <u>stubbornness</u>, <u>changeable moods or
attitudes</u>, <u>queer behavior</u>, <u>"nervousness,"</u> <u>question of hypophrenia</u>,
<u>lack of interest in school</u>, <u>poor work in school</u>, <u>inefficiency in
work, play</u>, etc., <u>absent-mindedness</u>, <u>worry over some specific fact</u>,
<u>bossy manner</u>, <u>fantastical lying</u>, <u>preference for younger children
as playmates</u>, and <u>headaches</u>.

        Only one notation, <u>bashfulness</u>, showed a negative correla-
tion of moderate size with <u>exclusion from school</u>, -.20 $\pm$ .04 among
boys.

        Among the six sex notations <u>overinterest in the opposite
sex</u>, for which only the girls' correlation was computed, showed the
substantial correlation of .33 $\pm$ .06. <u>Overinterest in sex matters</u>
and <u>masturbation</u> showed moderate correlations in the .20's among
both sexes.

        Among the seven physical or psychophysical notations <u>ques-
tion or diagnosis of encephalitis</u> yielded the fairly large correlation of .48 $\pm$ .08 among girls and a corresponding moderate coefficient of .24 $\pm$ .06 among boys. <u>Neurological defect (unspecified)</u>
among girls yielded the fairly substantial correlation of .30 $\pm$ .06.

        Among the four home or familial notations all correlations
were low or negligible, ranging from -.10 to .12.

CHAPTER LVII

ATTRACTIVE MANNER

Attractive manner was one of the four "desirable" behavior traits which were noted with sufficient frequency in our case-record material to justify correlational treatment. The other three "desirable" behavior notations, it will be recalled, were popularity (Table 28), clean habits (Table 90), and "leader" (Table 107). Attractive manner was noted among 307 of our 2,113 White boys, or 14.5 per cent, and among 165 of our 1,181 White girls, or 14.0 per cent. Its correlations with our three criteria of seriousness were low or negligible, ranging from -.08 to .16 (Table 115).

TABLE 115

CORRELATIONS WITH "ATTRACTIVE MANNER"

	Boys	Girls
Personality-total..............................	.16 ± .02	.05 + .03
Conduct-total.................................	.12 ± .02	.08 + .03
Police arrest.................................	.05 ± .03	-.08 + .05
	Larger Correlations (Positive)	
Popular.......................................	.36 ± .04	.36 ± .05 (1)*
Clean...	.32 ± .03	.30 ± .04 (2)
Vicious home conditions.......................	.27 ± .05	.21 ± .06 (5)
Underweight...................................	.26 ± .03	-.01
Grouped: sensitive or worrisome, etc.........	.25 ± .03	.17
Sex denied entirely...........................	.25 ± .05	.13
Worry over specific fact......................	.25 ± .05	.20 ± .07 (6-8)
Hatred or jealousy of sibling.................	.23 ± .05	.10
Sensitive over specific fact.................	.23 ± .03	.15
Spoiled child.................................	.23 ± .04	.20 ± .05 (6-8)
Former convulsions............................	.22 ± .04	.02
Headaches.....................................	.22 ± .04	.07
Sensitive (general)..........................	.22 ± .04	.19
Leader..	.21 ± .04	.23 ± .06 (4)
Absent-minded.................................	.20 ± .04	-.00

*Rank order of girls' correlations.

TABLE 115—Continued

	Boys	Girls
Irregular attendance at school...............	.01	.26 ± .05 (3)
Daydreaming....................................	.17	.20 ± .05 (6-8)
		Larger Correlations (Negative)
Retardation in school.........................	-.26 ± .03	-.16
Listless......................................	.06	-.34 ± .05
Unpopular.....................................	.02	-.23 ± .06

Other Correlations (Positive to Negative)

Boastful, "show-off," .19 and .09; Lazy, .19 and .05; Discord between parents, .19 and .14; Vocational guidance, .17 and .18; Fantastical lying, .16 and .12; Bossy, .15 and .06; Depressed, .15 and .05; Unhappy, .15 and .02; Grouped: depressed, etc., .14 and .07; Question of encephalitis, .14 and .09; Question of change of personality, .14 and .06; Inattentive in school, .14 and .02; Bad companions, .13 and -.01; Contrary, .13 and .04; Irregular sleep habits, .13 and .07; Poor work in school, .13 and .08; Inferiority feelings, .12 and -.10; Masturbation, .12 and .05; Teasing other children, .12 (boys); Defiant, .11 and .07; Loitering, .11 and .01; Selfish, .11 and .02; Excuse-forming, .10 and .05; Inefficient in work, play, etc., .10 and .06; Finicky food habits, .09 and .14; Leading others in bad conduct, .09 and -.09; Nail-biting, .09 and .06; Rude, .09 and .06; Smoking, .09 (boys); Stubborn, .09 and -.09; Sulky, .09 and .10; Apprehensive, .09 and -.02; Grouped: lack of interest in school, etc., .08 and .09; Complaining of bad treatment by other children, .08 (boys); Mental conflict, .08 and -.01; Lack of initiative, .08 and .04; Overinterest in sex matters, .08 and .19; Slovenly, .08 and -.04; Irresponsible, .08 and .12; Disturbing influence in school, .08 and -.02; Disobedient, .07 and .04; Lying, .07 and .13; Distractible, .07 and .08; Queer, .07 and -.05; Neurological defect, .07 and -.03; Restless in sleep, .06 and .03; Restless, .06 and .05; Crying spells, .06 and .10; Destructive, .05 and -.06; Grouped: disobedient, etc., .05 and -.05; Victim of sex abuse, .05 (girls); Grouped: swearing, etc., .04 and .09; Immoral home conditions, .04 and .15; Changeable moods, .04 and .02; Repressed, .04 and .03; Incorrigible, .04 and -.04; "Nervous," .03 and .07; Grouped: egocentric, etc., .02 and -.02; Grouped: dull, slow, etc., .02 and -.11; Grouped: "nervous," etc., .02 and .08; Brother in penal detention, .02 and .06; Speech defect, .02 and .06; Seclusive, .02 and -.09; Bashful, .02 and .10; Truancy from school, .02 and .12; Swearing (general), .02 (boys); Staying out late at night, .02 and .02; Refusal to attend school, .02 and -.11; Lack of interest in school, .02 and .15; Temper display, .01 and .02; Threatening violence, .01 (boys); Truancy from home, .01 and -.08; Stealing, .00 and -.01; Object of teasing, -.00 and .08; Exclusion from school, -.01 and .09; Quarrelsome, -.01 and -.08; Enuresis, -.01 and -.02; Sullen, -.01 and -.06; Slow, dull, -.02 and -.11; Emotional instability, -.02 and .10; Oversuggestible, -.03 and .06; Temper tantrums, -.03 and -.07; Gang, -.03 (boys); Overinterest in opposite sex, -.03 (girls); Irritable, -.04 and .02; Conduct prognosis bad, -.04 and -.10; Preference for younger children, -.04 and -.09; Question of hypophrenia, -.04 and -.18; Grouped: fighting, etc., -.04 and -.02; Grouped: temper, etc., -.06 and -.02; Fighting, -.07 and .02; Violence, -.08 and .09; Egocentric, -.09 and -.01; Follower, -.10 and .01; Feeble-minded sibling, -.10 and -.06; Lues, -.12 and -.09; Psychoneurotic, -.12 and -.11; Stuttering, -.14 (boys); Sex delinquency (coitus), -.14 and -.13

Its largest correlations (in the .30's) among both sexes were found for <u>popularity</u> and <u>clean habits</u>.

Moderate coefficients in the .20's among both sexes were found for four notations: "<u>leader</u>," "<u>spoiled child</u>," <u>worry over some specific fact</u>, and <u>vicious home conditions</u>. Eight notations among boys showed moderate correlations in the .20's but low or negligible coefficients below .20 among girls: <u>sensitiveness in general</u>, <u>sensitiveness over some specific fact</u>, <u>hatred or jealousy of sibling</u>, <u>absent-mindedness</u>, <u>sex misbehavior denied entirely</u>, <u>former convulsions</u>, <u>headaches</u>, and <u>underweight condition</u>. Among girls <u>daydreaming</u> and <u>irregular attendance at school</u> showed moderate correlations in the .20's but among boys low or negligible coefficients below .20.

<u>Attractive manner</u> showed three negative correlations of statistically significant size. <u>Listlessness</u> among girls yielded the substantial <u>negative</u> correlation of -.34 ± .05 but a negligible coefficient of .06 among boys. <u>Retardation in school</u> among boys and <u>unpopularity</u> among girls showed moderate negative correlations in the -.20's.

<u>Attractive manner</u> showed the moderate positive correlation of .25 ± .05 with <u>sex misbehavior denied entirely</u> among boys. All other correlations with sex notations were low or negligible.

Among the seven physical or psychophysical disabilities the only correlation of significant size was with <u>underweight condition</u> among boys, .26 ± .03.

Among the four home or familial notations moderate positive correlations in the .20's were found found for <u>vicious</u> (not "immoral") <u>home conditions</u> among both sexes.

CHAPTER LVIII

STUTTERING OR STAMMERING

In view of the widespread belief among speech pathologists
that the psychologic components in <u>stuttering or stammering</u> are important, it seems feasible to allot a separate chapter to its consideration. Although its correlation with <u>speech defect</u> (other
than stuttering) is substantial, .35 ± .06, its bi-serial correlations with all other notations are generally dissimilar to those
obtained for <u>speech defect</u> (Table 120, chap. llx). Since <u>speech
defect</u> appears to be correlated only with notations suggestive of
low intelligence or constitutional inadequacy, it has been rele-
gated to a subsequent chapter in which physical (or possibly "psychophysical") notations are considered. <u>Stuttering</u> was noted among
only 83 cases, or among 3.9 per cent, of our 2,113 White boys.
(Within our smaller population of 1,181 White girls there were not
sufficient cases to justify computing correlation coefficients.)
As an indicator of personality or conduct deviation, <u>stuttering</u>
appeared to be of little importance, its correlations (ranging
from -.05 to .10) with <u>personality-total</u>, <u>conduct-total</u>, and <u>po-
lice arrest</u> being low or negligible (Table 116).

Its largest correlation was with <u>speech defect</u> (other than
stuttering), .35 ± .06. Three notations—<u>psychoneurotic trends</u>,
<u>mental conflict</u>, and <u>staff notation of unfavorable conduct prog-
nosis</u>—showed moderate correlations in the .20's.

<u>Stuttering</u> showed moderate negative correlations in the
-.20's with six miscellaneous notations: <u>bad companions</u>, <u>running
with a gang</u>, <u>irregular attendance at school</u>, <u>leading others into
bad conduct</u>, <u>brother in penal detention</u>, and possibly with <u>sex delinquency (coitus)</u>.

Among the four sex notations for which boys' correlations
were calculated, all coefficients were negative and of negligible
size except possibly the dubious <u>negative</u> coefficient of -.20 ± .08
with <u>sex delinquency (coitus)</u>.

Among the six physical or psychophysical notations for

TABLE 116

CORRELATIONS WITH "STUTTERING"
(Boys Only)

```
Personality-total . . . . . . . . . . . . . . . .    .10 ± .03
Conduct-total . . . . . . . . . . . . . . . . . .   -.05 ± .03
Police arrest . . . . . . . . . . . . . . . . . .    .09 ± .05
```

Larger Correlations (Positive)

```
Speech defect . . . . . . . . . . . . . . . .    .35 ± .06
Psychoneurotic . . . . . . . . . . . . . . . .    .29 ± .07
Conduct prognosis bad . . . . . . . . . . . .    .28 ± .07
Mental conflict . . . . . . . . . . . . . . .    .22 ± .07
```

Larger Correlations (Negative)

```
Bad companions . . . . . . . . . . . . . . . .   -.27 ± .05
Gang . . . . . . . . . . . . . . . . . . . . .   -.24 ± .05
Irregular attendance at school . . . . . . . .   -.24 ± .06
Leading others into bad conduct . . . . . . .   -.20 ± .06
Sex delinquency (coitus) . . . . . . . . . . .   -.20 ± .08
Brother in penal detention . . . . . . . . . .   -.20 ± .06
```

Not Calculable

```
Vicious home conditions . . . . . . . . . . .    (n.c.)
```

Other Correlations (Positive to Negative)

Lack of initiative, .17; Inefficient in work, play, etc., .16; Object of teasing, .16; Inferiority feelings, .16; Listless, .13; Unpopular, .13; Grouped: sensitive or worrisome, etc., .12; Sensitive (general), .12; Restless in sleep, .12; "Nervous," .12; Crying spells, .11; Complaining of bad treatment by other children, .11; Former convulsions, .11; Headaches, .10; Emotional instability, .10; Sensitive over specific fact, .10; Queer, .10; Threatening violence, .10; Popular, .09; Grouped: "nervous," etc., .08; Distractible, .08; Selfish, .08; Bossy, .08; Absent-minded, .07; Lues, .07; Irregular sleep habits, .06; Bashful, .06; Lazy, .06; Fantastical lying, .06; Finicky food habits, .05; Oversuggestible, .05; Preference for younger children, .05; Spoiled child, .04; Smoking, .04; Slovenly, .04; Teasing other children, .03; Sulky, .03; Violence, .03; Apprehensive, .03; Irritable, .03; Repressed, .03; Question of hypophrenia, .02; Slow, dull, .02; Hatred or jealousy of sibling, .02; Refusal to attend school, .02; Irresponsible, .02; Disobedient, .02; Nail-biting, .01; Staying out late at night, .01; Daydreaming, .01; Depressed, .01; Grouped: dull, slow, etc., .01; Grouped: depressed, etc., .01; Grouped: swearing, etc., .00; Follower, .00; Immoral home conditions, -.00; Feebleminded sibling, -.01; Boastful, "show-off," -.02; Temper display, -.02; Retardation in school, -.02; Neurological defect, -.02; Grouped: egocentric, etc., -.02; Seclusive, -.03; Loitering, -.03; Enuresis, -.03; Sullen, -.04; Restless, -.04; Clean, -.04; Underweight, -.04; Vocational guidance,

TABLE 116—Continued

-.04; Grouped: disobedient, etc., -.04; Grouped: fighting, etc., -.05; Unhappy, -.05; Question of change of personality, -.05; Changeable moods, -.05; Temper tantrums, -.05; Fighting, - 05; Inattentive in school, -.06; Lying, -.06; Masturbation, -.06; Egocentric, -.06; Grouped: temper, etc., -.06; Question of encephalitis, -.07; Sex denied entirely, -.07; Excuse-forming, -.07; Swearing (general), -.07; Stubborn, -.07; Incorrigible, -.07; Defiant, -.08; Poor work in school, -.08; Leader, -.09; Truancy from home, -.09; Quarrelsome, -.09; Disturbing influence in school, -.09; Destructive, -.10; Stealing, -.10; Truancy from school, -.10; Overinterest in sex matters, -.10; Grouped: lack of interest in school, etc., -.11; Contrary, -.11; Lack of interest in school, -.12; Attractive manner, -.14; Discord between parents, -.14; Worry over specific fact, -.15; Exclusion from school, -.16; Rude, -.19

which correlations with <u>stuttering</u> were calculated, <u>speech defect</u> yielded the substantial positive correlation of .35 $\pm$ .06, all other correlations in this field being negligible, ranging from -.07 to .07.

Among the four home or familial notations <u>brother in penal detention</u> showed the moderate <u>negative</u> coefficient of -.20 $\pm$ .06, all other correlations in this field being low or negligible.

CHAPTER LIX

MISCELLANEOUS PHYSICAL AND PSYCHOPHYSICAL
NOTATIONS

In this chapter and the succeeding one are presented fourteen abbreviated tables concerning miscellaneous physical, psychophysical, home, familial, educational, and vocational notations
which are not "behavior traits" such as were considered in Tables
6-116, inclusive. A fuller discussion of these fourteen tables
would be appropriate in a separate study, in which emphasis could
be placed upon <u>causal analysis</u>. In the present volume the inten-
tion has been a study of intercorrelations among traits and a consideration of their relative importance or "seriousness." In these
fourteen tables all correlation coefficients less than ± .20 (ex-
cept those for <u>personality-total</u>, <u>conduct-total</u>, and <u>police arrest</u>)
have been omitted. These smaller coefficients may be found scat-
tered among Tables 6-116, inclusive.

Among these fourteen tables, <u>question or diagnosis of en-
cephalitis</u> is of especial interest because of its concomitants in
the personality and conduct fields. Because of the difficulty of
making a definite diagnosis among our cases in which actual hos-
pital records were so often lacking, we have employed the words
"question of" in order to emphasize the lack of certainty in our
consideration of its intercorrelations with other traits. In about
38 per cent of our "encephalitis cases" a definite staff notation
of encephalitis or "post-encephalitis" was made, while in the remaining 62 per cent the diagnosis was only tentative or conjec-
tural.[1]

It was noted among 70, or 3.3 per cent, of our 2,113 White
boys and among 37, or 3.1 per cent, of our 1,181 White girls. Its

---

[1]A more detailed analysis of our cases of encephalitis is given in
the article "The Behavior of Encephalitic Children" by R. L. Jenkins and Luton
Ackerson (<u>American Journal of Orthopsychiatry</u>, IV [1934], 499-507).

bi-serial correlations with <u>personality-total</u> were considerable, .41 ± .03 among boys and .52 ± .04 among girls. With <u>conduct-total</u> its correlation among girls was fairly substantial, .36 ± .04, but only moderate among boys, .20 ± .04. With <u>police arrest</u> its correlations were practically zero.

Question or diagnosis of encephalitis showed very high correlations in the .60's with <u>question of change of personality</u> among both sexes and large correlations in the .40's with staff notation of <u>emotional instability</u> (Table 117). It showed meaningful correlations ranging from the .20's to the .40's for such "nervous"

TABLE 117*

CORRELATIONS WITH "QUESTION OF ENCEPHALITIS"

	Boys	Girls
Personality-total.............................	.41 ± .03	.52 ± .04
Conduct-total.................................	.20 ± .04	.36 ± .04
Police arrest.................................	.03 ± .05	.00 ± .07
	Larger Correlations (Positive)	
Question of change of personality............	.65 ± .05	.66 ± .07 (1)[†]
Emotional instability.........................	.46 ± .06	.48 ± .08 (2-4)
Grouped: "nervous," etc......................	.35 ± .04	.48 ± .05 (2-4)
Grouped: temper, etc........................	.31 ± .04	.33 ± .06 (15-17)
Queer...	.30 ± .10	.29 ± .09 (24-27)
Irritable....................................	.30 ± .05	.31 ± .07 (19-22)
Irregular sleep habits.......................	.30 ± .07	.44 ± .09 (6-7)
Contrary.....................................	.29 ± .07	-.09
Listless.....................................	.27 ± .06	.03
Restless.....................................	.27 ± .05	.45 ± .06 (5)
Crying spells................................	.26 ± .05	.32 ± .06 (18)
Object of teasing...........................	.26 ± .05	.30 ± .08 (23)
Absent-minded................................	.25 ± .02	.31 ± .09 (19-22)
Exclusion from school........................	.24 ± .06	.48 ± .08 (2-4)
Complaining of bad treatment by other children	.23 ± .07	....
Grouped: fighting, etc......................	.23 ± .05	.29 ± .06 (24-27)
Threatening violence.........................	.22 ± .07	....
Depressed....................................	.20 ± .07	.08
Inefficient in work, play, etc..............	.20 ± .07	-.03
Distractible.................................	.17	.44 ± .07 (6-7)
Temper tantrums..............................	.04	.40 ± .07 (8-9)
"Nervous"....................................	.14	.40 ± .06 (8-9)

*Other coefficients smaller than ± .20 may be found in Tables 6-116.

[†]Rank order of girls' correlations.

TABLE 117—Continued

	Boys	Girls
Changeable moods	.09	.39 ± .07 (10-11)
Grouped: swearing, etc.	.10	.39 ± .08 (10-11)
Restless in sleep	.15	.36 ± .07 (12)
Finicky food habits	.14	.35 ± .08 (13-14)
Conduct prognosis bad	.13	.35 ± .10 (13-14)
Destructive	.05	.33 ± .10 (15-17)
Spoiled child	.06	.33 ± .08 (15-17)
Disturbing influence in school	.18	.31 ± .08 (19-22)
Incorrigible	.10	.31 ± .07 (19-22)
Daydreaming	-.02	.29 ± .08 (24-27)
Disobedient	.15	.29 ± .07 (24-27)
Masturbation	.18	.28 ± .07 (28)
Fighting	.09	.27 ± .04 (29-31)
Lying	-.10	.27 ± .06 (29-31)
Violence	.17	.27 ± .09 (29-31)
Stealing	.08	.26 ± .06 (32)
Defiant	.15	.25 ± .08 (33-34)
Loitering	.12	.25 ± .10 (33-34)
Grouped: disobedient, etc.	.14	.24 ± .06 (35-37)
Rude	-.02	.24 ± .07 (35-37)
Truancy from home	.02	.24 ± .07 (35-37)
Enuresis	.08	.22 ± .07 (38-41)
Unpopular	.09	.22 ± .10 (38-41)
Worry over specific fact	.02	.22 ± .11 (38-41)
Egocentric	-.11	.21 ± .08 (42-43)
Staying out late at night	.02	.21 ± .08 (42-43)
Grouped: lack of interest in school, etc.	.03	.20 ± .07 (44-45)
Boastful, "show-off"	.02	.20 ± .09 (44-45)
	Larger Correlations (Negative)	
Bossy	-.27 ± .07	.22 ± .09 (38-41)
Bashful	-.10	-.22 ± .07
Sex delinquency (coitus)	-.06	-.21 ± .07
Temper display	.14	-.21 ± .09

traits as "nervousness," restlessness, irritable temperament, temper tantrums or display (undifferentiated), crying spells, fighting, threatening violence, irregular sleep habits, queer behavior, object of teasing by other children, complaining of bad treatment by other children, and absent-mindedness. Among girls a large additional list of personality and conduct problems showed meaningful correlations ranging from the .20's to the .40's but low and generally positive coefficients below .20 among boys: changeable moods, restlessness in sleep, distractibility, disturbing influence

in school, incorrigibility, loitering or wandering, staying out
late at night, disobedience, violence, defiant attitude, rudeness,
egocentricity, boastful or "show-off" manner, unpopularity, destructiveness, swearing or bad language (undifferentiated), "spoiled
child," finicky food habits, daydreaming, stealing, lying, truancy
from home, enuresis, masturbation, and staff notation of unfavorable conduct prognosis.

The correlations for the heterogeneous category, neurological defect (other than formally diagnosed paralysis), drooping of
one side of face, dragging one leg, tremors, jerking of limbs,
twitching, tic, blinking eye, ptosis, nystagmus, "mask expression,"
dysdiadokokinesis, etc., are presented in Table 118. Since this

TABLE 118*

CORRELATIONS WITH "NEUROLOGICAL DEFECT" (UNSPECIFIED)

	Boys	Girls
Personality-total............................	.32 ± .02	.39 ± .03
Conduct-total................................	.07 ± .03	.12 ± .03
Police arrest................................	-.06 ± .03	-.19 ± .05
	Larger Correlations (Positive)	
Question of change of personality............	.36 ± .05	.42 ± .06 (2)[†]
"Nervous".....................................	.31 ± .04	.44 ± .04 (1)
Emotional instability........................	.29 ± .05	.25 ± .06 (14-15)
Restless in sleep............................	.28 ± .04	.32 ± .05 (6)
Grouped: "nervous," etc......................	.25 ± .03	.41 ± .04 (3)
Depressed....................................	.21 ± .05	.19
Absent-minded................................	.21 ± .05	.09
Changeable moods.............................	.20 ± .04	.33 ± .05 (5)
Restless.....................................	.20 ± .03	.28 ± .04 (9)
Irregular sleep habits.......................	.15	.36 ± .06 (4)
Exclusion from school........................	.08	.30 ± .06 (7)
Distractible.................................	.18	.29 ± .05 (8)
Object of teasing............................	.19	.27 ± .06 (10)
Nail-biting..................................	.11	.26 ± .05 (11-13)
Violence.....................................	.09	.26 ± .06 (11-13)
Worry over specific fact.....................	.16	.26 ± .08 (11-13)
Irritable....................................	.12	.25 ± .05 (14-15)

*Other coefficients smaller than ± .20 may be found in Tables 6-116.

†Rank order of girls' correlations.

TABLE 118—Continued

	Boys	Girls
Grouped: temper, etc..........................	.10	.24 ± .04 (16-17)
Selfish.......................................	.07	.24 ± .04 (16-17)
Spoiled child.................................	.10	.23 ± .06 (18-21)
Sensitive over specific fact..................	.10	.23 ± .05 (18-21)
Psychoneurotic................................	.10	.23 ± .07 (18-21)
Grouped: sensitive or worrisome, etc.........	.14	.23 ± .05 (18-21)
Inferiority feelings..........................	.06	.22 ± .07 (22)
Queer...	.16	.21 ± .07 (23-24)
Temper tantrums...............................	.03	.21 ± .05 (23-24)
Finicky food habits...........................	.05	.20 ± .06 (25-27)
Disturbing influence in school................	-.01	.20 ± .06 (25-27)
Listless......................................	.16	.20 ± .06 (25-27)
	Larger Correlations (Negative)	
Leader..	-.24 ± .05	.12
Sex delinquency (coitus)......................	.01	-.21 ± .05

category is so heterogeneous, the correlation coefficients calculated thereon are difficult of interpretation. Their resemblance
to those for question or diagnosis of encephalitis (Table 117) is
probably due to the fact that the questioned cases of encephalitis
form a substantial portion of those included under the rubric neurological defect (unspecified). Since only a very small fraction
of our cases showed neurological defects, it was not feasible to
obtain a more homogeneous grouping of cases.

The notation headaches or migraine appeared to be of moderate importance with respect to personality and conduct deviation
but of negligible significance so far as police arrest or overt
juvenile delinquency was concerned (Table 119). Headaches tended
to be materially correlated with neurotic and "nervous" behavior
traits. In our case-record material it was often difficult to ascertain whether the patient actually suffered physical pain when
complaining of headaches or was merely making neurotic complaints.

Speech defect (other than muteness or stuttering), e.g.,
infantile speech, lisping, mispronunciation, lalling, rhinolalia,
"scanning speech," etc., appeared to be of negligible importance

TABLE 119*

CORRELATIONS WITH "HEADACHES"

	Boys	Girls
Personality-total.............................	.31 ± .03	.25 ± .04
Conduct-total.................................	.14 ± .03	.30 ± .03
Police arrest.................................	.04	-.07 ± .06
	Larger Correlations (Positive)	
Restless in sleep.............................	.42 ± .04	.28 ± .06 (8)†
Absent-minded.................................	.32 ± .05	.24 ± .07 (14-15)
Finicky food habits...........................	.29 ± .05	.27 ± .06 (9-10)
Question of change of personality.............	.26 ± .06	.29 ± .07 (7)
Queer...	.24 ± .06	.18
Complaining of bad treatment by other children	.24 ± .06	....
Grouped: "nervous," etc......................	.23 ± .04	.26 ± .04 (11-12)
Temper tantrums...............................	.23 ± .05	.16
Attractive manner.............................	.22 ± .04	.07
Threatening violence..........................	.21 ± .06	....
Apprehensive..................................	.21 ± .04	-.14
Object of teasing.............................	.20 ± .04	.12
Listless......................................	.20 ± .05	.12
Worry over specific fact......................	.07	.36 ± .08 (1)
Mental conflict...............................	.01	.34 ± .08 (2)
Boastful, "show-off"..........................	.08	.33 ± .07 (3)
Violence......................................	.11	.31 ± .06 (4)
Overinterest in sex matters...................	-.04	.30 ± .07 (5-6)
Grouped: swearing, etc.......................	.06	.30 ± .06 (5-6)
Emotional instability.........................	.08	.27 ± .07 (9-10)
Hatred or jealousy of sibling.................	.11	.26 ± .07 (11-12)
Crying spells.................................	.17	.25 ± .05 (13)
Changeable moods..............................	.17	.24 ± .06 (14-15)
Restless......................................	.14	.23 ± .05 (16-19)
"Nervous".....................................	.19	.23 ± .05 (16-19)
Irritable.....................................	.18	.23 ± .05 (16-19)
Grouped: sensitive or worrisome, etc.........	.16	.23 ± .05 (16-19)
Fantastical lying.............................	-.02	.22 ± .07 (20)
Daydreaming...................................	.17	.21 ± .07 (21)
Inefficient in work, play, etc................	.19	.20 ± .07 (22-23)
Exclusion from school.........................	.03	.20 ± .07 (22-23)
	Larger Correlations (Negative)	
Smoking.......................................	-.20 ± .05	....

*Other coefficients smaller than ± .20 may be found in Tables 6-116.

†Rank order of girls' correlations.

so far as our three criteria of seriousness are concerned (Table 120). Its substantial correlation of .35 ± .06 with <u>stuttering</u> (calculated for boys only) in our data is questionable, since frequently it was difficult to distinguish from the case record whether

TABLE 120*

CORRELATIONS WITH "SPEECH DEFECT" (OTHER
THAN STUTTERING)

	Boys	Girls
Personality-total..............................	.18 ± .03	.11 ± .04
Conduct-total.................................	-.03 ± .03	.00 ± .04
Police arrest.................................	-.09	-.08 ± .05
	Larger Correlations (Positive)	
Stuttering....................................	.35 ± .06	....
Question of hypophrenia.......................	.22 ± .04	.15
Preference for younger children...............	.22 ± .05	.15
Follower......................................	.21 ± .04	.10
Sensitive (general)...........................	.21 ± .05	.04
Slow, dull....................................	.21 ± .03	.17
Grouped: dull, slow, etc.....................	.21 ± .03	.11
Grouped: "nervous," etc......................	.14	.22 ± .04
Enuresis......................................	.14	.22 ± .05
Object of teasing.............................	.15	.21 ± .06
Fighting......................................	-.02	.21 ± .04
Disturbing influence in school................	-.07	.20 ± .07
Queer...	.04	.20 ± .07
	Larger Correlations (Negative)	
Contrary......................................	-.22 ± .06	.06
Inefficient in work, play, etc................	.09	-.33 ± .07
Loitering.....................................	.02	-.31 ± .07
Repressed.....................................	.05	-.30 ± .08
Leading others into bad conduct...............	-.13	-.27 ± .08
Rude..	-.14	-.26 ± .05
Egocentric....................................	-.14	-.26 ± .06
Psychoneurotic................................	.03	-.21 ± .07

*Other coefficients smaller than ± .20 may be found in Tables 6-116.

the speech difficulty was a true stuttering or not. It appeared
to be characteristic of our younger children, its bi-serial correlations with chronological age among boys and girls respectively
being -.25 ± .03 and -.18 (Table 9, p. 128). It tended to show
some moderate correlations with behavior traits associated with
lower intelligence or "inadequate" personality.

Convulsions in the case-record material considered in the
present volume usually refers to "convulsions in infancy" or "former convulsions," and only seldom were they continuing at the time
of the child's examination in the clinic. In only a few instances
did they indicate a definite epilepsy. Former convulsions showed
only low or negligible correlations with personality or conduct
difficulties in our data (Table 121). Several correlations of moderate size ranging from .20 to .30 were found for various "nervous"
behavior traits.

TABLE 121*

CORRELATIONS WITH "FORMER CONVULSIONS"

	Boys	Girls
Personality-total..............................	.18 ± .03	.11 ± .04
Conduct-total.................................	.17 ± .03	.00 ± .04
Police arrest.................................	.07	-.19 ± .06
	Larger Correlations (Positive)	
Restless in sleep.............................	.29 ± .04	.26 ± .07
Attractive manner.............................	.22 ± .04	.02
Conduct prognosis bad.........................	.20 ± .06	.02
Temper display................................	.20 ± .04	.10
Grouped: temper, etc.........................	.20 ± .03	.02
Finicky food habits..........................	.06	.30 ± .07
Irregular sleep habits.......................	.15	.27 ± .08
Absent-minded.................................	.01	.23 ± .09
"Nervous".....................................	.19	.21 ± .06
Object of teasing............................	.05	.21 ± .08
Hatred or jealousy of sibling................	.15	.20 ± .09

*Other coefficients smaller than ± .20 may be found in Tables
6-116.

TABLE 121—Continued

	Boys	Girls
	Larger Correlations (Negative)	
Overinterest in sex matters....................	.15	-.21 ± .08
Preference for younger children..............	.16	-.20 ± .04

The children with <u>syphilis or lues (congenital or acquired)</u> <u>or with positive Wassermann</u> ("2-plus" or more) in our data formed a heterogeneous group because in some instances it was due to a prenatal or congenital infection while in other cases, especially among girls, it was acquired through specific sex acts by the patient   For this reason its correlation coefficients as shown in Table 122 are difficult to interpret.   Its correlations with our three criteria of seriousness were negligible.   Its only significant positive correlations were among girls for traits tending to be associated with sex acts.

TABLE 122*

CORRELATIONS WITH "LUES"

	Boys	Girls
Personality-total.............................	-.07 ± .03	.06 ± .04
Conduct-total.................................	-.03 ± .03	.12 ± .04
Police arrest.................................	.00 ± .04	.24 ± .05
	Larger Correlations (Positive)	
Sex delinquency (coitus)......................	.04	.23 ± .05
Question of hypophrenia.......................	.16	.22 ± .05
Object of teasing.............................	-.06	.22 ± .07
Overinterest in opposite sex.................	....	.21 ± .05
Follower......................................	.09	.21 ± .06
Violence......................................	-.00	.20 ± .07
Disturbing influence in school...............	-.05	.20 ± .07

*Other coefficients smaller than ± .20 may be found in Tables 6-116.

TABLE 122—Continued

	Boys	Girls
	Larger Correlations (Negative)	
Spoiled child	-.27 ± .05	-.05
Psychoneurotic	-.26 ± .07	-.19
Irregular sleep habits	-.23 ± .06	.03
Question of change of personality	.11	-.20 ± .07

Underweight condition (10 per cent or more) or "poor physical condition" (unspecified) appeared in our data to be of negligible clinical importance, only a few coefficients attaining moderate size in the .20's (Table 123).

TABLE 123*

CORRELATIONS WITH "UNDERWEIGHT"

	Boys	Girls
Personality-total	.09 ± .02	.11 ± .03
Conduct-total	-.04 ± .02	-.02 ± .03
Police arrest	-.12 ± .03	-.22 ± .04
	Larger Correlations (Positive)	
Attractive manner	.26 ± .03	-.01
Question of hypophrenia	.04	.25 ± .04
Sex delinquency (coitus)	-.12	.23 ± .04
Sex denied entirely	-.12	.21 ± .06
Unhappy	.12	.20 ± .06
	Larger Correlations (Negative)	
Threatening violence	-.20 ± .05	....

*Other coefficients smaller than ± .20 may be found in Tables 6-116.

CHAPTER LX

MISCELLANEOUS HOME, FAMILIAL, EDUCATIONAL, AND VOCATIONAL NOTATIONS

In this chapter seven abbreviated tables are presented, concerning home, familial, educational, and vocational notations, together with a brief discussion of each. Minor correlations falling between -.19 and +.19 may be found scattered throughout Tables 6-116, inclusive. The populations upon which these correlations were based are listed in Table 3, p. 55.

Vicious home conditions (exclusive of "immorality"), such as moonshining, bootlegging, gambling, begging, or planning burglaries or hold-ups within the home, showed only low positive correlations ranging from .06 to .18 with our three criteria of seriousness or "ominousness." Among girls there were four positive correlations of substantial size ranging from .32 to .41 with low positive correlations below .20 among boys: staying out late at night, swearing or bad language (undifferentiated), truancy from school, and (calculated for girls only) victim of sex abuse by older child or person (Table 124). A few additional conduct and personality problems showed moderate correlations in the .20's among both sexes.

Immoral home conditions (such as prostitution of parent, or sibling living in adultery in the home) among girls showed the moderate tetrachoric correlation of .30 ± .05 with police arrest (Table 125). All other correlations with personality-total, conduct-total, and police arrest were quite negligible. It showed moderate correlations among girls with sex delinquency (coitus), .29 ± .03, and among boys with overinterest in sex matters, .30 ± .07. Among behavior notations of nonsexual nature there were a few moderate correlations in the .20's.

The notation brother or half-brother in penal or correctional institution or with police arrest among boys showed the

551

TABLE 124*

CORRELATIONS WITH "VICIOUS HOME CONDITIONS"

	Boys	Girls
Personality-total..............................	.13 ± .03	.06 ± .04
Conduct-total.................................	.12 ± .03	.18 ± .04
Police arrest.................................	.18 ± .05	.15 ± .06
	Larger Correlations (Positive)	
Victim of sex abuse...........................	....	.33 ± .06 (3)[†]
Irregular sleep habits........................	.29 ± .06	.13
Attractive manner.............................	.27 ± .05	.21 ± .06 (9-11)
Worry over specific fact......................	.26 ± .07	-.17
Bad companions................................	.26 ± .05	.28 ± .06 (5)
Emotional instability.........................	.21 ± .07	-.20 ± .07
Staying out late at night.....................	.14	.41 ± .06 (1)
Grouped: swearing, etc........................	.05	.35 ± .07 (2)
Truancy from school...........................	.18	.32 ± .06 (4)
Leading others into bad conduct...............	.13	.25 ± .08 (6)
Stealing......................................	.17	.24 ± .05 (7)
Slovenly......................................	.10	.22 ± .06 (8)
Truancy from home.............................	.18	.21 ± .06 (9-11)
Retardation in school.........................	-.04	.21 ± .05 (9-11)
	Larger Correlations (Negative)	
Egocentric....................................	-.08	-.33 ± .05
Grouped: egocentric, etc.....................	-.03	-.29 ± .05
Popular.......................................	-.05	-.29 ± .07
Irresponsible.................................	.11	-.27 ± .08
Inferiority feelings..........................	.05	-.27 ± .08
Destructive...................................	.10	-.26 ± .08
Hatred or jealousy of sibling.................	.18	-.25 ± .08
Irritable.....................................	.06	-.24 ± .06
Distractible..................................	.07	-.21 ± .07
Sex denied entirely...........................	.07	-.20 ± .09

*Other coefficients smaller than ± .20 may be found in Tables 6-116.

[†]Rank order of girls' correlations.

substantial tetrachoric correlation of .33 ± .04 with <u>police ar-</u>
rest (Table 126). All other correlations with our three criteria
of seriousness or "ominousness" were low or negligible. Among
boys there were a few moderate positive correlations ranging from
.20 to .32 with the overt conduct difficulties, <u>stealing, truancy</u>
<u>from school, truancy from home, bad companions, running with a</u>

TABLE 125*

CORRELATIONS WITH "IMMORAL HOME CONDITIONS"

	Boys	Girls
Personality-total............................	-.00 ± .03	-.03 ± .04
Conduct-total................................	.01 ± .03	.10 ± .03
Police arrest................................	-.00 ± .04	.30 ± .05
	Larger Correlations (Positive)	
Overinterest in sex matters..................	.30 ± .07	.17
Irresponsible................................	.23 ± .06	-.05
Sex delinquency (coitus).....................	.13	.29 ± .03
Inefficient in work, play, etc..............	-.11	.23 ± .07
Truancy from school..........................	.05	.20 ± .06
	Larger Correlations (Negative)	
Temper tantrums..............................	-.22 ± .05	-.03
Irritable....................................	-.19	-.26 ± .05
Poor work in school.........................	-.12	-.26 ± .04
Question of hypophrenia......................	-.19	-.24 ± .05
Object of teasing...........................	-.16	-.23 ± .06
Leader.......................................	.04	-.20 ± .07

*Other coefficients smaller than ± .20 may be found in Tables 6-116.

TABLE 126*

CORRELATIONS WITH "BROTHER IN PENAL DETENTION"

	Boys	Girls
Personality-total............................	-.08 ± .03	-.12 ± .03
Conduct-total................................	.10 ± .03	-.01 ± .04
Police arrest................................	.33 ± .04	.00 ± .05
	Larger Correlations (Positive)	
Truancy from school..........................	.32 ± .03	.18
Stealing.....................................	.28 ± .03	.02

*Other coefficients smaller than ± .20 may be found in Tables 6-116.

TABLE 126—Continued

	Boys	Girls
Leading others into bad conduct........	.27 ± .05	.22 ± .08
Bad companions.........................	.25 ± .07	.07
Truancy from home......................	.23 ± .04	.07
Gang...................................	.20 ± .05	....
	Larger Correlations (Negative)	
Temper tantrums........................	-.26 ± .05	-.17
Daydreaming............................	-.22 ± .05	-.32 ± .06
Psychoneurotic.........................	-.22 ± .06	-.34 ± .07
"Nervous"..............................	-.20 ± .04	-.30 ± .05
Stuttering.............................	-.20 ± .06	....
Spoiled child..........................	-.11	-.36 ± .05
Hatred or jealousy of sibling..........	.10	-.32 ± .07
Sensitive (general)....................	-.04	-.31 ± .06
Grouped: "nervous," etc................	-.14	-.27 ± .04
Worry over specific fact...............	-.17	-.26 ± .08
Changeable moods.......................	-.12	-.25 ± .05
Question of change of personality......	.03	-.24 ± .08
Irregular sleep habits.................	.09	-.23 ± .07
Grouped: temper, etc...................	-.08	-.22 ± .05
Irritable..............................	-.00	-.22 ± .05

gang, and leading others into bad conduct. Curiously enough, there
were more negative than positive correlations with behavior problems in the personality sphere.

The notation mental deficiency or feeble-mindedness among
siblings showed low negative bi-serial correlations with the personality-total and conduct-total and negligible tetrachoric r's
with police arrest (Table 127). Among the separate behavior notations it showed a few positive coefficients of significant size
with such notations as question of hypophrenia, slow or dull manner, and retardation in school; but the majority of its correlations of significant size were negative in sign.

Discord between parents or foster-parents was noted among
525, or 24.8 per cent, of our 2,113 White boys and among 285, or
24.1 per cent, of our 1,181 White girls. Its correlations with
our three criteria of seriousness were low or negligible, ranging

TABLE 127*

CORRELATIONS WITH "FEEBLE-MINDED SIBLING"

	Boys	Girls
Personality-total..........................	-.20 ± .03	- 12 ± .03
Conduct-total.............................	-.15 ± .03	-.16 ± .03
Police arrest.............................	.05 ± .04	.09 ± .05
	Larger Correlations (Positive)	
Retardation in school......................	.25 ± .04	.31 ± .04
Question of hypophrenia....................	.20 ± .04	.27 ± .05
Slow, dull................................	.07	.26 ± .05
Grouped: dull, slow, etc..................	.04	.25 ± .04
	Larger Correlations (Negative)	
Inattentive in school......................	-.28 ± .05	-.22 ± .06
"Nervous".................................	-.28 ± .04	-.15
Refusal to attend school...................	-.28 ± .06	-.06
Temper tantrums...........................	-.27 ± .05	-.14
Preference for younger children............	-.27 ± .05	-.08
Popular...................................	-.25 ± .12	.06
Grouped: "nervous," etc..................	-.24 ± .04	-.11
Destructive...............................	-.24 ± .05	-.14
Queer.....................................	-.23 ± .06	-.04
Disturbing influence in school.............	-.23 ± .04	-.09
Grouped: depressed, etc..................	-.22 ± .05	-.25 ± .06
Sulky.....................................	-.22 ± .06	-.25 ± .07
Question of change of personality..........	-.22 ± .06	.06
Grouped: disobedient, etc................	-.20 ± .04	-.27 ± .04
Spoiled child.............................	-.17	-.45 ± .05
Boastful, "show-off"......................	-.05	-.38 ± .06
Inferiority feelings......................	-.09	-.33 ± .07
Daydreaming...............................	-.09	-.32 ± .06
Defiant...................................	-.19	-.32 ± .06
Temper display............................	.02	-.31 ± .06
Repressed.................................	-.10	-.30 ± .08
Mental conflict...........................	-.13	-.29 ± .08
Fantastical lying.........................	.11	-.27 ± .06
Bad companions............................	.02	-.26 ± .06
Selfish...................................	-.13	-.26 ± .04
Worry over specific fact..................	-.08	-.26 ± .08
Clean.....................................	-.18	-.26 ± .05
Stubborn..................................	-.15	-.24 ± .05
Psychoneurotic............................	-.16	-.23 ± .07

*Other coefficients smaller than ± .20 may be found in Tables 6-116.

TABLE 127—Continued

	Boys	Girls
Leader..	-.11	-.21 ± .07
Overinterest in sex matters....................	-.03	-.21 ± .06
Grouped: sensitive or worrisome, etc.........	-.16	-.21 ± .05
Grouped: egocentric, etc.....................	-.07	-.20 ± .05
Excuse-forming................................	-.02	-.20 ± .06
	Not Calculable	
Irresponsible.................................	-.23 ± .06	(n.c.)
Hatred or jealousy of sibling.................	(n.c.)	-.32 ± .07

from -.01 to .19 (Table 128). It showed moderate positive correlations in the .20's among boys with <u>unhappiness</u> and <u>restlessness</u>
<u>in sleep</u> and among girls with the three notations, <u>destructiveness</u>,
<u>finicky food habits</u>, and (calculated for girls only) <u>victim of sex</u>

TABLE 128*

CORRELATIONS WITH "DISCORD BETWEEN PARENTS"

	Boys	Girls
Personality-total.............................	.19 ± .02	.08 ± .03
Conduct-total.................................	.02 ± .02	.16 ± .03
Police arrest.................................	.13 ± .03	-.01 ± .04
	Larger Correlations (Positive)	
Unhappy.......................................	.23 ± .04	.11
Grouped: depressed, etc......................	.21 ± .03	.07
Restless in sleep.............................	.20 ± .03	-.04
Finicky food habits...........................	.06	.21 ± .05
Destructive...................................	.12	.20 ± .06
Victim of sex abuse...........................	....	.20 ± .05
	Larger Correlations (Negative)	
Absent-minded.................................	.02	-.20 ± .05

    *Other coefficients smaller than ± .20 may be found in Tables
6-116.

abuse by older child or person. The fact that in our case-record material discord between parents showed so negligible a relation-ship with personality and conduct problems among our children is contrary to the frequently expressed belief among students of child behavior that parental or familial discord is a potent cause of un-desirable behavior. The present writer does not attempt to explain or interpret these correlational results at this time.

Irregular attendance at school or frequent change of school in our data was a heterogeneous notation which, on the one hand, included instances in which a child's truancies may have been so extensive that the continuity of his school career may have been seriously interrupted and, on the other hand, instances in which these irregularities may have been due to inability or unwilling-ness of the child's parents to keep him in regular attendance. Its correlations with our three criteria of seriousness were low, or at best only moderate (Table 129). The majority of its significant

TABLE 129*

CORRELATIONS WITH "IRREGULAR ATTENDANCE AT SCHOOL"

	Boys	Girls
Personality-total...............................	.07 ± .03	-.02 ± .04
Conduct-total..................................	.15 ± .03	.01 ± .04
Police arrest...................................	.20 ± .04	-.22 ± .05
	Larger Correlations (Positive)	
Truancy from school............................	.35 ± .03	.26 ± .05 (3-4)[†]
Refusal to attend school.......................	.34 ± .05	.32 ± .07 (2)
Loitering......................................	.27 ± .05	.16
Poor work in school............................	.20 ± .03	.03
Slovenly.......................................	.20 ± .04	.09
Irregular sleep habits.........................	.14	.34 ± .07 (1)
Attractive manner..............................	.01	.26 ± .05 (3-4)
Grouped: swearing, etc........................	.08	.25 ± .06 (5)
Finicky food habits............................	-.08	.23 ± .06 (6-7)
Retardation in school..........................	.17	.23 ± .04 (6-7)

*Other coefficients smaller than ± .20 may be found in Tables 6-116.

[†]Rank order of girls' correlations.

TABLE 129—Continued

	Boys	Girls
	Larger Correlations (Negative)	
Stuttering..	-.24 ± .06	....
Sex delinquency (coitus).......................	-.21 ± .06	-.14
Selfish...	.02	-.26 ± .04
Sullen..	.07	-.20 ± .06
Inefficient in work, play, etc.................	-.07	-.20 ± .07

correlations were for problems associated with his school life, such as <u>refusal to attend school</u>, <u>truancy from school</u>, <u>poor work in school</u>, <u>retardation in school</u>, and traits denoting inadequacy, such as <u>loitering or wandering</u> and <u>slovenliness</u>.

    The children for whom a <u>request for vocational guidance</u> appeared in the case records formed a vaguely defined group. In some cases the <u>request for vocational guidance</u> was the chief reason for the clinic examination, while in other cases the request was secondary to some behavior or educational problem. Its correlations (Table 130) are reproduced in this volume for the sake of completeness. The present writer at this time is unable to make any interpretations concerning these obtained correlations.

TABLE 130*

CORRELATIONS WITH "REQUEST FOR VOCATIONAL GUIDANCE"

	Boys	Girls
Personality-total.............................	.02 ± .02	.02 ± .03
Conduct-total.................................	-.10 ± .02	-.17 ± .03
Police arrest.................................	-.35 ± .03	-.34 ± .04
	Larger Correlations (Positive)	
Lack of initiative............................	.23 ± .05	.14
Lazy..	.11	.21 ± .06
Refusal to attend school......................	.03	.20 ± .07

    * Other coefficients smaller than ± .20 may be found in Tables 6-116.

TABLE 130—Continued

	Boys	Girls
	Larger Correlations (Negative)	
Sex delinquency (coitus)........................	-.39 ± .05	-.41 ± .04
Retardation in school.........................	-.31 ± .03	-.32 ± .04
Stealing......................................	-.22 ± .02	-.31 ± .04
Gang..	-.21 ± .04	....
Fantastical lying.............................	-.17	-.44 ± .05
Masturbation..................................	-.10	-.37 ± .04
Loitering.....................................	.11	-.34 ± .06
Lying...	-.13	-.31 ± .04
Truancy from home.............................	-.16	-.29 ± .04
Grouped: "nervous," etc......................	-.01	-.27 ± .04
Bossy...	.01	-.25 ± .05
Truancy from school..........................	.02	-.25 ± .05
Question of hypophrenia.......................	-.10	-.23 ± .04
Staying out late at night....................	-.08	-.23 ± .04
Temper display...............................	-.06	-.22 ± .05
Object of teasing............................	-.05	-.22 ± .05
"Nervous"....................................	-.03	-.21 ± .04
Incorrigible.................................	-.17	-.21 ± .04

INDEX

Date Due